*Hawaiian
Natural History,
Ecology, and Evolution*

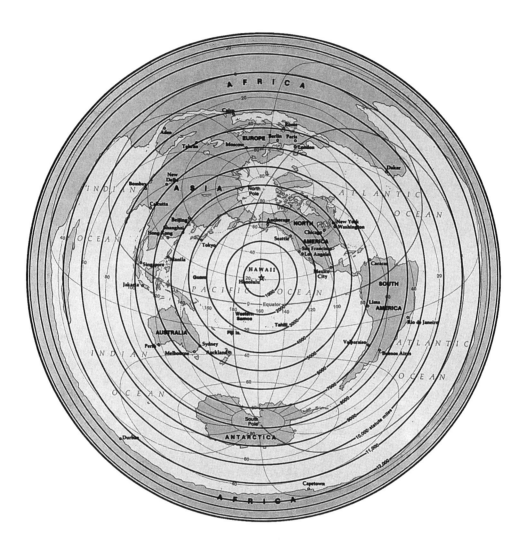

The perpetually isolated location of the main Hawaiian Islands. On this map, known as an azimuthal equidistant projection, the concentric circles radiating from Honolulu indicate units of 1,600 km (1,000 miles). (Unnumbered figure on p. 9 of Armstrong [ed.] [1983], used with permission of University of Hawai'i Press.)

Hawaiian
Natural History,
Ecology, and Evolution

Alan C. Ziegler

University of Hawai'i Press
Honolulu

Library of Congress Cataloging-in-Publication Data

Ziegler, Alan C.
    Hawaiian natural history, ecology, and evolution / Alan C. Ziegler.
        p. cm.
    Includes bibliographical references (p.) and index.
    ISBN 0-8248-2190-4
    1. Natural history—Hawaii. 2. Ecology—Hawaii. I. Title.

QH198.H3 Z54 2002
508.9969—dc21   2001048094

Designed by David Alcorn, Alcorn Publication Design,
Graeagle, California

Printed by The Maple-Vail Book Manufacturing Group

Dedicated to all those who have worked in the past, who are presently working,
and who will work in the future toward understanding
and preserving Hawai'i's natural heritage.

Contents

Figures

Plates

Plates appear after page 126.

Tables

Acknowledgments

A lmost no one preparing a work like this one has extensive expertise in more than one or two of the subjects covered, and I am no exception. Thus, a number of extremely obliging colleagues and other scholars have most generously reviewed each of the chapters. In fact, their work in this task has been so thorough that they should collectively be recognized as essentially coauthors of this book. Because, however, I may not always have faithfully followed each of their numerous suggestions, any resultant shortcomings in the book are due solely to this inaction on my part and not to these colleagues' studied advice. These reviewers of the individual chapters or portions thereof are as follows:

Chapter 1. Introduction: Emily A. Hawkins.

Chapters 2, 3, 4. Plate Tectonics, Hawaiian Archipelago Formation, Volcanism: Floyd W. McCoy, John M. Sinton.

Chapter 5. Hawaiian Topography: Floyd W. McCoy, John M. Sinton, Goro Uehara.

Chapter 6. Actions of the Ocean: Stephen V. Smith.

Chapter 7. Climatology: Glenn Bauer, Thomas A. Schroeder, Stephen V. Smith.

Chapter 8. Freshwater: Glenn Bauer, Scot K. Izuka, William Meyer.

Chapter 9. Ecological Principles: Robert A. Kinzie III, Charles H. Lamoureux.

Chapter 10. Evolutionary Principles: Hampton L. Carson, E. Alison Kay.

Chapter 11. The Marine Environment: Isabella A. Abbott, E. Alison Kay, James E. Maragos.

Chapter 12. Marine and Freshwater Fishes: William S. Devick, Robert A. Kinzie III, Bruce C. Mundy, John E. Randall, Arnold Y. Suzumoto.

Chapter 13. Dispersal and Establishment: Francis G. Howarth, Charles H. Lamoureux.

Chapter 14. The Terrestrial Environment: William S. Devick, Lorin T. Gill, Derral R. Herbst, Francis G. Howarth, Robert A. Kinzie III, Dieter Mueller-Dombois.

Chapter 15. Flowering Plants: Gerald D. Carr, Derral R. Herbst, Charles H. Lamoureux.

Chapter 16. Terrestrial Arthropods: Francis G. Howarth, Gordon M. Nishida.

Chapter 17. Picture-Winged Flies: Hampton L. Carson, Kenneth Y. Kaneshiro.

Chapter 18. Nonmarine Snails: Robert H. Cowie, Michael G. Hadfield.

Chapter 19. Amphibians, Reptiles, and Mammals: George H. Balazs, Carla H. Kishinami, P. Quentin Tomich.

Chapters 20, 21, 22. Birds, Hawaiian Honeycreepers, Flightless Birds and Fossil Sites: Sheila Conant, Helen F. James, Storrs L. Olson, Robert L. Pyle.

Chapter 23. The Northwestern Hawaiian Islands: Sheila Conant, Charles H. Lamoureux.

Chapters 24, 25. Polynesian Origin and Migration, Polynesian Ecology: Thomas S. Dye, Ben R. Finney, Lorin T. Gill, Patrick V. Kirch.

Chapter 26. Historic Ecology: Thomas S. Dye, Patrick V. Kirch, Linda W. Pratt.

Chapter 27. Natural Resource Protection: Samuel M. Gon III, Barbara A. Maxfield, Marjorie F. Y. Ziegler.

Chapter 28. Historic Hawaiian Naturalists: E. Alison Kay.

Glossary of Hawaiian Place Names: Emily A. Hawkins.

Many scientists in addition to the chapter reviewers have similarly freely shared their knowledge in particular fields of Hawaiian natural history, as well as, often, unpublished data or personal photographs. Among all of these indispensable colleagues, I must especially acknowledge my indebtedness to E. Alison Kay and the late Charles H. Lamoureux, who for many years have jointly taught an upper-division course on Natural History of the Hawaiian Islands at the University of Hawai'i Mānoa Campus (in which while auditing the course I first became aware of the full spectrum of Hawaiian natural history phenomena). The general system of subject coverage used in this book has been drawn almost unaltered from their course outline. These two, as well as Isabella A. Abbott and two anonymous reviewers, spent long hours reading early drafts of the entire manuscript and provided a great number of helpful suggestions for improvement. Hawai'i artist and educator Keith Krueger skillfully prepared several of the figures. Eileen D'Araujo did her usual superb job of copyediting for the University of Hawai'i Press. Finally, the staff librarians of the Bishop Museum were consistently and cheerfully of great aid in recommending or locating a diverse array of sometimes obscure references that might otherwise have been overlooked.

Introduction

This book is intended as a relatively condensed guide to the natural history of the Hawaiian Islands, a vast and complex—but fascinating—field. In addition to providing general reading and reference material, it may also prove useful as a text for college-level courses on the natural history of the archipelago.

In teaching such classes at both the university and community college levels in Hawai'i, I found that various books or parts of them provided excellent coverage of a number of Hawaiian natural history subjects. An early classic is the monumental 1915 work by William A. Bryan, a few parts of which were updated by Elwood C. Zimmerman in his 1948 publication. Among the most comprehensive recent publications are the slightly revised 1980 edition of Sherwin Carlquist's book (although essentially the entire text was completed in 1968); an evocative 1988 work by John L. Culliney; the 1972 and 1994 compilations edited by E. Alison Kay; and the 1998 edition of the *Atlas of Hawai'i,* with Sonia P. Juvik and James O. Juvik as editors.

No single one of these publications, however, contains up-to-date coverage of all of the relevant subjects, including related ecological and evolutionary aspects. Nor do most simultaneously maintain the depth of discussion at a relatively uniform level. Thus, this volume was prepared in an attempt to fill these perceived needs.

PLAN OF WORK

Content

Each chapter focuses on a relatively discrete subject, with the depth of coverage approximating what might be appropriate for a single college lecture. To keep the volume a manageable length, the chapters on biology often concentrate on a few representative cases, rather than attempting to cover a large number of examples in a superficial fashion. If the volume is used as a text, this necessary loss of detail will be inconsequential because many instructors will undoubtedly base their lectures on their own considerable knowledge of various natural history subjects and assign corresponding chapters only as introductory or supplemental reading.

References

Pertinent publications suggested for further reading are listed at the end of each chapter. Full bibliographic information regarding these, as well as those cited in the illustration legends and table titles, is given in the annotated References Cited section near the end of the volume.

Audiovisual Aids

An attempt has been made to list at least a few pertinent audiovisual sources at the end of each chapter. Equally good or better programs, however, may have been overlooked, and excellent additional ones will undoubtedly appear in the future. Full bibliographic information on these works appears in the annotated Audiovisual Aids section. Because the form (that is, film, cassette, compact disk) varies among such programs and may change through time for any given one, no format is listed.

In 1991 the Moanalua Gardens Foundation in Honolulu assembled a collection of two hundred 35-mm color slides on Hawaiian natural history subjects, with an index containing much information about each slide, and a color print of each. Sets are available for loan from each Hawai'i Department of Education District Office, or by special arrangement from any Regional Library in the state.

DATABASES

Essentially all of the numerical and other data appearing in this volume reflect information available as of the end of 1999. In a number of instances, however, this information had already become outdated while the work was in press and will, of course, continue to change. Fortunately, under current plans of the Bernice Pauahi Bishop Museum in Honolulu, timely data updates for many biotic groups will be available through the museum's maintenance of the Hawaii Biological Survey databases. Significant portions of these information sources are now available on the museum's website on the World Wide Web at:

>   http://www.bishopmuseum.org/bishop/HBS/

Further information may be obtained from the museum through the electronic mail address:

>   hbs@bishopmuseum.org

TERMINOLOGY AND BIOLOGICAL NOMENCLATURE

Words and terms considered especially important in the understanding of a subject are printed in **boldface type,** usually the first time they appear. When available in standard biological reference works, both English and Hawaiian names of organisms have been listed along with their scientific designations. Also, a list of Hawaiian terms for members of various biotic groups, conveniently arranged under English-name categories, was prepared by Harold W. Kent in 1986.

HAWAIIAN LANGUAGE

Spelling and Glossing

The orthography and meanings of Hawaiian words given here, other than locality names, are *italicized* and follow, as much as possible, the slightly revised 1991 third printing of the revised and enlarged 1986 edition of the Hawaiian-English dictionary of Mary K. Pukui and Samuel H. Elbert. A guide to Hawaiian grammar is available (Elbert and Pukui 1979), with an abbreviated version included in Pukui et al. (1975).

Place Names

In the citing of Hawaiian localities an attempt has been made to conform to the most commonly used current orthography. Thus, the spelling in the 1974 gazetteer of Pukui and colleagues is followed, but the hyphens appearing in most of their compound terms have been omitted and the parts of the terms joined. Exceptions have been made in the case of a few place names, however, primarily involving those beginning with "Mauna" (mountain), "Puʻu" (hill), and the like. In these, the earlier hyphens have been omitted, but the parts of the term left separated.

Glossary
Because this *is* a book about Hawaiʻi, a Glossary of Hawaiian Place Names mentioned is included near the end of the volume. These original Hawaiian terms are not only inherently interesting in a linguistic sense, but many of them also allow insight regarding matters that were important in the daily life of ancient Hawaiians, as well as about traditional beliefs in the complex interrelationship of humans, nature, and religion.

English Transcription
Hawaiian was originally only a spoken language, and the spelling used today was largely standardized by American missionaries in the mid-1820s. To transcribe the spoken language, they used only eleven of the twenty-six letters in the English alphabet: five vowels and seven consonants, even though some of the latter did not exactly reproduce the Hawaiian sounds that they were purported to represent. For example, "k" was used to indicate an original Hawaiian spoken consonant that lay somewhere between the English "t" and "k"—perhaps even closer to the former. In very early historic writing, the "t" was used relatively frequently, as is illustrated by the almost invariable pre-1820 historic spelling of the name of Kamehameha I as "Tamehameha." Beginning in the later 1820s, however, the written "k" replaced "t." The letters "r" and "l" seem to have had a similar history, with "l" becoming the one chosen.

Diacriticals
In addition, usually beginning only after about the mid-1900s, two diacritical marks not used by the missionaries were added in writing to accurately reflect the original Hawaiian pronunciation. These are the *ʻokina* or glottal stop (also known in English as hamza) and the *kahakō* or macron. The marks have been included here for all Hawaiian words; because their presence is essential, not only for proper pronunciation, but also for correct translation or understanding of meaning, their significance should be explained.

The *ʻokina,* which is effectively an additional consonant, always immediately precedes a vowel, and is indicated by a reversed apostrophe (ʻ). In speaking, this is rendered by momentarily closing the glottis, then suddenly releasing the breath when pronouncing the vowel, much as the sound used before each of the two syllables in the English exclamation "oh-oh!" In a Hawaiian word the *ʻokina* indicates that a "k"-like sound present in an earlier Polynesian spoken word (and usually still maintained in Polynesian-based speech of areas outside Hawaiʻi) has been omitted. For example, the ancestral Polynesian word for lizard (and a mythical water dragon) was *"moko,"* but in Hawaiian this became *"moʻo."* In very occasional instances, however, the original pronunciation has been retained, as in the name of an islet off Oʻahu: Mokoliʻi or "little *(liʻi)* lizard."

It is interesting that this propensity for ancient Hawaiians to shorten words was sometimes carried even further, as by use of the *kahakō* (see below) to change the already abbreviated *moʻo* to *mō,* seen in the Oʻahu locality name Mōʻiliʻili or "pebble *(ʻiliʻili)* lizard." Words with identical series of letters, but with and without the *ʻokina,* have different meanings (and, of course, pronunciations): *"pau"* (finished) and *"paʻu"* (soot).

The *kahakō* or macron, which is used only with a vowel, is represented by a mark (-) above the letter and is indicated in speaking by drawing out the vowel sound somewhat. This diacritical mark is used in written Hawaiian to differentiate between the sounds of long and short vowels as used in the parent Austronesian and derivative Polynesian languages. It effectively replaces one of two consecutive vowels (usually identical, but occasionally different; see Lā'ie in the Glossary). That is, the Hawaiian *"mū"* (destructive insect) (among other meanings) is the derivative or reflex of the ancestral *muu.* Also, this diacritical mark, just as in the case of the *'okina,* can be used to signify the deletion of one or even more syllables following the marked vowel. This is evinced by the comparison of two treatments of the Hawaiian term *"moku,"* one of whose common meanings is "island." The word is usually used in its complete form, as in the locality name Mokumanu or "bird *(manu)* island," but occasionally the final syllable is replaced by a *kahakō,* as in Mōkōlea or "plover *(kōlea)* island." Just as in the case of the *'okina,* presence or absence of the *kahakō* completely changes the meaning of an identical series of letters; compare, for instance, *"pa'ū"* (moist) and *"pā'ū"* (sarong) with each other, and with the two similar words at the end of the preceding paragraph.

Miscellany

As a final note to interpreting the language, the peruser of any significantly long list of Hawaiian proper nouns may be puzzled by the noticeable frequency of words beginning with *"ka-"* (and, less often, *"ke-,"* depending on the following letter or syllable). This prefix is simply the Hawaiian singular definite article "the," traditionally commonly incorporated into the names of people and places. The corresponding plural article is always *"nā-."*

SUGGESTED REFERENCES

W. A. Bryan 1915; Carlquist 1980; Culliney 1988; Elbert and Pukui 1979; Juvik and Juvik (eds.) 1998; Kay (ed.) 1972, 1994; Kent 1986; Pukui and Elbert 1986; Pukui et al. 1974, 1975; Zimmerman 1948.

AUDIOVISUAL AIDS

The house of science; Island of Aldabra; Slide bank of Hawai'i's native biota.

2

Plate Tectonics

All aspects of movement of large portions of the earth's surface are included under the broad term **"plate tectonics"** (Greek *"tektonikos"* [builder]). Through most of the history of science it was assumed that the continents of the earth had always held their current positions. In the early 1900s, however, the Austrian meteorologist Alfred L. Wegener put forth the radical theory that at one time all of the land of this planet had been a single huge mass, which he termed **"Pangaea"** (Greek *"pantos"* [whole] and *"gaia"* [earth]), but had subsequently broken into northern and southern portions and then further split into smaller units that dispersed or "drifted" through the surrounding ocean to form the various current continents (Figure 2.1).

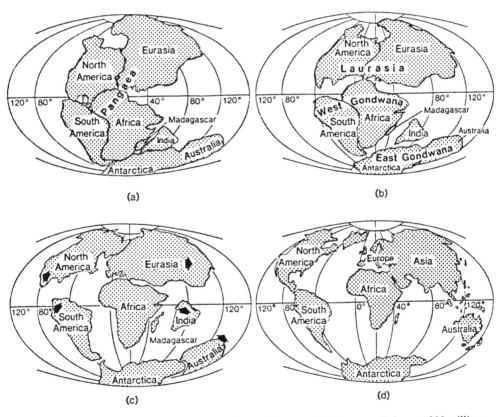

Figure 2.1. Continental drift following the breakup of Pangaea. *(a)* Pangaea a little over 200 million years ago; *(b)* formation of Laurasia and Gondwana about 135 million years ago; *(c)* completed fragmentation of Gondwana approximately 65 million years ago; and *(d)* current configuration of continents. The times and, to some extent, the sequence of landmass separations are still subject to some debate. (Fig. 27.1A of Johnson [1983], used with permission of The McGraw-Hill Companies.)

For many years, Wegener's theory was usually not seriously considered, but scientific discoveries made since the mid-1900s now show that his idea is basically correct. Theories to explain the details and exact mechanisms of plate tectonics phenomena, however, have gone through various revisions, and many are still being actively debated; undoubtedly they will continue to be changed or refined. Also, recent research has demonstrated that continent-sized landmasses have probably been alternately separating and coalescing ever since the solidification of the earth from gaseous matter some 4.6 billion years ago. Wegener's Pangaea simply represented the continental configuration that existed at a particular time well along in Earth's history: roughly 200 or so million years ago.

SEAFLOOR SPREADING

Paleomagnetism

Probably the event most responsible for finally convincing the scientific world that plate tectonics must be a reality, and for stimulating further research, was formulation of the theory of **seafloor spreading.** This was interpreted from geological and geophysical studies of ocean basins and necessitated an understanding of the magnetic properties of volcanic rock. When melted rock, existing as **magma** (Greek, salve) below the earth's surface, is extruded as **lava** (Italian, a rain torrent overflowing the streets) from a volcanic opening, the iron-bearing particles in the molten material are free to move. Attracted by the earth's magnetic field, the particles align north and south with it, becoming fixed in this position as the lava hardens. Any unit of lava rock thus constitutes essentially a gigantic bar magnet, and enough of this original **paleomagnetism** is retained to yield detectable north- and south-seeking poles. For unknown reasons, the north-south magnetic field of the earth occasionally reverses polarity, having done so a dozen or more times during the last several million years. During such periods of reversed polarity, the normally north-seeking arrow of a modern compass would, instead, point south. These alternations of "normal" and "reversed" world polarity are also accurately reflected by corresponding polarity reversals or **magnetic anomalies** in lava deposits formed during the same time periods. (Although lava is the lithic material used in this explanation of paleomagnetism, most types of sedimentary rocks also undergo this same process during their formation.)

Midocean Ridges

Extending from north to south through much of the Atlantic Ocean basin is the **Mid-Atlantic Ridge** (Figure 2.2), a massive submarine elevation bearing along its entire midline a volcanically active seam or **rift zone.** For years, scientists studying this ridge and the surrounding ocean basin had been independently amassing seemingly unrelated data pertaining to the paleomagnetism and various other physical characteristics of the region. About 1960, in what proved to be only the beginning of an intriguing episode of scientific detective work, a few investigators started integrating unusual similarities noticed in such information.

It had been found, for instance, that lava located at any particular spot equidistant east and west of the Mid-Atlantic Ridge possessed identical presence or absence of reversed polarity; that is, this pattern of magnetic anomalies traced in one direction from the ridge was a mirror image of that traced in the other (Figure 2.3). There was no way these identical magnetic anomaly series could have occurred unless each pair of equidistant lava areas tested had been formed at the same time. Thus, the lava being extruded along the rift zone was not only producing the

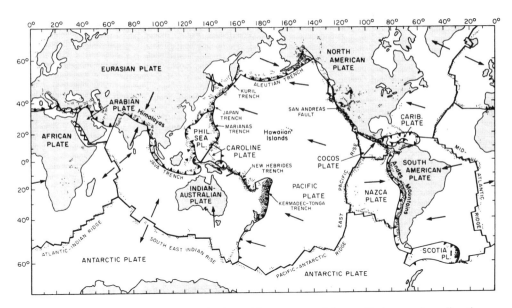

Figure 2.2. Tectonic plates and related physiographic structures of the world. Arrows show direction of plate movement, and barbs on plate margins at subduction zones point toward the overriding plate. Note, especially, the steplike nature of the various midocean rises, indicating the existence of transform faults (Figure 2.4). The numerous small dots along the rises and faults designate areas of extensive seismic activity. (Fig. 18.4 of Macdonald et al. [1983], used with permission of Frank L. Peterson.)

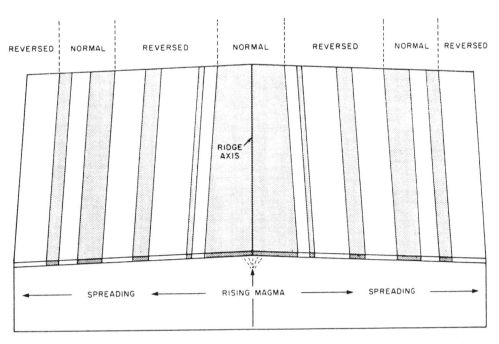

Figure 2.3. "Mirror-image" pattern of magnetic anomaly. Obvious are the identical paleomagnetic reversals of various tested (stippled) segments of seafloor material at equal distances on either side of a midocean ridge or spreading zone. (Slightly modified from Fig. 18.3 of Macdonald et al. [1983], used with permission of Frank L. Peterson.)

ridge itself, but, upon hardening, was continually being forced outward on both sides of the ridge. And, if new seafloor was spreading east and west from the ridge, so were the continents of Africa and South America at opposite sides of the ocean floor. Other equally important geological clues, such as ever-greater lava age and increasing thickness of overlying marine sediment as testing progressively moved out to either side of the Mid-Atlantic rift, were also successfully incorporated into this theory of seafloor spreading.

East Pacific Rise

Some of the information was also derived from studies related to that portion of a similar Pacific Ocean north-south submarine ridge located far out from the western coast of South America and termed the **East Pacific Rise** (Figure 2.2; see also the ever-increasing ages for marine sediments located successively farther northwest of this rise shown in Figure 4.1). In fact, it has now become obvious that the Mid-Atlantic Ridge is only one segment of a continuous gigantic submarine volcanic mountain chain, at places as much as 3,000 m (9,900 feet) high and 2,000 km (1,240 miles) wide, with occasional side branches. As shown in Figure 2.2, this chain stretches about 65,000 km (40,300 miles) around the world from the Arctic Ocean north of Iceland to southeastern Alaska. Active volcanism marks a rift along the midline of this entire ocean ridge system, and it is here that new crust under all the oceans is continually being produced by extruded magma.

CONTINENT MOVEMENTS

Supportive Evidence

Acceptance of the general plate tectonics theory meant that continents could move, so additional evidence available from the continents themselves was more closely examined. For example, even long before Wegener's work it had been recognized that the outline of the west coast of Africa "fits" very well into that of the east coast of South America if the two continents are imagined swung together. But, more definitively, geologists now realized the significance of earlier studies that had shown areas of identical volcanic or sedimentary rocks of about the same age in particular coastal areas of the two continents that would have been in contact if the continents were so joined. Each of these corresponding pairs of lithic material presumably originally resulted from the same episode of geological activity before the two land areas separated.

Also, the formerly puzzling evidence of ancient glaciers in lowland areas near the equator was now enlisted to reinforce the idea that some continents had moved far north or south of their earlier positions. And biogeographers and paleontologists could point to the present or past extensive distribution of certain Southern Hemisphere plants and animals, such as the southern beeches (genus *Nothofagus*) and various extinct or extant animals including marsupials, in South America, Antarctica, and Australia, as reasonably indicating that these continents probably were derived from a common parent landmass. Acceptance of this new theory proved more comfortable to many scientists than their having to defend an earlier postulate—that now-vanished land bridges must once have linked such widely separated and presumably immobile areas of the earth. This was an idea almost impossible to support because it would have required that portions of continents somehow were destroyed without trace in midocean.

Paleomagnetism, so important in the formulation of the seafloor spreading theory, played a further role in elucidating plate tectonics. If continents never moved, the volcanic and much sedimentary rock of all continents would always exhibit a paleomagnetic orientation (whether normal or reversed) parallel to the earth's north-south magnetic field. On a number of continents or portions of them, however, many rocks show various paleomagnetic alignments that do not correspond with this expected magnetic-field orientation. Thus, the continents must have rotated since these rocks were formed, presumably through global drift. It is true that the earth's magnetic poles, themselves, "wander," but it is thought that the geographic shift has never been more than perhaps 2,000 km (1,240 miles) from their current locations, not enough to account for the disparity evident in many continental paleomagnetic alignments.

EARTH COMPOSITION

To return to the example of Atlantic seafloor spreading, as the continents of Africa and South America move apart, new seafloor material forms from the molten rock extruding into the Mid-Atlantic rift. But if an increase in size of the earth's surface is occurring here at spreading areas in this and other oceans, an equal amount of surface area must simultaneously be in the process of loss elsewhere, because there is no convincing evidence that the earth is expanding (or contracting).

To explain this phenomenon of compensatory surface loss, however, it is first necessary to provide a general idea of the physical makeup of the earth itself. The commonly used classic geological categorization recognizes a central **core,** its inner portion almost certainly solid but its outer molten. This is surrounded by the **mantle,** which is heated to extremely high temperatures by the core. Most of its material is probably not liquid, but is still fluid enough to deform and flow very slowly. Overlying the mantle is a relatively very thin **crust,** consisting of the rigid rock of the seafloors and the continents.

A second, variant, classification is used here, and this also envisions three components. In addition to the core, there is the **asthenosphere** (Greek *"asthenes"* [weak], in allusion to the relatively more rigid layer overlying it), which includes almost all of the mantle of the first classification, and the **lithosphere** (Greek *"lithos"* [stone]), made up of the continental and oceanic crusts along with a very thin layer of partially molten mantle material immediately underlying these crusts.

Essentially all of the crust material is of volcanic origin, but that of the continents is primarily less-dense granitic rock and reworked lithic material from continental-plate volcanoes (see chapter 4), lighter in weight than the denser seafloor volcanic rock and thus tending to "float" higher above the upper asthenosphere than does the latter.

LITHOSPHERIC PLATES

Types

The movement of Africa and South America away from each other can be used to illustrate the concept of mobile **lithospheric plates.** Each of these continents along with its conjoined portion of Atlantic Ocean floor out to the midocean rift zone constitutes a separate lithospheric plate. Such continents firmly embedded in a partially surrounding area of seafloor have been aptly compared to a raft locked in the ice of a frozen river. About fourteen lithospheric plates are currently recognized (Figure 2.2). Their continental thickness has been estimated to range from about 55 to 100 km (34 to 62 miles). The conjoined ocean-floor portion as well as wholly oceanic plates are noticeably thinner, sometimes being as little as 5 km (3 miles) thick.

Motion

The rate of motion differs between plates, ranging from about 1 to more than 15 cm (about 0.4 to 6.0 inches) per year. Although it is possible that the partially molten underside of the lithosphere facilitates plate movement around the surface of the earth, just what causes this movement is unclear. Many geologists and geophysicists think the driving force may well be gigantic slow thermal convection currents in the underlying asthenosphere, produced as mobile material rises after being heated near the core, spreads under the lithosphere, then cools and sinks to repeat the cycle. All of the earth's plates are in at least relative motion with each other, even if one or two may not currently be in absolute motion.

Ocean Trenches

Especially important in formulating a plausible explanation of plate movement was oceanographers' knowledge that in various oceans there were exceptionally deep linear areas or trenches, the deepest probably being the Western Pacific's Marianas Trench, at places as much as 13 km (8 miles) deep. For some then-unknown reason, these were most often found extending along the convex ocean-facing side of curved strings of islands whose volcanic eruptions were typically quite explosive, such as those making up the Japanese and Aleutian chains (Figure 2.2). Also, it was noted that, enigmatically, zones of deep-seated earthquakes similarly closely parallelled the trenches.

Seafloor Age

In still another scientific field, investigators specializing in dating volcanic and sedimentary deposits had long been perplexed by the fact that, although they could date continental rocks to almost 4 billion years old, the oldest deep ocean-basin material found was less than 5 percent of that age: no more than about 180 million years. Certain perceptive researchers then realized that although seafloor was constantly being added to the earth's surface in some areas, it might also be seafloor—rather than continental land—that was being subtracted in others.

Subduction Zones

Ultimately, from consideration of all of the foregoing seemingly unrelated information regarding lithospheric plates—especially their ocean portions—scientists developed the concept of **subduction zones.** If the "leading" edge of an ocean-floor plate, expanding from a rift zone at its "trailing" edge, is colliding with the oceanic portion of a continent-bearing plate, the denser ocean-floor plate will be forced under the lighter continental one, forming a deep submarine trench along the line of contact, and will be destroyed as the subducting portion melts upon entering the asthenosphere (Plate 2.1, *A, B*). In other words, processes at ocean-plate margins are, indeed, responsible for essentially all of both the gain and the loss of surface area worldwide. And the time from midocean-rift origin to destructive subduction of such plates must be less than 180 million years or so, which would satisfactorily explain why no seafloor material older than this could be found. The relationship of the curved strings of volcanic islands and accompanying earthquake zones to subduction zones was also determined, as explained further in the next section.

PLATE COLLISIONS

There are at least three general possibilities that could result from plate collisions: (1) a volcanically active island arc will be formed, (2) a volcanic coastal or continent-edge mountain range will appear, or (3) a nonvolcanic interior continental mountain range will result. Formation of each is explained here in a greatly oversimplified fashion.

Island Arcs

As a moving ocean plate subducts beneath a peripheral submerged portion of a continental one, there is enormous friction between the surface of the ocean-plate lithosphere and the semiliquid undersurface of the continental-plate lithosphere. This causes the latter to fully melt and volcanically build up to the ocean surface all along the contact border, resulting in a line of volcanic islands situated on the continent side of, and paralleling, the deep-ocean trench. Because depression of a spherical surface such as the ocean plate always results in a circular concavity—as can be seen when pressing a tennis ball with a finger—the emergent volcanic material will be arranged in a curved line or island arc (Plate 2.1, *A*) with its concave side toward the continent. Two good examples in the Pacific Basin are the Aleutian and Japanese island chains, both formed by subduction of the Pacific Plate under the oceanic portion of the Eurasian Plate (Figure 2.2). In the instance of the collision of two wholly oceanic plates, one will subduct and an island arc will similarly be created. For instance, the subduction of the Pacific Plate beneath the Philippine Sea Plate formed the arcuate land pattern of the Mariana Islands apparent in Figures 2.2 and 24.1.

Coastal Mountain Ranges

If a continental plate with little or no peripheral submerged portion overrides, or is underridden by, a subducting oceanic plate, molten continental-plate material erupts through the overlying continental rocks to form a line of volcanically active mountains paralleling the coast (Plate 2.1, *B*). On the eastern rim of the Pacific, the Andes of South America have resulted from such tectonic action, as has also the more-or-less continuous string of western North American mountains that includes the Coast, Cascade, and Sierra Nevada Ranges. The Pacific Basin is often said to be encircled by a "Ring of Fire" because much of its rim contains strings of either island-arc volcanoes or coastal ranges of volcanically active mountains.

Interior Mountain Ranges

When the continental portions of two plates collide, neither subducts, but the enormous force they exert on one another causes a massive mountain range to build as the appressed plate margins buckle upward. The usual orientation of such a cordillera is perpendicular to the direction of plate movement, and the mountains are not volcanically active (Plate 2.1, *C*). Formation of the still-rising Tibetan Himalayas was initiated when the India portion of the vagrant Indian-Australian Plate collided with the Eurasian one (Figure 2.1)

SEISMOLOGY

Earthquakes

Most significant **earthquakes** or violent seismic (Greek *"seismos"* [earthquake]) activities are directly related to plate tectonics. Because the earth's lithospheric plates are in constant relative motion, the opposing margins of two may sometimes be sliding against one another along a **fault,** rather than directly colliding. Friction between them causes the apposed rocks to bind together, resulting in a gradual buildup of tension at the edge of each plate. Periodically, this tension becomes great enough either to break a large rock section or to cause one of the entire lithic units to suddenly slip along the fault. Such a violent movement is immediately radiated from this epicenter through the surrounding region as the shock waves of an earthquake.

Plate Rotation

Sliding-motion earthquakes also commonly occur in small portions of the same plate in the vicinity of midocean ridges, although such deep-ocean disturbances are seldom felt on land. Because the motion of all lithospheric plates is essentially one of rotation, with the pivot point or axis usually located outside the plate itself, the plate can be likened to a wedge-shaped segment of a turning phonograph record. The portions of the rotating plate farther from its axis must move faster than those located more proximally. But friction, contact with other plates, or additional factors often prevent all portions of a rotating plate from moving at the same angular velocity. As a result, certain concentric bands of plate material lag behind others until two adjacent ones break apart, and the more centrally located one periodically slips forward past the outer one, producing an earthquake. This unequal movement of concentric bands causes the originally linear rift along which the plate is forming to be broken into a zigzag pattern of short offset segments, quite obvious in the ocean rift zones of Figures 2.2 and 4.1.

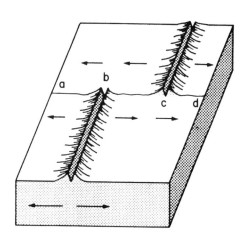

Figure 2.4. Seafloor movements along a transform fault. The two stippled grooves are offset segments of the same rift zone, and arrows show direction of plate spreading. Points b and c mark ends of a single transform fault, and a and d note proximal portions of the related fracture zone. (Adapted from Fig. 18.5 of Macdonald et al. [1983], used with permission of Frank L. Peterson.)

Fracture Zones

The fracture that extends between each of the pairs of dislocated rift segments is a **transform fault,** along which the plate material on either side is moving in opposite directions, as depicted in Figure 2.4. In this figure, the transform fault extends from point b to point c and is seismically quite active, as indicated by the concentrations of small seismic-activity dots along the ocean-rise transform faults in Figure 2.2. The infamous San Andreas Fault of coastal California is thought to be of this transform type, although it is located in a portion of the Pacific Plate currently elevated above sea level. Beyond each end of the transform fault shown in Figure 2.4, points a and d indicate the proximal portions of the two halves of a long, groovelike seafloor **fracture zone,** which is just a continuous vestige of the transform fault. The Pacific Plate fracture zones situated between western North America and the Hawaiian Archipelago are shown in Figure 4.1. Such zones are seismically inactive because, in contrast to the centrally located transform-fault portions, spreading plate material on either side of them is now moving in the same direction and at the same speed.

Subduction-Zone Earthquakes

A second common type of seismic activity associated with subducting ocean plates is typified by the major destructive earthquakes that frequently affect Japan and many other lands around the Pacific Rim. During subduction, violent earth tremors result as the upper surface of the moving ocean plate is compressed against the rigid crustal portion of the continental one and alternately seizes and suddenly releases. The relatively enormous number of earthquakes caused may be appreciated by noting in Figure 2.2 the great density of seismic-activity dots along, for example, the Kermadec-Tonga Trench of the Southwest Pacific. Thus, the distribution of this type of earthquake activity coincides with the Pacific Rim "Ring of Fire" (as well as with the Andesite Line to be discussed in chapter 4 on volcanism).

Other Earthquakes

Another type of earthquake associated with plate tectonics results from the opposing motion—more often in a vertical than a horizontal plane—of compressed faulting rock masses during the building of interior mountain ranges such as the Himalayas. There are also numbers of small earthquakes occurring relatively constantly all along midocean rift zones. Apparently, these are

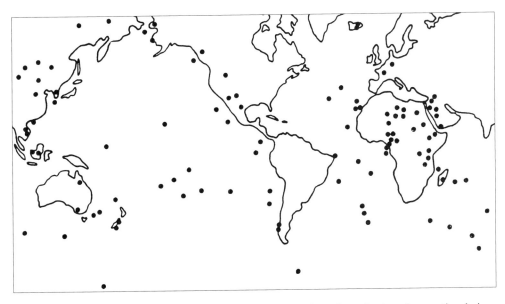

Figure 2.5. Known and suspected world hot spots. The dots indicate those that have been active during the past 10 million years. Not shown are about eleven additional hot spots on or near the Antarctic continent. (Fig. 43 of Erickson [1992]; copyright 1992 by Jon Erickson, used with permission of Facts On File, Inc.)

produced as some portions of previously hardened rock near the rift zone are forced away from others at slightly different rates by the new lava continually being extruded. Most remaining kinds of seismic movements are related to quite localized volcanic processes (chapters 4, 5), rather than to plate-tectonic phenomena.

HOT SPOTS

Lava Characteristics

Around the world there are currently over one hundred areas of localized volcanism that have been termed hot spots (Figure 2.5). The total amount of lava currently produced by these hot spots is relatively insignificant (although it was apparently considerably greater at various times in the very distant past), constituting probably less than 1 percent of all the volcanic material now being extruded worldwide. But such lava sources are of great relevance in the context of this book because they are responsible for the formation of a number of midocean island chains, including the Hawaiian Archipelago. The lava produced at a hot spot is usually quite fluid and can be distinguished from that extruded at either seafloor spreading rifts or subduction zones by its different chemical composition. Hot-spot magma is presumably received directly from a "plume" welling up from the core-asthenosphere boundary. Judging from the chemical discrepancy, this source is not the same as that providing magma for most portions of midocean rift zones.

Rifts

Through thermal expansion, the rising molten material of a hot spot causes a pronounced dome to form on an overlying plate's surface. This prominence either is eventually melted through or ruptures to produce rifts through which lava is extruded and built up into one or more active volcanic peaks. For reasons still somewhat obscure, the hot-spot rifts most often occur in a three-armed or "Y" pattern, less often in a two- or four-armed one. The significance of the positioning of hot-spot rift arms in relation to the distribution of primary eruption areas of Hawaiian volcanoes will become clear in chapter 4.

Stability

Only a few dozen of the so-called hot spots of Figure 2.5 appear to have remained relatively stationary, at least for many tens of millions of years (and many workers restrict application of the term to only these). These particular essentially immobile hot spots can thus be extremely important tools in determining the rate of movement of lithospheric plates throughout the world, including the one that forms a major portion of the Pacific Basin and bears the Hawaiian Islands.

RADIOMETRIC DATING

The ages of a few geologic events have already been mentioned, and many more such references are made in chapter 3 dealing with Hawaiian Archipelago formation, so a description is presented here of the method most commonly used to date ancient occurrences.

Half-Lives

Radiometric dating is based on the following principle. Many chemical elements occur in slightly differing physicochemical forms called isotopes, a few of which are radioactive. The latter isotopes are unstable, gradually but uniformly giving off subatomic particles as they "decay" into one or more nonradioactive isotopes of the same or different elements. The time required for half of a given amount of a "parent" radioactive isotope to decay into its "daughter" isotope(s) is known as its **half-life.** For elements existing naturally, rather than created in the laboratory, isotope half-lives range from a matter of months to thousands—or even millions or billions—of years. Radioactive decay of a given isotope occurs at a constant and well-known rate, so dating will be very precise if amounts of the isotope in a substance can be accurately measured.

Radiocarbon Dating

The radioactive carbon isotope ^{14}C has a half-life of 5,750 years in decaying to normal ^{12}C, the nonradioactive form of the element. The ratio of ^{14}C to ^{12}C in the atmosphere varies over time, but this ratio has been determined back for almost a dozen ^{14}C half-lives, and a calibration curve has been produced for use with tested material of different ages. Because all living plants and animals contain a substantial amount of carbon and constantly take in and give off this element as a constituent of chemical compounds produced throughout their lifetime, at any given time the ^{14}C:^{12}C ratio in their tissues is the same as that in the atmosphere. When an organism dies it ceases to take in carbon, and by the end of each succeeding 5,750-year period, half of the radioactive isotope ^{14}C originally in its tissues has decayed. In **radiocarbon dating,** a procedure known as mass spectrometry is used to measure the relative amount of the radioactive carbon isotope in the remains of the organism and, utilizing the calibration curve, quite accurately determine the time elapsed since its death. Although ^{14}C is a useful isotope for fixing the age of geologically relatively young material, because the ratio of ^{14}C to ^{12}C in nature is so low, the amount of the radioactive isotope left in dead organic material after only six or so half-lives is too small to measure accurately. Thus, satisfactory radiocarbon dating is limited to samples less than about 35,000 years old.

Potassium-Argon Dating

In radiometric dating of older material such as ancient lava, a frequently used isotope is one of potassium: ^{40}K, which has a precisely known half-life of over a billion years in decaying into calcium and normal argon gas, ^{40}Ar. ^{40}K is a constituent of newly formed lava, which contains essentially no argon gas because any that was present in the parent magma usually escaped when the liquid magma was extruded. The **potassium-argon (K-Ar)** dating method compares the ratio of subsequently produced trapped ^{40}Ar to remaining ^{40}K in a sample of lava to reveal the length of time since the lava was either originally erupted or last completely melted.

DENDROCHRONOLOGY

A quite different technique can often be used for dating rather recent events, although it is subject to a number of limitations in addition to those detailed here. **Dendrochronology** (Greek *"dendron"* [tree] and *"chronos"* [time]) involves dating by means of the trunk rings in well-preserved wood. Many tree species add a detectable peripheral growth area each year, and the thickness of this varies directly with the favorableness of the year's growing conditions. Thus, a trunk cross section shows a concentric series of growth rings of various thicknesses, and the same temporally unique ring-width sequence appears in most or all trees of the general region living during the same time period.

Even though very few types of trees live for a thousand or more years, the tree-ring sequences obtained from a number of successively older trunks of living and long-dead trees of a given region can be overlapped to form a continuous ring-width record extending back several thousand years (a 6,000-year sequence has been obtained for at least one continental area). The age, or age span, represented by a trunk section can then be determined exactly by fitting its particular ring-width sequence along this chronological gauge or template.

Unfortunately, dendrochronology cannot usually be employed in tropical and subtropical areas such as the Hawaiian Islands. Under the essentially continuous growing conditions provided by year-round warm temperatures and frequent rainfall, discrete tree rings are usually not discernible in most species. Even if obvious rings are formed in certain Hawaiian trees under particular topographic and climatic conditions, once they die their wood tends to rot quickly in the warm, moist environment or to be relatively quickly destroyed by insects, thus preventing extension of the requisite ring-width sequence back any significant number of years in the Islands.

SUGGESTED REFERENCES

Burke and Wilson 1976; Clague and Dalrymple 1987, 1989; Decker et al. (eds.) 1987; Macdonald et al. 1983.

AUDIOVISUAL AIDS

Earthquakes: Predicting the big one!; Earth science: Continental drift-theory of plate tectonics; Geology; Geology: Science studies the moving continents; History, layer by layer (earth and ocean); Inside Hawaiian volcanoes; Radioactive dating.

3

Hawaiian Archipelago Formation

The Hawaiian Archipelago comprises eight so-called **main islands,** which make up over 99 percent of the chain's emergent land area, and about the same number of clusters of small, mostly uninhabited low landmasses of the **Northwestern Hawaiian Islands** (see chapter 23). As shown in Figure 3.1, all these large and small islands form a long, essentially straight alignment, extending from the southeast to the northwest for approximately 2,400 km (1,500 miles). The nearest landmass outside the chain is isolated Johnston Atoll, about 800 km (500 miles) to the south of the center of the chain, with no continent closer than about 3,200 km (2,000 miles) (Frontispiece; Figure 11.1).

The profile at the top of Figure 3.1 shows that the individual Hawaiian Islands (or, occasionally, a small group of closely situated ones) are merely the emergent summits of enormous mountains whose bases are in the neighborhood of 5,000 m (16,500 feet) below sea level. This is also true of the lava foundation of the numerous sandy islets, shoals, and submerged banks making up the Northwestern Hawaiian Islands. These mountains are all volcanic peaks, although only on the southernmost main island, the "Big Island" of Hawai'i, is one currently erupting.

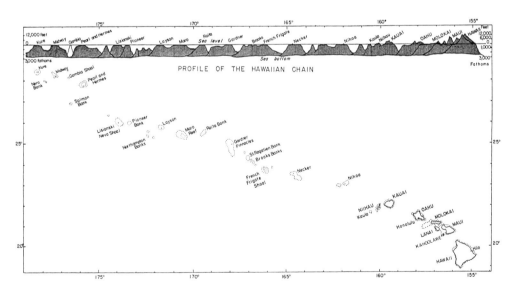

Figure 3.1. Islands, banks, reefs, and shoals of the Hawaiian chain. The vertical scale of the profile is exaggerated about twenty times. The distance from the center of Hawai'i to that of Kaua'i is approximately 515 km (320 miles). Dotted lines indicate the 180-m (595-foot) submarine contour around each island. (Unnumbered figure on p. 2 of E. H. Bryan Jr. [1954], used with permission of Bishop Museum Press.)

Table 3.1 lists the ages of the various islands; most of these ages were obtained using the potassium-argon radiometric procedure (see chapter 2). The islands become progressively and uniformly older as the chain is followed to the northwest, although the seafloor around each island is from 20 to 90 million years older than the island itself. The island age sequence as well as the discrepancies between island and seafloor ages will become clear in the following discussion.

HAWAIIAN HOT-SPOT VOLCANISM

Island-Chain Formation

The Hawaiian Islands were formed by the **Hawaiian hot spot,** currently centered at about the middle of the southeast coast of Hawai'i Island. Magma is emitted through a portion of the Pacific Plate that has taken about 20 million years to move northwest from its place of formation on the East Pacific Rise (see chapter 2). This newly extruded lava eventually builds up into a volcano that is steadily carried away from the hot spot as the plate moves toward its subduc-

Table 3.1. Radiometric ages of various Hawaiian islands. The ages (mostly obtained using the potassium-argon procedure) represent those of the oldest lava yet found on each island. The meaning and significance of the rejuvenation-lava ages are discussed in the text. A range of ages usually indicates testing of different major volcanoes on the same island. (Data primarily from Clague and Dalrymple [1987].)

Island	Age (in millions of years)
Hawai'i	0.00–0.60
Maui	1.00–1.75
	(rejuvenation lava <0.001–1.1)
Kaho'olawe	1.03
Lāna'i	1.60
Moloka'i	1.90–2.10
	(rejuvenation lava 0.4–0.5)
O'ahu	2.75–4.00
	(rejuvenation lava 0.006–0.8)
Kaua'i	5.25
	(rejuvenation lava 0.5–2.8)
Ni'ihau	5.55
	(rejuvenation lava 0.4–2.5)
Nihoa	7.50
Necker	10.7
La Pérouse Rock	12.4
Gardner Pinnacles	13.3
Laysan	20.2
Pearl and Hermes Reef	21.1
Midway Atoll	28.3

tion zone in the North Pacific (Figure 2.2). The stationary hot spot continues to extrude magma, but either the supply of this is sporadic or its flow to the surface of the plate is intermittently slowed or blocked. Thus, a line of discrete volcanic islands rather than a continuous ridge is produced.

Lōʻihi

In 1980, an actively building submarine volcano was found about 30 km (19 miles) off the southeastern coast of Hawaiʻi Island and was named **Lōʻihi** (Figure 5.1). Because Lōʻihi is only about 45 km (28 miles) from Kīlauea Volcano, and both are so actively adding lava to this region, it is quite possible that the facing slopes of these two young volcanoes will coalesce

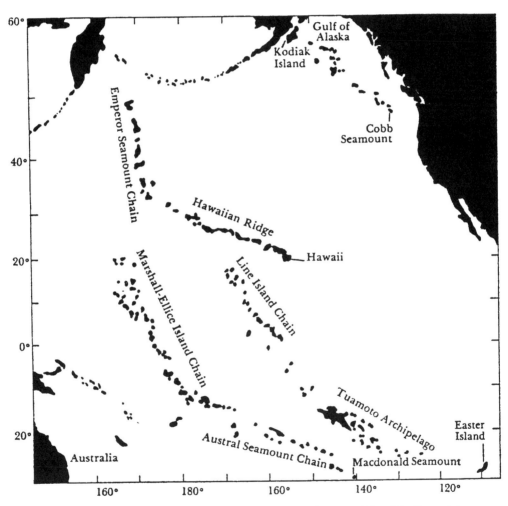

Figure 3.2. Island and seamount chains of the Pacific Plate. At the upper right of the figure, it is thought that the line of islands extending northwest and then north from the Cobb Seamount may also have been formed in the same manner as the central ocean-plate chains. (Fig. 10 of Dalrymple et al. [1973], used with permission of *American Scientist.*)

before Lō'ihi emerges above sea level. Lō'ihi would then form a sixth volcanic peak on Hawai'i rather than a separate island. Such submarine coalescence was probably the case with the other five volcanoes currently visible on Hawai'i, although the oldest (Kohala) could possibly have once constituted a distinct island.

Hot-Spot Conduits

The fact that Lō'ihi, Kīlauea, and neighboring Mauna Loa are all active at essentially the same time indicates that magma from a (presumed) single hot spot can simultaneously service more than one volcano. There could conceivably be some confluence of their magma conduits and thus intermixture of the magma supplying each volcano, although this has yet to be conclusively demonstrated. At any rate, each magma conduit initially leading directly vertically from the hot spot's opening in the ocean floor apparently remains open and capable of transmitting lava for perhaps a million years as it is being drawn out to the northwest by plate movement. Evidently, the magma in the conduit eventually cools enough to solidify, and the volcano to which the conduit leads becomes dormant and finally extinct. Before this happens, however, one or more newer conduits develop and provide magma to younger volcanoes located to the southeast.

EMPEROR SEAMOUNT CHAIN

Although only the islands from Hawai'i to Kure are shown in Figure 3.1, study of the North Pacific seafloor has shown that extending this so-called Hawaiian Ridge farther to the northwest are at least a half dozen submerged seamounts. From the northwesternmost of these a continuing line of still more seamounts undergoes a pronounced bend to the north, and these twenty-five or more similar structures form the **Emperor Seamount Chain** leading to the Pacific Plate subduction zone at the Aleutian Trench (Figure 3.2). The ages of lava dredged at selected seamounts of the ridge and chain progressively increase from about 30 million years just beyond Kure, through approximately 43 million years at the bend itself, to at least 75 or 80 million years near the Aleutian Trench.

Pacific Plate Rotation

Most investigators believe that the Emperor Seamounts represent earlier productions of the Hawaiian hot spot, with yet-older similarly submerged volcanic mountains already destroyed by progressive plate subduction. If this is correct, while a major portion of the Emperor Seamount chain was being developed, the location of the pivot point or rotational axis of the plate was such that they were transported in a rather northerly direction. A little over 40 million years ago, however, the plate axis shifted far northeast, from a little south of the tip of Baja California to just off the west coast of Greenland, so that the line described by all subsequently formed Hawaiian Islands extended in a northwesterly direction. It is not known for certain what caused the shift in rotational axis of the Pacific Plate, but it is suspected that the collision of the India portion of the Indian-Australian Plate with the Eurasian Plate (Figures 2.1, 2.2) somehow indirectly affected the directional movement of plates contiguous with one or both of them.

The orientation of at least two other isolated Pacific Plate island chains seems to support the theory of shift in rotational axis. These are the Tuamotu-Line Islands and the Austral-Marshall-Ellice Islands (Figure 3.2). Both are similar to the Hawaiian-Emperor chain in the exis-

tence of an active hot spot at the southeastern end and a linear arrangement of apparently successively older islands and seamounts stretching from southeast to northwest in the southern
segment, but abruptly bending more to the north near their midpoint. Their bend, like the
Hawaiian-Emperor one, is radiometrically dated at approximately 40 million years.

RATE OF PLATE MOVEMENT

Assuming the Hawaiian hot spot has remained essentially stationary during formation of the
Hawaiian-Emperor chain, at least a rough idea of the rate of Pacific Plate movement can be
obtained by dividing the distance between the hot spot and a particular included island or
seamount by the age of the latter. For example, Midway Atoll is about 2,500 km (1,550 miles)
from the hot spot, and its greatest radiometrically determined age is roughly 28 million years.
The pertinent division yields a plate-movement rate of a little under 9 cm (3.6 inches) per year.
The rates similarly obtained for approximately three dozen other islands and seamounts of the
chain average 8.6 cm (3.4 inches) per year, with most of the rates falling within about 10 percent of that figure. These rates, however, must be regarded as absolute maximum ones because
it is unlikely that in any case the oldest lava of each island was recovered for dating.

LAND–SEA LEVEL RELATIONSHIPS

Although present-day maps show that the main Hawaiian Islands comprise eight discrete major
landmasses, rather slight differences in levels of land and sea can easily alter this number in
the case of those islands separated by relatively shallow channels. Past changes in these levels
apparently spanned the surprising range of 365 m (1,205 feet) above current sea level to about
1,000 m (3,300 feet) below. Such changes can occur if the absolute elevation of the land fluctuates while that of the ocean remains constant, or vice versa. Or the two elevations may simultaneously move in opposite directions to produce the greater differences in relative levels.

Vertical Land Movements
In **tectonic** change, only the land varies in elevation. One tectonic-change type may be due to
thermal-expansion doming near a hot spot of the ancient ocean plate underlying an island and
subsequent lowering of the island as the plate cools and thins while moving away from the area.
A second type of tectonic change also of significance in the Hawaiian Islands is the initial
depression and eventual reelevation of the ocean plate under the great weight of a large volcano, which first builds on it and then slowly erodes away. This latter tectonic phenomenon, in
which the changing weight of an island is in equilibrium with the upward resisting force of the
underlying ocean plate at any given time, is usually subclassified as an **isostatic** (Greek *"isos"*
[equal] and *"statikos"* [causing to stand, or staying]) change.

Vertical Sea Movements
During **eustatic** (Greek *"eu"* [original] and *"statikos"*) changes, only the sea level fluctuates,
as when the oceans rise during interglacial or melting periods of continental ice sheets and fall
during glacial or accretion periods of the thick ice layers. To illustrate the potential magnitude
of eustatic change, if all the present-day glaciers melted, it has been estimated that the ocean
worldwide would rise 60 m (198 feet). And, because these continental ice sheets may have been

close to three times as large during some of their previous dozen or so maxima of the past 1.8 million years, eustatic changes were undoubtedly substantially greater then.

Effects on the Hawaiian Islands

The Hawaiian Islands have certainly undergone the first type of tectonic movement as they subsided while being carried away from the hot spot, but to what degree—and exactly when—they have also been simultaneously affected by the isostatic type of tectonic change is still not fully determined. At any rate, the *average* tectonic lowering apparent for all the main islands is about 2 cm (0.8 inches) per 1,000 years. In regard to eustatic changes, there seems to be general agreement that relative changes of sea level around the main islands in the range of at least 75 m (248 feet) above to possibly 90 m (297 feet) or more below the current ocean level have occurred during the past 2 million years or so.

During this time period if sea level rose only about 30 m (99 feet) the eastern and western halves of Maui would have become separate islands. Conversely, with a sea level drop of only 80 m (263 feet), the current islands of Maui, Lāna'i, and Moloka'i would have been consolidated; a fall of another 60 m (198 feet) would have added Kaho'olawe to this landmass. At least the first three of these four islands have been unified as a single one (informally called **"Maui Nui"** [Big Maui] (Figure 3.3), about half the size of current Hawai'i Island, at least once and possibly several times during their existence. The ocean around the older islands of O'ahu,

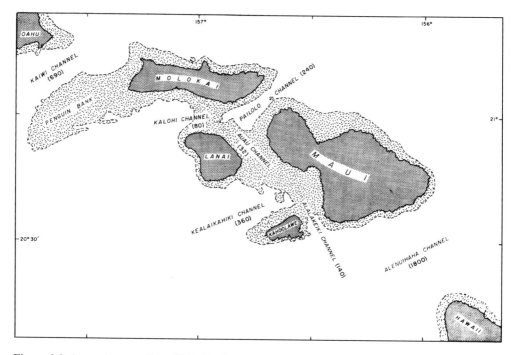

Figure 3.3. Approximate outline of Maui Nui (stippled area). This large ancient island was formed during the past 1 to 2 million years whenever relative sea level dropped at least 140 m (460 feet) below current height. The dashed line enclosing the stippled area is the 180-m (595-foot) submarine contour. Channel depths are in meters. (Fig. 20.1 of Macdonald et al. [1983], used with permission of Frank L. Peterson.)

Kaua'i, and Ni'ihau is deep enough to have prevented any similar coalitions among them during at least this period.

HAWAIIAN ISLAND LIFE HISTORY

The life-history sequence of a Hawaiian island from a deep submarine volcano to a drowned reef-topped island is depicted in Figure 3.4, but it must be emphasized that this is an idealized arrangement because some of the islands may not have undergone every one of the stages shown. The manner in which a single island can be formed from more than one volcano and attain its current physiographic characteristics is additionally illustrated by diagrams of O'ahu's geologic growth in Figure 3.5.

Deep Submarine Stage
Lō'ihi corresponds with the **Deep Submarine Stage** of Figure 3.4, *A*. It extends approximately 4,000 m (13,200 feet) above the ocean floor, with its summit currently about 950 m (3,135 feet) below sea level. The upward growth rate of a submarine volcano should be relatively rapid compared with that of a subaerial one because, upon contact with water under such high pressure, the extruded magma forms somewhat billowy or pillowlike dense lava masses that tend to pile up near the point of extrusion rather than flowing freely away. The exact growth rate of Lō'ihi has yet to be determined, but it probably at least equals that of the subaerial portions of Mauna Loa and Kīlauea, which average perhaps 1 to 2 cm (0.4 to 0.8 inches) per year. Thus, the newest Hawaiian volcano should appear above the sea in about 40,000 or 50,000 years, if not somewhat sooner.

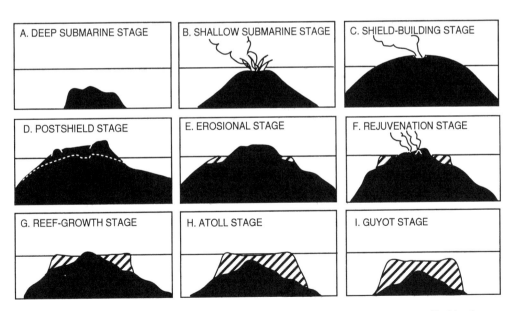

Figure 3.4. Idealized life history of a Hawaiian island. All of the stages except *B* are typified by the current islands and seamounts of the Hawaiian-Emperor chain. (Figure by Keith Krueger.)

Shallow Submarine Stage

When a submarine volcano has grown to within about 100 m (330 feet) of the ocean surface it enters the **Shallow Submarine Stage** (Figure 3.4, *B*). There is no Hawaiian volcano currently in this growth stage, but the well-studied activity of an Icelandic hot-spot volcano named Surtsey that reached sea level in the early 1960s may be used to illustrate it. As the summit nears the surface, the water pressure progressively decreases, so the steam and other gases in the magma can come out of solution. Seawater also contacts the extruding magma, producing enormous amounts of additional steam, and the combined pressure of the gases results in explosive eruptions. Contact of just-extruded lava with seawater fragments it into various-sized pieces, and great amounts of the sand-grain-sized ones are carried aloft by steam. This fine material then rains down from the steam clouds to pile up around the point of eruption, although initially most of it is washed away by waves soon after each eruptive episode.

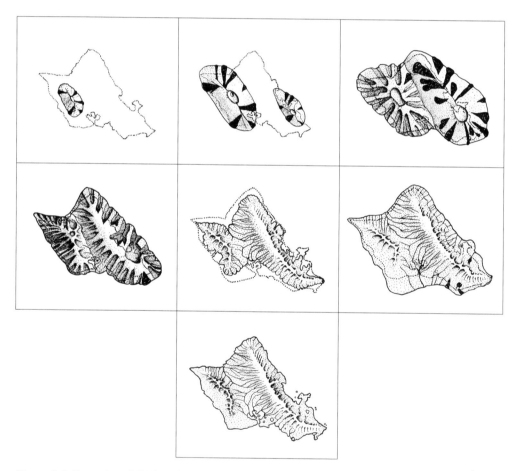

Figure 3.5. Formation of Oʻahu Island. This series shows the development of a Hawaiian island from the coalescence of more than one volcano. (Adapted from unnumbered figures on pp. 6–7 of Carlquist [1980], used with permission of the National Tropical Botanical Garden.)

Shield-Building Stage

Finally, however, the summit region of the emerging volcano broadens and its center builds far enough above the sea to prevent freshly extruded lava from being reached by the waves. The typical low, rounded, subaerial (above-sea) portion of a shield volcano is then able to grow from the almost countless thin flows of very fluid lava (Plate 4.1). This initiates an extended **Shield-building Stage** (Figure 3.4, *C*), which is exemplified by Kīlauea and Mauna Loa. It is usually the period of most active eruption—and growth—of an emergent island, with well over 95 percent of the subaerial volume of the volcano being produced. As the volcano continues to grow from summit flows, lava also increasingly begins to issue from often-numerous secondary openings along rift zones radiating great distances from the summit (Figure 3.6).

Also, as the volcano's mass increases, it isostatically subsides by downward deformation of the underlying ocean floor. The growing Hawai'i Island, for example, is sinking at an aver-

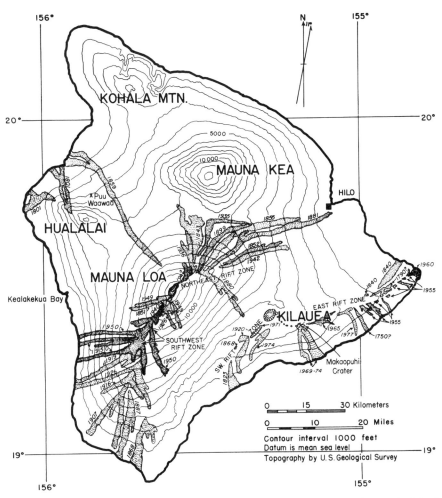

Figure 3.6. Topographic map of Hawai'i Island. Five major volcanoes making up the island are shown, as well as the locations and dates of lava flows occurring between about 1750 and 1977. (Fig. 3.2 of Macdonald et al. [1983], used with permission of Frank L. Peterson.)

age rate of about 0.35 cm (0.14 inches) yearly. In general, this subsidence progressively lessens substantially, but still continues (initially at perhaps 0.002 cm [0.008 inches] per year) after the volcanic island is carried slightly away from the mounded hot-spot area, as the moving ocean lithosphere itself continues to thin from its previous thermally induced thickness over the hot spot.

With time, periodic withdrawals of magma underlying the volcanic summit area cause its center to sink, after which lava rimming the depression may also sink in concentric rings, forming stairlike "step faults." This subsidence forms a broad caldera, such as that currently present on both Kīlauea and Mauna Loa. A caldera may never develop on some Island volcanoes, and the caldera of others can apparently disappear through lava filling, only to redevelop elsewhere in the summit area. Caldera formation may possibly begin much earlier than the Shield-building Stage, however, because very recent submarine photography reveals that Lōʻihi already has one or more large summit depressions. Calderas crowning Island volcanoes are usually quite impressive structures; that of Kīlauea is 3 km (1.9 miles) wide and 4 km (2.5 miles) long, and Mauna Loa's is 2.5 by 5 km (1.6 by 3.1 miles). The step faulting in both of these is quite obvious.

Postshield Stage

After perhaps a half million years of active subaerial growth, however, an Island volcano enters what may be considered its senescent period, during which eruptions become progressively less frequent and any caldera present slowly disappears, signifying the beginning of the **Postshield Stage** (Figure 3.4, *D*). The magma extruded gradually changes to a more viscous and dense type that, after filling in the caldera, continues to build up until the summit area itself has been extended noticeably above the now-buried caldera rim. The total amount of lava produced during this entire Postshield Stage is slight, however, probably amounting to only between 1 and 3 percent of the total subaerial volume of the volcano. The production of fair numbers of symmetrical cratered cinder cones both near the volcano's summit and scattered over its flanks (but not along the earlier rift zones) is frequently typical of postshield time. Mauna Kea on Hawaiʻi provides an excellent example of the Postshield Stage, and the numerous good-sized cinder cones are a conspicuous feature of its current summit and upper slopes (Plate 7.1). Hualālai of the same island has probably at least entered this stage.

Beginning at perhaps some point in the preceding Shield-building Stage, however, and continuing through at least the Postshield Stage, substantial parts of a volcano—sometimes as much as half of the subaerial volume—are periodically lost, as also depicted in Figure 3.4, *D*. Such diminutions are caused by truly giant earth slumps in which the ocean-facing slopes of the mountain massively slide into the sea, sometimes at avalanche speed (see chapter 5). Such dislocations are presumably usually triggered by a combination of swelling of the volcanic summit or flanks through magma injection and gravitational force on the continually thickening and unbuttressed slopes.

Erosional Stage

From the moment an Island volcano first appeared above the sea, water erosion as well as physical and chemical weathering have acted to wear down each new building lava flow. The net gain, however, only shifts to a net loss caused by these various destructive forces toward the end of the Postshield Stage. In the ensuing **Erosional Stage** (Figure 3.4, *E*), during which it has been estimated that the subaerial height of an Island volcano may sometimes be erosionally reduced at the geologically rapid rate of about 8 cm (3.2 inches) every 1,000 years, the volcanic slopes quickly begin to be deeply furrowed by stream channels.

Formation of soil through physical and chemical weathering of older lava (see chapter 5) also proceeds at a relatively swift pace. Erosion as well as extensive soil slumping and rock avalanches continue to move material to the lowlands, and in many places this erosion results in the formation of giant valleys (Plate 8.1). Also, especially during periods of heightened sea level, the ocean inexorably wears away at the volcano's lower flanks and levels off broad coastal areas while producing steep sea cliffs (Figure 6.5, Plate 6.1). Kohala Volcano (Figure 3.6) on northwestern Hawai'i is in the Erosional Stage.

The enormous depressed summit area of Maui's Haleakalā is often called a "crater," but, in reality, this developed its current form only during and after the Erosional Stage. Some geologists think the volcanic summit covering the ultimately filled caldera may originally have reached some 1,000 m (3,300 feet) higher than the mountain's current 3,055 m (10,082 feet), but others feel it was never significantly higher than at present. At any rate, eventual meeting of the heads of the two great stream-eroded valleys of Ke'anae and Kaupō during the Erosional Stage removed the caldera fill and cover, which left a new deep summit basin. Subsequent volcanic episodes beginning about 100,000 years ago largely filled this with lava flows and ash, and also produced the cinder cones now dotting the current basin floor.

Rejuvenation Stage

The islands of Maui, Moloka'i, O'ahu, Kaua'i, and Ni'ihau have all experienced eruptions during or after the late Erosional Stage, with one on million-year-old East Maui's Haleakalā occurring in historic time. Those of O'ahu's Ko'olau Volcano occurred between about 2.0 and 2.7 million years after the volcano first appeared above water, and those of Wai'ale'ale on Kaua'i at least 5.0 million years after emergence. Thus, even though an island may be as many as 5 million years old, it can still experience at least localized volcanic activity in the **Rejuvenation Stage** (Figure 3.4, *F*; sometimes called Posterosional Eruption Stage). This means that all main island volcanoes of at least Erosional-Stage age must be considered only dormant rather than extinct, including those of Lāna'i and Kaho'olawe, although these latter two have apparently never experienced Rejuvenation-Stage eruptions.

Incidentally, although subaerial eruptions of this stage on Maui, Moloka'i, O'ahu, Kaua'i, and Ni'ihau are geologically well documented, published reports of historic submarine eruptions between these islands, as well as farther northwest of Ni'ihau, are either in error or still subject to scientific confirmation. In one case, a reputed 1956 submarine eruption in the channel between O'ahu and Kaua'i was said to have produced masses of floating pumice and clouds of "sulfurous fumes." Upon testing, however, the recovered pumice proved to be from an earlier distant eruption off the Mexican coast. A little farther up the chain, what may have been a submarine eruption was said to have been witnessed a year earlier by passengers and crew of an airliner passing over a locality about 90 km (56 miles) east of 10.7-million-year-old Necker Island. Thus far, however, no physical evidence has come to light that either confirms or refutes this claim.

Hawaiian Rejuvenation-Stage eruptions usually consist of temporally and spatially limited episodes of isolated volcanic activity occurring on the heavily eroded lower slopes of old volcanoes. Their locations almost never show any relationship to the orientation of earlier volcanic rift zones. These eruptions often produce highly visible Island structures such as cinder cones, but in most cases do not significantly alter the overall shape of the original volcano. Apparently, although the hot-spot conduit to an island may have long ago been effectively plugged, some pockets of magma deep within various parts of a volcano remain molten for millions of years. These magmatic remnants occasionally come in contact with underground fresh- or saltwater, apparently either by rising toward the surface or more likely through subsidence of the island. The resulting eruptions are often quite explosive, and such an occurrence in a populated area today could cause considerable damage and possible loss of life.

On Oʻahu, these sporadic late eruptions began about 0.8 million years ago (Table 3.1, rejuvenation lava dates), with the most recent one possibly occurring as few as 6,000 years ago. Cratered cones resulting primarily from ash and cinder eruptions, such as Diamond Head, Punchbowl, and a number of others (Figure 5.5), were formed during this stage, but other Rejuvenation-Stage activity on both Oʻahu and other islands occasionally included substantial flows of quite fluid lava.

Reef-Growth Stage

In Figure 3.4, although the **Reef-growth Stage** *(G)* is placed after the Erosional and Rejuvenation Stages, it was proceeding simultaneously with them. Whenever the nearshore waters were free from destructive lava flows, extensive coral-algal growth (see chapter 11) encircling an island had been building a **fringing reef.** The portion of this reef closer to the shore, however, especially in areas where shallow water extends out considerable distances and seawater circulation is limited, may be retarded in growth by both freshwater runoff and the sediment it carries. The coral farther out along the seaward perimeter, though, grows more rapidly because of its proximity to clearer, freely circulating ocean water with more oxygen and nutrients. This latter coral forms a **barrier reef,** which often essentially reaches sea level, in contrast to the shoreward fringing-reef "floor," which may be from 3 to 30 m (9.9 to 99 feet) or more below the ocean surface. Around the main islands a barrier reef is best developed in Oʻahu's Kāneʻohe Bay, about 3 km (1.9 miles) offshore. In the Northwestern Hawaiian Islands, at least Nihoa and Necker with their limited amount of volcanic land still above sea level probably qualify for the Reef-growth Stage.

Atoll Stage

During the entire time a northwesterly moving Hawaiian island has been sinking as it moved off the thermally domed area at the hot spot, the surrounding coral-algal reef has been simultaneously growing upward; this growth is as much as 1.5 cm (0.6 inches) or more per year under the relatively favorable water temperatures and other conditions prevailing at the latitude of Hawaiʻi Island. This is more than enough to allow the living reef to maintain its upper level a little below the ocean surface as the sinking continues. As the island drifts farther north into colder water, reef growth progressively slows, but the reef has already attained a considerable thickness over the original volcanic base. For example, drilling at two localities on Midway Atoll revealed reef thicknesses of 155 and 378 m (512 and 1,247 feet).

When the last lava prominence of the island disappears beneath the sea through subsidence and subaerial erosion, it becomes covered with reef growth and the island enters the **Atoll Stage** (Figure 3.4, *H*). In place of the planed-down former summit area, there is now—ideally—only a shallow central reef basin with the higher peripheral barrier reef dropping off steeply into the surrounding ocean depths. The enclosed **lagoon** thus formed most often averages about 10 m (33 feet) in depth, with its deepest portions usually extending down no more than approximately 100 m (330 feet). Its geographic extent, however, is usually vast because its perimeter was originally determined by the shoreline shape of the island in its maximum growth stage. Such extensive shallow lagoon areas are also variously known as "banks," "reefs," or "shoals." Important **reef passages** allowing entrance of vessels into the calmer lagoon water are gaps and channels in the barrier and fringing reefs formed long before when watercourses of the volcanic island discharged substantial streams of sediment-laden fresh water into the immediate area, inhibiting reef growth.

In many instances, enough wave-broken reef fragments accumulate on higher segments of the barrier reef to build up slightly above the ocean surface. Still more coral-algal debris, along with sand and occasionally driftwood, then continue to increase the size and elevation of this incipient islet, and ocean birds as well as migratory shorebirds begin to use it for nesting or roosting. Plant seeds washed ashore or brought in by the birds begin to grow, and soon a small, vegetated sandy island has been formed. All of the islands thus developed, together with the lagoon around which they are arranged, make up an **atoll.** ("Atoll" is the term used for such an island-lagoon arrangement by Maldive Islanders of the Indian Ocean; this term quite possibly is the only Maldivian word to be used worldwide.) In other parts of Polynesia, where atolls are more prevalent than in Hawai'i, the atoll islands are called *motu,* of which the Hawaiian word *moku* (used for a district, island, section, fragment, or other delimited land entity) is a cognate. Hawaiian atolls—although seldom as symmetrical as in the idealized description given here—are represented by French Frigate Shoals, Maro Reef, Laysan and Lisianski Atolls, and Pearl and Hermes Reef, as well as Midway and Kure (Plate 3.1) Atolls, all in the Northwestern Chain (see chapter 23).

As long as at least a small volcanic part of an island remains above the sea, it is often informally termed a **"high island,"** to distinguish it from a sandy atoll *motu* or **"low island."** In regard to the locations of atolls worldwide, because the reef-building species of coral and many calcareous algae are warm-water organisms, atolls can only be formed from those oceanic-plate volcanoes situated in tropical or near-tropical waters. As a result of this temperature restraint, the current distribution of atolls is limited as follows: one in the open Atlantic Ocean, about twenty-five in the Caribbean, seventy-five in the Indian Ocean, and perhaps more than three hundred in the Pacific.

Guyot Stage

As a Hawaiian atoll continues its northwestward movement, ocean-water temperature steadily decreases, until the water becomes too cold (below approximately 20°C [68°F]) for reef growth to keep up with atoll subsidence. The usual reef wave-erosion rate of between 0.1 and 0.2 cm (0.04 and 0.08 inches) per year also continues, and the entire atoll sinks progressively farther beneath the surface. When the highest portion of the drowning atoll's reef reaches the critical lower limit of sufficient light for photosynthesis, the coral-algal growth finally ceases.

In terms of biological processes, this particular point of cessation of reef growth is a specific physiological one, rather than a fixed geographical one. That is, if the ocean warms through geologic time, the latitude where coral-algal growth stops moves correspondingly north; if the ocean cools, the pertinent latitude moves south (or the reverse of these directions in the Southern Hemisphere). This physiological boundary is so important in determining the eventual

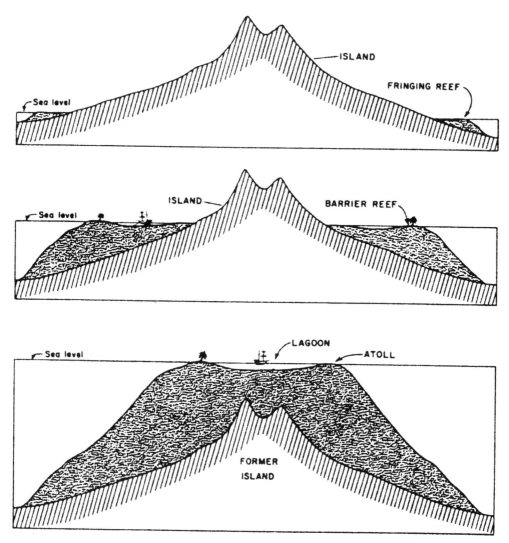

Figure 3.7. Progressive stages in atoll formation. The development of such a structure from a subsiding volcanic island and its surrounding coral-algal reef was correctly interpreted by Charles Darwin in 1839. (Slightly modified from Fig. 14.19 of Macdonald et al. [1983], used with permission of Frank L. Peterson.)

drowning of ocean-plate islands after the Atoll Stage that it has been given a special name: the **Darwin Point,** in recognition of Charles Darwin's important contribution in first envisioning the formation mechanics of atolls (Figure 3.7).

Moving past the Darwin Point, the drowned former atoll becomes a flat-topped seamount or **guyot** (Figure 3.4, *I;* named [indirectly] for Arnold H. Guyot, a nineteenth-century Swiss-American geologist and geographer). The current location of the Darwin Point is somewhere between the northernmost atoll, Kure, and the youngest guyot of substantial size, Hancock Seamount, less than 100 km (62 miles) to the northwest. Occasional seamounts are peaked rather than truncated, but these presumably represent submarine volcanoes that never reached the ocean surface before becoming extinct. There are almost three dozen guyots and peaked seamounts making up the northernmost part of the Hawaiian-Emperor Chain. This **Guyot Stage** represents the last change in the shape of a Hawaiian island until it melts upon subduction, and the Meiji Seamount is the one now poised on the brink of the Aleutian Trench just before being lost.

SUGGESTED REFERENCES

Burke and Wilson 1976; Carson and Clague 1995; Clague 1998; Clague and Dalrymple 1987, 1989; Dalrymple et al. 1973; Decker and Decker 1997; Decker et al. (eds.) 1987; Macdonald et al. 1983; Moore et al. 1994; Walker 1990.

AUDIOVISUAL AIDS

Earth science: Continental drift-theory of plate tectonics; Geology; Hawaii: A chain; Hawaii and planet Earth: The Hawaiian geography; Hawaii: Islands of the Fire Goddess; Hawaii's low islands; Inside Hawaiian volcanoes; Volcano Surtsey.

4

Volcanism

Volcanism is characteristic of three areas on the earth: subduction zones, hot spots, and midocean rifts.

LAVA COMPOSITION

The general chemical composition or mineral content of lava from each type of area tends to be distinctive, and the physical characteristics of lava extruded or hardened under various conditions may also differ. Thus, knowledge of these two qualities of volcanic material is extremely useful to geologists and volcanologists. For example, it may allow determination of locations and types of volcanic activity that cannot now be directly observed, as in the case of geologically long-extinct volcanic areas of the earth or possibly even on other planets. Further, for various reasons, lava produced during each of the developmental stages of at least hot-spot volcanoes (see chapter 3) is often chemically distinct also, so at least the relative age of an isolated lava sample from a particular volcano of Hawai'i and other hot-spot areas can usually be determined. Although not further discussed, the chemical and physical properties of lava also have a significant effect on how and at what rate the lava will be affected by various weathering processes.

In recent years, archaeologists working with geologists have been geochemically documenting artifactual raw material from specific prehistoric quarries or other exploited sources. This information is then used to trace previously unknown ancient trade routes involving this material by matching the composition of an excavated stone artifact with that unique to a particular source. Through this procedure Southeast Polynesian stone adzes from Henderson Island have been traced to a source on distant Pitcairn Island. And, within the Hawaiian Islands, material that must have been quarried on Kaho'olawe was found represented by prehistoric adzes on Kaua'i.

Andesite and Basalt

There are certain generalities that seem almost globally true regarding chemical composition of products from the three types of volcanic areas on earth. The magma produced by melting of the lower portion of a continental plate during subduction of an oceanic plate rises through the overlying portion of the plate, melting and incorporating sedimentary and earlier volcanic material as it ascends. As extruded lava, it thus tends to show relatively high amounts of the common continental-rock elements silicon, calcium, sodium, and potassium, along with relatively low amounts of iron and magnesium. This general type of continental igneous rock is termed **andesite,** in reference to the Andes Mountains, which are typical subduction-zone lava productions. If andesite occurrence is plotted in the Pacific Basin area, it is found to coincide with the Pacific "Ring of Fire" and the subduction-zone earthquake belt (see chapter 2), so this **Andesite Line** obviously outlines the junction of continental and ocean tectonic plates around this ocean (Figure 4.1). If subduction-zone magma solidifies within a continental plate instead of being extruded, granite is produced, so a large amount of continental crust is granitic.

The chemistry of magma welling up at hot spots differs slightly from that of ocean spreading zones, but both types usually contain less silicon as well as more iron and magnesium than does andesite. Volcanologists consider this general kind of lava chemically distinct enough from andesite to warrant a separate terminology, a major category of which is **basalt.**

There are several hundred kinds of volcanic rock recognized worldwide; most of their names are applied because of chemical composition, but some refer solely to the physical characteristics of a product regardless of chemical content. Dozens of these chemically differing lithic materials are commonly found in Hawai'i. In this book, however, it seems desirable to avoid overly involving readers in the complex field of geochemistry, but at the same time to have some convenient method of differentiating Hawaiian and other hot-spot lava and that from mid-ocean rifts from that of subduction zones in discussions. Thus, in most cases, the term "basalt" is used here in an overly broad and sometimes technically incorrect manner for the hot-spot and midocean rift products, and "andesite" is similarly used for all subduction-zone lava.

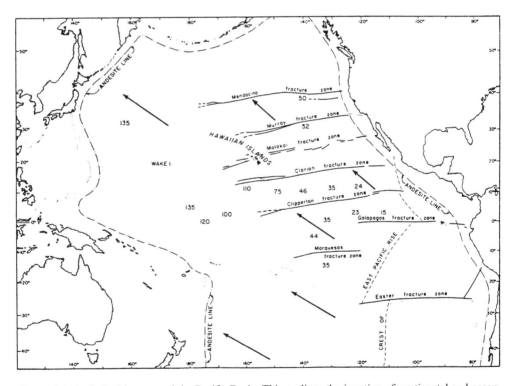

Figure 4.1. Andesite Line around the Pacific Basin. This outlines the junction of continental and ocean tectonic plates here. The solid line between offset portions of the dashed East Pacific Rise in the Easter, Galápagos, and Clipperton Fracture Zones is a transform fault (see Figure 2.4). Arrows indicate the current direction of Pacific Plate movement, and numbers give the age in millions of years of the oldest ocean sediments on various portions. (Slightly modified from Fig. 18.9 of Macdonald et al. [1983], used with permission of Frank L. Peterson.)

Magmatic Gases

All types of magma contain dissolved gases, although most of these escape when the magma is extruded. The most abundant is steam, constituting up to 70 percent of the gas content, with nitrogen and carbon dioxide (both odorless), hydrogen sulfide (with a "rotten egg" scent), sulfur dioxide (causing a choking sensation when inhaled), and a few trace gases making up the remainder. It is the amount of dissolved gas—especially steam—in combination with magma viscosity (often directly related to chemical composition) that primarily determines the type and force of a volcanic eruption.

VOLCANIC STRUCTURE

Little is known of the structure and eruption mechanics of volcanic sites along the deep-ocean spreading zones, but many of these characteristics of both subduction-zone and hot-spot volcanoes have been well studied. A typical volcano (Figure 4.2) possesses a **magma chamber** or reservoir, possibly sometimes being simply a pool of magma but more often likely consisting of a great mass of rather "spongy" rock material, saturated with fluid or semifluid molten material. A long linear passage connects an extensive underlying deep source of magma with this chamber, and a **pipe conduit** forms the final path from the chamber to a summit **vent.** The generally circular depression surrounding the vent is a **crater,** and, by one often-observed convention, a summit crater more than about 1.6 km (1.0 miles) in diameter is called a **caldera.**

Swelling of the chamber as it is filled with upwardly forced magma, along with some accompanying thermal expansion of the surrounding earth, often causes cracks through which magma is forced away from the chamber other than through the pipe conduit. Those cracks

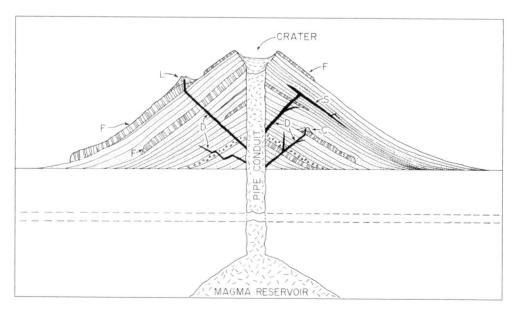

Figure 4.2. Cross section of a typical volcano. Shown in this idealized subduction-zone volcano are *(D)*, vertical dikes; *(S)*, a horizontal sill; *(F)*, various lava flows; and *(L)*, a flank cone. Also indicated is *(C)*, an old now-buried flank cone. (Fig. 7.2 of Macdonald et al. [1983], used with permission of Frank L. Peterson.)

leading more-or-less vertically are **dikes,** and those extending rather horizontally are **sills.** Dikes usually occur in large numbers, and these **dike swarms** may form a conspicuous topographic feature when exposed in excavations (Figure 4.3). Some magma moving through dikes or sills may reach the caldera but most attains the surface on the slopes of the volcano, producing **flank eruptions** and cones (Figure 4.2).

COMPOSITE VOLCANOES

Shape

Subduction-zone volcanoes are characterized by their generally well-recognized shape; Fuji-yama or Fuji-san of Japan's Honshu Island is a familiar example. Such volcanoes appear relatively tall, with a somewhat limited summit depression surrounding the vent and slopes that are usually slightly concave upward, often forming an angle as great as 30 or 35 degrees with the horizontal (Figure 4.4). This steepness occurs because of the alternation between expulsion of solid heat-fractured or pyroclastic lithic material and flows of relatively fluid lava that plaster this over and prevent it from slumping. The dual nature of the erupted material constituting the stratified cone is responsible for the term **composite volcano** (or stratovolcano). Another distinctive characteristic of these continental-plate volcanoes is their lack of extended eruptive rift zones radiating from the summit.

Figure 4.3. Part of a volcanic dike swarm. The feature shown is exposed in a road cut on Windward Oʻahu. The individual dikes are the vertical darker columns in the lighter-colored volcanically derived soil. (Photograph by Frank L. Peterson, used with permission.)

Eruption Mechanics

Most people around the world envision volcanic action as enormous periodic explosions, hurling molten lava and other **ejecta** (when solid, alternatively called tephra or pyroclastic rock) for great distances. Although this is not typical of Hawaiian volcanism, it is often true of the actions of the subduction-zone volcanoes of island arcs and continents. Magma already in a chamber is kept under constant pressure by additional magma being forced up from below, and the gases dissolved in the molten material cannot expand as long as this pressure is maintained. The containment of the chamber magma is often brought about through occlusion of the pipe conduit and dikes by semifluid magma or solidified lava. If the opposing pressure of such blockage is somehow overcome, the dissolved gases begin to come out of solution, and these can expand to between 100 and 150 times the volume of the magma that contained them. This increasing gas pressure then serves to propel the molten rock through any opening to the surface with tremendous force. The pressure continues to build as ever-decreasing external pressure allows the gases to expand even more, thus accelerating the continuing magma expulsion.

This gas-release phenomenon is sometimes aptly termed the **"soda pop model,"** in which the erupting lava is likened to a carbonated beverage spewing from its container under pressure of dissolved carbon dioxide that immediately begins to come out of solution when the cap is removed. One of the more spectacular types of subduction-zone volcanic eruptions is the dangerous *"nuée ardente"* (French [glowing cloud]): a particularly destructive flow of super-heated minute bits of lava that glides down a volcano's slope on a cushion of gas escaping from the particles along with suddenly heated underlying air. Such a red-hot stream can reach down-slope speeds of between 160 and 450 km (100 and 280 miles) per hour, depending on variation of the eruptive angle between vertical and horizontal.

The above-surface activity of composite volcanoes may take a number of other quite varied forms. Subduction-zone magma tends to be of relatively great viscosity due primarily to its high silicon content, so eruptions also involving a high steam content can be truly cataclysmic, often including solid material of substantial bulk torn off the walls of subterranean passages. Volcanologists have applied different terms to various types of these catastrophic eruptions. These may be based on the name of a volcano typically showing the particular action ("Vulcanian" for the Italian Mount Vulcano, and "Peléan" for Mont Pelée of Martinique in the Caribbean), or on its location ("Strombolian" for the Italian volcanic island of Stromboli), or

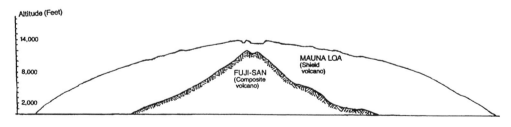

Figure 4.4. Comparison of typical volcano profiles. Note, especially, the steep and upwardly concave slopes of the composite or subduction-zone volcano, and the substantially flatter and upwardly convex slopes of the shield or hot-spot one. (Adapted from unnumbered figure on p. 25 of Decker and Decker [1997], used with permission of Hawaii Natural History Association.)

even on a historical personage associated with a particular type of eruption ("Plinian" for the Roman naturalist Pliny the Elder, killed while investigating an especially violent eruption of Mount Vesuvius in A.D. 79). Sometimes, however, eruptions may consist of only quiet flows of quite fluid lava, or of long-continued production of simply a column of smoke or very fine ash, and so on. Obviously, though, the initiation of any activity by a subduction-zone volcano should always be considered at least potentially dangerous.

SHIELD VOLCANOES

Shape
Hot-spot volcanoes differ markedly from subduction-zone volcanoes in external shape (Figure 4.4). The general subaerial profile is relatively low and broad, with slopes inclined at angles as small as 6 to 12 degrees and usually showing a slight upwardly convex curve, with the entire summit region occasionally rather flattened or even somewhat depressed. The slopes built up below sea level are steeper than the ones above, but are still of a noticeably lesser inclination than the subaerial ones of composite volcanoes. The fancied resemblance of the above-sea shape of hot-spot volcanoes to an ancient low-domed Teutonic battle shield lying face up led to the name **shield volcano.**

The distinctive subaerial shield-volcano profile is primarily the result of the relatively non-viscous nature of the low-silicon magma extruded throughout most of the volcano's active life, as well as the usual lack of solid ejecta. This type of lava yields very fluid flows that tend to spread out in thin sheets rather widely from the vent (Plate 4.1). The depressed summit area usually evident during the primary growth stages is the result of repeated caldera collapse.

It is interesting that, because the subaerial slopes of a mature shield volcano like Hawai'i Island's Mauna Loa are so gentle and extend so far in every direction, it is difficult to discern that it is actually a volcano. The first-time visitor looking in the direction of the immense mountain from a vantage point on neighboring Mauna Kea, probably expecting to see the familiar shape of a composite volcanic cone, is usually quick to ask "Where's the volcano?"

Size
Shield volcanoes visible above the ocean surface are usually truly enormous structures. Mauna Kea and Mauna Loa extend over 4,100 m (13,450 feet) above sea level and, because the base of Hawai'i Island is about 5,000 m (16,400 feet) below sea level, the total distance these volcanoes have built up is at least 9,000 m (29,500 feet). For those who prefer to measure the height of mountains by the distance above the seafloor, both of these Hawaiian mountains exceed the height above sea level of nonvolcanic Mount Everest by about 300 m (1,000 feet). Measured in this manner, Mauna Loa is not only the second tallest mountain in the world (after Mauna Kea), but it is probably also the largest in volume, having one hundred times the bulk of, for example, the good-sized Fuji-san (Figure 4.4).

Rift Zones
Early in its history, a shield volcano characteristically develops rift zones in the form of two to four long, deep cracks radiating from its summit. All of the eruption types seen at the caldera can also occur anywhere along these rift zones. In fact, the rift-zone eruptive activities ulti-

mately produce so much lava that the volcano's shape, viewed from above (Figure 5.1), is quite asymmetrical compared with the typically circular outline of a composite volcano. The rift zones also extend the already extremely broad profile of a shield volcano.

Eruptions

The gas content of magma involved in at least early eruptions of Hawaiian volcanoes may sometimes be almost as high as that in most subduction-zone volcanoes, and so the very fluid lava can be thrown to great heights as it is extruded. When the point of such ejection is a single vent, a "fire fountain" can hurl lava as high as 600 m (1,980 feet) for days on end. When this occurs along extended sections of a rift zone, a spectacular "curtain of fire" is produced.

Usually, however, the gas content is significantly lower than that of subduction-zone magma. This characteristic, along with the low viscosity of hot-spot magma, prevents most cataclysmic explosions related to sudden unplugging of conduits and explosive ejection of huge amounts of high-viscosity lava and pyroclastic rock. The difference in force and danger of eruptions of the two volcano types may best be illustrated by an analogy. If dry oatmeal is stirred into a pan of boiling water, the escaping bubbles of steam at first cause no significant spattering of the thin mixture, which corresponds to hot-spot magma. After it thickens, however, the mixture can be considered to represent subduction-zone magma, because the same amount of escaping steam causes violent and potentially injurious ejection of semisolid material from the cooking vessel.

Mauna Loa and Kīlauea are two of the four Island volcanoes known to have erupted since the 1778 arrival of the first recorded non-Polynesian, the English explorer Captain James Cook (see chapter 25). Mauna Loa's most recent eruption occurred in 1984, and in the past 100 years lava flows have added an impressive 1.8 m (6.0 feet) of height to certain slope areas. The activity of Kīlauea has been especially striking since Mauna Loa's latest eruption, particularly along its east rift zone. Here, voluminous lava flows, many reaching the ocean, have caused extensive property loss among historic structures as well as destruction of a number of prehistoric Hawaiian coastal sites. The other two volcanoes with post-1778 eruptions are Hualālai, also on Hawai'i, 1800–1801 (Figure 3.6), and Maui's Haleakalā, about 1790 (see chapter 5).

Flowing lava is not the only hazard associated with Hawaiian volcanic activity. During an apparent hydromagmatic eruption (see below) of Halema'uma'u Crater in Kīlauea's caldera about 1790, part of the army of the South Hawai'i chief Keōua, comprising probably several hundred warriors along with family members and domestic animals, set out on a well-used trail along the southwest rift zone. A few hours later a following unit found the entire group of people dead on the line of march, with no external injuries, although some of the accompanying pigs were still alive. Because of the lack of injuries, it seems that eruption of possibly either or both suffocating fine ash and accompanying poisonous gas was responsible for this tragedy. Incidentally, in several areas along that trail, human footprints left in various layers of this same type of fine ash and preserved by eventual natural cementing are often pointed out as those of the ill-fated military group, although many could just as well be of earlier or later travelers that frequently passed that way.

Magma-Water Reactions

A rather special type of volcanic explosion that may occur at either subduction-zone or hot-spot volcanoes is especially characteristic of Hawaiian Rejuvenation-Stage eruptions (see chapter 3). If contact is made between a shallowly buried magma pocket and a substantial quantity of underground water, the sudden generation of steam often provides enough pressure to produce an explosion reaching the surface, occasionally a quite destructive one. Such water-related eruptions are called **hydromagmatic** if magma is erupted along with the cloud of steam, mud, and pyroclastic debris, or **phreatic** (Greek *"phreatos"* [of a well]) if little or no magma accompanies the eruption. Either kind may at times result in the seemingly anomalous expulsion of nonvolcanic substrate fragments as, for example, when a surface or buried fossil coral-algal reef happens to overlie the magma pocket.

ERUPTION "FORECASTING"

The eruption of a volcano is often initiated by a completely unpredictable event, such as a landslide near the summit, a great influx of magma from the source deep below the chamber, or (rarely) by some external force as slight as an increase in the gravitational tidal pull of the sun and moon. The great 1980 eruption of Mount St. Helens in the northwestern United States was set off by a major landslide involving a third of the mountain summit, which released the pressure on the volcano's magma chamber. In other instances, however, potentially imminent eruptions can be accurately predicted. Scientists working at a number of volcano study centers such as Hawaiian Volcano Observatory, of the U.S. Geological Survey, on Kīlauca's caldera rim have had a large measure of success in such forecasting.

This forecasting is based on observations considered to have indicated, primarily, underground magmatic activity preceding past eruptions. When additional magma moves into a chamber, the upper portion of the volcanic cone begins to swell, thus increasing slope angle and summit width. This movement, called tumescence, can be detected by accurate survey equipment, including a **tiltmeter.** The instrument operates on the same principle as a carpenter's water-bubble level, but is sensitive enough to measure a change of 0.1 cm (0.04 inches) per km (0.6 miles) of slope. Minute changes in distance across a caldera can be detected and measured by use of a **geodimeter,** originally simply a very long wire or tape stretched across the depression, but now replaced by more efficient laser-beam instruments.

Two types of subterranean earth movements also signal the possibility of an impending eruption, and both of these are detected and monitored with a **seismograph.** The swelling of a volcano often leads to a number of discrete, mostly small, earth movements collectively called an **earthquake swarm,** caused by frequent displacements of rock units along underground faults (see chapter 2). In addition, the renewed movement of magma in subterranean passages produces a distinctive series of often long-continued small-magnitude seismic disturbances, usually referred to as **harmonic tremor.**

VOLCANIC PRODUCTS

Many of the same volcanic products result from various eruptions of both hot-spot and subduction-zone volcanoes. As previously noted, the term "ejecta" is used here to include all fluid or solid material thrown out by a volcano. Fluid ejecta that solidifies before it reaches the ground, if classified by size, is either **ash** (with particles up to about rice-grain size), **lapilli** (Italian [little stones] to about golf-ball size), or rounded **bombs** and angular **blocks** (up to the size of a house).

When classified by physical character, hardened fluid ejecta fragments of any size that are of a quite porous and relatively lightweight nature are usually called **cinder** or scoria (Latin [slag]). Smaller teardrop-shaped lapilli with glassy black exteriors, formed from quickly cooled high-flung magma, are sometimes found in great numbers around an eruption site. Because Pele is the Hawaiian goddess of volcanoes, these are known in the Islands as "Pele's tears" (Figure 4.5). When exceptionally fluid magma is thrown high into the air it is often drawn into long, golden brown glasslike threads ("Pele's hair"). These may drift on the wind for 50 km (31 miles) or more before descending, then appearing like glistening cobwebs spread over the surface or collected into small windrows.

At times, forcefully ejected magma is still somewhat plastic when it falls to earth, and the various-sized pieces may flatten and build up on one another to form **spatter,** with larger isolated units often descriptively called "cow-dung bombs." When erupted magma is exceptionally gas-laden, the cinderlike product **pumice** may sometimes result. This is so filled with gas cavities that most types will float in water, and eruptions taking place in very shallow ocean-floor sites are often detected through pumice masses washing up on beaches. Thick layers of ash usually become cemented after a period of years, forming a weakly to strongly consolidated lithic material known as **tuff** (Latin *"tofus"* [a soft porous rock]).

Volcanic Glass

If extruded lava is cooled very rapidly, the growth of macroscopic crystals usually found in slower-cooling material is terminated, and the resultant product is glasslike. An appropriate analogy is that of pouring chocolate fudge on a cold marble slab immediately after removing it from heat, with the rapid cooling preventing formation of large sugar crystals and also producing a shiny exposed surface. In the case of basalt, this blackish opaque material is usually called **volcanic glass,** and the equivalent product of andesite is called obsidian (and may occur in a variety of colors, including green and red).

Lava-Flow Types

The particular flow mechanics of molten lava yields two noticeably different physical forms of hardened material: *pāhoehoe* and *'a'ā* lava (Plate 4.2). It is interesting that these same Hawaiian words—without the diacritical marks—have been adopted by most volcanologists to describe identical flow types around the world. *Pāhoehoe* is a solid lava sheet, often possessing many lobular marginal extensions called "toes" and sometimes twisted into great ropy masses. It typically has an extremely thin, shiny surface layer of volcanic glass. An *'a'ā* flow, on the other hand, consists of a jumble of separate rough-surfaced clinkerlike elements, from the size of pebbles to boulders, mostly lacking a volcanic-glass coating.

In forming *pāhoehoe,* lava maintains its smooth flow movement until it solidifies, but the mechanics of *'a'ā* formation are still subject to some debate. A reasonable explanation often offered is that extruded lava initially flowing smoothly in the form of *pāhoehoe* is somehow caused to begin "tumbling," as when slowed by some obstacle or when dropping over a small precipice, in the process breaking into fragments that each quickly harden and coat the flow's core. Regardless of formation method, however, an *'a'ā* flow is propelled by the hidden, barely molten lava core, which slowly advances by riding on the hardened fragments being dragged over and under its leading edge, much like a tank moves forward on its continuous track. Macroscopically, the internal structure of *pāhoehoe* displays gas cavities or vesicles of a quite regular spherical shape; those in *'a'ā* are usually greatly deformed as a result of the lava fragments' distortion due to continued plastic flow immediately before hardening.

Pillow Lava

Lava that results from either submarine extrusion of magma or flow of fluid lava into water under certain conditions is termed **pillow lava.** The issuing magma or flowing lava is almost immediately hardened (without a steam explosion) into rounded, often discrete billowy masses up to about 4 m (13 feet) in length and diameter. Macroscopic vesicles are absent in at least deep-submarine pillow lava because the great hydrostatic pressure prevents gas expansion in the extruded magma before it solidifies. Discovery of a pillow-lava outcrop at a site far from an ocean or body of fresh water obviously reveals that such an aquatic environment once existed there.

Columnar Lava

Another occasionally seen type of volcanic product consists of clusters of usually upright lava prisms, most often hexagonal, each up to about 1 m (3.3 feet) in thickness. The columnar configuration results when the interior of an exceptionally massive lava flow remains undisturbed as it slowly cools. Substantial shrinkage occurs, causing cracks or "joints" to develop and extend

Figure 4.5. Two eruption products of very fluid magma. *Left,* "Pele's tears"; *right,* "Pele's hair." Both of these are frequently found in the vicinity of active Kīlauea Volcano on Hawai'i. The coin diameter is 1.8 cm (0.7 inches). (Photograph by Frank L. Peterson, used with permission.)

through the flow at roughly right angles to the coolest surface, in somewhat the same manner that polygons of hardened earth are formed from a deep layer of mud in drying and shrinking. One well-known columnar basalt formation is the "Devils Postpile" of California, and such material is conveniently accessible to viewers on Hawai'i at the area called "Boiling Pots" along the Wailuku River near Hilo, and on Kaua'i just inland from the dock at Nāwiliwili.

SUGGESTED REFERENCES

Decker and Decker 1997; Macdonald et al. 1983; Sinton and Sinoto 1997; Time-Life Books 1982.

AUDIOVISUAL AIDS

Eruption at the sea; Fire under the sea: The origin of pillow lava; Hawaii: Born of fire; Hawaii: Volcanoes; Heartbeat of a volcano; Inside Hawaiian volcanoes; Volcano.

Hawaiian Topography

In 1840, the renowned American geologist James D. Dana (see chapter 28) correctly deduced that the main Hawaiian Islands decreased in age from northwest to southeast by observing the lessening degree of erosion of volcanic peaks from Kauaʻi to Hawaiʻi. But, in antiquity, Hawaiians had already recognized the same age sequence and explained it in various versions of the **Pele legend.**

PELE'S WORK

The volcano goddess and her family emigrated from Kahiki (literally Tahiti, but also used for a distant mythical land) and first landed on Niʻihau. Pele dug to establish the family home and kindle her volcanic fires, but groundwater rose in the pit and extinguished the flames. She then continued these efforts south through the islands with the same result. Finally, however, on Hawaiʻi, pits dug in both Mauna Loa's caldera Mokuʻāweoweo and the "Fire Pit" Halemaʻumaʻu of Kīlauea's caldera remained free of water, so Pele was able to establish permanent fiery homes there.

The natural antipathy between forces of fire and water frequently appears in traditional folklore around the world. It is interesting that in Hawaiian legends this same antagonistic relationship is acknowledged not only in the extinguishing of Pele's fires but also in repeated instances of conflict between her family and *moʻo* or dragons (see chapter 19) typically closely associated with water (see, for example, the meanings of Mōʻiliʻili and Mokoliʻi in the Glossary).

Pele's flooded earlier residences may be seen in such forms as Oʻahu's **Salt Lake** (Figure 8.5; originally Āliapaʻakai, once 1.5 km or 0.9 miles in diameter but now mostly filled for a golf course) and the pond-bottomed 300-m-(990-foot-)deep crater of Kauhakō (Lua o Pele or "Pele's Pit") on Kalaupapa Peninsula of Molokaʻi. Because Pele dug deep in her searches, it is not surprising that legend held that Salt Lake was bottomless, so the geologist Dana had a canoe carried up from the coast and paddled to the lake center with the longest sounding line he could find. He lowered the line only to discover that the deepest point measured 0.4 m (1.3 feet). Hawaiian legends are always interesting and are certainly worth studying because of their value in providing information on many aspects of ancient Hawaiian life not available from any other source. Obviously, however, not all can be accepted uncritically.

RIFT ZONES

Lines of cinder or spatter cones in the southeastern portion of Hawaiʻi Island are also said to be the mid-fourteenth-century work of Pele: some of these are masses of molten lava she hurled at a fleeing chief, Kahawali, who had displeased her. Such linear arrangements of cones usually trace the rift of a Hawaiian volcano, although most rift-zone activity is usually much more extensive. Rift zones on Hawai'i are shown in Figure 5.1, but certain of these are not especially obvious in the field because they have been obscured by lava flows of younger volcanoes. For example, the south rift of Mauna Kea is covered by Mauna Loa's flows, with the latter lavas that abut the older mountain forming the broad **Humu'ula Saddle** or "Saddle Area" between the two peaks at about 1,800 m (5,940 feet).

O'ahu shows an extreme development of rift zones; apart from the immediate volcanic summit areas (Figure 5.2), the entire Ko'olau and Wai'anae Ranges were formed by rift erup-

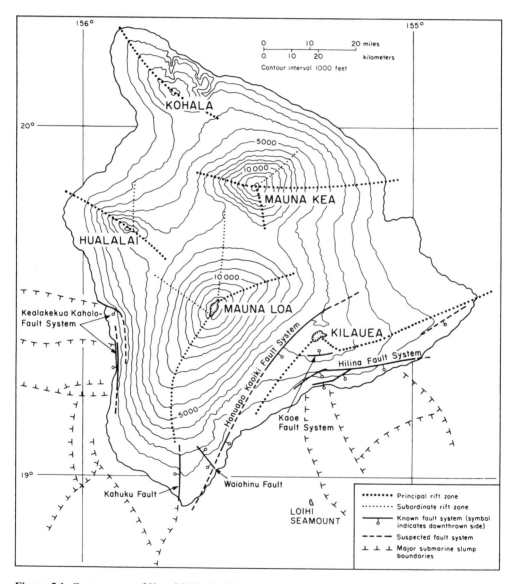

Figure 5.1. Contour map of Hawai'i Island. Volcanic rift zones and tangential faults on land, as well as submarine slumps and the location of the submarine volcano Lō'ihi are also shown. (Fig. 19.6 of Macdonald et al. [1983], used with permission of Frank L. Peterson.)

tions. Lava flowing west from the Koʻolau summit and rift zone partially covered the eastern slopes of the older Waiʻanae Range (Figure 3.5), producing the elevated Schofield Plateau. The summit areas of these two volcanoes, on each of which two or more calderas formed at different times, are no longer present, but quite likely reached between 3,050 and 4,575 m (10,000 and 15,000 feet) above sea level at maximum volcano growth. The upper subaerial two-thirds or more of each volcano, however, was subsequently lost to giant land slumps (see next section), erosion, and island subsidence (see chapter 3).

PALI, FAULTS, AND MASSIVE SLUMPS

Especially noticeable on the south and southeast slopes of Kīlauea and Mauna Loa are several long lines of cliffs or *pali.* These are termed **tangential faults** because their geometric relationship to the general volcanic contours is that of a tangent to a circle (Figure 5.1). They were formed when subaerial and upper submarine slopes of a growing mountain slumped down the unbuttressed ocean side of the island, either suddenly or incrementally over an extended period of time. In these landslides, substantial portions of a volcano were sometimes lost. One gigantic slump on the north side of East Molokaʻi, which carried away perhaps half of the original

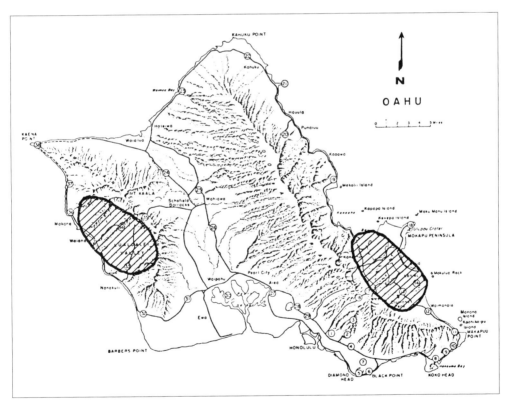

Figure 5.2. Relief map of Oʻahu. The Waiʻanae *(left)* and Koʻolau *(right)* Ranges built up along rift zones of two ancient volcanoes, whose original caldera-bearing summits (cross-hatched areas) and upper slopes have long since collapsed or eroded away. (Base map from Fig. 5.1 of Stearns [1985], used with permission of Pacific Books, Publishers.)

volcano there and scattered debris out over the ocean floor for well over 160 km (100 miles), is said to be among the largest landslides on earth. These slumps may also involve parts of the volcano's rift zones and are very likely responsible for the initial formation of high elongate escarpments such as, for example, the Koʻolau Pali of Windward Oʻahu (Figure 5.3). Wave action during subsequent heightened sea stands and, on the windward side of islands, prolonged freshwater erosion have accentuated such impressive clifflike alignments.

When such great landslides occur suddenly, they invariably produce earthquakes, of which the largest one recorded in Hawaiʻi during the last hundred years, 7.2 on the Richter scale, occurred in November 1975. It apparently resulted from seaward land slumping along the Hilina fault system (Figure 5.1) of Kīlauea's east rift zone. This early morning earthquake caused shoreside Halapē Campground of Hawaiʻi Volcanoes National Park to drop 4 m (13 feet) into the ocean, with the inrushing water from a series of immediately following tsunami waves (see chapter 6) killing two of the thirty-two campers sleeping there, as well as four horses.

The larger of ancient slump-related earthquakes, much more powerful than any subsequently witnessed in Hawaiʻi, would have generated enormous waves that devastated nearby

Figure 5.3. The great Koʻolau Pali of Windward Oʻahu. The southern half of this escarpment between Waimānalo (center foreground) and Kāneʻohe (right background) is shown. The forked peak in the large cloud shadow is Olomana. (Photograph by Agatin T. Abbott; Fig. 21.12 of Macdonald et al. [1983], used with permission of Frank L. Peterson.)

main islands. For example, numerous coral reef fragments enigmatically situated at about 325 m (1,073 feet) on southeastern Lāna'i and at 70 m (231 feet) on Moloka'i are thought by some investigators to have been washed there on such tsunamis produced by major slides occurring along the western coast of Hawai'i between about 100,000 and 200,000 years ago.

CALDERA-FILL REMNANTS

The basalt that filled calderas of senescent Hawaiian volcanoes is so dense that portions of it may occasionally remain as isolated jutting structures long after the rest of the summit region has eroded away. The striking forked peak of Olomana on Windward O'ahu (Figure 5.3) and 'Īao Needle of West Maui are considered to be such remnants. Although water easily penetrates most lava formations, caldera-fill basalt is relatively impervious. On Kaua'i, a large, flat portion of the fill of Wai'ale'ale Volcano's caldera (originally the largest in the Islands, about 15 to 20 km or 9.3 to 12.4 miles across) remains on the island's summit (Figure 5.4). Here, the area's abundant rainwater collecting on this thick basalt maintains the anomalous high-elevation Alaka'i Swamp.

REJUVENATION-STAGE ERUPTION FEATURES

O'ahu

Most of the more-obvious O'ahu Rejuvenation-Stage features (see chapter 3) are located in the southeastern part of the Ko'olau Volcano complex and were commonly formed by large hydromagmatic and phreatic explosions (see chapter 4). Such eruptions, probably sometimes extending over several days, formed a number of prominent cratered cones, made up primarily of the cemented fine-ash rock known as tuff. Punchbowl (originally Pūowaina), Diamond Head (Lē'ahi), Koko Head, Koko Crater (Kohelepelepe), Rabbit (Mānana) Islet, as well as Ulupa'u Head and Mokumanu Islet of the Windward Mōkapu Peninsula, are examples of such structures. Even Hanauma Bay appears to be the remnant of a tuff cone, with its original seaward rim eroded away and its crater now flooded (Figure 5.5). When formed on land, cones of this and other types are almost invariably called ***pu'u,*** the general Hawaiian term for an isolated protuberance of essentially any type or size. Incidentally, the fact that the southwestern rim of at least some of these tuff cones (Diamond Head, for example) is higher than that on the north-

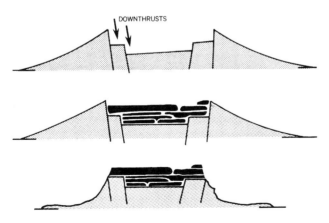

Figure 5.4. Development of Kaua'i Island's flat summit. *Top,* formation of original Wai'ale'ale Volcano caldera; *middle,* filling of caldera by dense basalt; *bottom,* erosion of surrounding summit basalt. The low permeability of the dense caldera fill material to rainwater contributed significantly to development of the high-elevation Alaka'i Swamp. (Unnumbered figure on p. 54 of Carlquist [1980], used with permission of the National Tropical Botanical Garden.)

eastern side indicates that the primary trade wind direction while they were formed was probably the same as at present.

A few other Oʻahu Rejuvenation-Stage eruptions included lava flows along with ash production, such as those forming Mount Tantalus (originally Puʻu ʻŌhiʻa) and Sugarloaf (Puʻu Kākea), as well as possibly also Round Top (Puʻu ʻUalakaʻa), above Mānoa Valley. Lava from Sugarloaf streamed down Mānoa Valley to form both the flat floor of the lower valley and the deposit of basalt that was extracted from the "Quarry Area" of the University of Hawaiʻi campus. The small Kaimukī shield volcano, in the eastern Honolulu section of that name, formed from lava flows of the Rejuvenation Stage.

Other Islands

On Maui, the most recent volcanic activity occurred low on the southwest rift zone of Haleakalā and resulted in the formation of two spatter cones and at least two partially coalesced lava flows that entered the ocean at La Pérouse Bay to form the present Cape Kīnaʻu. No written record documents the actual event, but information obtained from local informants about

Figure 5.5. Rejuvenation-Stage tuff cones and craters of southeastern Oʻahu. The flooded crater in the right center is Hanauma Bay; below it is Koko Head, and above it Koko Crater. The similarly created Rabbit (Mānana) Islet is visible in the far left background. (Photograph by Agatin T. Abbott; Fig. 21.18 of Macdonald et al. [1983], used with permission of Frank L. Peterson.)

1900 suggested that the date was somewhere between 1750 and 1770. The establishment of a more precise time for this eruption is most interesting. In 1786, the exploring French sea captain Jean-François G. de La Pérouse mapped the extensive Maui embayment that now bears his name; then, in 1793, the British captain George Vancouver again mapped the area. Both maps have been preserved, and comparison shows an obvious lava peninsula in the center of the bay on Vancouver's map that was not on La Pérouse's earlier one. The eruption and lava flow that formed the peninsula thus took place sometime between the dates of the two mappings, or approximately 1790.

Earlier Rejuvenation-Stage eruptions formed the many cinder cones and lava flows that partially filled the Erosional-Stage summit depression of Maui's Haleakalā (see chapter 3). Volcanic activity of this stage also produced Molokini Islet, between East Maui and Kahoʻolawe, now reduced to a crescent-shaped remnant of a tuff-cone crater rim. The Kalaupapa Peninsula midway along the north coast of Molokaʻi, to which victims of Hansen's Disease were once exiled, formed from lava flows of a miniature Rejuvenation-Stage shield volcano that developed immediately off the island's shore and whose vent is still visible as Kauhakō Crater. On Kauaʻi, prominent Kīlauea Hill of the north coast is primarily a tuff cone of this same stage, and the islets Kaʻula and Lehua near neighboring Niʻihau are both, like Molokini, tuff-cone remnants with partially eroded crater rims.

MINERALS AND ADZE BASALT

Calcite and Olivine

Hawaiian basalt of the late Shield-building Stage usually differs from earlier and, especially, later material by containing greater numbers of macroscopic crystals. Clear crystals of yellowish green **olivine** are relatively common among those found, and small fractured examples can be picked up at scattered localities, including the area immediately to the south of the Makapuʻu Point Overlook parking lot on southeastern Oʻahu.

Scarcity of olivine and other crystals in at least most Rejuvenation-Stage lavas could possibly result from an effective screening out of previously formed crystals as this late lava is forced to the surface through quite-restricted channels. Or there may be differential formation and/or layering of crystals in later-stage magma, so that there are very few in magma reaching the surface at this stage. One mineral occasionally evident in Rejuvenation-Stage lava, however, is calcite in the form of clear discrete calcium carbonate crystals. The discovery of these on Diamond Head by early British sailors, and the seamen's mistake in considering them the more valuable gem, yielded the modern name of this tuff cone.

Volcanic Glass

Although not a precious stone by historic standards, volcanic glass (see chapter 4) was an extremely valuable commodity to pre-Contact Hawaiians, who used the razor-sharp flaked-off chips of this dense black material for small cutting implements. A layer of volcanic glass may be found on the outer surfaces of some dike and sill basalt, but this is usually much less than 1 cm (0.4 inches) thick. Significantly larger pieces of volcanic glass can be found scattered among the pumicelike ejecta of a particular type of lava (trachyte), such as that forming Puʻu Waʻawaʻa, a Postshield-Stage cone on the north rift zone of Hualālai on Hawaiʻi.

Adze Basalt

Another extremely useful lithic material in prehistoric Hawai'i was fine-grained, nonvesicular basalt. The very dense nature of this favored adze raw material was often produced by a combination of rapid cooling and unrelieved pressure so that neither macroscopic gas bubbles nor large crystals were formed. This is often true of dike basalt, but thick cores of *'a'ā* flows consisting of low-gas, relatively viscous lava can provide this same general kind of material. Areas of exposure of either of these lava types typically constituted sites of prehistoric quarrying operations. The frequent occurrence of the place names Kaluako'i (the adze pit) and Keanakāko'i (the cave of the adze maker[s]) and suggests the importance of this activity to ancient Hawaiians. Also, archaeological investigations have revealed that, in spite of an extremely inhospitable environment, there was an otherwise unrecorded extensive adze-stone quarry and workshop complex near the south summit of Mauna Kea. For reasons entirely unclear, however, the former intensive seasonal utilization of this site with its seemingly most desirable raw material was evidently discontinued less than a century before European Contact in 1778.

LAVA FIELDS

Trails

The often-vast flows of relatively new lava, as now especially evident on Hawai'i, tend to lack distinctive features to serve as landmarks for foot travelers. Prehistoric Hawaiians, as well as post-Contact hunters and hikers, usually erected small lava-block cairns or *ahu* at intervals to serve as guideposts, and a number of these can be seen from the Saddle Road on prehistoric and historic lava flows between Hilo and Mauna Kea.

Long-continued travel over the generally smooth *pāhoehoe* flows broke the thin volcanic-glass crust, forming a dull-appearing trail through the shiny untrod lava to either side, and these paths are visible at great distances. Walking the rough *'a'ā* flows is much more difficult than travel over *pāhoehoe* (Plate 4.2); the clinkery lava blocks soon wore out sandals of vegetable material used by ancient Hawaiians, as they do the soles and even edges of the uppers of modern footwear, and the frequent falls resulting from missteps on this loose material can cause serious lacerations. On well-used coastal trails, large waterworn basalt stones were commonly carried from the shore and laid on leveled *'a'ā* to serve as stepping-stones. Also, many of the coastal paths were marked at frequent intervals with white coralline-reef cobbles, visible at close range to travelers without lights even on moonless nights.

Kīpuka

One of the more obvious features created by lava flows is a **kīpuka:** essentially an island of land left uncovered but surrounded by a widespread new flow. In ancient Hawai'i, such isolated areas containing soil were culturally important land parcels suitable for agriculture in the midst of an expanse of unproductive bare lava, and their significance is reflected by the fact that at least three dozen Hawai'i Island localities have names prefixed by "Kīpuka." These remnant pieces of land also have aided in survival of many native species of plants and smaller or more sedentary animals, most of whose populations were destroyed by the lava flow. Further, the *kīpuka* undoubtedly facilitated and hastened development of new species among such organisms, acting—although on a much smaller scale—like the separate islands of an isolated archipelago (see chapter 10).

LAVA TUBES

Pāhoehoe flows give rise to a number of interesting structures. As one major example, when a thick stream of lava moves away from its source, its surface and other peripheral portions tend to solidify. This greatly diminishes heat loss from the centrally located fluid material, allowing it to continue to stream like an underground river through a **lava tube** toward the leading edge of the flow (Figure 5.6). The subterranean stream may sometimes be visible through a **skylight** (Plate 5.1). Burning of escaping gases within the partially filled active tube apparently sometimes produces temperatures high enough to remelt lava on the ceiling, perhaps producing some of the skylights but more often only causing formation of lava stalactites. As the issuance of lava at the source ceases, the molten material continues to flow out of the lava tunnel, and the portion remaining in the tube finally hardens into a flat floor. "Shelves" along the tube walls may be formed through erosion by the moving stream, by slumping, or from hardening of lateral surface portions of the flow.

Lava-tube skylights in revegetated areas constitute a great danger to off-trail hikers, because the openings are often concealed by vinelike ferns or other ground-covering plants. The fact that the skylights can serve as trap openings has one scientific benefit, however, because paleontologists have recovered a great variety of remains of prehistoric ground-living birds and invertebrates such as land snails that fell through them over thousands of years (see chapter 22). Lava-tube ceilings, themselves, may occasionally collapse under the weight of a heavy passing vehicle such as a bulldozer, dropping the machine into the hidden tube.

Lava tubes may be seen fairly commonly at younger volcanoes such as Kīlauea, where, for example, the large Thurston Lava Tube of Hawai‘i Volcanoes National Park is a popular visitor attraction. On the older main islands, however, few of the original tubes are now evident because these structures tend to be obliterated by collapse and rubble filling within a relatively short geologic time—usually only a few hundred thousand years.

OTHER LAVA-FLOW PHENOMENA

Tree Molds

Very fluid lava flowing into a forested area often produces intriguing structures called **tree molds,** which occur in two forms. The lava immediately surrounding a living tree trunk frequently is cooled enough by the trunk's moisture to solidify around it and, if the remaining lava then drains away, this encasing lava is left behind as an upright column, its interior hollow if the original trunk burned away or is eventually lost to decay. A "forest" of such pillars has been set aside as the Lava Tree State Monument near Pāhoa in the southeastern corner of Hawai‘i Island. In the second type of tree mold, the entire flow of lava enveloping the tree trunk cools in place. After disintegration of the trunk, each tree mold remains as a cylindrical pit, which, although not as dangerous as lava-tube skylights, can still cause injury to an unwary person stepping into one. In a few instances, trees uprooted or with trunks burned through by a lava flow have fallen onto the cooling surface, leaving imprints clear enough to identify the type of tree involved.

"Birth Pebbles"

An ancient *pāhoehoe* flow in the vicinity of Punalu‘u near the southern tip of Hawai‘i Island was ultimately responsible for one of the most charming of Hawaiian legends: that of the *‘ili ‘ili*

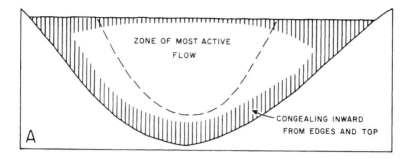

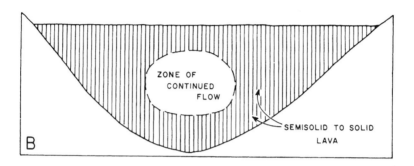

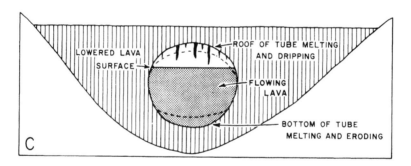

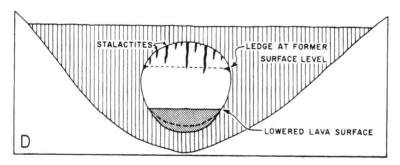

Figure 5.6. Stages in formation of a lava tube. The *pāhoehoe* flow shown here is confined to a valley, although a tube can similarly form in any thick, long-continued *pāhoehoe* flow. (Fig. 2.21 of Macdonald et al. [1983], used with permission of Frank L. Peterson.)

hānau or "birth pebbles." Two types of waterworn basalt cobbles or small boulders occurred on a beach there: completely smooth ones (males) and ones with small circular pits in their surface (females). These two kinds mated and produced as their children the innumerable small pebbles making up a major portion of the beach; these pebbles could often still be seen in the superficial maternal cavities, and occasionally even in the process of being forced out (born). The neonates slowly grew and replaced their parents to perpetuate the life cycle. Because most of the beach material in this area has been removed for historic construction and other purposes, the process probably no longer occurs.

Sadly, geologists have to explain this phenomenon in a less-engaging manner. A portion of a *pāhoehoe* flow in the area traversed a stream channel or beach filled with small waterworn pebbles, incorporating many of them into the flow to form conglomerate basalt. Upon hardening and eventually being broken up and smoothly waterworn, the pebble-containing fragments became the mothers, while fragments from nonconglomerate portions of the flow became the fathers. Further water erosion of the female stones freed the contained pebbles, perhaps sometimes being aided by solar thermal expansion of water in the pebble-containing pits that resulted in periodic expulsion of these smaller stones.

PETROGLYPHS

Smoother portions of lava flows provided early Hawaiians a long-lasting base on which to use a pointed basalt fragment to occasionally "peck" human or other animal figures and various other designs. Those formed on *pāhoehoe* surfaces are especially noticeable because they stand out against the surrounding unbroken thin crust of shiny volcanic glass. These **petroglyphs** (Greek *"petros"* [rock] and *"glypho"* [to carve]) or *kiʻi pōhaku* (stone picture) were also often placed on boulders or vertical basalt outcroppings. An excellent array of primarily geometric designs may be viewed on Puʻu Loa, a low, weathered *pāhoehoe* mound a short distance off the lower Chain of Craters Road in Hawaiʻi Volcanoes National Park. Local informants state that this particular petroglyph concentration, which includes a great number of pecked-out small cuplike depressions, was primarily related to a traditional Hawaiian disposal method of the umbilical-cord stumps or *piko* of infants. In this, the cord remnant was placed in the depression and a cobble placed over it to prevent removal by Polynesian Rats. All types of petroglyphs occur, although usually rather sparingly, at widely scattered localities throughout the main islands. Even though undoubtedly important to the individual makers, the lack of uniformity in any aspect of petroglyphs statewide—or even on a single island—suggests that these creations did not have a universally important cultural function in ancient Hawaiʻi.

BOULDERS

Significance

Ancient (and some modern) Hawaiians attached special importance to certain stones, especially ones of larger size or particular configuration. As just a few of numerous examples, one or more somewhat distinctive-appearing stones seem to have placed upright at almost every type of religious shrine, and numerous isolated boulders or rock formations are frequently identified in legends as the embodiments of deities and lesser personages. A few so-called "bell stones" are also known; these give out a sonorous ringing tone when struck in a certain manner. Phallic stones were recognized and visited in now-obscure fertility rituals, as were stones with patterns suggesting female genitalia. A few natural(?) groupings of larger boulders obviously once held special significance because they were visited near the end of confinement by pregnant chiefesses or other female royalty, who often reclined on individual "birthing stones" during parturition. One such set of boulders has been preserved at the place known as Kūkaniloko, immediately north of the present central Oʻahu community of Wahiawā.

WINDBLOWN SAND

Sand dunes occur in certain low-lying coastal areas of most main islands, with an extensive collection at Moʻomomi Beach on the north coast of western Molokaʻi sometimes being referred to as the **"Desert Strip."** Great quantities of calcareous sand from the disintegrating fringing reef exposed at geologic times of lowered sea level were blown inland for 2 km (1.2 miles) or more. The action of rainwater made slightly acidic by dissolved carbon dioxide has cemented some of this wind-transported sand into rock called eolianite, often forming **lithified dunes.** Much of the sand in surrounding areas remains loose and continues to be blown about by the wind, giving rise to the old Hawaiian name of Keonelele (the flying sand) for one part of the Moʻomomi area. Fragments of basalt here gradually develop the appearance of having been somewhat smoothed and then coated with varnish as their exposed surface is polished by the windblown sand. Such extensive dune areas often contain remains of prehistorically extinct birds and ancient species of land snails, which are periodically exposed in the shifting sand (see chapter 22).

SOILS

Definition
Two often-used definitions of soil are (1) any part of the earth's surface in which plants are anchored, or (2) the weathered superficial layer of the earth's crust with which are mingled living organisms and the products of their decay. Either of these definitions is acceptable. But in this era of travel to the moon and, eventually, other members of our solar system that possess "soil" but not life, both meanings have become dated. It has thus been suggested that a more appropriate definition of soil may now be an older, somewhat facetious one: any surface material of a planet that can be removed without blasting. (Although "earth" may be an acceptable alternative word for "soil," most soil scientists prefer that the term "dirt" be restricted to the type of material found in a vacuum cleaner's collection bag.)

SOIL FORMATION

Formation of soil or **pedogenesis** occurs more rapidly in tropical areas than in temperate ones because the year-round warmth of the former allows chemical reactions to occur with greater consistency and speed, and the generally higher rainfall facilitates solution and leaching of chemical components. Four primary factors determine the type of soil that will be formed: (1) parent material, (2) precipitation and topography, (3) associated plant and animal life, and (4) time.

Parent Material

The basic manner of soil formation can be relatively straightforward, as when a soil develops in situ (that is, while remaining in the same place). In one of the simplest cases, assume that a new 'a'ā lava flow occurs in a relatively high-rainfall area of the young island of Hawai'i. Acting most immediately on the upper surface of this jumbled mass, rainwater, atmospheric gases, and periodic temperature changes progressively weather it, chemically altering the basalt through extraction of original chemical components and formation of new ones, while at the same time physically fragmenting larger pieces into increasingly smaller particles.

Within, usually, less than 100,000 years, three intergrading layers or horizons have developed (Figure 5.7). The basal horizon (R) consists almost entirely of the parent 'a'ā, little if at

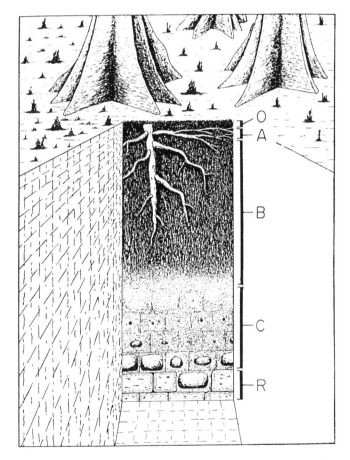

Figure 5.7. Schematic representation of in situ soil formation. The five intergrading horizons are, from top to bottom: O, fresh organic plant and animal litter; A, mixed decomposed organic and minerally leached inorganic matter; B, pure mineral-rich inorganic soil; C, mixed soil and decomposing parental basalt fragments; and R, essentially unaltered basalt rock. (Modified from Fig. 1.2 of Fitz-Patrick [1980], used with permission of Pearson Education Ltd.)

all changed from its original state. This grades above into a layer (C) in which already disintegrated fine lithic material surrounds portions of the basalt less susceptible to weathering. This intermediate horizon then progresses into an overlying one (B) consisting entirely of finely divided soil that bears little or no resemblance to the original *'a'ā,* but still retains much of the lava's original mineral content.

Precipitation and Topography

A substantial amount of the silicon (mostly in the form of soluble compounds), as well as a few of the metallic compounds, supplied by the basalt are progressively leached out and lost from the young soil. Relatively great amounts of reddish or yellow oxides of iron are formed and give the soils of various areas their distinctive colors as well as somewhat high acidity. Oxides of different hues developed from aluminum, titanium, and manganese originally present may also become common components of the soil; in fact, a few Hawaiian soils, such as one covering the wetter areas of eastern Kaua'i, are probably rich enough in aluminum oxide (bauxite) to be mined commercially for extraction of the metal. Under at least moderately wet climatic conditions, various of the elements leached out of the young soil may sometimes be redeposited as compounds a little below the surface, forming a dense "hardpan" or caliche. On Kaho'olawe, such a hardpan developed under the high-rainfall regime of an earlier geologic period, and this layer is apparent in many places on the now-dry island where wind erosion has laid it bare.

Different slope angles control the amount of water able to sink into the ground, as well as the quantity of developing soil lost to erosion. In addition, since the time of the initial *'a'ā* flow, older soils of different types (even dust from Central Asian deserts carried on high-elevation winds) have usually been blowing and washing into the area to mix with the more recently formed material.

Plant and Animal Life

Plant cover inevitably developing on the transforming lava flow provides vegetable material that enters the soil, resulting in a higher fourth horizon (A) of mixed decomposed organic and minerally leached inorganic matter (Figure 5.7). Typically, a fifth and final horizon (O) is recognized: a superficial one represented by the surface layer of dead but not yet decomposed plant litter. Numerous types of animals that live in and on the upper two horizons also contribute their metabolic wastes and dead bodies to the soil.

Time

The Hawai'i Island soil of this example will necessarily change in both chemical and physical composition over the succeeding few million years. Even if a soil now present on the quite old island of Kaua'i had originally formed in exactly the same manner as the Hawai'i one, it would now be noticeably different from the younger one in various characteristics solely because of the several million additional years that pedogenic processes had been affecting it. The material on Kaua'i would be termed an old or "senile" soil and would have lost much of its earlier agricultural fertility because of substantial mineral loss through chemical reactions and leaching. That on Hawai'i would represent a young or "juvenile" soil; the equivalent but variously aged soils on the intervening islands generally are characterized as mature or "virile" ones.

SOIL CLASSIFICATION

There are a number of familiar, but quite informal, terms commonly used to describe soils: "sandy," "loamy," "clayey," and the like. For scientific use, however, it is necessary to employ some type of formal and standardized classification that can be applied and understood worldwide, analogous to that used for classifying plants and animals (see chapter 10). At least two such arrangements that classify soils by a combination of their chemical and physical properties as well as other pedogenic factors are currently in use, and the more recent of these is employed by most workers in the Hawaiian Islands. In this arrangement, all of the world's soils are divided into twelve "orders," with four named categories of increasing restrictiveness interposed between the highest category and the sixth or lowest category of "series." The state of Hawai'i, with its varied rainfall, diverse topography, and altitudinally differing temperatures, possesses eleven of the dozen soil orders. In the Islands these contain 190 soil series, all of which take their names from Hawaiian places (leaving out diacritical marks). This is a relatively very large number of series for such a small total land area—about the same as designated for each of several of the larger mainland states.

Categories

No more than a very brief sampling of the multitudinous criteria characterizing each of the six levels of this classification is given here. For instance, the order Oxisol encompasses all well-weathered soils usually developed under tropical climatic conditions on rather flat land and that contain relatively high percentages of oxides of iron and certain other metals along with quite limited amounts of silicon. At the lowest classification level within this order, a Hawaiian example is the soil series termed Wahiawa. This name indicates a unique soil found and originally described at O'ahu's Wahiawā on the Schofield Plateau, where this distinctive reddish earth has historically supported vast fields of Pineapple.

Classification Use

The scientific classification of soils is valuable in a variety of ways. A soil expert, knowing the complete classification of the predominant soil in an area, will be able to predict its behavior under various conditions without ever having to see the soil. This allows informed decisions regarding actions or uses contemplated for the land. For instance, certain soils derived from volcanic ash (and thus classified within the order Andisol) that contain a great amount of humus and have developed under continually wet subsurface conditions are characteristic of the Rain Forest Zone (see chapter 14). They are relatively quite resistant to erosion because they have great ability to convey water from the surface to underlying layers. It can be further determined from the classification of these soils that they are of a generally gelatinous and "smeary" nature and, if allowed to dry out, are never again capable of reabsorbing the same amount of water they originally could. In the past certain rain-forest tracts of the main islands were clear-cut without consideration of their soil's qualities. Now, some such places may be so desiccated that it is difficult for natural succession of plant growth to proceed, or even for attempted reforestation with the original native trees to be entirely satisfactory.

Of more immediate concern to everyday life in the state is the inappropriate use of land consisting of a mature blackish, sticky soil type containing a high percentage of a physicochemically active clay mineral and other aluminum compounds. Just as is characteristic of all other soils classified in the order Vertisol, the chemical content of this one causes it readily to dry out during times of low precipitation, with the substantial shrinkage yielding large and deep surface cracks, but allows it equally readily to reabsorb water in rainy weather, noticeably swelling in the process. Houses unadvisedly constructed on this type of soil, such as in the 'Āina Haina subdivision of eastern Honolulu, are notoriously susceptible to movement during these volume alternations, with foundations cracking and even entire buildings sometimes progressively sliding down very modest slopes.

SUGGESTED REFERENCES

Becket and Singer (eds. and comps.) 1999; Clark 1980, 1985a,b, 1990; Cox and Stasack 1970; Decker and Decker 1997; Decker et al. (eds.) 1987; FitzPatrick 1980; Gavenda et al. 1998; Hazlett and Hyndman 1996; Macdonald 1972; Macdonald et al. 1983; Moore et al. 1989, 1994; Stearns 1985; Uehara 1983.

AUDIOVISUAL AIDS

Hawaii: A chain; Hawai'i and planet Earth: The Hawaiian geography; Hawaii: Born of fire; The living soil; Soil and decomposition.

6

Actions of the Ocean

This chapter covers primarily only the physical ocean actions that most directly affect the Hawaiian Islands. Not considered are many important broad aspects of the ocean such as salinity, temperature, nutrient content, and water mixing, which may be found in any standard oceanography text. The effect of the Pacific Ocean in general, and its extensive North Pacific Current or Gyre in particular, on Hawaiian climate is discussed in chapter 7 and the gyre's role in transporting marine and terrestrial founding organisms to the archipelago in chapters 11 and 13.

TRADE-WIND AND TIDAL CURRENTS

Two seawater movements of lesser magnitude than the North Pacific Current are obvious in Hawai'i. The persistent northeast trade winds (see chapter 7) produce a current almost continually flowing southwest through the archipelago. This, however, is generally masked by slightly swifter localized tidal currents, whose speed along the coast is usually about 0.5 km (0.3 miles) per hour, although it increases by three or four times that around certain points and headlands. This water may move in one direction for about 5 or 6 km (3 or 4 miles) along the coast as the tide is rising and the same distance in the opposite direction as it is falling. The interaction of trade-wind and tidal currents yields a quite erratic pattern of water movement, with eddies and countercurrents transporting floating material in a largely unpredictable manner among the main islands. Ephemeral or periodic eddies so produced can sometimes have interesting effects; for example, if two canoes are racing only 100 m (330 feet) apart on either side of an eddy, one is helped by the circling water, and the other hindered.

TIDAL ACTIVITY

Cause

Tides are produced by the gravitational pull of both moon and sun on the solid earth and its oceans, with the moon exerting a much greater force than the larger but more distant sun, and the land shape being essentially unaffected compared with that of the ocean. The seawater nearest the moon receives the greatest gravitational pull. Here a bulge develops, while 90 degrees around the earth to either side the ocean is flattened out or lowered, leaving another bulge 180 degrees from the first.

The mounded water of each bulge is carried a certain distance by the revolving earth before it has time to recede fully, so the two tidal bulges are displaced somewhat from the line between the two planets (Figure 6.1). As the earth turns, all its land masses are moved through these raised and lowered ocean areas, and the water at the shore rises and falls approximately twice a day. In essence, the tides constitute a pair of enormously broad waves continually circling the world's oceans.

Variability

This seemingly regular tidal process, however, is complicated by several factors. The earth's revolution in relation to the sun takes 24 hours, but in relation to the moon almost 25 hours, precluding synchronization of solar and lunar tides most of the time. Also, the sun is seldom in line with the earth and moon, and this constantly changing relative position causes its gravitational pull to interact with that of the moon in a varying (although predictable) manner. Every 2 weeks, however, at the times of new and full moon, the three bodies are in line, and the combined effects of moon and sun result in exceptionally high or **spring tides.** When, at the time of first- and third-quarter moon, the sun is oriented 90 degrees to the line between earth and moon, its gravitation pull maximally reduces the two lunar-caused ocean bulges, causing exceptionally low or **neap tides.** Tides in the Hawaiian Islands follow the more typical cycle of two low and two high daily, as opposed to a single one of each that may occur in some parts of the world due to local coastal physiographic conditions. The amplitudinal tidal range in Hawai'i tends to be quite low, however—usually only about 0.3 to 0.6 m (1 to 2 feet).

TSUNAMIS

"Tidal waves" have nothing to do with tides, but like earthquakes are mostly related to massive displacement of lithic material along faults (see chapter 2). Such ocean phenomena are properly termed **tsunamis** (Japanese [long harbor wave]). When sudden rock movement such as an

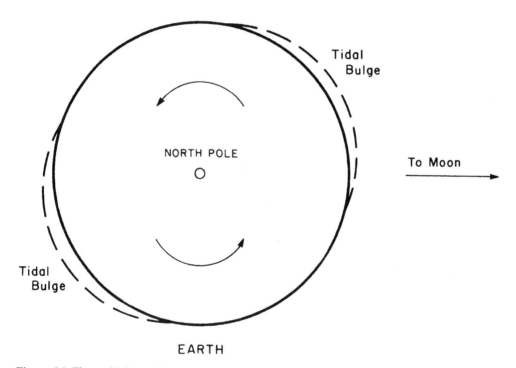

Figure 6.1. The earth's lunar tidal bulges. The diagram is idealized in that the sun's similar, but weaker, gravitational influence is not included. Note that the earth's rotation carries the bulges slightly past a direct line to the moon before the mounded ocean water has time to recede. (Fig. 14.1 of Macdonald et al. [1983], used with permission of Frank L. Peterson.)

earthquake displaces large amounts of seawater, this disturbance is usually translated into one or more powerful wave motions that move across the open ocean as swells at amazing speeds: up to 400–500 km (250–310 miles) per hour. Thus, tsunamis generated on continental coasts of the Pacific Basin can reach Hawai'i in between 5 and 10 hours. Being swells (see description later in this chapter), such wave motions are not especially obvious at sea; the crests there are perhaps only 1 m (3.3 feet) in height. Upon reaching shore, however, the tsunami waves can build up to great size.

During the past 200 years, noticeable tsunamis from continental areas have reached the Hawaiian Islands about once every 4 years on average, although over half of these have caused little or no damage. About half a dozen, however, have been responsible for considerable death and destruction. Physiographic characteristics of the inshore seafloor and adjoining shore, as well as direction of the tsunami swells, primarily determine how large the breaking waves moving inland will be at any particular locality. The configuration of the nearshore area around Hilo, on the northeastern coast of Hawai'i, is especially conducive to damage from tsunamis originating along the northern and eastern Pacific Rim. The urban area was very heavily damaged in both 1946 and 1960 by waves almost 10 and 11 m (33 and 36 feet) high, respectively, although the waves of both tsunamis at certain other points on Hawai'i and the remaining main islands were well under a meter (3.3 feet) in height. It is odd that tsunamis originating along the western Pacific Rim have done little recorded damage in Hawai'i. This, however, is quite possibly due to chance and does not indicate that a devastating West Pacific tsunami will never reach the Islands.

Modern methods of detecting and monitoring tsunamis originating far from the Islands now provide residents with adequate warning. Tsunamis generated within the archipelago itself, however, may strike nearby islands within a matter of minutes. Thus, upon feeling or being informed of a nearby earthquake, or upon hearing neighborhood warning sirens sound, persons in Hawai'i should immediately tune in local radio or television stations for any Civil Defense warnings. Also, maps in telephone books for each island show coastal areas likely to be inundated by tsunamis.

WAVE ACTIVITY

Breakers

The truly large waves normal along Hawaiian coasts are produced by major storms, which are usually located far from the archipelago except in the case of an occasional closely approaching hurricane. Wave motions set up by these large, distant storms travel great distances in the form of **swells,** losing little energy because the water affected by the wave motion is only moving a short distance up and down in small circles (Figure 6.2) rather than being carried along by the swell. Far at sea, the wave motions are apparent only as slow, massive surface undulations, seldom cresting there, but upon nearing land they build into a succession of huge, crashing breakers. The transformation begins when the wave motion reaches water depths about half the swell's wavelength (distance between two adjacent crests), where it is said to "feel bottom." Frictional drag on the shallow bottom then slows the swells so that the wave crests move closer together and increase in height until the advancing uplifted water can no longer be supported and collapses forward as a breaker.

Smaller swells are relatively consistently generated year-round by the northeast trade winds, and still another source of occasionally substantial swells are nearby *kona* (leeward or opposite the trade winds) storms to the south or southwest of the Islands. Breakers produced by either of these types of swells tend to be rather small and somewhat closely spaced or "choppy."

Wave Sets

There may often be more than one large storm occurring in the Pacific, so there can be two or more series of swells moving across the ocean simultaneously. These wave motions interact by canceling or reinforcing each other, producing variation in the heights of successively breaking waves or **wave sets.** Although there may be some degree of regularity in appearance of the larger waves in these sets, prediction of their exact occurrence by a surfer waiting in the "lineup" is generally not especially successful.

Surfing Spots

When "surf's up" in Hawai'i, variations in coastal sea-bottom profiles as well as differences in type of swells produce the particular kinds of waves characterizing different surfing areas. These range from the frequent 7.5- to 9.0-m (25- to 30-foot) sloping giants of Waimea Bay on O'ahu's "North Shore" (occasionally even reaching 10.5 m [35 feet] and then reputedly the world's largest surfable waves) to the lower but uniquely tubelike waves often found at the "Pipeline" of nearby 'Ehukai Beach. As every surfer knows, the location of the best waves tends to change with the season. In summer, frequent large swells from storms of the austral winter in the Southern Hemisphere Pacific give southern shores of the Islands the largest waves; in winter, numerous North Pacific storms furnish the largest surf to northern shores.

Undertows and Shorebreaks

The immediate backwash of waves moving onto a beach is an **undertow,** easily felt when standing in shallow water just off the beach. Undertows are usually not a serious hazard to beachgoers because their flow is ordinarily of limited strength and promptly cancelled by the next

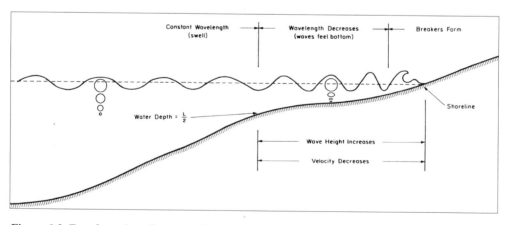

Figure 6.2. Transformation of ocean swells to breaking waves. Breakers form when the swells reach water about half their wavelength deep. The series of circles indicates the very limited movement of water produced by each swell in the open ocean. (Fig. 14.2 of Macdonald et al. [1983], used with permission of Frank L. Peterson.)

incoming wave. When waves are large, a dangerous **shorebreak** may result if they are not cresting until they almost reach the beach. The shorebreak itself may dash a swimmer against the bottom, or the subsequent undertow may pull an unsuspecting wader off balance and allow injury by the next break. Large shorebreaks often occur at Makapuʻu and Sandy Beaches of Oʻahu's southeast tip and, although they provide good bodysurfing for the experienced person, can be quite hazardous to the uninitiated.

Rip Currents

Whenever waves of considerable size are washing ashore, the incoming water continually returns offshore. Its course typically follows close to and parallel with the shore until some bottom irregularity such as a channel or a point causes the current to turn seaward. This outward flow is a **rip current** and is usually identifiable in the midst of rougher inshore water as a relatively smooth corridor with foam moving seaward. Surfers utilize these rips to paddle more easily out to the breaker line, but they can prove dangerous for inexperienced beachgoers. A swimmer unwittingly entering one can be carried helplessly toward the open sea at as great a speed as 3 or 4 km (1.9 to 2.5 miles) per hour. This is too fast to swim against, and individuals caught in a rip current sometimes drown after exhausting themselves trying to swim directly back to shore.

There is no need for such loss of life, however, because rip currents extend only about 50 m (165 feet) out from shore, at which point they simply dissipate. If caught in one, a swimmer should passively ride the current out to its termination, then either wait for rescue if necessary or enter the onshore-moving water to either side to be carried back to the beach. If any swimming is done while in the rip current, it should only be across it to reach incoming water.

Wave Refraction

No matter from what direction major swells are approaching an island, the waves on all of its beaches are moving toward the shore; this is the result of **wave refraction.** The portion of an incoming swell that encounters shallow water first is slowed most, and the portions successively farther away to either side are slowed less and less because they are over increasingly deeper water. Thus, the originally straight swell is refracted or bent around both sides of the island, being transformed into waves reaching the shore at almost right angles.

BEACH-SAND MOVEMENTS

Longshore Currents

Even when there are no breakers at a beach, there is almost always a littoral or **longshore current** caused by refracted or other waves approaching the shore other than perpendicularly (Figure 6.3). On sand beaches, the oblique movement of each wave moves roiled sand only a very short distance, but the overall result is a continuing migration of sand from one end of the beach to the other. Eventually, the moving sand is deposited in some area offshore of the downcurrent beach end, and this place is sometimes too deep for seasonal waves to move the sand back onto the beach (see discussion later in this chapter). Sand is always being either produced by disintegration of coastal reef or carried into the shore area by rivers and streams, so that lost at one end of a beach is usually replaced by new sand entering at the other. This continual movement of constituent material along beaches is why they are often called **"rivers of sand."**

Groins

Various human activities sometimes prevent new sand from being moved into upcurrent beach areas, and waterfront property owners find their unreplenished beaches gradually being lost. They attempt to stop the depleting flow by building **groins** or walls extending at right angles into the ocean at the downcurrent end of the property. At least some sand is retained by building up at the groin, but this process prevents sand from replenishing properties downcurrent, and landowners there similarly have to build groins to retain what they can of their beaches. Sand will still slowly be lost from all the beaches, however, unless some way can be found to restore or duplicate the original new sand source. On Oʻahu's Waikīkī Beach, for example, hotels have resorted to trucking in sand to replace that continually lost from their fronting beaches. A beach's sand source may also be lost naturally, as in the case of rising sea levels over several thousand years that turn a basaltic headland into an effective groin. Such a barrier at the upcurrent end of the surfing beach at Oʻahu's Waimea Bay has caused the still-eroding beach to narrow by well over 60 m (197 feet) during only the past century.

Sea Walls

Although still incompletely understood, there is a long-term cycle involving degradation and accretion of beaches. In this, a single episode of beach loss or gain sometimes extends over dozens of years, often simultaneously affecting two parts of a long beach in the opposite manner. The north and south ends of 4-km-long (2.5-mile-long) Kailua Beach of Windward Oʻahu have alternately advanced and retreated several times over a 30-year period, one moving seaward while the other moved inland. The maximum range of movement during this period has been substantial: 24 m (79 feet) for the north end and 53 m (175 feet) for the south end. Some beachfront residents there have constructed **sea walls** along the eroding ocean edge of their property. Such structures, however, through changing the characteristics of the upwashing

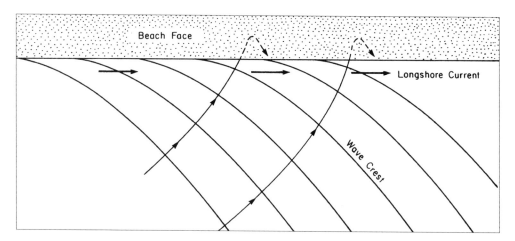

Figure 6.3. Generation of a longshore current. This water movement is produced by incompletely refracted waves (see text), whose crests reach the shore at other than a right angle. The slight downcurrent transport path of sand disturbed by each incoming wave is indicated by dashed lines. (Fig. 14.4 of Macdonald et al. [1983], used with permission of Frank L. Peterson.)

waves, serve only to accelerate the loss of sand at the lots. All Hawaiian beaches are public property up to the vegetation line, so sea walls have denied everyone in Hawai'i availability of many beach stretches. Changes in the design of sea walls, as well as use of structures colloquially called "sand grabbers" to diffuse wave force and promote deposition of suspended sand, are currently being tested as solutions. Also, obviously, limits should be set on how close future structures can be placed to beaches.

Berms

Both long- and short-term sand movements by waves may build up a sand wall or **berm** on the higher borders of beaches. This is especially troublesome where streams enter the ocean, because the berms often cause the streams to back up and flood surrounding areas or present other problems. In the ancient past, development of a large berm on the shore of northern Kailua Bay formed the present Kawainui Marsh from an original ocean embayment. Currently, a small berm that periodically builds up and blocks drainage of a portion of the marsh into the south bay through Ka'elepulu Stream has to be bulldozed open two or three times yearly to release the stagnating water.

Seasonal Loss and Gain

Even without human modification of beaches, much sand on the side of an island receiving seasonal high storm waves may be lost as it is washed out into deeper water, often leaving only a boulder-covered shoreline. The portion of this sand that is deposited in water less than about 9 m (30 feet) deep, however, is retrieved by gentler waves during other seasons and redeposited to restore the beach. But if exceptional ocean conditions such as a tsunami massively sweep sand from a beach and deposit it in offshore areas deeper than this, the beach may be lost for the foreseeable future.

BEACH-SAND TYPES

White Sand

Some beaches in Hawai'i and around the world consist entirely of accumulations of larger lithic material, such as pebbles, cobbles, or even boulders. Sand, however, is the common beach constituent, but this may be of quite different materials. On continents, fine fragments of ubiquitous granitic rock form the buff-colored silicon dioxide "quartz" sand of most beaches. On isolated oceanic islands, however, where granite is scarce or absent, the whitish material making up most beaches is calcium carbonate "calcareous" sand of marine origin. Although this is usually termed **coral sand,** by far the greatest number of its particles are formed not from coral animal skeletons, but from bits of calcareous algae (see chapter 11) and exoskeleton material of marine invertebrates such as foraminiferans, echinoderms, and mollusks. It is much less dense than quartz sand and, for certain Hawaiian construction uses requiring strong concrete, the continental material must be imported.

Black Sand

On volcanic islands, the brownish sand and much of the blackish sand present on some beaches is formed through chemical and physical weathering of various types of older basalt, but a certain type of distinctly glossy **black sand** is formed from contact of fluid lava with seawater. When lava flows into the ocean, the resultant steam explosion produces tiny particles with an outer coating of volcanic glass. The black sand so created during Kīlauea's almost continuous flows of the 1980s and 1990s has been transported at least 20 km (12 miles) southwest along the Hawai'i coast by longshore currents to form almost a continuous beach where previously there had existed mostly only low sea cliffs. Upon cessation of a flow that produces it, such a beach is progressively lost to storm-wave erosion within a century or two; the famed black-sand beach at Punalu'u near the southern tip of Hawai'i was gradually diminished in this manner.

When lava flows into the ocean for a relatively extended period, depending largely on the prevailing wind direction, some of the sand, ash, and cinder borne aloft by the steam clouds is deposited on the shore nearby. This may build up into a **littoral cone** (Latin *"litoris"* [of the shore]), and occasionally even twin cones are formed, one to either side of the flow's mouth. Wave action often washes away lower-lying cones, but a few on slightly higher ground survive. The aptly named Pu'u Hou (New Hill), 8 km (5 miles) northwest of South Point (or Ka Lae) on Hawai'i, was formed in 1868 by a Mauna Loa flow reaching the ocean there (Figure 3.6).

Green Sand

About 4.5 km (2.8 miles) northeast of South Point is the much older Pu'u Mahana, which evidently formed from a subaerial ash eruption at a shoreline vent. The cone is greatly eroded on its ocean side, with much of the finer ash fraction washed out to sea, and primarily only fragmented olivine crystals (see chapter 5) left on the shore. This is sometimes called Papakōlea Beach after a nearby inland locality and forms one of the finest of the state's few **green sand** beaches.

SHORELINE LITHIC FEATURES

Sea Stacks

A number of the small islets off the coast of various main islands are sometimes mistaken for volcanic cones (for example, Mokoli'i or "Chinaman's Hat" and the paired Mokulua Islets of Windward O'ahu). In reality, these are the result of ocean erosion of large land-related basalt units. As diagrammed in Figure 6.4, waves may erode softer portions of a partially submerged basalt ridge, especially an *'a'ā* unit sandwiched between *pāhoehoe* flows, to form a **sea cave.** This cave may subsequently be extended completely through narrower ridges as a **sea arch,** and eventual collapse of the upper part of this produces a **sea stack.** This can be distinguished from an offshore volcanic cone by its possession of the same series of lava layers evident in the wave-eroded face of the shore portion of the original ridge.

Blowholes

Waves sometimes transform a sea cave or shore-opening lava tube (see chapter 5) into a **blowhole,** good examples of which are Hālona Blowhole near O'ahu's Koko Crater and the larger "Spouting Horn" near Kōloa on Kaua'i. A blowhole becomes operative when the roof of the cave or tube develops a small opening to the surface. Then each time a wave rushes into and fills the cavern, air trapped inside is greatly compressed and explosively forced out of the ceiling opening, usually carrying with it some seawater to form a high spray plume.

Nips and Benches

Ocean action during a constant-height sea stand over at least a few thousand years typically results in a wave-cut notch or **nip** in shore rock at about sea level (Figure 6.5). If the slope of the land extending into the sea is not too great, a broad wave-cut **terrace** or bench may also be formed. Old nips and terraces at various distances above and below current sea level are often relied upon to determine the levels of previous extended ocean stands, although there is sometimes difficulty in eliminating isostatic or other tectonic changes (see chapter 3) as the true cause. The generally consistent positions of at least certain nips and terraces on several main islands (for example, those at +1.5, +3.6, and approximately +7.5 m [5, 12, and 25 feet]), how-

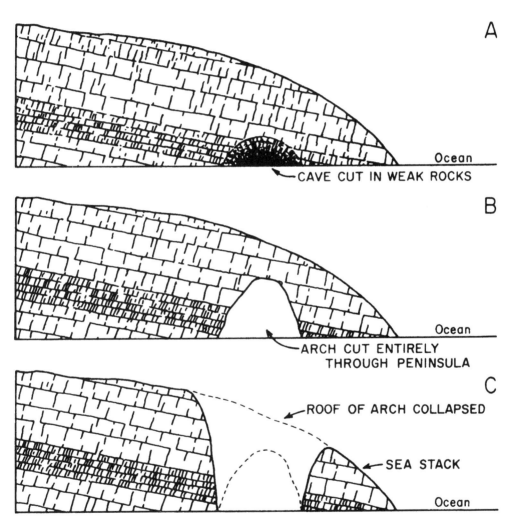

Figure 6.4. Formation of a sea cave, arch, and stack. Note the correspondence in lava layers of the sea stack and the adjacent shore promontory, which serves to distinguish the former structure from an isolated offshore volcanic cone. (Fig. 14.12 of Macdonald et al. [1983], used with permission of Frank L. Peterson.)

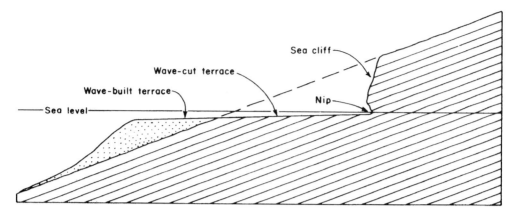

Figure 6.5. A wave-cut terrace, nip, and sea cliff. The relationships among the three are shown here along a relatively gently sloping shoreline. An offshore submarine terrace formed of material eroded from the land is also indicated. (Fig. 14.6 of Macdonald et al. [1983], used with permission of Frank L. Peterson.)

ever, seem to indicate that eustatic or sea level changes were responsible, rather than tectonic adjustments simultaneously and equally affecting all the pertinent islands.

Sea Cliffs

As relative sea level continues to remain constant, the inland extent of a nip progressively increases while the rock material immediately above it continues to collapse and be washed away, thus yielding a **sea cliff.** These actions are especially rapid along coasts where the land enters the ocean at a very steep angle and the sea depth immediately offshore is also relatively so great that little or no terrace is formed. These are conditions that would have prevailed after the giant coastal earth slumps that affected most of the main island volcanoes (see chapters 3, 5). Together, these two processes produced and often maintained such immense sea cliffs as those of northeastern Moloka'i, with their higher points well over 1,000 m (3,300 feet) above the ocean. These are among the highest sea cliffs in the world, and some of those of the Nāpali coast of northwestern Kaua'i (Plate 6.1) are almost as spectacular.

SUGGESTED REFERENCES

Bascom 1960; Bathen 1978; Clark 1980, 1985a,b, 1990; Flament et al. 1998; Macdonald et al. 1983.

AUDIOVISUAL AIDS

The beach: A river of sand; Hawaii's ocean: The Pacific; Hawaii: Surf and sea; Oceanography.

7

Climatology

There is sometimes uncertainty over the difference in the terms "weather" and "climate." **Weather** refers to the atmospheric conditions prevailing at the moment or over a short period of time, as: "We've had very nice weather this week." The study of weather is termed meteorology. **Climate** denotes the weather of an area in a long-term or overall sense, and its study is climatology. The climate of Hawai'i is subtropical; the main islands lie between approximately 19° and 22° north latitude, at the northern border of the Tropics or Torrid Zone. This is the same general latitudinal position as Cuba; Mexico's Yucatán; and Calcutta, India, but Hawai'i is not as oppressively hot and humid as those places. The generally agreeable Hawaiian climate is primarily the result of four factors: (1) latitude, (2) ocean setting, (3) position in the global wind pattern, and (4) presence of local mountains.

LATITUDE

Seasonality

A year in the Hawaiian Islands does not show an obvious division into the four temperate-region seasons. It consists of only two climatological periods, perceptively delimited by ancient Hawaiians as the times of *kau wela* and *ho'oilo*. **Kau wela** (hot season) lasted from the modern months of May through October, and during this period the sun was highest in the sky, the weather warmer, the rainfall typically less, and the trade winds more nearly constant. ***Ho'oilo*** extended from November through April, when the sun's arc was lowest, the weather cooler, rain more frequent, and the northeasterly trades more often replaced by winds from other directions. The fact that the rain of this period is necessary for satisfactory crop growth during the following *kau wela* likely explains its name: *ho'o-* is a causative prefix, and *ilo* means to sprout or germinate.

Day Length

Because the sun's yearly north-south shift between the tropics of Cancer and Capricorn is centered on the equator, areas at low latitudes like the main Hawaiian Islands experience relatively little seasonal difference in day length; the longest summer day in Hawai'i is a little over 13 hours and the shortest winter one just under 11 hours, a difference of only about 2½ hours. By comparison, the difference in length between these days in Washington, D.C., is approximately 6 hours. This means that the reduced amount of solar radiation or sunshine reaching the Islands in winter is still two-thirds of that received in summer, but for Washington, D.C., it is only one-third.

Temperature

At a leeward lowland locality such as O'ahu's Honolulu the average year-round temperature is about 24°C (75°F). The warmest month is August, with an average temperature of about

25.8°C (78.4°F), and the coolest is February, at approximately 22.2°C (72.0°F); the range between these two is only 3.6°C (6.5°F). In Washington, D.C., the difference between the hottest and coldest monthly averages is over 22°C (40°F); this relatively great range is partially a result of the seasonal difference in the amount of sunshine.

On a daily basis in the Islands, the average difference in highest daytime and lowest nighttime temperatures generally far exceeds that for warmest and coldest months of the year, corroborating the old observation that "nighttime is the winter of the Tropics." There is a 4.4° to 11°C (8° to 20°F) difference in these daily averages for various Hawaiian localities. Lowland areas on the windward side of main islands fall in the lower part of this range, and localities of leeward lowlands shielded from the trade winds in the middle portion, with localities above 1,500 m (4,920 feet) experiencing the greatest daily range. For example, even in summer the upper slopes of Mauna Kea on Hawai'i experience frost many nights, but daytime temperatures often rise enough for coatless dress.

The highest temperature recorded in the Hawaiian Islands is 37.8°C (100°F), taken on 27 April 1931, at Pāhala on lowland leeward Hawai'i, but even in such dry, sunny areas readings over 32°C (90°F) are unusual. The lowest recorded temperatures for such leeward coastal areas are usually a little above 10°C (50°F), but such low figures are also extremely unusual, being generally restricted to localities shielded from the warmer trade winds and occurring only every few years. Temperature drops with elevation, and the lowest recorded temperature for the state is –12.8°C (9°F), presumably occurring in late winter, on the summit of Mauna Kea (4,207 m or 13,796 feet).

OCEAN INFLUENCE

Thermal Characteristics

Oceans cover about 70 percent of the earth's surface and have an important effect on climate of the land, particularly that bordering the sea. Effects of the Pacific Ocean on small isolated islands such as those of the Hawaiian Archipelago are especially profound, particularly because no point in the Islands is more than 43 km (27 miles) from the shore. Relative to most other substances, water has high latent heat (that is, the transfer of a great amount of heat energy is necessary to alter its temperature). The enormous Pacific Ocean, thus, can easily release and absorb large amounts of heat to and from air passing over it without its own average temperature changing substantially. An extreme example of this is seen in the amelioration of icy Arctic winds sometimes blowing south over the northern Pacific, which can be warmed as much as 56°C (100°F). The Arctic, however, does have a significant effect on ocean temperature around Hawai'i in another respect.

The **North Pacific Current or Gyre** (Figure 11.1; see chapter 13) can be traced from off Japan, through the northern Pacific, along the western North American coast, west just above the equator, and north off the Philippines. This current receives masses of cold water from the Bering Sea, and its southerly moving currents bring some of this cold water to the archipelago. This results in a sea temperature around the Islands several degrees lower than expected for a current in a tropical setting. Cooler trade winds moving over the eastern loop of the current gradually warm to about the same sea temperature, and warmer ones cool to it, subsequently serving to provide the archipelago with an equable ambient temperature.

Thermostatic Function

In spite of intense solar radiation during the day, the ocean around the Hawaiian Islands is heated very little compared with the land; the variation between daytime and nighttime sea temperatures is only about 0.6°C (1°F). Similarly, on a yearly basis in the vicinity of the main islands, the ocean's thermal response to differences in winter and summer solar heating is a change of as little as 3.3°C (6°F): from about 22.8° to 26.1°C (73° to 79°F). Because of this relative stability in temperature, the ocean water acts as a giant thermostat, buffering extreme changes in ambient land temperature. On a main island, when there are essentially no cooling trades or other sea breezes, the land air temperature may be driven up considerably higher than that of the ocean by solar radiation. Most of the time, however, the relatively steady ocean winds keep the temperatures within about 5.6°C (10°F) of the maximum and minimum ocean figures.

It is interesting, however, that because of the ocean's high latent heat, there is a noticeable lag in reaching its seasonal temperature extremes. As a result of the ocean/trade-wind heat exchange, the Islands' highest ambient temperatures do not occur during the period of most intense solar radiation, but, rather, about 2 months later, in August or September. Similarly, the lowest air temperatures are not reached around December when solar radiation is at a minimum, but in February or March.

WIND PATTERNS AND STORMS

Trade Winds

Significant air movements and storms in the Hawaiian Islands are governed by the archipelago's position in the global wind pattern. A massive high-pressure system known as the **North Pacific High** or Anticyclone is semipermanently positioned generally northeast of the Islands (Figure 7.1). Winds constantly spiral out of this system in a clockwise direction, those issuing from the southern side of the High constituting the **trade winds** that blow over the archipelago from a general northeastern direction. (These winds received their name from early European merchantmen who sailed before them from the American Pacific Northwest in the extensive "China Trade"; see chapter 26.) The trades are remarkably consistent, blowing over 80 percent of days in summer and from 50 to 80 percent in winter. This relative constancy is reflected by the Hawaiian term *"koʻolau,"* usually now translated simply as "windward," but which was possibly originally more specific in that it may have meant toward the northeast, the source of the trades. Trade winds are usually relatively gentle, exceeding 19 km (12 miles) per hour only about half of the time throughout the year, and even then the velocity almost always remains below 40 km (25 miles) per hour.

The North Pacific High, however, annually shifts with the sun, moving north in the summer and south (or southeast) in the winter. In the High's summer position, the main Hawaiian Islands are in the mainstream of the trade winds, but its winter shift moves the center of the trades south of the archipelago. The High also tends to weaken in the winter, thus further lessening the intensity of the trades then.

Aleutian Low

The winter southward movement and weakening of the High has another important effect. Moving east across the ocean north of the North Pacific High there is usually a mass of air known

Seasonal High Pressure Systems and Wind Patterns

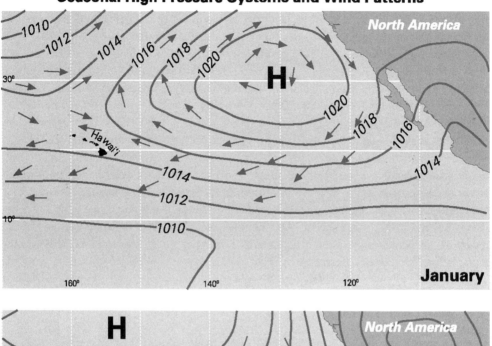

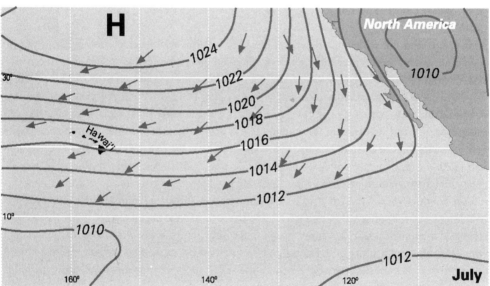

Figure 7.1. Typical seasonal positions of the North Pacific High. *Top,* winter; *bottom,* summer. In the former season, note the High's shift to the southeast and its decreased pressure (in millibars), which allow winter storms of the easterly moving Aleutian Low to approach or reach Hawai'i. (Unnumbered figures on p. 54 of Giambelluca and Schroeder [1998], used with permission of University of Hawai'i Press.)

as the **Aleutian Low** or Cyclone (termed the "Westerlies" by mariners formerly sailing with it). Imbedded in this air mass are both high- and low-pressure systems, thus constituting a "storm track" or easterly moving band of frequently changing weather. At its high summer strength and latitude, the North Pacific High, which represents an area of relatively stable meteorological conditions, keeps the Low's storm track far north of Hawai'i. In winter, however, as the High weakens and moves to the south the air disturbances coming from the west are allowed to shift southward and approach or sometimes reach the Islands. This effective strengthening of the Aleutian Low is responsible for the higher winter surf experienced on north and, often, west Island shores. The high summer surf of the south shores, incidentally, is related to the High's summer shift back to the north, which permits storms of the Southern Hemisphere winter to move closer to Hawai'i.

When the Aleutian Low is situated close to the Hawaiian Islands, at least two types of major meteorological disturbances are likely to occur: Kona storms and cold-front storms.

Kona Storms

In the Northern Hemisphere, air spirals counterclockwise into low-pressure systems such as those of the Aleutian Low. The low-pressure air is then continually forced upward by additional incoming air, so that clouds form and rain results as this elevated mass is cooled. As an easterly moving low approaches the Islands, the predominant wind shifts through various directions, depending on the relative position of the system's center. Any of these directions differing from *ko'olau*, or that of the usual northeasterly trades, was termed ***"kona"*** by ancient Hawaiians. The arrival of such a **Kona storm,** which may occur two or three times each winter, usually results in greater than usual rainfall on at least the typically dry leeward areas of the Islands, and the accompanying winds may occasionally be quite strong. Most often, however, a Kona storm is relatively quite gentle and slow-moving; its rainfall may be prolonged and can affect an entire island for several days, and the barely moving air results in a overall muggy atmosphere. The absence of trade winds and occurrence of a slight Kona wind from the southeast sometimes also causes fumes from any current volcanic activity on Hawai'i to spread to the other main islands as a bluish haze locally called "vog."

Cold-Front Storms

If the temperature of a storm-track air mass reaching the Islands is relatively low, this dense air wedges under the warmer, lighter air over an island so that a **cold-front storm** is produced (Figure 7.2), and the Islands' temperature can be reduced to near-record lows. These storms arrive in Hawai'i on average about five times a year, but many of them weaken or disappear after passing over Kaua'i and sometimes O'ahu. Winds of such a storm are typically strong to very strong, occasionally producing gusts in the vicinity of 153 km (95 miles) per hour. Interaction with topographic or contemporaneous meteorological conditions may sometimes produce such anomalous events as short-lived waterspouts or minor tornadoes on land. Cold-front storm precipitation may be variable, but is nevertheless important to leeward Island areas in supplementing that of the occasional Kona storms.

Thunderstorms

These atmospheric disturbances occur most often in winter, generally when trade winds and the included inversion layer (see discussion later in this chapter) are weaker and there is also a

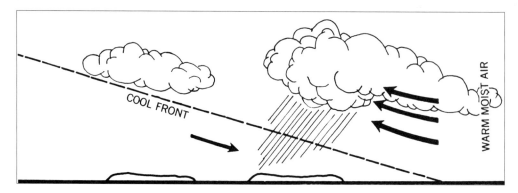

Figure 7.2. Schematic representation of production of a cold-front storm. A mass of cold air ("cool front") is shown moving over islands from the west, causing elevation of warm, moist air to yield the associated rainfall. Leeward regions of the Hawaiian Islands receive most of their yearly precipitation through these and Kona storms. (Unnumbered figure on p. 66 of Carlquist [1980], used with permission of the National Tropical Botanical Garden.)

low-pressure air system over the archipelago. Under such conditions, which are often characteristic of Kona storms and certain cold-front ones, warm moisture-laden trade-wind air is drawn into the low and forced upward. The towering billowy cumulus clouds then formed sometimes reach between 9,000 and 15,000 m (29,700 and 49,500 feet). Greatly cooled at these high elevations, the clouds release moisture in torrential rains, causing devastating flash floods. Strong winds usually do not accompany such rains, but lightning, of course, is a component of every thunderstorm.

Hurricanes

Other tropical storms have essentially no relationship to the North Pacific High and the various storms previously discussed, but are spawned by a complex interaction between sea-level low-pressure systems moving west from the far eastern Pacific and upper ocean-water temperatures. Those disturbances in which the winds are less than 119 km (74 miles) per hour are called tropical storms, and those with stronger winds are classified as **hurricanes** (or "typhoons" west of the 180th meridian) (Figure 7.3). Hurricanes occur mostly between June and November, sometimes termed the "Official Hawaiian Hurricane Season," when the ocean is warm enough to sustain them. These are the storms that do the most damage in the Hawaiian Islands because of their strong winds and heavy rainfall, along with the high surf produced. Fortunately, however, these cyclonal storms are relatively infrequent in the archipelago, usually severely impacting it only once every 10 years or so, because most past well to the south.

MOUNTAIN EFFECTS

Orographic Winds

Hawaiian mountains substantially affect the strength and direction of wind, as well as the distribution and amount of rainfall. The velocity of trade winds may be greatly increased and their direction variously changed as they move in or out of narrow upland valleys. Such mountain-affected air patterns are called **orographic winds** (Greek *"oros"* [mountain] and *"graphikos"*

Figure 7.3. Satellite view of Hurricane 'Iniki. The storm is outlined by clouds being drawn counterclockwise into the low-pressure center or "eye." 'Iniki passed almost directly over Kaua'i on 11 September 1992, causing extensive damage to property and the natural environment. (Photograph courtesy of U.S. National Oceanic and Atmospheric Administration.)

[a dealing with]) and under usual trade-wind conditions are most evident to the lee side of Hawaiian peaks. In the Kula District on the western slopes of East Maui's Haleakalā, for example, once or twice a year modified trades blow downslope at speeds of 64 km (40 miles) per hour, and every four or five years these "Kula winds" may be expected to reach 97 km (60 miles) per hour. Similar winds affect Lahaina at the leeward base of the West Maui mountains, very occasionally reaching between 129 and 161 km (80 and 100 miles) per hour; they are sometimes called "*lehua* winds" because of the red blossoms of the *'Ōhi'a lehua* tree swept downslope on them.

When funneled between two large mountains trades may also gain considerable speed and strength. The channel between Hawai'i and Maui, bordered by the former's Mauna Kea and the latter's Haleakalā, is often made quite rough in this manner; its name, 'Alenuihāhā (great billows smashing), undoubtedly reflects this turbulence. Just to the west, the designation of the channel between Maui and Kaho'olawe as 'Alalākeiki (child's wail) could possibly have resulted from a family's attempt to navigate the passage by canoe during a period of high wind.

Orographic Precipitation

Hawaiian mountains also strongly influence the distribution and amount of precipitation, which furnishes the major portion of freshwater to the Islands (see chapter 8). Evaporation of water from the ocean's surface, which has been estimated at about 1 m (3.3 feet) of ocean depth per year worldwide, provides the air with this moisture in the form of water vapor. Moist air traveling at a uniform elevation over the ocean loses little if any of this water; average yearly rainfall at sea is about 62.5 cm (25 inches), with a range of 50 to 75 cm (20 to 30 inches). When the moisture-laden winds are cooled by elevation over Hawaiian mountains, however, **orographic rainfall** occurs, resulting in a yearly average for the main Hawaiian Islands of about 175 cm (70 inches). The range is very great, with a few areas receiving less than one-seventh of this (25 cm or 10 inches) and others more than six times as much (1,050 cm or 420 inches) (Table 7.1, Figure 7.4).

By the time incoming ocean air has risen to between about 1,525 and 1,830 m (5,000 and 6,000 feet) it has lost most of the water that can be extracted by natural cooling (Figure 7.5). Hawaiian localities in this elevational range, such as the summits of Pu'u Kukui (1,765 m or 5,788 feet) on West Maui and Mount Wai'ale'ale (1,570 m or 5,148 feet) on Kaua'i, thus receive the greatest amounts of rainfall. (The Wai'ale'ale summit and its Alaka'i Swamp may well hold the world record for annual rainfall, although an Indian locality of very similar topographic setting may receive slightly more.)

Inversion Layer

As evident from Table 7.1, elevations above about 2,000 m (6,600 feet) receive considerably less rain than those below. This is due to an interesting meteorological phenomenon known as the **inversion layer,** which is inherent to much of the trade-wind air mass moving out of the North Pacific High. Usually, moisture-laden trade-wind air warmed by the sun-heated surface of a Hawaiian island rises unimpeded, becoming progressively cooled at an average of 1.7°C (3°F) per 300 m (990 feet) of elevation. It happens, however, that at about the latitude of the main islands, relatively dry air is descending from very high elevations after ascending above the equator and moving north in an oval circulatory pattern called the Hadley Cell (named after an English scientist who first described the phenomenon). This air is heated by compression as it descends and suppresses the cooling air rising below it, thus producing a temperature-

Table 7.1. Average yearly rainfall of selected higher-elevation Hawaiian localities. An asterisk (*) following the elevation indicates the highest point of the island. Because of lack of recording stations at some of the actual summit altitudes listed, their rainfall figures are estimated ("est."). In the case of mountains less than about 1,800 m (5,940 feet) the rainfall figures are usually also from stations below the highest points and therefore are probably considerably less than summit precipitation. (Data from various sources.)

Island and Locality	Elevation		Station Rainfall	
	m	(feet)	cm	(inches)
Hawai'i				
Mauna Kea (summit)	4,207	(13,792)*	est. <38	(<15)
" (Halepōhaku)	2,812	(9,220)	70	(28)
Mauna Loa (summit)	4,171	(13,677)	est. <38	(<15)
" (Observatory)	3,401	(11,150)	53	(21)
Hualālai (summit)	2,523	(8,271)	60	(24)
Kohala	1,655	(5,425)	295	(118)
Kīlauea	1,240	(4,049)	158	(63)
Maui				
East Maui (Haleakalā)	3,057	(10,023)*	est. <75	(<30)
" (Kūhiwa Gulch)	1,830±	(6,000±)	913	(365)
West Maui (Pu'u Kukui)	1,765	(5,788)	998	(399)
Kaho'olawe				
Moa'ulanui	450	(1,477)*	est. <75	(<30)
Lāna'i				
Lāna'ihale (summit)	1,028	(3,370)*	100	(40)
Moloka'i				
East Moloka'i (Kamakou)	1,516	(4,970)*	378	(151)
West Moloka'i (Pu'u Nānā)	421	(1,381)	70	(28)
O'ahu				
Ko'olau Range (Kōnāhuanui)	961	(3,150)	218	(87)
" (Punalu'u Stream)	787	(2,580)	843	(337)
" (Pauoa Flats)	549	(1,800)	415	(166)
Wai'anae Range (Mount Ka'ala)	1,226	(4,020)*	203	(81)
Kaua'i				
Mount Wai'ale'ale (Kawaikini)	1,570	(5,148)*	1,215	(486)
Ni'ihau				
Pāni'au	391	(1,281)*	est. <75	(<30)

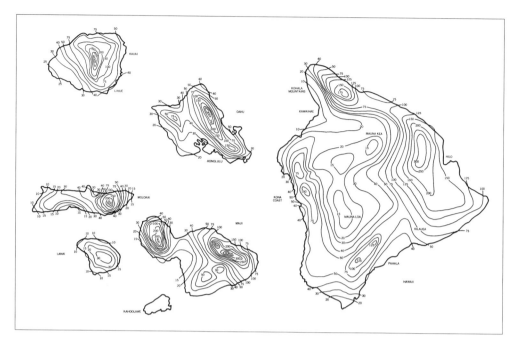

Figure 7.4. Rainfall distribution in the main Hawaiian Islands. (The islands are not shown in their true geographical relationships.) The isohyetal lines connect points of approximately equal values of annual precipitation (in inches; 1 inch = 2.54 cm). No data are available for Ni'ihau (not shown) and Kaho'o-lawe; they each probably receive less than 30 inches (76 cm) yearly. (Unnumbered figures on pp. 76–77 of Carlquist [1980], used with permission of the National Tropical Botanical Garden.)

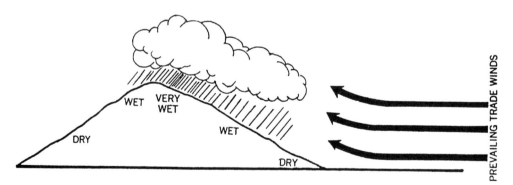

Figure 7.5. Schematic representation of trade-wind rainfall on a mountain. The distribution of such precipitation is shown as the warm moisture-laden air passes over a Hawaiian peak about 1,525 to 1,830 m (5,000 to 6,000 feet) in height, such as Pu'u Kukui on West Maui or Wai'ale'ale on Kaua'i. (Slightly modified from unnumbered figure on p. 68 of Carlquist [1980], used with permission of the National Tropical Botanical Garden.)

inverted layer with warm air anomalously overlying cool. The inversion-layer's elevation may vary daily, but is most often between about 1,525 and 2,135 m (5,000 and 7,000 feet), often exceeding the Hawaiian mountain summits receiving maximum rainfall. Thus, additional warm moist air continuing to rise above the land encounters the previously trapped cool stratum at the inversion layer base and is also cooled, eventually forming there a level **cloud blanket** with an often-rainy zone about 100 m (330 feet) or more in thickness (Figure 7.6).

This inversion layer is present in Hawai'i between half and three-quarters of the time, and by keeping most of the moist trade-wind air from reaching greater heights, severely limits precipitation above the layer. The very low annual rainfall figures for such high-elevation localities as the summits of Mauna Kea (less than 38 cm or 15 inches) and Haleakalā (less than 75 cm or 30 inches) attest to the effectiveness of this altitudinal precipitation barrier. The summit area of Mauna Kea, especially, has aptly been termed an "alpine desert" because of this scarcity of moisture (see chapter 14); in fact, it is primarily only the winter storms occurring when the trade winds and associated inversion-layer system are weakest that bring any appreciable amount of precipitation to the area, most often as small, soft hail or snow (Plate 7.1). Further, the usual absence of trade-wind air, hazy with water vapor and lower-elevation air contaminants—along with the volcano's dormancy—make the mountain's crest an excellent site for the thirteen astronomical observatories already established or under construction there as of 1999.

On some days, however, moist air moving up the sunlit lower slopes of Mauna Kea becomes so heated that it can either seep or be blown by strong trades through the inversion layer to form towering clouds as it cools. Then, usually beginning in early afternoon, an observer at the summit can watch these billowing shapes building up from various spots on the cloud blanket spread out far below, sometimes reaching 4,500 m (14,850 feet). Because the air above the inversion layer is relatively so dry, however, the water vapor making up these clouds is largely lost to it, and the clouds dissipate without precipitation occurring.

Hilo Rain

Areas at essentially sea level on windward coasts would be expected to receive only about the same amount of rainfall as the open ocean: about 62.5 cm (25 inches) annually. The port city of Hilo on the east coast of Hawai'i, however, is notoriously wet, having the remarkable yearly

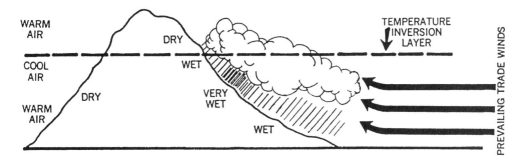

Figure 7.6. Schematic representation of inversion layer–trade winds interaction. The inversion layer is situated between about 1,525 and 2,135 m (5,000 and 7,000 feet), and the mountain diagrammed is greater than about 2,400 m (7,870 feet) in height, such as Mauna Kea on Hawai'i or Haleakalā on Maui. (Slightly modified from unnumbered figure on p. 68 of Carlquist [1980], used with permission of the National Tropical Botanical Garden.)

rainfall average of 350 cm (140 inches) (Figure 7.4). The trade winds passing over the city build up as they are blocked by massive Mauna Loa and Mauna Kea just downwind, forcing the following air to rise and cool almost at the coast, thus yielding the abundant precipitation. Also, the heating of the broad slopes of these two great mountains causes an upward convection current that draws in a substantial amount of moist ocean air in addition to that of the trades. This consistent rainfall is one of the primary reasons that Hilo has been surpassed by the relatively dry leeward Hawai'i Kona coast as a tourist destination and retirement community.

Pali Rainfall

In contrast to Hilo, Kailua, occupying an essentially identical coastal position and elevation on Windward O'ahu, receives only about 100 cm (40 inches) of annual rainfall because the Ko'olau Range only a short distance downwind is considerably lower in elevation and bulk than the Hawai'i mountains. Certain parts of this elongate Ko'olau escarpment, however, receive rather great amounts of rainfall, even though they are much lower than the potential maximum rainfall zone of about 1,525 to 1,830 m (5,000 to 6,000 feet) mentioned earlier. Note in Table 7.1, for example, the relatively high annual rainfall figure of 843 cm (337 inches) for the range's Punalu'u Stream at only 787 m (2,580 feet). In this section of the Ko'olaus, the windward slopes are relatively gradual rather than steep, and the ascending trades have time enough to cool and lose much of their water content at the intermediate height before passing over the range crest.

Somewhat special wind and rainfall patterns result as trade winds meet an abrupt rather than a gradual elevational rise on the Windward Ko'olau face, such as the steep, but only moderately high *pali* in the Kāne'ohe-Kailua area (Figures 5.3, 7.7). A normal trade breeze strengthens to such an extent when its air is compressed against and forced over the sheer cliff here that it is often difficult to stand against the wind at the Pali Lookout off the highway between Honolulu's Nu'uanu Valley and Windward O'ahu. In fact, after rains, a few of the nearby ephemeral waterfalls sometimes have their water blown back upward, thus being billed as "upside-down

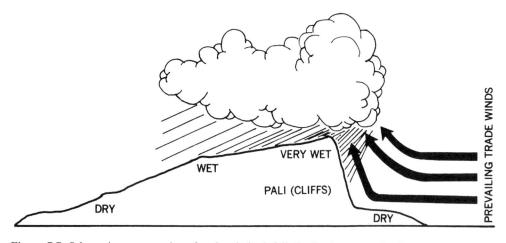

Figure 7.7. Schematic representation of trade-wind rainfall distribution at a *pali*. The steep ocean-facing cliff diagrammed is about 915 m (3,000 feet) in elevation, such as parts of the Windward Pali along the Ko'olau Range on O'ahu. (Unnumbered figure on p. 68 of Carlquist [1980], used with permission of the National Tropical Botanical Garden.)

waterfalls." When the moist air reaches the crest of the *pali,* the rapid cooling often causes immediate cloud formation and heavy precipitation. Some of this rain falls on the sheer seaward face, but because of the force of the wind, most of it is blown farther to the leeward side. The difference in amount of rain over such a short horizontal distance is obvious from a comparison of the annual rainfall figures in Table 7.1 of only about 218 cm (87 inches) for Kōnāhuanui (961 m or 3,150 feet) at the *pali* crest as opposed to the almost double figure of 415 cm (166 inches) at the lower-elevation Pauoa Flats (549 m or 1,800 feet) about 3 km (1.8 miles) directly leeward.

Rain Shadows

The extension of this trade-wind precipitation into the leeward Koʻolau valleys yields the mist and typically brief showers, along with frequent rainbows, of places like upper Mānoa and Nuʻuanu Valleys. But as it moves farther leeward, the air that has passed over the Koʻolau Range

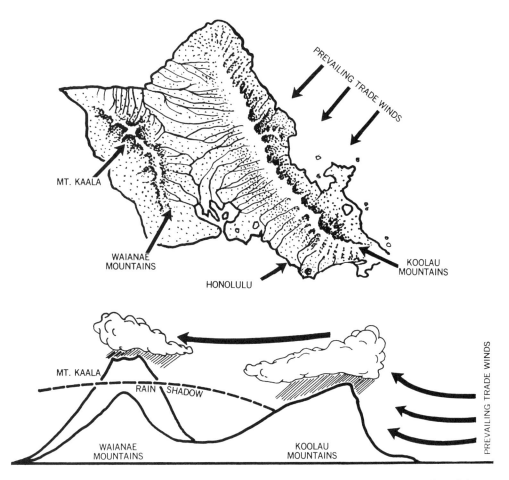

Figure 7.8. Schematic representation of the rain-shadow phenomenon on Oʻahu. The section of the Koʻolau Mountains shown in the profile is about 915 m (3,000 feet) in elevation, that of the lower Waiʻanae Mountains about 795 m (2,600 feet), and Mount Kaʻala is 1,226 m (4,020 feet). (Unnumbered figure on p. 70 of Carlquist [1980], used with permission of the National Tropical Botanical Garden.)

follows the continuing decline in surface elevation. Because this air is now in lower, warmer areas, rain ceases to fall from it; in fact, no more water can be lost unless the air is again cooled by reaching an elevation greater than that of the Koʻolau crest. Thus, as shown in Figure 7.8, a **rain shadow** is produced that keeps most of Oʻahu's leeward areas quite dry, as evidenced by the very low annual rainfall average of about 57.5 cm (23 inches) for Waikīkī, downtown Honolulu, and the International Airport.

Although the lower portions of the Waiʻanae Mountains are in the rain shadow of the Koʻolaus, higher parts of this range such as Mount Kaʻala at 1,226 m (4,020 feet) receive a relatively fair amount of rain. When passing over any Waiʻanae elevations higher than the maximum elevation of the Koʻolaus, the air is cooled to a lower temperature and additional water vapor thus condenses and precipitates. The amount of rainfall here, however, is noticeably less than if a large amount of the water vapor had not already been lost at the Koʻolau crossing.

The previously mentioned Kona coast of Hawaiʻi, and popular similar leeward Maui coastal tourist destinations such as Kāʻanapali and Lahaina, as well as Kīhei, owe their low rainfall to their positions in the rain shadows of high West and East Maui mountains, respectively (Figure 7.4). Noticeably dry West Molokaʻi, as exemplified by Puʻu Nānā near the community of Maunaloa with only 70 cm (28 inches) annual rainfall (Table 7.1), is in the rain shadow of the high eastern half of the island. This rain-shadow phenomenon affects not only different portions of a single island, but also entire islands. As may be seen in Figure 3.1, rain-poor Niʻihau is shaded by Kauaʻi to the northeast, and parched Kahoʻolawe by similarly positioned East Maui.

Fog Drip

Lānaʻi is also partially in the rain shadow of Maui, and most of the lower parts of the island are, indeed, quite dry. The trade winds moving over its higher elevations of approximately 1,000 m (3,300 feet), however, still contain enough moisture to form a fairly consistent cloud mass there. In fact, the name Mauna Lei (lei mountain), given to a community and large gulch draining the high center of the island, is said to refer to the garland of clouds often surrounding this summit area. Although the greatest annual rainfall as measured by gauges on Lānaʻi is only about 100 cm (40 inches), at the island's highest point, Lānaʻihale, there is considerable **fog drip,** which results from condensation of moist ocean air on night-cooled vegetation. The name of Hauola (dew of life) for a large Lānaʻi gulch was quite likely bestowed because the ancient inhabitants there are said to have obtained drinking water by shaking dew from dense plant cover into containers or by collecting that condensing on oiled tapa (bark cloth) spread on the ground overnight. It has been estimated that in certain localities throughout the main islands this unmeasured fog drip may amount to at least twice the amount of rainfall officially recorded by gauges.

Convective-Uplift Rainfall

Certain leeward coasts, especially the Kona coast of Hawaiʻi, consistently receive a higher annual rainfall than would be expected from their rain-shadow location by another means: **convective uplift** of moist air. The Kona coast is so well shielded from the trades by Mauna Loa and, to some extent, Hualālai that it has essentially its own wind and rain regimes, at least other than during the winter westerly storm periods. In fact, it is the only Hawaiian location at which summer rainfall exceeds that of winter. As diagrammed in Figure 7.9, when the broad western slopes of Mauna Loa and Hualālai are progressively heated by the sun each day, the air over them begins to rise by convection, creating a partial vacuum into which is drawn moisture-laden ocean air from the west. This incoming air is obvious as an afternoon onshore breeze, and when drawn up the mountain slopes it is cooled enough to produce a substantial cloud cover and, usually, attendant afternoon rain. After the sun sets, however, the slopes and the air over them gradually cool, and the wind pattern is reversed, so throughout the evening there is typically a steady offshore breeze.

This combination of afternoon shading cloud cover and rain has historically made the Kona coast an ideal place to grow introduced coffee species, marketed as the well-known "Kona Coffee." This must be partially shaded for successful production, and in many other coffee-growing areas of the world the requisite shade is provided instead by the expensive planting of taller broad-canopied trees in the coffee groves.

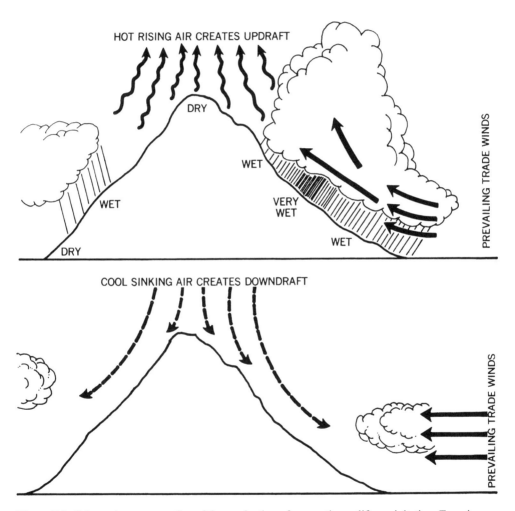

Figure 7.9. Schematic representation of the production of convective-uplift precipitation. *Top,* air movement during the afternoon; *bottom,* during the night and early morning. This process characteristically occurs daily along Hawaiʻi Island's western or Kona coast (situated on the left side of the diagrams). The mountain illustrated could represent either Mauna Loa or Hualālai. (Unnumbered figures on p. 74 of Carlquist [1980], used with permission of the National Tropical Botanical Garden.)

EL NIÑO

Although the subject cannot be discussed in any great detail here, a mention should be made of the meteorologically related oceanic phenomenon known as *El Niño* that periodically affects Hawaiian climate. This is basically a major surface current of relatively quite warm ocean water that for incompletely understood reasons develops in the far western Pacific every few years. The mass of warm water moves eastward across the ocean in equatorial latitudes, usually reaching the northwestern coast of South America about Christmastime (thus its Spanish name of The Child, in reference to the newborn Christ). This flow of warm ocean water is massive enough to influence weather patterns worldwide in a predictable manner: usually dry areas tend to receive heavy rainfall and storms, and usually wet areas often undergo droughts; at the same time colder areas usually become unseasonably warm, and warmer ones cold. As far as Hawai'i is concerned, an *El Niño* episode typically causes lower than usual rainfall and fosters the development of hurricanes. Also, it allows the previously described Aleutian Low storm track to move even farther south, thus often bringing higher and more prolonged surf to the north and west shores of the Islands.

SUGGESTED REFERENCES

Armstrong (ed.) 1983; Carlquist 1980; Giambelluca and Schroeder 1998; Price 1972; Sanderson (ed.) 1993; Schroeder 1993.

AUDIOVISUAL AIDS

Hawaii: Kona storms; Hawaii: Mauka showers; Hawaii's climate.

Freshwater

ost people on the main Hawaiian Islands give little thought to the ready availability of freshwater. This commodity, however, should be of much greater concern to people of isolated and relatively small, densely populated, ocean islands than to those of a continental area with ready access to more abundant water resources. As an indication of the importance of freshwater to Hawai'i, a greater part of the very considerable geological knowledge of the Hawaiian Islands gathered in the first half of the twentieth century, other than that dealing directly with volcanic activity, was obtained primarily for purposes of locating and most efficiently utilizing groundwater sources.

THE HYDROLOGIC CYCLE

Before discussing dynamics of freshwater in the Hawaiian Islands specifically, it should be explained that all of the earth's water is involved in a continuous **hydrologic cycle** (Figure 8.1), which is powered by the sun's heat energy. Water vapor enters the atmosphere primarily through evaporation of warmed sea water, is moved around the earth by winds, then condenses and returns to the surface as precipitation (see chapter 7). It is a dynamic system, with the water deposited on land either temporarily collecting on the surface as freshwater bodies or below the surface as groundwater. Eventually, however, all of it continues in the cycle by either flowing into the ocean or entering the atmosphere through both direct evaporation and transpiration by plants and animals. In Hawai'i, all of the freshwater necessary for life on each island is currently supplied by precipitation on the same island. Although the proportions vary between islands, on average about a third of this falling water flows directly to the ocean, another third leaves as vapor, and the remaining third infiltrates to become groundwater.

GROUNDWATER

Basal Lens
A major portion of the groundwater on a Hawaiian island forms a **basal lens,** or Ghyben-Herzberg lens after the Dutch and German scientists who first correctly explained the phenomenon. The basal lens floats on top of slightly denser salt water that saturates the deeper portion of an island base, with a relatively thin transition zone of mixed fresh and salt water between them. The basal lens is typically thickest under the center of an island, where its upper surface is mounded above sea level, and thinnest at the coast, where this surface usually approaches sea level (Figure 8.2). The difference between the upper-surface elevation and any lower one is known as "head," and the hydrostatic pressure it provides causes constant natural discharge of freshwater from lower-elevation subaerial as well as submarine springs. Under natural conditions, the size of the lens at any given time represents a long-term equilibrium between the amount of water recharging it and the equivalent amount of water discharged to the ocean and

atmosphere. If, however, water is artificially withdrawn, as through wells, the lens decreases in size until a new equilibrium is reached in which water loss through both natural and artificial means again equals natural recharge.

The freshwater dynamics of Oʻahu may be used as an example of the previously mentioned phenomena. About 16 percent of the island's precipitation is lost as surface runoff to the ocean, 44 percent evaporates or is transpired after sinking into the ground, and the remaining 40 percent that also infiltrates serves as groundwater recharge. The island's basal lens is about 550 m (1,815 feet) in maximum thickness, and the transitional freshwater/saltwater zone averages perhaps 30 or 60 m (100 or 200 feet) thick. The upper surface of the basal lens reaches as high as 13 m (43 feet) above sea level in places. The recharge of groundwater on Oʻahu is about 34.8 cubic meters per second (m³/s) or 792 million gallons per day (mg/d). At least 80 percent of

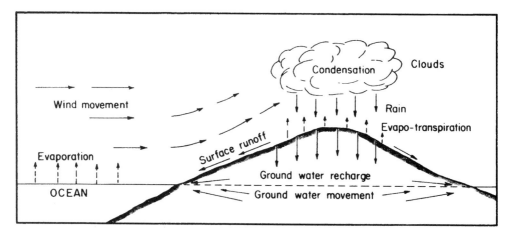

Figure 8.1. Generalized illustration of the hydrologic cycle. Precipitation deposited on land continues in the cycle through ultimate runoff to the ocean, direct evaporation, and transpiration by vegetation. (Fig. 10.1 of Macdonald et al. [1983], used with permission of Frank L. Peterson.)

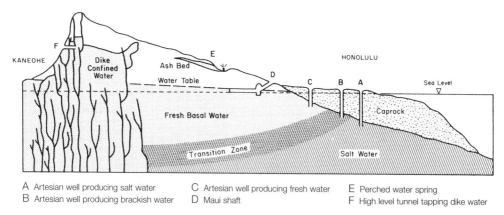

A Artesian well producing salt water   C Artesian well producing fresh water   E Perched water spring
B Artesian well producing brackish water D Maui shaft   F High level tunnel tapping dike water

Figure 8.2. Generalized cross section showing occurrence of groundwater in southeastern Oʻahu. The island is viewed in profile from the north. The term "Maui shaft" (D) refers to a particular type of pumped-well design. (Fig. 11.6 of Macdonald et al. [1983], used with permission of Frank L. Peterson.)

the approximately 14.3 m³/s (325 mg/d) of freshwater used on the island is currently pumped from basal groundwater sources. The remainder, as is discussed later in this chapter, is derived from tunnels tapping or "developing" dike-confined and perched water, pumpage of isolated lenses in caprock, and artesian or free-flowing wells.

Dike-Confined Water

Just as horizontal layers of dense caldera-fill basalt greatly impede passage of rainwater (see chapter 5), similarly dense but vertically oriented dikes (see chapter 4) slow the lateral movement of infiltrating water. This **dike-confined water** typically builds up to high levels in the more permeable substrate between dikes. It can be obtained by tunneling horizontally through the dikes to lead it off (Figure 8.2, *F*) or by sinking a well between the dikes and pumping out the water. In either case, further expense in transporting it is largely avoided because much of this water is located at relatively high elevations and gravity alone powers its movement to the areas of use.

Perched Water

Some infiltrating rainwater is greatly impeded in its downward movement to the basal lens because it encounters a buried horizon of various types of fine material of low permeability, such as ash or certain kinds of clayey soil, although a less-common dense basalt sill (see chapter 4) can also accomplish this. The water collecting on the low-permeability layer or perching member is known as **perched water,** and water of this type eventually flowing to and escaping at the layer's lowest edge may form a "perched spring" (Figure 8.2, *E*). Such springs are sometimes situated high on valley walls where erosion has intersected this part of the perching member. Much as in the case of dike-confined water, perched water can be extracted through tunnels or wells, but these extend only to the upper surface of the perching member.

Wells

Similar low-permeability layers are located on parts of the coastal plain of Oʻahu and a few other main islands, forming what is known as **caprock.** The basal freshwater that stands higher than the freshwater and saltwater beneath the caprock exerts considerable hydrostatic pressure on this peripheral portion of the lens. Because of the pressure, drilling through the caprock to freshwater from a surface elevation below the upper level of the basal lens will result in an artesian well, here meaning one from which water flows without need of pumping (Figure 8.2, *A, B, C*). In 1879, an enterprising James Campbell drilled the first Hawaiian artesian wells at Honouliuli in the southwestern Oʻahu ʻEwa Plain and used this abundant water to raise immense crops of Sugarcane, thus amassing the present-day Campbell Estate fortune. In many areas, the caprock itself contains small fresh-to-brackish water lenses, but, thus far, these remain essentially unutilized as potable water sources although many are used as a source of irrigation water.

Withdrawal of water from the basal lens through either artesian or pumped wells lowers its upper surface (that is, the water table), sometimes to such an extent that water of higher-elevation artesian wells no longer comes all the way to the surface and must then be pumped from them. At least the shallower of inland pumped wells can obviously go completely dry as the water table drops. Also, as the basal lens decreases in size, the transition zone of mixed freshwater and saltwater moves inland and closer to the surface. Depending on well depths, pumping rates, and various related factors, former freshwater wells of both artesian and pumped type nearest the coast may then begin yielding brackish water. This latter problem is compounded by the fact that the portion of the basal freshwater lens directly beneath the intake of an active well is thinned more than other areas, so that transition-zone water can even more readily approach and contaminate the well.

WATER TRANSPORT

Background

The windward sides of most main islands are wetter and therefore have more abundant water resources than the leeward sides (see chapter 7). In historic times, however, vast agricultural development has often been greatest on the leeward side of these islands, and it has been necessary to devise means of moving some of the initially abundant windward water to irrigate this drier region. An example of how this has been accomplished is provided by a description of the primary water-diversion system of Oʻahu.

Waiāhole Ditch System

In the early 1900s, sugar companies were growing ever-increasing amounts of Sugarcane in rain-shadowed south-central Oʻahu (Figure 5.2; see chapter 7). Irrigation water from pumped and artesian wells as well as a few nearby streams was becoming insufficient there because the combined rate of usage and natural discharge had long exceeded the rate of natural recharge. On then-sparsely populated Windward Oʻahu, however, there was a large amount of rainwater flowing—seemingly mostly unused—off the trade wind–facing Koʻolau slopes as streams to the ocean. The sugar growers then understandably looked to this potentially obtainable freshwater as a solution to their problem.

On other main islands, in the latter half of the 1800s and early 1900s at least three commercially successful water-diversion systems involving tunnels and ditches had been constructed to supply mountain stream water for irrigating lowland Sugarcane fields. This prompted the Oʻahu growers to attempt the same sort of development. Thus, from 1913 to 1916, great numbers of Japanese laborers were employed by the Oʻahu Sugar Company to construct a remarkable water-retrieval and transport complex known as the **Waiāhole Ditch System.** On the steep *pali* face of the Koʻolaus, a series of ridge-piercing tunnels and contoured ditches 8 km (5 miles) long was dug from an elevation of 241 m (795 feet) in upper Kahana Valley south to the head of Waiāhole Valley at 213 m (703 feet) on the northern edge of Kāneʻohe.

This portion of the system not only intercepted water from about three dozen streams and a number of perched springs, but also received water developed along the way by means of branch tunnels excavated to dike-confined Koʻolau Range water. Incidentally, although completely unexpected when the project was designed, this dike-confined water proved to constitute by far the greatest amount of water flowing into the system. Then, at the southern Windward terminus, all of this gravity-powered water was led west through the Koʻolau Range by a tunnel 4,450 m (14,685 feet) long, dug by round-the-clock shifts of laborers. Thence, the water flowed through a series of more tunnels, large pipes, and open ditches to Sugarcane fields of south-central Oʻahu.

The entire Waiāhole Ditch System is approximately 43.5 km (27 miles) long, and since its opening in 1916 has had an average water flow of over 1.4 m³/s (32 mg/d), although the actual annual yield has consistently diminished because of continuing depletion of the transitory dike-confined water. Of the average flow over the life of the project, 1.2 m³/s (27 mg/d) is estimated to have been groundwater. The average amount of surface water the system collected from streams and perched springs might thus seem to be 0.2 m³/s (4.5 mg/d). Because the withdrawal of high-level groundwater caused less to seep out to these surface sources, however, the reduction from predevelopment Windward surface water flow was substantially greater than this amount, conceivably at least twice as much, although no exact figures are available.

This entire water-diversion project, although benefitting south-central Oʻahu agriculture, has had certain socially and environmentally detrimental consequences for the rest of the island. Before the system's construction, essentially all of the Windward surface freshwater had flowed in stream channels, maintaining the native ecosystem there and nourishing prehistoric and historic lowland Taro pondfields before forming extensive Kāneʻohe Bay estuaries. By the mid-1900s, however, the significant diminution in this original surface flow had noticeably dewatered Windward streams, pondfields, and estuaries. Also, withdrawal of the dike-confined Windward groundwater has resulted in ultimate shrinkage of the entire island's basal fresh-water lens, with the previously described attendant problems of such shrinkage. In recent years, though, because foreign competition has made growing Hawaiian Sugarcane increasingly unprofitable, this former major crop will be phased out on at least most main islands by early in the twenty-first century. On Oʻahu, this cessation, with no major replacement crop definitely planned thus far, has raised the possibility that a certain amount of water collected by the Wai-āhole Ditch System can be kept on Windward Oʻahu so that surface-water flow to lowland areas will be substantially increased and the island's basal lens at least somewhat augmented.

SURFACE WATER

Rivers and Streams

In the main Hawaiian Islands, about five hundred rivers, streams, and major tributaries of both are generally recognized as watercourses. About a quarter of these are only intermittently active; the remaining 376 have at least one segment that is perennial, or carrying water year-round. Essentially all Hawaiian watercourses are characterized by gentle flow, although some with relatively narrow channels and steep banks can carry dangerous torrents of rushing water after local cloudbursts.

Few Hawaiian watercourses are of considerable size. The two largest in terms of water transported are the Wailuku River at Hilo on Hawaiʻi and the Hanalei River on north-central Kauaʻi, with year-round average flows of 8.1 and 6.6 m³/s (184 and 151 mg/d), respectively. Only five or six other rivers, all on Kauaʻi, have a flow equalling or exceeding 2.4 m³/s (55 mg/d). Oʻahu's Kaukonahua Stream at 48.3 km (30 miles) is the longest perennial watercourse; the Wailuku River is second at about 36.5 km (22.7 miles). Less than a dozen others have perennial segments greater than 16 km (10 miles) in length. Approximately 86 percent of the perennial rivers and streams have been physically altered from their natural condition in one or more of several ways during historic times. For example, 53 percent now have some amount of their water diverted, 15 percent have been artificially channelized by having bottom and sides concreted or otherwise armored, and so on.

Amphitheater-Headed Valleys

Surface freshwater is basically responsible for probably the largest topographic features of the Hawaiian Islands other than the volcanoes themselves. These are the giant **amphitheater-headed valleys,** so named because of their rounded and steep-sided upper reaches, which are usually wider than their mouths (Plate 8.1). During the Postshield Stage of a Hawaiian island's life history (see chapter 3), numerous small streams carry water radially from mountain summits, each gradually cutting its own V-shaped valley down the mountain, with narrow knife-edged ridges separating each of the gorges (Plate 8.1, Figure 8.3). The chemical weathering of the aging basalt allows this erosion to proceed considerably more rapidly than it would in the case of fresh volcanic material. As the valleys erode farther toward the summit, some of the intervening ridges are worn down, causing portions of the headwater drainage of streams flowing down one valley to be diverted into an adjacent one in a process known as "stream capture" or **stream piracy.** As a result, a relatively few augmented stream courses become dominant, and their individual valleys undergo a greatly increased rate of erosion as the streams progressively wear back into the mass of the old volcano. The capture of increasing numbers of secondary streams at higher elevations eventually produces the distinctive circular outline of the upper amphitheater-headed valley.

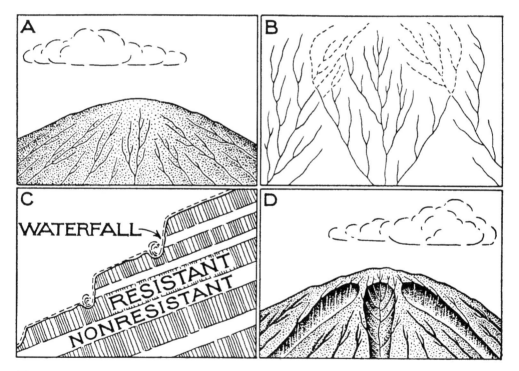

Figure 8.3. Formation of amphitheater-headed valleys. *A,* radial stream drainage near the summit of a shield volcano at the Postshield Stage; *B,* subsequent development of a dominant watercourse through stream piracy; *D,* ultimate appearance of the much-eroded volcano with three major valleys. *C* depicts the role of alternating layers of different basaltic substrate types in formation and maintenance of spectacular high waterfalls at valley heads. (Fig. 2.2 of Stearns [1985], used with permission of Pacific Books, Publishers.)

Although the actual period of time is unknown, it seems likely that 100,000 years or more must be required to produce an amphitheater-headed valley. And such an impressive structure can only be formed after the active life of a volcano, otherwise new lava flows entering the stream gorges would constantly compensate for erosional loss. Thus, on the relatively young island of Hawai'i, only four amphitheater-headed valleys have been formed so far: Waipi'o, Waimanu, and the lesser Pololū and twin-mouthed Honokāne Valleys, all leading to the ocean from the wet windward slopes of 600,000-year-old Kohala, the oldest of the island's original volcanoes (Figure 8.4).

Waterfalls

Many of the streams flowing into, especially, the upper ends of fully formed amphitheater-headed valleys do so in the form of narrow waterfalls, often of great height. As diagrammed in Figure 8.3, *C,* the alternation of layers of relatively erosion-resistant and erosion-susceptible basalt are responsible for this. A stream flowing into the valley erodes relatively quickly through softer material in its bed, but when exceptionally hard substrate is reached erosion slows greatly, and the stream flows on top of the layer until it reaches and flows over an exposed edge, forming a waterfall of moderate height. The softer material directly beneath the falling water con-

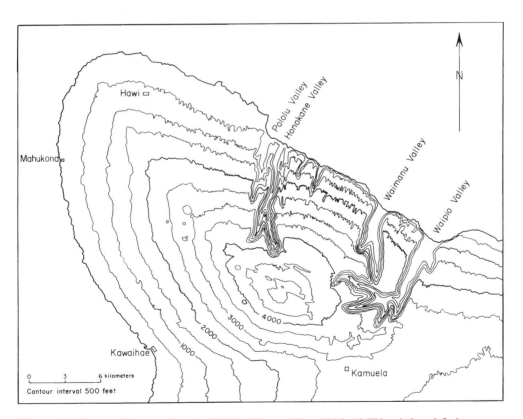

Figure 8.4. Topographic map of ancient Kohala Volcano, Hawai'i Island. This windward-facing area of northwestern Hawai'i possesses the only four amphitheater-headed valleys yet formed on this relatively young island. (Fig. 19.8 of Macdonald et al. [1983], used with permission of Frank L. Peterson.)

tinues to be rather quickly worn away until the next layer of resistant bedrock is reached, at which time the process is repeated. A deep **plunge pool** is formed in the resistant material at the spot where the falling water impacts it. Because of their usual elevated position, these interesting cuplike "hanging" plunge pools are often not visible from the valley floor, and must be viewed from either the air or the upper valley rim to be fully appreciated. Eventually, however, a plunge pool deepens enough to penetrate its resistant basalt layer, and a waterfall of great height results when a number of resistant layers have similarly been worn through.

Drowned Watercourses

As streams issuing from the confines of major valleys flow through lower, relatively flat coastal areas they are often free to meander, and sometimes divide and coalesce in various patterns before entering the ocean. Such configurations of lowland watercourses are usually not especially evident during geologic periods of relatively low sea level, but at high sea stands the coastal outline produced by the formations sometimes becomes quite noticeable. For example, the intricate shoreline pattern of O'ahu's Pearl Harbor, with its long narrow entrance and varied lobular inner reaches or lochs, can easily be understood when it is realized that the area is simply a system of eroded watercourse beds developed during lower stands of the sea, now drowned by the current relatively elevated sea level (Figure 8.5). Similarly, submarine canyons recently discovered offshore of major Island stream valleys allow tracing of former land watercourses there.

Lakes and Marshes

Natural Hawaiian lakes and ponds as well as inland marshes and swamps tend to be rather rare. In many Island areas that are above the local water table and where the original basalt has been

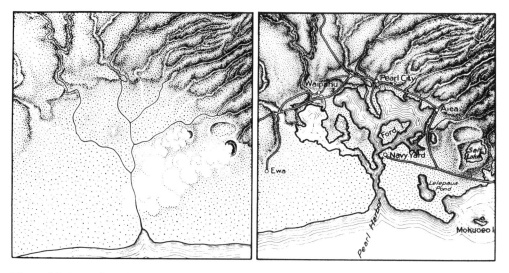

Figure 8.5. Formation of Pearl Harbor on O'ahu. *Left,* stream drainage system of the area during an earlier geologic time of relatively lower sea level; *right,* present-day embayment configuration after a relative ocean rise of about 18 m (60 feet). (Fig. 21.4 of Macdonald et al. [1983], used with permission of Frank L. Peterson.)

little physically and chemically altered, natural impoundments cannot form because surface water is too quickly lost through the permeable substrate. Most high-elevation bodies of water that do exist, like Mauna Kea's Lake Waiau on Hawai'i, the Alaka'i Swamp on Kaua'i, and a very few smaller bog areas (Figure 14.4), are present only because their substrate has relatively very low permeability. Most of the naturally wet areas are at low elevations, such as the swampy tract found in Honolulu's Waikīkī district before historic draining, and exist because the local water table intersects a permeable land surface there.

Also, many ground depressions that might collect water tend geologically to fill in rather rapidly with soil eroded from higher elevations. For example, between 7,000 and 8,000 years ago an ocean embayment existed at the site of the present Kawainui Marsh between Kāne'ohe and Kailua on Windward O'ahu, into which drained at least two streams of considerable size. A slight lowering of the ocean about 2,000 years ago resulted in a broad sand berm being built up at the embayment's mouth, eventually separating it from the ocean. Siltation through upland soil erosion, along with growth of marsh vegetation, then produced the current sloughlike area. Without the current human clearing actions, in another century or so the marsh would probably have become a broad, dry field traversed by a meandering stream or two.

SUBSURFACE FRESHWATER PHENOMENA

Hot Springs

On a volcanically active island such as Hawai'i, some groundwater is heated to high temperatures by contiguous subterranean rock that encloses magma. This water may then reach the surface as a hot spring, a number of which, mostly small in size, are located along the coast of Hawai'i bordering Kīlauea's east rift zone (Figure 5.1). Some of these at Isaac Hale Beach Park near the community of 'Opihikao are evident as warm currents felt when wading in shallow water along the shore, and a locally popular onshore freshwater pocket in the lava is large enough to accommodate a dozen or so people in water about the temperature of a hot bath.

Geysers and Fumaroles

In many other volcanically active areas worldwide, geysers are a well-known feature, so it may be surprising that none is present in Hawai'i. Geysers are much like hot springs because their water is heated by underground volcanic lithic material, but differ in that their conduit to the surface is relatively very long and narrow. As the water confined at the bottom of the conduit is heated above sea-level boiling temperature, its thermal expansion steadily forces up the overlying column of cooler liquid until the hydrostatic pressure decreases enough to allow this superheated lower water to suddenly transform or "flash" into steam. The resultant enormous volumetric increase then impels the overlying water and associated steam out of the conduit's vent, yielding the characteristic fountaining action. Once the steam and water of the column have been temporarily expended, cool water again seeps into the conduit, and its temperature begins to increase until the cycle is repeated. It is uncertain why there are no geysers in Hawai'i, although possibly the lack of sufficiently deep conduits and/or suitably located superheated water is responsible.

Perhaps the closest approach to geysers in Hawai'i are **fumaroles,** or volcanic vents emitting only gases, such as those of the "Steaming Flats" area of Kīlauea Caldera. Most of the constant clouds quietly issuing there are steam derived from geothermally heated, locally infiltrating rainwater rather than from deep groundwater. The nearby and easily accessible "Sulphur Bank" on the north rim of the caldera is of interest because hydrogen sulfide gas emitted along with steam is oxidized to crystalline sulfur and water, leaving gleaming yellow deposits of the element around the fumarole openings.

Geothermal Energy

The great amount of subterranean volcanic heat energy is successfully utilized in several countries around the world (for example, Iceland and New Zealand). Obtaining a usable form of this **geothermal energy** often involves only drilling down to the level of steam trapped within dense rock material and leading this to the surface to propel electricity-producing turbines or for use in heating and other energy-related activities. On Hawai'i, test drillings at the summit of Kīlauea indicated, for various reasons including apparent retarded circulation in low-permeability rock of the water needed for continued steam production, that this particular area was not a feasible geothermal energy source. A similar test 34 km (21 miles) from the summit on the east rift zone, near the community of Pāhoa, indicated that although the underground rock material was too permeable to trap steam, there was sufficient superheated groundwater in it to be successfully tapped for near-surface steam production, and commercial development of the area began about 1980.

This steam-producing operation somewhat parallels the mechanics of a geyser, in that any overlying cooler water is removed so that the superheated water below is relieved of pressure and can transform into steam. The major technical problems involve successfully capturing and controlling the explosively escaping steam, along with the nuisance and safety factors of suppressing the excessive noise and noxious gases such as hydrogen sulfide that accompany the steam. Also, to certain native Hawaiians, the social problem of this alleged but undefined defilement of their volcano goddess Pele (see chapter 5) is no less important.

GLACIERS

Formation

At the opposite extreme from superheated bodies of water are glaciers formerly present in the Hawaiian Islands. On the higher mountains of the islands of Hawai'i and, occasionally, Maui, winter precipitation usually takes the form of snow (Plate 7.1). During past glacial periods this snowfall was apparently greater (and/or annual temperatures slightly lower) than at present, so that a portion of the winter snowpack persisted from year to year. In fact, even today the ground only a few meters below the surface of the Mauna Kea summit area is permanently frozen, and it has been postulated that the waters of its Lake Waiau, at 3,970 m (13,020 feet) the highest lake in the Islands and the third highest in the United States, are prevented from being lost through the substrate by the presence of such permafrost. Continued accumulation of snow, and its pressure transformation into ice, led to the formation of a prehistoric glacier on at least Mauna Kea. In fact, up to four successive glaciers, probably ranging in thickness from 100 to 170 m (330 to 560 feet), are thought to have existed on the upper 300 to 600 m (990 to 1,980 feet) or so of the summit at different ice-age periods somewhere between about 9,000 or 30,000 and 280,000 years ago (Figure 8.6).

Glacial Traces

In the life of a glacier, ice is continually added to its higher-elevation center, while previously formed ice slowly flows radially downslope, where it is constantly lost through melting at the glacier's lower margin. Because a glacier picks up material from the rock or other substrate over which it flows, melting of the lowest-elevation ice results in deposition of an easily identified accumulation of lithic debris or soil, called a **terminal moraine.** Another indication of prior glaciation is the presence of distinctive parallel grooves or **striations** on bedrock of an area, caused by flow of the thick rock-laden ice over its surface. Both of these glacial indicators are present on the upper slopes of Mauna Kea and, in addition, glacial meltwater is thought to be almost certainly responsible for the substantial erosion necessary to have formed the deep Pōhakuloa Gulch on the south slope of the mountain.

Possible Glaciers

On the same island, the almost equally high, but younger, Mauna Loa was in existence during at least part of the time of the Mauna Kea glaciations, but its summit was possibly kept too

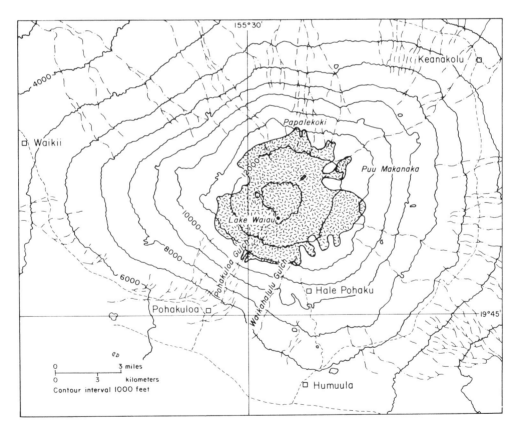

Figure 8.6. Ice-age glaciation on Mauna Kea, Hawai'i Island. The stippled area indicates the apparent maximum extent of ice sheets that covered the summit during various glacial periods. (Fig. 13.3 of Macdonald et al. [1983], used with permission of Frank L. Peterson.)

warm by surface and subterranean volcanic activity to sustain year-round snowpack. Small amounts of permanent ice can currently be found in sheltered high-elevation caves, however, so it may be that traces of any past glaciation on Mauna Loa have been obliterated by more-recent lava flows. Maui's Haleakalā may have been slightly too low in elevation for glacier formation or, if a glacier was ever present, all traces of it could have been lost during the massive erosion that subsequently took place at the mountain's summit (see chapter 3). Recently, though, investigators have found possible glacial striations on high-elevation Haleakalā bedrock, as well as what might be part of a terminal moraine. It is interesting that throughout all these glacial periods, climatologists consider that temperatures at sea level in the Hawaiian Islands were probably no more than about 3 to 5.5°C (5 to 10°F) less than at present, so that at least the lower portions of the Islands would still have possessed a subtropical climate.

KARST TOPOGRAPHY

Freshwater in the form of rain has substantially affected Hawaiian coastal substrates consisting primarily of exposed fossil coral-algal reef, as explained below.

Emergent-Reef Formation

Of the various past high sea stands, each produced during an interglacial period when there was a net loss of water from continental glaciers, the most recent occurred approximately 120,000 years ago and formed a shoreline about 7.5 m (24.6 feet) above current sea level around all of the main Hawaiian Islands. This is known as the **Waimānalo Sea Stand,** because the height of the sea then was first discerned through prominent nips (see chapter 6) on lithified sand dunes located at the Windward Oʻahu community of this name. (In reality, there were probably two prolonged periods of elevated sea level around this time, as indicated by twin nips in the Waimānalo dunes: one at 6.6 m or 21.8 feet, and the other at 8.1 m or 26.7 feet.) As the sea gradually rose to these heights, the fringing coral-algal reef grew with it, remaining perhaps 1 m (3.3 feet) or so below the surface. Then, when the sea retreated to—and at least a number of meters below—its current level during the succeeding glacial period, the reef was left exposed wherever it had formed around the Islands.

Subsequently, primarily marine erosion scoured this particular reef formation from most Hawaiian coasts, but considerable portions of it still remain exposed on flatter coastal areas of some islands, where they frequently qualify as the earlier-mentioned caprock. On the southwest corner of Oʻahu the emergent reef forms the extensive ʻEwa Plain. This same reef also deeply underlies present downtown Honolulu and Waikīkī, and lesser surface remnants may be found on the windward side of the island, notably in the Kahuku area; on the east coast of Mōkapu Peninsula; and in the form of a small islet in Kailua Bay and probably also others near Lāʻie.

Sinkholes

Rainwater is acidified to very weak carbonic acid through natural absorption of atmospheric carbon dioxide. Any calcareous substrate such as an emergent reef or exposed ancient seafloor on which this mildly corrosive liquid falls is eventually greatly corroded by it, whereupon the substrate forms **karst topography** (from the German name of such an eroded limestone plateau in northwestern Yugoslavia).

On the ʻEwa Plain, rainwater has gradually dissolved **sinkholes** in more soluble portions of the exposed fossil reef. Typically, these sinkholes are bell-shaped in profile; the surface opening often is about 1 m (3.3 feet) or so in diameter, with the interior usually increasing to perhaps two or three times that. This particular shape is attained because the rainwater at and near the surface opening evaporates rather quickly, redepositing previously dissolved calcium carbonate there as crystals that are relatively resistant to subsequent solution. Also, rainwater reaching the sinkhole interior evaporates more slowly, and when entering any soil there picks up additional carbon dioxide from it, thus increasing the water's dissolving power. Solution of the reefal material proceeds downward until the underlying water table is reached, usually about 2 to 3 m (6.6 to 9.9 feet) or so below the entrance on many parts of the ʻEwa Plain, where a flat floor results. This groundwater is near saturated with calcium carbonate and thus effectively neutralizes the acidified rainwater contacting its surface.

Originally, there were tens of thousands of these sinkholes exposed on Oʻahu; those of the ʻEwa Plain extend south from the Waiʻanae area of the Leeward coast through the Barbers Point region, then east to well beyond the community of ʻEwa Beach. At least 99 percent of these, however, have been filled or covered in the last century or so by agricultural and developmental projects, but attempts continue to permanently preserve at least a small area of the few remaining sinkholes. These cavities have been found to contain innumerable bones of endemic Hawaiian birds (many of the species prehistorically extinct) as well as many other scientifically and educationally important animal and plant remains (see chapter 22).

It might also be noted that, in dissolving downward from the surface, the Hawaiian sinkholes differ from structures of the same name formed in most areas of limestone or other calcareous substrate. For example, the karstic sinkholes usually thought of as typical, such as those of Florida, most often develop primarily from the bottom up. Infiltrating surface water entering a deep crack progressively dissolves out a long, narrow shaft to a subterranean watercourse flowing through a cave. The shaft is additionally enlarged by undissolved lithic material falling from the walls to its base, to be continually carried away by the underground stream. The ceiling of the shaft becomes increasingly thinner until it eventually collapses, usually without any surface indication that this is imminent.

Caves

Extensive subterranean passages are usually typical of karstic regions, but their formation requires underground streams or rivers. The Hawaiian Islands have essentially no such subterranean watercourses, so karstic caves are usually lacking in the chain; most structures of this shape are either lava tubes (see chapter 5) or sea caves (see chapter 6).

SUGGESTED REFERENCES

Hunt 1996; Macdonald et al. 1983; Mink and Bauer 1998; Nichols et al. 1996; Sanderson (ed.) 1993; Stearns 1985; Stemmermann 1981; U.S. Department of the Interior 1990; Wilcox 1998.

AUDIOVISUAL AIDS

Earth science: Water cycle, 2d ed.; Hawaiian waters: Mauka/makai lifeline; Hawaii's streams; Hawaii's water resources; Kalo paʻa o Waiāhole [The hard taro of Waiāhole].

9

Ecological Principles

The term "ecology" was coined in the later 1800s from the two ancient Greek words *"oikos"* (house) and *"logos"* (discourse), thus literally meaning "study of the house." In practice, **ecology** is the study of not only the "house" (environment) but also of the interrelationships of all living (biotic) and nonliving (abiotic) components of our planet. The term **"ecosystem"** is normally used to designate any particular interactive group of these biotic and abiotic units (for example, the stream ecosystem shown in Figure 9.1).

Microcosm Concept
To help illustrate the successful perpetuation of all life on earth, the example of a very simple ecosystem or **microcosm** (Greek *"mikros"* [small] and *"kosmos"* [world]) might be described. A large glass jug is partially filled with fresh pond water, and a small amount of growing algae along with a few tiny algae-eating shrimp are added. The jug is then stoppered and left exposed to the sun, so that nothing enters the jug except sunlight and nothing leaves except radiated heat. In the first week or so, either part of the algae or some of the shrimp will die off, but then the amount of plant material and number of shrimp stabilize, and the microcosm will perpetuate itself in this form essentially indefinitely. It may be recognized that this is the same principle behind the early 1990s Biosphere II experiment ("Biosphere I" is the whole earth) carried out near Oracle, Arizona, in which six humans attempted two years of isolated existence in a sealed and self-sustaining structure containing various ecosystems. Although the operation was not completely successful—primarily because of the relatively limited variety of organisms included—the underlying theory being tested is undoubtedly sound.

Communities and Populations
Two other basic ecological terms should be introduced here. A **biological community** consists of all the interacting plants and animals in a given habitat. In the case of the microcosm, this is the limited freshwater pond assemblage; on a much larger scale, this could be a coral reef and its related organisms or the interdependent plants and animals of a temperate deciduous forest. **Population** is a more restrictive term, meaning all of the actually or potentially inter-breeding individuals of a particular kind in a given biological community (for example, all the shrimp of the same species in the microcosm).

ECOLOGICAL CYCLES

Perpetuation of life in the microcosm and, indeed, on the entire earth is dependent on a number of cycles involving abiotic components. Although each of these cycles is usually discussed as an independent process, most usually overlap or intersect. For example, the cycling of carbon dioxide cannot be completed without plant photosynthesis, but this photosynthesis cannot take place without chlorophyll, and chlorophyll cannot be manufactured unless the cycling of nitrogen is proceeding properly.

ENERGY

Ultimate Source

Only a few cycles that clearly affect all or essentially all (see following paragraph) of the world's organisms will be described. In what might be (technically incorrectly) termed the **energy cycle,** the ultimate source of the energy for life on earth is sunlight, both visible and invisible, reaching here in the form of radiant energy. About half of this radiation does not strike the earth's surface because it is either reflected back into space by clouds or absorbed by the atmosphere as heat energy. Of that reaching the surface, almost all serves to elevate the temperature of the land and ocean, with attendant evaporation of water, and less than 1 percent is utilized in the essential metabolism or body chemistry of organisms.

There are, however, certain single-celled organisms whose metabolic energy is not received either directly or indirectly from sunlight. These organisms may generally represent the earliest form of life on earth, and so they are collectively termed the **Archaea** (Greek *"arche"* [beginning]). Over five hundred archaean species have been found in certain deep caves, high-temperature hot springs, and around deep-ocean volcanic vents. They all use either thermal or chemical-reaction energy to metabolize various elements and simple chemical compounds.

Heat Transfer

In contrast to all "true" ecological cycles, however, that of energy is not completely self-contained, because energy in the form of sunlight must continually be added to it. The energy content of neither the microcosm nor the earth is increasing; thus, an amount of energy equal to that

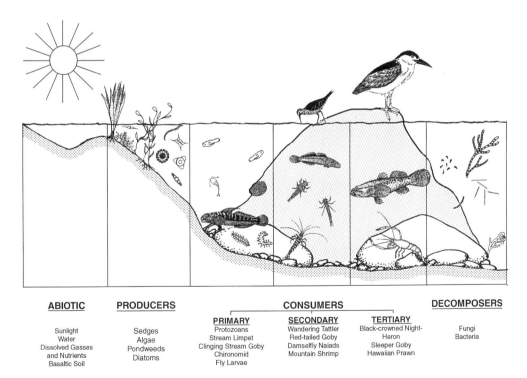

ABIOTIC	PRODUCERS	CONSUMERS			DECOMPOSERS
		PRIMARY	**SECONDARY**	**TERTIARY**	
Sunlight	Sedges	Protozoans	Wandering Tattler	Black-crowned Night-	Fungi
Water	Algae	Stream Limpet	Red-tailed Goby	Heron	Bacteria
Dissolved Gasses	Pondweeds	Clinging Stream Goby	Damselfly Naiads	Sleeper Goby	
and Nutrients	Diatoms	Chironomid	Mountain Shrimp	Hawaiian Prawn	
Basaltic Soil		Fly Larvae			

Figure 9.1. A simplified ecosystem as exemplified by a Hawaiian stream. Many representative native organisms are not illustrated. The meaning and significance of the different levels of consumers, as well as certain other biotic and abiotic components shown, are explained in the text. (Fig. by Keith Krueger.)

reaching each must *ultimately* be leaving them. In the microcosm, this loss takes place primarily through radiation into the surrounding air of the combined heat from metabolism of the contained organisms, abiotic chemical reactions, and solar heating of the system. For the earth, the similarly derived heat, as well as that from other sources such as fires, is lost by continual radiation into space. (Omitted from the foregoing discussion is the important mathematical concept of subsequent unavailability to the two systems of some entering free energy through the constant tendency toward a state of maximum entropy or molecular disorganization.)

Photosynthesis

Solar energy is *directly* utilized for metabolism only by plants, algae, and some bacteria. This is accomplished through **photosynthesis.** The chemical reaction for this process is as follows (numbers preceding the chemical symbols indicate that the number of atoms on both sides of the equation do balance):

$$\text{Sunlight} + \frac{\text{Carbon}}{\text{Dioxide}} + \text{Water} \xrightarrow[\text{(catalyst)}]{\text{Chlorophyll}} \frac{\text{Simple}}{\text{Sugar}} + \text{Oxygen}$$

$$\text{energy} + 6\,CO_2 + 6\,H_2O \longrightarrow C_6H_{12}O_6 + 6\,O_2$$

Carbon dioxide is readily available from the atmosphere, and water from precipitation. Chlorophyll is a green chemical compound that acts as a catalyst in photosynthesis (that is, it promotes this unique chemical reaction without itself being changed). The simple sugar produced is either stored unchanged within the plants or converted into more complex organic (carbon-containing) compounds such as the carbohydrates starch and cellulose, and the oxygen is released into the atmosphere.

Plant-eating (herbivorous) animals burn or oxidize these carbohydrates for energy and also for growth and other vital processes, producing carbon dioxide and water as waste products. Plants themselves use this same process for their own metabolism, converting about one-fifth of their photosynthesized products for this purpose. The chemical formula for this metabolic reaction in organisms is as follows:

$$\frac{\text{Simple}}{\text{Sugar}} + \text{Oxygen} \xrightarrow[\text{enzymes}]{\text{Digestive}} \text{Metabolism} + \frac{\text{Carbon}}{\text{Dioxide}} + \text{Water}$$

$$C_6H_{12}O_6 + 6\,O_2 \longrightarrow \text{energy} + 6\,CO_2 + 6\,H_2O$$

Comparison of these two formulas reveals that one is simply the reverse of the other, and, depending on the particular catalyst or catalytic enzyme, the chemical reactions can proceed in either direction. Except for the Archaea mentioned earlier, this reversible reaction can be regarded as the basic formula for all life on earth. Thus, in the self-sustaining microcosm, the photosynthesizing algae provide carbohydrates and oxygen to the shrimp, and the metabolizing shrimp provide carbon dioxide to the algae.

CHEMICAL CYCLES

Nitrogen Cycle

Both plants and animals require cycling of a number of other common chemical compounds or nutrients as well as rarer trace elements. One of the more important of these processes is the **nitrogen cycle,** because this element forms an indispensable part of all plant and animal proteins as well as many other biological molecules (including chlorophyll). Although almost 80 percent of the earth's atmosphere is gaseous nitrogen, most plants and animals cannot utilize the element in this form. Nitrogen-fixing bacteria, however, are able to convert it into substances that can be used by plants. Small additional amounts of nitrogenous compounds are formed by lightning and other natural processes, and today a great amount of nitrogen is fixed in the industrial production of fertilizers. Many of the nitrogen-fixing bacteria live in nodules on the roots of legumes (members of the pea family), which are commonly grown as rotational crops if artificial fertilizers are not used to provide nitrogen for commercial agricultural operations. Nitrogen chemically bound in animal metabolic wastes such as uric acid, urea, and ammonia is returned to the cycle by other bacteria and fungi, as is also the nitrogen in plant and animal protein upon its decomposition. In the microcosm the continued cycling of nitrogen is made possible by these same microorganisms.

Carbon Dioxide Cycle

Although there are immense amounts of chemically bound carbon available in "sinks" such as ocean water, limestone rocks, and fossil fuel deposits, photosynthesis and the reverse organic metabolism reaction are the processes most active in the **carbon dioxide cycle** (Figure 9.2). Volcanic activity and natural vegetation fires have also always recycled a certain amount of carbon dioxide to the atmosphere, but their contribution is relatively small compared with the amount humans are now adding through burning of fossil fuels for both industrial purposes and operation of internal-combustion engines. This unnatural overloading of the atmosphere with carbon dioxide has produced a **greenhouse effect,** which reduces the amount of solar energy radiated from the earth and is widely alleged to be resulting in gradual global warming. If true, this temperature increase will lead to accelerated glacier and ice pack melting, with attendant rising sea levels, among numerous other problems.

FOOD WEBS

The documentation by modern science of the intricate and extensive interrelationship of ecological events was presaged many years ago by the early California naturalist and Sierra Club founder John Muir, who mused: "When we try to pick out anything by itself we find it hitched to everything else in the universe." The **food web** shown in Figure 9.3 is a prime example of this ecological complexity, and even the involved diagram of this figure is incomplete because scavengers and decomposers are not included. **Scavengers** are animals of any type and size that feed primarily on the dead bodies of other individuals, and these feeding activities facilitate ecological recycling. **Decomposers** or "reducers" are usually either microscopic forms such as bacteria or fungi of any size, both of which subsist on animal waste products and remains of all kinds of organisms. Food webs consist of a number of interconnected **food chains;** in Figure 9.3 one such chain is indicated by the lines leading to the right from the core plant segment of "leaves, twigs" to, successively, "insects," "skunk," "red fox," and "wolf."

ECOLOGICAL PYRAMIDS

Trophic Levels

A food web or a food chain is often portrayed in the form of an ecological or **Eltonian pyramid,** named for the pioneer British ecologist Charles S. Elton. Such structures are variously titled "pyramids of numbers," "pyramids of biomass," "pyramids of energy," and so on, depending on just what units of measurement are employed. (The generalized pictorial pyramids of Figure 9.4 are unitless, but are possibly best regarded as ones of numbers or of biomass.) The different steps of a pyramid are termed **trophic levels** (Greek *"trophe"* [food]). The plants that manufacture and store carbohydrates constitute the base level as **producers.** These are eaten by herbivorous **consumers** of the second trophic level, and the abbreviated pyramid of the microcosm ends here. In natural ecosystems, however, there are also those animals (and occasional "insect-eating" plants) that occupy the third trophic level because they feed on consumers of the second trophic level. The second-level animals must now be termed **primary consumers,** and the carnivorous third-level ones **secondary consumers.** Many food chains exist in which there are **tertiary consumers** (also carnivores, of course), and, occasionally, even animals of one or two still-higher trophic levels. Certain types of organisms such as parasites and omnivores could be assigned to essentially any level of an Eltonian pyramid, but are usually not portrayed because they do not fit in well with the typical overly simplistic format. Also, corals with producer-level symbiotic algae (see chapter 11) and consumer polyps of primary/secondary trophic-level status cannot be satisfactorily accommodated.

Trophic Limits
There is, however, a practical limit to the number of steps in any ecological pyramid, because the *available* energy drops drastically with each ascending trophic level (with this drop being

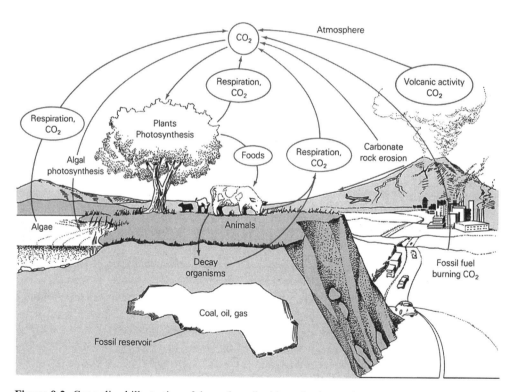

Figure 9.2. Generalized illustration of the carbon dioxide cycle. A certain amount of carbon dioxide is also recycled from the atmosphere through absorption in upper ocean levels and incorporation into the calcareous exoskeletons of marine invertebrates. (Fig. 41.10 of Wallace et al. [1986]; copyright 1986, 1981, Scott, Foresman and Co., used with permission of Addison-Wesley Educational Publishers, Inc.)

due to ultimate loss of heat, as noted in the earlier discussion of the energy "cycle"). An animal must utilize most of the energy obtained from food just to metabolically maintain its usual activities, with only a relatively small percentage of the total energy taken in throughout life being stored as body parts that can be utilized by a predator of the next-higher trophic level. Even in the most efficient food chains, the metabolic energy represented by plants decreases by a factor of about ten in moving to the primary consumer level, and by a factor of between perhaps five and ten for each successive step. Thus, if there are 1,000 kilocalories (kcal) of metabolic energy available in a particular biomass of green plants, only about 100 to 200 kcal will ultimately be available in the bodies of the many primary consumers that have eaten this plant material, only 10 to 40 kcal in the lesser number of secondary consumers, and only 1 to 8 kcal in the still-fewer tertiary consumers.

Also, consumers of any higher trophic level, being extremely low in numbers, have great difficulty in covering and maintaining hunting territories large enough to contain the high number of lower-level consumers necessary to satisfy the great metabolic needs of such **"top carnivores."** Some animals often—and usually incorrectly—regarded as top carnivores, such as most bear species and, for that matter, humans, have evolutionarily "solved" this problem by developing omnivorous feeding and scavenging habits that involve both plant material and pri-

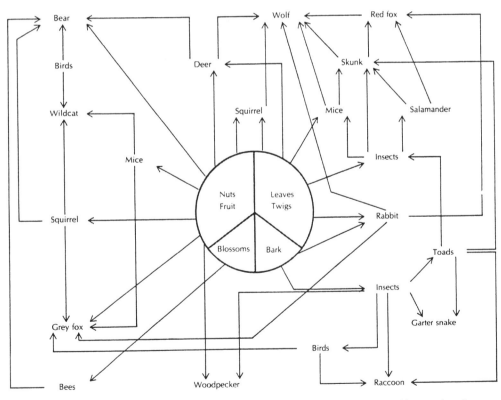

Figure 9.3. Diagram of food web in a temperate deciduous forest. Note that even this complex diagram is incomplete because many organisms constituting the scavengers and decomposers are not included. (Fig. 45.8 of Johnson et al. [1977]; copyright 1977, Holt, Rinehart and Winston, used with permission.)

mary consumers, instead of having to rely solely on carnivores usually placed immediately below them in a food chain or pyramid.

Vegetables Versus Meat

The interpretation of an Eltonian pyramid explains why inhabitants of most populous undeveloped countries subsist largely on vegetable substances rather than on animals. At least five to ten times as many humans can be supported by consumption of grains, legumes, and other vegetable products than could be if all that plant material was fed to animals that were then used as the sole food of the people.

Substance Concentration

Such pyramids also help explain how a harmful substance becomes concentrated in higher-level carnivores. In Hawai'i, for example, occasional high populations or "blooms" of a one-celled photosynthesizing organism carrying poisonous ciguatoxin (see chapter 12) introduces the poison to the food chain through primary-consumer fishes. Although the level of toxicity of these herbivores is usually—but not invariably—not dangerously high, by the time the trophic level of larger predators such as Skipjack Tuna *(Katsuwonus pelamis)* and moray eels

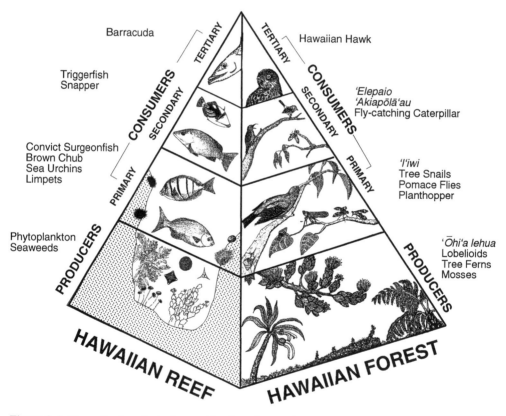

Figure 9.4. Generalized ecological pyramids of numbers or biomass. These presented for the Hawaiian reef and forest communities are obviously greatly simplified, showing only a few typical native organisms. (Figure by Keith Krueger.)

(*Gymnothorax* spp.) is reached, the toxin may be concentrated enough to cause death when eaten by humans and Hawaiian Monk Seals *(Monachus schauinslandi)*.

ECOSYSTEMS GLOBALLY

Biomes

If ecosystems are examined worldwide, it will be found that certain generally similar types tend to exist in either the same latitudinal band and/or the same elevational range. These very extensive ecosystems are given the special designation of **biomes** and are typically described by their dominant type of vegetation. Two of the several methods used to portray global distribution of land biomes are shown in Figure 9.5. It must be emphasized that the *species* of major plants are not necessarily the same in all regions supporting a particular biome; it is just that the growth forms of the dominant plants are generally the same everywhere the biome occurs. In the case of the Taiga biome, for instance, the major trees are coniferous types (that is, nonflowering evergreen ones such as fir, spruce, hemlock, and so on), the individuals of which share the same general growth form.

   To briefly characterize the other biomes appearing in the much-abridged lower diagram of Figure 9.5, Tundra consists entirely of low-growing vegetation, dominated by dwarf woody or perennial plants only a fraction of a meter (a few inches) tall, with abundant lichens and mosses. Temperate Deciduous Forest is made up primarily of true flowering plants (see chapter 15), often with a more-or-less single-layered canopy and usually a shrubby understory. Tropical Rain Forest consists of an exceptionally large assortment of primarily nonconiferous tree species, forming a two- or three-layered canopy containing many epiphytes, with vines and shorter plants often forming a very dense undergrowth.

   An appreciation of the interaction of latitude and elevation in determining biome distribution may be gained from this same lower portion of Figure 9.5. Taiga, for example, can potentially exist worldwide between 68° north and 68° south latitude, but, altitudinally, is able to extend down to sea level only in the latitudinal band of about 46° to 68° both north and south of the equator. On the other hand, at low latitudes of 0° to 23° it can only be found at the high elevational range of about 2,000 to 3,000 m (6,600 to 9,900 feet). There are, of course, many modifying factors that disrupt this idealized portrayal of biome distribution—rainfall, soil type, and so on—but the overall scheme tends to hold fairly well for at least large portions of continents, especially those of the Northern Hemisphere.

Vegetation Zones

On a smaller scale, within the very broad range of environmental conditions of a given biome, plant occurrences are considered in terms of **vegetation zones.** As in the case of biomes, the different plant assemblages of vegetation zones are basically also the result of the same differences in climatic conditions; thus, variation in the typical vegetation throughout an area may similarly be expected to occur with changes in both elevation and precipitation. The Hawaiian Archipelago possesses most of the biomes occurring elsewhere, but their geographic extent in the Islands is often so limited as to cause them to be relatively inconspicuous. The higher of the main islands, however, with their varied topography and rainfall, show plant zonation very clearly. More detailed discussion of this subject and the immediately following one of succession is reserved for chapter 14 on the Hawaiian terrestrial environment.

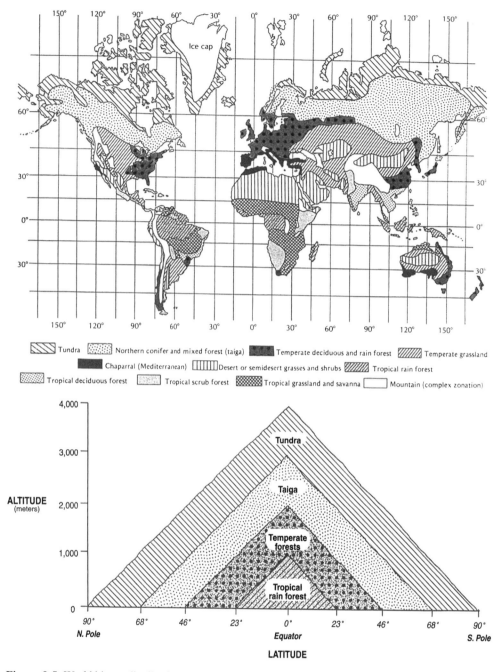

Figure 9.5. World biome distribution portrayed in two ways. Altitudinal occurrence is available only from the lower diagram, which is limited to a few biome types for presentation. See text for further details. (Upper illustration slightly modified from Fig. 45.13 of Johnson et al. [1977]; copyright 1977, Holt, Rinehart and Winston, used with permission.)

ADDITIONAL ECOLOGICAL CONCEPTS

Succession

Finally, two more important ecological concepts should be explained. The first is **ecological succession,** which, like biomes and vegetation zones, is usually described in terms of plants, although animals essentially mirror the vegetational phenomena. Succession describes changes in vegetation with time, rather than with geography and/or elevation as do biomes and vegetation zones. If there is an area newly cleared of vegetation, such as a fresh lava flow or, perhaps, the site of a massive landslide or bulldozing operation, one or more species of plants inevitably soon colonize it. These constitute the **pioneer vegetation,** and this initial group of plants serves to prepare the area for an assemblage of succeeding species that is adapted to largely replace it.

For example, ferns and lichens first developing from windblown spores on a new lava flow slowly build up small pockets of soil in which seeds of flowering plant species arriving by various means are able to grow. The additional soil and shade provided by this second plant wave then allows a physically larger and often more-varied vegetation to develop in its place. This repetitive appearance of different suites of **successional species** continues until development of a particular plant community that does not change with time, which is known as the **climax vegetation.** The entire process from pioneer to climax vegetation, which may take several centuries or more, is usually known as a **sere,** and each generally discernible major step within it as a **seral stage.**

NICHES

Definition and Number

The second major concept it is necessary to introduce here is that of **ecological niches.** In theory, the ecological niche of a plant or animal species comprises the totality of its interaction with its functional ecosystem; therefore, by definition, no two species that differ in any life attribute can occupy the same niche. In practice, however, the ecological niche is considered in a considerably more circumscribed manner, in the case of animals very often being limited primarily to the species' diet, manner of obtaining it, and sometimes the habitat occupied. For example, it is usually acceptable to make the oversimplified statement that certain Australian kangaroos subsisting on vegetation along forest edges occupy the same niche as do North American deer and certain African antelopes. This most-lenient interpretation of the term should be assumed whenever it is encountered subsequently in this book.

It is important to realize that the number of ecological niches present in a habitat may vary greatly, depending on geographic location and size of the area considered. There are relatively few niches (and thus occupying species) in the perpetually frozen polar regions, but many niches (and species) in the tropical rain forests; also, there are necessarily fewer niches on small oceanic islands than on continents.

Niche Competition

One use of the ecological niche concept in ecological (and evolutionary) thought may be illustrated by the following example. If, somehow, two types of organisms with the same general way of life are placed in competition for a particular niche (as, for instance, when faunal exchange between continents occurs over a newly formed land bridge), one of the two organisms will inevitably prove slightly more efficient in exploitation of the niche and will eventually supplant the other. Also, if it happens that one of the newly met competing forms possesses some novel major adaptive characteristic of relatively great selective advantage, the replacement of prior niche occupant(s) may be of spectacular scope, as evidenced in the widespread occupation of reptiles' niches by birds and mammals some 100 million years ago.

Occupant Identity

The two or more types of animals putatively occupying similar ecological niches in different parts of the world need not all be of the same vertebrate class (that is, one could be a reptile, another a bird, and the third a mammal). A good example of this is the occupancy of a large herbivore's niche on isolated oceanic islands. In the Galápagos Islands this niche was originally filled by gigantic tortoises and in the Hawaiian Islands by large, flightless, gooselike birds (see chapters 20, 22), but in historic times mammals such as alien goats have largely usurped this way of life in both archipelagos.

Finally, it might be noted that in considering an ecosystem that has been functioning essentially undisturbed for at least tens—if not hundreds—of thousands of years, the assumption is frequently made that all *possible* niches are occupied. This is not at all universally accepted and, in fact, may be quite an untenable supposition. For example, the niche filled by flightless ibises on ancient Maui Nui of the Hawaiian Islands (see chapter 20) may not have been filled on the other islands of the archipelago. Or, to take a most extreme worldwide case, although there are a great number of animal species that spend their entire lives in water without direct dependence on solid ground, there is not one that similarly utilizes air.

SUGGESTED REFERENCES

Doty 1967, 1973a,b; Gosline 1965; Mueller-Dombois 1975; Yamamoto and Tagawa 2000.

AUDIOVISUAL AIDS

Behavior and ecology of coral reef fishes; The coral reef community; Ecology; Energy; The food web and energy transfer; Hawaiian waters: House of the shark; Hawaiian waters: Mauka/makai lifeline; Pond communities in Hawaii; Succession on lava.

10

Evolutionary Principles

A number of terms applicable to **taxonomy** (the science of classifying and naming plants and animals) are described here. The taxonomic classification of an organism indicates both its relative level of evolutionary development and its relationship to other organisms. As an example, that of the *'iole (Rattus exulans hawaiiensis),* the Hawaiian Islands' representative of the widespread Pacific Region Polynesian Rat is presented below. (Note that only the scientific names of genus, species, and subspecies are italicized.)

KINGDOM: Animalia
  PHYLUM: Chordata
    SUBPHYLUM: Vertebrata
      CLASS: Mammalia
        ORDER: Rodentia   *Primate*
          FAMILY: Muridae   —   *Ape*   *great apes ?*
            SUBFAMILY: Murinae
              GENUS: *Rattus*   — *Homo*
                SPECIES: *Rattus exulans*   *H.s.*
                  SUBSPECIES: *Rattus exulans hawaiiensis*

A number of intermediate steps sometimes used between the higher taxonomic levels listed here have been omitted. Also, botanical classification uses the levels division and subdivision rather than phylum and subphylum. The term "subspecies" (or "race") is usually based on biogeography. "Variety" and "breed" may occasionally be used in somewhat this same sense, but are most often applied only to domesticated plants and animals. The plural of "phylum" is "phyla"; that of "genus" is "genera"; and "species" is both singular and plural. The abbreviations "sp." or "spp." following a generic name indicate one or multiple undetermined species of the group. The words "form," "kind," "type," and **"taxon"** (plural "taxa"), often used in discussions in this volume, are informal terms and can refer to organisms at any taxonomic level. Finally, "biota" (plural "biotas") means a joint taxa complement of plants ("flora," plural "floras") and animals ("fauna," plural "faunas").

In regard to occurrence of an organism, **"native"** means occurring naturally in an area. **"Endemic"** means native to a relatively small geographic area (such as an island or archipelago), and **"indigenous"** means native to a larger geographic region (such as a continent). **"Alien," "introduced,"** or **"exotic"** mean transported to an area by humans.

BINOMIAL NOMENCLATURE

A species name has two parts, both based on or synthesized from classical Latin or Greek: a capitalized generic name *(Rattus)* followed by an uncapitalized specific one *(exulans).* This concise system constitutes **binomial nomenclature.** The generic name indicates that the species involved is closely interrelated with others of the genus, and the specific name shows that the taxon is reproductively isolated from all others of the genus.

The Swedish naturalist Karl von Linné (better known by the Latinized name of **Carolus Linnaeus**) is considered the "Father of Taxonomy." He recognized the advantages of binomial nomenclature and was the first to use it consistently throughout an encyclopedic biological work: the 10th edition of his monumental *Systema naturae,* published in 1758. This edition was eventually accepted as the basis for the binomials of all organisms named up to that time. To be scientifically acceptable the name of each additional plant and animal subsequently described has to adhere to the binomial system.

SPECIES OR SUBSPECIES?

The Problem

The word **"species"** as used in this volume conforms to this generally accepted definition: a group of individual organisms that can actually or potentially successfully interbreed *in nature.* There are sometimes, however, geographically isolated populations of individuals effectively separated from populations of morphologically quite similar organisms. It obviously cannot be known whether individuals belonging to any one population are able to interbreed successfully with those of another because they have no opportunity for contact, at least under natural conditions. Thus, the question is whether to consider all the isolated similar populations the same species or whether to apply different species names to each (Figure 10.1).

"Lumpers" and "Splitters"

There is no completely satisfactory solution to this problem; some taxonomists consistently tend to regard two or more separated but morphologically similar populations as the same species and are known informally as "lumpers." Other equally competent workers, often called "splitters," usually recognize each of the isolated groups as separate species. For instance, a lumper would probably consider the Hawaiian population of *Rattus exulans* merely the subspecies *hawaiiensis,* as it appears in the arrangement given earlier, but a splitter would likely consider it the distinct species *Rattus hawaiiensis.* This contrast in taxonomic philosophy explains at least some of the discrepancies in numbers of native Hawaiian "species" that may be encountered in various references.

EVOLUTION AND DARWIN

Biological Evolution

That all of the different types of native organisms are always so well adapted to their various ways of life did not come about by chance; it is the result of almost countless years of **biological evolution.** This process, sometimes alternatively referred to as "descent with change," results from genetic changes occurring in a population over time. These changes can yield easily observed differences in morphology or physical attributes (body size, coloration, leaf shape, and so on) or less obvious ones such as an alteration of physiology (for example, ability to metabolize a particular substance or tolerance to water of various salinities). In animals, the changes may even be in psychological or behavioral traits (degree of sociability, perhaps, or improved capability to learn certain tasks). It should be realized that evolution is never "directed" toward any particular goal, but is an inevitable natural process over which no plants or animals except modern humans have any degree of conscious control, or even awareness.

Neo-Darwinism

The basic principles of biological evolution as accepted today date back to the 1859 publication of a book usually known as *The origin of species* (more meaningfully, the complete title is *On the origin of species by means of natural selection, or the preservation of favoured races in the struggle for life*) by the Englishman **Charles R. Darwin.** This initial concept of **Darwinian evolution** was greatly expanded and modified in the twentieth century as the result of new scientific discoveries, especially in the field of genetics and heredity (see later in this chapter), so that this "modern synthesis" is now known as **Neo-Darwinism.**

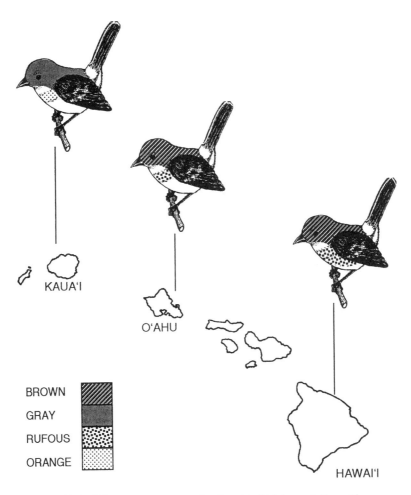

BROWN

GRAY

RUFOUS

ORANGE

KAUA'I

O'AHU

HAWAI'I

Figure 10.1. Color patterns among closely related bird populations. These island forms are usually considered only subspecies of the Hawaiian 'Elepaio *(Chasiempis sandwichensis),* although taxonomists who are extreme "splitters" might call them three separate species. The variation in color pattern is likely due to founder effect and/or genetic drift. (Figure by Keith Krueger.)

THE *BEAGLE* CRUISE

During the six years of university instruction insisted upon by his family, Darwin had showed no special interest in his subjects of, first, medicine, then, theology, preferring his own largely informal natural history investigations. Upon graduation in 1831 at 22, he promptly accepted the unpaid position of naturalist aboard the sailing ship HMS *Beagle* on a five-year exploring voyage around the world. Despite chronic and often debilitating seasickness, his extensive journal entries throughout these years reveal a desire to record as much natural history information as possible. Darwin's geological insight in regard to development of atolls has already been noted in chapter 3, but a great number of his biological observations were crucial to eventual formulation of his evolutionary theory. His studies of the land birds of the dozen small Galápagos Islands, 970 km (600 miles) off the Pacific coast of Ecuador (see the next section), are often cited as having played a major role in eventual formulation of his theory. These animals, however, are actually given scant notice in the 1859 publication. But, with Darwin's keen powers of observation and reasoning, it seems almost certain that the birds must sometimes have come to mind as he thought along evolutionary lines.

Special Creation

In Darwin's time, the widely—but not universally—accepted view of what are now considered biological species was that each was the result of **special creation** by a divine power, with each specifically designed to carry out a particular way of life. Also, each different type of organism created was thought to be immutable (not subject to change). Darwin probably originally had no great argument with this doctrine; certainly, he had no thought of specifically attempting to show that all of his religious training was wrong in regard to special creation.

Whenever the *Beagle* stopped at a foreign coastal or insular locality, Darwin was free to go ashore and explore at will. During his investigations on the first Galápagos island visited, Darwin observed at least two groups of birds exhibiting different morphology and, apparently, feeding habits. The bird types of one group all had finchlike bills and seemed to eat primarily seeds, and those of the other all had smaller or slender bills and possibly fed mostly on insects. Upon visiting other islands in the archipelago, he found the same general groups of birds on each. But Darwin noted that each of the species within a group on one island differed slightly in morphological characters, especially bill size, from species in the equivalent group on another. These fourteen species making up the various groups, now collectively but informally known as **"Darwin's finches,"** are illustrated in Figure 10.2. This situation in which a number of species of birds of very similar, but not identical, morphology and ecology inhabited each of several neighboring islands is not what scientists of the day might have expected from special creation. Why should an omnipotent power not have produced the *same* suite of species within each group on all islands, rather than slightly different species in the groups of each island?

At the time, Darwin was unable to determine the correct interrelationship of these groups of Galápagos birds and apparently decided to consider all of the species making up each group as collective members of one or another of common families known elsewhere in the world. By a half dozen years after the trip, however, Darwin had come to a slightly different conclusion. In a report on his *Beagle* voyage findings, he had reached the point of at least suspecting that a single species of, for example, the finch-billed type might possibly somehow have been modified to produce all of the current Galápagos birds with this same general bill shape. It is sad that Darwin was never to learn the amazing fact that not only were the birds within this group related, but that essentially all of the birds he observed, of whatever group, had evolved from a *single* immigrant species. (This ancestor proved to be a South American member of the finch family Fringillidae, but fully elucidating this and other details of relationships among "Darwin's finches" would take a century of work by scientists after his death in 1882.)

Other natural history observations made by Darwin in the course of the voyage were similarly not easily explained by the doctrine of special creation. Rabbits (order Lagomorpha) were

Figure 10.2. Diversity among "Darwin's finches" of the various Galápagos Islands. Observation of the great variation in bill types and other characteristics of these birds undoubtedly greatly influenced Charles Darwin in developing his theory of evolution. These birds, all fourteen species of which evolved from a single ancestral type, also provide an excellent example of adaptive radiation. (Fig. 17.7 of Wallace et al. [1986]; copyright 1986, 1981, Scott, Foresman and Co., used with permission of Addison-Wesley Educational Publishers, Inc.)

absent from the grasslands of Argentina he explored while the *Beagle* and its crew were off-shore surveying the coastline. The countryside seemed ideally suited for these animals he knew so well from his native England, but it was inhabited instead by a member of the order Rodentia, related to the Guinea Pig, that looked and acted essentially the same as a rabbit. Darwin puzzled as to why this latter animal would have been created especially for South America, when a rabbit created for Europe would have done perfectly well for South America as well. Also, he was further perplexed that a fossil giant armadillo excavated there no longer existed in the area, but a much smaller extant South American animal was very similar to it. Once created, what had happened to the ancient giant species? Was it possible that, through time, it had somehow decreased in size to become the living smaller relative? If so, why and how?

From all of these and many similar novel natural history observations he had made, Darwin was ultimately forced to the fundamental conclusion that some organisms could, indeed, change through time, and thus every one found today was not necessarily the result of special creation. For example, some of the numerous similar species of Galápagos birds he had observed could have developed their slight but consistent differences only after being separated on different islands of the archipelago, on each of which they were confronted with somewhat different ecological requirements. (The Galápagos are young volcanic islands much like the main ones of Hawai'i, but the *Beagle* did not visit the Hawaiian Archipelago. If it had, Darwin would undoubtedly have recognized that the same evolutionary phenomenon was even better demonstrated by the amazingly varied Hawaiian honeycreepers discussed in chapter 21.)

Age of the Earth

During long sailing months on the *Beagle,* Darwin also had ample time to study the classic text of **Charles Lyell,** a founder of the newly developing field of geology. From this work he became aware that the earth could be many million years old, rather than only a few thousand as his earlier religious instruction had maintained. If this were so, there would have been an immense amount of time for organisms to become extinct before the advent of humans, or to somehow develop into different ones, or to move to new areas. This great age for the planet might then explain why the giant armadillo and several other types of fossil South American mammals he discovered were not known alive, and also why similar extant, possibly descendant, forms of some were found in the same or different places. Lyell's work also proposed that in the distant past parts of the earth had risen above their original position, while others had sunk below it. This assertion further increased Darwin's confidence in Lyell's theories, because he personally had come upon fossil seashells 3,050 m (10,000 feet) above current sea level while climbing in the Andes Mountains.

THEORY FORMULATION

Upon returning to England in 1836, Darwin married into the wealthy Wedgwood family of pottery eminence and for the next 20 years or so was free to pursue the life of a country gentleman. He leisurely carried out and published on a wide variety of plant and animal natural history investigations. But throughout this entire period he continued to develop his ideas on how species could come to be morphologically modified—or even how new ones might be formed—in nature, always seeking additional lines of evidence to explain and confirm his slowly developing theory.

Survival of the Fittest

Also greatly influencing Darwin's thinking in the years after his return was his chance reading of an old treatise on human population by **Reverend Thomas R. Malthus.** Malthus argued that because the reproductive potential of humans was enormous, the numbers of people could increase faster than their food supply. But a human population eventually became limited by some factor, be it a natural disaster such as famine or pestilence, or a conscious decision to limit reproduction or wage war. If this premise were extended to include populations of all other organisms, they too could increase so rapidly as to outstrip either their food supply or some other essential environmental variable. One natural selective factor or another, however, would inevitably limit their numbers. Darwin thus considered that, in effect, there was—literally or figuratively—a "struggle for life," with the fittest members of a population most likely to overcome or outcompete others of their kind and thus survive to reproduce.

Domestic Breeding

In addition, as the owner of a country estate Darwin followed with great interest the development and maintenance of various lines of farm animals such as sheep, cattle, and horses, as well as those of other familiar domestic animal types like dogs and domestic pigeons. He knew well that animal breeders did not allow all the animals born or hatched each year to produce young for the next. Rather, the breeders examined all of the progeny and picked for breeding stock only those individuals showing the variations considered most desirable: for example, sheep with superior wool, or pigeons with unusually long and decorative neck feathers. Then, from each succeeding generation only the most favorable individuals were similarly selected for mating to perpetuate and improve the desired line. In some cases, Darwin noted that the process had ultimately yielded a population whose individuals diverged markedly from the original variety, as, for example, in the case of the numerous widely differing breeds of dogs. And, of course, he was aware that the same selective breeding had long been carried out with a variety of agricultural and ornamental plants.

All of these observations were, of course, made through many years following the *Beagle* voyage and involved domesticated organisms rather than wild types. But they were a great and long-continued source of interest to Darwin, and it seems likely that they played an important—perhaps even major—role in the final formulation of his evolutionary theory.

The Basic Premises

By at least the mid-1840s, the three major points of his theory of biological evolution were fairly well crystallized in Darwin's mind. First, every species produces many more young than survive to reproduce. Second, although most of these young individuals closely resemble their parents, a few show a certain amount of random (but presumably inheritable) variation in physical and other characteristics. Third, the biotic or abiotic factors that cause elimination of most of the progeny do not act entirely by chance, but tend to favor survival of those young whose slightly differing characteristics happen to best fit the current ecological and/or environmental requirements. In presenting these premises, Darwin was only substituting **natural selection** in wild populations for the principles of human "artificial" selection of domestic animals and plants. (In years to come, Neo-Darwinists would realize that although individual survival was, of course, essential, the major driving force in evolution of wild organisms was most often the *increased* number of young provided the population by its better-fit members.)

THE WALLACE IMPETUS

By 1858 Darwin had finally been persuaded by the geologist Lyell (now Sir Charles) and the botanist **Joseph D. Hooker** (later Sir Joseph) to begin drafting a manuscript that would fully explain his theory. Darwin, however, procrastinated extensively, and it is not at all certain that he would ever have published his theory except for a most unusual and unexpected event. In the post one day he received for comment a manuscript by a young naturalist and biological collector named **Alfred R. Wallace,** who had previously worked in the jungles of Brazil and was then employed in the Malay Archipelago. Darwin was astonished to find that Wallace had independently conceived almost exactly the same evolutionary theory as his own. He under-standably felt that he could not then publicly announce his own theory because it might seem that he had taken it from Wallace's work. So he passed the younger naturalist's paper on to offi-cials of the prominent Linnean Society, asking that it be read at the next meeting, which would mean that Wallace alone would receive credit for the theory.

The Origin of Species

Fortunately, Lyell and Hooker would not allow Darwin to relinquish all of the credit to Wal-lace and arranged for a joint presentation of the work of the two before the Society, so that each deservedly received credit. The startling appearance of Wallace's work, however, finally galva-nized Darwin. Before the end of the following year he had completed and published *The ori-gin of species,* a much-abbreviated version of what he had originally planned would be a fully definitive and extensively documented multivolumed treatise on evolution. Darwin must have been little short of astounded at the reception of his work; the entire first edition of the book sold out the day it appeared. Wallace did not similarly expound his evolutionary ideas in print, although he did go on to make important fundamental contributions to the field of zoogeogra-phy, or distribution of animals, so the name of Darwin is the one usually associated with the basic concept of evolution by natural selection.

As a matter of fact, although this does not in the least lessen the credit due to both men, scientific knowledge had advanced to such a stage by the late 1850s that the formulation of this specific type of evolutionary theory was probably inevitable; if it had not been Darwin and Wallace who did it, it would have been some other equally perceptive scientist soon thereafter. Even in the early 1850s, the missionary and Hawaiian land-snail student John T. Gulick (see chapter 28) was already publicly questioning the doctrine of special creation and immutability of species. The readiness of the contemporary scientific community for acceptance of such a theory is perhaps best illustrated by **Thomas H. Huxley,** a well-known zoologist of the time and subsequent pugnacious champion of Darwinism in word and print ("Darwin's Bulldog"). Upon reading *The origin of species* he is said to have exclaimed in self-reproach: "How extremely stupid not to have thought of that!"

Theory Shortcomings

The Darwinian theory of that time, as its proposer fully realized, lacked two critical pieces of evidence: a satisfactory explanation of how variations of parental organisms could be passed on to their young, and an actual example of the evolution of one species into another. It is inter-esting that the initial investigative work on the biological process that would ultimately provide the answer to the first of these wants was being carried out at just about the same time that Dar-win was publishing his theory.

GREGOR MENDEL AND GENETICS

In mid-nineteenth-century Austria, the Augustinian monk **Gregor (formerly Johann) Mendel** had for years been meticulously recording results of his interbreeding of varieties of common Green Peas *(Pisum sativum).* His studies revealed that many parental characteristics of these plants (flower and seed color, plant height, and the like) were inherited by their progeny in certain predictable ratios, but the significance of his astute observations would not to be recognized until the early twentieth century, when the science of genetics was formally established.

Far-reaching discoveries in this field have since revealed that parental characteristics are passed to offspring primarily by means of chromosomes, of which the young typically receive an equal number from each parent in the uniting gametes or sex cells. Modern geneticists, working with cell biologists and other investigators, have also elucidated the means by which the inheritable variations are themselves produced within the chromosomes. This is by naturally occurring changes in the normal physicochemical composition of, primarily, **genes** or segments of the extremely complex molecule (deoxyribonucleic acid or DNA) making up each chromosome. Such various alterations of a single gene are collectively termed **alleles,** and their inheritance leads to mutant individuals, many of which can easily be distinguished morphologically, physiologically, or psychologically from others of their species. These gene mutations are unpredictable, may occur at any one of a number of regions of the chromosome, and can be brought about by a variety of factors, including natural or artificial radiation and mutagenic chemical substances.

THE FINAL MISSING EVIDENCE

Elimination of the second perceived deficiency in the Darwinian theory was a near impossibility because of the time required for a new species to develop. The entire elapsed history of science would probably not be long enough to observe and record the evolution of one species into another, a process presumably taking at least several thousand years.

Peppered Moths

One interesting and important example of morphological change in a wild organism, however, was discovered and eventually explained in the mid-1900s, and this is typically offered as an example of "Darwin's missing evidence." Although this case does not constitute *total* evolution of a new species, it does rather satisfactorily illustrate the work of natural selection in bringing about a major genetic change in a population—in this case one that produced a shift in its most commonly observed coloration.

Throughout the 1800s, the Industrial Revolution had brought an increasing number of factories with coal-burning furnaces to English manufacturing cities, and the fallout of soot eventually darkened essentially everything in the surrounding countryside. In most of Britain there was a common light-colored lepidopteran, the **Peppered Moth** *(Biston betularia),* and this species spent the day resting on similarly colored lichen-covered tree trunks and rocks. Birds preyed on these resting moths, but many escaped detection because of their protective coloration. As the resting places became darker and darker because of the industrial pollution, however, the light-colored moths became increasingly visible on them and were thus more easily seen and taken by birds (Figure 10.3).

Figure 10.3. Protective coloration in two forms of Peppered Moth *(Biston betularia). Top,* a clean lichen-covered tree trunk with the conspicuous dark variant on the left, and the common light-colored moth practically invisible on the right; *bottom,* a soot-covered trunk with the dark variant to the left hardly apparent, and the light form very obvious. (Unnumbered figures on pp. 49–50 of Kettlewell [1959], used with permission of Oxford University Museum of Natural History.)

Evolutionary Reversal

In 1848, dark-colored mutants of the species were reported for the first time, and this variant form matched its sooty background so well that a smaller percentage of it than of the common light-colored form was taken by birds. In fact, this natural selection favored the dark or melanistic (Greek *"melanos"* [black]) mutants so heavily that during the next 100 years the populations of Peppered Moth around industrial towns steadily changed until they were made up of approximately 90 percent dark-colored individuals. It is interesting that in the latter half of the twentieth century, Britain initiated steps to substantially reduce such industrial pollution. With this, the selective color advantage began to reverse as the landscape commenced loss of its soot covering, and the percentage of light-colored variants relative to dark-colored ones in Peppered Moth populations soon began to increase.

LAMARCKISM

This Neo-Darwinian explanation of Peppered Moth evolutionary change provides an opportunity to introduce a major alternative scientific theory: that of the illustrious early French biologist **Jean Baptiste de Lamarck.**

Lamarckian Theories

Fifty years before the appearance of *The origin of species* Lamarck had proposed, as Darwin would, that species were not immutable. Part of his belief, however, was that some environmental factor caused an organism to acquire certain characteristics and pass these on to its progeny, a process now usually referred to as the **inheritance of acquired characteristics.** For example, if the Peppered Moth phenomenon had occurred during Lamarck's time, he might well have explained that the originally light-colored moths kept constantly blackened by the soot were somehow affected internally so that they were then able to pass on this same dark coloration to their young. Lamarck further postulated that the physical activities of an organism enabled it to acquire and pass on to its young particular characteristics; this often was known as the **use and disuse** component of his theory.

For its time—a full half century before Darwin's landmark publication—Lamarck's theory was an excellent proposition and not at all the fanciful notion that it is sometimes portrayed to be. It deservedly had many adherents among those scientists seeking alternatives to the doctrine of special creation. Before the development of Darwinism, in the relatively unsophisticated scientific thinking of the time, biological examples easily explained by Lamarckism did, indeed, appear to abound. Some sons of blacksmiths did seem to have inherited the same muscular arms that their fathers were, presumably, able to acquire only after years of vigorous hammer use. Or, because to survive among the myriad of other herbivores on the African savanna giraffes constantly had to stretch their neck to obtain foliage from tall trees, could it not be that this habitual physical activity alone was responsible for their young possessing similar long necks?

Neo-Darwinian Explanation

The exact *mechanism* of how the giraffe's lengthened neck was passed on to progeny was not explained by Lamarck's theory, but, it should be remembered, even by 1859 Darwin could still provide no explanation for such transmission. It is probably obvious, however, how Neo-Darwinism would explain the two foregoing examples. Natural mutation of ancestral genetic material had resulted in transmission of unusually large arm musculature to certain individuals in the blacksmith trade (as a matter of fact, this may well have been why a number of them originally entered and successfully exploited this line of work), and this same morphological characteristic was then genetically passed on to some or all of their offspring. The arm size of these particular children, however, would still have been equally substantial whether or not the strong-armed father had decided to become a blacksmith. As for the giraffes, natural selection resulted in enhanced survival and subsequent increased reproductive output of the occasional longer-necked mutants among litters of a normally proportioned ancestral form, especially during those periods when availability of tree foliage became a limiting factor. And continued similar selection for long-necked, and resultingly higher-producing, individuals through innumerable generations (as taller and taller trees evolved) yielded the typical giraffe of today.

Lamarckian Experiments

Although proponents of Lamarckism persisted well into the twentieth century, in the view of most scientists the theory has been convincingly discredited by a great number of experiments, one of the first of which was carried out in the late 1800s. A German researcher measured the tail lengths of mice of an inbreeding laboratory colony, then cut off their tails, as well as those of each successive litter. After many generations, he allowed all current animals to mature without caudal amputation and found that tail length of the mouse colony had not diminished in the slightest. Although this particular experiment is probably not the most appropriate one to present as a refutation of Lamarckism, primarily because it does not very closely replicate any naturally occurring phenomenon, it is nevertheless habitually cited (as here), perhaps because of its somewhat naive scientific approach and rather ludicrous nature.

Soviets and Lamarckism

To argue which is correct, Lamarckism or Darwinism, may seem a purely academic exercise, but adherence to one or the other concept can have dire consequences for some human populations, as for ones who might be reduced nearly or quite to starvation by crop failures. For example, in the Soviet Union under Premier Joseph V. Stalin, the sciences of genetics and agronomy were under the control of politically favored Lamarckians, primarily the autocratic Trofim D. Lysenko. Instead of allowing Neo-Darwinian principles to be applied to production and selection of stock or seeds for critically needed expanded agricultural ventures, the Lamarckian doctrine of inheritance of acquired characteristics had to be followed. For instance, in Lysenko's view, if seed for wheat to be grown on the cold dry Siberian steppes was needed, this should be provided only by the most luxuriant of wheat plants grown under optimal climatic conditions elsewhere in the country. As any Neo-Darwinian could have told Stalin, this seed would undoubtedly be the worst choice for the opposite climatic conditions of Siberia, but it was many years before Lamarckism lost favor in the Soviet Union and agronomy was finally again able to provide the populace with sufficient food.

PUNCTUATED EQUILIBRIUM

A Newer Concept

In the last quarter of the twentieth century the stimulating concept of a process termed **"punctuated equilibrium"** was introduced into evolutionary theory. Briefly stated, this premise attributes essentially all the evolutionary modification of a biological lineage to occasional periods of relatively rapid change, without constant mediation by natural selective pressures. This is largely opposed to the generally held traditional view that evolution usually (but, as a few workers have shown, not invariably) proceeds in the form of very gradual changes resulting largely from continual natural selection. The proposers of the punctuated equilibrium theory were prompted to advance it after noticing that there are many types of organisms in the fossil record, especially among marine invertebrates, that remained unchanged for millions of years, even if it appeared that environmental conditions had changed substantially during that period. Most of these specific animal types eventually seemed to vanish abruptly from the geological sediments and in their places appeared new and noticeably different—but apparently descendant—forms.

The Phenomenon

Primarily because of this observation, it was quite radically theorized that, for obscure reasons, a species population tends to be resistant to assumption of available mutations for much of its existence. Occasionally, however, in peripheral portions of the geographic range, daughter species develop very rapidly in terms of geological time. Then, one among these that happens to be best adapted to the current environmental conditions survives to establish a long-lasting lineage, while the other new peripheral species soon accompany the parental one into extinction. The new lineage, like its parent one, then undergoes a long period without change ("equilibrium") until its course of evolution, too, is altered drastically ("punctuated") by a new episode of speciation.

Gradualism Versus Punctuationism

Thus, the new premise alleges that evolution of a biological line is more strongly influenced by character changes at the species level than either below it at the individual level or above it at the level of the population. Perhaps the difference in the classic Darwinian concept and the punctuated equilibrium one can best be illustrated by comparing the *most extreme* hypothetical example of each. In the former or **gradualism** model, a present-day species is the product of untold millions of years of very gradual changes in an unbranching lineage whose characteristics evolved by natural selection of the environmentally best-suited individuals in each generation. In the latter or **punctuationism** model, a present-day species evolved in a saltatorial or sporadic manner, its lineage undergoing long periods with no discernible change in characteristics, interspersed with episodes of abrupt transformation to a quite different form. This newer theory is currently the subject of some debate and research, but it may well be that the actual process of evolution in most biological lines lies somewhere between these two extremes. The problem for students of evolution is thus now to determine for any given taxon which of these evolutionary models its lineage most closely resembles.

INSULAR EVOLUTION

Several generally accepted classic Darwinian principles and processes that are especially pertinent to the biological history of the Hawaiian Islands are discussed in the remainder of this chapter.

Advantages of Island Studies

Isolated groups of oceanic islands have very appropriately been termed "natural laboratories for the study of evolution." Organisms reaching and populating such islands undergo essentially all of the same evolutionary processes that occur on continent-sized land masses, but these events usually proceed more rapidly and frequently in an insular setting. Also, the results are almost always more clearly scientifically evident than those from most much older continental areas, where the temporal and geographic superposition of many past evolutionary bouts greatly hinders interpretation of the current biological situation.

Facilitation of Speciation

If two populations of a species become geographically separated, through thousands of years natural random mutation of genes results in differences in their genetic compositions. If the populations subsequently are reunited, this differentiation may have proceeded far enough to prevent successful interbreeding completely because of such factors as gamete incompatibility, incongruous breeding behavior, and the like. Thus, any mutations subsequently occurring in either of the overlapping groups that tend to discourage interbreeding and lessen ecological competition will be favored by natural selection, and the groups may soon constitute two reproductively isolated and morphologically distinct species.

This speciation process can occur more easily in an archipelago than on the large continuous land area of a continent because the several islands are somewhat isolated from each other, but at the same time close enough to allow at least occasional chance biotic exchange among them. That is, after a species has successfully populated the first island, it eventually is usually able to establish a daughter population on a second, and that isolated group then typically undergoes its own differentiation. With time, interchange between the two islands may occur again, in which case a second species could then be developed on at least one of the islands. Over the period of only a million years or so, repeated episodes of such alternate separation and renewed contact of members of an evolving lineage, especially if a number of islands are involved, can result in an extensive array of species on each of the land masses of the archipelago (witness Darwin's finches). In the case of a continent, such relative isolation of one segment of a population from another is much less likely, and all individuals of the species usually remain an integral interbreeding and morphologically similar unit. Even if separation does occur, as in a tectonic division of the continent by a new mountain range, the time elapsing before possible secondary contact may be so great that the two isolated groups will probably be so different morphologically that they cannot be surely recognized as having once been of the same species.

Biotic Disharmony

Another reason that isolated oceanic islands are so interesting and informative in evolutionary studies is that their biotas are always **disharmonic.** This word is used here to mean that entire higher *taxonomic* groups (usually class, order, or family) of organisms playing a major ecological role on continents that provided the various founding species to islands are absent from the new areas. (Although long widely used in this manner, "disharmonic" is perhaps an unfortunate term because it may imply to some that island biotas have an undesirable quality, one that can—and should be—corrected by human action. Still, there seems no better one available; "depauperate," "impoverished," "truncated," "incongruent," and the like all have the same disadvantage.)

As a result of biotic disharmony, certain of those relatively few plant and animal groups that do manage to colonize isolated islands are able to evolve into diverse and often radically different forms that effectively take the place of the missing organisms (see the discussion of adaptive radiation in the next section). It is interesting that study of insular disharmony can frequently show that a particular morphological or other characteristic of a continental species must be closely related to its survival. A good botanical example is that of immigrant continental species with thorny or bitter bark that, upon colonizing islands where the disharmonic fauna contains few or no large plant-eating animals, evolve into endemic species lacking such characteristics. This process provides seemingly sound evidence that the lost characters serve as protection against such vertebrate herbivores in the continental setting.

At the lower taxonomic levels (species and, sometimes, genus), the terms "depauperate" and "attenuate" are here used only in connection with a *specific* taxonomic group. The former is usually understood to mean that the group is present in an insular assemblage, but is represented by considerably fewer taxa than on continents. The latter signifies that the number of species (or genera) of the group progressively decreases as traced from a continent or other geographic source through successively more-distant islands (see the beginning of chapter 11 for additional discussion of this biotic attenuation).

SOME MAJOR EVOLUTIONARY PHENOMENA

Adaptive Radiation

Whenever an organism is able to colonize a new area, if most or all of the ecological niches are unfilled, only partially filled, or occupied by competitively inferior forms, this founding species will almost invariably evolve into a number of forms exploiting many of these available ways of life. (New niche occupants are usually of the same general taxonomic type as any old ones [that is, for example, both are mammals] although this does not always have to be so. A mammal may be replaced by a bird, or a reptile by a mammal, and so on.) This dispersive evolution of a single species of colonizing organism is **adaptive radiation.** Such an evolutionary diversification of "Darwin's finches" and Hawaiian honeycreepers has already been mentioned, and the remarkable adaptive radiation of early marsupials in Australia in the essential absence of other mammals there is another well-known case. Note that all three of these prime examples involve islands, and in each case the adaptive radiation of the newer arrivals was allowed by the faunal disharmony of the isolated areas.

Adaptive Shifts

In the adaptive radiation of the Galápagos finches, the feeding specialty of some forms changed from the ancestral seed-eating type to an insectivorous one, as may be gathered from the different beak types shown in Figure 10.2. Such a significant alteration in some aspect of the ecology of an organism is an **adaptive shift.** Many such shifts in Hawaiian plants and animals are covered in several later chapters, but it may be said here that they include such phenomena as changes in plant pollination agent from insects to birds, in insect diet from vegetable to animal material, and in bird locomotion from volancy to flightlessness.

Convergent Evolution

As organisms in one part of the world adaptively radiate into various ecological niches, their various morphological and other characteristics come to resemble those of organisms occupying similar niches elsewhere. This is **convergent evolution** and is well illustrated by abundant examples in both the fossil and recent biological record.

Figure 10.4. Convergent evolution in birds. *Left,* Hawaiian Honeycreepers; *right,* ecologically equivalent birds native elsewhere. The lower two Hawaiian birds are prehistorically extinct, so their ecology is deduced primarily from bill morphology. (Figure by Keith Krueger.)

As just one of these examples, in forested parts of the world there is a way of life open for a small bird that can avoid competition with other species by feeding on invertebrates hidden quite deeply in moss, dense leaf clumps, and tree-trunk cavities. Among the Hawaiian honeycreepers (finch subfamily Drepanidinae), the Kaua'i *'Akialoa (#Akialoa stejnegeri),* with exceptionally long downcurved bill, short tail, and dull green coloration occupied this niche. In these and many other characteristics it is closely convergent with such ecologically equivalent forms as the spider-hunters (*Arachnothera* spp.; sunbird family Nectariniidae) of Southeast Asia. This and other cases of notable Hawaiian honeycreeper convergence with birds of different families elsewhere are illustrated in Figure 10.4.

Instances of convergent evolution among plants are probably equally common and as scientifically interesting. The remarkable evolutionary convergence in certain alpine plants such as a Hawaiian silversword (*Argyroxiphium sandwicense;* sunflower family Asteraceae) and an African Giant Lobelia (*Lobelia keniensis;* bellflower family Campanulaceae) is shown in Figure 10.5. This particular growth form, including a dense basal rosette of narrow, pointed leaves surmounted by a crowded columnar inflorescence, is evidently well suited to low-latitude alpine conditions because it has evolved in a number of unrelated high-mountain plants in various parts of the world's Tropics.

Figure 10.5. Convergent evolution in two spectacular subtropical alpine plants. *Left,* Haleakalā Silversword (*Argyroxiphium sandwicense* [sunflower family Asteraceae]) of the Hawaiian Islands; *right,* Giant Lobelia (*Lobelia keniensis* [bellflower family Campanulaceae]) of Kenya, Africa. Both plants are in the early stage of flowering, standing a little less than 1 m (3.3 feet) tall. (*Left,* photograph by Betsy H. Gagné, used with permission; *right,* Fig. 56 of Hedberg [1964], used with permission of *Acta Phytogeographica Suecica.*)

Founder Effect

When only one or a very few individuals of a species reach a new geographic area, a **founder effect** is necessarily introduced. The small immigrant component can carry only a limited number of the multitudinous alleles present in its parental population. Thus, barring possible novel interaction between the genes possessed (see discussion later in this chapter), the morphological, physiological, or other expressions of most genes are correspondingly limited in the new population.

Genetic Drift

The allelic composition of this immigrant population may subsequently become further biased by **genetic drift.** An originally uncommon morphological or other characteristic can easily become a typical one because, in the interbreeding of the small population, certain of the already limited number of alleles of a particular gene may be lost purely by chance, leaving only one or a few in the gene pool. This is especially liable to occur if none of the characteristics produced by the various alleles of the immigrants is of significant selective advantage—or disadvantage—in the new environment. For example, genetic drift, possibly along with founder effect, may be responsible for the differences in color pattern found among dispersed Hawaiian populations of the *'Elepaio (Chasiempis sandwichensis)* shown in Figure 10.1.

Multi-Gene Interactions

A disclaimer of sorts should be made here. The explanations just given regarding loss or fixation of particular characteristics through founder effect or genetic drift hold very well for those controlled by a single gene. Other characteristics, however, may be the expression of complex and variable interactions among genes. Thus, a particular characteristic differing between a daughter and parent population may be due solely to a mutant, now selectively advantageous, alteration in interaction among retained parental alleles. Much important information regarding this gene-interaction phenomenon has been gained from recent study of mating behavior and genetic composition of chromosomes in Hawaiian picture-winged flies of the family Drosophilidae, which are covered in chapter 17.

SUGGESTED REFERENCES

Carlquist 1965, 1974, 1980; Carson 1987a, b, 1989; Darwin 1859; Desmond and Moore 1991; Eiseley 1956; Kettlewell 1959; Medveden 1969; Somit and Peterson (eds.) 1992.

AUDIOVISUAL AIDS

Darwin; Darwin and the theory of natural selection; Genetics and populations; Heredity and genetics; Natural selection; New species from old; The riddle of heredity.

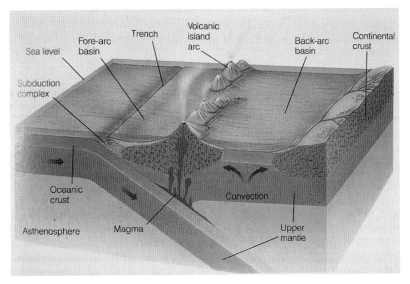

A

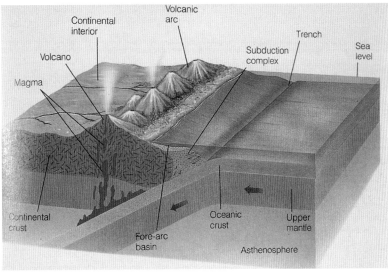

B

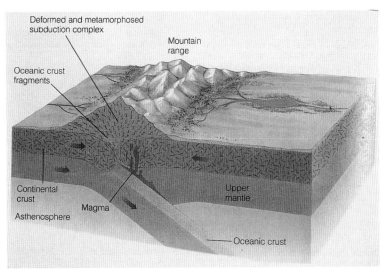

Plate 2.1. Formation of mountain ranges and ocean trenches through tectonic-plate collisions. *A,* Volcanic island arc; *B,* volcanic coastal continental range; *C,* nonvolcanic interior continental range. (Figs. 13-18, 13-19, and 13-20 of Monroe and Wicander [1992]; used with permission of Brooks/ Cole, a division of Thomson Learning.)

C

Plate 3.1. Green Island, a *motu* of Kure Atoll, Northwestern Hawaiian Islands. The open ocean is in the foreground, and the atoll's extensive lagoon in the background; the low sandy *motu* has formed on the barrier reef separating the two. The structures are military, including primarily a crushed-coral airstrip and LORAN station. All of these had been abandoned by 1994, and much of the *motu* has largely returned to its natural state. (Photograph by George H. Balazs, used with permission.)

Plate 4.1. A typical lava flow from a hot-spot volcano. Shown is lava from Mauna Ulu cascading into 'Alae Crater, east rift zone of Kīlauea, Hawai'i Island, on the evening of 5 August 1969. Thousands of these extensive, thin, and very fluid flows form the subaerial portion of a shield volcano. (Photograph courtesy of Hawaiian Volcano Observatory.)

Plate 4.2. Comparison of *pāhoehoe* and *ʻaʻā* lava flows. *Foreground, pāhoehoe,* whose shiny coating is a microscopically thin layer of volcanic glass; *background, ʻaʻā,* showing the typical fragmented condition and generally dull coloration. (Photograph by Barbara Decker, used with permission.)

Plate 5.1. Skylight of an active lava tube. The structure shown is near Mauna Ulu on the east rift zone of Kīlauea, Hawaiʻi Island. Lava stalactites visible at the top of the photograph resulted from melting of the tube's ceiling by escaping gases burning above the flowing lava. (Photograph courtesy of Hawaiian Volcano Observatory.)

Plate 6.1. Sea cliff and sea arch on the Nāpali coast of northwestern Kauaʻi. The cliff backing the two beaches, as well as the arch between them, were formed during a slightly higher sea stand. Rain erosion produced the sharp, deeply fissured ridge extending inland from the cliff. The "hanging" Honopū Valley appears at the right of the photograph. (Photograph by Bev Harter, used with permission.)

Plate 7.1. Winter snow on the summit of Mauna Kea, Hawai'i Island. Also visible are a number of large cinder cones or *pu'u* and, center far background, one of the many astronomical observatories located there. (Photograph by Don Swanson, courtesy of Hawaiian Volcano Observatory.)

Plate 8.1. View up a typical amphitheater-headed valley. Shown is Olokele Canyon of southwestern Kaua'i. (Photograph by Bev Harter, used with permission.)

Plate 12.1. The endemic Hawaiian Clinging Stream Goby or *'O'opu nōpili (Sicyopterus stimpsoni).* The individual shown is ascending the moist exposed rocks of a streambed, using the suction organ formed by its partially fused pelvic fins. The species reaches about 15 cm (6 inches) in length and can travel approximately 1 m (3.3 feet) or more per minute in this manner. (Photograph by Raymond A. Mendez, used with permission.)

Plate 13.1. External transport of plant fruits by a bird. The viscid fruits are probably those of the indigenous Hawaiian *Alena (Boerhavia repens)* and are adhering to the body and wing plumage of a Red-tailed Tropicbird or *koa'e 'ula (Phaethon rubricauda).* (Photograph by David Cavagnaro, used with permission.)

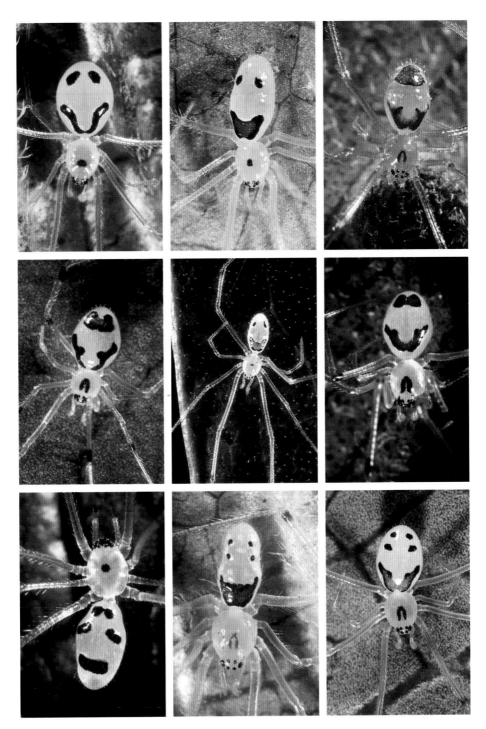

Plate 16.1. Individual variation in abdominal pattern of the Happyface Spider *(Theridion grallator)*. Students of Hawaiian invertebrates sometimes take a few moments off from work with less colorful species to typify the various visages: at upper left is Caspar the Ghost, at lower left Charlie Chaplin, at lower right could be Uncle Toshi, and so on. Head-and-body length of this species is 0.4–0.6 cm (0.16–0.24 inches). (Photographs by William P. Mull, used with permission.)

Plate 17.1. Size comparison of two *Drosophila* species. *Above,* an endemic Hawaiian picture-winged fly *(D. conspicua); below,* the alien Common Pomace Fly *(D. melanogaster).* The latter is only about 0.2 cm (0.08 inches) in head-and-body length, probably about the size of colonists yielding all Hawaiian drosophilids. (Photograph by William P. Mull, used with permission.)

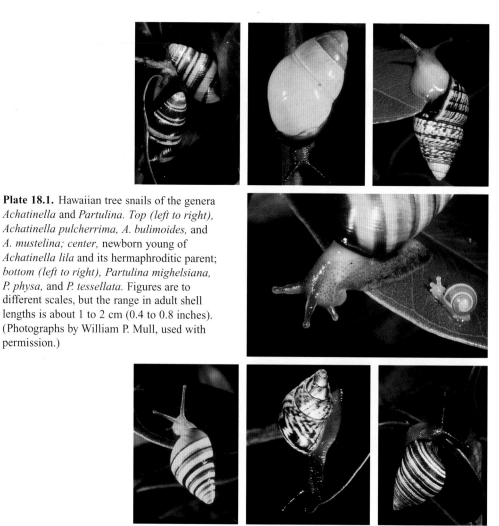

Plate 18.1. Hawaiian tree snails of the genera *Achatinella* and *Partulina. Top (left to right),* *Achatinella pulcherrima, A. bulimoides,* and *A. mustelina; center,* newborn young of *Achatinella lila* and its hermaphroditic parent; *bottom (left to right), Partulina mighelsiana, P. physa,* and *P. tessellata.* Figures are to different scales, but the range in adult shell lengths is about 1 to 2 cm (0.4 to 0.8 inches). (Photographs by William P. Mull, used with permission.)

Plate 19.1. Green and Black Poison-dart Frog *(Dendrobates auratus)*. The adult body length of this historically introduced amphibian is about 3.5 cm (1.4 inches). (Photograph by H. Douglas Pratt, used with permission.)

Plate 20.1. Endemic Hawaiian species of the honeyeater family Meliphagidae. Scientific names are as follows: *Kioea, #Chaetoptila angustipluma;* Hawai'i *'Ō'ō, #Moho nobilis;* O'ahu *'Ō'ō, #Moho apicalis;* Kaua'i *'Ō'ō, #Moho braccatus;* Bishop's *'Ō'ō, #Moho bishopi.* Plumage variation among at least the four *'Ō'ō* is quite likely due to genetic drift in isolated populations after dispersal to different main islands. (Painting by H. Douglas Pratt; adapted from Plate 36 of Pratt et al. [1987]; copyright 1987, Princeton University Press, used with permission.)

KIOEA

HAWAII OO

BISHOP'S OO

OAHU OO

KAUAI OO

Plate 21.1. Selected bill types of historically known Hawaiian honeycreepers. *A*, Hawai'i Mamo (#*Drepanis pacifica*); *B*, 'I'iwi *(Vestiaria coccinea)*; *C*, 'Ākohekohe *(Palmeria dolei)*; *D*, 'Ula'aihāwane (#*Ciridops anna*); *E*, 'Apapane *(Himatione sanguinea)*; *F*, 'Akiapōlā'au *(Hemignathus wilsoni)*; *G*, Kaua'i 'Akialoa (#*Akialoa stejnegeri*); *H*, Hawai'i 'Ākepa *(Loxops coccineus coccineus)*; *I*, Hawai'i 'Amakihi *(Loxops virens virens)*; *J*, 'Akikiki *(Oreomystis bairdi)*; *K*, Maui Parrotbill *(Pseudonestor xanthophrys)*; *L*, 'Ō'ū *(Psittirostra psittacea)*; *M*, Kona Grosbeak (#*Chloridops kona*); *N*, Nihoa Finch *(Telespiza ultima)*; *O*, Po'ouli *(Melamprosops phaeosoma)*. (Painting by H. Douglas Pratt; Fig. 1 of Freed et al. [1987]; copyright 1987, Elsevier Science, used with permission of the artist and Elsevier Science. Scientific nomenclature from James and Olson [1991].)

Plate 22.1. Artist's conception of three prehistorically extinct, flightless Maui birds. *Left,* Upland Maui Ibis (†*Apteribis brevis*); *center foreground,* Medium Maui Rail (†*Porzana* sp.); *right,* Large Maui Rail (†*Porzana severnsi*). The skeletons of all three were first discovered in the same lava tube. At least the Medium Maui Rail was probably heavily preyed upon by the Maui Stilt-Owl (†*Grallistrix erdmani*), so the blackish plumage may well represent protective coloration selectively evolved for life on the shaded forest floor. (Painting by H. Douglas Pratt; Fig. 2 of Freed et al. [1987]; copyright 1987, Elsevier Science, used with permission of the artist and Elsevier Science.)

Plate 23.1. Green Turtle or *honu (Chelonia mydas)* and Hawaiian Monk Seal or *ʻīlio holoikauaua (Monachus schauinslandi).* These are shown basking on a beach of East Island at French Frigate Shoals, with the basaltic remnant known as La Pérouse Rock visible in the far background. (Photograph by George H. Balazs, used with permission.)

Plate 24.1. Artist's rendition of a traditional double-hulled Polynesian voyaging canoe. This is probably a relatively late form of the craft used on voyages of discovery and settlement throughout the central Pacific. The painting is by Herb K. Kāne, who was the general designer, construction supervisor, and first captain of the similar modern *Hōkūleʻa* (see text). (Used with permission of the artist.)

Plate 25.1. Present-day wetland Taro fields or *lo'i*. This pondfield system in lowland Hanalei Valley of Kaua'i was apparently equally extensive in late prehistoric times. (Photograph by Greg Vaughn, used with permission.)

Plate 26.1. A sheep exclosure in the Mauna Kea Forest Reserve on Hawai'i. Photographed in 1975; the area in the center was fenced off 12 years earlier at the then-current treeline of approximately 2,900 m (9,500 feet). This protection from alien hoofed game mammals has allowed abundant regeneration of endemic *Māmane (Sophora chrysophylla)* trees and native understory plants, while similar vegetation outside of the fence has been eliminated by the feral animals. (Photo by Gerald D. "Jerry" Rothstein, used with permission.)

Plate 27.1. The endemic *Palila (Loxioides bailleui).* This endangered Hawaiian honeycreeper, now found only high on Hawai'i Island's Mauna Kea, is shown picking a green seed pod of *Māmane (Sophora chrysophylla),* from which it extracts its primary food. A landmark 1978 lawsuit brought by the Sierra Club (now Earthjustice) Legal Defense Fund on behalf of the bird and other plaintiffs as its "next friends" forced the state to cease maintenance of alien game mammals in its devastated critical habitat. (Photograph by Jack Jeffrey, used with permission.)

Plate 28.1. A typical bird illustration of the Professional Naturalist Period. Endemic Hawai'i 'Ō'ō (#*Moho nobilis*) painted by John G. Keulemans from specimens and field notes of Henry C. Palmer, who worked in the Hawaiian Archipelago from 1890 to 1893. (Plate 38 of Rothschild [1893–1900].)

11

The Marine Environment

Although this chapter focuses primarily on only seaweeds and mollusks, with a brief treatment of corals, many of the facts presented regarding these organisms also hold true for almost all others of the Hawaiian marine biota.

GEOGRAPHIC SOURCES

The primary source of founding Hawaiian marine biota has been the **Indo-West Pacific,** as considered here an area extending as far west as Indonesia and the Philippines and north to the Ryukyu Islands of southern Japan (Figure 11.1). Roughly half of the native Hawaiian marine species are indigenous taxa also occurring in the Indo-West Pacific, perhaps another 10 to 15 percent are shared only with the west coast of the Americas, and about 13 percent or so are pantropical indigenous forms. The remaining 20 to 25 percent of Hawaiian forms are endemic.

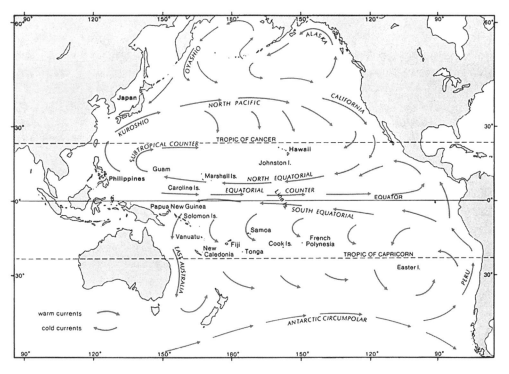

Figure 11.1. Major ocean currents of the Pacific. Note the different flow directions among the three Equatorial currents. (Unnumbered figure on p. 16 of Fielding and Robinson [1987], used with permission of Ann Fielding.)

DISPERSAL

Biotic Attenuation

It may be seen from a map of the Pacific (especially Figure 24.1) that there are quite a number of widely separated island groups situated between the Indo-West Pacific and the Hawaiian Archipelago as well as the Polynesian islands farther to the south. The numbers of marine species steadily decrease along this eastwardly extending line, resulting in **biotic attenuation.** This species diminution can be visualized as a **"filter funnel,"** with its large opening to the far west and the small end at the easternmost islands. The colonizing of successively more-distant islands can be said to be via a "sweepstakes" or **"lottery route,"** because a great many individuals may initiate the journey, but only a lucky few complete it. Specific examples of attenuation, as well as disharmony above the species level, are given in discussions of three major marine groups later in this chapter.

Currents and "Stepping-Stones"

The Kūrōshio Current from the Philippines and southern Japanese islands and the succeeding North Pacific Current has been most important in at least the initial stage of transport from the far west, with periodic eddies from these two major currents probably ultimately bringing most biota to the Hawaiian Archipelago. The North Equatorial and Subtropical Counter Currents, especially their various eddies, have performed a similar function in biotic transport from southwestern island groups such as the Marshalls, Carolines, and others (Figure 11.1). Figures 11.2 and 24.1 show that between these archipelagos and the Hawaiian Chain there are several tiny isolated central Pacific atolls such as Wake and Johnston. There are also the Line Islands (Palmyra Atoll and others to the southeast) interposed roughly midway between the southern Polynesian island groups and Hawaiʻi. In many cases, these intervening atolls may have served as "stepping-stones" to the Hawaiian chain by providing intermediate homes for colonizing populations whose descendants eventually continued dispersal to the archipelago.

To judge from the high degree of similarity between both the reef-building coral and fish faunas of the Hawaiian Islands and those of Johnston Atoll (about 800 km or 500 miles southwest of the center of the archipelago), there has been relatively frequent reciprocal faunal exchange between the two areas. Studies of sporadic appropriately directed central Pacific subcurrents and eddies have produced estimates of about 30–50 and 187 days as the time it would take organisms to be floated from, respectively, Johnston and Wake to the Hawaiian Archipelago. These periods are well within the survival spans of the passively dispersed planktonic (see discussion in the next section) larval forms characteristic of many marine animals. And an unusual "fast track" current occurring only once every few hundred thousand years would have allowed transport to Hawaiʻi of even shorter-lived young.

The ancient high islands now represented by guyots and seamounts (see chapter 3) to the south and west of the Hawaiian Islands also undoubtedly similarly greatly facilitated the northward and eastward travel of Hawaiian marine founders in the geologic past. Conversely, the virtual absence of such submarine elevations between the Hawaiian Islands and the entire west coast of the Americas indicates that westward "island hopping" by New World coastal marine organisms was effectively inhibited. Also, although the currents such as the California and Peru (or Humboldt; Figure 11.1) that wash these American shores are ideally directed to transport marine organisms to Hawaiʻi, no substantial number of species has apparently arrived via them. These relatively cold currents from higher latitudes to both the north and south support coastal biotas of temperate species, few of which would be good candidates for establishment upon reaching the subtropical waters of most Polynesian islands.

Ocean Transport

Seaweeds propagate by spores, male and female gametes, or vegetative fragments. These plants obtain nutrients from surrounding seawater, so all of these types of propagules can exist for long periods while being carried as **plankton** (Greek *"planktos"* [wandering]) or passively drifting plant and animal life, often microscopic, as long as they remain close enough to the surface to receive enough sunlight to photosynthesize. In fact, air-filled sacs or bladders have evolved in the mature plants of a few widespread seaweed types, thus ensuring that their vegetative propagules float.

Essentially the entire native Hawaiian shore and nearshore marine fauna was also undoubtedly carried to the Islands as plankton, most species as larvae. About half of the plankton hauls

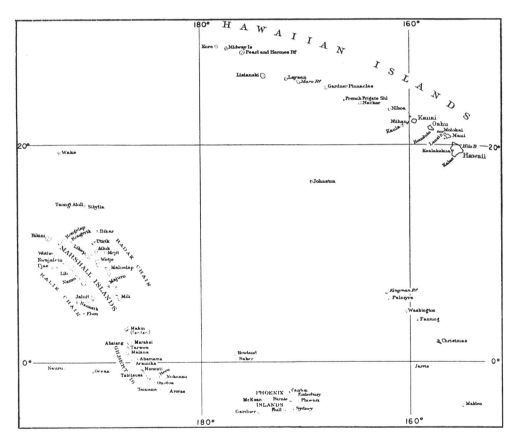

Figure 11.2. Map of the central Pacific. The small landmasses to the lower right, extending from Kingman Reef through Malden, along with Howland and Baker at the lower center of the map, represent the northern portion of the Line or Equatorial Islands. (Fig. 1 of Gosline [1955], used with permission of *Pacific Science*.)

made off the Line Islands contain molluscan larvae, and 92 percent made throughout the open Pacific include larval forms of some sort of inshore marine organism. Larvae can survive for differing lengths of time while being so transported; for example, some molluscan larvae for between about 200 and 320 days, but others only a week or so, and various coral larvae for periods between 45 and 212 days. Apparently, various fish larvae remain viable for at least several months, feeding on even smaller plankton as they drift.

There have been various types of wood and other vegetal debris drifting around the Pacific for untold millions of years and, in the last century or two, also various types of manufactured material, much eventually washing ashore on islands. Larvae or even adults of many types of marine organisms, especially those not well suited for transport as free plankton, may have arrived in Hawai'i associated with or attached to such buoyant material. For instance, sexually mature coral colonies have been found growing on floating pumice, and even occasionally somehow floating unaided. Inshore mollusks are seen attached to marine turtle shells, and it is possible that certain larger whales could also serve in a similar manner. In the latter half of the twentieth century, a tremendous increase occurred in both number and size of Pacific drift items, especially because of the widespread use of drift nets of buoyant synthetic material. There has been at least one report of a group of small fish of an inshore type inhabiting the immediate environs of a free-floating drift net remnant.

Other marine plants and animals seem to have been introduced historically to Hawai'i as part of the fouling on hulls of towed-in barges or in discharged seawater ballast. Also, the oil supertankers now plying the oceans can entrain floating debris in their wakes, thus hastening and directing the passage of any associated biota even to ports outside the usual ocean-current paths.

BIOTIC COMPOSITION

Marine Disharmony

The Hawaiian marine biota is not at all as disharmonic (see chapter 10) as that of the land and freshwater. Almost without exception, every order and higher taxonomic group as well as most important families of, at least, Indo-West Pacific marine organisms also occur in Hawai'i, so the disharmony occurs mostly at the generic level. The filter-funnel attenuation of the Indo-West Pacific marine biota reaching Hawai'i is such that, depending on the particular marine group, between 20 and 85 percent of the species typical of the insular Pacific west and south of the Hawaiian Islands has never established in the archipelago. The current absence of certain marine taxa must, however, be considered with caution. Fossil finds among only corals and mollusks have shown that a few currently missing species and even genera had inhabited the Hawaiian Islands in the distant past, but were subsequently lost, probably due to long-term fluctuations in local ocean characteristics.

Endemism

The degree of species endemicity among the native Hawaiian marine biota as a whole averages about 25–30 percent (range 4–80 percent for specific groups). This is low compared with the greater than 90 percent average for the terrestrial native Hawaiian biota, but is still apparently the greatest marine endemism of all Pacific island groups. Table 11.1 lists four major groups of the Hawaiian marine biota and their percentages of native and alien species. The small numbers of alien species for the major groups in the table mirror the situation in the Hawaiian marine biota as a whole; far fewer marine than terrestrial organisms have been either intentionally or inadvertently introduced (compare Table 13.1).

Speciation Rates

This collective Hawaiian marine endemism is not due to substantial adaptive radiation among a relatively few immigrant groups as it is on land, but to very limited speciation among a rather great number of founders.

Among all Hawaiian marine groups, the average number of endemic species per genus is only about two, whereas the average is at least eight for the major terrestrial biotic groups listed in Table 13.1. This higher number of species produced on land is even more remarkable when it is realized that the terrestrial forms currently known had only about 30 million years available for speciation (considering the hiatus of approximately 10 million years in availability of *upland* habitat before this time; see chapter 13), while the marine forms had more than 80 million. Although, as is shown in the next section, the average number of years between successful establishments in the archipelago is quite similar for at least the three groups of terrestrial and marine biota with the greatest number of founders, subsequent production of new species by each marine founder was undoubtedly greatly inhibited relative to that by most terrestrial ones. One reason may be that conspecific individuals of founding marine species continued to arrive in the Islands at more frequent intervals than did those of founding terrestrial organisms. Also, the coastal marine environment of most marine groups is essentially continuous around, and often among, islands of an archipelago. This provides essentially no means by which potentially speciating populations can become geographically isolated from conspecifics either already present or newly arriving, whereas the land offers many such opportunities. Thus, constant gene flow among individuals of a marine species results in a "swamping out" of incipient genetic drift (see chapter 10) and significantly inhibits any new adaptive features from appearing in island populations. It is unknown how great the rate of influx of additional individuals of a founding species must be to prevent genetic drift and/or speciation. One long-time genetics investigator has suggested that an average rate of only one individual per generation for every thousand

Table 11.1. Approximate species numbers of selected major Hawaiian marine biota. Percentages of native and alien species within each of these four groups are listed in parentheses. Figures for abyssal fishes are not included in totals because they are either estimated or unknown. (Data from various sources.)

Biota	Total	Endemic	Indigenous	Alien
Seaweeds	505	77 (15%)	420 (83%)	8 (2%)
Stony corals	51	13 (25%)	38 (75%)	—
Mollusks	790	190 (24%)	592 (75%)	8 (1%)
Bony fishes				
Abyssal	300	?	?	—
Pelagic	300	—	300 (100%)	—
Inshore	530	131 (25%)	391 (73%)	8 (2%)
Total[a]	2,176	411 (19%)	1,741 (80%)	24 (1%)

[a] Not including abyssal fishes.

organisms in an isolated moderately sized population might suffice to prevent such genetic differentiation.

Establishment Rates

If the average figure of two new species per founder is applied to the numbers for endemic taxa of the selected marine forms in Table 11.1, there must have been about thirty-nine founders for Hawaiian seaweeds, six for shallow-water stony (or reef-building) corals, ninety-five for mollusks, and sixty-seven for inshore fishes. These founder estimates can be added to the numbers of respective indigenous species (that is, presumably nonspeciating colonizers) to gain a rough idea of the average number of years needed for establishment by a species in each of these four groups (assuming 80 million years as the time available for colonizing *inshore* marine habitats in the entire Emperor Seamount–Hawaiian Island chain; see chapter 3), as has been done in Table 11.2. From comparisons of the paired founder-species numbers and years per establishment in this table, it is obvious that it is extremely difficult for many corals to successfully reach and colonize the Hawaiian Archipelago (see further discussion in the corals section later in this chapter) compared with members of the three other marine groups listed. If the corals are excluded from consideration, the average years per establishment for any one of the three remaining major marine groups in Table 11.2 is approximately 155,000 years. This figure compares fairly closely with that of about 147,000 for the three groups of Hawaiian terrestrial biota with the greatest number of founders shown in Table 13.4.

MARINE HABITATS

Terms

A commonly used classification of marine habitats appears in Figures 11.3 and 11.4. The terms **"reef," "littoral"** (or neritic), and **"pelagic"** all refer to the upper ocean waters and indicate increasing distances from shore; **"benthic"** signifies the bottom habitat in water less than about 200 m (660 feet) deep, and the term **"abyssal"** (or bathyal; not shown in the figures) means the ocean floor and near-bottom habitat at greater depths. The **intertidal** is the longshore bottom area alternately covered and uncovered by the tides, and this is essentially synonymous with

Table 11.2. Approximate establishment rates for selected major native Hawaiian marine biota. The founder numbers represent estimated endemic-species ancestors plus indigenous species. Abyssal and pelagic fishes are not included because numbers of endemic and indigenous species of the former are unknown, and all of the latter are quite likely essentially Pacific-wide in distribution. The age of *inshore* marine habitat in the archipelago, including the remaining Emperor Seamounts, is taken as 80 million years. (Data from various sources.)

Biota	Founder			Average Years per Establishment
Seaweeds	39 +	420 =	459	175,000
Stony corals	6 +	38 =	44	1,820,000
Mollusks	95 +	592 =	687	115,000
Bony fishes (inshore)	67 +	391 =	458	175,000
Total	207 +	1,441 =	1,648	570,000

the **surge zone** noted in both figures. There are also **tide pools** (or surge pools) above the highest intertidal along rocky coasts, but, because tides in the Hawaiian Islands range considerably less than 1 m (3.3 feet), the pool water is typically supplied and changed almost entirely by wave surge, which may be at least two or three times as high as the tides.

Brackish Pools

In coastal lava flows and ancient emergent coral-algal reefs there is the quasi-marine habitat of **anchialine ponds** (Greek *"anchialos"* [near the sea]; Figure 27.1). These generally small, shallow ponds have no surface connection with the ocean, but contain brackish water supplied by subterranean flows from both the freshwater table and the sea. A few intertidal fish species are occasionally found in these ponds, although perhaps the most characteristic animal of their limited but largely endemic fauna is a tiny red (or occasionally white) shrimp or ʻŌpae ʻula *(Halocaridina rubra).* As an island ages, anchialine ponds are typically lost as they fill in with soil and organic matter.

Coastal Reef

The living reef surrounding all except the youngest of the Hawaiian islands is usually referred to as a "coral reef." This is correct in the case of calmer bays and offshore depths below heavy wave action, where corals predominate as reef builders. But along shores exposed to open-ocean conditions, including heavy surf, the reef is more properly termed a "coral-algal" one, because the major portion of it is formed by encrusting species of **calcareous algae** or calcium carbonate–secreting seaweeds (see discussion later in this chapter). The crustose and stonelike seaweeds not only constitute most of the barrier reef (see chapter 3), but also maintain and build up much of the fringing reef by cementing together sand, broken coral fragments, and other loose material, as well as by filling in many cavities.

CORALS

Biotic Composition and Disharmony

Species endemicity in the shallow-water Hawaiian reef-coral fauna, representing sixteen genera, is about 25 percent. Three of these species here considered Hawaiian endemics are also found at Johnston Atoll and/or the northern Line Islands, but just as in the case of inshore fishes (see chapter 12) the coral fauna of this southern region is regarded as only an extension of the Hawaiian one. The current absence of some four dozen other Indo-West Pacific genera from Hawaiian waters results in a disharmony greater than that for most other marine groups. This absence is due partially to the current relatively low ocean temperature of Hawaiʻi, but probably more to the relative difficulty that certain potential founding or recolonizing coral species have in reaching the archipelago because of the short life of their planktonic larvae and the general inability of adults to raft or float.

Reef Corals

The **stony** or **reef-building corals** (order Scleractinia, phylum Coelenterata) that have built a significant portion of the Hawaiian coastal reef display several types of branching, shelflike, and encrusting growth forms. The more abundant among the fifty-one Island species are the finger and lobe corals (*Porites* spp.), rice corals (*Montipora* spp.), moosehorn and cauliflower or

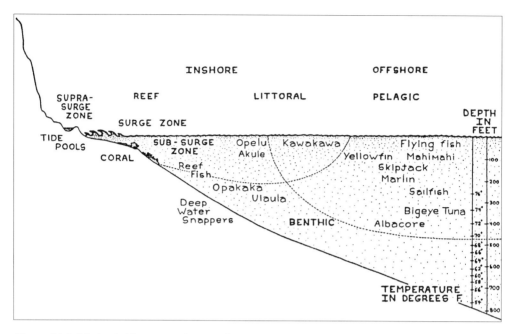

Figure 11.3. Marine habitats around a Hawaiian island. Certain kinds of fishes typical of each habitat are also noted. The coral in shallower water comprises primarily reef-building species, with admixed calcareous algae. That shown in deeper water is of nonreef-building species. (Fig. 1 of Gosline and Brock [1960], used with permission of William A. Gosline.)

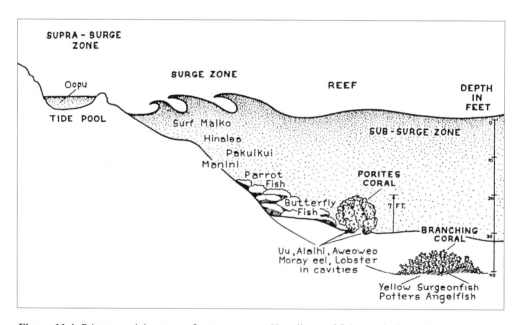

Figure 11.4. Primary activity areas of some common Hawaiian reef fishes and other animals. The corals are all of the reef-building type. (Fig. 2 of Gosline and Brock [1960], used with permission of William A. Gosline.)

rose corals (*Pocillopora* spp.), and false brain corals (*Pavona* spp.). The genus *Acropora,* with many species in Pacific island groups to the far south and southwest, is represented in Hawai'i by only four species, mostly confined to the Northwestern Hawaiian Islands. Fossil remains, however, indicate that *Acropora* and at least six other now-missing reef-coral genera were common in the Islands about 15 to 20 million years before the present, some of these surviving until only 1 or 2 million years ago.

Ecology

Corals consist of small, colonial, plankton-eating animals or **polyps.** Those of stony species secrete around themselves calcareous cups or calyces making up the coral exoskeleton. Also, the polyps of shallow-water reef-building species have unicellular algae living symbiotically in their tissues. Photosynthesis (see chapter 9) by these algae produces an excess amount of nutrient material, which is necessary to supplement that produced by the host animals themselves. The algal metabolism also removes excretory carbon dioxide from the polyps' tissue, lowering its acidity and allowing the calcareous exoskeleton material to be laid down more readily than without such removal. It is important to note that the presence of these algae determines the maximum depth at which reef-building corals can live. The water must be shallow enough for sufficient sunlight to reach the photosynthesizing algae. The depth limit is usually about 100 m (330 feet) or so, but may be up to twice this in exceptionally clear water. The few nonreef-forming abyssal types, primarily the black corals (order Antipatharia) and semiprecious pink corals (order Gorgonacea), are found below this depth because they can exist without symbiotic algae.

MARINE ALGAE

Classification

Seaweeds have traditionally been classified in four divisions, based primarily on the particular plant color produced by the contained photosynthetic pigments. All four groups are found along most world coasts, with a few members of each also found in freshwater and other moist terrestrial environments; this is especially true of blue-green "algae" (or Cyanobacteria; see below). The four divisions classically recognized are the **green algae** (Chlorophyta), **brown algae** (Phaeophyta), **red algae** (Rhodophyta), and **blue-green "algae"** (Cyanophyta).

The blue-green "algae," however, are truly puzzling organisms, and it is now thought that they are not closely related to the other three groups listed above. For example, their cells lack a defined nucleus with delimited chromosomes and show certain other (presumably) quite primitive characteristics. In fact, some scientists think that these "algae" are best considered only structurally advanced colonial bacteria, and so they are currently termed **Cyanobacteria.** There are no figures available for the possible total of marine species of this group, although there are estimated to be about one hundred land and freshwater taxa. For these reasons, the blue-green "algae" are not included in the tables or discussed elsewhere in this chapter. They are not without interest, however, because some marine forms have the unusual habit of boring into corals and stony species of typical algae by dissolving the calcium carbonate of these organisms. And one, without a common name but known scientifically as *Lyngbya majuscula,* occasionally receives attention because floating fragments of it produce "swimmer's itch."

Limu is the general Hawaiian term for essentially all of these algal types (as well as for any other plant growing under either freshwater or saltwater). The approximate numbers of Hawaiian marine algal species in each of the three typical groups are shown in Table 11.3. A single marine flowering plant, the small indigenous Sea Wrack or Hawaiian Seagrass (*Halophila hawaiiana* [frogs-bit family Hydrocharitaceae]) grows on certain Hawaiian shallow reef floors among various seaweeds and is often mistaken for one of them.

Calcareous Algae

Certain marine algae deposit in their tissue calcium carbonate extracted from seawater. The green and brown algae include few such forms, with calcification occurring only in parts of the plant body in these upright forms. The red algae also possess a few upright species of this same partially calcified type, but in addition include many calcareous encrusting or nodular species. These latter two types of red algae are typified by such genera as *Hydrolithon* (formerly known as *Porolithon*), *Lithophyllum,* and *Lithothamnion* (the "lithon" part of these names is from the Greek *"lithos"* [stone]). In fact, species of the first-named genus form such a predominant part of the barrier reef that this structure was often termed the "Porolithon ridge." Presumably, the hardening function of the independently evolved calcification in the three typical algal groups serves as protection of softer parts from fatal overgrazing by marine herbivores.

Geographic Source

There are a number of widespread tropical or subtropical seaweeds whose range includes the Hawaiian Islands. The ancestral species yielding four common endemic Hawaiian species of brown *limu kala* (*Sargassum* spp.) was apparently a subtropical American coast form, but the source area of most or all other Hawaiian seaweeds seems to have been the Indo-West Pacific. Species attenuation is relatively slight when traced from west to east. For example, a recent survey has shown that the various Northwestern Hawaiian Islands have an approximate total of 204 species of macroscopic marine algae, while the physiographically equivalent several *motu* of Eniwetak Atoll in the Marshall Islands to the west have about 222. The relative frequency ranking of species number within each of the three algal types, however, is the same for the two atoll groups. Thus, vagaries of dispersal and establishment are more likely responsible for the modest discrepancy between number of species than are differences in the two areas' environments.

Biotic Disharmony

As with essentially all other Hawaiian marine groups, disharmony in taxa of marine algae is primarily at only the generic rather than higher taxonomic level. One example among algae is

Table 11.3. Approximate species numbers of Hawaiian marine algae. The blue-green "algae" are not included (see text). Percentages of native species and of alien taxa now evidently established in the wild are indicated in parentheses. (Data primarily from Isabella A. Abbott [1999 and personal communication, November 1999].)

Division	Total	Endemic	Indigenous	Alien
Green algae (Chlorophyta)	84	5 (6%)	77 (92%)	2? (2%)
Brown algae (Phaeophyta)	46	5 (11%)	41 (89%)	—
Red algae (Rhodophyta)	375	67 (18%)	302 (80%)	6 (2%)
Total	505	77 (15%)	420 (83%)	8 (2%)

especially noticeable: the absence in Hawai'i of several genera of the often strikingly large and abundant brown kelps so characteristic of the temperate American and Asian coasts. It is generally accepted that the Hawaiian ocean water is too warm to support these and many other such colder-water forms of marine biota.

There are no additional significant absences of at least major taxonomic groups of marine algae from Hawai'i, although there is some suggestion that Hawai'i is on the northern edge of the ocean-temperature range of certain typical warm-water Indo-West Pacific seaweeds. For instance, indigenous Island species of the green alga *Caulerpa* grow only about half as large as their conspecifics in warmer parts of the Pacific, and a few species of the genus common nearer the equator are lacking in Hawai'i.

Evolutionary Phenomena

Studies to date seem to show that endemism among Hawaiian seaweeds is low even for a marine group, being only about 15 percent (Tables 11.1, 11.3). The paucity of pertinent Pacific-wide studies, however, currently makes it impossible to describe examples of founder effect and genetic drift that may have occurred among Hawaiian marine algae. Adaptive radiation and adaptive shifts among Hawaiian seaweeds have also been little investigated, although probably there are essentially no examples of either phenomenon in the archipelago. For instance, no Hawaiian forms have adaptively radiated into the ecological niche of the large continental-margin kelps previously noted as missing from the Islands. The closest approximation to these large kelps seems to be found among species of the brown *limu kala* (*Sargassum* spp.), some of which may reach 30 cm (12 inches) in height. The reason for this failure of any algae to evolve larger forms in Hawaiian waters may well be related to the earlier mentioned evolutionary "difficulty" in speciation of marine biota because of the probable continual arrival of additional parental stock.

Hawaiian Ecology

Seaweeds are producers, representing the basal trophic level filled by terrestrial green plants (see chapter 9). They are consumed by a large number of herbivores (both fishes and various invertebrates) of the second trophic level, which in turn sustain higher-level carnivorous fishes and other predators.

No algal division exclusively occupies a Hawaiian marine habitat, although certain brown algae such as *Sargassum* spp. and, seasonally, *limu līpoa* (*Dictyopteris* spp.) often constitute a majority of the vegetation in relatively deeper reef areas. In the Islands, many noncrustose species of all three seaweed groups are commonly found attached to firm substrate from the tidepool level down as far as there is sufficient sunlight for photosynthesis. A few marine algae of low and spreading growth form, for example the common green Rats-foot Seaweed or *limu wāwae'iole (Codium edule)*, can remain so securely anchored by partial burial in sand that they do not require a hard attachment surface. Periodically, however, an exceptionally strong, deep current, possibly in combination with a particular type of wave action, tears loose this and many other kinds of seaweed, and some beaches may then become covered with a thick and soon-odious layer of mixed species as this plant material washes ashore.

The number of algal species per island changes throughout the island's life history because this abundance is necessarily directly related to the number of circumisland habitats available at any given stage. Thus, the relatively limited variety of habitats around the young still-building island of Hawaiʻi, comprising primarily lava benches with few well-developed reefal or other distinctive inshore areas, supports fewer *limu* species than does an older island such as Oʻahu. Around the latter island, lava benches are still present in some areas, but elsewhere there has been time for development of a great variety of reef flats and other areas of different marine substrate. This variety of habitats allows support of the maximum number of algal types. As an island erodes and subsides to become an atoll, the algal species variety decreases to the general low level of that of the original young high island (although the taxa may differ) because the only coastal substrate now available is the relatively uniform surrounding calcareous reef.

Alien Seaweeds

Many types of seaweeds important to ancient Hawaiians are still used today as ingredients of Island dishes and as relishes, seasonings, and culinary thickening agents. A few additional species historically introduced to Hawaiʻi as food or mariculture crops have established. The native red *Limu manauea (Gracilaria coronopifolia)* and a very similar native species with the (Japanese-derived) name of *Ogo (G. parvispora)* are so popular that the North American congener, *G. tikvahiae,* had to be imported for cultivation to meet the commercial demand. Two Filipino red algae, the robust *tambalang* (*Kappaphycus alvarezii* and *K. striatum* [formerly placed in the genus *Eucheuma*]), were introduced during the 1970s to experiment with production of **carrageenan,** a colloid gel used as a food and drug additive. At about that same time, the red *Hypnea musciformis* was (illegally) imported for the same purpose, but its branches were found to be too delicate to process properly.

At least four other possibly alien forms have established in Hawaiʻi in the past 100 years or so. The two red algae *Acanthophora spicifera* and *Gracilaria salicornia* were first noted in the mid-1900s after apparently arriving via the fouled hulls or ballast water of vessels. Two green algae, Reticulate Sea Lettuce *(Ulva reticulata),* as well as *Avrainvillea amadelpha,* could also have been imported, although some authorities think one or both may be indigenous.

Harmful Seaweeds

With the exception of the earlier mentioned irritating cyanobacterium *Lyngbya majuscula,* no Hawaiian marine plant life is generally regarded as noxious, although a few algal species may prove internally so to the occasional allergic person. There is, however, a toxic colonial animal, the sea-anemonelike coelenterate *Palythoa toxica,* which bears the taxonomically inaccurate but apt Hawaiian name *Limu make o Hāna* (deadly seaweed of Hāna [on far East Maui]). This is apparently not only lethal if eaten, but its toxin can also cause prolonged debilitating symptoms if it enters through skin abrasions. Certain branched colonial hydrozoans of the animal phylum Coelenterata may be mistaken for seaweeds, but the immediate stinging sensation upon handling them is an obvious indication that the organism is not a *limu.*

MARINE MOLLUSKS

Classification

The most recent published accounting indicates there are at least 790 marine species of the phylum **Mollusca** currently found in the Hawaiian Islands. As shown in Table 11.4, these are divided among six classes, of which the snail-like **Gastropoda** and clamlike **Bivalvia** are by far the most numerous, together comprising almost 90 percent of Hawaiian marine molluscans.

In the class Cephalopoda, two kinds of octopus or *heʻe* (*Octopus* spp.) are especially notice-able on Hawaiian reef flats and slightly deeper benthic areas. In the Islands these are known as "squid" rather than "octopus," but the Hawaiian true squid or cuttlefish of this same class, the Pacific Reef Squid or *mūheʻe (Sepioteuthis lessoniana)*, is a free-swimming littoral and pelagic animal. There are two pelagic species of a rather small paper nautilus or *ʻauwaʻalālua* (*Argonauta* spp.), whose thin and very fragile white flotation organ or "shell" occasionally washes up on Island beaches, but the more familiar chambered nautilus forms (*Nautilus* spp.) do not occur in Hawaiʻi. Chitons (class Polyplacophora) are typically small, flat, oval animals protected by a series of eight overlapping dorsal calcareous plates. They are usually found attached to firm reef substrates, but tend to be somewhat scarce in the Islands. The remaining two molluscan classes found in Hawaiʻi are tooth shells or Scaphopoda, and solenogasters or Aplacophora, but both are represented here by only a few small benthic and, possibly, abyssal species.

Geographic Source

The Hawaiian molluscan fauna is derived essentially entirely from the Indo-West Pacific area. More endemic species and subspecies seem closely related to taxa of that region than to those of the central Pacific island groups to the south of the Islands. Taxonomic disharmony involving groups at the generic and higher levels is not particularly noticeable, because almost all of the important Indo-West Pacific families are represented. The disharmony that does exist, however, includes absence of the family Tridachnidae containing the giant clams, a common Indo-West Pacific group. Also noticeably lacking is the primarily continental-coast gastropod abalone family, a few species of which are found on some other isolated Pacific islands closer to continents. The Hawaiian Islands have slightly less than 80 percent of the inshore gastropod genera found in Micronesia. Attenuation is evidenced by the fact that Hawaiʻi has fewer than eight hundred molluscan species, while in, for example, the Japanese Ryukyu Islands there are almost twenty-five hundred.

Biotic Composition

There are 106 Hawaiian gastropod families comprising approximately 572 species, but the significantly fewer 40 bivalve families contain only about 132 species. Tables 11.5 and 11.6 list the more common families of these two molluscan classes, along with numbers of native species.

Table 11.4. Approximate species numbers of Hawaiian marine mollusks. Percentages of native and alien taxa are indicated in parentheses. (Data primarily from Eldredge and Miller [1995] and Kay [1979].)

Class	Total	Endemic	Indigenous	Alien
Snails, etc. (Gastrododa)	572	119 (21%)	449 (78%)	4 (1%)
Clams, etc. (Bivalvia)	132	66 (50%)	62 (47%)	4 (3%)
Octopus, etc. (Cephalopoda)	73	2 (3%)	71 (97%)	—
Tooth shells (Scaphopoda)	3	—	3 (100%)	—
Aplacophorans (Aplacophora)	6	—	6 (100%)	—
Chitons (Polyplacophora)	4	3 (75%)	1 (25%)	—
Total	790	190 (24%)	592 (75%)	8 (1%)

Marine Gastropods

Gastropods are almost all relatively mobile animals and, unlike most bivalves, are well suited to life on the coral-algal reefs and underwater lava substrates of the Hawaiian Islands. A few gastropods, however, are completely pelagic, usually seen only when they occasionally wash or blow ashore. The violet snails or *pūpū pani* (*Janthina* spp. [family Janthinidae]) float attached to a raft of self-produced bubbles and prey on similarly colored drifting Portuguese-man-of-war or *pa'imalau* (genera *Physalia* and *Velella* [phylum Coelenterata]). Many species of several gastropod families around the world have apparently evolutionarily lost their shell, and among those represented in Hawai'i are nudibranchs of the Dorididae and other closely related families. These shell-less gastropod types are carnivorous and are usually found associated with specific algae or on certain marine substrates. Some species may occasionally be seen swimming higher in the water column, and a few are pelagic. Most shelled gastropods are snail-like and are known collectively as *pūpū* in Hawaiian. The members of at least three families, however,

Table 11.5. The ten Hawaiian marine gastropod families containing the most native species. The percentage of the entire native Hawaiian marine complement (572 species) of this class represented by each family is indicated in parentheses, as are also the percentages of endemic and indigenous species within each family. (Data from Kay [1979].)

Family	Total	Endemic	Indigenous
Towers (Turridae)	65 (11%)	34 (52%)	31 (48%)
Miters (Mitridae)	50 (9%)	6 (12%)	44 (88%)
Triphorids (Triphoridae)	46 (8%)	19 (41%)	27 (59%)
Costellariids (Costellariidae)	44 (8%)	6 (14%)	38 (86%)
Cones (Conidae)	43 (8%)	2 (5%)	41 (95%)
Terebrids (Terebridae)	42 (7%)	10 (24%)	32 (76%)
Cowries (Cypraeidae)	38 (7%)	6 (16%)	32 (84%)
Doridids (Dorididae)	34 (6%)	17 (50%)	17 (50%)
Drupes (Thaididae)	27 (5%)	4 (15%)	23 (85%)
Pyramidellids (Pyramidellidae)	26 (5%)	13 (50%)	13 (50%)
Total	415 (73%)	117 (28%)	298 (72%)

Table 11.6. The five Hawaiian marine bivalve families containing the most native species. The percentage of the entire native Hawaiian marine complement (132 species) of this class represented by each family is indicated in parentheses, as are also the percentages of endemic and indigenous species within each family. There are no alien species in these families. (Data from Kay [1979].)

Family	Total	Endemic	Indigenous
Mussels (Mytilidae)	14 (11%)	10 (71%)	4 (29%)
Arks (Arcidae)	13 (10%)	4 (31%)	9 (69%)
Scallops (Pectinidae)	10 (8%)	4 (40%)	6 (60%)
Shipworms (Teredinidae)	10 (8%)	3 (30%)	7 (70%)
Tellens (Tellinidae)	9 (7%)	3 (33%)	6 (67%)
Total	56 (42%)	24 (43%)	32 (57%)

have evolved a relatively low conical or limpetlike shell and a large muscular "foot," both adaptations well suited to withstanding the force of waves breaking on exposed coastal rocks to which they cling. Species of these three families usually have Hawaiian names incorporating the general term *'opihi.*

Ecologically, most gastropods are primary-level consumers, grazing on low-growing or coating noncrustose seaweeds. An ecologically significant minority, however, are carnivores at the secondary or higher consumer level, almost without exception feeding on other mollusks or different marine invertebrates. Essentially all herbivorous gastropods use the **radula,** a rasping organ bearing a series of hard toothlike processes, for feeding on algae. Certain carnivorous types, however, use the radula to drill through the shells of invertebrate prey, some even secreting chemicals that dissolve calcium carbonate, which aids in drilling. In the **cone shells** or *pūpū 'alā* (*Conus* spp. [family Conidae]), the radula teeth have evolved into often-enlarged barbs. These teeth are hollow, connected by a tube to a toxin-producing gland, and are used for stunning and securing prey (including occasional small fishes). Several species can inflict a painful poisoned wound on an unsuspecting person handling the animal. In the natural food web, many mollusks of various types are eaten by larger predators including octopus and several types of powerful-jawed fishes (see chapter 12).

Marine Bivalves

Hawaiian species of the class Bivalvia are noticeably less numerous than those of the class Gastropoda, probably primarily because of the scarcity of extensive sandy or muddy shoreline flats in which most of the world's bivalves live. A majority of the Island bivalves permanently or semipermanently attach themselves to firmer marine substrates or occasionally burrow into these. In the softer bottoms of the few well-protected bays in Hawai'i, however, such as O'ahu's Pearl Harbor and Kāne'ohe Bay, certain native and alien bivalves potentially flourish (see discussion later in this chapter). Bivalves are filter feeders, straining planktonic plants and animals out of the water with an elaborate gill system; thus, ecologically, they include both primary and secondary consumers.

Evolutionary Phenomena

There are no endemic Hawaiian families of either Gastropoda or Bivalvia and just three genera that thus far seem restricted to the archipelago. At most, only about a fifth of the species of gastropods, and half of the bivalves, may be endemic. It is not certain why only a few families shown in Tables 11.5 and 11.6 should have evolved a relatively large percentage of apparently endemic species (for example, the gastropod tower shells [Turridae] and some nudibranchs [Dorididae] as well as the bivalve mussels [Mytilidae]). It may be that such families of high Island endemicity have shorter-lived larvae than those with fewer endemic species, thus reducing the number of subsequent conspecific immigrants reaching the archipelago to inhibit speciation, but this is largely speculative.

Some molluscan families that are not especially speciose in Hawai'i nevertheless exhibit a relatively high degree of endemism. Probable examples include the various *'opihi* of the family Patellidae (four species of *Cellana,* all endemic) and the marine and freshwater members of the family **Neritidae** (ten species in five genera, six endemic). In the patellids, endemism seems to have resulted from an adaptive shift of particular species to an existence high in or just above the intertidal. In the neritids, the shift in habitat (discussed further later in this chapter) has been from seawater to, ultimately, freshwater. Such selective adaptation moved the original Hawaiian Patellidae and at least some of the evolving Neritidae progressively farther away from their former purely marine habitat. This change in habitat presumably fostered evolution of endemic forms by reducing or preventing gene flow between differentiating lineages and any newly arriving individuals of the founders' stock.

Founder effect and/or genetic drift presumably explains the occasional instances of differences in shell color pattern, size, and shape of certain Hawaiian mollusks. For example, in most parts of its extensive oceanic range, the Snakehead Cowrie or *āleaalea* (*Cypraea caputserpentis* [family Cypraeidae]) has white spaces between the teeth bordering the shell opening, but in Hawai'i (and the Marquesas Islands) these areas are dull orange or brown. The Hawaiian Turban or *'alīlea* (*Turbo sandwicensis* [family Turbinidae]) in the Northwestern Hawaiian Islands reaches almost twice the length of those in the main islands, and its whorls are separated somewhat like a corkscrew rather than being contiguous as in the latter form.

There is no spectacular example of Hawaiian molluscan adaptive radiation. For the very few marine genera with as many as several endemic species, most of these endemics seem to have evolved from an almost equal number of founders, rather than from only one or two immigrant species. For instance, the four endemic *'opihi* are thought to have evolved from three different founders, and the six endemic cowries or *leho* from either five or six immigrant species.

There is, though, a subdued version of adaptive radiation involving salinity tolerance and shell configuration evident among Hawaiian species of Neritidae. (It is presumed here that this minor radiation resulted from adaptive shifts in habitat of several evolving species of a single Island lineage, rather than from independent establishment of several different brackish-water and freshwater ancestors.) Indigenous members of the family such as the Black Nerite or *pipipi* (*Nerita picea*) and Polished Nerite or *kūpe'e* (*N. polita*) live in full-salinity water of the high intertidal and have globose snail-like shells. The overlapping habitats occupied by a succession of six derivative endemic species, however, span the entire salinity range: from normal seawater, through brackish estuarine water, to the freshwater of mountain streams. The species tolerating a wide variety of salinity are termed **euryhaline** (Greek *"eurys"* [wide or broad] and *"hals"* [salt]). Also, the shells of these six endemic taxa progressively shift from snail-like to limpetlike with change in habitat; that of the **Stream Limpet** or *hīhīwai* (*Neritina granosa*), whose range extends highest up freshwater streams, generally is the most flattened.

It is interesting that, within the entire stream habitat, shell characteristics of Stream Limpets change with habitat variations. Individuals in swift high-elevation water have a thin-walled, smooth, unwinged shell; those in usually slower low-elevation water have a thicker, rugose, laterally winged one. However, if a smooth-shelled animal is relocated from upper to lower stream reaches, it will thenceforth produce only thick, rough-textured shell material and will develop wings as it grows.

It might reasonably be expected that the upper-stream shell configuration (or, at least the ability to produce it) had been naturally selected to prevent the animal from being detached by the strong water flow there. Studies suggest, however, that overall metabolic demands, rather than stream dynamics, primarily determine shell morphology. Development and maintenance of both the shell and the muscular clinging foot represent major expenditures of metabolic energy. The swifter the water, the larger the foot must be, so selection has favored those variant Stream Limpet individuals that can divert, as necessary, more metabolic energy to developing and operating the foot than to constantly producing a more massive shell structure. Also, there may be less food available on the scoured substrate of higher stream reaches than on that of less-disturbed lower segments, thus additionally favoring this ability to divert metabolic energy from shell production as long as physically stressed.

Alien Mollusks

At least one marine gastropod seems to have been legally liberated in Hawaiian waters: the Nile Top Shell, *Trochus niloticus,* of the family Trochidae. This was introduced to Oʻahu's Kāne-ʻohe Bay about the end of the 1960s as an anticipated source of shell material for button manufacturing, but the population seems now to have died out. Several alien species of bivalves were introduced in the nineteenth and twentieth centuries as food items. The American and Japanese Oysters (*Crassostrea virginica* and *C. gigas* [family Ostreidae]) were successfully established in Kāneʻohe and Kailua Bays as well as in Pearl Harbor. The introduced Japanese Littleneck Clam *(Tapes japonica)* and the Eastern North American Quahog *(Mercenaria mercenaria),* both of the family Veneridae, also thrived for a time in Kāneʻohe Bay and Pearl Harbor, as well as in shallow water of Kauaʻi. None of these four alien bivalves is currently legally harvested, however, primarily because of either greatly depleted (if not extirpated) populations or polluted habitat conditions.

SUGGESTED REFERENCES

Abbott 1989, 1999; Beletsky 2000; Carleton 1987; Culliney 1988; Doty 1967, 1973a, b; Fielding and Robinson 1987; Fortner 1978; Grigg 1983, 1988; Gulko 1999; Hourigan and Reese 1987; Jokiel 1987; Kay 1979, 1987; Kay and Palumbi 1987; Magruder and Hunt 1979; Maragos 1977, 1995, 1998; Maragos and Jokiel 1986; Scheltema 1986; C. M. Smith 1992; Titcomb 1978.

AUDIOVISUAL AIDS

Coral; The coral reef community; Hawaii: Surf and sea; Hawaiian seafood: Limu; Hawaii's coral: Dead or alive; Life at Salt Point; Life on the sandy shore and the rocky shore; Places in the sea.

12

Marine and Freshwater Fishes

Marine fishes found in the central Pacific represent two taxonomic classes: **Chondrichthyes,** the cartilaginous-skeletoned forms, comprising sharks, rays, and the rare, little-known abyssal family Chimaeridae; and **Osteichthyes,** the bony-skeletoned fishes.

BIOTIC COMPOSITION

Johnston Atoll

In this volume, the inshore fish fauna of **Johnston Atoll** (800 km or 500 miles southwest of the Hawaiian Archipelago midpoint; Figures 11.1, 11.2) is considered along with that of Hawai'i, following the current practice of most ichthyologists. The 300 or so recorded Johnston species are somewhat over half the number found in the Hawaiian Archipelago, and 285 of these are common to the two areas. Of these mutually possessed species, forty-five or more are found only at Johnston and in the Hawaiian chain. Four species here called Hawaiian endemics are apparently restricted to Johnston Atoll, although the identification and putative endemic status of three of these still have to be verified because they have been viewed only from submersibles.

Cartilaginous Fishes

In Hawai'i there are fifteen shark families with approximately forty-two species, and five ray families comprising about nine species. The sharks are essentially all predators of high trophic levels, usually feeding on living vertebrates and invertebrates but also scavenging dead ones. Most of the various types of rays either eat benthic mollusks by crushing their shells using massive dental plates or strain plankton by means of a specialized oral apparatus.

Bony Fishes

The bony fishes are much more numerous and ecologically diverse than the cartilaginous ones. Among the almost two hundred families of bony fishes found within approximately 322 km (200 miles) of the Hawaiian Islands, there are well over 1,100 native abyssal, pelagic, and inshore species. The bony species here somewhat arbitrarily termed inshore (or shore) fishes are those that may usually be found in water shallower than about 200 m (660 feet) and include members of approximately one hundred families. The native and alien inshore bony species number about 530 (Table 11.1) and, along with a few of the more common pelagic bony fishes, are essentially the only marine taxa further considered in this chapter. Table 12.1 lists the ten most speciose families of Hawaiian inshore fishes.

Many of these inshore species are primary consumers, living on seaweeds or smaller planktonic and benthic algae, but a considerable number of them, as well as most of the pelagic forms, are consumers of higher trophic levels, preying on other fishes and a great variety of invertebrates.

GEOGRAPHIC SOURCE

The source of the Hawaiian inshore fish fauna is largely the Indo-West Pacific, with very likely less than ten or so founders from the East Pacific. The extensive deep-water gap and the ocean-temperature difference between Hawai'i and the American continents were described in chapter 11. Their joint effectiveness in restricting interchange of shore fishes among these areas is further suggested by the fact that, of the more than 380 indigenous inshore species reaching Hawai'i from the entire Pacific region to the west and south, only between 20 and 30 are also found along the American coasts (presumably reaching there, along with about 70 additional species of inshore fishes from the Indo-West Pacific, by way of the Equatorial Counter Current [Fig. 11.1], rather than directly from Hawai'i). Dispersal from New World coasts west through the Pacific is even more difficult, judging from the fact that only six or seven shore-fish species of East Pacific origin have reached Hawai'i.

DISHARMONY AND ATTENUATION

Although many inshore fish families of significant speciosity in the Indo-West Pacific are also fairly well represented in Hawai'i, a few exceptions introduce a limited amount of disharmony. For example, among herbivorous families, rabbitfishes (Siganidae) are lacking in the Islands.

Within families, however, the substantial effect of filter-funnel attenuation (see chapter 11) on the Hawaiian fish fauna becomes especially evident if the total number of native inshore species in various far-West Pacific island groups is traced eastward. There are approximately 2,500 such species of bony fishes in the Philippines, some 940 in Micronesia, but only about 530 in the Hawaiian Islands. The native Hawaiian amphidromous gobies (families Gobiidae and Eleotridae; see discussion later in this chapter) provide a more specific example. Although there are

Table 12.1. The ten Hawaiian primarily inshore fish families containing the most native species. Waifs and alien species are not included. The percentage of the entire native inshore bony fish fauna of approximately 530 species represented by each family is indicated in parentheses, as are the percentages of endemic and indigenous species within each family. (Data primarily from Bruce C. Mundy and John E. Randall, personal communication, January 1999.)

Family	Total	Endemic	Indigenous
Wrasses (Labridae)	45 (8%)	17 (38%)	28 (62%)
Moray eels (Muraenidae)	45 (8%)	5 (11%)	40 (89%)
True gobies (Gobiidae)	32 (6%)	12 (38%)	20 (62%)
Scorpionfishes (Scorpaenidae)	27 (5%)	8 (30%)	19 (70%)
Jacks (Carangidae)	24 (5%)	0 (0%)	24 (100%)
Surgeonfishes (Acanthuridae)	24 (5%)	0 (0%)	24 (100%)
Butterflyfishes (Chaetodontidae)	23 (4%)	4 (17%)	19 (83%)
Groupers (Serranidae)	22 (4%)	6 (27%)	16 (73%)
Snake eels (Ophichthidae)	21 (4%)	6 (29%)	15 (71%)
Squirrelfishes (Holocentridae)	20 (4%)	1 (5%)	19 (95%)
Total	283 (53%)	59 (21%)	224 (79%)

approximately fifty-six such species among the Indonesian-Malaysian islands, this number has already attenuated to eighteen by the time the Philippines are reached, with only a dozen or fewer found farther east in such places as Guam and Samoa, and only five continuing on to the Hawaiian Islands. Species attenuation is generally most obvious in certain predatory groups. Emperors (Lethrinidae), so numerous and characteristic of Southwest Pacific islands, are represented in Hawaiian waters by only a single somewhat atypical species. The elsewhere-abundant snappers (Lutjanidae) include only two inshore species and a few primarily deep-water forms in Hawai'i, and at least shallow-water species of the grouper family Serranidae also tend to be very scarce in the Islands.

EVOLUTIONARY PHENOMENA

Endemism

As listed in Table 11.1, endemism among *only* Hawaiian inshore bony fishes is approximately 25 percent, which is apparently the highest of any Pacific archipelago or isolated island. In fact, only Easter Island of the Southeast Pacific (Figure 24.1) with perhaps 22 percent endemism rivals the Hawaiian Archipelago. The Easter Island fish fauna, however, has not been as well sampled as that of the Hawaiian Islands, so future collecting there will likely lower this percentage because there will probably be many more indigenous than endemic bony species among new discoveries. The Marquesas group, halfway between Easter Island and Hawai'i, ranks third in endemicity with a relatively low figure of about 10 percent.

The substantial amount of speciation exhibited among its shore fishes has undoubtedly resulted from the isolation of the Hawaiian Archipelago, through many millions of years being widely separated from primary potential sources of colonists. This isolation has often allowed certain founders arriving in the Islands to remain separated from ancestral populations elsewhere in the Pacific long enough to evolve into new species. Some of these endemics became the most abundant members of their respective families in the archipelago, as in the case of the **Saddle Wrasse** or *hīnālea lauwili* (*Thalassoma duperrey* [Labridae]) and the **Milletseed Butterflyfish** or *lauwiliwili* (*Chaetodon miliaris* [Chaetodontidae]). Such abundance as that of these two endemics is most often attributed to the fact that, having evolved in the Islands, they are maximally adapted to the Hawaiian environment and are thus more successful than later-arriving related indigenous species or any endemic taxa derived from these. Alternatively, the ancestor of each may simply have been among the earliest members of its family to colonize the archipelago, thus giving these ancestors ample opportunity and time to become widespread in the chain as they speciated into the two endemics. Some endemic species, however, remain rare, at least around the main islands. In the case of at least such species as the **Lined Coris** or *mālamalama* (*Coris ballieui* [Labridae]) that are most abundant in the Northwestern Hawaiian Islands, it may be that these taxa evolved there, and adaptation to the colder northern water produced a form poorly suited for life in warmer southern waters, even if small main island populations are established.

Although speciation of shore fishes and other marine organisms upon ancestral arrival in the Hawaiian Islands may have been relatively common, further differentiation entirely within the archipelago has probably been minimal. Or at least it has been much less frequent than that occurring among terrestrial organisms (see chapter 10). In contrast to the terrestrial habitats divided among several separate islands, the general marine habitat is essentially continuous throughout the archipelago. This allows relatively more frequent gene flow among marine populations around all of the various islands, thus greatly inhibiting buildup of unique genetic combinations necessary for incipient speciation to proceed.

Founder Effect and Genetic Drift

Just as in the case of most other native Hawaiian organisms, any original founder effect and subsequent genetic drift among marine fishes is now largely impossible to demonstrate. Instances of possible founder effect have been disguised by speciation occurring long ago, and most genetic drift in populations has been either prevented or largely overridden by continued influx of conspecific individuals. One of the few examples of probable genetic drift currently evident among Hawaiian fishes involves the variation in pectoral fin base marking among central Pacific populations of the **Convict Surgeonfish** or ***manini*** (*Acanthurus triostegus* [Acanthuridae]) illustrated in Figure 12.1.

The high percentage of entirely dark brown individuals in the population of the normally yellow Longnose Butterflyfish or *lauwiliwili nukunuku 'oi 'oi* (*Forcipiger longirostris* [Chaetodontidae]) along the Hawai'i Island west coast could possibly represent another case of genetic drift. Much of the marine substrate in that area, however, consists of dark basalt that the dark fishes' color somewhat matches. Such similarity may provide protective coloration against predation for at least part of the species population there and thus be responsible for selective retention of its color dimorphism. In addition, in several other fish species, Hawaiian and Johnston Atoll members show slight differences in color pattern and fin-ray numbers, which suggests at least minimal genetic drift in one or both of the two areas' populations. Again, though, it is not possible to state with certainty that genetic drift is indicated. In a few apparently similar cases, ecological variables such as geographical differences in water temperature have been suggested as a developmental cause of such morphological variation.

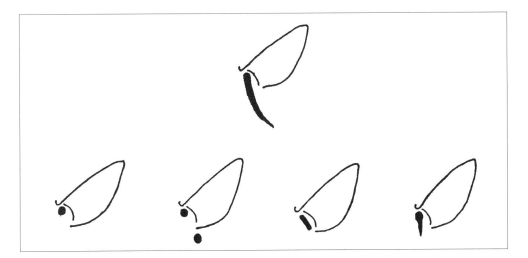

Figure 12.1. Differences in color markings of the Convict Surgeonfish or *manini (Acanthurus triostegus).* The upper diagram shows the long dark mark at the pectoral fin base typical of Hawaiian chain forms, and the four lower depict variations found in different subspecific populations of the Line and Phoenix Islands. These differences are probably the result of genetic drift. (Adapted from Fig. 3 of Gosline and Brock [1960], used with permission of William A. Gosline.)

Adaptive Radiation

Aside from a moderate amount of speciation and subsequent ecological diversification of Island wrasses (seventeen of the forty-five species are endemic), notable adaptive radiation is not apparent among Hawaiian fishes. Very likely, the immigration of various species of numerous families, along with very slight adaptive shifts by many of their descendant species, have not allowed any important ecological niches to remain unfilled long enough for at least major evolutionary diversification by any one group. Also, the relative ease with which various fish types can reach all portions of the archipelago's marine habitat undoubtedly ensured that any new niches that became available were quickly occupied by the most suitable species among the many competing families.

Although many freshwater alien fishes have readily established in, primarily, the lower reaches of Hawaiian watercourses (see discussion later in this chapter), not a single line of *entirely* marine fish colonists has radiated into the higher-elevation Hawaiian freshwater habitat (as, for example, the neritid mollusks discussed in chapter 11 probably did). This failure is likely due to the occupation of the upper watercourse habitat by certain preadapted and competitively superior gobies discussed later in this chapter: four **true gobies** or *'o'opu* (Gobiidae), of which three are endemic, and the endemic **Hawaiian Sleeper Goby** or *'o'opu 'akupa* (Eleotridae). These are all **amphidromous** (Greek *"amphi"* [double] and *"dromos"* [a running]). Adults of most species are specialized for life in freshwater streams experiencing periodic torrential flows that would sweep away most types of fishes. Their eggs are laid there, but the tiny newly hatched larvae descend into the ocean and are carried about by currents for a growth period of up to a few months before those young able to find the mouth of a stream ascend it (as *hinana*) to mature.

This development of endemic Island goby species, however, does not represent adaptive radiation, because each of them apparently evolved directly from different congeneric colonists of Indo-West Pacific species with identical amphidromous habits. Goby adults can live only a few days in ocean water, so the ancestral immigration was accomplished by planktonic young, the characteristic larval seaward migration facilitating such dispersal.

The absence of freshwater eels of the family Anguillidae from Hawai'i, however, is somewhat surprising. Members of this family occur in coastal watercourses of several continents and are also present in the streams of a number of isolated Pacific islands; Guam in the Mariana Islands apparently is the closest to the Hawaiian Archipelago. Adults of most anguillid species spend the greater part of their life in fresh or brackish water, migrating to offshore ocean areas when sexually mature to spawn and die. Much as in the case of amphidromous gobies, the dispersing young that reach shores are able to locate mouths of rivers and streams and ascend them to mature. Why, in the course of millions of years, none has reached and successfully established in the Hawaiian Islands is difficult to understand.

HAWAIIAN ECOLOGY

Deeper-Water Fishes

General fish habitats around a Hawaiian island are shown in Figure 11.3. In the pelagic area the bony fishes are all carnivores of relatively high trophic levels, feeding on other fishes and near-surface invertebrates of various sizes, from plankton to squid. These pelagics are typified by several genera of flyingfishes or *mālolo* (Exocoetidae), **Yellowfin Tuna** or *'ahi* (*Thunnus* *albacares* [Scombridae]), and Dolphin or *mahimahi* (*Coryphaena hippurus* [Coryphaenidae]). Nearer shore but still mostly outside the shallow reef area are the smaller, littoral-zone jacks of the family Carangidae such as schooling **Mackerel Scad** or *'ōpelu (Decapterus macarellus)* that feed on larger zooplankton, as well as medium-sized scombrids like Little Tuna or *kawakawa (Euthynnus affinis),* with a diet of fishes and benthic crustaceans including crabs. Among the typical "bottomfishes" of the benthic habitat are found members of the Lutjanidae, for example, **Smallscale Snapper** or *'ōpakapaka (Pristipomoides filamentosus)* and **Red Snapper** or *'ula'ula (Etelis carbunculus),* which feed primarily on other fishes.

Inshore Herbivores

It is in the relatively shallow reef waters (Figure 11.4) that by far the greatest variety of fishes occurs. Among the more common seaweed eaters are most **surgeonfishes** (Acanthuridae) of the genus *Acanthurus,* including the Blue-lined Surgeonfish or *maiko (A. nigroris),* Achilles Tang or *pāku'iku'i (A. achilles),* and small schools of Convict Surgeonfish or *manini,* as well as sea chubs (alternatively called rudderfishes) or *nenue* (*Kyphosus* spp. [Kyphosidae]). Various **parrotfishes** or *uhu* (Scaridae) use their stout "beaks" to harvest mostly larger algae, often taking along part of the underlying reef, with some larger species even including live coral in their diet. These generally good-sized and bright-hued fishes then use plates of stout ridgelike teeth in the pharyngeal region just beyond the mouth to grind the ingested material into fine particles, which facilitates digestion of the metabolizable biotic material. The undigested calcareous residue almost incessantly voided is a major source of sand, and each adult parrotfish is estimated to produce perhaps 900 kg (1 ton) of sand per year.

Primarily because it periodically becomes an item of interest to beachgoers, mention should be made of the small (15 cm or 6 inches) omnivorous Fantail Filefish or *'ō'ili 'uwī'uwī (Pervagor spilosoma* [Monacanthidae]). Every few years thousands of this attractively colored endemic species die naturally at sea and drift ashore, forming noticeable windrows of dried carcasses along Hawaiian beaches. The cause of such die-offs is uncertain, but it may be that at times such a large number of animals is produced that the inshore environment cannot support them all, and many eventually die from starvation.

Inshore Carnivores

Wrasses of a few species eat larger zooplankton or smaller fishes high in the reef water column. The previously mentioned Mackerel Scad as well as similar schools of **Bigeye Scad** or *akule (Selar crumenophthalmus)* that subsist on smaller plankton frequently visit the same water layers from littoral areas farther offshore. Periodically sweeping into shallower waters to seize reef fishes are fast-swimming and very efficient predators such as larger **jacks** or **ulua** (*Caranx* spp. [Carangidae]) and **barracudas** or *kākū* (*Sphyraena* spp. [Sphyraenidae]). Certain wrasses as well as several kinds of triggerfishes or *humuhumu* (Balistidae) prey on bottom-living crustaceans, echinoderms, and similar reef invertebrates. Other bottom dwellers include strange colonial Hawaiian Garden Eels (*Gorgasia hawaiiensis* [Congridae]) that strain zooplankton while extended high out of their sand burrows like a field of reeds, and several razorfishes or *laenihi* (*Xyrichtys* spp.) of the wrasse family that feed carnivorously near the ocean floor and dive into the sand to escape danger.

Two largely predatory families have beaklike jaws similar to those of the primarily herbivorous parrotfishes: a variety of small and large bristly skinned puffers, some called *'o'opu hue*

(Tetraodontidae), and spine-covered porcupinefishes or *kōkala* (primarily *Diodon* spp. [Diodontidae]). Tetraodontids include many kinds of invertebrates in their diet along with some algae, although the latter material is possibly mostly taken inadvertently. Diodontids, with massive dental crushing plates immediately behind the beak, eat almost entirely harder-shelled animals such as mollusks, echinoderms, and crustaceans. If seized by a larger predator or human, these two types of fishes balloon the body by gulping in water or, if removed from the sea, utilizing air in the same manner. Potential handlers should be aware of the extremely powerful bite of members of both these families; larger individuals are capable of crushing a finger bone.

Close in around coral heads various colorful butterflyfishes with bristlelike teeth concentrate on eating the tiny coral polyps, although a few species also include a small amount of algal tissue in their diet. Other smaller fishes in this same area feed primarily on coral-associated planktonic and benthic invertebrates. Most noticeable among these are many of the diurnal and sometimes territorial **damselfishes** including the Blackspot Sergeant or *kūpīpī* and Hawaiian Sergeant or *mamo* (*Abudefduf sordidus* and *A. abdominalis,* respectively [Pomacentridae]), Angelfishes of three genera (Pomacanthidae), and additional species of the ubiquitous wrasse family. At night, this feeding niche is taken over primarily by **squirrelfishes** such as *ʻūʻū* and *ʻalaʻihi* (genera *Myripristis* and *Sargocentron,* respectively [Holocentridae]), bigeyes or *ʻāweoweo* (*Heteropriacanthus cruentatus* and *Priacanthus meeki* [Priacanthidae]), and cardinalfishes or *ʻupāpalu* (*Apogon* spp. [Apogonidae]). Many members of these nocturnally feeding families are red, which provides protective coloration not only at night but also during daylight hours when they rest in deep water or dark underwater caves and crevices. Red lies in the portion of the spectrum most effectively filtered out by water, so under conditions of very low illumination a reddish fish appears gray, rendering the individual less obvious to predators.

Certain fishes are large-mouthed ambush predators on other fishes and crustaceans. While awaiting prey, they perch motionless on the reef floor or coral outcroppings, blending in almost perfectly with the background because of their cryptic coloration and, in many species, epidermal frills. In Hawaiʻi these predators comprise primarily several kinds of scorpionfishes or *nohu* (Scorpaenidae), frogfishes (*Antennarius* spp. [Antennariidae]), and various **hawkfishes** (especially genera *Cirrhitops, Cirrhitus,* and *Paracirrhites* [Cirrhitidae]) generally known as *poʻopaʻa* and *pilikoʻa.* Most of the different lizardfishes or *ʻulae* (Synodontidae), with a relatively large and formidable dentition, rest on sand, mud, or rubble bottoms waiting to dart upward and seize small fish prey. Flounders or *pākiʻi* (*Bothus* spp. [Bothidae]; as well as similar species of other families), with both eyes on the upturned side of the head, lie on the sand or reef substrate, where their generally brownish mottled coloration conceals them from both predators and prey fishes. **Goatfishes** such as *weke* and the Whitesaddle Goatfish or *kūmū* (*Mulloidichthys* spp. and *Parupeneus porphyreus* [Mullidae]) use a pair of specialized chin barbels (reminiscent of a goat's beard, but laid back under the throat when not in use) to probe the sand for smaller invertebrates.

More fearsome predators inhabit holes and crevices in the reef: primarily the large **moray eels** of the genus *Gymnothorax* (Muraenidae) with long, sharply pointed teeth, which are included with most other snakelike fishes in the collective Hawaiian term *puhi.* The similar-sized but smaller-toothed Mustache Conger Eel or *puhi ūhā* (*Conger cinereus* [Congridae]) is also relatively common. Although none of these eels will usually approach a person, either type is liable to inflict a serious bite on a swimmer or diver who suddenly or unsuspectingly places a hand or foot close to the fish's resting area. A few moray eels of other genera have low, rounded teeth and feed primarily on crabs, lobsters, and other hard-shelled crustaceans. Snake eels such as the Magnificent Snake Eel or *puhi lā'au* (*Myrichthys magnificus* [Ophichthidae]) are smaller predators, taking mostly crustaceans, with many species lying concealed in sand with only the head exposed. Because all of these types of eels tend to remain hidden during the day and only hunt the reef floors in the late afternoon and evening, their relatively enormous abundance is usually greatly underestimated. Some studies place their true biomass at about 10 percent that of the entire reef fish fauna. The fact that the diurnal wrasses spend nocturnal hours either buried in sand or in reef crevices, during which time they surround themselves with a cocoon of skin-secreted mucus, suggests that this wrapping was evolutionarily developed to help prevent night-hunting eels from either sighting or smelling these potential prey species. Sleeping parrotfishes also develop a mucus coating overnight, which may serve the same protective function. Some investigators, however, feel that, if the nighttime mucus covering does indeed provide such protection, this is entirely fortuitous. Mucus may be constantly externally secreted by fishes of these two families to serve some unrelated more important function, and the material is continually washed away as an animal swims during the day, but collects around a sleeping individual at night.

FEEDING SPECIALIZATIONS

The small Hawaiian Cleaner Wrasse *(Labroides phthirophagus)* approaches larger fishes of both herbivorous and carnivorous types with impunity, apparently being recognized because of its distinctive striped color pattern of yellow, blue, black, and magenta, as well as its movements. For food, the species removes from these fishes presumably irritating crustacean parasites attached to both the exterior and accessible interior areas such as gills. The individuals being cleaned seem to learn to rely on the Cleaner Wrasse, repeatedly visiting the cleaning station and even waiting in line if other fishes have preceded them. The diminutive fangblennies or *pāo'o* (*Plagiotremus* spp. [Blenniidae]) stalk other fishes (and occasional swimmers), suddenly rushing to nip off and eat mucus and bits of skin, although such contact with a human is hardly noticed. The relatively large sticklike **Trumpetfish** (*Aulostomus chinensis* [Aulostomidae]) and **Cornetfish** (*Fistularia commersonii* [Fistulariidae]), both usually known as *nūnū,* use their long, tubular snouts like a hydraulic vacuum-cleaner wand, sucking a stream of water containing small fishes into their mouths. These predators sometimes travel among schools of herbivorous surgeonfishes to capture small fishes disturbed by the latter or swim alongside larger fishes apparently to approach prey more closely.

VENOMOUS FISHES

The sharp spines of the camouflaged, bottom-resting **scorpionfishes** can give very painful puncture wounds to humans. In many species these spines are grooved and associated with poison glands in such a manner that venom can easily enter the wound. The dreaded scorpaenid stonefishes (genus *Synanceia*) of the Southwest Pacific, whose venom is strong enough to cause the death of a human, fortunately do not occur in the Hawaiian Islands. There are present, however, the Hawaiian Lionfish *(Dendrochirus barberi)* and Hawaiian Turkeyfish or *nohu pinao (Pterois sphex),* which both have numerous spines that can cause extremely painful (but not fatal) wounds. These particular scorpionfishes usually rest under ledges or in caves, so putting a hand or foot in such a place without first examining the area should be avoided. The only other fishes in Hawai'i that possess venomous spines are the squirrelfishes, but because just a posteriorly directed cheek spine is involved it is rather unlikely that a handler would be accidentally injured.

The foregoing fishes, like the entire remaining Hawaiian fish fauna, are safe to eat, with two different kinds of exceptions. Both the puffers and porcupinefishes possess a powerful intrinsic poison at all times, which may vary in concentration in different portions of their bodies. Individuals of at least the former family are commonly eaten in Japan, but only after being prepared by someone experienced in their proper culinary handling. Occasional mullets (Mugilidae) and goatfishes may contain a toxin inducing hallucinations or nightmares when eaten, but even if experienced, these symptoms are so mild that essentially no one is deterred from eating fishes of these families.

Ciguatera Poisoning

The second instance in which Hawaiian fishes may not be safe to eat involves **ciguatera** (New World Spanish, apparently from Caribbean Indian *"cigua"* [(a particular?) marine gastropod], which was supposed to contain this toxin). This term designates poisoning from consumption of, primarily, carnivorous fish species from certain areas and/or at particular times (although, occasionally, herbivorous species may also become toxic). In general terms, the alkaloid ciguatoxin (which is not destroyed by cooking) is produced in a single-celled, planktonic, dinoflagellate organism, which periodically undergoes a great population increase or "bloom" and settles thickly on macroscopic brown and red algae. As these seaweeds are eaten by many types of herbivorous fishes, the toxin is successively passed up the marine food chain and becomes concentrated in carnivorous fishes of the higher trophic levels. This toxicity, however, is great primarily in only nonpelagic, territorial predators, because they continually feed on herbivores in a limited affected area. Pelagic species have little chance of building up high ciguatoxin levels because they forage over a wide ocean expanse and prey on a great variety of smaller fishes, most of which have not been feeding in areas harboring affected algae. A little-understood but possibly related toxin that produces similar symptoms can occasionally be found in small, inshore plankton feeders of the herring and sardine family Clupeidae.

When any of these fishes build up high levels of poison it becomes especially concentrated in the viscera and head. Because among several cultures represented in Hawai'i it is traditional practice to eat internal organs along with the head and body of a fish, the possibility of serious or even fatal cases of ciguatera or clupeid poisoning is considerably increased. In fact, one well-known Honolulu fish market insists on cleaning all reef fishes sold, apparently as a precaution against the occurrence of any poisoning in customers. Also, whenever state agencies become aware of the appearance of high ciguatoxin levels in particular fish species from certain coastal areas, an appropriate warning is issued.

SURGE-POOL AND BRACKISH-WATER FISHES

Although a great variety of smaller reef fishes may be encountered in tide pools from time to time, such pools are the usual habitat of only certain smaller blennies and saltwater species of true gobies. Most of these fishes are generally omnivorous and many, especially blennies, may sometimes skitter over the pool surface or even the surrounding dry substrate to another pool when disturbed. Estuaries and some anchialine ponds (see chapter 11) support several types of fishes adapted to water of variable salinity. Among the more obvious of these are the **Striped Mullet** or *'ama'ama (Mugil cephalus)* and the **Hawaiian Flagtail** or *āholehole* (*Kuhlia sandvicensis* [Kuhliidae]).

ALIEN MARINE FISHES

Among the fairly large number of alien marine species introduced to Hawai'i, only eight have established successfully (Table 12.2), but the individuals of some now collectively constitute a substantial proportion of all inshore Island fishes. The introduction of half of these established species was intentional. For example, the **Bluestripe Snapper** or (in Tahitian) *ta'ape (Lutjanus kasmira)* typifies importations to supplement a presumed impoverished nearshore sport and commercial fishery. The ta'ape has become extremely abundant since its release in 1958, apparently causing population diminution among certain more desirable native carnivorous species. The four species unintentionally introduced arrived primarily through their biological contamination of stock of intentionally imported marine organisms. At least three of these accidentally introduced species are relatively small forms of little or no commercial or other value, but in fact are quite likely detrimental to native fishes.

FRESHWATER FISHES

Native Species

Five amphidromous gobies are the Hawaiian Islands' only native freshwater species; they are individually listed in Table 12.3. Most of these *'o'opu* typically attain only small to medium size, with adult length ranging from 5 to 35 cm (2 to 14 inches), although there are old historic

Table 12.2. Alien marine fishes established in Hawaiian waters. See Table 12.4 for typically freshwater species occasionally also found in brackish habitats. (Data primarily from Randall [1987].)

Family and Species	Type of Establishment	Purpose or Source
Blennies (Blenniidae)		
Tasseled Blenny *(Parablennius thysanius)*	Unplanned	Accompanying live imported seaweed?
Herrings and sardines (Clupeidae)		
Goldspot Sardine *(Herklotsichthys quadrimaculatus)*	Unplanned	From bait well of research vessel
Marquesan Sardine *(Sardinella marquesensis)*	Planned	Tuna bait fish
Snappers (Lutjanidae)		
Blacktail Snapper or to'au *(Lutjanus fulvus)*	Planned	Sport and commercial fishing
Bluestripe Snapper or ta'ape *(Lutjanus kasmira)*	Planned	Sport and commercial fishing
Gray mullets (Mugilidae)		
"Trash Mullet" or kanda *(Moolgarda engeli)*	Unplanned	Accompanying alien tuna bait fish
Goatfishes (Mullidae)		
Yellowbanded Goatfish *(Upeneus vittatus)*	Unplanned	Accompanying alien tuna bait fish
Groupers (Serranidae)		
Peacock Grouper or roi *(Cephalopholis argus)*	Planned	Sport and commercial fishing

reports of Giant Stream Goby individuals reaching 75 cm (30 inches). All four true gobies (Gobiidae), like their purely marine relatives in Hawai'i, have partially fused pelvic fins that form a suction-cup organ, which enables individuals to maintain themselves on—and move up —the beds of swiftly flowing streams (Plate 12.1). The two gobiid species inhabiting higher watercourse reaches, the Clinging and Red-tailed Stream Gobies, are even capable of ascending perpendicular rock faces at the sides of waterfalls by means of this structure. The Hawaiian Sleeper Goby (Eleotridae) lacks the fused pelvic fins and thus cannot move up streams beyond the first sheer rise of the channel. The five native gobies can reproduce only in streams and usually spend most of their lives there, although the Giant Stream Goby is sometimes also present in abundance in shallow artificial reservoirs.

Table 12.3. The five native Hawaiian freshwater fishes. The Giant Stream Goby is indigenous and the other four are endemic. (Data from various sources.)

Family and Species	Hawaiian Name	Scientific Name
True gobies (Gobiidae)		
Giant Stream Goby	'O'opu nākea	*Awaous guamensis*
Red-tailed Stream Goby	'O'opu hi'u kole or 'o'opu 'alamo'o	*Lentipes concolor*
Clinging Stream Goby	'O'opu nōpili	*Sicyopterus stimpsoni*
Black-headed Stream Goby	'O'opu naniha	*Stenogobius hawaiiensis*
Sleeper gobies (Eleotridae)		
Hawaiian Sleeper Goby	'O'opu 'akupa	*Eleotris sandwicensis*

Table 12.4. Alien freshwater fishes established in Hawai'i. Species noted with an asterisk (*) may also be found in brackish habitats, and a question mark (?) indicates a species not definitely established. (Data primarily from Devick [1991].)

Family and Species	Type of Establishment	Purpose or Source	Primary Habitat
Needlefishes (Belonidae)			
Stickfish (*Xenentodon cancila*)	Unplanned	Home aquarium	Reservoir
Sunfishes (Centrarchidae)			
Bluegill Sunfish (*Lepomis macrochirus*)	Planned	Sport fishing	Reservoir
Green Sunfish (*Lepomis cyanellus*)?	Unplanned	Home aquarium	Reservoir
Bass (*Micropterus*, 2 spp.)	Planned	Sport fishing	Stream, reservoir
Snakeheads (Channidae)			
Snakehead (*Channa striata*)	Planned	Food	Reservoir
Cichlids (Cichlidae)			
Oscar (*Astronotus ocellatus*)	Planned	Sport fishing	Reservoir
Tucunare (*Cichla ocellaris*)	Planned	Sport fishing	Reservoir
Cichlid ("*Cichlasoma*," 5 spp.)	Unplanned	Home aquarium	Stream, reservoir
Pelvicachromis (*Pelvicachromis pulcher*)	Unplanned	Home aquarium	Reservoir

(Continued on the following page)

Table 12.4. *(continued)* Alien freshwater fishes established in Hawaiʻi. Species noted with an asterisk (*) may also be found in brackish habitats, and a question mark (?) indicates a species not definitely established. (Data primarily from Devick [1991].)

Family and Species	Type of Establishment	Purpose or Source	Primary Habitat
Tilapia (*"Tilapia,"* 5 spp.) [2 of them*]	Planned Unplanned	Aquaculture, plant control, sport fishing, tuna bait fish aquaculture, home aquarium	Stream, reservoir
Chinese catfishes (Clariidae)			
Chinese Catfish (*Clarias fuscus*)	Planned	Food	Reservoir
Loaches (Cobitidae)			
Do-jo (*Misgurnus anguillicaudatus*)	Planned	Food	Stream
Threadfin Shad (Clupeidae)			
Threadfin Shad (*Dorosoma petenense*)*	Planned	Research	Stream?, reservoir
Carp (Cyprinidae)			
Blackspot Barb (*Puntius filamentosus*)	Unplanned	Home aquarium	Reservoir
Green Barb (*Puntius semifasciolatus*)	Unplanned	Home aquarium	Reservoir
Goldfish (*Carassius auratus*)	Planned	Decoration, food	Reservoir
Carp or koi (*Cyprinus carpio*)	Planned	Decoration, food	Reservoir
True gobies (Gobiidae)			
Small Goby (*Mugilogobius cavifrons*)*	Unplanned	Ballast water?	Stream
Goby (*Mugilogobius* sp.)	Unplanned	Home aquarium	Stream
Typical catfishes (Ictaluridae)			
Channel Catfish (*Ictalurus punctatus*)	Planned	Sport fishing	Reservoir
Plated catfishes (Callichthyidae)			
Bronze Corydoras (*Corydoras aeneus*)	Planned	Sport fishing	Stream
Suckermouth catfishes (Loricariidae)			
Bristlenose Catfish (*Ancistrus*, 2 spp.)	Unplanned	Home aquarium	Stream, reservoir
Suckermouth Catfish (*Hypostomus*, 2 spp.)	Unplanned	Home aquarium	Stream, reservoir
Radiated Ptero (*Liposarcus multiradiatus*)	Unplanned	Home aquarium	Stream?, reservoir
Top minnows (Poeciliidae)			
Mosquitofish (*Gambusia affinis*)	Planned	Mosquito control	Stream, reservoir
Mollies (*Poecilia*, 4 spp.) [3 of them*]	Planned Unplanned	Mosquito control Home aquarium	Stream
Swordtail (*Xiphophorous*, 2 spp.)	Planned	Mosquito control	Stream
Salmonids (Salmonidae)			
Rainbow Trout (*Oncorhynchus mykiss*)	Planned	Sport fishing	Stream
Swamp eels (Synbranchidae)			
Rice-paddy Eel (*Monopterus albus*)	Planned	Food	Reservoir

Alien Species

Although the Hawaiian Islands have almost no natural freshwater impoundments of substantial size (see chapter 8), a number of large bodies of water have been created within the past two centuries, essentially all of which are reservoirs for irrigation and domestic water storage. Also, before being drained in the past 80 years or so, Taro and Rice pondfields along with a few duck and inland fish ponds represented a large portion of the human-produced freshwater habitat. Many alien freshwater fish species have been released by government agencies, primarily to stock the larger bodies of water, but also for biological-control purposes. Other nonmarine alien fishes have either escaped from aquaculture ventures or been illegally released by freshwater aquarists. Those taxa known to have established Island breeding populations are listed in Table 12.4. In this table, the term "reservoir" includes all historically constructed freshwater impoundments, and "food" fishes are those imported primarily by various Asian cultures for stocking artificial ponds and pondfields. Most of the "home aquarium" fishes are small species, but a few grow to considerable size, which may well be why many owners were prompted to provide them more spacious quarters, in doing so seriously disturbing native stream ecosystems.

SUGGESTED REFERENCES

Beletsky 2000; Culliney 1988; Devick 1991; Devick (ed.) 1991, 1993; Ford and Kinzie 1982; Gosline 1965; Gosline and Brock 1960; Hoover 1993; Hourigan and Reese 1987; Kinzie 1991; Kosaki et al. 1991; Randall 1987, 1996; State of Hawai'i, Department of Land and Natural Resources 1996; Titcomb 1972.

AUDIOVISUAL AIDS

Behavior and ecology of coral reef fishes; Flowing to the sea; Hawaiian waters: House of the shark; Hawaiian waters: Mauka/makai lifeline; Hawaii: Islands of the Fire Goddess; Hawaii's streams; Life at Salt Point; Life in Lost Creek.

13

Dispersal and Establishment

The populating of the Hawaiian Islands by marine organisms was covered in the two preceding chapters; this one discusses the same aspect of the terrestrial biota. There have been islands of one size or another in this immediate area for at least 80 million years (see chapter 3). The currently known Hawaiian terrestrial biotic lines, however, apparently did not have this much time for colonizing the archipelago. Koko Volcano (now reduced to a seamount in the southern part of the Emperor chain) formed a large high island at the Hawaiian hot spot approximately 48 million years ago. As it was becoming an atoll and losing all of at least its upland biotic lines, it appears no other *high* island was available for colonization until the formation of Kure about 30 million years ago.

Through these 30 million years, however, a considerable number of land and freshwater plant and animal species managed to reach and establish breeding populations on at least one of the Hawaiian Islands. A major portion of the endemic biota of each newly formed Hawaiian island was probably made up of members of many of these lineages that were able to "island hop" southward as their original islands disappeared. Undoubtedly, though, some new immigrants established first on younger islands and then moved northward to older islands.

BIOTIC COMPOSITION

Selected major groups of Hawaiian land and freshwater organisms are listed in Table 13.1. In contrast to marine forms (see, for example, Tables 11.1, 12.1), certain of these terrestrial groups

Table 13.1. Approximate species numbers of selected major Hawaiian terrestrial biota. Among species listed as indigenous, three birds and the mammal (a bat) are currently considered endemic at the subspecies level. Figures for snails, birds, and mammals include extinct species, but not migrant shorebirds. Thirteen insect species and two spider species of uncertain native/alien status are included in the totals. (Data from various sources.)

Biota	Total	Endemic	Indigenous	Alien
Ferns (and allies)	205	125 (61%)	53 (26%)	27 (13%)
Flowering plants	2,059	907 (44%)	113 (5%)	1,039 (51%)
Insects	7,982	5,293 (66%)	84 (1%)	2,592 (33%)
Spiders	205	126 (62%)	—	77 (38%)
Snails	804	762 (95%)	8 (1%)	34 (4%)
Fishes	49	4 (8%)	1 (2%)	44 (90%)
Amphibians	6	—	—	6 (100%)
Reptiles	21	—	—	21 (100%)
Birds	158	98 (62%)	6 (4%)	54 (34%)
Mammals	22	1 (5%)	1 (5%)	20 (90%)
Total	11,511	7,316 (64%)	260 (2%)	3,914 (34%)

contain very large numbers of species, and in almost all cases this abundance is due to the presence of numerous endemic taxa rather than to any substantial percentage of indigenous species. Also, the high degree of terrestrial endemicity of Hawaiian flowering plants and certain animal types is the result of remarkable adaptive radiation, often involving only a very small proportion of the collective founder complement.

BIOTIC DISHARMONY

The "filter-funnel" dispersal phenomenon so important in determining the Hawaiian Archipelago's marine biota (see chapter 11) was equally influential in producing the biotic disharmony and attenuation (see chapter 10) evident among the terrestrial flora and fauna.

Plants

Disharmony among the native Hawaiian flora is clear. As just two examples, there is a single native genus of palm, the *loulu* (*Pritchardia* spp.), whereas there are up to one hundred genera of the family among the Southwest Pacific island groups; and bamboos or *'ohe* (genera *Phyllostachys* and *Schizostachyum*), so characteristic of eastern Asia, never reached the Hawaiian Archipelago on their own. In regard to species attenuation, although there are a multitude of orchids associated with most tropical and subtropical areas worldwide, there are only three rather inconspicuous native species in the Hawaiian Islands (although there is an enormous number of showy alien ones).

Animals

At the level of vertebrate class, disharmony is especially apparent in the absence of native amphibians, and at the ordinal level, in lack of nonmarine reptiles and land mammals except

Table 13.2. Founders and dispersal methods of selected major native Hawaiian terrestrial biota. The founder numbers represent estimated endemic-species ancestors plus indigenous species. When more exact dispersal data are not available, the probable relative importance of each transportation mode is indicated by the number of plus (+) signs. Percentage figures in the Native column represent their proportion of the total species (including alien and those of uncertain status) of the group established in Hawai'i. Figures for snails, birds, and mammals include extinct species, but not migrant shorebirds. (Data from various sources.)

Biota	Native	Founder	Species per Founder	Sea	Wind	Birds
Ferns (and allies)	178 (87%)	114	1.6	—	95%	5%
Flowering plants	1,014 (49%)	291	3.5	23%	2%	75%
Insects	5,377 (67%)	434	12.4	++	+++	+
Spiders	126 (62%)	13	9.7	++	+++	+
Snails	770 (96%)	29	26.6	++	+	+++
Fishes	5 (10%)	5	1.0	100%	—	—
Birds	104 (66%)	26	4.0	—	100%	—
Mammals	2 (9%)	2	1.0	—	100%	—
Total	**7,576 (66%)**	÷ 914	= 8.3 (avg.)	++	+++	+

for two bats. Disharmony and attenuation of Hawaiian terrestrial and freshwater animals is discussed in more detail in later chapters devoted to the major faunal groups.

FOUNDING ORGANISMS

Table 13.2 lists the estimates of various specialists as to how many founder species (including indigenous ones) were responsible for yielding the native species of selected major Hawaiian terrestrial plant and animal groups. Although the listed numbers of native species may be influenced by whether the specialist relied upon is a "lumper" or a "splitter" (see chapter 10), this does not significantly affect the reported number of founding species, because workers of either philosophy tend to agree on these totals. The average of about eight for the number of species originating from each terrestrial founder tends to be quite high compared with the mean of perhaps two for each marine founder (see chapter 11). Table 13.2 also presents an estimate of percentages of founders that reached the Hawaiian Islands via sea, wind, and birds.

OCEAN DISPERSAL

Major Pacific Currents
An extensive ocean current of significant biological importance to the Hawaiian Islands is a gigantic, roughly oval one termed the **North Pacific Current or Gyre** (Greek *"gyros"* [circle]). As shown in Figure 11.1, the complete gyre can be traced from off Japan, east through the northern Pacific, south along the western North American coast, west just above the equator, then north from off the Philippines. The movement usually involves only the upper 100 m (330 feet) or so of seawater, and its average speed is about 0.5 to 1.0 km (0.3 to 0.6 miles) per hour, with rates in different portions varying by a factor of three or more. The segments of the gyre that brought most marine colonists to the Hawaiian Islands (see chapter 11) were also crucial in transporting certain terrestrial biota to the archipelago.

Although the Hawaiian Islands lie in the "eye" of the North Pacific Current rather than directly in its course, items such as glass net floats from Japan and lumber products from the American Northwest coast frequently wash ashore in the chain. This seeming anomaly results from the fact that the current is, in reality, not a clearly defined unidirectional one, but rather a complex mass of eddies and back-currents. Most of the material from continental and distant insular shores deposited on Hawaiian beaches has been separated from the current mainstream by these erratic secondary water movements, sometimes after making multiple circuits of the entire gyre.

The westward-moving portion of the gyre south of the Hawaiian Islands is known as the North Equatorial Current, with the Subtropical Counter Current as an extension that loops north in the western Pacific and heads back east toward Hawai'i (refer to Figure 11.1). South of these is the eastward-moving Equatorial Counter Current, and still farther south the westward-moving South Equatorial Current. The combination of alternating west-east-west flows of the three equatorial currents would seem to form an impenetrable barrier to direct northward flotation to Hawai'i of materials from anywhere in the Southern Hemisphere Pacific. Surprisingly, however, a fair number of seaborne organisms of southern island-group affinity have reached the Hawaiian Islands. Some of these, including the ancestors of probably all of the freshwater gobies (see chapter 12), were evidently carried (usually as larvae) in eddies perpendicular to the general direction of the three equatorial currents. Many land organisms such as propagules of certain flowering plants, however, may have come to the Islands as flotsam occasionally simply blown across these currents by extended strong winds.

Suitable Candidates

To be viably transported in the ocean, seeds or vegetative portions of plants must both float and be resistant to osmotic damage by saltwater. The relatively large buoyant seeds or occasional branches of a number of widely distributed South Pacific shoreline plants floated to the Hawaiian Islands and established; in fact, it has been found that soaking seeds of some such species in seawater actually improves germination. Fallen trees and other substantial woody material flushed out to sea by rivers of Pacific Rim areas have washed up on Hawaiian beaches throughout the archipelago's existence. It is doubtful, however, that plants (for example, certain ferns) originally growing on such larger drift items would survive the subsequent extended exposure to seawater. Even if a few did, it is difficult to imagine how they would be able to reach suitable inland forest habitat from an Island beach.

Among animals, all life stages of insects, spiders, and other terrestrial arthropods could easily survive transportation to Hawaiʻi by such "rafting." Similarly, land or freshwater snails on a large floating object would firmly attach themselves to emergent portions by means of mucus, effectively preventing passage of fluids in or out of the shell, and could survive for many months in such a dormant condition. Any frogs or salamanders on even a large buoyant item, however, would have little chance of survival because of osmotic dehydration by saltwater or spray; thus, almost no isolated oceanic island has any native amphibian. Reptiles, on the other hand, have skin highly adapted to prevent water passage, and this permits lengthy exposure to seawater. It may be that even eggs of some tree-dwelling species such as geckos possess this same adaptation. No terrestrial reptile, however, has apparently naturally colonized the Hawaiian Archipelago. Among mammals, smaller rodents can apparently raft almost as successfully as some reptiles, as evidenced by several endemic species of these (as well as lizards) on the Galápagos Islands 965 km (600 miles) off the coast of South America. But no rodents or other nonvolant land mammals reached the Hawaiian Archipelago until brought by humans.

Successful Colonizers

As shown in Table 13.2, almost one-fourth of the founding species of Hawaiian flowering plants are thought to have arrived by sea. Just a few of the more familiar of such plants are the Screw Pine or *hala (Pandanus tectorius),* Beach *Naupaka* or *naupaka kahakai (Scaevola taccada; formerly S. sericea),* and the Purslane or *ʻihi (Portulaca lutea).* It is interesting that although fruit of the Coconut or *niu (Cocos nucifera)* floats well and remains viable for 110 days in saltwater, for some obscure reason this species has not colonized isolated islands; all populations throughout the insular Pacific apparently are of prehistoric human introduction. Among animals, it seems certain that most of at least those terrestrial colonizing insects, spiders, and other arthropods too large to have been transported by winds, and not parasitic on (or benignly attached to) birds, arrived through ocean rafting. A number of inshore marine insects and other arthropods, some of which subsequently yielded endemic terrestrial species, also undoubtedly arrived in the same manner. Determining the relative importance of ocean travel to Hawaiian terrestrial snail colonists is difficult, and there are no previously published estimates. At least a certain number, including relatively larger species, likely arrived by rafting. As already noted, the amphidromous freshwater goby ancestors almost certainly arrived by sea.

AERIAL DISPERSAL

Unaided Fliers

Most birds, bats, and such insects as dragonflies and some butterflies are quite capable of flights to the Hawaiian Islands from either other Pacific island groups or bordering continents. A number among these three faunal types are migratory, and occasional individuals with a faulty internal migratory regulating mechanism probably undertook flights in other than normal directions. Most perished, but a few whose errant paths extended out to sea occasionally reached the archipelago.

Winds

Other potential founders, however, even including many flighted ones, would very likely have been unable to reach Hawai'i without some aid from strong air currents. The trade winds (see chapter 7) seem scarcely strong enough to bodily transport any except the smallest organisms. In addition, these winds do not blow directly over North America, but typically originate from the North Pacific High system some distance southwest of the North American Pacific coast (see Figure 7.1). Westward-moving hurricanes seem strong and sustained enough to carry any individuals or groups of volant or smaller nonvolant organisms able to survive them from at least southern North America and Central America to the Hawaiian Islands.

Intermittent storm winds from the west, however, may sometimes be stronger than, at least, the trade winds, and would presumably be capable of carrying some organisms to the archipelago. To test this possibility, in the latter 1950s and early 1960s J. Linsley Gressitt and colleagues at Honolulu's Bishop Museum (see chapter 28) sampled the air over the open Pacific by means of nets attached to surface vessels as well as to long-range aircraft. They found numerous small flying and passively floating invertebrates in various parts of the air column. It is interesting that the different orders and families of insects and spiders captured were generally of the same kinds and in the same proportions as those of the native Hawaiian invertebrate fauna, thus tending to support the premise of wind transport of at least these types of arthropods to the archipelago.

Jet Stream

What seems to be the most effective air carrier of organisms to Hawai'i, however, is the **jet stream,** a swift, high-elevation eastward air current that partially encircles the Northern Hemisphere between about 9,150 and 12,200 m (30,000 and 40,000 feet). For a few months each year a portion of the jet stream's arc extends between Southeast Asia and the general region of Hawai'i (Figure 13.1). The winds may be as great as 195 km (122 miles) per hour over the western end of this segment, but slow to less than two-thirds this over the Hawaiian area. Warm air is drawn upward along the stream's southern border, while cold air flows down from its northern edge. This is potentially a very efficient mechanism for picking up relatively small Asian and Indo-West Pacific plant and animal life, transporting it to the North-central Pacific in as little as 2 days, and then depositing at least some of it on the Hawaiian Islands as the wind decelerated. Gressitt and his team were not able to sample the jet stream itself, so its efficiency in transporting founders is unknown. The freezing temperature of the stream, however, may well limit the types of organisms that can be carried without mortality.

Suitable Candidates

Ferns, mosses, algae, and fungi can reproduce by means of spores, and the majority of these propagules that are microscopic are easily carried by air currents. The very small seeds of orchids and a number of other flowering plants such as *'Ōhi'a lehua (Metrosideros polymorpha)* are almost as easily transported. Even the relatively larger seeds of some plants such as dandelions, milkweeds, and maples can undoubtedly be conveyed at least moderately long distances because they possess the aerial-flotation enhancers of fluffy tufts of long, fine bristles or thin, winglike appurtenances. Among animals, insect eggs, immature forms, and wingless adults typically do not possess structures specifically adapted to wind dispersal. The small size of some or all of these life stages in a number of species, however, results in a high surface-to-weight ratio that greatly facilitates this type of transport. Spiders are very often carried on air currents by "hang gliding" or "ballooning" attached to their easily lofted web material.

Successful Colonizers

The great majority of native Hawaiian ferns (and fern allies) were very likely wind-transported in the form of microscopic spores. The spores that produce the female gametes in a few gen-

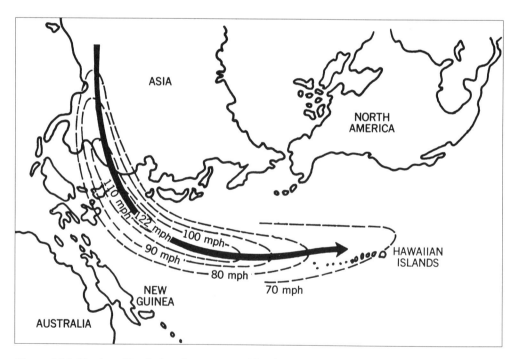

Figure 13.1. Northern Hemisphere jet stream position in January. The average maximum speed of 122 miles per hour equals approximately 195 km per hour. (Unnumbered figure from p. 87 of Carlquist [1980], used with permission of the National Tropical Botanical Garden.)

era, as well as the enclosing sporocarps of water-clover ferns or *'ihi'ihilauākea* (*Marsilia* spp.) and a few other taxa, however, are too large for this type of dispersal. These were probably carried variously attached to birds, as undoubtedly also were some smaller spores of these and other species. The very low average of less than two endemic species per fern/fern ally founder (Table 13.2) undoubtedly reflects the relatively great frequency with which additional spores of founder populations continued to arrive and inhibit speciation in Hawai'i.

Flowering plants whose propagules have morphological adaptations for wind transport make up only about 2 percent of the total native Hawaiian complement of this group. Evidently, the air-flotation structures of most seeds are not efficient enough to ensure truly long-distance transport. Even without exact figures, it seems safe to say that a majority of colonizing insects and spiders reached Hawai'i on winds. In the case of the latter arthropod type, hang gliding is apparently a very successful dispersal method. Species of at least seven among the fifteen spider families native to the Hawaiian Islands are excellent travelers by this means, and most of the remaining families include at least some species that are often similarly transported. Presumably no terrestrial snails (or their eggs), and certainly no fish ancestors, arrived on air currents, although, of course, all ancestors of native Hawaiian avian and bat taxa originally populated the Islands via flight (albeit probably sometimes wind-assisted).

AVIAN DISPERSAL

Potential Vectors

Bird-borne terrestrial plant founders have traveled to Hawai'i either in the alimentary tract or attached to external surfaces. Although the low figure of twenty-six for founding Hawaiian bird species in Table 13.2 may suggest that few birds ever reach these islands, this is not at all correct; many types of birds periodically arrive in the archipelago, but few are able to establish permanent populations. There are about fifty varied bird species that appear in the Islands on such a regular seasonal basis that they are usually termed migrants. In addition, during the past century at least 108 "accidental" avian species have been recorded in Hawai'i, including such diverse forms as herons, ibises, many ducks and geese, hawks and eagles, plovers and sandpipers, gulls and terns, and even ten kinds of small songbirds.

Among the migrant birds, the **Pacific Golden-Plover** or *kōlea (Pluvialis fulva)*, along with four members of the sandpiper family Scolopacidae (Table 20.3), are likely to be frequent transporters of organisms. Not only are some of these shorebirds relatively abundant but all five migrate from nesting grounds in the New or Old World Arctic to winter in Hawai'i. These birds undoubtedly occasionally carry Arctic plant propagules or smaller invertebrates to the archipelago. Some of the migrating individuals also usually overfly Hawai'i and travel on to South Pacific islands, including the Society group, New Zealand, and even Tasmania. Although most of these latter individuals do not usually land in the Hawaiian Islands, once every few centuries an individual might well do so before flying on, thus potentially introducing South Pacific biotic materials to Hawai'i (or vice versa).

Suitable Candidates

Among the diverse birds recorded in Hawai'i, only certain songbirds have a diet consisting largely of seeds, but other avian types—including, for example, the five common migrant shorebirds—occasionally add seeds as well as small fruits to their usual animal fare. Such small propagules that are not destroyed during the digestive process could easily be transported during the 2- or 3-day flight to the Hawaiian Islands. Various seeds or even entire plants of minute forms such as water ferns (*Azolla* spp.) and duckweeds (*Lemna* spp.) can be carried long distances attached to different parts of water- and shorebirds in a layer of dried algae or mud. The seventy or more species of ducks, geese, and shorebirds sporadically or regularly visiting Hawai'i seem to ensure that, given enough time, almost all small or small-seeded plants growing in the birds' continental habitats would also arrive.

Adaptive characteristics of many other plants even more surely provide for their dispersal by birds (and mammals). Numerous continental plant species have evolutionarily developed seed- or fruit-attachment devices such as hooks, barbed bristles, and stiff straight hairs or awns (Figure 15.1). Such propagules are readily spread by birds and mammals that come in contact with the fruiting plants, as is well known by hikers attempting to clean their clothing after outings through weedy areas. Birds reaching the Hawaiian Islands carrying such seeds or fruits would similarly preen them out of their plumage, or the propagules would be deposited if the bird died after arrival. In addition, as indicated in Plate 13.1, fruits or seeds of certain other plants are covered with a sticky coating—or one that becomes gluelike when wet—resulting in adhesion to almost anything that touches them. Finally, the pulp of any large, fleshy fruit that contains relatively small seeds could serve to affix such seeds to birds eating the fruit.

Land and freshwater snails can also be transported by birds; successful colonists potentially carried would primarily represent either young individuals or adults of small species and eggs of oviparous ones. The ability of terrestrial gastropods to attach the shell firmly to flotsam was noted earlier, and very occasional individuals might become similarly anchored to birds subsequently flying to the Hawaiian Islands. There is at least one report of an apparently migrant duck found in the archipelago with one or more attached snails, and there are a number of similar reports from elsewhere in the world involving other types of birds. Birds can also be expected to carry their usual complement of parasitic insects, such as body and feather lice and certain bloodsucking flies, ticks, and fleas, as well as an occasional "hitchhiking" pseudoscorpion.

Successful Colonizers

In general, plant and animal species carried by birds have a better chance of establishing than do species transported by wind. A bird would most often acquire a transported organism in habitat common to the two. Upon arriving in the Hawaiian Islands, the bird would seek similar habitat, thus likely depositing the associated organism in a favorable place to establish.

The probability that a few fern ancestors arrived in the Hawaiian Islands in the form of bird-attached spores has already been mentioned. Of all the immigrant species of flowering plants reaching the Islands naturally, an estimated three-fourths were transported by birds. Of this number, a little more than half probably arrived in—rather than on—birds. It is likely that only a negligible percentage of the colonizing insect total was naturally flown in attached to birds, and probably even fewer spider colonists immigrated in this manner. A minority of terrestrial snail ancestors probably arrived via birds, but there is no estimate of the actual species number.

GEOGRAPHIC SOURCE

Table 13.3 presents information regarding percentages of terrestrial Hawaiian founding plants and animals that may have been supplied by different geographic areas. In reality, the source is undetermined for a large percentage of native biota, primarily because the usual high degree of endemism in the more speciose groups largely prevents determination of the exact ancestral species of most Island taxa. This uncertainty is especially great in the case of insects, as indicated by the questioned figures in Table 13.3. The data that are available, however, including knowledge of the source of indigenous species, suggest that a substantial majority of insects (and of most other major terrestrial biotic groups) arrived from Southeast Asia and the insular Southwest Pacific. Much of this geographic dominance probably demonstrates primarily the greater transporting efficiency of eastward winds as opposed to westward ones. But this aerial transportation has almost surely been enhanced and complemented by the number of "stepping-stone" high-island clusters in the Southwest Pacific, structures largely lacking during either the past or the present in the East Pacific (see chapter 11).

Although it was noted in the previous two chapters that very few American marine species of plants and animals had dispersed to Hawai'i, Table 13.3 shows that the New World has possibly provided more than its share of native nonmarine bird species (but note that the origin of over one third is undetermined). If this apparent high degree of New World avian contribution is real, it would evidently reflect the effectiveness of the trade winds in assisting or facilitating arrival of these volant animals in the Hawaiian Islands, at least for birds that were somehow able to reach the trade winds' mid-East Pacific origin. For birds of subtropical and tropical American regions, the westward-moving Pacific hurricane track could serve in the same manner, although surviving the air turbulence would undoubtedly be a problem (see also chapter 20). The relatively lower number of Asiatic and Indo-West Pacific bird founders suggests that various characteristics of, at least, the high-elevation jet stream render it unsuitable for similar

Table 13.3. Geographic source of selected major native Hawaiian terrestrial biota. Founder numbers represent estimated endemic-species ancestors plus indigenous species. Figures for snails, birds, and mammals include extinct species, but not migrant shorebirds. See text for explanation of the questioned insect numbers. The Asian designation includes the Indo-West Pacific region. (Data from various sources.)

Biota	Founder	Asian	American	Unknown
Ferns (and allies)	114	59 (52%)	14 (12%)	41 (36%)
Flowering plants	291	163 (56%)	54 (19%)	74 (25%)
Insects	448	<426? (<95%)	22? (<5%)	?
Spiders	13	1 (8%)	1 (8%)	11 (84%)
Snails	29	13 (45%)	1 (3%)	15 (52%)
Fishes	5	5 (100%)	—	—
Birds	26	7 (27%)	10 (38%)	9 (35%)
Mammals	2	—	2 (100%)	—
Total	928	674 (73%)	104 (11%)	150 (16%)

transportation of relatively large and warm-blooded vertebrates. Apart from the potential role of storms and other substantial air movements in aiding avian dispersal, a glance at the map of Fig. 24.1 will show that migratory birds leaving at least the more northern part of North America for southern wintering grounds could relatively easily reach Hawai'i if they became disoriented. Birds similarly leaving most parts of northern Asia, however, would have considerably less chance of encountering the Islands.

It seems unusual that the numerous high Pacific islands to the south and southwest of Hawai'i have not contributed more to the native avifauna, because they are home to a number of subtropical bird types that it seems would have occasionally errantly flown to the Hawaiian Islands (for example, certain herons, doves and fruit-eating pigeons, parrots, and kingfishers).

ESTABLISHMENT RATES

Table 13.4 provides a rough idea of how often a founder of a given type of upland terrestrial organism reached and established on some Hawaiian island. (It seems almost certain that additional species—perhaps many—of the listed biotic groups were also successful colonists, but that their descendant lines became extinct in ancient times, leaving no currently available record; in that case, the average number of years required for each successful establishment would be substantially lowered.) Flowering plants and insects exhibit the most rapid establishment rates; their species successfully colonized the archipelago at roughly thirty to fifty times the average rate for all the groups considered. This relative proficiency in colonization undoubtedly reflects their (or their propagules') generally small size, as well as the resultant relative ease with which immigrants of these two groups are passively transported in various ways. But it seems obvious that colonization by even the flowering plants and insects has not been easy, because in each group it has taken an average period of, respectively, 105,000 and 70,000 years for each successful establishment.

Table 13.4. Approximate establishment rates for selected major native Hawaiian terrestrial biota. The founder numbers represent estimated endemic-species ancestors plus indigenous species. No amphibians or land reptiles are considered native. Figures for snails, birds, and mammals include extinct species, but not migrant shorebirds. The time available for *upland* terrestrial colonization of the archipelago is considered to be 30 million years. (Data from various sources.)

Biota	Founder	Average Years per Establishment
Ferns (and allies)	61 + 53 = 114	265,000
Flowering plants	178 + 113 = 291	105,000
Insects	350 + 84 = 434	70,000
Spiders	13 + 0 = 13	2,310,000
Snails	21 + 8 = 29	1,035,000
Fishes	4 + 1 = 5	6,000,000
Birds	20 + 6 = 26	1,155,000
Mammals	1 + 1 = 2	15,000,000
Total	648 + 266 = 914	3,240,000

The establishment rate of one Hawaiian colonization every 6 million years for (amphidro-mous) freshwater fishes seems, intuitively, rather low, but undoubtedly this attests to the effectiveness of the "filter funnel" in regulating biotic dispersal from the Indo-West Pacific Region eastward into the central Pacific. Mammals show the lowest rate of terrestrial establishment, as might be expected from the combination of their generally large size, relatively poor ability to survive any type of long-distance ocean transport, and limitation of flight to bats.

ESTABLISHMENT

A vastly greater number of plant and animal species unquestionably reached the Hawaiian Islands than were able to subsequently establish a population. No one has the least idea of what the percentage of such unproductive arrivals might have been, but it would not be surprising if it exceeded 95 percent or even 99 percent.

Immediate Requirements

An organism successfully dispersing to Hawai'i would still have to reach suitable habitat even to have a chance of establishment. For example, an epiphytic fern spore deposited on a dry, open lava flow would be quite unlikely to produce a colony, and a forest snail attached to a beach-washed log might well never reach properly vegetated habitat. For immigrant species with individuals of opposite sexes, at least one of each would have to be present—or a single arriving animal would have to be an impregnated female. Eggs or other growth stages of most introduced parasitic animals would perish unless proper intermediate as well as final hosts were soon located.

Long-Term Requirements

Even if an immigrant individual did manage to satisfy these immediate requirements, a variety of obstacles would still have to be overcome before a population could become permanently established. Biotic disharmony and attenuation might well present a major problem. A matured immigrant plant that required a rather specific pollination agent (for example, a certain type of insect, bird, or even flower-visiting bat) would promptly be lost except in the unlikely event that some local animal was able to pollinate it. For self-fertilizing or vegetatively propagating plants there would be no similar short-term problem, but deleterious and possibly even fatal genetic problems arising from such founder inbreeding in some might eventually result in decreased viability and ultimate loss of the young population (see chapter 15 for further discussion of this problem).

Although a wide variety of climatic regimes exist in the Hawaiian Islands—from near-desert to alpine (see chapter 14)—the major portion of the Islands' land area has always been essentially subtropical. Thus, organisms arriving from the relatively wet and warm islands of the Southwest Pacific would most likely be better adapted for establishment than would species from the generally drier and often-cooler New and Old World coasts. In the case of a number of such temperate plants, the new subtropical climatic and other abiotic factors would probably prevent maturation or successful seed germination, and in animals from similar environments, normal progression of life cycles might well be disrupted. Continued survival of immigrant bird species would be dependent on the chance presence of suitable food for both adults and young, available at just the proper times of year. And, finally, an initially established population of either plant or animal might die out because it proved unable to adequately exploit an ecological niche occupied by a previously established species.

In fact, considering the fantastic odds against almost any new plant and animal ever reaching an isolated archipelago like Hawai'i and then finding suitable habitat, in conjunction with *potential* bars to continued population existence in such a biotically disharmonic and attenuated area, the number of organisms that did successfully establish in the archipelago is little short of amazing.

SUGGESTED REFERENCES

Carlquist 1974, 1980, 1982; Carson and Clague 1995; Cowie 1998; Cowie et al. 1995; Eldredge and Miller 1995; Howarth 1990; Howarth and Mull 1992; James and Olson 1991; Kinzie 1991; Miller and Eldredge 1996; Mueller-Dombois 1975; Olson and James 1991; Sohmer and Gustafson 1987; Wagner and Funk (eds.) 1995; Wagner et al. 1999.

AUDIOVISUAL AIDS

Hawaii: An island community; Islands within islands within islands; Succession on lava.

The Terrestrial Environment

The general phenomenon of succession was explained in chapter 9 on ecological principles. It should, however, be reiterated that, although animals similarly undergo succession (in fact, are usually the first organisms to arrive in a new environment), the phenomenon is typically illustrated using plants. A specific example of vegetational succession in terms of a Hawaiian ecosystem is presented in this chapter.

PLANT SUCCESSION

As each island in the Hawaiian Archipelago was formed, the initial terrestrial ecosystem had to begin on new volcanic material. The following description outlines the vegetation changes occurring at about 1,200 m (4,000 feet) in a relatively moist area newly coated by volcanic ejecta. This portrayal is necessarily somewhat generalized because plant species and rate of succession differ somewhat under the different climatic regimes of windward and leeward island sides, as well as between land covered by *pāhoehoe, ʻaʻā,* or ash. As just one example, mature forest can take many times as long to develop on *pāhoehoe* as on the other two volcanic substrates.

Pioneer Stage

A new lava flow may require many months to cool sufficiently to allow invasion of vegetation. Even after the surface of the basalt nears air temperature, water seeps down to still-heated depths after each heavy rain and is turned to rising steam that kills any germinating propagules. When, however, the flow interior has cooled enough to allow plant growth, the general native vegetational sequence typically begins with colonization by blue-green "algae" (or Cyanobacteria; see chapter 11). In cracks or under lava shelves, moisture is retained long enough to support spore germination and growth of mosses and various ferns, including sword ferns or *kupukupu* of the genus *Nephrolepis.* Lichens, which are symbiotic associations of an alga and a fungus, establish soon thereafter. A very common lichen species of this seral stage is *Stereocaulon vulcani,* and after 4 or 5 years it has sometimes largely covered lava surfaces. (The "moss rocks" so favored in Hawaiʻi for stone walls and garden decoration are simply basalt cobbles and boulders laden with lichens of one species or another.)

Intermediate Seral Stages

Along with the nonflowering pioneers, various flowering plants also appear during the early years. These are typically led by the tree *ʻŌhiʻa lehua (Metrosideros polymorpha).* (Many of the native Hawaiian plants such as this one have no English common name; the family names of most flowering plants mentioned here are supplied in chapter 15.) A few alien plant species may invade or regenerate on substrates partially covered by ejecta, but in completely devegetated areas native pioneers are in the majority. Native shrubs, including Hawaiian blueberry or *'ōhelo* (*Vaccinium* spp.), the sturdy *Pūkiawe (Styphelia tameiameiae),* and various Hawaiian tarweeds or *na'ena'e* (*Dubautia* spp.), establish in small pockets of soil developing from organic material and disintegrating basalt. Red tree ferns or *'ama'u* (*Sadleria* spp.) are scattered throughout. (Species of this genus had long been called small tree ferns, but this now seems inappropriate because it has been determined that individuals apparently grew to a considerably greater size before becoming host to a damaging historically introduced weevil.) After only a few more years, a layer of the False Staghorn Fern or *uluhe (Dicranopteris linearis)* usually begins to develop and after many years provides unbroken ground cover 1 to 2 m (3.3 to 6.6 feet) high for the unshaded areas. When fully covered by this fern, the underlying lichens die, but among the tangled vinelike fern branches appear a few erect plants such as the fern relative Christmas Tree Club Moss or *wāwae'iole (Palhinhaea cernua;* formerly known as *Lycopodium cernuum).*

Later Seral Stages

In 100 to 150 years or so, *'Ōhi'a lehua* have so increased in size and number that a great deal of the False Staghorn Fern, as well as the red tree ferns, begin to be shaded out. A different type of large fern, the Hawaiian tree fern or *hāpu'u* (*Cibotium* spp.), with thick trunk and tall fronds sometimes reaching a height of more than 5 m (17 feet), now provides a substantial understory. A few of the earlier shrub species have been replaced by a greater variety of similar-sized plants. Smaller trees such as the Bastard Sandalwood or *naio (Myoporum sandwicense)* as well as occasional small groves of the true sandalwood or *'iliahi* (*Santalum* spp.) have appeared. In wetter areas, the Screw Pine relative *'Ie'ie (Freycinetia arborea)* climbs tree trunks, with its long adventitious aerial roots extending toward the ground. Also, a substantial layer of mosses has come to cover tree trunks and branches as well as parts of the forest floor. After the deaths of a substantial number of trees, the fleshy Ear Fungus or *pepeiao akua (Auricularia polytricha)* grows on their fallen trunks and dead stumps as a decomposer.

Eventually, in this preclimax community, a large percentage of the mature *'Ōhi'a lehua* trees, which are typically mostly of the same generation in a given area, may experience an extensive dieback. This seems to be a normal long-term process periodically undergone by these and a few other forest trees. It is apparently due to a number of contributing and interacting factors and not to a calamitous outbreak of some epidemic disease or a sudden massive infection by insects or other harmful organisms. As currently theorized, the advancing age of this first cohort of trees eventually leads to some loss of crown foliage, and this defoliation increasingly predisposes the individuals of the cohort to susceptibility to other physiological stresses that hasten their demise. These stresses are induced primarily by extended periods of extreme weather conditions, as well as by long-term changes in **edaphic** or soil-related conditions, including gradual alteration in texture, waterlogging, depletion of essential nutrients (see chapter 5), and natural buildup of toxic materials. Possibly, attacks by pathogens or other debilitating biotic agents also contribute to development of physiological stress.

This natural death of many old trees opens the canopy, however, and in areas where the Hawaiian tree-fern canopy is not too dense a new generation of *'Ōhi'a lehua* is able to grow as seedlings receive sufficient sunlight. This second assemblage of individuals, however, typically consists largely of a different variety or subspecies, morphologically distinguishable from the original lava colonizers primarily by having smooth leaves rather than somewhat hairy ones. Also, these replacing trees seem to have a root system better adapted to growth on old rotting logs and in the now-developed soil than in crevices of the original lava substrate. It is at this stage, however, that the area is especially subject to invasion by alien trees or other plants that are adapted to just some of the factors that contributed to the *'Ōhi'a lehua* dieback (for example, the wet-soil Paperbark [*Melaleuca quinquenervia*] and the nitrogen-fixing Firetree [*Myrica faya*]). In at least scattered patches these aliens completely or largely prevent the development of the second variety of *'Ōhi'a lehua* mentioned, as well as alter many other subsequent aspects of the successional process.

Climax Stage

After 300 or 400 years additional shrubs and trees of different sizes, including such species as Pacific Holly or *kāwa'u (Ilex anomala), 'olapa (Cheirodendron* spp.), and sometimes *Koa (Acacia koa),* have established. Among these, a few restricted to the understory may now rival *'Ōhi'a lehua* in abundance. Various epiphytes grow high in larger trees and include the relatively large and showy Bird's Nest Fern or *'ēkaha (Asplenium nidus).* The natural sere for this area can now be considered complete, because a climax rain forest has been formed, with *'Ōhi'a lehua* and Hawaiian tree ferns as codominants.

Although this rain forest is here called a climax one, it differs from most continental climax assemblages because the final dominant species are largely the same ones originally pioneering the sere, instead of being completely different ones. Further, at least the Hawaiian Rain Forest Zone (see vegetation-zone descriptions in the next sections) typically is much less diverse in species than rain forests in continental areas with similar climatic conditions, probably reflecting the disharmonic and attenuated nature of the Hawaiian biota (see chapters 10, 11). It may also be noted that in this Island vegetation zone, as in rain forests everywhere, few native species are seasonally deciduous; thus, unlike many continental nonconiferous areas, there are never periods when essentially all the plants are leafless.

VEGETATION ZONES

Zonation

Changes in vegetation (as well as in entire ecosystems) occur not only temporally but also geographically (that is, from one part of an island to another), and this is known as **zonation.** These areal and elevational differences in flora are due not only to climatic factors, such as variations in temperature and precipitation, but also to edaphic factors such as dissimilarities in soil texture or chemical composition. This floral variation is perhaps best described in terms of vegetation zones, which are here considered subunits of the worldwide biomes discussed in chapter 9 and, similarly, are typically named for the climax vegetation type.

A great number of classification schemes describing Hawaiian plant assemblages have been devised over the years, most of them more complex than the general one used here. Figure 14.1 shows this classification of vegetation zones on a typical main island in profile (although only Hawai'i and Maui are still high enough to possess all of the zones). The elevational skewing of most zones in relation to the wetter windward and drier leeward sides of the island should be especially noted. Figure 14.2 shows essentially the same zones, but in a plan view of the actual main Hawaiian Islands. (It may be of interest to compare these historically designated zones with those recognized by ancient Hawaiians, as shown in Table 25.3.)

STRAND ZONE

The **Strand Zone** is limited to that part of the coastal area fairly consistently receiving ocean spray. Its substrate is often entirely loose or cemented sand, but in a few areas is composed essentially of only lava flows or emergent ancient coral-algal reef (see chapter 8). Although the plant assemblages vary greatly according to the substrate type, all species are necessarily those that can withstand or counteract osmotic water loss to salt contacting foliage or roots. Many of the native species are indigenous ocean-dispersed ones found throughout most of the Pacific. Typical among these are the shrubby Beach *Naupaka* or *naupaka kahakai* (*Scaevola taccada;* formerly *S. sericea*) and the often-prostrate variety of *'ilima ('Ilima papa [Sida fallax]),* along with the trailing vines of Beach Morning Glory or *pōhuehue (Ipomoea pes-caprae)* and the spiny-fruited Caltrop or *nohu (Tribulus cistoides)*. There are also a number of smaller broad-leafed plants, many with noticeably fleshy or succulent foliage, as well as a few tough-stemmed grasses, but, typically, no native trees.

A number of salt-tolerant alien species are now common, such as the Polynesian-

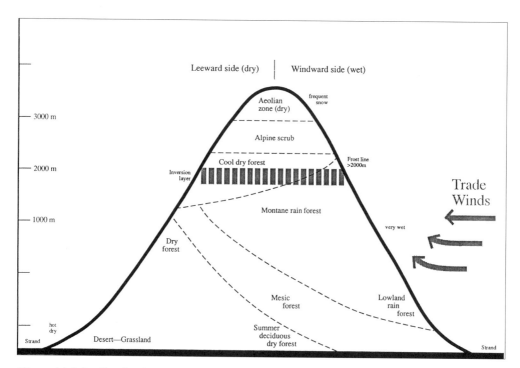

Figure 14.1. Profile of major Hawaiian vegetation zones. A very high mountain such as Mauna Kea or Mauna Loa on Hawai'i is illustrated. The Coastal Zone is not indicated in this diagram, and the zone labeled Aeolian is that discussed in the text as the Alpine Stone Desert Zone. (Unnumbered figure on p. 11 of Howarth and Mull [1992], used with permission of Francis G. Howarth.)

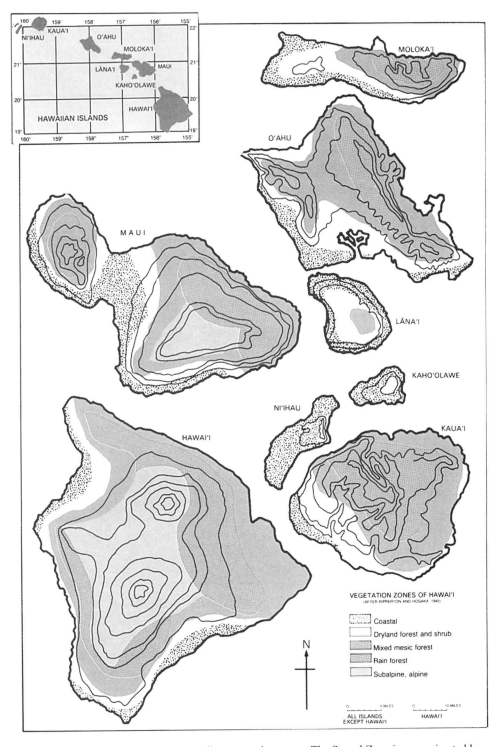

Figure 14.2. Plan view of major Hawaiian vegetation zones. The Strand Zone is approximated by the heavy outline of each island. Trade winds approach from the direction of the upper right corner of the map. (Unnumbered figure on p. 41 of Sohmer and Gustafson [1987], used with permission of Seymour H. Sohmer.)

introduced Coconut or *niu (Cocos nucifera)* and Alexandrian Laurel or *kamani (Calophyllum inophyllum)*. Historically imported species include Tree Heliotrope *(Tournefortia argentea)* and Tropical Almond or False *Kamani, kamani haole (Terminalia catappa)*. Another tree commonly found in this vegetation zone, especially around many former traditional Hawaiian villages, is *Kou (Cordia subcordata)*. This species was long thought to have been introduced by early Polynesians, but it may be indigenous instead. Its seeds have been recovered from Island coastal deposits predating Polynesian arrival, but it is still uncertain whether these represent only propagules rendered nonviable during unassisted ocean passage here or whether they are seeds of a successfully established population of the species predating humans.

Certain other trees characteristic of more inland localities are also capable of thriving in the Strand Zone, specifically, the historically introduced ironwood or *paina* (the Hawaiian transliteration of "pine" [*Casuarina* spp.]) and the thorn-clad algaroba or mesquite, *kiawe (Prosopis* spp.). Among shrubs, the alien Indian Fleabane *(Pluchea indica)* is a common species throughout much of the drier portion of the zone. Historically imported mangroves *(Rhizophora mangle* and *Bruguiera sexangula)* flourish as dense "swamps" in a few protected muddy shore and shallow estuarine areas.

COASTAL ZONE

In drier lowland areas beyond the reach of salt spray, with substrates often firmer than sand and extending as high as about 300 m (1,000 feet) in some areas, is the **Coastal Zone.** The drier leeward main island coasts that receive annual rainfall of between perhaps only 38 and 75 cm (15 and 30 inches) produce this type of vegetation zone. It also extends completely through the low isthmus between East and West Maui, encircles Lānaʻi, and occupies much of the entire islands of Kahoʻolawe and Niʻihau (Figure 14.2).

Small- to medium-sized native trees are interspersed among shrubs and grasses, giving the region a quite open appearance. The zone's plants and animals have been so disturbed by both ancient and modern humans that it is difficult to say how closely its current native floral complement approximates the condition before human arrival. Pollen deposits extending back several thousand years, however, indicate that the endemic Hawaiian palms or *loulu* of the genus *Pritchardia* once occurred throughout much of this zone. These were accompanied by a bushlike member of the pea family probably closely related to *Kanaloa kahoolaweensis,* a new genus and species found growing on the island of Kahoʻolawe in 1992. These two plant taxa were mostly extirpated sometime between middle Polynesian and very early historic times. The native trees characteristically found in the zone today are Hawaiian Coral Tree or *wiliwili (Erythrina sandwicensis),* the formerly more abundant lowland Coast Sandalwood or *ʻiliahi aloʻe (Santalum ellipticum),* and the essentially ubiquitous Bastard Sandalwood. The common, thorny-leaved Screw Pine or *hala (Pandanus tectorius)* is evidently indigenous rather than Polynesian introduced. Shrubs include an upright variety of *ʻilima (ʻIlima kū kula)* as well as such low and spreading plants as Hawaiian Cotton or *maʻo (Gossypium tomentosum)* and the beautifully flowered but now-rare pea family member *ʻOhai (Sesbania tomentosa).*

Almost countless alien plants have been imported for cultivation in the Coastal Zone, especially around residential and other developed areas. The early Hawaiians planted primarily imported species essential for their way of life (see chapter 25), probably including the medicinally important, large, shrublike Indian Mulberry or *noni (Morinda citrifolia)*. Among the more noticeable historically introduced trees are Monkeypod *(Samanea saman),* False *Koa* or *koa haole (Leucaena leucocephala),* and the ornamental plumeria (*Plumeria* spp.).

DRY FOREST ZONE

The **Dry Forest Zone** or, alternatively, the Dryland Forest and Shrub Zone, lies between the Coastal Zone and the beginning of moderately moist forested areas above. The lower and upper limits are about 200 and 1,000 m (660 and 3,300 feet), respectively, at least on the leeward sides of the larger Islands, where it is best developed. It is also found over much of the middle-elevation interior of Lānaʻi and on the summits of Kahoʻolawe and Niʻihau. Its rainfall is relatively scarce, ranging from about 75 to 100 cm (30 to 40 inches) annually. Like the Coastal Zone, the region appears somewhat parklike, but with the shrubs and trees a little more closely spaced. The original Hawaiian Dry Forest Zone has similarly been greatly disturbed by human activities, primarily prehistoric burning and historic ranching, so its current vegetation probably does not portray the original diversity of the area. On Leeward Oʻahu, small remnant areas of native vegetation in lower areas of the Waiʻanae Mountains are now highly informative because they appear to represent the general floral composition of this zone before human arrival.

Certain Coastal Zone native trees such as Hawaiian Coral Tree and Bastard Sandalwood also extend up into this zone, but more typical are Hawaiian Persimmon or *lama (Diospyros sandwicensis), nīoi (Eugenia* spp.), and soapberries or *aʻe* and *āulu (Sapindus* spp.). Endemic shrubs include several species of *nehe (Lipochaeta* spp.). The Oʻahu pollen-deposit investigations mentioned for the Coastal Zone indicate that Hawaiian palms and the same associated pea-family member also once occurred in the lower portion of the zone, along with a species of the altitudinally wide-ranging shrubby *ʻAʻaliʻi (Dodonaea viscosa)* on the wetter windward sides of the main islands.

Common alien trees and smaller plants currently dominate much of this zone. The trees are exemplified by False Koa, Christmas Berry or *wilelaiki* (a transliteration of "Willie Rice," a former Island politician who campaigned wearing the red berries as a hat lei [*Schinus terebinthifolius*]), and algaroba. The more common shrubs are the thorny verbena relative Common Lantana or *lākana (Lantana camara),* and Prickly Pear Cactus or *pānini* ("fence-wall"; rows of the large spiny plants often were grown as domestic stock barriers [*Opuntia ficus-indica*]). Molasses Grass *(Melinis minutiflora)* forms large brakes here. In the early historic period, extensive areas of this zone were reported covered with the upright Twisted Beard-Grass or *pili (Heteropogon contortus),* but it is still not certain whether this species is indigenous or a Polynesian introduction. Beginning in the later 1800s, vast stretches of this zone, as well as the Coastal Zone below and lower portions of the Mesic Forest Zone above, were cleared and planted in commercial varieties of irrigated Sugarcane or *kō (Saccharum officinarum* and congeneric hybrids) as well as Pineapple or *hala kahiki* ("foreign *hala*" [*Ananas comosus*]) (Figure 26.1).

MESIC FOREST ZONE

The elevational mountain band between about 750 and 1,250 m (2,475 and 4,125 feet) of the larger Islands, and the summit of Lānaʻi, support the **Mesic Forest Zone.** The climatic factors producing this vegetation zone seldom include prolonged droughts as do those of the Dry Forest Zone below it. Annual rainfall, though, is less than that of the Rain Forest Zone above it, varying rather widely from about 100 to 250 cm (40 to 100 inches) or slightly more.

The original vegetation of this zone was quite possibly the most diverse of all Hawaiian vegetation zones, but, like that of most lower ones, has been greatly depleted in variety, with the native species extensively replaced by alien ones. Also, this zone, along with the next-higher Rain Forest Zone, apparently once contained the greatest number of endemic Hawaiian plant species (although the next-lower Dry Forest Zone could possibly have closely rivaled them). The canopy is not completely closed although its trees and shrubs are usually rather closely spaced. The two most abundant native trees are now scattered giant *Koa* and large individuals of *'Ōhi'a lehua,* although the latter becomes even more abundant in the Rain Forest Zone. An endemic sandalwood *(Santalum freycinetianum)* is also noticeable, in the company of various endemic tree lobelias, many known by the collective names of *'ōhā* and *hāhā,* as well as shrub- and tree-sized endemic amaranths or *pāpala* (*Charpentiera* spp.) and the common *'A'ali'i.* Other notable endemic and usually now-rare plants include several showy-flowered hibiscus relatives such as *koki'o* (*Kokia* spp.) and *hau kuahiwi* (*Hibiscadelphis* spp.).

Polynesian-introduced Candlenut or *kukui (Aleurites moluccana)* is especially abundant along streambeds and in wet gulches, but historically introduced species now occupy extensive areas elsewhere, many of these taxa forming dense closed-canopy stands. Historically imported species include Common Guava or *kuawa* and Strawberry Guava or *waiawī 'ula'ula* (*Psidium guajava* and *P. cattleianum,* respectively), as well as Mango or *manakō (Mangifera indica).* Orchards of Macadamia Nuts (almost entirely *Macadamia integrifolia*) are now present on Hawai'i and, to a lesser extent, other main islands. Among other historic introductions, the immense vines of the climbing passionflower Banana Poka *(Passiflora mollissima)* drape even the largest trees, Prickly Florida Blackberry or *'ōhelo 'ele'ele* ("black *'ōhelo"* [*Rubus argutus*]) forms often-impenetrable understory patches, and Kikuyu Grass *(Pennisetum clandestinum)* thickly covers deforested areas. Some higher areas cleared in the early twentieth century contain monocultures of such historically introduced watershed-protection or potential timber species as various eucalyptus or *'eukalikia* (sometimes *palepiwa* [ward off fever] [*Eucalyptus* spp.]), Silk Oak or *'oka kilika* (the transliterated English common name [*Grevillea robusta*]), and Norfolk or related Southern Hemisphere "pines" (*Araucaria* spp.).

RAIN FOREST ZONE

The **Rain Forest Zone** is most typically developed at about the inversion layer (see chapter 7), roughly 1,700 to 2,000 m (5,610 to 6,600 feet), but in a few exceptionally wet windward areas such as Hawai'i Island's Hilo may extend down to as low as 200 m (660 feet) or so. Rainfall is frequent and ranges between approximately 300 and 1,125 cm (120 and 450 inches) or more per year, with upper elevations of the zone shrouded by clouds much of the time. In fact, this latter perpetually wet and dripping area, with mossy and epiphytic vegetation covering the forest floor and larger plants (Plate 14.1), is often referred to as the "cloud forest." The canopy tends to be more nearly closed than that of any other zone, but is still not unbroken.

The climatic conditions of this zone are not especially suitable for most residential or agricultural purposes, so large portions of it still retain a semblance of their condition before human arrival. Many of the typical trees and other native plants of the Rain Forest Zone were noted in the discussion of the later stages in Hawaiian plant succession at the beginning of this chapter. *Koa* trees are found sporadically, but are more characteristic of the drier zones immediately below and above. A few more plants of particular interest might be noted. Six of the eight endemic species of mountain *naupaka* or *naupaka kuahiwi* (*Scaevola* spp.) are found in the Rain Forest Zone, and the three endemic Hawaiian orchids are restricted to it. The zone is also the primary home of numerous species of four endemic lobelioid genera of the bellflower subfamily Lobelioideae.

Some lower-elevation parts have been cleared and replaced by groves of the same alien trees mentioned for the preceding Mesic Forest Zone. The shrubby alien Koster's Curse *(Clidemia hirta)* is found thickly covering disturbed parts of the forest floor in many areas, and Common and Strawberry Guavas as well as Prickly Florida Blackberry have also become well established.

COOL DRY FOREST ZONE

On Hawai'i and Maui, beginning just above the inversion layer on the windward side and just below it on the drier leeward side, is the **Cool Dry Forest Zone,** sometimes termed the Subalpine Forest Zone. The elevational limits are very roughly 1,700 to 2,400 m (5,610 to 7,920 feet) depending on the island's side. Because of the zone's position largely above the inversion layer, its rainfall is considerably lower than that producing the Rain Forest Zone just below, varying between about 50 and 125 cm (20 and 50 inches) annually, although substantial additional moisture is obtained from fog drip (see chapter 7). The zone's climate is temperate rather than subtropical, and at least its upper half experiences frequent frost and sometimes snow during the winter.

The predominant tree species tend to change gradually between lower and upper parts of the zone; in the lowest areas many scattered *Koa* occur, often mixed with a few *'Ōhi'a lehua* extending up from the Rain Forest Zone, but in the higher portion a very distinctive open parkland forest appears, consisting almost entirely of the yellow-flowered leguminous *Māmane (Sophora chrysophylla)* and Bastard Sandalwood. Other areas, such as the extensive high-elevation "Saddle Area" between Mauna Kea and Mauna Loa on Hawai'i (see chapter 5), tend to lack such trees, although it is not certain that this was the condition before human arrival. These places currently support a somewhat crowded endemic shrubland vegetation consisting primarily of the relatively large and elevationally widely distributed endemic goosefoot *'Āheahea (Chenopodium oahuense),* various Hawaiian tarweeds of the almost equally widespread genus *Dubautia,* and on Maui a small sandalwood *(Santalum haleakalae).* Grass species of several native and alien genera cover a portion of the space between the shrubs, and a few introduced plants of larger size are also found in this forest zone.

ALPINE SCRUB ZONE

Treeline in Hawai'i occurs along an undulating line centered on about 2,750 m (9,000 feet), and the **Alpine Scrub Zone** (sometimes considered only subalpine) extends from this level to the upper limit of significant plant life at perhaps 3,450 m (11,300 feet). The zone is found only on Hawai'i and Maui, and its vegetation consists entirely of shrubs and smaller plants. The sparse precipitation that limits the stature of this above-treeline flora is usually no more than about 40 cm (16 inches) annually, with occasional years bringing Maui as much as 75 cm (30 inches). On Hawai'i, at least, the zone's precipitation is received largely in the form of winter snows. Frost occurs nightly almost year-round, but solar radiation (especially ultraviolet) here above most clouds is quite intense. By far the most spectacular plants are the endemic silverswords or *'āhinahina* (*Argyroxiphium* spp. [see chapter 15]). There are also the native Hawaiian blueberry and *Pūkiawe,* as well as two or three endemic Hawaiian mints (*Stenogyne* spp.), and both herbaceous alien and shrublike Hawaiian species of cranesbill or *nohoanu* (*Geranium* spp.). Although now rare, even an endemic subspecies of strawberry or *'ōhelo papa* ("prostrate *'ōhelo*" [*Fragaria chiloensis sandwicensis*]) is part of the flora. Rounded clumps of native bunchgrasses of the genera *Deschampsia, Panicum,* and *Trisetum* are also scattered throughout. The alien Woolly Mullein *(Verbascum thapsus)* along with the small dandelionlike Hairy Cat's Ear *(Hypochoeris radicata)* are perhaps the most noticeable exotic plants of this generally rather barren elevational band.

ALPINE STONE DESERT ZONE

Between the upper limits of the Alpine Scrub Zone and the summits of approximately 4,250 m (14,000 feet) of Mauna Kea and Mauna Loa on Hawai'i, as well as on the summit of Maui's 3,057-m (10,023-foot) Haleakalā, occurs the **Alpine Stone Desert Zone.** The substrate is almost entirely unweathered volcanic ejecta such as fine ash, cinders, and occasional bare lava flows. Annual precipitation is quite low, consisting almost entirely of winter snows equivalent to about 38 to, occasionally, 75 cm (15 to 30 inches) of rain; frost is a nightly occurrence, and the ground a little below the surface in some areas on at least Mauna Kea apparently remains permanently frozen. There are numerous small lichens and frequently also mosses, as well as, among the few endemic flowering plants, an occasional high-ranging silversword.

High-Altitude Aeolian Ecosystem

Recent zoological studies of the Hawaiian Alpine Stone Desert Zone have revealed that an unusual biotic and abiotic assemblage there constitutes a **High-Altitude Aeolian Ecosystem** (Latin *"Aeolus"* [god of the winds]). The primary productivity base of the ecosystem is not on-site vegetation but plant and animal material carried up to these great elevations by daytime convection currents. Although wind-transported leaves of shrubs of the Alpine Scrub Zone may provide sustenance for the few herbivores in this ecosystem, most of the available food material consists of similarly conveyed insects and other small arthropods (as well as even an occasional small bird). Such animals reaching the Alpine Stone Desert Zone are usually soon immobilized or killed by the low temperatures. These are preyed upon or scavenged by native arthropods that possess unique selective adaptations (such as body fluids with a freezing point below that of water) allowing survival in this seemingly most forbidding environment. Because the endemic fauna of this ecosystem, as well as that of the one described next, are so unusual, a fuller discussion of their animal types is reserved for chapter 16 on terrestrial arthropods.

SELECTED ADDITIONAL HAWAIIAN ECOSYSTEMS

Lava Tube Ecosystem

Like the High-Altitude Aeolian Ecosystem, another Hawaiian biotic land assemblage contains rather few noticeable plant species and is dominated by varied small animal forms. This is the

Lava Tube Ecosystem. Formation of lava tubes was described in chapter 5 and, with the exception of an occasional exposed former sea cave and an extremely limited number of elongated horizontal passages in fossil-reef substrate, lava tubes form the only extensive natural tunnel-like formations in the Hawaiian Islands. Because lava tubes disappear rather rapidly in geologic terms through collapse or filling, relatively few are now evident on older Kaua'i and O'ahu. A number, however, may still be found on the slopes of Haleakalā as well as on other islands of ancient Maui Nui (Figure 3.3), and additional ones are constantly being formed on volcanically active Hawai'i. In more interior segments of intact lava tubes the atmosphere is perpetually saturated with moisture, and there is seldom any appreciable soil buildup on the bare lava floor before the formation of "skylights" or surface openings (Plate 5.1).

A few fungi, being decomposers without chlorophyll, can grow in the completely dark zones of these tubes, but this is not possible for photosynthesizing plants (see chapter 9). Green plants are, however, still the ultimate source of energy in the ecosystem, primarily in the form of tree roots, especially those of *'Ōhi'a lehua,* which may grow down through 10 m (33 feet) of lava and penetrate the tube ceilings (Figure 14.3). A small amount of additional organic material is supplied to the ecosystem by plant and animal debris that occasionally finds its way from the surface into the tubes.

Figure 14.3. Roots of *'Ōhi'a lehua (Metrosideros polymorpha)* in a lava tube. This organic material penetrating the ceiling represents the primary energy source in such a sunless ecosystem. Shown is Kazumura Lava Tube on the east slope of Kīlauea Volcano of Hawai'i. This tube is of great scientific value because it supports at least a dozen endemic species of subterranean invertebrates. (Photograph by Francis G. Howarth; Fig. 2 of Howarth [1987], copyright 1987 by Elsevier Science, used with permission of the photographer and Elsevier Science.)

At least ninety-five endemic animal species—all invertebrates—have been found living in Hawaiian lava tubes. All of the *exclusively* lava-tube ones were derived from surface ancestors entirely within the archipelago. In fact, each must have evolved on the same island—or, sometimes, even in the same isolated lava-tube system—where it is now found, because once adapted to a subterranean existence, such a species could not have dispersed to other Hawaiian Islands or even to distant lava tubes on the same island.

Bog Ecosystem

In relatively wetter areas of the Islands and not restricted to any particular vegetation zone are small, isolated, permanently wet areas supporting a Bog Ecosystem. These tend to be very scarce, with each of the larger main islands having only one or two. The substrate remains saturated because it is primarily either very dense basalt or low-permeability clay, or both in the case of the Alaka'i Swamp surmounting Kaua'i.

Small hummocks typically covering the ground in bogs are formed largely of various low-growing native sedges (Figure 14.4). The most unusual floral aspect of bogs is probably the presence of dwarf individuals or varieties of such common tree and shrub species as *'Ōhi'a lehua* and Hawaiian blueberry; both of these flower and fruit in this ecosystem even though often less than about 10 cm (4 inches) high. Also, although most endemic Hawaiian members of the violet family have evolved into shrub size, the single small, endemic, herblike one is restricted to bogs. A widespread Northern Hemisphere bog species of "insect-eating" Sundew or *mikinalo* (to suck flies [*Drosera anglica*]) has also naturally colonized certain Kaua'i bogs.

FRESHWATER ECOSYSTEMS

Streams and their biota constituted essentially the only type of freshwater ecosystem in Hawai'i before human arrival, although a very occasional large natural pond or small lake did occur.

Stream Dynamics

As noted in chapter 8, water flow of a typical unaltered Hawaiian **Stream Ecosystem** may sometimes be seasonally variable, especially in lower portions of watercourses. During any time of the year, however, cloudbursts in associated mountain watersheds can quickly turn even dry segments of stream courses into raging and life-threatening torrents. Thus, streambeds of any considerable elevational grade tend to be constantly scoured of sediments, with the substrate consisting only of larger rounded stones and solid basalt. Also, because of the interbedding of underlying layers of harder and softer types of lava, the upland portions of most mature streams are broken into relatively flatter sections separated from one another by waterfalls of various heights, rather than forming a uniformly descending gradient (Figure 8.3, *C*). In lower, more-level, coastal reaches, streams may widen or coalesce to form a river-sized watercourse, such as the Wailuku on Hawai'i and the Hanalei of Kaua'i. If the current of the low-elevation segments of waterways tends to be rather weak, their paths may meander somewhat, and a moderate deposit of silt with associated organic matter tends to accumulate in their beds and around their mouths. Also, many segments of at least smaller or shallower Hawaiian streams are routinely subjected to relatively great fluctuations in water temperature because of periodic changes in amount or speed of flow, thus environmentally stressing their biota considerably.

Stream Biota

Typical plant and animal types of a Hawaiian Stream Ecosystem are depicted in Figure 9.1. Other Stream (and Pond) Ecosystem arthropods and snails are mentioned in chapters 16 and 18, respectively. The only three freshwater bivalve mollusks found in the Hawaiian Islands are alien and occur in both lower-elevation stream segments and, more typically, ponds. The Asiatic Clam (*Corbicula fluminea* [family Corbiculidae]) was introduced as a food species in 1981 and now occurs on the four largest main islands. In the late 1990s two alien freshwater bivalve species were found in Taro pondfields on Maui: the Swamp Fingernail Clam *(Musculium partumeium)* and the Ubiquitous Pea Clam *(Pisidium casertanum)*, both of the family Sphaeriidae. These last two species are too small to have been introduced for food purposes, but it is not known how or when they did arrive, nor whether they occur on additional main islands.

Freshwater fishes are covered in chapter 12, and the entirely alien amphibian and reptile complement in chapter 19. In regard to insects, many of the common orders of continental areas whose immature stages are aquatic never naturally colonized the Hawaiian Islands. Among orders that did reach the archipelago, however, many dozens of new species with aquatic larvae

Figure 14.4. Hawaiian Bog Ecosystem on East Maui. Shown is the high-elevation (2,290-m or 7,500-foot) Greensword Bog of Haleakalā National Park. The numerous hummocks are primarily of the endemic sedge *Oreobolus furcatus.* Dwarfed individuals of a few native plants such as *'Ōhi'a lehua (Metrosideros polymorpha)* and Hawaiian blueberry or *'ōhelo (Vaccinium* spp.) are also typical members of such communities. (Photograph by Wayne C. Gagné, used with permission of Betsy H. Gagné.)

have evolved. Most notable of these orders are true flies (order Diptera) as well as the dragonflies and damselflies (Odonata). The true bugs (Heteroptera), beetles (Coleoptera), moths and butterflies (Lepidoptera), and wasps (Hymenoptera) are also represented in the archipelago by a few native species whose immatures live in streams. Stream-adapted crustaceans are most noticeably represented by two native amphidromous shrimp, both omnivorous feeders on stream detritus. The smaller of the two is the endemic Mountain Shrimp or *ʻōpae kalaʻole (Atyoida bisulcata),* which reaches all stream elevations because its young can surmount waterfalls by crawling up the low vegetation at the sides of the cascade. This species apparently filters food out of the water when stream flow is swift and scrapes food from the substrate when it is slow. The larger is the indigenous Hawaiian Prawn or *ʻōpae ʻoehaʻa (Macrobrachium grandimanus),* which may attain a head-and-body length of 10 cm (4 inches) and is restricted to lower sections of streams. The amphidromous Tahitian Prawn *(Macrobrachium lar),* introduced in the 1950s, is also common below first waterfalls, and there is some indication that it can occasionally overcome at least moderate falls and populate higher stream segments. A second alien freshwater crustacean, the Grass Shrimp *(Neocaridina denticulata),* was first noticed in Nuʻuanu Stream on Oʻahu in 1990.

Pond Dynamics

The various historically developed water reservoirs and new or old flooded agricultural fields, along with their biota, constitute the Hawaiian freshwater **Pond Ecosystem.** Because of the essential lack of freshwater impoundments in the Islands before human arrival, the pond biota includes very few endemic species, being composed primarily of indigenous and alien taxa. Because the abiotic environment of a Hawaiian Pond Ecosystem can be—and usually is—controlled by humans, these nonbiological factors tend to be more stable than those of an unaltered Hawaiian stream. Occasional major perturbations, however, do disrupt the pond biota, as when depth and oxygen content of water are dramatically decreased because of a need to draw out large amounts of water, but many of the established alien pond species are those adapted to surviving just such environmental fluctuations.

Pond Biota

Typical nonagricultural vegetation of the Pond Ecosystem includes, primarily, floating mats of alien Water Hyacinth *(Eichhornia crassipes)* and Water Lettuce *(Pistia stratiotes);* a great variety of native and alien sedges and grasses grow along untended banks. A definitive list of native and alien pond-adapted insects has not yet been prepared. Among crustaceans, the introduced North American Crayfish *(Procambarus clarkii)* has invaded many freshwater bodies, and in recent times entire pond "farms" have been constructed for commercial production of the alien Tahitian Prawn. Native birds of the Pond Ecosystem are covered in chapter 20, and a number of migratory or accidental species of continental ducks and geese also utilize these bodies of water.

SUGGESTED REFERENCES

Akashi and Mueller-Dombois 1995; Beletsky 2000; Daws 1988; Devick 1991; Devick (ed.) 1991, 1993; Howarth 1987; Kitayama et al. 1995; Mueller-Dombois 1975, 1987; Mueller-Dombois and Fosberg 1998; Pratt and Gon 1998; Smathers and Mueller-Dombois 1972;

Sohmer and Gustafson 1987; Stemmermann 1981; Stone et al. (eds.) 1992; Valier 1995; Wagner et al. 1999; Yamamoto and Tagawa 2000.

AUDIOVISUAL AIDS

A bog community in Hawaii; Ecology; Flowing to the sea; Hawaii: A mountain community; Hawaiian waters: Mauka/makai lifeline; Hawaii: Born of fire; Hawaii: Crucible of life; Hawaii's forests; Hawaii's streams; In the middle of the sea; Islands within islands within islands; Life in Lost Creek; Pond communities in Hawaii; Species and evolution; Succession on lava.

15

Flowering Plants

The geographic sources, dispersal, and establishment of plants colonizing the Hawaiian Islands were discussed in chapters 11 and 13. In this chapter dispersal and salient evolutionary processes of native flowering plants are investigated further. A final discussion deals with the remarkable "Silversword Alliance."

Classification

Seed-producing plants are usually arranged in two taxonomic divisions: **Gymnospermae** (Greek *"gymnos"* [naked] and *"sperma"* [seed]; primarily pines, firs, and similar cone-bearing plants), and **Angiospermae** (Greek *"angeion"* [container]; flowering plants). The angiosperms comprise two classes: **Liliopsida** or **Monocotyledonae,** typified by grasses, sedges, palms, irises, and orchids, and **Magnoliopsida** or **Dicotyledonae** ("broad-leafed" plants), containing the remaining herbs, shrubs, and nonconiferous trees. Monocots typically have parallel leaf veins, flower parts in threes, and a single initial "embryonic leaf" or cotyledon in the sprouting plant. Dicots usually have networklike leaf venation, flower parts in fours or fives, and a pair of cotyledons.

Table 15.1. The fifteen Hawaiian flowering plant families containing the most native species. The percentages of native and established alien species in each appear in parentheses. All are dicots except for the grass, sedge, and palm groups. (Data from Wagner et al. [1999].)

Family	Native	Alien	Total
Bellflower (Campanulaceae)	123 (97%)	4 (3%)	127
Sunflower (Asteraceae)	94 (49%)	96 (51%)	190
Mint (Lamiaceae)	60 (78%)	17 (22%)	77
African violet (Gesneriaceae)	57 (100%)	—	57
Coffee (Rubiaceae)	55 (75%)	18 (25%)	73
Rue (Rutaceae)	53 (98%)	1 (2%)	54
Grass (Poaceae)	47 (23%)	161 (77%)	208
Sedge (Cyperaceae)	45 (56%)	36 (44%)	81
Pink (Caryophyllaceae)	40 (78%)	11 (22%)	51
Mallow (Malvaceae)	25 (48%)	27 (52%)	52
Pepper (Piperaceae)	25 (93%)	2 (7%)	27
Pea (Fabaceae)	23 (18%)	105 (82%)	128
Spurge (Euphorbiaceae)	22 (46%)	26 (54%)	48
Palm (Arecaceae)	22 (88%)	3 (12%)	25
Myrsine (Myrsinaceae)	21 (88%)	3 (12%)	24

BIOTIC COMPOSITION

Native Hawaiian flowering plants represent fourteen families of monocots and seventy-three of dicots. Of the 137 monocot species, 94 or 69 percent are endemic and 43 or 31 percent indigenous; corresponding figures for the 877 dicots are 813 (93 percent) and 64 (7 percent). The fifteen plant families containing the most native Hawaiian species are listed in Table 15.1; all of these families are among the ones also best represented elsewhere in the world.

SPECIATION

The fifteen genera of plants containing the largest number of endemic Hawaiian species are listed in Table 15.2; fourteen of these belong to the fifteen common families in Table 15.1. The small number of colonists yielding the endemic species of each Table 15.2 genus reflects explosive speciation by only a very few founding species, rather than limited speciation by a large number of immigrant taxa. The reasons that certain families so speciose in other parts of the world, such as orchid (Orchidaceae), pea (Fabaceae), myrtle (Myrtaceae), and nightshade (Solanaceae), have evolved relatively few endemic species in Hawai‘i are obscure, but probably

Table 15.2. The fifteen Hawaiian flowering plant genera containing the most endemic species. The number of founders from which their species' complements apparently evolved are also listed. *Cyanea* and *Clermontia,* as well as *Phyllostegia* and *Stenogyne,* likely each arose from a single founder. (Data from Wagner et al. [1999].)

Genus (and Family)	Endemic	Founding	Genus (and Family)	Endemic	Founding
Cyanea Bellflower (Campanulaceae)	73	1	*Clermontia* Bellflower (Campanulaceae)	22	—
Cyrtandra African violet (Gesneriaceae)	58	4 to 6	*Hedyotis* Coffee (Rubiaceae)	21	1 or 2
Melicope Rue (Rutaceae)	45	1	*Stenogyne* Mint (Lamiaceae)	21	—
Phyllostegia Mint (Lamiaceae)	32	1	*Myrsine* Myrsine (Myrsinaceae)	20	1 or 2
Schiedea Pink (Caryophyllaceae)	29	1	*Bidens* Sunflower (Asteraceae)	19	1
Dubautia Sunflower (Asteraceae)	23	1	*Chamaesyce* Spurge (Euphorbiaceae)	16	1 or 2
Peperomia Pepper (Piperaceae)	23	3	*Labordia* Logania (Loganiaceae)	16	1
Pritchardia Palm (Arecaceae)	22	1			

include scarcity of appropriate animal pollinators and dispersing agents, as well as a shortage of suitable ecological niches (see chapter 9), especially for later-arriving founders.

FOUNDER EFFECT AND GENETIC DRIFT

Most of the species groups evolving from a single or only a few plant founders have become so morphologically varied that it is now difficult to determine to what extent founder effect and genetic drift (see chapter 10), as opposed to natural selection alone, may have been responsible for observed changes.

Cyrtandra *Evolution*

A good example of the difficulty faced in making such a determination is provided by the *ha'i-wale* (as in the case of many native plant taxa, there is no well-accepted English common name) of the genus *Cyrtandra* (Gesneriaceae). The fifty-eight endemic species are the most of any Hawaiian plant genus except *Cyanea* (Campanulaceae) (Table 15.2). All have white flowers, but other floral characteristics as well as fruits and many vegetative parts show a great amount of variation, even among species occurring in the same vegetation zone or habitat. Among these various endemic *ha'iwale* species, the flowers are either smooth or hairy and borne on either branch tips, upright stems, or ground-level shoots; the fruits may be either rounded or greatly elongated; and the leaves vary from broad to narrow, with different degrees of hairiness. Possibly, some such variations have resulted from differences in species ecology rather than genetic drift; for instance, the varied positions of flowers may have evolved in response to differing locomotor activities of a particular insect pollinator (for example, crawling beetles versus flying moths). Until more research is carried out, however, this and similar matters cannot be satisfactorily elucidated.

DISPERSAL MECHANISM CHANGES

Before human arrival, Hawaiian plant founders had to travel by means of either ocean currents, wind, or birds (see chapter 13), although the pertinent transportation method in the case of a number of colonizing species is still subject to conjecture. After establishment, however, some of the most profound adaptive shifts (see chapter 10) in speciating lines involved changes in presumed dispersal adaptations of the ancestor. Except for many ocean-transported plant species of the Strand Zone (see chapter 14), probably extremely few arriving propagules were deposited in just the proper habitat necessary for their establishment. Among those that were, however, it would usually then be advantageous if their propagules were *not* easily dispersed from the newly occupied habitat, but remained in the same suitable area. Such sedentariness is especially important on oceanic islands of limited size, whose various habitat types tend to be similarly restricted in extent instead of often stretching unbroken over many hundreds of square kilometers or square miles as on continents.

Ocean Flotation

The majority of the Hawaiian plant founders arriving via the ocean were undoubtedly transported as buoyant seeds or fruits. Most of these species were common Pacific-wide Strand Zone plants and still maintain their specific identity in the Hawaiian Islands, likely because conspecific individuals continue to occasionally arrive, establish, and maintain the same ancestral gene pool. A few of these beach plants, however, were somehow eventually able to move inland to yield endemic species inhabiting not only the neighboring Coastal Zone but also various higher forest vegetation zones. Flotation of propagules of these inland endemics would then be of no great advantage and, in fact, would undoubtedly quite often be disadvantageous, because seeds or fruits carried downslope by freshwater or offshore by ocean currents would be removed from suitable habitat. The large seeds of the various coral trees (*Erythrina* spp. [Fabaceae]) of lowland Southeast Asia float well, and so the ancestor of the Hawaiian Coral Tree or *wiliwili (E. sandwicensis)* very likely reached the Islands by sea. However, this endemic Hawaiian species of Coastal and Dry Forest Zones has evolved nonbouyant seeds, thus enhancing the plant's continued existence in its new inland habitat.

Wind Transport

Although ferns and fern allies are not flowering plants, a subsequent evolutionary change in wind dispersal of spores of most after reaching Hawai'i is instructive. The endemic Hawaiian forms have adaptively shifted to spore sizes greater than those of their ancestors. Most continental fern spores range between 20 and 40 μm (micrometers) or 0.0008 and 0.0016 inches in size, but those of the endemic red tree ferns or *'ama'u (Sadleria* spp. [Blechnaceae]) have increased to approximately 50 μm (0.002 inches) in the Mesic Forest Zone species, and to as much as 62 μm (0.0025 inches) in the sole Rain Forest Zone species. This larger size reduces the average distance the propagules of these ferns (and of similarly dispersed flowering plants) are blown away from the parent and its favorable habitat.

Among the relatively few flowering plant ancestors presumably reaching Hawai'i on the wind, the most likely so transported are orchids, because of the extremely small size and typically immense number of their seeds. Also, this family is represented by an extremely large number of species in at least most tropical and subtropical land masses bordering the Pacific. There are, however, only three endemic Hawaiian orchid species and no indigenous ones. This paucity is almost certainly not due to failure of seeds to arrive in the Islands, but to the fact that either or both a symbiotic fungus and an insect (or other) pollinator specific to various species were absent in the areas where their seeds were deposited. In regard to the three orchids that did manage to establish in the Islands, it would be interesting to know if there has been an adaptive shift to increased seed size in any, but apparently this possibility has not been investigated. The very small seeds of the myrtle family endemic *'Ōhi'a lehua (Metrosideros polymorpha)* may conceivably also have been blown to the archipelago. Those of the current Hawaiian species are lightweight and measure only about 0.3 by 1.5 mm (0.0012 by 0.006 inches); in fact, it has been found that a wind as slight as 9.7 km or 6 miles per hour can keep them aloft. But if the original propagules were about the same size and were indeed blown to Hawai'i, one reason for the apparent failure of Island seeds to increase in size could possibly be the selective advantage of the endemic Hawaiian propagules' being blown fair distances onto frequent new lava flows.

Bird Transport

A majority of the continental ancestors of endemic Island flowering plants reaching Hawai'i through the agency of birds were variously attached to feathers or body parts. Some of the seeds or fruits may have been fortuitously included in a layer of dried algae or mud or adherent due to mucilaginous coatings, and others were affixed to plumage by such mechanical devices as hooks, barbed awns, or stiff bristles. A fruit ("seed") admirably so adapted is one like that of the alien Spanish Needle or Beggartick (*Bidens pilosa* [Asteraceae]). There are nineteen endemic Hawaiian species of the genus, collectively known as *ko'oko'olau,* occupying various vegetation zones. In many, especially the Rain Forest Zone species, the barbed awns and bristles on the fruit have become diversely modified or lost, as illustrated in Figure 15.1. In fact, some of the Hawaiian fruit types shown appear to be the result of an adaptive shift to dispersal by wind, with flattened or spiraled winglike bodies.

The minority of avian-transported Hawaiian flowering plant founders were probably carried internally. Most propagules potentially carried to the Islands in seed eaters such as finches would already have been digested upon arrival, but a few might occasionally survive to germinate. There are also founding, migrant, or visitant birds such as crows, thrushes, rails, waterbirds, shorebirds, and even certain seabirds that either swallow entire fruits or pick up seeds mistaken for gizzard stones or food items. These propagules would later be excreted or regurgitated (or could germinate from the body of a bird dying soon after arrival) to possibly establish populations. Shiny black seeds resembling small stones and attractive to birds are characteristic of such endemic plants as *alani* (*Melicope* spp., formerly known as *Pelea* [Rutaceae]) and *hō'awa* (*Pittosporum* spp. [Pittosporaceae]). Floating seeds of at least the Polynesian-introduced Candlenut or *kukui* (*Aleurites moluccana* [Euphorbiaceae]) are currently brought back to nests by albatrosses (*Diomedea* spp. [Figure 23.3]), and founder species may well have been similarly transported great distances to the archipelago in the distant past by these birds while foraging throughout the entire Pacific.

Small seeds of plants with fleshy fruits could have been transported to the Islands either in the digestive system of birds or in fruit pulp that became attached to them during feeding. A number of endemic plants whose presumed ancestors outside of Hawai'i have fleshy fruit containing small seeds generally seem to have retained this characteristic, so such propagules remain susceptible to transport by Hawaiian birds. Included in this category are many endemic species of *Clermontia* (Campanulaceae), most known as *'ōhā,* and related members of the subfamily Lobelioideae. Most continental members of the mint family Lamiaceae have dry fruits, although all species of the essentially endemic genera *Phyllostegia* and *Stenogyne* possess fleshy fruits with seeds easily transported in or on birds. Presumably, the common ancestor of these two Hawaiian plant taxa was among the minority of continental fleshy-fruited mint species and was carried to the Islands by birds. The nine endemic species of so-called mountain *naupaka* or *naupaka kuahiwi* of the genus *Scaevola* (Goodeniaceae), most found in areas away from the shore, differ from the single indigenous, ocean-transported, Strand Zone Beach *Naupaka (S. taccada;* formerly *S. sericea)* in having moist instead of dry fruits. The moist fruits are evidently attractive to frugivorous birds, so the apparent three ancestors of this inland suite of species likely originally reached the Hawaiian Islands through avian transport rather than by ocean flotation.

This retention of susceptibility to avian dispersal by all of the above-mentioned plants may not be as disadvantageous as it first appears. A native bird species feeding on fruit of a native plant species typical of a particular upland habitat is usually part of the same ecosystem, so would not tend to carry the seeds to areas differing radically in ecological attributes.

There are, however, some fleshy-fruited native Hawaiian plant types in which transportation of presumably bird-ingested fruits or seeds *away* from proper habitats could have proved to be an evolutionary "problem." The endemic Hawaiian palms or *loulu* (*Pritchardia* spp. [Areca-

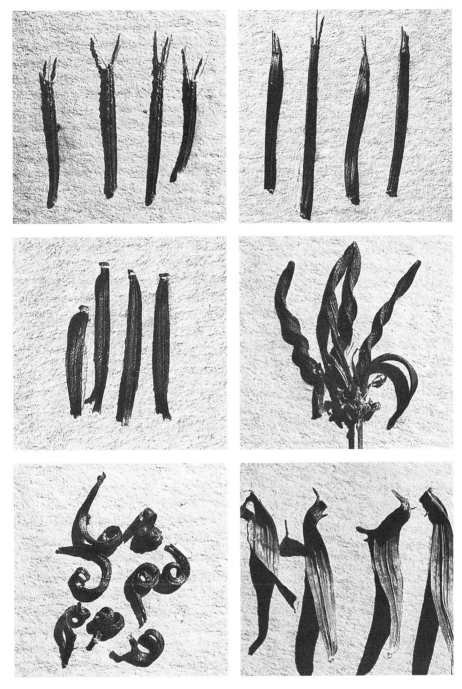

Figure 15.1. Loss of avian dispersal characteristics in endemic Hawaiian *Bidens*. The presumed ancestor could be either Spanish Needle *(B. pilosa)* of the Americas *(upper left)* or another species showing the same type of terminal barbed awns and stiff hairs on the fruit body. The fruits are shown at various enlargements, but the range of lengths is from 0.5 to 2.0 cm (0.2 to 0.8 inches). (Unnumbered figure on p. 164 of Carlquist [1980], used with permission of the National Tropical Botanical Garden.)

ceae]) may provide an example of the solution to such a problem through an adaptive shift in fruit size. As shown in Figure 15.2, the fruit of the series of native *Pritchardia* species from various Pacific island groups extending east from Fiji to the Hawaiian Archipelago becomes progressively larger. Many investigators believe that the *Pritchardia* line reached the Hawaiian Islands in the form of floating fruits or seeds, subsequently establishing large lowland populations, which then yielded upland species with increasingly larger fruit less susceptible to dispersal. The validity of this quite plausible ocean-arrival hypothesis, however, has yet to be proven. If it happens to be incorrect, there is a seemingly equally reasonable alternative scenario. In Fiji and even Samoa the fruit of some *Pritchardia* species is small enough to be swallowed whole by a medium-sized bird, but the propagules in the main Hawaiian Islands are too large to be carried by even a large flighted bird (at least a land one, although albatrosses could easily pick up and transport floating fruits). The intermediate size of the fruit of the Nihoa Palm *P. remota,* restricted to the Northwestern Hawaiian Island of Nihoa (see chapter 23), is problematical. It could represent a slightly enlarged descendant of a small-fruited founder (bird-transported?) from the Southwest Pacific, or it could equally well be the result of genetic drift to smaller size in an endemic large-fruited main island form somehow reaching Nihoa.

The same progressive size increase in fruits and seeds along assumed ancestral dispersal routes can be seen in a number of indigenous Hawaiian genera, such as the *māhoe* (*Alectryon* spp. [Sapindaceae]), *hōʻawa* (*Pittosporum* spp.), and the *aʻe* (*Zanthoxylum* spp. [Rutaceae]). Among the main islands, the propagules of many Kauaʻi and Oʻahu plant species of these

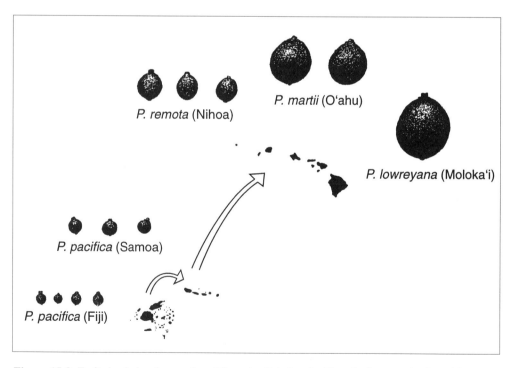

Figure 15.2. Fruit size in insular species of the palm *Pritchardia.* Note the increase in size with increasing distance east of the Southwest Pacific emigrant region. The largest fruit shown is about 5 cm (2 inches) in diameter. (Figure by Keith Krueger.)

groups are larger than those of closely related taxa on younger islands like Maui and Hawai'i. Probably, the smaller ancestral types of fruits or seeds have continued to be intermittently brought to the archipelago (presumably by birds rather than ocean flotation). Such arriving propagules establishing on each newly formed island yielded a small-propaguled colony, but those successfully establishing on older islands either quickly lost this morphological attribute through interbreeding with a large-propaguled relative or failed to establish at all because of competition with such a relative. Incidentally, a second and perhaps additional reason for increased fruit and seed size—as least in the case of forest species—is that this provides a greater amount of stored nutrients for the shaded seedling, allowing it to grow far enough through surrounding vegetation to obtain sufficient sunlight for photosynthesis before exhausting its initial energy supply.

INBREEDING PROBLEMS AND SOLUTIONS

Self- and Cross-Fertilization

The successful colonizing complement of a majority of native Hawaiian species probably consisted of a single individual. In contrast to most evolutionarily advanced animals, there are seed-producing plants in which the same individual produces both male and female gametes (the flower's pollen grains and ovules, respectively). When both sexes are contained in the same flower, the flowers are termed perfect, and if the male and female components mature at the same time *and* there are no genetically based self-incompatibility barriers in the species, the plants are capable of self-fertilization. If flowers contain only one sex they are termed imperfect. When imperfect flowers of both sexes occur on the same plant, the species is **monoecious** (Greek *"mono"* [one] and *"oekos"* [house]); when the male and female flowers occur on different plants the species is **dioecious.** Thus, because a single individual of many of the species that either possess perfect flowers or are monoecious can potentially self-fertilize, and one of a dioecious species cannot, most of the successful Island colonists would have been other than dioecious. In fact, botanical studies indicate that between 80 and 90 percent of Hawaiian colonizing flowering-plant species were probably capable of self-fertilization.

Each plant in subsequent generations of a perfect-flowered or monoecious founder, however, would potentially remain self-fertilizing or **inbreeding.** This is almost always deleterious —and usually ultimately fatal—because of the retention and accumulation of numerous unfavorable genetic alterations in the inbred population. Also, because of founder effect, the number of alleles of many genes is already severely restricted in new insular populations, limiting the amount of morphological and other variation available. This makes the lineage less able to utilize any novel ecological opportunities that arise, with inbreeding further lowering the probability of appearance of such evolutionarily desirable variant individuals. If, however, mutation somehow provides a mechanism favoring or obligating **outbreeding** or gamete exchange between different individual plants, the buildup of unfavorable characteristics would be decreased, and the originally perfect-flowered or monoecious lineage may be able to survive.

There are several ways in which outbreeding may become obligatory in an originally self-fertilizing lineage, and one of the most common is evolution of dioecy. Although only about 4 percent of flowering plants worldwide are fully dioecious, the proportion in the total native Hawaiian flora is almost 15 percent, the highest known percentage for any region of comparable or larger size. Some of the more common endemic Island plants exhibiting full dioecy are the thirteen endemic *pilo* (*Coprosma* spp. [Rubiaceae]) and over three-fourths of the forty-five endemic *alani* (*Melicope* spp.), although the colonizing ancestors of these particular genera were among the estimated 10 percent or so of founders that were either already fully dioecious or possessed one of three breeding systems approaching this condition (see discussion later in this section).

Many of the other fully dioecious Hawaiian species, however, developed this condition only after speciating from self-fertilizing ancestors. Examples of such endemic species are the eleven *kōpiko* (*Psychotria* spp. [Rubiaceae]) and the five *ma'aloa* (*Neraudia* spp. [Urticaceae]). Fully dioecious species such as these, plus those developing one of the following three breeding systems approaching dioecy after also speciating from self-fertilizing ancestors, make up the relatively high proportion of about a third of the 21 percent or so of native Hawaiian plants that are either dioecious or dioeciouslike.

The 6 percent of all native Hawaiian plants that have evolved approaches to full dioecy have done so by developing three kinds of breeding systems. In one system (subdioecy), a species has three different kinds of plants: a few retaining only perfect flowers, but the majority bearing either only female or only male flowers. This system is found in, for example, a few species of *Schiedea* (Caryophyllaceae) and *'ākia* (*Wikstroemia* [Thymelaeaceae]). In another system (polygamodioecy), there are only two types of plants: all bearing a few perfect flowers, but with the many remaining flowers of only one or the other sex. Typifying this system is the *Olomea* (*Perrottetia sandwicensis* [Celastraceae]). The third system (gynodioecy) also involves two types of plants: most with only perfect flowers, but a few bearing only female flowers. Nine of the nineteen Hawaiian species of Spanish Needle relatives or *ko'oko'olau* (*Bidens* spp.) and at least fourteen of the twenty-one species of *Hedyotis* (Rubiaceae) possess this system. (No endemic species seems to have developed a system featuring perfect flowers on some plants, and only male ones on the rest.)

Another common means by which outbreeding can be brought about in a formerly self-fertilizing colonizing lineage is development of some type of genetic self-incompatibility that ultimately prevents or drastically lowers progeny production and thus necessitates outbreeding for survival. This has recently been shown true of certain species of the Silversword Alliance.

Hybridization

A great amount of hybridization or cross-fertilization of species within the same genus or even family is also characteristic of the collective endemic Hawaiian flowering plant flora. Under most circumstances, such crosses between two relatively closely related species is selectively disadvantageous because the hybrid offspring—if produced at all—are less well-adapted to current ecological requirements than is either parental type. Such progeny are thus outcompeted in various ways and usually either fail to survive until reproductive age or yield substantially fewer offspring upon breeding than individuals of the parental species. In fact, even the morphologically or physiologically aberrant traits of the hybridizing parent individuals undergoing this **"gamete wastage"** in producing hybrids tend to be eliminated because of the lack or decreased number of successful offspring that would perpetuate the "unsuitable" genotypes.

On islands, however, in spite of some inherent disadvantages, hybridization has apparently often been a successful mechanism for combating the debilitating effects of inbreeding. This breeding among species serves essentially the same function as outbreeding within a species: the production of new genetic combinations in populations or lineages. Opportunities for hybridization on larger Hawaiian islands are relatively great because of the proximity of either several different ecosystems or disjunct areas of the same ecosystem, each containing distinct but closely related species. This allows pollen of a plant in one such location to be relatively easily blown, or carried by an animal pollinator, to the flowers of a close relative in another.

Some botanists feel that the great variation in morphology (and probably physiology) among the numerous forms of *'Ōhi'a lehua* grouped under the single binomial *Metrosideros polymorpha* (Myrtaceae; fittingly, the specific name means "many-formed" in Greek) of different vegetation zones, ecosystems, or seral stages is due to recurrent episodes of hybridization between populations of a taxonomic level below the species. Hybridization among the many morphologically varied endemic Hawaiian species of the previously mentioned *ko'oko'olau* has apparently been relatively extensive, because somewhere between nine and seventeen possible natural hybrid forms seem to exist, and all potential hybrids among the nineteen endemic species have been produced in the greenhouse. Similar striking ability to hybridize has been recognized in several other groups of endemic Hawaiian plants, two of the primary ones being members of the previously discussed genus *Cyrtandra* and the Silversword Alliance.

ARBORESCENCE

The evolution of treelike species from small herbaceous ancestral taxa is **arborescence** (Latin *"arbor"* [tree]). This has occurred in a number of Hawaiian flowering plant families, most notably spurge (Euphorbiaceae), amaranth, goosefoot (Chenopodiaceae), bellflower, goodenia (Goodeniaceae), and even violet (Violaceae).

'Akoko

There are apparently sixteen endemic species of Hawaiian spurge or *'akoko* (*Chamaesyce* spp.; formerly included in the genus *Euphorbia*), all derived from one—or, less likely, two—colonizers. Although *C. degeneri* is a low and spreading Strand Zone species, most other Hawaiian endemics of the genus grow farther inland and differ in a number of other respects. Certain of these upland species can be used to illustrate the probable morphological stages in an adaptive shift to arborescence. The several subspecies or varieties of the widespread *C. celastroides* on various main islands exhibit growth forms ranging from a large but low, quite-tangled, mat of branches; through a somewhat spreading shrub; to a multitrunked small tree. And, in relatively dry forest areas both above and below the Rain Forest Zone of Maui and Hawai'i, *C. olowaluana* truly qualifies as a tree, growing to 9 m (30 feet) high and occasionally reaching 30 cm (12 inches) in trunk diameter. Also definitely treelike is *C. herbstii* in the Mesic Forest Zone of O'ahu's Wai'anae Mountains, reaching about 8 m (26 feet) in height.

Bases of Arborescence

There are probably several reasons for the obvious adaptive selection of arborescence in Hawaiian and other insular floras. The large fruit and seeds of relatively few continental species of forest trees were able to reach the Islands. Thus, many upland treelike ecological niches were left unfilled, and species of a few originally herbaceous lineages became arborescent while adaptively radiating into them. Additional herbaceous species formed an understory in the new forests, and selectively favored among them were some with growth mutations producing a taller plant whose leaves could capture more sunlight. Further, although a number of the Hawaiian colonists may initially have been annuals (living only a year), the absence of many perennial (multiyeared) forms in the disharmonic Island flora strongly favored selection of lineages living several years, thus giving these variants more time to grow to a larger size. And in the equable Hawaiian climate their growth could be year-round rather than only seasonal.

The continental relatives of at least three endemic Hawaiian plant types—two genera of the family Amaranthaceae, *kuluʻī* (*Nototrichium* spp.) and *pāpala* (*Charpentiera* spp.), as well as the goosefoot species *ʻĀheahea (Chenopodium oahuense)*—are typically quite small herbs. In Hawaiʻi, however, the last-named species, as well as at least one taxon in each of the two genera, is arborescent. The trunks of these various species, though, do not consist of the normal dense wood of other native Hawaiian trees, but are composed of thin layers of woody material separated by very thick layers of much-softer material. This yields a very light and quick-burning wood, and an ancient Hawaiian form of occasional evening entertainment on Kauaʻi consisted of setting fire to sections of *pāpala* logs and throwing them off sea cliffs into a strong wind, so that the blazing lightweight material was swept around and kept aloft for relatively extended periods, providing a spectacular fireworks display.

POLLINATION SHIFTS

Agents

Wind-pollinated flowers are usually small and greenish. The endemic Hawaiian flora contains a large number of species with such modest blossoms, so probably many of these have retained their ancestral pollination method. Plants with small to moderate-sized white flowers tend to be pollinated by small insects such as short-tongued bees, true flies, true bugs, nocturnal moths, and crawling beetles (see chapter 16), which visit the flowers to extract nectar or eat pollen. Also, the transfer of pollen by such invertebrates is most efficiently accomplished if the flower visited is relatively simple in structure (for example, with a corolla of open petals or only a very short basal tubular section). But plants with large and showy flowers of bright colors, especially those with long, often-curved corollas, are almost always pollinated by nectar-seeking birds such as certain endemic Hawaiian honeycreepers (see chapter 21) and larger flying insects such as long-tongued bees, butterflies, and diurnal hawk moths.

Insects to Birds

For reasons not clear, there has been a tendency in endemic Hawaiian plant lines to adaptively shift from pollination by small insects to that by the above-named birds and larger flying insects. In fact, this shift has been primarily to the vertebrate taxa, probably because larger flying forms are relatively rare in the endemic insect fauna of Hawaiʻi.

The flowers of five endemic species of cranesbill or *nohoanu* (*Geranium* spp. [Geraniaceae]) are adapted to pollination by moths, being relatively simple funnel-shaped structures, white in color. The sixth endemic species, *G. arboreum,* however, has long, curved, tubular flowers, which are bright red. These characteristics seem unquestionably morphological and visual adaptations to pollination by a nectar-feeding bird with a long downcurved beak. This same floral change has occurred in a number of other Hawaiian endemics, although many have either purple or only partially red flowers. Among the more noticeable of these are many species of *kokiʻo* and *hau kuahiwi* (*Kokia* spp. and *Hibiscadelphus* spp., respectively [Malvaceae]). *Clermontia* and various other native Hawaiian lobelioid genera also possess flowers similarly adapted to bird pollination, but some workers believe these particular taxa may well have evolved from immigrant ancestors that had already evolved this pollination method.

LOSS OF PROTECTIVE MECHANISMS

Flowering plants on all continents have necessarily evolved protective mechanisms to survive browsing, bark stripping, and similar damage by herbivorous vertebrates. Such characteristics are primarily thorns, spines, or prickles; poisonous or heavily scented foliage; and bitter bark. Most isolated island groups lack native mammals or other vertebrates that eat large plants, so there is natural selection for loss of these adaptations in certain colonizing plant lines. Metabolic energy saved by suppression of these once-protective characteristics can then be utilized for development of other attributes proving to be of survival value in the new environment.

Thorns, Spines, and Prickles

In the Hawaiian Archipelago, examples of evolutionary loss of plant physical armament abound. Some genera of the nettle family Urticaceae elsewhere in the world bear sharp, easily broken, hollow hairs filled with stinging formic acid that deter smaller herbivores, but the endemic *Olonā (Touchardia latifolia)* and two of the remaining thirteen endemic Hawaiian species of the family have lost such specialized ancestral hairs. The thorns of such continental rose family (Rosaceae) species as raspberries (*Rubus* spp.) are reduced to innocuous deciduous vestiges in the endemic Hawaiian raspberries or *'ākala* (*R. hawaiensis* and *R. macraei*).

It is interesting that a few endemic Hawaiian species do have obvious sharp-pointed structures of various types, including the Hawaiian Coral Tree with thorn-shaped prickles and the Hawaiian Prickly Poppy or *pua kala* (spiny flower; *Argemone glauca* [Papaveraceae]). It is quite likely that the respective morphologically similar ancestors of these two were relatively recent Island immigrants, and there has not been time enough for natural selection to bring about loss of the armament. Also, the poppy is reported to be one of the very few Hawaiian species that is biennial (living 2 years, as opposed to many years in most endemic plant taxa), another suggestion that it may represent a relatively recently established line, presumably from an annual colonist. The seaside Caltrop or *nohu* (*Tribulus cistoides* [Zygophyllaceae]) is well known to barefoot beachgoers along certain Hawaiian coasts through its long-spined seed cases, but this is an indigenous rather than an endemic species. Constant influx of ancestral genetic material in the form of ocean-carried conspecific propagules undoubtedly prevents loss of these sharp-pointed structures on the seed cases, whatever their original purpose.

Protective Neoteny

The only other native Hawaiian plant group in which a significant number of species display thorns, spines, or prickles is the bellflower subfamily Lobelioideae, with this character restricted to the genus *Cyanea* (including *Rollandia*). Of the seventy-three species of this endemic genus, many collectively known as *hāhā,* twenty (representing at least four evolving lineages) possess prickles, which may be up to 1 cm (0.4 inches) long. The growth form of most of these twenty consists of a single stem topped with a leaf clump. The prickles, however, are more numerous and better developed on the early stem and young leaves of the plant, and are either lacking or fewer and smaller on parts developing after the individual grows about 1 m (3.3 feet) or so tall. The prickles would hardly deter small insects from eating the young herbaceous material between them, and land snails would not harm the vegetation because they eat only fungi and algae on leaf surfaces; therefore, there must be some other predator involved.

In the past quarter century, remains of prehistorically extinct, flightless and herbivorous true geese and large gooselike duck relatives have been discovered on most of the main islands (see chapters 20, 22). These ground birds had a vertical reach of up to 1.2 m (4 feet). Thus, because the tender young *hāhā* stem and leaves up to this height would have been subject to severe and often fatal browsing pressure by these birds, the prickles quite possibly evolved as a defense. Older portions of the plant would have grown beyond the reach of the birds and thus would not need these putatively protective structures.

This explanation gains credence when it is considered that the puzzling phenomenon of **heteroblasty** (Greek *"heteros"* [different] and *"blastos"* [sprout]; sometimes termed hetero-phylly, Greek *"phyllon"* [leaf]) or marked differences in juvenile and adult leaf shape, is found in thirteen of the twenty *Cyanea* species bearing juvenile prickles. This high degree of associ-ation at least implies that there is some sort of direct relationship between these two phenom-ena. (Although heteroblasty is relatively common on oceanic islands, especially those that once possessed large flightless birds, it must be noted that it also occurs on continents, and in both places often in various plant groups that do *not* have prickles.)

The young leaves of heteroblastic *Cyanea* are relatively finely dissected, some even fern-like, and in the small immature plant are located close to the ground. The replacing adult leaves of most *hāhā* are entire and, of course, occur relatively high above the ground in the older plant. It seems that the flightless birds would probably have learned, through eating the occasional adult leaf that they were able to reach, that this part of *Cyanea* plants constituted desirable food. They would also learn that the accessible young divided leaves of at least the prickly species were not acceptable fare. In fact, the browsers might not even recognize the young dissected leaves as belonging to the same species as the palatable older entire ones. This could provide additional protection to the plant because the birds might be less inclined to even attempt eat-ing the young foliage (along with the juvenile stem tip) and thus seriously injure or kill the immature plant.

The fact that the unarmed adult leaves of a few species of *Cyanea* retain the dissected con-figuration of juvenile prickly ones (Figure 15.3) is probably the evolutionary result of presumed visual recognition and learned aversion to young dissected prickly leaves by the herbivorous birds, so that any accessible dissected adult foliage was also offered considerable protection by this mimicry. Or it could be that, because in ancient Hawai'i there were no vertebrate foliage predators that could forage higher than these flightless birds, there was no substantial selective pressure in these particular *Cyanea* species to change the shape of adult leaves from that of immature ones. Why, however, all *Cyanea* species with finely dissected, prickly young leaves would not have similarly kept this same leaf shape in adulthood is not apparent. (There is some evidence that finely dissected leaves may be an adaptive response of plants in general to shady, moist habitats, but this possible explanation of the adult fernlike leaf shape in certain *Cyanea* species has yet to be explored.)

The only endemic Hawaiian plant other than species of *Cyanea* that bears prickles on stems and leaves of young plants, but not of adult ones, is *Pōpolo kumai* (*Solanum incompletum* [Solanaceae]). It seems significant that this species, although not as obviously heteroblastic as the pertinent *Cyanea* ones, still shows at least a limited degree of difference in shape of the small-prickled young leaves and unarmed adult ones. This retention of any juvenile characteristic in the adult of an organism is generally known as **neoteny** (Greek *"neos"* [young] and *"tein"* [to extend]), and it will be encountered again in the discussion in chapter 22 on loss of flight by certain Hawaiian birds.

Poisons

Poisonous taxa occur with some regularity in a number of continental plant families, so a number of founding species almost surely possessed one or more toxic parts on arrival. In spite of many centuries of Polynesian—and over 200 years of historic—familiarity with the hundreds of native Hawaiian plants, however, members of apparently less than half a dozen genera are known or alleged to have some degree of toxicity, at least to vertebrates. One, and possibly more, of the twelve endemic species of *ʻākia* (*Wikstroemia* spp. [Thymelaeaceae]), many of

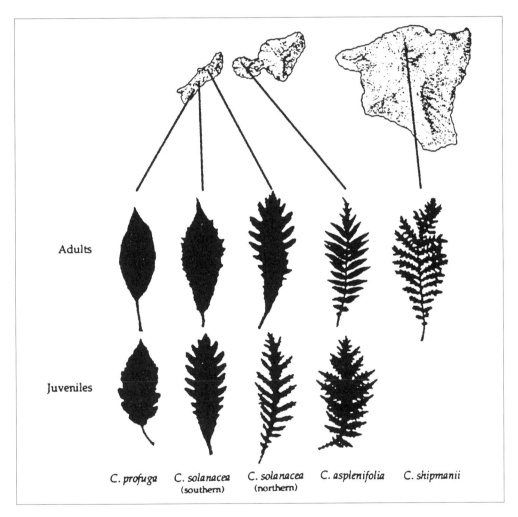

Figure 15.3. Probable protective neoteny in a lineage of the lobelioid genus *Cyanea. Left to right:* leaves of progressively descendant heteroblastic species from Molokaʻi, Maui, and Hawaiʻi. Note the adult leaf of each closely resembles the juvenile one of the immediately ancestral species. (Fig. 5 of Givnish et al. [1994]; copyright 1994, National Academy of Sciences, U.S.A., used with permission.)

whose continental congeners are notoriously poisonous, still possesses enough toxin to stun fish when, as in an ancient Hawaiian fishing method, plants of this genus were pulverized and placed in tide pools. A root and bark infusion of some undetermined species of *'ākia* was also said to have been part of a poisonous drink used to execute criminals in pre-Contact Hawai'i. Roots of the nineteen endemic Hawaiian species of *ko'oko'olau* (Figure 15.1), along with the leaves of about half of these, contain a small amount of poison, but because a tea is traditionally made from the foliage of most or all species, it seems this generic toxicity is of little danger or concern to humans. Roots of the endemic *Hao* (*Rauvolfia sandwicensis* [Apocynaceae]) and the indigenous *Huehue* (*Cocculus trilobus* [Menispermaceae]) are reputed to contain certain amounts of a poisonous substance, but the usual absence of human dietary utilization of any portions of these plants should obviate any potential consequences of their toxicity. Many species of the spurge family in other parts of the world contain white latexlike sap that is quite irritating to the skin or poisonous if ingested. It may well be that the still-untested white sap of endemic Hawaiian spurges retains this characteristic, so it would be prudent to avoid contact with any Island member. (See related discussion of the spurge-feeding endemic planthopper *Dictyophorodelphax mirabilis* in chapter 16.)

This ancestral characteristic of poisonous qualities was apparently lost in all other descendant plant lines of the Hawaiian Islands because it was of little or no selective advantage due to the scarcity of not only herbivorous vertebrates but also former continental invertebrate predators. Although not poisonous, the aromatic oils found in the leaves and stems of many continental plants such as mints (Lamiaceae) are apparently at least potent enough to discourage consumption of any significant amount of vegetation by either vertebrate or invertebrate predators. (Although humans may relish in their food small amounts of such pungent continental mints as Basil, Oregano, Sage, and Spearmint, a meal composed largely or entirely of these or any other such highly aromatic herbs could undoubtedly not be finished.) In the Hawaiian Islands, however, all of the fifty-eight endemic mints have lost this common continental characteristic of the family. Like the absence of poisons in almost all endemic Island plants, this loss of aromatic oils is presumably due to lack of ancestral predators.

Conversely, some endemic plant species could possess newly evolved chemical (or other) defenses evolved against novel Hawaiian invertebrate predators, although this possibility remains essentially uninvestigated. The endemic Hawaiian Cotton or *ma'o* (*Gossypium tomentosum* [Malvaceae]), in the absence of ancestrally associated beneficial insects in the Islands, has evolutionarily decreased the number of leaf glands producing substances that also attracted the damaging Pink Boll Worm *(Pectinophora gossypiella)* and virus-carrying aphids to continental *Gossypium* species. Because of this desirable quality of the endemic Island species, it has been interbred with commercial cottons to provide them the same protective characteristic.

In regard to toxic alien plants in the Hawaiian Islands, there are many with poisonous sap, foliage, or reproductive parts, and some of these are highly dangerous to humans. For example, sap of the common yellow-flowered Be-still Tree or *nohomālie* (*Cascabela thevetia* [Apocynaceae]), as well as of the equally ornamental Oleander or *'oliana* (*Nerium oleander* [also Apocynaceae]), is so potent that picnic food cooked on skewers of their branches has sickened people. In fact, such use of the latter species is reported to have caused the death of some affected individuals. Of a much lower level of concern is the milky sap of various historically introduced *Plumeria* species (Apocynaceae) and, especially, Mango or *manakō* (*Mangifera indica* [Anacardiaceae]), which promptly produces a localized skin rash in many people if contacted.

SILVERSWORD ALLIANCE

Two botanically well-known, and probably the best studied, examples of Hawaiian plant adaptive radiation and resultant convergent evolution involve members of the bellflower and sunflower (Asteraceae) families. Only three endemic genera of the latter are discussed here: the Hawaiian tarweeds or *naʻenaʻe* (*Dubautia;* twenty-three species), the Kauaʻi greenswords or *iliau* (*Wilkesia;* two species), as well as silverswords or *ʻāhinahina* and Maui greenswords (*Argyroxiphium;* five species). This tripartite group is usually referred to as the **Silversword Alliance** and seems to have evolved from a single tarweed species of, probably, either the genus *Madia* or *Raillardiopsis* (or closely related ancestral taxon) of the general California region.

Hawaiian Tarweeds

Certain drier-area species of Hawaiian *Dubautia* are still rather similar to the apparent ancestral tarweed, being rather nondescript, medium-sized subshrubs with somewhat narrow leaves and a number of small yellowish or white flowers. Other endemic species of the genus, however, have adaptively radiated remarkably, ranging from sprawling or shrublike plants occupying new lava flows and lowland scrub areas, to forms with somewhat succulent water-retaining leaves living in the dry and inhospitable Alpine Scrub Zone (Figure 15.4). Some Hawaiian tarweeds of the Mesic Forest and Rain Forest Zones have attained arborescent proportions with heights of 3 to 6 m (10 to 20 feet), but others with downcurved stems almost creep over the forest floors, and a broad-leafed species is even a vine. At least one *Dubautia* in the Rain Forest Zone has evolved pendant flowering heads, a characteristic shared with species of several other families in the zone and presumably of selective importance in preventing precipitation from flooding the flowers.

Kauaʻi Greenswords

The two Kauaʻi greenswords or *iliau* constitute the genus *Wilkesia,* and neither of these occurs off the island. Both differ noticeably from *Dubautia,* with *W. gymnoxiphium* possessing a single or a few slender woody stems up to 5 m (16.5 feet) high, topped by a rosette of long and narrow, green, short-haired leaves (Figure 15.4). *Wilkesia hobdyi* (sometimes known as the Dwarf *Iliau*) branches from near the base and grows to only about 0.7 m (2.3 feet), although the leaves on each branch are similarly arranged in an apical rosette. The greenswords also differ from the annually blooming perennial Hawaiian tarweeds of the genus *Dubautia* because several years of growth are required before they flower, and each individual branch bearing flowers dies after this single reproductive event.

Silverswords and Maui Greenswords

The three species of silverswords and one of the two Maui greenswords of the genus *Argyroxiphium* are even more morphologically divergent from their tarweed ancestor. These four species all initially grow as a single basal or relatively short-stemmed, cushion-shaped rosette of long, narrow, and usually thickened leaves (Figure 15.4). In the silverswords, the leaves are densely clothed with silvery hairs, which serve to protect the leaf bodies from the strong solar radiation of high elevations, as well as to reduce moisture loss through air movement over the leaf surface. The Hawaiian name *ʻāhinahina,* meaning very gray, alludes to the color produced by this dense pubescence. The leaves also contain a gelatinous substance that stores water; this moisture apparently is required to ultimately produce the magnificent columnar inflorescence.

Figure 15.4. Growth forms in the Silversword Alliance. *Top left,* Hawaiian Tarweed or *naʻenaʻe (Dubautia menziesii); top right,* Silversword or *ʻāhinahina (Argyroxiphium sandwicense); bottom left,* flowering natural hybrid between the two; *bottom right,* Kauaʻi Greensword or *iliau (Wilkesia gymnoxiphium). (Bottom left* photograph by Kenneth M. Nagata, remainder by Gerald D. Carr; all used with permission.)

This flower stalk is up to 2.25 m (7.4 feet) tall in one species and bears up to five hundred separate flower heads (Plate 15.1); like that of one Maui greensword, it develops only after several years of growth and the entire plant dies after flower production.

As a botanist would predict from their leaf characteristics, two of the three silversword taxa are desertlike-ecosystem plants, growing primarily in intense sunlight and dry conditions of the higher Alpine Scrub Zone of Maui's Haleakalā and the two higher volcanoes on Hawai'i Island. In this adaptation, they are morphologically and physiologically convergent with a number of plants of the same and other families that have successfully colonized arid alpine habitats throughout the world's Tropics and subtropics (Figure 10.5). The third silversword species *(Argyroxiphium caliginis)* is, quite surprisingly, found only in an extremely wet habitat: that of the 'Eke and Pu'u Kukui bogs of West Maui, at the lowest moisture-laden level of the inversion layer (see chapter 7). Although notably modified in some respects from the two "typical" silverswords, this Bog Ecosystem species seems to have evolved from the Alpine Scrub Zone silversword on the eastern end of Maui. It may be that the acid water of bogs causes osmotic water loss to plants growing there, so the putative dry-area alpine ancestor of this bog silversword may have been preadapted to this new habitat in terms of water conservation.

Alliance Hybridization

Natural cross-fertilization with successful production of hybrids is an exceptionally common phenomenon among species of the three Silversword Alliance genera, as well as within two of the genera. No intrageneric *Wilkesia* hybrids have been found in the wild, but a total of more than thirty crosses between species within *Dubautia* and *Argyroxiphium* have been identified in nature, as well as ten between members representing all three genera (Figure 15.4). An additional thirty-eight hybrids within genera, including *Wilkesia,* and nineteen more between such groups have been produced artificially. This facile ability to hybridize is obviously due to the failure by members of the complex to develop effective reproductive isolating mechanisms. This failure, in turn, is probably the result of two interacting evolutionary phenomena. First, the entire Silversword Alliance has only relatively recently evolved from a common founding ancestor and, thus, has not yet had time enough to become especially diverse genetically. Second, constantly changing characteristics of the Hawaiian environment (the sudden appearance of a new local habitat in the form of a lava flow through a climax forest ecosystem, for example) has placed a survival premium on the ability of the group to quickly produce new forms—that is, hybrids—capable of exploiting such novel ecological situations.

SUGGESTED REFERENCES

Baldwin and Robichaux 1995; Carlquist 1974, 1980; Carr 1985, 1987; Givnish et al. 1994, 1995; James and Burney 1997; Lammers 1990; Sohmer and Gustafson 1987; Wagner and Funk (eds.) 1995; Wagner et al. 1999.

AUDIOVISUAL AIDS

The adaptive radiation of the silversword alliance; In the middle of the sea; Islands within islands within islands; Species and evolution; Succession on lava.

16

Terrestrial Arthropods

Insects constitute the vast majority of invertebrate species worldwide. Because of their great individual numbers they are the most important to humans in ecological and economic terms, so this chapter's discussion is devoted largely to them.

CLASSIFICATION

Invertebrates are divided among several phyla, the five best-known ones with terrestrial members being the three containing generally wormlike animals, comprising the flatworms (phylum Platyhelminthes), roundworms (Aschelminthes), and segmented worms (Annelida), as well as the molluscs (Mollusca; see chapters 11, 18) and the joint-limbed invertebrates (Arthropoda). The phylum **Arthropoda** contains more species than in all other phyla combined and is usually divided into twelve classes. Seven of these are either extinct, entirely marine, or possess very few species. Of the remaining five classes, **Crustacea** are primarily marine and freshwater, although there are a few terrestrial exceptions, including sandhoppers and sowbugs of the orders Amphipoda and Isopoda, respectively. Only the other four arthropod classes are considered here: the insects **(Insecta)** and, to a much more limited extent, the spiders, mites, scorpions, and allies **(Arachnida)**; as well as centipedes **(Chilopoda)** and millipedes **(Diplopoda)**.

GEOGRAPHIC SOURCE AND DISPERSAL

Approximately 95 percent of Hawaiian terrestrial arthropod founders apparently originated in the Indo-West Pacific or nearby Asian region, rather than in the Americas. A small percentage of the successful colonizers, especially shoreline species as well as most chilopods and diplopods, very likely reached the archipelago on ocean-borne debris. Certain other smaller terrestrial arthropods may have survived transport on the frigid jet stream (see chapter 13), but probably the majority of all arthropods were carried on warmer lower-elevation air currents. Among arachnids, most spiders doubtless came by "hang gliding" or "ballooning" on wind-borne web material, and parasitic mites, ticks, and insects came primarily with their bird hosts. A few larger founding insect species—less than fifty—may well have actively flown to the Islands.

BIOTIC DISHARMONY

The class Insecta is a phenomenally successful group worldwide in terms of evolutionary diversification, estimated to comprise between 10 and 30 million species, of which probably only about 10 percent have been formally described. Taxonomic disharmony (see chapter 10) in Hawai'i is quite apparent in this class, with only about half of the approximately three dozen world insect orders occurring naturally in the Islands. And the 140 or so families represented by native Hawaiian species make up only about 15 percent of the earth's family total. A few orders or families of insects generally numerous or conspicuous on continents are absent from the *native* fauna, perhaps most noticeably the cockroaches (order Blattaria), termites (Isoptera), preying mantises (Mantodea), and mayflies (Ephemeroptera). And there is only one native flea (Siphonaptera). Scarab beetles (family Scarabaeidae, order Coleoptera), swallowtail butterflies (Papilionidae, Lepidoptera), horse flies (Tabanidae, Diptera), as well as bumblebees and ants (Apidae and Formicidae, Hymenoptera), are also missing. The ease with which many of these types of insects and other arthropods have spread through the Hawaiian Islands after historic introduction indicates that this taxonomic disharmony is due simply to the failure of natural colonizers of each group to reach the archipelago, rather than to lack of suitable conditions for establishment.

BIOTIC COMPOSITION

In the Hawaiian Archipelago there are 7,982 insect species (all terrestrial except for about 50 marine forms) recorded to date, of which at least 5,293 (66 percent) are endemic, 84 (1 percent) indigenous, and 2,592 (33 percent) alien, with the relatively insignificant number of 13 species being of uncertain status. Among the native insect species, over 98 percent are endemic (Table 13.1). (These and the following species counts may well eventually be almost doubled when the Island arthropod fauna is fully investigated.) Among the 792 arachnids (all terrestrial except for about 19 marine mites), a minimum of 260 (33 percent) is endemic, 12 (2 percent)

Table 16.1. The ten Hawaiian insect orders containing the most native species. The two equivalent orders of arachnids, as well as the classes of chilopods and diplopods, are also listed, and numbers of alien species for all groups are included. In parentheses are the percentages that endemic and indigenous species represent in each group's native component. (Data from Gordon M. Nishida [ed.] [1997] and personal communication, November 1999.)

Class (and Order)	Total	Endemic	Indigenous	Alien	Status?
Insects (Insecta)					
Beetles (Coleoptera)	1,983	1,367 (99%)	11 (1%)	602	3
True flies (Diptera)	1,449	1,060 (99%)	12 (1%)	377	0
Moths and butterflies (Lepidoptera)	1,148	957 (100%)	—	191	0
Wasps, bees, and ants (Hymenoptera)	1,270	652 (100%)	—	609	9
Plant- and leafhoppers (Homoptera)	695	386 (100%)	—	309	0
True bugs (Heteroptera)	408	304 (99%)	2 (1%)	102	0
Grasshoppers and crickets (Orthoptera)	287	259 (99%)	1 (1%)	27	0
Springtails (Collembola)	169	95 (100%)	—	73	1
Barklice (Psocoptera)	134	89 (97%)	3 (3%)	42	0
Chewing lice (Mallophaga)	109	5 (9%)	52 (91%)	52	0
Spiders and Allies (Arachnida)					
Mites and ticks (Acari)	572	122 (91%)	12 (9%)	388	50
Spiders (Araneae)	205	126 (100%)	—	77	2
Centipedes (Chilopoda)	24	12 (100%)	—	12	0
Millipedes (Diplopoda)	28	16 (100%)	—	12	0

indigenous, and 468 (59 percent) alien, with 52 (6 percent) of uncertain status. Endemics thus form close to 96 percent of the native arachnid complement. Table 16.1 lists the orders of Insecta and Arachnida best represented in the native Hawaiian fauna. There are twenty-four recorded chilopods: twelve (50 percent) endemic, none indigenous, and twelve (50 percent) alien. Of the twenty-eight diplopods, sixteen (57 percent) are endemic, none indigenous, and twelve (43 percent) alien. The chilopod and diplopod assemblages before human arrival were thus 100 percent endemic.

SPECIATION

Particular native insect genera have speciated explosively in Hawai'i, and the ten of these yielding the highest numbers of endemic species are listed in Table 16.2. The 492 Hawaiian pomace fly species so far named in the two listed genera of the family Drosophilidae (discussed further in chapter 17), along with probably 200 or so still-unnamed endemic species, represent over one-fourth of the world's drosophilids. It is not known for certain why these and a few other insect genera speciated so exceptionally in the Hawaiian Islands. The multitude of ecological niches (see chapter 9) available because of taxonomic disharmony and species attenuation undoubtedly partially explains the proliferation of species from some founding types, as does also the fact that an archipelago provides more opportunities for extreme speciation than does a continental land mass (see chapter 10). These cannot be the only reasons, however, because neither satisfactorily explains the truly extraordinary instances of species proliferation as that in, for example, the two drosophilid genera. On the other hand, a few native insects have undergone little or no speciation even though each has colonized several of the main islands. It is unknown why this is so, but in many cases it may well be because additional individuals of these species are able to reinvade one island from another often enough to prevent full speciation on each.

Table 16.2. The ten Hawaiian insect genera containing the most endemic species. The family and order of each are also listed. Figures with a + symbol designate possible numbers of undescribed species. (Data primarily from Gordon M. Nishida, personal communication, April 1999.)

Genus	Family and Order	Endemic Species
Drosophila (including Idiomyia)	Pomace flies (Drosophilidae, Diptera)	356 (+100)
Hyposmocoma	Cosmopterigid moths (Cosmopterigidae, Lepidoptera)	350 (+100)
Scaptomyza (including Celidosoma, Grimshawomyia, and Titanochaeta)	Pomace flies (Drosophilidae, Diptera)	136 (+100)
Sierola	Bethylid wasps (Bethylidae, Hymenoptera)	180
Proterhinus	Primitive weevils (Aglycyderidae, Coleoptera)	177
Plagithmysus	Long-horned beetles (Cerambycidae, Coleoptera)	139
Campsicnemus	Long-legged flies (Dolichopodidae, Diptera)	136
Trigonidium	Crickets (Gryllidae, Orthoptera)	130
Lispocephala	House flies (Muscidae, Diptera)	102
Odynerus	Potter wasps (Vespidae, Hymenoptera)	99

FOUNDER EFFECT AND GENETIC DRIFT

Founder effect and genetic drift are difficult to demonstrate convincingly among native insects (although the picture-winged flies discussed in chapter 17 are a notable exception). Because of the short generation times of almost all insects and their usual large numbers of young, as well as accompanying high mortality rates through severe natural selection, initial founding populations are potentially able to speciate rapidly. Thus, the course of putative morphological and other changes from ancestor through descendant lines is usually obscure, especially if the ancestor is not surely known. And the ecology of a majority of endemic insects is so little known that it is often not possible to determine whether character differences within or among species are related to various selective advantages or to random genetic drift (see chapter 10). A few examples of insects exhibiting such still-unexplained changes are given here.

The strong-flying Koa Bug (*Coleotichus blackburniae* [shield-backed bug family Scutelleridae; order Heteroptera]) occurs on all main islands. The basic dorsal coloration is green, but a great variety of admixtures of red or blue are found on various islands and even on the same island. Somewhat the same situation is found in two lepidopterans: one of the two endemic butterflies, along with at least one species of an endemic moth genus. The former is the Kamehameha Butterfly or *pulelehua* (*Vanessa tameamea* [brush-footed butterfly family Nymphalidae; order Lepidoptera]), showing essentially the same dorsal wing coloration on all main islands, but with the underwing color pattern varying greatly among islands. (Incidentally, the second endemic butterfly is the small and relatively inconspicuous Blackburn Butterfly [*Udara blackburni* (blue butterfly family Lycaenidae)], which shows no appreciable geographic variation.) The moth is *Eupithecia craterias* (inchworm family Geometridae; order Lepidoptera), of Molokaʻi, Maui, and Hawaiʻi, with both adults and ambush-predator larvae (see discussion later in this chapter) showing inter- and intraisland color variation.

ADAPTIVE SHIFTS

The different changes in way of life undergone by endemic insects are multitudinous; only some of the more extreme can be described in this section, with further examples provided in the two discussions dealing with the High-Altitude Aeolian and Lava Tube Ecosystem faunas later in this chapter. Many insects of evolving Hawaiian lineages probably selectively acquired these changes as they moved into niches filled on continents by close relatives or insects of different taxonomic groups missing from the attenuated and disharmonic Hawaiian fauna.

Flightlessness

Most insects colonizing the Hawaiian Islands, like those of the world in general, were flighted, but loss of volancy subsequently occurred within all of the ten orders of winged insects colonizing the archipelago naturally except for the dragonflies and damselflies (Odonata). There are endemic nonvolant katydids and crickets (order Orthoptera), barklice (Psocoptera), thrips (Thysanoptera), true bugs (Heteroptera), planthoppers (Homoptera), lacewings (Neuroptera), at least four species of moths (Lepidoptera), various species within eight families of beetles (Coleoptera), smaller wasps (Hymenoptera) of several families, and even a few true flies (Diptera).

The Hawaiian brown lacewings (family Hemerobiidae) provide a good example of progressive changes in wing structure and flight ability. Some volant endemic species have retained the two pairs of normal large, flat, filmy ancestral wings, but a few other still-volant forms have developed irregularly shaped wings, especially those of the anterior pair, which may become somewhat cuplike. Some of the rest of the brown lacewings have reduced the hind wings so much that flight is no longer possible, and others have completely lost this pair. In these flight-less forms, the front wings have become somewhat reduced in size and also so variously thick-ened or heavily ridged that in several species they seem convergent with the protective elytra or greatly modified forewings of most beetles.

Habitat

Several endemic insect taxa have adaptively shifted from aquatic to terrestrial habitat; others have made the opposite transition. Immature forms or naiads (Latin *"naiadis"* [water nymphs]) of narrow-winged damselflies (Damselfly family Coenagrionidae) usually live on the bottoms of streams and ponds. The habitats of the young (*lohelohe* [Figure 16.1]) of Hawaiian damsel-flies of the genus *Megalagrion* range from the ancestral aquatic one, through exposed wet rocks beside streams, to the damp leaf axils of native wet-forest plants, and even to the forest leaf lit-ter. Similarly, certain endemic species of the genus *Saldula* (shore bug family Saldidae), a group usually living along continental stream margins, are found in leaf litter and trees in Hawai'i. On the other hand, within the same order, the endemic Gagnés' Damsel Bug, *Nabis gagneorum* (damsel bug family Nabidae), has abandoned the dry forest environment typical of many of its native relatives to seek prey along the wet edges of streams.

Diet

Elsewhere in the world all caterpillars ("inchworms") of small geometrid moths in the genus *Eupithecia* are herbivorous, eating leaves, flower parts, and pollen. In Hawai'i, however, an amazing adaptive shift to carnivory by the larvae of a number of species was made early in the adaptive radiation of the lineage, yielding a group of at least eighteen carnivorous taxa among the twenty-two or so endemic *Eupithecia*. The caterpillars of these carnivorous species perch motionless on leaves or twigs, being variously modified to match the different colors and tex-tures of these parts of their particular plant host. When an exploring fly or other small arthro-pod happens to touch specialized posterior sensory hairs, the predator whips its anterior end toward the prey and seizes it with sturdy long-clawed forelimbs before devouring it (Figure 16.2). The immediate ancestor of this group was likely a geometrid species whose caterpillar ate concentrated protein-rich food such as pollen rather than bulky high-cellulose leaf material. The transition to digestion of animal protein would then probably not have required especially radical physiological modification.

Host

On continents, blow flies of the family Calliphoridae (order Diptera) lay eggs on the dead bod-ies of vertebrates, and the hatched larvae (maggots) subsist on this carrion. Undoubtedly, colo-nizing calliphorids originally utilized the carcasses of dead seabirds, primarily in coastal rook-eries, but in most other parts of Hawai'i before human arrival the usual egg-deposition sites were limited because of the virtual or complete absence of nonvolant terrestrial vertebrates. It is surprising, though, that there is an endemic Hawaiian calliphorid genus containing twenty-five species, as well as one endemic species of a primarily continental genus. Most of these spe-ciating Hawaiian taxa apparently were successful only because of the evolution of a new reproductive strategy. The female produces only a single egg, rather than numerous ones, and this is retained internally until it hatches into a larva that continues to develop almost to the stage of pupation. This advanced larva is then deposited in a protected site, including the shell cavities of living or dead land snails, animals that were once extremely plentiful in the Hawaiian Archipelago (see chapter 18). In fact, there is possible evidence that some of these endemic blow flies adaptively evolved a behavior in which they habitually remained near native land snail colonies.

OTHER EVOLUTIONARY PHENOMENA

Morphology

One of the most unusual structural developments involves the endemic planthopper genus *Dictyophorodelphax* (family Delphacidae). In these small plant-sap feeders, the elongated head equals the remaining body in length and houses a long loop of the alimentary system (Figure 16.3). The hosts are Hawaiian spurges or *'akoko* (*Chamaesyce* spp.), and because these and

Figure 16.1. Naiad of the endemic Hawaiian narrow-winged damselfly *Megalagrion koelense*. This immature form or *lohelohe* has adaptively shifted from the ancestral stream-bottom habitat to one of damp leaf axils of wet-forest plants. The animal shown is approximately 1.5 cm (0.6 inches) long. (Photograph by William P. Mull, used with permission.)

Figure 16.2. Caterpillar of the endemic Hawaiian geometrid moth *Eupithecia staurophragma*. The predatory animal is holding a just-captured Hawaiian picture-winged fly *(Drosophila heteroneura)* in its enlarged and clawed forelimbs. The caterpillar is approximately 2.5 cm (1.0 inches) long. (Photograph by William P. Mull, used with permission.)

many other spurges worldwide possess latexlike and sometimes irritating or toxic sap (see chapter 15), the long cephalic gut extension may somehow be related to either rendering this food harmless or preparing it for digestion. Or perhaps the great amount of ingested sap in the extension may serve a protective function by rendering the species unpalatable to bird predators. Still another possibility is that the elongated head is protection against such predation because it makes the insect perched on a plant stem resemble a thorn or small twig.

Size

Gigantism is found in several endemic Hawaiian insects, most notably the largest main island species, the Giant Hawaiian Dragonfly (*Anax strenuus* [dragonfly family Aeshnidae]), with a 15-cm (6-inch) wingspan, and a 5-cm (2-inch) wood-boring beetle *(Megopis reflexa)*. No single explanation of the advantage of gigantism on islands, where it is most commonly encountered, is completely satisfactory or applicable in all cases. On continents, small size may be of selective advantage in hiding or escaping from predators, and lack of these types of enemies (especially certain families of birds) in disharmonic island faunas could have allowed some species of immigrant lineages to become larger. Or perhaps the lack of related insects with similar diets due to species attenuation resulted in a greater availability of food (or an increased size range of prey in carnivorous types) that, in turn, allowed this larger and metabolically costlier body size.

Figure 16.3. The endemic Hawaiian planthopper *Dictyophorodelphax mirabilis*. The enormously lengthened head contains an extension of the alimentary system, which is still of undetermined function. The animal is 0.8 cm (0.32 inches) long. (Photograph by William P. Mull, used with permission.)

"Happyface Spider"

No discussion of endemic Hawaiian arthropods would be complete without a mention of the Happyface Spider (*Theridion grallator* [comb-footed spider family Theridiidae]), aptly designated because of the humorous (to humans, at least) facelike markings of red, black, and white on the dorsal surface of the pale yellow abdomen (Plate 16.1). Apparently, these peculiar markings serve as disruptive coloration to help conceal the animal from predatory birds in its typical daytime resting location on the underside of leaves. As noticeable in the plate, there is a great deal of variation in this patterning among various populations, and about 15–20 percent of the individuals in certain populations may be unmarked. That is, the species is **polymorphic** in terms of the particular type of abdominal markings present and **dimorphic** in regard to presence or absence of a patterned abdomen.

It is possible, however, that the percentages of marked and unmarked spiders in a population may be continually altered by predation. When marked individuals constitute a majority of a population, birds would learn to recognize the patterned animal as a food item and take more of them than of the unpatterned ones, allowing the latter to increase in numbers. Then, by the time the patterned individuals had become relatively scarce, birds would have gradually become conditioned to perceiving primarily the unmarked individuals as prey; when these had again become scarce, the cycle would repeat. Presumably, the species possesses some sort of genetic mechanism that results in retention of this pattern dimorphism, which has evolved because of its survival value to the species.

HIGH-ALTITUDE AEOLIAN FAUNA

The environmental and general ecological characteristics of the High-Altitude Aeolian Ecosystem were presented in chapter 14, so primarily only its fauna will be examined here.

Especially notable among the dozen and a half endemic invertebrates thus far known to be adapted to this essentially unvegetated mountain-summit ecosystem is, on Maui's Haleakalā, a flightless moth (*Thyrocopa apatela* [family Oecophoridae]). Its caterpillars survive on drifting dead leaves caught in their webs spun in rock crevices; many of the adults inhabiting this alpine zone have apparently reached such suitable egg-deposition sites by themselves being blown helplessly across the substrate. There are also one or more High-Altitude Aeolian spiders that may either take over the caterpillar's web or spin their own to entrap insects wind-carried from lower elevations.

First found at Mauna Kea's summit cinder cone of Pu'u Wēkiu on Hawai'i is the Mauna Kea Wēkiu Bug (*Nysius wekiuicola* [seed bug family Lygaeidae; order Heteroptera]). A similar species, the Mauna Loa Wēkiu Bug *(N. aa)*, was subsequently found living at the summit of the large neighboring volcano. These extremely specialized insects of this alpine ecosystem have not only lost the power of flight but have also undergone a dietary shift from the vegetable-sap food of their lower-elevation relatives. They subsist on body fluids obtained from cold-numbed moribund or dead arthropods searched out on the ground. In addition, a physiological shift has resulted in development of a substance in the blood of the species that prevents freezing in the usual low temperatures at this great elevation. In fact, this particular adaptation to the cold is so extreme that wēkiu bugs can be killed by the heat of a human hand holding them. There is also a miniature chilopod peculiar to the High-Altitude Aeolian Ecosystem: a black rock centipede (undescribed species [family Lithobiidae]), only 1 cm (0.4 inches) long, that may be found seeking prey among the substrate cinders.

LAVA TUBE FAUNA

Significance

The general characteristics of the Lava Tube Ecosystem, like those of the preceding one, were described in chapter 14. An amazing array of endemic arthropods has been found in Hawaiian lava tubes. Because it is almost certain that no subterranean forms were among the animals colonizing the Hawaiian Islands, these species all necessarily had to have evolved from surface relatives within the archipelago and in a geologically very short time. On Hawai'i Island, for example, it is obvious that this period could have been no more than a few hundred thousand years, the maximum time that presumably inhabitable lava tubes have existed there. This underground fauna has thus shown that the conventional notion that cave-adapted animals always represent relict forms, taking many millions of years to evolve after extinction of their surface ancestors, obviously does not hold true for, at least, Hawaiian subterranean taxa.

Troglobites

Animals completely adapted to life in subterranean passages are termed **troglobites** (Greek *"trogle"* [hole] and *"biote"* [a living]) or obligate cavernicoles. Of the approximately two hundred invertebrate species known to be members of the Hawaiian Lava Tube Ecosystem as of 1999, seventy-five are fully adapted to such an existence. Each of these latter taxa is restricted to a single island or even the tube system of a single lava flow. Although the Hawaiian troglobites can disperse at least limited distances between suitable habitats through crevices and other spaces in the surrounding basalt, as previously noted in chapter 14 the troglobites on one Hawaiian Island or isolated lava-tube system on an island would have no chance of reaching other islands or lava tubes. Thus, those of each island evolved there and will become extinct when all lava tubes of the island are finally lost (see chapter 5).

Adaptive Shifts

An excellent example of a progressive transition from a surface existence to one in a lava tube is apparently provided by the endemic rock cricket genus *Caconemobius* (family Gryllidae). The Hawaiian Beach Cricket *(C. sandwichiensis)* is found scavenging on wave-splashed boulders of all main island coasts and is quite similar to its presumably ocean-borne ancestor. Probably derived from it is a type adapted to relatively new unvegetated lava flows stretching inland from the shore, such as the Lava Flow Cricket *(C. fori)* of Hawai'i Island, which emerges only at night from the moistness of deep lava cracks to feed on wind-carried surface plant debris. Then, from this near-surface type evidently evolved a species found in the dark, wet zones of lava tubes, for example, Hawai'i Island's Lava Tube Cricket *(C. varius)* with small eyes and noticeably reduced body pigmentation. Presumably, this same suite of three ecological types has independently evolved on each newly formed Hawaiian Island, with one or both of the two inland kinds of cricket being lost on the island as lava flows became vegetated and lava tubes disappeared.

Morphological Changes

A number of other types of Hawaiian insects, spiders, centipedes, and millipedes derived from surface-dwelling ancestors have also successfully adapted to life in the darker regions of lava tubes, usually becoming flightless, blind, and/or pale-colored in the process. As might be expected, this has produced a number of cases of parallel evolution as different ancestral species evolved to fill the same ecological niche in separate lava-tube systems. Predatory species include the Howarth Earwig (*Anisolabis howarthi* [family Carcinophoridae; order Dermaptera]), three species of ground beetles (*Atelothrus aaae, A. howarthi,* and an undescribed species of the genus *Tachys* [family Carabidae]), as well as an unnamed cave rock centipede of the genus *Lithobius.* One of the most unusually modified predators is the Lava Tube Thread-legged Bug (*Nesidiolestes ana* [family Reduviidae]), whose two hind pairs of exceptionally elongated thin legs serve a function somewhat analogous to that of a spider's web. The blind insect spans cracks or roots with widespread hind limbs as it waits in ambush to seize prey with its pair of mantislike forelegs.

Wolf or big-eyed hunting spiders of the family Lycosidae are typically sharp-eyed active nonweb predators of surface arthropods, but adaptation of one species to subterranean life on Hawai'i has so reduced its vision that the animal is known as the Small-eyed Big-eyed Hunting Spider *(Lycosa howarthi).* An even more extreme development of this phenomenon in a lycosid known from only three small remnant tubes of a Kaua'i lava flow has yielded *Adelocosa anops,* the No-eyed Big-eyed Hunting Spider. (It seems possible that at least this latter species has evolved the ability to locate prey by sound, using some sort of specialized organs in the anteriormost pair of legs, but this possibility has yet to be proven.)

Among Hawaiian troglobites that feed primarily on roots or whatever other vegetable material they occasionally find are at least eight blind cave planthoppers (*Oliarus* spp. [family Cixiidae]) and the undescribed Hawai'i cave moth (*Schrankia* sp. [family Noctuidae]), the female of which is flightless. Blind and essentially unpigmented cave springtails (order Collembola) and similarly sightless and light-colored cave millipedes (*Nannolene* spp. [family Cambalidae]) survive on a diet of subterranean fungi. And, occupying a different ecological niche, the blind Lava-tube Water Treader (*Cavaticovelia aaa* [family Mesoveliidae; order Heteroptera]) has forsaken its ancestral aquatic-surface existence for one on lava-tube floors, where it scavenges for dead invertebrates.

Facultative Cavernicoles

Not only the obligate cavernicoles but an even larger number of other native invertebrates—and even alien vertebrates—also utilize different resources of lava tubes during at least part of their daily or life cycle. No alien species can utilize the Lava Tube Ecosystem as efficiently as subterranean-adapted native ones, but some such animals are at least occasionally seen in this habitat. These aliens, which prey on, and/or compete for food with, the native species include several taxa of cockroaches (family Blattidae) and, among vertebrates, the Roof Rat or *'iole nui (Rattus rattus).*

ALIEN TERRESTRIAL ARTHROPODS

There are occurrence records of at least 3,993 alien insect species and about 524 other nonmarine arthropods for the Hawaiian Islands, although, as a rough estimate, probably only about two-thirds of this number have established permanent populations. A majority of these aliens arrived inadvertently as a result of (primarily historic) human activities. Many of the inadvertent introductions have resulted in great economic loss (as in the case of termites and cockroaches) and biological harm (some ants and wasps) in Hawai'i, as is mentioned again in chapter 26. From 1890 to 1999, 649 of the alien arthropod species (mostly insects) were purposely imported and released in attempts to biologically control noxious alien plants and a few damaging exotic insects or to pollinate commercial plants. Only about 420 of these biocontrol or pollinating agents established successfully, however. A number of them have exerted at least some measure of control on the target hosts, although a few have additionally proved damaging to native species.

SUGGESTED REFERENCES

Carlquist 1974, 1980; Eldredge and Miller 1995; Howarth 1987, 1990; Howarth and Mull 1992; Miller and Eldredge 1996; Montgomery 1983; Mull 1975; Nishida (ed.) 1997; Yamamoto and Tagawa 2000; Zimmerman 1948, 1970.

AUDIOVISUAL AIDS

Hawaii: A mountain community; Hawaii: Born of fire; Hawaii: Crucible of life; Hawaii: Strangers in paradise; Islands within islands within islands.

Picture-Winged Flies

The nearly cosmopolitan Common Pomace Fly (*Drosophila melanogaster* [pomace fly family Drosophilidae, order Diptera]) has been used since 1910 as an experimental animal in genetics. Housing and rearing large numbers of such a small, quickly reproducing organism is simple, and chromosomal genetic composition easily examined (see discussion later in this chapter).

HAWAIIAN *DROSOPHILA*

Apparently only one or, at most, two colonizing continental species of this family yielded all native Hawaiian drosophilids, comprising 492 endemic species described to date, with perhaps 300 more still unnamed. As detailed in Table 17.1, the named endemic species and the thirty alien ones in Hawai'i are distributed among seven genera: five minor ones with a total of less than a dozen species and the two major groups *Drosophila* and *Scaptomyza*. *Drosophila* is the most speciose native Hawaiian insect genus (Table 16.2), and its 356 endemic Island species described so far represent over a tenth of the world's complement of this genus.

Within the Hawaiian Evolutionary Biology Program of the University of Hawai'i at Mānoa in Honolulu there is a Hawaiian Drosophila Research Project devoted solely to study of endemic *Drosophila*. Probably the most interesting and valuable of all the scientific information these Hawaiian flies have provided involves the relationship of mating behavior to speciation. Especially well studied have been a group of at least 106 generally large species informally termed

Table 17.1. Genera and species numbers of Hawaiian pomace flies (family Drosophilidae). The one hundred or so picture-winged species are all members of the genus *Drosophila*. An additional number of species of, especially, the larger two genera are still awaiting formal description. (Data from various sources.)

Genus	Total	Endemic	Indigenous	Alien
Cacoxenus	1	—	—	1
Chymomyza	1	—	—	1
Dettopsomyia	2	—	—	2
Drosophila (including *Idiomyia*)	373	356	—	17
Leucophenga	1	—	—	1
Pseudiastata	4	—	—	4
Scaptomyza (including Celidosoma, Grimshawomyia, and *Titanochaeta*)	140	136	—	4
Total	522	492	—	30

"picture-winged flies" in reference to the varied patterns of black markings appearing on the usually clear wing panels (Plate 17.1). Most picture-winged species are endemic to a single Hawaiian island.

PHYLOGENY

Chromosomal Inversions

A method used extensively for determining **phylogeny** or evolutionary interrelationships among the numerous picture-winged species should be mentioned. Certain cells, especially in the salivary glands of larvae, cease dividing at a certain stage and grow in size. At an advanced larval stage, five of the six pairs of chromosomes in the salivary gland cells are extremely large and readily visible microscopically when stained. Each chromosome shows along its length a series of a hundred or more bands of differing darkness and thickness, probably consisting of genetic material (see chapter 10; Figure 17.1). Sections of a chromosome that occasionally break loose may rejoin the remaining chromosome portion, but in some cases only after rotating 180 degrees, resulting in so-called inversions. Inversions thus produce a distinctive difference from the original sequence of bands. The usual banding sequences of the endemic Hawaiian *Drosophila grimshawi* are arbitrarily taken as the "standard" with which to compare the banding order of other Island species to determine if an inversion has occurred.

There are over 225 inversions recorded among picture-winged flies. Because these take place at random locations along a chromosome, and exactly the same inversion is not likely to occur independently in another species, each such abnormality is considered originally unique to a particular species or, indeed, sometimes to only a single population of a species. Such a chromosome mutation is passed on to any daughter species or population, but such a derived group may undergo a second inversion at a different location on the chromosome, so that both

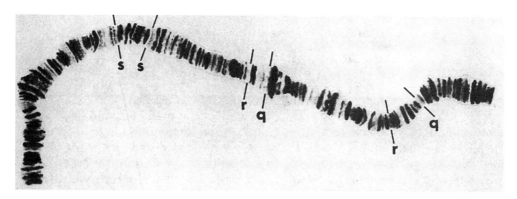

Figure 17.1. Stained chromosome of a Hawaiian picture-winged fly (*Drosophila* sp.). The varied dark bands represent genetic material, and the endpoints of three banded chromosomal segments that are commonly found inverted or reversed are indicated by the paired letters q, r, and s. Over 225 different inversions have been recorded in the Hawaiian picture-winged flies and are used in tracing phylogenetic relationships. (Adapted from Fig. 2 of Carson [1987a]; copyright 1987, Elsevier Science, used with permission of Hampton L. Carson and Elsevier Science.)

band-sequence aberrations then appear in any of its own descendant populations. Thus, through chromosome examination, the phylogeny of the youngest of the three species in the foregoing sequence can be traced back through its parental and grandparental species. Even more extensive evolutionary lineages can similarly be determined for any further derived species in which additional inversions have occurred.

The original drosophilid colonists apparently arrived in the Hawaiian Archipelago about 5 million years ago, when Kaua'i and the next two or three islands to the north were the only large landmasses in the chain. Thus, much of the subsequent dispersal of picture-winged flies and other Hawaiian *Drosophila* undoubtedly occurred from old to newly formed islands. (Particular sets of chromosomal inversion sequences have shown, however, that there has also been occasional backmigration of newly evolved species from younger to older islands.) By combining the chromosomal-inversion data for various drosophilid species with the foregoing assumption of the usual direction of interisland movement, a working phylogeny of the entire picture-winged complex has been developed. More recent work involving such biochemical characteristics as proteins and DNA components has allowed refinement of this phylogeny. When interpreted within the framework of Island geological dating, this phylogenetic sequence also provides a partial temporal scale for speciation in Hawaiian *Drosophila*.

SEXUAL SELECTION

Mating Behavior

The Hawaiian Drosophila Research Project has pioneered another approach to determining the phylogeny and dynamic change in species populations of picture-winged flies. The usual mating pattern of *Drosophila* species worldwide is for males and females to congregate at overripe fruit or similar feeding sites and mate in the immediate vicinity. In the picture-winged flies, however, most males establish territories within a mating arena or **lek** site (Swedish [mating ground]) rather than at a feeding locality. The male defends his territory and drives away other males and then engages in elaborate courtship behavior to induce visiting females into copulation. Females tend to be quite discriminating, however, usually not mating with males of another species and, within their own, often visiting a number of territories and rejecting several males before finally accepting one whose courtship activity and related morphology is evidently found satisfactory.

This mating behavior is quite similar to that of certain avian types (for example, the birds of paradise and bower birds of the Australian Region). Whenever this lek-type mating occurs, the rather unusual situation exists in which female selection of mates to perpetuate the population seems based almost entirely on the superior quality of a male's mating behavior, rather than on how well adapted the male may be to all of the other ecological and environmental demands on the species. It is quite possible, however, that this superiority is simply the result of a particular male's being exceptionally well adapted in Darwinian terms (see chapter 10) to all other such selective factors (and the successfully reproducing female must, of course, similarly have qualities allowing it to survive until at least this stage of the life cycle). At any rate, judging from the explosive speciation that has occurred among picture-winged flies and many other lek-utilizing animals, this particular mating-behavior pattern seems a quite successful evolutionary strategy for them, even though it is not characteristic of the majority of animal species.

Species Maintenance

As a specific illustration of this sexual-selection process and its apparent role in maintaining distinct species in picture-winged flies, the case of two among the twenty-six or so Hawai'i Island taxa is cited. *Drosophila silvestris* and *D. heteroneura* appear very closely related on the basis of chromosomal banding-inversion sequences as well as DNA and other molecular studies. The two are partially **sympatric** (occurring in the same geographic area) and are also extremely similar in microhabitat preference, often being found on the same individual plant. The females of both feed on and lay eggs in rotting bark of endemic *Clermontia* species (many known as 'ōhā wai [subfamily Lobelioideae; bellflower family Campanulaceae]) where the hatched larvae feed and grow before dropping off to pupate in the soil below. In fact, these two species are so closely related that hybrids are occasionally found, although possibly such hybridization occurs only when population size has greatly diminished or some other aspect of normal ecology of one or both has been disrupted, as in the event of a major habitat disturbance.

Interspecific Differences

Apparently, the sole factor allowing the two sympatric populations to maintain their separate specific identities is the marked difference in male sexual behavior, in concert with related female sexual preferences for both this behavior and associated male morphological characteristics.

Male *Drosophila silvestris* combat conspecific males to control a mating territory, using primarily a stiffly outstretched left wing and upright body encounters in the contest. Once a *D. silvestris* male has gained possession of a territory, it is visited by females visually or otherwise recognizing certain characteristics peculiar to males of their own species. The male effort to entice a female to mate first entails a frontal approach to her with wings extended noticeably far forward and body moving from side to side. If she does not then attack the male or vacate the territory, the male circles to her rear and, while constantly vibrating his wings in a particular fashion, places his folded forelegs bearing rows of bristles on top of the female's abdomen. The forelegs are then also vibrated, after which the female may permit copulation, although the male is often rejected even at this late stage in the mating ritual.

Males of the second species, *Drosophila heteroneura,* engage with conspecific males in an entirely different type of contest for a mating territory. In contrast to the normally proportioned head of *D. silvestris,* this species has a broad mallet-shaped one, which is used along with exaggerated wing waving in butting contests with other males to control the territory. After female recognition of the male as the same species, successful copulation involves only slight, but apparently crucial, variations of the male behavior described for *D. silvestris.* For example, the wings are not extended so far forward, and the body is not moved from side to side.

SPECIATION

Geographic Separation

The question is where and how did speciation of these two closely related *Drosophila* originally occur, and exactly what is the role of differences in the elaborate sexual behavior in this speciation. In a scenario that would *traditionally* be favored by most biologists, it would generally be assumed that the two picture-winged flies developed from the same ancestral species—or from phylogenetically very close ones—as two populations became **allopatric** (geographically separated). Such separation could have come about through, for instance, transport of insemi-nated females to different previously uninhabited portions of Hawai'i Island on a strong wind. Particular mutant morphological and physiological qualities of the two sets of founders would then be adaptively selected by differing ecological and environmental requirements of their respective habitats. This differentiation, along with possible genetic drift (see chapter 10), would ultimately raise each allopatric population to the approximate level of a full species.

Behavioral Changes

Subsequently, as one or both of these populations increased in numbers, their ranges might come to overlap. If some degree of successful interbreeding were still possible, there would then be a great selective advantage (to both populations) of mechanisms preventing such interbreed-ing, the latter of which would constitute "gamete wastage" (see chapter 15). Subsequently, com-plete reproductive isolation could be attained very efficiently through development of widely divergent mating-behavior patterns, as might easily come about through selective enhancement of particular sexually related random behavioral mutations already present in the formerly iso-lated groups. That is, within each of the two potential species, those males that exhibited the more extreme development of sexually related morphological and behavioral characteristics would be most favored for parenthood, along with those conspecific females most discrimina-tory in choosing to mate only with males possessing the extreme sexual differences.

The most important point in the foregoing *traditional* explanation of speciation is that the differences in mating behavior and related morphology—or at least the extreme development of them—in the two populations did not become fixed until *after* one or both of them had already proceeded well toward full speciation through the adaptive selection of various non-sexual mutations. Although this particular theorized sequence seems quite reasonable, it has not been completely without critics, some of whom point out that little actual work has been done to test it. An intriguing and scientifically very important finding of studies by the Hawaiian Drosophila Research Project is that, in cases involving intricate sexual encounters such as those of the picture-winged flies, the development of a unique mating-behavior pattern through sex-ual selection in an incipient species may *precede* most or all changes in nonsexual character-istics, as recounted below.

The Kaneshiro Hypothesis

After some years of work on various aspects of *Drosophila,* especially performance of a series of laboratory mate-preference experiments with closely related picture-winged flies, Kenneth Y. Kaneshiro of the project proposed a method by which mating behavior could initially deter-mine the path of evolution among members of the genus. The original **Kaneshiro Hypothesis** stated that when a species with a complicated mating ritual provides a small number of indi-viduals as stock for an incipient species, only a limited amount of the full range of parental male sexual behavior may be carried over to the daughter population.

Because of this founder effect (see chapter 10), derived males displaying the precise mat-ing behavior that was optimal in the parental species will be scarce, and natural selection will tend to favor those derived females that accept a less than optimal version of this routine. In fact, females of a newly derived population that are as discriminating as the average breeding female of the parental one are quite likely not to produce any young because they cannot easily find a male who satisfies their strict mating-behavior requirements.

Reconsideration of the hypothesis during a quarter century of subsequent research involving *Drosophila* population genetics, however, has led to the conclusion that, even in the case of a founding event entailing very few individuals, most of the variety of genetically controlled mating behavior of the parental population will probably still be represented among them. But, again, due to the small number of males available in this daughter population, there is still favorable selection for reproduction by less-discriminating females. Thus, the average inherited preference shown by females in the daughter population will, as the hypothesis originally predicted, quickly become considerably less discriminatory in terms of acceptable male sexual behavior. (As the period of geographic isolation of the derived group increases beyond the time period considered here, however, the group will undoubtedly develop its own unique variation of optimal male courtship routine and attendant characteristics, with its females progressively showing less and less preference for those most favorable in the parental population.)

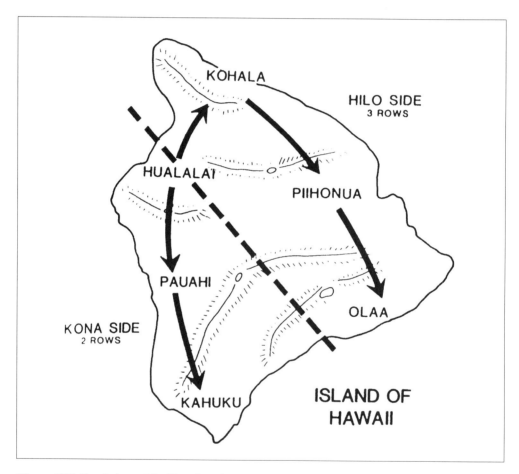

Figure 17.2. Populations of the Hawaiian picture-winged fly *Drosophila silvestris*. The dashed line separates "Kona-side" and "Hilo-side" groups. Arrows indicate initially suggested directions of dispersal and sequence of establishment of the five groups derived from the putative founding Hualālai population. As explained in the text, the first dispersal to the Hilo side could conceivably have been to Pi'ihonua instead of Kohala. (Fig. 2 of Carson [1983], as modified from Fig. 1 of Kaneshiro and Kurihara [1981]; copyright 1983, Kluwer Academic Publishers, used with permission.)

The hypothesis thus goes on to propose that there will be an observable difference or asymmetry in the degree of sexual discrimination shown by ancestral females as opposed to derived ones. That is, given a mating choice between parental- and daughter-population males, females of the parent population will largely (but not completely) spurn the inferior courtship routine of most males of the daughter population and mate primarily with parental-population males. Daughter-population females, on the other hand, will accept parental-population males at least as readily as those of their own population. This part of the hypothesis logically extends to inclusion of additional descendant populations or species in an evolving lineage. It would then be anticipated in a series of such progressively younger descendant groups that the females of the oldest will show a decreasing inclination to mate with males of groups increasingly further derived from this ancestral one.

DROSOPHILA SILVESTRIS STUDY

In addition to demonstrating evolutionary relationships among several populations or species of a lineage, the Kaneshiro Hypothesis can also help elucidate the temporal sequence in which different geographic populations of a dispersing species were established, as explained by the following study.

Populations

Drosophila silvestris occurs only on Hawai'i, represented by populations in six isolated areas, as shown in Figure 17.2. Hualālai, Pauahi, and Kahuku are referred to as the "Kona-side" group; and Kohala, Pi'ihonua, and 'Ōla'a the "Hilo-side" one. There seem to be no significant differences in the ecology or nonsexual characteristics of the two groups. In fact, even differences in secondary sexual body characteristics are slight: Kona-side males have two rows of bristles along the tibial segment of the forelegs used in courtship behavior, and Hilo-side males have a third row of various completeness between these two. On the basis of this characteristic, the collective Kona-side populations of *D. silvestris* seem obviously descended from a Maui species possessing the same two bristle rows, and the Hilo-side populations are presumed derived from one of the Kona-side groups, developing the extra bristle row after the separation.

It is not determinable from any nonbehavioral characteristics which of the three Kona-side populations is the oldest, or which of them provided the founder of the Hilo-side complement. To answer these questions, laboratory mate-preference experiments based on tenets of the Kaneshiro Hypothesis were performed. Among the three Kona-side groups, Hualālai females tended to reject both Pauahi and Kahuku males, but both Pauahi and Kahuku females readily accepted Hualālai males, indicating that the Pauahi and Kahuku populations were derived from the Hualālai one. Comparison of these two derived populations showed that Pauahi females largely rejected Kahuku males but Kahuku females accepted Pauahi males, so the Kahuku population was considered derived from the Pauahi group. Thus, on the basis of these studies, the Hualālai group seems to be the oldest Kona-side population and, if so, would presumably represent the island's founding population of *Drosophila silvestris*. Also, the fact that the Pauahi and Kahuku populations occupy very recent Mauna Loa lava flows, much younger than almost all of the Hualālai ones, increases the possibility that they are the derived Kona-side groups.

To substantiate the initial premise based on number of tibial bristle rows that the three-rowed (Hilo-side) group had been derived from the two-rowed (Kona-side) one, it was necessary to show that the oldest Hilo-side population was younger than at least one of the three Kona-side populations. Experimental mate-preference procedures previously carried out among a limited number of individuals from the three Hilo-side populations had suggested that Kohala was the oldest and ʻŌlaʻa the youngest. Consequently, the same type of experiments were performed using Kohala and Kona-side Hualālai individuals. These indicated that Hualālai females tended to reject Kohala males, but Kohala females readily accepted Hualālai males, thus confirming that the Kohala population was younger.

It might be of interest to note that subsequent—and still ongoing—research has suggested to some investigators the need for a slight revision of relative ages among the three Hilo-side populations. Primarily, the Piʻihonua group has been found much more variable in mating behavior, morphology, and genetics than previously realized, being quite similar to the Kohala one in many of these characteristics. Thus, it, rather than the Kohala population, may represent the original Hilo-side immigrant. Further mate-preference experiments or other future investigations will probably be needed to elucidate this possibility.

In spite of their ongoing nature and the sometimes conflicting interpretation of results when combined with other research data, these mate-preference laboratory experiments on Hawaiian *Drosophila* utilizing the Kaneshiro Hypothesis have already convincingly demonstrated the value of the procedure. It should prove of at least equal worth in obtaining the same type of phylogenetic information on certain other animal groups exhibiting similarly complicated mating behavior.

SUGGESTED REFERENCES

Carson 1983, 1987a, 1997; DeSalle 1995; Giddings and Templeton 1983; Kaneshiro 1976, 1988; Kaneshiro and Kurihara 1981; Kaneshiro et al. 1995; Montgomery 1975; Spieth 1984.

AUDIOVISUAL AIDS

Ecology; Genetics and populations; Hawaii: Crucible of life; The picture wings of Hawaii.

Nonmarine Snails

Within the phylum Mollusca, all nonmarine snails of the world (comprising both land and freshwater species) are included in the class Gastropoda (see chapter 11). Just as in the case of marine mollusks, worldwide there are far fewer nonmarine species of bivalves than of gastropods. All nonmarine bivalves are freshwater forms, but none is native to Hawai'i, and the three alien species have already been noted in chapter 14. Land and freshwater snails began evolving from marine ancestors well over 250 million years ago, and the marine respiratory gill was replaced by a "lung" in the form of a highly vascularized internal body cavity, which allowed oxygen to be absorbed directly from the air. Once evolved, the shell morphology of many nonmarine snails tended to be quite conservative; 200-million-year-old fossil shells from continents are practically indistinguishable from those of living members of the family Achatinellidae of the Pacific Basin.

CLASSIFICATION

Of the several gastropod subclasses worldwide, only two contain land and freshwater species. The **Prosobranchia** (possibly an artificial group encompassing unrelated taxa), commonly called operculates, still maintain the marine ancestor's keratinous or calcareous **operculum** used to seal the shell aperture. Operculates are represented in Hawai'i by only the land families Helicinidae and Hydrocenidae. The **Pulmonata,** or pulmonates, have lost the operculum, and in the slugs even the shell. Ten pulmonate families, representing both land and freshwater types, occur naturally in the Islands. As a further differentiation between operculates and pulmonates, the sexes are separate in the former subclass. All species of the latter subclass are **hermaphroditic,** each individual possessing both male and female reproductive systems (although pair copulation is the usual, but not exclusive, breeding method).

GENERAL ECOLOGY

Some species of the world's nonmarine snails have become adapted to freshwater habitats, and a few have even reinvaded the ocean, but all of these must either periodically return to the surface to breathe or occupy only intertidal habitats where they are exposed to air during low tides. A few additional land groups worldwide have adapted to life very close to the seashore, where they are constantly exposed to spray from breaking waves. Several of these coastal forms (primarily of the family Ellobiidae) are among the nonmarine snails that naturally colonized the Hawaiian Archipelago. Most of the world's nonmarine snails are herbivorous and, like their ocean ancestors, use a filelike radula (see chapter 11) to rasp different types of vegetable matter to ingestible-sized fragments. The few that have become carnivorous similarly use the radula in preying on other gastropods. A majority of land and freshwater snails lay eggs rather than giving birth to live young.

GEOGRAPHIC SOURCE AND DISPERSAL

The geographic source of a majority of the native Hawaiian nonmarine snail fauna seems over-whelmingly to have been the general West Pacific and Southeast Asia region rather than the Americas, although the source of about half of the founders is still uncertain (Table 13.3). The relative importance of various transport methods is not completely clear (Table 13.2). The great-est number of founders could have been transported attached to birds, and a somewhat lesser number possibly arrived on emergent portions of floating ocean debris. Transportation of very small species (or even somewhat larger ones attached to loose leaves) from the western Pacific area by strong winds such as those of the jet stream (see chapter 13) or westerly storms (see chapter 7) is a possibility, although snail survival in at least the jet stream's freezing tempera-ture is questionable. Hurricanes (also chapter 7) would provide a more favorable temperature, but the fact that most founders apparently did not arrive from the eastern Pacific region where these storms originate argues against their importance in snail transport.

Regardless of transport method, the fact that pulmonates are hermaphroditic could have facilitated establishment of an arriving immigrant, because in the case of at least some species a single individual can self-fertilize and initiate a population. Various nonmarine snails first reached the Hawaiian Archipelago many millions of years ago; shells of some have been recov-ered in drill-core material from the surface of the deeply buried basalt of Midway Atoll, dat-ing back at least 28 million years (see chapter 3).

DISHARMONY AND ATTENUATION

Taxonomic disharmony (see chapter 10) in Hawaiian nonmarine snails is most apparent at the family level. There are about one hundred such snail families (with over 20,000 species) world-wide, but only a little over twenty families occur naturally in the Pacific Basin, with just twelve of these reaching Hawai'i. The native Island fauna lacks members of such widespread or com-mon continental families as the Southeast Asian Camaenidae, Eurasian Bradybaenidae, Euro-pean Helicidae, and North American Polygyridae, as well as slugs of any family and members of any carnivorous group. Hawai'i does not even have a representative of the relatively speciose family Partulidae, so widespread in the South and Southwest Pacific.

Attenuation in the Hawaiian nonmarine snail fauna is difficult to portray solely by citing total species numbers, primarily because of the bias introduced by the relatively enormous num-ber of endemic Island taxa. Judging, however, from the rather low total of twenty-one founders, as well as the very small number of eight indigenous species, filter-funnel action (see chapter 11) must have severely restricted dispersal of nonmarine snails to the Hawaiian Archipelago.

BIOTIC COMPOSITION

Both morphologically and numerically, the native Hawaiian nonmarine snail fauna was once perhaps the world's most diverse relative to the size of the Islands. The twelve families repre-sented by native Hawaiian land and freshwater snails are listed in Table 18.1, along with the twenty-four apparently represented only by alien forms. The primarily marine Neritidae, with at least one species successfully invading freshwater (see chapter 11), are omitted from the table and further discussion here. Similarly omitted are the two native limpetlike species of the fam-ily Siphonariidae because it is uncertain whether they have retained their immediate ancestors' marine habitat or have become secondarily marine after earlier leaving the sea.

Table 18.1. Families of nonmarine snails established in Hawai'i. The Neritidae and Siphonariidae are excluded (see text). Species numbers of the various categories, as well as estimated numbers of founders yielding the endemic complement, are noted. Questioned figures in the Endemic column indicate species possibly erroneously reported from Hawai'i, and in the Alien column species perhaps not established. A ± symbol designates estimated numbers of undescribed species. (Data from Cowie [1997] and Cowie et al. [1995].)

Family	Endemic	Founding	Indigenous	Alien
Land forms				
Achatinellidae	212	4	—	1
Achatinidae	—	—	—	1
Amastridae	325 (+1?)	1	—	—
Arionidae	—	—	—	— (+1?)
Ariophantidae	—	—	—	— (+1?)
Athoracophoridae	—	—	—	— (+1?)
Bradybaenidae	—	—	—	1
Ellobiidae	6	1	4	—
Endodontidae	33 (+190±)	1	—	—
Ferussaciidae	—	—	—	— (+1?)
Helicarionidae	60	1	—	— (+1?)
Helicidae	—	—	—	1
Helicinidae	14 (+5?)	1	—	—
Hydrocenidae	2	1	—	—
Limacidae	—	—	—	2 (+5?)
Milacidae	—	—	—	1
Philomycidae	—	—	—	1
Polygyridae	—	—	—	— (+1?)
Punctidae	1 (+5±)	1	—	—
Pupillidae	55 (+1?)	3	1	1 (+2?)
Spiraxidae	—	—	—	1
Streptaxidae	—	—	—	2 (+3?)
Strobilopsidae	—	—	—	— (+1?)
Subulinidae	—	—	—	4 (+4?)
Succineidae	41 (+3?)	1	1	—
Veronicellidae	—	—	—	2 (+1?)
Zonitidae	8 (+1?)	5	2	4 (+1?)
Freshwater forms				
Ampullariidae	—	—	—	3 (+1?)
Ancylidae	—	—	—	1
Bithyniidae	—	—	—	— (+1?)
Hydrobiidae	—	—	—	1 (+1?)
Lymnaeidae	5	1	—	2
Physidae	—	—	—	1 (+2?)
Planorbidae	—	—	—	1
Thiaridae	—	—	—	2 (+5?)
Viviparidae	—	—	—	1
Total 36 families	762 (+11?+195±)	21	8	34 (+33?)

HAWAIIAN NAMES

Ancient Hawaiians undoubtedly had a number of discrete names for the various types of land snails—especially the more colorful and easily observed ones—but very few have been recorded. The term most often associated with land gastropods in general seems to be *pūpū kuahiwi* (high-hill snails), which is still appropriate for species inhabiting relatively undisturbed upland vegetation zones. Many other now-extinct species, however, were known to live in lowland areas, so the retention of this one name may simply reflect the preferential loss of lowland native flora and fauna after human arrival. The collective term *pūpū kani oe* (snails with the long sound) is also encountered and alludes to the early Hawaiian belief that native arboreal snails (probably mostly of the family Achatinellidae discussed later in this chapter) were able to sing. Early historic observers ascribed the "song" heard to the scraping of the shells during movement of large numbers of the animals; in reality, the sound was quite likely a chorus of distant chirping forest crickets.

ENDEMISM

Although endemism in Hawaiian marine mollusks is relatively low (approximately 24 percent [Table 11.1]), that in nonmarine snails is extremely high, at least 95 percent. There is one endemic family, the Amastridae, in addition to at least fifty-five endemic genera among the dozen naturally occurring families, which collectively contain over 760 endemic species named thus far. Many of these species are usually considered single-island endemics (that is, restricted to one Hawaiian island). This endemic status is undoubtedly true for a majority of these, but further studies may well reveal that some are actually only representatives of the same species that have relatively recently spread to one or more other islands.

Few indigenous nonmarine snails are found in the Hawaiian Islands; only eight species have been identified to date (Table 18.1). This low number is probably due to a combination of the great average time that elapsed between natural colonization events (about a million years [Table 13.4]) and the apparent fact that an isolated establishing snail species usually evolves into a morphologically distinct one (that is, an endemic species) within a relatively short geologic time, perhaps only a few tens of thousands of years. That the four nonendemic Hawaiian species of Ellobiidae constitute the most numerous indigenous forms is undoubtedly the collective result of this family's shoreline habitat, apparent saltwater tolerance, and possession of free-swimming marine larvae by some species. These family characteristics greatly increase the likelihood of additional individuals of an established species arriving and prevented speciation through continual influx of ancestral genetic material.

FOUNDER EFFECT AND GENETIC DRIFT

Founder effect and genetic drift (see chapter 10) occurring in original nonmarine snail colonists and their initial populations of millions of years ago are, understandably, essentially completely obscured by time. It may be relevant, however, to note that the size ranges of land snails on various isolated oceanic islands are mostly at the smaller end of the worldwide scale, with about 60 percent of insular species being less than 1 cm (0.4 inches) in shell length. This is undoubtedly due largely to the greater ease with which small species can be transported by birds and winds, but the fact that smaller individuals within a given population of a species would similarly be more easily transported than larger conspecifics means that founder effect may also have played a part in this size diminution.

Other evidence of possible founder effect, as well as of almost certain genetic drift, is abundant among certain closely related taxa of Hawaiian land snails. Probably the most dramatic is provided by the relatively enormous color-pattern variation in the several dozen geographically isolated populations of species of the endemic Oʻahu tree snail genus *Achatinella* (family Achatinellidae [Figure 18.1]). The recognition of many of the different forms shown in the figure as separate species is largely arbitrary, because "lumpers" (see chapter 10) would consider many of these simply varieties of between only about twelve and sixteen species (as in this volume), but "splitters" might recognize at least all of the forty-two "species" indicated by the figure labels, if not further segregating some of their populations as additional species.

The original recognition of the relatively enormous number of apparently different Hawaiian morphological "species" of the family is of historical interest, because it called into question the notions of special creation and immutability of species. In fact, one early Hawaiian naturalist, the missionary son John T. Gulick (see chapter 28), examining a particularly varied group of this family at least 5 years before Darwin's theory of evolution appeared, was led to proclaim: "All these *Achatinellae* never came from Noah's Ark!"

Not only is this color variation in certain achatinellids (primarily of the genera *Achatinella* and *Partulina*) striking when separate populations of a species are compared, but it is also noticeable within many individual populations. None of this diversity can be clearly attributed to ecological requirements or environmental conditions. It also seems unrelated to sexual selection because, in the case of cross-fertilization, copulating partners are presumably incapable of seeing each other's distinctive color pattern. So the variability within a single population probably represents genetic drift, which results in preservation of random, selectively neutral color mutations. The variability among different populations could possibly be due to a combination of founder effect and the appearance of additional selectively neutral color mutations. A number of the instances of the shells' spiraling in opposite directions (dextral or "right-handed" and sinistral or "left-handed" [obvious in Figure 18.1]) may also represent founder effect rather than genetic drift. In this case, however, the population providing the founding stock must obviously have contained both dextral and sinistral individuals, presumably often derived through genetic drift.

ADAPTIVE SHIFTS

Habitat

Major adaptive shifts are uncommon among endemic Hawaiian nonmarine snails, with only limited radiation into ecological niches (see chapter 9) substantially different from ancestral ones. No Hawaiian species has developed carnivory, nor apparently forsaken an arboreal or other land habitat for a completely aquatic one. There have been, however, instances of a less-extreme habitat shift from one terrestrial ecosystem to another. This is especially obvious among the Hawaiian Succineidae, which in other parts of the world typically dwell along the margins of bodies of freshwater and, occasionally, even saltwater. A single colonizing form has adaptively radiated into over forty endemic ground and arboreal species that occupy Hawaiian habitats ranging from sand dunes and associated low vegetation to upland rain forests, all generally away from aquatic areas.

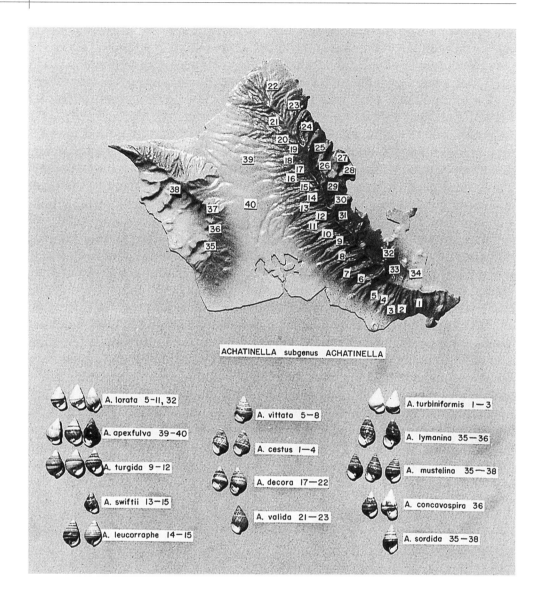

ACHATINELLA subgenus ACHATINELLA

A. lorata 5-11, 32
A. apexfulva 39-40
A. turgida 9-12
A. swiftii 13-15
A. leucorraphe 14-15

A. vittata 5-8
A. cestus 1-4
A. decora 17-22
A. valida 21-23

A. turbiniformis 1-3
A. lymanina 35-36
A. mustelina 35-38
A. concavospira 36
A. sordida 35-38

Reproduction

Most of the very few endemic Hawaiian nonmarine snail species that have been satisfactorily studied—both morphologically and behaviorally—belong to the achatinellid land genera *Achatinella* and *Partulina* of the subfamily Achatinellinae. Data from these genera have been heavily relied upon in this and other sections of this chapter, although it is not known how typical this information is of the endemic Hawaiian land-snail fauna in general.

There has probably been a change in reproductive strategy among at least some endemic Hawaiian snails compared with many continental ones. This involves an increase in reproductive age, a decrease in annual number of young, and a slowed growth rate of immatures. For example, certain *Achatinella* and *Partulina* range in age from about three and a half to seven

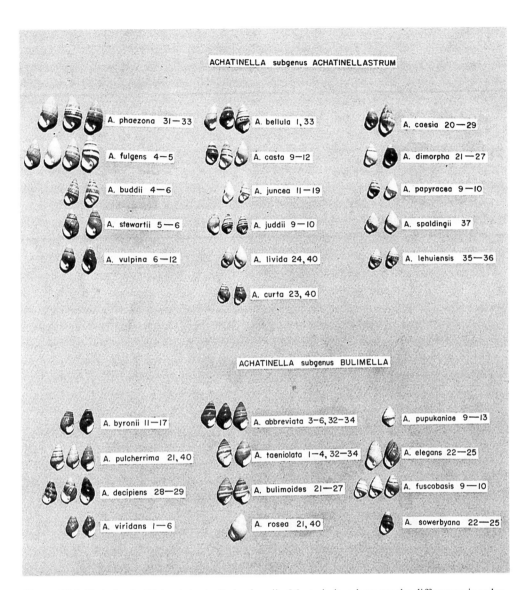

Figure 18.1. Variation in Oʻahu *Achatinella* land snails. Most obvious here are the differences in color pattern and direction of shell spiraling. These many previously named taxa are currently considered to represent only between twelve and sixteen valid species. The individual numbers beside each species' name correspond to locality numbers on the map. Lengths of the particular shells shown range from about 1.5 to 2.0 cm (0.6 to 0.8 inches). (Unnumbered figure on pp. 182–183 of Carlquist [1980], used with permission of the National Tropical Botanical Garden.)

years at first reproduction and usually produce only four to seven young annually. These young then grow at the rate of 0.2 to 0.4 cm (0.08 to 0.16 inches) in shell length yearly.

These data may be compared with those of a very successful alien form, the **Giant African Snail,** *Achatina fulica* (family Achatinidae), whose reproductive and growth characteristics are generally similar in many respects to those of several other continental land snails studied. The Giant African Snail typically begins reproduction within its first year and yields about six hundred eggs annually. The hatchlings then increase at least 2.5 cm (1.0 inches) in length each year. The investigated endemic Hawaiian species of *Achatinella* and the closely related genus *Partulina,* however, live to a maximum age of between 10 and 19 years, but the alien species reaches only 4 or 5.

Evolution of the subdued but extended reproductive effort of at least these particular achatinellids quite possibly resulted from a lack of predation by carnivorous snails and essentially all other invertebrates (but see the case of blow flies in chapter 16). Also, there presumably was decreased vertebrate predation in the group's insular environment, compared with that affecting species such as the Giant African Snail in a continental setting. In Hawai'i before human arrival, probably only a small number of endemic birds (chapters 20–22), possibly mostly flightless ones, included land snails in their diet. The fact, however, that a few endemic land snail species without conspicuous color patterns have a sculptured shell surface somewhat matching their typical habitat backgrounds suggests that this vertebrate predator pressure may have been significant in evolution (or retention) of this texture. Certain ground-living Hawaiian species of the family Amastridae retain the ancestral characteristic of secreting quantities of mucus to which enough debris adheres to disguise the animals quite effectively, further suggesting the existence of one or more visually dependent Hawaiian predators.

Size

Almost all native Hawaiian nonmarine snails are relatively small, less than about 1.0–2.0 cm (0.4–0.8 inches) in greatest height and width, but there are a few considerably larger species. The shell height of four in the (now extinct?) amastrid genus *Carelia* of Kaua'i and Ni'ihau reaches almost 8 cm (3.2 inches). That of three other (also probably now extinct) amastrid species, one each on Kaua'i, Moloka'i, and Maui, may equal this. It is possible that this gigantism signifies an ecological niche radically different from that of other Hawaiian land snails. But, if so, it is most surprising that the same possible way of life has not been filled on the remaining main islands by species of Amastridae or other families. Incidentally, it seems that snails of this relatively great size could have furnished a prehistoric dietary item, although there is no evidence regarding this possibility from either archaeological or ethnological sources.

Shape

The shell shapes of endemic Hawaiian land snails represent primarily two types: most species of a majority of families are relatively tall and somewhat narrow, but those of a substantial minority are quite low and broad. A very few remaining species of particular families are roughly globular. These differences in shape are not closely correlated with island of occurrence or, to some extent, taxonomic group. The two primary shapes are each well represented on all of the main islands, and at least the speciose family Amastridae (see discussion later in this chapter) has numerous species of both shell configurations.

Presumably, then, this variation in shell shape is related to ecological niche, although the details of such a putative relationship have yet to be elucidated. Unfortunately, the extinction of up to 75 percent of the endemic Hawaiian nonmarine snail species within the last two millennia (probably mostly during just the last two centuries) has removed the possibility of pertinent ecological studies of most taxa. It has been speculated that shell shape may be determined by usual locomotion or posture. For example, a tall narrow shape might well be advantageous to burrowing species as well as to those that must consistently draw the shell behind them over near-vertical surfaces such as plant trunks or pendant leaves. On the other hand, a low, broad shell could possibly be best suited for life under forest duff and other loose ground litter. All of these possibilities need to be explored through studies on still-extant species of Hawaiian nonmarine snails.

NOTABLE FAMILIES

As indicated in Table 18.1, at least three families have speciated extensively in Hawai'i: the **Achatinellidae** (212 endemic species), **Amastridae** (326±), and **Endodontidae** (220±). Representatives of all three are found on each main Hawaiian Island, although there are some marked interfamilial differences in numbers of species per island.

Achatinellidae

The center of Hawaiian achatinellid species abundance and taxonomic diversity is O'ahu, which has well over a third of the 212 endemic species, representing eight of the twelve Island genera. From O'ahu, speciosity progressively decreases to both the northwest and southeast in the main island chain, being especially low on Kaua'i.

Shell size is generally greater among species of the endemic Hawaiian subfamily Achatinellinae than in any other world population of the family (suggesting an adaptive shift to larger individuals after Island colonization and evolution of the subfamily). The size and shape of shells among achatinelline species tend to have similar ranges, the height usually being from about 0.5 to 2.0 cm (0.2 to 0.8 inches), and the rather moderate width from approximately 0.1 to 1.0 or 1.1 cm (0.04 to 0.44 inches). As discussed earlier, among species of *Achatinella* and *Partulina* enormous variation has evolved in color and pattern (as well as direction of spiraling in at least *Achatinella* [Figure 18.1]). The varied shell colors of most *Achatinella,* especially the arrangement of these hues in spiral bands, and the shell's polished appearance, has given rise to the alternative common name of little agate shells (which is also the Latin meaning of the scientific name). The occasionally encountered Hawaiian term *"pūpū hinuhinu"* (very shiny shells) is similarly appropriate. Examples of *Achatinella* and *Partulina* are shown in Plate 18.1, and these two groups are by far the Hawaiian land snails best known among collectors and scientific investigators.

A majority of Hawaiian Achatinellidae are arboreal, living in trees and lower vegetation of often moister areas and, apparently like many other arboreal snails worldwide, eating mostly fungi and algae growing on foliage and branches rather than the leaves themselves. Most Hawaiian achatinellid species resorb the eggshell within the body and subsequently give birth to the young, but some are egg layers. The coloration of immatures is similar to that of the apical shell region of the adult, and the young apparently receives no parental care.

Amastridae

Amastrid species numbers are highest on Kaua'i and O'ahu and lowest on Hawai'i. This endemic family may well be the oldest land-snail group in the archipelago, judging primarily from the fact that it is the most diversified morphologically. Evolutionary radiation in shell morphology has involved changes in shape and size rather than variation from the typical dull coloration and general surface smoothness. The original colonist yielding the family may have been a rather small species with a shell of only moderate height and width. This putative "primitive" shell type, averaging possibly a little less than 1.0 cm (0.4 inches) high and 0.5 cm (0.2 inches) wide, is still characteristic of many, although not a majority of, Hawaiian Amastridae.

From this possible original shell type, certain species of the ten amastrid genera have developed some striking evolutionary variations, which include a relatively tall and somewhat narrow shape, as well as a quite low and broad one. Some small O'ahu amastrid species possess the low and broad type of shell, rather like that of the Endodontidae (discussed next), but most on all islands show a tall, narrow shell; a few become almost awl-like. Occasional species undergo a noted increase in size, as in the case of the earlier-mentioned *Carelia*. In contrast to the many tree- and shrub-inhabiting species of Achatinellidae with which they share the same general geographic areas, most Amastridae are either leaf-litter species or denizens of ferns. The members of these two highly speciose families evidently avoid a great deal of potential food competition in this partitioning of primary habitat. One of the two amastrid subfamilies lays eggs; the other produces live young.

Endodontidae

Among the numerous native endodontid taxa, the thirty-three species described thus far are more or less evenly distributed among the main islands. But, because there are probably about 190 yet-unnamed ones, this reputed distribution pattern must be considered tentative. Hawaiian Endodontidae are generally quite small species found on the ground, boulders, or low tree stumps. The shell forms a very flat spiral only 0.1 or 0.2 cm (0.04 or 0.08 inches) high and between 0.4 and 0.8 or 0.9 cm (0.16 and 0.34 inches) wide. The shell is generally dull-colored in most forms but is notable for great species diversity in surface sculpturing. A few species are found in moister upland situations, but the areas more usually occupied are within the drier Coastal Zone (see chapter 14), including grassland. All species of endodontids lay eggs.

ALIEN NONMARINE SNAILS

Of the numerous species of alien land and freshwater snails either inadvertently or intentionally brought to the Hawaiian Islands by humans, at least thirty-four are known to have become established, as enumerated in Tables 18.1 through 18.3. Many of these are small, inconspicuous forms, doubtless arriving unnoticed in vegetable and other material imported mostly during historic times, but certain others are large, conspicuous snails intentionally imported for specific purposes.

Various reasons have been given for the private importation in 1930 of the previously mentioned Giant African Snail. With a shell reaching 15 to 20 cm (6 to 8 inches) in length, it seemed a good potential food animal and/or one of putative value in folk medicine. It has also been stated that the large animal was brought in just as a garden ornamental. Although this species

Table 18.2. Alien land snails established in Hawai'i. The probable type, purpose, and/or source of introduction are noted. An asterisk (*) signifies a possibly indigenous species, and a question mark (?) one perhaps not established. (Data from Cowie [1997].)

Family Species	Type of Establishment	Purpose or Source
Achatinellidae		
Lamellidea oblonga	Inadvertent	Polynesian (?) transport
Achatinidae		
Achatina fulica	Planned	Various
Arionidae		
Arion sp.?	Inadvertent	Historic transport
Ariophantidae		
Parmarion martensi?	Inadvertent	Historic transport
Athoracophoridae		
Athoracophorus sp.?	Inadvertent	Historic transport
Bradybaenidae		
Bradybaena similaris	Inadvertent	Historic transport
Ferussaciidae		
Cecilioides aperta?	Inadvertent	Historic transport
Helicarionidae		
Undetermined genus and sp.	Inadvertent	Historic transport
Helicidae		
Helix aspersa	Inadvertent (?)	Historic transport (?)
Limacidae		
Deroceras laeve	Inadvertent	Historic transport
Deroceras reticulatum?	Inadvertent	Historic transport
Limax flavus?	Inadvertent	Historic transport
Limax maximus	Inadvertent	Historic transport
Limax sandwichensis?	Inadvertent	Historic transport
Limax tenellus?	Inadvertent	Historic transport
Limax valentianus?	Inadvertent	Historic transport
Milacidae		
Milax gagates	Inadvertent	Historic transport
Philomycidae		
Meghimatium striatum	Inadvertent	Historic transport
Polygyridae		
Polygyra cereolus?	Inadvertent	Historic transport
Pupillidae		
Gastrocopta pediculus?	Inadvertent	Historic transport
Gastrocopta servilis	Inadvertent	Historic transport
Pupisoma orcula?	Inadvertent	Historic transport

(Continued on following page)

Table 18.2. *(continued)* Alien land snails established in Hawai'i. The probable type, purpose, and/or source of introduction are noted. An asterisk (*) signifies a possibly indigenous species, and a question mark (?) one perhaps not established. (Data from Cowie [1997].)

Family Species	Type of Establishment	Purpose or Source
Spiraxidae		
Euglandina rosea	Planned	Biocontrol
Streptaxidae		
Gonaxis kibweziensis	Planned	Biocontrol
Gonaxis quadrilateralis	Planned	Biocontrol
Gulella wahlbergi?	Planned	Biocontrol
Ptychotrema walikalense?	Planned	Biocontrol
Ptychotrema sp.?	Planned	Biocontrol
Strobilopsidae		
Strobilops aenea?	Inadvertent	Historic transport
Subulinidae		
Allopeas clavulinum	Inadvertent	Historic transport
Allopeas gracile	Inadvertent	Polynesian transport
Opeas beckianum?	Inadvertent	Historic transport
Opeas hannense?	Inadvertent	Historic transport
Opeas mauritianum?	Inadvertent	Historic transport
Opeas opella	Inadvertent	Historic transport
Paropeas achatinaceum?	Inadvertent	Historic transport
Subulina octona	Inadvertent	Historic transport
Veronicellidae		
Laevicaulis alte	Inadvertent	Historic transport
Vaginula plebeia	Inadvertent	Historic transport
Veronicella cubensis?	Inadvertent	Historic transport
Zonitidae		
Hawaiia minuscula	Inadvertent	Historic transport
Oxychilus alliarius	Inadvertent	Historic transport
Oxychilus cellarius?	Inadvertent	Historic transport
*Striatura sp.**	Inadvertent (?)	Historic (?) transport (?)
Zonitoides arboreus	Inadvertent	Historic transport

grows rapidly and reproduces abundantly in Hawai'i, it was not a commercial success. It did, however, cause noticeable damage to, primarily, garden plants. Thus, in the later 1950s and early 1960s, a total of twenty-three species of alien carnivorous snails from various parts of the world were introduced by the State in a vain effort to biologically control this voracious giant snail.

Most of these introduced predatory species did not establish in the Islands, with the exception of at least the two species of *Gonaxis* (family Streptaxidae) listed in Table 18.2 and, most

Table 18.3. Alien freshwater snails established in Hawai'i. The probable type, purpose, and/or source of introduction are noted. An asterisk (*) signifies a possibly indigenous species, and a question mark (?) one perhaps not established. (Data from Cowie [1997].)

Family Species	Type of Establishment	Purpose or Source
Ampullariidae		
Pila conica	Planned	Historic food
Pomacea bridgesii	Planned	Home aquarium
Pomacea canaliculata	Planned	Historic food
Pomacea paludosa?	Planned	Home aquarium
Ancylidae		
Ferrissia sharpi *	Inadvertent (?)	Historic (?) transport (?)
Bithyniidae		
Bithynia robusta?	Inadvertent (?)	Historic transport
Hydrobiidae		
*Tryonia protea**	Inadvertent (?)	Polynesian (?) transport (?)
(Uncertain genus) *porrecta?*	Inadvertent	Historic transport
Lymnaeidae		
Fosasaria viridis	Inadvertent (?)	Historic transport
Pseudosuccinea columella	Inadvertent (?)	Historic transport
Physidae		
*Physa compacta?**	Inadvertent (?)	Historic (?) transport (?)
Physa elliptica?	Inadvertent (?)	Historic transport
Physa virgata	Inadvertent	Historic transport
Planorbidae		
Planorbella duryi	Planned	Home aquarium
Thiaridae		
Melanoides tuberculata	Inadvertent	Historic (?) transport
Tarebia granifera	Inadvertent	Historic (?) transport
Tarebia lateritia?	Inadvertent	Historic transport
Thiara baldwini?	Inadvertent	Historic transport
Thiara indefinita?	Inadvertent	Historic transport
Thiara kauaiensis?	Inadvertent	Historic transport
Thiara verrauiana?	Inadvertent	Historic transport
Viviparidae		
Cipangopaludina chinensis	Planned	Historic food

notably, the relatively large and aggressive **Rosy Cannibal Snail,** *Euglandina rosea* (family Spiraxidae). None of these established species seems to have significantly reduced Giant African Snail populations, however, and most of these predators survive in Hawai'i by feeding partly on endemic nonmarine snails, including freshwater forms. At least ten alien herbivorous freshwater snail species historically introduced for either food or home aquarium use are also now established in many parts of the state. For instance, at least three of the four imported apple snails (genera *Pila* and *Pomacea* [family Ampullariidae]) are known to have succeeded in becoming established as of 1999. One of these, the Channeled Apple Snail *(Pomacea canaliculata),* is becoming increasingly abundant as a serious pest of commercial pondfield crops, such as Taro *(Colocasia esculenta)* and Watercress *(Nasturtium officinale).*

SUGGESTED REFERENCES

Cowie 1995, 1997, 1998; Cowie et al. 1995; Hadfield 1986; Hadfield et al. 1993; Hart 1978; Kobayashi and Hadfield 1996; Solem 1990; Yamamoto and Tagawa 2000.

AUDIOVISUAL AIDS

Listen to the forest.

19

Amphibians, Reptiles, and Mammals

Of the six classes of vertebrates, the two comprising fishes were covered in chapter 12, and another (birds) is examined in chapters 20–22. The remaining three, amphibians, reptiles, and mammals, are discussed in this chapter. (The first two of these are sometimes collectively referred to as "herps," in reference to their joint study in **herpetology;** Greek *"herpetos"* [crawling things].)

AMPHIBIANS

Background
Almost all members of the class **Amphibia** (Greek *"amphi"* [double] and *"bios"* [life]) lead an existence partly on land and partly in freshwater. All are egg producing or **oviparous;** the eggs most often are deposited in water. These hatch into aquatic larvae that, upon metamorphosis or transformation into adults, typically emerge to spend at least part of their life on land. Only two of the five living orders are well known: the frogs and toads (order Anura) and the salamanders (Caudata). Most of those anurans known loosely as "frogs," as well as many of the salamanders, have thin, smooth skin through which internal water can rapidly be lost; the animals soon die if not remaining in relatively moist surroundings. "Toads," especially those of the essentially cosmopolitan family Bufonidae, and a few types of salamanders have thickened, rough skin on at least their dorsal surface that resists water loss, so these can survive for longer periods in drier habitats. Amphibian larvae are herbivorous or omnivorous, and the adults are carnivorous, being consumers of secondary or higher trophic levels of the ecological pyramid (see chapter 9). Adult food ranges from insects and other arthropods, through various types of worms, to occasional smaller vertebrates.

Biotic Composition
No amphibians have been able to naturally colonize isolated oceanic islands such as those of Hawai'i. A number of alien amphibians are mentioned in the literature as having been found in the wild in the Islands, but only those that seem surely to have established sustained breeding populations are discussed here (Table 19.1).

Frogs and Toads
Frogs of the genus *Eleutherodactylus* from the Caribbean region, where they are known as "coquis," apparently established colonies on various main islands in the early 1990s. These are the Common Coqui (*E. coqui* [thus far found only on Maui and Hawai'i]) and the Greenhouse Frog (*E. planirostris* [O'ahu and Hawai'i]). A third species, the Martinique Coqui *(E. martinicensis)* was also originally reported from Maui, but further examination of the specimens indicates that they may only be additional individuals of *E. coqui,* so this possible third species tentatively is unlisted here. Coquis are small forest frogs, with head-and-body lengths between

about 1.3 and 3.8 cm (0.5 and 1.5 inches), not requiring a standing water habitat. They remain quietly perched during the day and then are usually not obvious to the casual observer. At night, however, when the frogs come out to feed, they make their presence abundantly clear by the call of the males, which is amazingly loud for the animals' size. The first two species forage in trees and some lower vegetation, and the last feeds in leaf litter and other ground habitats. All of these species seem to have been inadvertently brought to the Islands—and further spread among them—while hidden in nursery shipments of plants or soil.

The almost entirely terrestrial **Marine Toad** *(Bufo marinus)* is well known to most residents of all main islands as "bufo." It reaches a maximum head-and-body length of at least 17 cm (6.8 inches), with females a third larger than males. The primary impetus for its introduction was anticipated control of insects injurious to Island Sugarcane crops. During breeding periods, males station themselves in or near temporary or permanent shallow bodies of freshwater and give a trilling call to attract females. Eggs are fertilized during amplexus or prolonged dorsal clasping of the female by the male and hatch in the water, where the tadpoles feed and grow until metamorphosis. The milky secretions extruded by disturbed adults from large glands on the sides of the head are highly irritating or toxic if brought into contact with the eyes or ingested, and the poison is known to have killed a small dog that had persistently bitten a bufo.

Skin secretions of poison-dart frogs are used by indigenous peoples of their American Tropics homeland to poison tips of blow darts or arrows for killing small game. These secretions are not harmful to humans unless introduced into a skin cut or the eyes. The **Green and Black Poison-dart Frog** *(Dendrobates auratus* [Plate 19.1]) was originally introduced to Mānoa Valley on Oʻahu and is now also found in Waiāhole Valley on the windward side of the island. This small frog, only about 3.5 cm (1.4 inches) long, lives in moist surroundings and seldom spends time in water. The species shows most unusual behavior in producing and rearing young. The eggs are not fertilized during amplexus as in the case of most other frogs and toads, but rather by extrusion of sperm onto the eggs only after they have been laid in a damp terres-

Table 19.1. Amphibians established in Hawaiʻi. All of these are alien species, and details relating to their introductions are also listed. (Data from Banks et al. [eds.] [1987] and McKeown [1996].)

Family Species	Year of Introduction	Original Source	Purpose of Introduction
Leptodactylid frogs (Leptodactylidae)			
Common Coqui *(Eleutherodactylus coqui)*	Early 1990s	Caribbean	Inadvertent?
Greenhouse Frog *(Eleutherodactylus planirostris)*	Early 1990s	Caribbean	Inadvertent?
True toads (Bufonidae)			
Marine Toad *(Bufo marinus)*	1932	Puerto Rico	Insect control
Poison-dart frogs (Dendrobatidae)			
Green and Black Poison-dart Frog *(Dendrobates auratus)*	1932	Panama	Mosquito control
True frogs (Ranidae)			
Bullfrog *(Rana catesbiana)*	1880s?	California	Food
Wrinkled Frog *(Rana rugosa)*	1896	Japan	Insect control

trial location. The male then remains near the eggs until they hatch, whereupon he transports the tadpoles to water on his back and may subsequently move these young between pools in the same manner.

The **Bullfrog** or **poloka** *(Rana catesbiana)* has become common in lower streams and reservoirs of all main islands since its introduction in the late 1800s. (The Hawaiian name is sometimes claimed to be an onomatopoeic term based on the animal's deep croaking call, although it is more likely simply the Hawaiian transliteration of "frog.") The species reaches the quite great head-and-body length of about 17.5 cm (7 inches), and can ingest animals as large as adult mice and young chicks of waterbirds. The **Wrinkled Frog** *(Rana rugosa)* is noticeably smaller than the Bullfrog, reaching only about a third of its length. It is found in many upland stream habitats on all main islands, usually being absent from quieter lower-stream and reservoir situations, quite possibly because of predation by the Bullfrog. The Green Frog *(Rana clamitans)* is not included in the tabulations here. This species established an O'ahu breeding population after being introduced from eastern North America about 1935, but has not been reported for a half century, so has quite possibly died out in the Islands.

REPTILES

Background
Living members of the class **Reptilia** are divided into four orders: the tuataras of New Zealand (sole survivors of the ancient order Rhynchocephalia), alligators and crocodiles (Crocodilia), turtles (Chelonia), and the lizards and snakes (Squamata). Reptiles are found in all tropical and temperate areas but, like amphibians, being "cold-blooded" or **ectothermic** (having their internal temperature regulated by an external source), are lacking in more northern regions where temperatures during a major portion of the year are too low to allow normal metabolism.

In contrast to amphibians, reptiles have skin highly specialized to prevent passage of water, either in or out, and nitrogenous wastes are voided as a water-conserving paste of uric acid crystals rather than as an aqueous solution of urea. These characteristics have allowed numerous reptiles to occupy not only arid habitats such as deserts but also the marine ecosystem, where osmotic loss through the skin of internal water to the saltwater would be fatal. Evolutionary changes in the reptilian egg, including attainment of a shell, result in its being well able to protect the embryo when laid in varied terrestrial habitats, rather than requiring deposition in freshwater. A number of lizards and snakes have even developed **ovovivipary,** in which the eggs hatch within the female's body and the young are "born" alive. Many turtles and a few lizards are herbivorous, thus being primary consumers, and the remaining reptiles are carnivorous at various higher trophic levels; a few (crocodilians, for example) are "top predators" in their particular food chains.

Biotic Composition
With the ability to resist osmotic water loss, terrestrial reptiles can survive extensive ocean transport and so have been able to colonize a number of isolated island groups. The animals, especially lizards, can be conveyed by currents while clinging to drifting trees and other plant material or, as has apparently been the case in a few types of land tortoises, can even float unaided while being so transported. Probably no terrestrial reptile reached the Hawaiian Islands in these ways, however, likely because of a combination of chance and the extreme isolation of

the archipelago. Other than species known to have been historically introduced, the Hawaiian nonmarine reptilian fauna consists solely of small lizards of the gecko and skink families; probably a majority of species arrived with early Polynesians (Table 19.2).

Turtles

Among the five species of marine turtles found in the central Pacific, only two regularly nest in the Hawaiian Islands. The **Green Turtle** or *honu* (*Chelonia mydas* [Plate 23.1]) is the common Island egg layer, and more than 90 percent of this summer activity occurs in the Northwestern Hawaiian Islands (see chapter 23), primarily on French Frigate Shoals. A few animals, however, currently lay eggs on northwestern Moloka'i, and there formerly was limited historic nesting on northern Lāna'i. About five hundred females nest in any given year; this number perhaps represents approximately a third of all adult females in the Hawaiian population. Extension of marine turtle nesting to unutilized islands is quite rare because turtles hatching on a particular beach apparently usually return only there to lay eggs when adult. Immature Green Turtles, as well as adults of both sexes not engaged in mating and nesting in the Northwestern Hawaiian Islands during a particular year, are commonly seen in all months around the main islands, where they feed exclusively on marine algae. As a matter of fact, the greenish-tinged fat of this formerly much-eaten species is the result of this algal diet and is responsible for the animal's English name. Adults weigh between 68 and 180 kg (150 and 400 pounds) and have shells from about 80 to 108 cm (32 to 43 inches) long.

After over two decades of protection under the U.S. Endangered Species Act (see chapter 27), the Hawaiian Green Turtle population is noticeably increasing, with the total number of breeding-age males and females in 1999 estimated at around 4,000 and the number of immature animals conceivably as many as forty or fifty times that figure. Since the late 1950s, however, increasing numbers of Green Turtles in Hawai'i and elsewhere have been found with external and internal epithelial tumors (fibropapillomas) reaching considerable size. These growths also now appear widely in other species of the same family around the world. Because the tumors are often located in the head area as well as in the oral cavity, sighting and ingesting food is sometimes greatly impaired. Also, the disease may be directly responsible for the notable physiologically stressed condition of many afflicted individuals. Fibropapillomas of various sizes are now annually recorded in between 40 and 65 percent of Hawaiian Green Turtles. The cause of this disease is strongly suspected to be a yet-unidentified virus, but involvement of one or more other factors such as internal or external parasites and environmental pollution has not been ruled out.

The **Hawksbill Turtle** or *'ea* (*Eretmochelys imbricata*) is much less common in Hawaiian waters than the preceding species and is currently known to nest in the archipelago on only about a dozen beaches, distributed around the islands of Hawai'i, Maui, Moloka'i, and (most sparingly) O'ahu. Only between about five and twenty or so females can be found nesting in any given year. Adults of this invertebrate-consuming species in the Hawaiian Islands are noticeably smaller than those of the Green Turtle, being between 34 and 68 kg (75 and 150 pounds) in weight and about 80 cm (32 inches) in average length. The Hawksbill is not usually eaten because its flesh is reputedly poisonous, at least during certain times of the year throughout most parts of its worldwide ocean range. It was formerly prized, however, for the relatively thick and attractively patterned horny scutes or "tortoiseshell" overlying the bony shell, used for manufacture of artifacts and jewelry before the advent of plastics. Perhaps one hundred individuals

Table 19.2. Reptiles established in Hawai‘i. There are no endemic species. The approximate probable establishment times for alien taxa are indicated. (Nomenclature from Banks et al. [eds.] [1987], with other data primarily from McKeown [1996].)

Family Species	Time of Establishment
Turtles	
Typical sea turtles (Cheloniidae)	
Green Turtle or *honu (Chelonia mydas)*	(Indigenous)
Hawksbill Turtle or *‘ea (Eretmochelys imbricata)*	(Indigenous)
Olive Ridley Turtle *(Lepidochelys olivacea)*	(Indigenous)
Loggerhead Turtle *(Caretta caretta)*	(Indigenous)
Leatherback sea turtles (Dermochelyidae)	
Leatherback Turtle *(Dermochelys coriacea)*	(Indigenous)
Softshell turtles (Trionychidae)	
Chinese Softshell Turtle *(Pelodiscus sinensis)*	1800s
Wattle-necked Softshell Turtle *(Palea steindachneri)*	1800s
Typical freshwater and land turtles (Testudinidae)	
Red-eared Slider *(Trachemys scripta)*	1980±?
Lizards	
Iguanid lizards (Iguanidae)	
Green Iguana *(Iguana iguana)*	1950s
Green Anole *(Anolis carolinensis)*	1950s
Knight Anole *(Anolis equestris)*	Early 1980s
Brown Anole *(Anolis sagrei)*	Early 1980s
True chameleons (Chamaeleonidae)	
Jackson's Chameleon *(Chamaeleo jacksonii)*	1970±?
Geckos (Gekkonidae)	
Mourning Gecko *(Lepidodactylus lugubris)*	Polynesian?
Stump-toed Gecko *(Gehyra mutilata)*	Polynesian?
Small Tree Gecko *(Hemiphyllodactylus typus)*	Polynesian?
Fox Gecko *(Hemidactylus garnotii)*	Polynesian?
Common House Gecko *(Hemidactylus frenatus)*	Mid-1940s
Orange-spotted Day Gecko *(Phelsuma guimbeaui)*	Mid-1980s
Gold-dust Day Gecko *(Phelsuma laticauda)*	Mid-1970s
Skinks (Scincidae)	
Snake-eyed Skink *(Cryptoblepharus poecilopleurus)*	Polynesian?
Moth Skink *(Lipinia noctua)*	Polynesian?
Copper-tailed Skink *(Emoia cyanura)*	Polynesian?
Azure-tailed Skink *(Emoia impar)*	Polynesian?
Garden Skink *(Lampropholis delicata)*	1910±?
Snakes	
Sea snakes (Elapidae)	
Yellow-bellied Sea Snake *(Pelamis platurus)*	(Indigenous)
Blind snakes (Typhlopidae)	
Brahminy Blind Snake *(Rhamphotyphlops braminus)*	1930

is a generous estimate of adult Hawksbills residing in Hawaiian waters as of 1999, although there are probably also at least several times that many immature individuals.

Two other marine turtles occur pelagically in the central Pacific around the Hawaiian Archipelago, but are relatively rare in coastal Island waters. Almost all of the few reported individuals of these have been found stranded on Island beaches, either entangled in marine debris or physiologically or morphologically debilitated in some manner. The Olive Ridley Turtle *(Lepidochelys olivacea)* is known to have nested a single time on northeastern Maui in 1985. The eggs were salvaged from a precarious location, and most hatched in captivity although none of the young survived to be released. This is the smallest sea turtle around the archipelago; adults weigh from 36 to 45 kg (80 to 100 pounds) and measure 58 to 75 cm (23 to 30 inches) long. The Loggerhead Turtle *(Caretta caretta)* also seems to be a completely pelagic animal in the central Pacific. Adults of this large species are usually between 77 and 158 kg (170 and 350 pounds) in weight and 80 to 115 cm (32 to 46 inches) in length, but an exceptionally large individual is reported to have weighed over 225 kg (500 pounds) and to have been 213 cm (85 inches) long. Apparently, both of these species as well as the following one feed almost entirely on jellyfish and other larger pelagic and benthic marine invertebrates, as well as, possibly, occasional fishes and algae.

The Leatherback Turtle *(Dermochelys coriacea)* is sparingly but consistently reported among the Islands, usually when it is taken on commercial fishing vessel longline hooks in off-shore waters. Pacific-region Leatherbacks normally nest on warmer coasts of both sides of the Pacific Basin, but in 1997 a female laid eggs on a Lānaʻi beach. All of these eggs proved to be infertile, however, and this nesting seems obviously to have been an anomalous event. This is the largest of all sea turtles, reaching the startling size of 630 to 675 kg (1,400 to 1,500 pounds) and 210 to 240 cm (84 to 96 inches). The species differs from all of the world's other marine turtles because it lacks a bony shell and horny scutes; the body is covered with thick, leathery skin in which are embedded numerous small, discrete bony plates.

Freshwater species constitute the remaining three turtles commonly found in the Hawaiian Islands (Table 19.2). All are alien species and represent forms either historically introduced for food or released from home aquariums.

Lizards

Which, if any, of the geckos and skinks (Figure 19.1) questionably listed as Polynesian introductions in Table 19.2 may actually have reached the Hawaiian Archipelago unaided before human arrival is undetermined. All of these species now occur on many other islands of the Pacific, but the fact that none has undergone any discernible evolutionary change either there or in Hawaiʻi suggests that little if any colonization occurred before human arrival. Once Polynesian voyages in large oceangoing canoes began, however, there is little doubt that most of these small lizards were easily transported and widely spread throughout the central Pacific (see chapters 24, 25). Two of the Island geckos, the **Mourning Gecko** *(Lepidodactylus lugubris)* and the **Fox Gecko** *(Hemidactylus garnotii),* are **parthenogenic,** meaning that a single transported individual can produce viable eggs and thus establish a population (all female). This characteristic would obviously greatly facilitate colonization of isolated islands. Geckos, incidentally, are among the very few reptiles capable of vocalization, and the rapid series of somewhat birdlike chirps of one or more of the Hawaiian species are often heard around Island homes. The number of historically introduced and illegally released lizards is much greater than that indicated in Table 19.2, but only those species known to have established breeding populations are listed.

Although the ancient Hawaiian name ***mo'o*** may today be applied to these and other small lizards, the application is perhaps inappropriate. As used in Hawaiian mythology (and sometimes even modern folklore), this term almost invariably denotes a fearsome, almost dragonlike creature, usually associated with water. Thus, this *mo'o* concept may well have been derived originally from the experience of early Polynesians who were undoubtedly acquainted with the large and dangerous Saltwater Crocodile *(Crocodylus porosus)* of the Southwest Pacific, which has also been recorded as far east as Fiji and, allegedly but questionably, the Tuamotus.

Snakes

Of the four dozen or so species of marine snakes found in various areas in the Pacific, the pelagic Yellow-bellied Sea Snake *(Pelamis platurus)* is the sole taxon reported from Hawaiian waters. Only between about ten and twenty specimens appear to be on definite record for the archipelago; at least four of these were individuals taken at sea rather than on beaches. Young of marine snakes are born alive, usually in the open ocean. The venom of this and other sea snakes is extremely toxic, and the fangs administering it are advantageously located in the anterior portion of the upper jaw. The usual nonaggressive nature of the snakes, however, along with their rarity, keeps human injuries from them to a minimum. All sea snakes may be distinguished from eels by the snakes' possession of a scaled, nonslimy skin and lack of a gill opening. The Yellow-bellied Sea Snake has a purplish black dorsal surface with yellow to orange lateral and ventral surfaces, and the tail is banded with these same colors; no eel or similarly shaped fish shows this same overall color pattern.

Figure 19.1. Four common terrestrial reptiles in Hawai'i. All of these small species are alien. *Clockwise from upper left:* Stump-toed Gecko *(Gehyra mutilata),* Snake-eyed Skink *(Cryptoblepharus poecilopleurus),* Green Anole *(Anolis carolinensis),* Brahminy Blind Snake (*Rhamphotyphlops braminus;* [head to left]). The anole is shown one-half natural size; the others are approximately life size. (Photographs by Allen Allison, used with permission.)

The nonvenomous **Brahminy Blind Snake** (*Rhamphotyphlops braminus* [Figure 19.1]) was first noted in 1930 on the (then) campus of The Kamehameha School for Boys in the lower Kalihi Valley of Honolulu. It is supposed that this earthworm-sized burrowing snake was inadvertently carried in soil around the roots of plants recently transported from the Philippines to landscape the school grounds. The species, which is often called the "Flowerpot Snake" because of its ease in traveling in this manner, subsequently became established on all other main islands. This originally Southeast Asian species is the only known parthenogenic (see earlier discussion on geckos) snake, which helps explain its historic colonization of most isolated Pacific and Indian Ocean islands, as well as of southern parts of Mexico and Africa. The animal is uniform dark brown to black (but becoming light bluish gray preparatory to shedding the skin), has very small eyes barely visible beneath the overlying head scales, and a short spine at the tail tip apparently used to anchor the body when burrowing.

MAMMALS

Background

Even leaving humans out of consideration, members of the class **Mammalia** are now the dominant animals of the world's terrestrial habitats—at least in terms of major environmental effects by individuals. Also, in the oceans, marine mammals are often large, and thus play a significant role in near-surface pelagic and coastal ecosystems. Essentially all mammals, like birds, are "warm-blooded" or **endothermic** (generating and regulating their temperature internally). Thus, mammals and birds are the only vertebrates capable of inhabiting polar regions in addition to all lower-latitude ones.

Mammals typically possess hair at some life stage, and the females of almost all species exhibit **vivipary,** giving birth to live young, and nurse them with milk transmitted through nipples. (The spiny "anteaters" [family Tachyglossidae] and Duck-billed Platypus [family Ornithorhynchidae]) of the order Monotremata lay eggs, but still nourish the hatched young with milk.) The skin of mammals, like that of their reptilian ancestors, is highly resistant to passage of water, although the unique mammalian sweat glands can release internal moisture, whose evaporation aids in lowering body temperature. Various mammals figure prominently in each possible consumer step of the ecological pyramid, from herbivorous rodents and rabbits through the highest-level carnivores such as lions and tigers, larger bears, and the many toothed whales.

Living mammals are usually divided taxonomically into about twenty orders, with the average large continent containing native species of at least a dozen of these. The native Hawaiian Island land-mammal fauna, however, is noticeably disharmonic. In addition to indigenous humans (order Primates), only two other orders are represented naturally: one terrestrial (bats) and one nearshore marine (seals and allies), each containing a single extant Island species (Table 19.3). The additional two native Hawaiian orders (both whales; discussed further in the next section) are entirely pelagic. Six more orders are represented in the Hawaiian Islands only by alien species.

Order Pinnipedia

The archipelago's only living mammal endemic at the species level is the **Hawaiian Monk Seal** or *'īlio holoikauaua* (*Monachus schauinslandi* [Plate 23.1]). The Hawaiian name means "dog running in the toughness [or rough elements]," presumably referring to the animal's long-

Table 19.3. Terrestrial and nonpelagic marine mammals established in Hawai'i. The time of introduction for alien species is also indicated; the Water Buffalo may no longer exist in the wild on any island. The dagger (†) preceding a name indicates an apparent prehistorically extinct endemic taxon. (Data primarily from Tomich [1986].)

Order
  Family
    Species
	Time of Initial
	Introduction

Pouched mammals (Marsupialia)	
Kangaroos and wallabies (Macropodidae)	
Brush-tailed Rock-wallaby *(Petrogale penicillata) kanakalū*	1916
Bats (Chiroptera)	
Common bats (Vespertilionidae)	
Hoary Bat *(Lasiurus cinereus) 'ōpe'ape'a*	(Indigenous)
†Undescribed genus and species *'ōpe'ape'a (?)*	(Endemic)
Rabbits (Lagomorpha)	
Hares and rabbits (Leporidae)	
European Rabbit *(Oryctolagus cuniculus) lāpaki*	pre-1825
Rodents (Rodentia)	
Old World rats and mice (Muridae)	
Polynesian Rat *(Rattus exulans) 'iole*	Polynesian
Norway Rat *(Rattus norvegicus) 'iole nui*	Pre-1860?
Roof Rat *(Rattus rattus) 'iole nui*	1870s?
House Mouse *(Mus musculus) 'iole li'ili'i*	Pre-1825
Carnivores (Carnivora)	
Dogs, wolves, and foxes (Canidae)	
Domestic Dog *(Canis familiaris) 'īlio*	Polynesian
Mongooses and civets (Viverridae)	
Small Indian Mongoose *(Herpestes auropunctatus) manakuke*	1883
Cats, lions, and tigers (Felidae)	
House Cat *(Felis catus) pōpoki*	1800±?
Seals, sea lions, and walruses (Pinnipedia)	
Hair seals (Phocidae)	
Hawaiian Monk Seal *(Monachus schauinslandi) 'īlio holoikauaua*	(Endemic)
Odd-toed hoofed mammals (Perissodactyla)	
Horses, donkeys, and zebras (Equidae)	
Domestic Horse *(Equus caballus) lio*	1803
Donkey *(Equus asinus) kēkake*	1825
Mule *(Equus caballus x Equus asinus) hoki*	Pre-1847
Even-toed hoofed mammals (Artiodactyla)	
Pigs, babirusa, and wart hogs (Suidae)	
Pig *(Sus scrofa) pua'a*	Polynesian

(Continued on following page)

Table 19.3. *(continued)* Terrestrial and nonpelagic marine mammals established in Hawai‘i. The time of introduction for alien species is also indicated; the Water Buffalo may no longer exist in the wild on any island. The dagger (†) preceding a name indicates an apparent prehistorically extinct endemic taxon. (Data primarily from Tomich [1986].)

Order Family Species	Time of Initial Introduction
Deer, elk, moose, caribou, etc. (Cervidae)	
Axis Deer *(Axis axis)* kia	1867
Black-tailed Deer *(Odocoileus hemionus)* kia	1961
American antelope (Antilocapridae)	
Pronghorn *(Antilocapra americana)* ‘anekelopa	1959
Cattle, goats, sheep, African antelopes, etc. (Bovidae)	
Domestic Cattle *(Bos taurus)* pipi	1793
Water Buffalo *(Bubalus bubalis)* pipi pākē	1881
Domestic Goat *(Capra hircus)* kao	1778
Domestic Sheep *(Ovis aries)* hipa	1791
Mouflon *(Ovis musimon)* hipa	1954

shore swimming activities in the surf. Females attain about 2.4 m (8 feet) in length and 257 kg (570 pounds) in weight; the males reach only 173 kg (385 pounds). The population in 1999 was thought to number about 1,300 to 1,400 individuals.

The Hawaiian Monk Seal currently gives birth almost entirely on the isolated beaches of the Northwestern Hawaiian Islands. Occasional animals are, however, seen along shores of the main islands, especially since the late 1980s, with females pupping on both Kaua‘i and O‘ahu. Single wandering animals have been seen at various localities up to 3,700 km (2,300 miles) from Hawai‘i: at the atolls of Johnston, Palmyra, and Wake, as well as Bikini in the Marshall Islands (Figure 24.1). The absence of skeletal material from both paleontological and archaeological sites on the main Hawaiian Islands suggests that, for obscure reasons, the species may always have been scarce in the vicinity of large young islands of the archipelago, preferring instead the small sandy atolls. The only other members of its subtropical genus are a now-rare insular Mediterranean species and a recently extinct Caribbean one.

Order Chiroptera

The large, strong-flying, fruit- and blossom-eating bats that successfully expanded their range from tropical Southeast Asia to as far east as the Mariana Islands and Samoa never reached Hawai‘i. The only bat species now extant in the archipelago is the smaller, insectivorous **Hoary Bat** or *‘ōpe‘ape‘a (Lasiurus cinereus)*. Bats of this New World genus are accomplished long-distance fliers and at least some species are migratory, characteristics that doubtless aided colonization of the Hawaiian Islands. The species probably occurs on all main islands, although currently quite sparingly on most. The archipelago population has been named as an endemic subspecies although only very slight (if any) average differences in size and coloration separate it from conspecific continental populations. This essential lack of differentiation suggests that the length of Island residency of the Hawaiian animal has been in the range of hundreds of thousands—rather than millions—of years. Unlike many insectivorous bats that roost colonially in caves, the Hoary Bat and its several continental congeners are typically solitary daytime roosters in trees and other vegetation, although remains of individuals are occasionally found in caves.

In the early 1980s, a number of (undated) skeletons of a second, smaller taxon of apparently prehistorically extinct insectivorous bat were discovered on the floors of Hawai'i, Maui, and Moloka'i lava tubes (along with a few Hoary Bat skeletons). Lack of bat-excrement deposits ("guano") in Hawaiian lava tubes, however, indicate that neither of these native chiropterans ever utilized this habitat in substantial numbers. The extinct bat is still awaiting formal naming. It, however, evidently belongs to the same large and cosmopolitan family (Vespertilionidae) as the Hoary Bat and may represent a relatively closely related genus, thus presumably also being derived from the Americas. The time period that the smaller bat existed in the Islands is incompletely known, as is the exact time that the Hoary Bat first arrived. Bones of the two forms have subsequently been recovered from Kaua'i and O'ahu paleontological deposits that are much less than 100,000 years old. And at least the smaller bat is represented in an O'ahu crater-fill deposit substantially more than 130,000 years in age (Ulupa'u Head; see chapter 22).

Polynesian Mammals

The **Polynesian Rat** or *'iole* (*Rattus exulans* [Figure 19.2]), **Domestic Dog** or *'īlio (Canis familiaris)*, and **Pig** or *pua'a (Sus scrofa)* were the three species of mammals brought to the Hawaiian Islands by ancient Polynesians (see chapter 25). The latter two have extensively interbred with individuals of the same species continually introduced after foreign contact with the Islands, so it is difficult to determine the total range of morphological variation present in the original Polynesian forms. To judge from archaeological skeletal evidence and early historical records, however, both the ancient Domestic Dog and Pig seem to have been significantly smaller and more lightly built than even average-sized, often domestically selected, historic animals. The Polynesian Rat, evidently carried by Polynesians to all Pacific island groups they colonized, perhaps provides an example of founder effect and/or genetic drift in Hawai'i. The genotype producing the blackish or melanistic dimorphic color phase evident on certain other Pacific archipelagos (at least the Solomons, Marshalls, and Samoa) is not represented in the Hawaiian population.

Historic Mammals

Most of the larger mammals introduced to Hawai'i in the early historic period were intended either for food or beast-of-burden purposes. Among the smaller alien species, the **House Mouse** or *'iole li'ili'i (Mus musculus)* as well as the larger **Norway and Roof Rats** or *'iole nui (Rattus norvegicus* and *R. rattus)* first arrived in the Islands as unintended travelers on early historic sailing ships. One or more **House Cats** or *pōpoki (Felis catus)* were usually carried aboard many of these same vessels, primarily to control the rodent infestations. Undoubtedly, some of these felids or members of their ship-born litters were given to Hawaiian residents at Island ports, where the entire native populace was understandably fascinated by this strange and completely new kind of animal. The more recently imported **Small Indian Mongoose** or *manakuke (Herpestes auropunctatus)* was intended as a control agent of alien rats in Sugarcane fields.

The incongruous presence of a marsupial in the Islands is due to the chance escape from a private zoo of a single pair of the **Brush-tailed Rock-wallaby** or *kanakalū (Petrogale peni-*

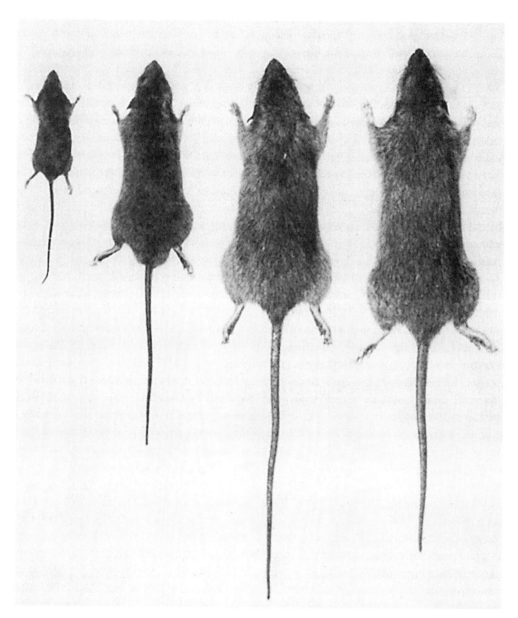

Figure 19.2. Comparison of the four introduced murid rodents in Hawai'i. *Left to right:* House Mouse *(Mus musculus),* Polynesian Rat *(Rattus exulans),* Roof Rat *(Rattus rattus),* and Norway Rat *(Rattus norvegicus).* Note the distinctive external characteristics of significantly smaller size of the House Mouse (approximately 15 cm or 6 inches in total length) and exceptionally long tail of the Roof Rat. (Photograph by William S. Devick; Fig. 12 of Tomich [1986], used with permission of Bishop Museum Press.)

cillata) early in the twentieth century. For almost 80 years the population derived from this pair has managed to maintain a small population on the steep, rocky slopes of lower Kalihi Valley on O'ahu. It is interesting that when specimens taken from this colony in 1979 were compared with various populations in the species' Australian homeland, they were found to be noticeably smaller, and several of their biochemical characteristics could not be matched in any of the living Australian groups tested. It is a still-unanswered question whether these differences in the Hawaiian form (whose exact ancestral source area within Australia is unknown) resulted from genetic drift, or whether the particular original population from which the colonizing pair came is now extinct.

A novel and sometimes amusing set of Hawaiian names developed as alien historic species were introduced. The early Island term for the cat, *pōpoki,* was apparently the Hawaiian transliteration of "poor pussy." Certain other names that came to be applied were elaborations of traditional terms for similar animals; for example, *'iole* was the long-familiar Polynesian Rat, so the smaller alien House Mouse quite naturally became *'iole li'ili'i* or "little rat," and the two new larger Norway and Roof Rats were each *'iole nui* or "big rat." Most other such appellations merely represented Hawaiian pronunciations of English names, as *manakuke* and *kanakalū* for "mongoose" and "kangaroo," respectively, as well as *kēkake* for "donkey," *hipa* for "sheep," and *pipi* for "beef" (= cattle). Occasional curious name transpositions and combinations also appeared: for example, *kao* for the Domestic Goat instead of for "cow," and *pipi pākē* or "Chinese cattle" for Water Buffalo *(Bubalus bubalis).*

Whales, Dolphins, and Porpoises

The pelagic marine mammals or **cetaceans** are divided into two orders: the Mysticeti or baleen whales; and the Odontoceti or toothed whales, including dolphins and porpoises. All mysticetes feed on "krill" or concentrations of small planktonic crustaceans, straining these (and occasional accompanying schools of small fishes) out of great mouthfuls of water by means of close-set series of internally frayed keratinous plates (baleen or "whalebone") that line the inside of the upper jaw. Even the largest baleen whales are not "top carnivores" in the food chain because they are preyed upon by certain sharks. All of the cetaceans for which there seem reliable records of Hawaiian occurrence are among those Pacific species listed in Table 19.4.

Of the half dozen or so baleen whales found in the central Pacific, only the **Humpback Whale** or *koholā (Megaptera novaeangliae)* is usually seen in nearshore Hawaiian waters. (The term *"koholā"* was quite possibly a generalized one in ancient Hawai'i, applying to any large cetacean; see further information in the discussion on the Sperm Whale below.) The entire North Pacific Humpback population, currently numbering at least several thousand animals, feeds during the warmer half of the year in Arctic waters. In winter, the animals divide into three discrete units that migrate south to calve along, respectively, the American and Asian coasts as well as among the main Hawaiian Islands. The Hawaiian complement is present among the Islands from about December through May or June, its conspicuous blowing ("spouting") and leaping activities forming a popular attraction. This Hawaiian population is estimated as between 1,500 and 3,000 individuals, and the number of calves born in the archipelago each season appears to range from about 75 to 150.

The toothed whales are represented by about three dozen species throughout the Pacific as a whole; half of these are relatively small, between about 2 and 5 m (7 and 16 feet) in length, and only one of the remaining species exceeds 9 m (30 feet). Most of the toothed whales occupy a relatively high trophic level, feeding on fishes, large squid, and occasionally larger benthic invertebrates, and at least the Killer Whale *(Orcinus orca)* takes smaller dolphins and porpoises as well as seals and sea lions. The largest odontocete worldwide is the **Sperm Whale** *(Physeter macrocephalus),* whose males reach 19 m (63 feet) in length, with females about two-thirds that long. The species is almost never seen alive in Hawaiian waters. Dead or dying individuals, however, occasionally wash ashore, although such occurrences were doubtless very infrequent before about 1820, when historic whaling began in the central Pacific.

Table 19.4. Cetaceans in or near Hawaiian waters. Undoubtedly, a few additional species very occasionally visit the archipelago. The approximate maximum lengths attained are listed. An asterisk (*) precedes the names of the species most often seen around the main islands and a question mark (?) those of uncertain occurrence. (Data from various sources.)

Order Family Species	Maximum Length in Meters (Feet)
Baleen whales (Mysticeti)	
Fin-back whales (Balaenopteridae)	
*Humpback Whale *(Megaptera novaeangliae)*	15 (50)
Fin Whale *(Balaenoptera physalus)*	18 (60)
Bryde's Whale *(Balaenoptera edeni)*	14 (45)
Minke Whale *(Balaenoptera acutorostrata)*	8 (27)
Right whales (Balaenidae)	
Right Whale *(Eubalaena glacialis)*	18 (60)
Toothed Whales (Odontoceti)	
Sperm whales (Physeteridae)	
Sperm Whale *(Physeter macrocephalus)*	Male, 19 (63); female, 12 (40)
Pygmy Sperm Whale *(Kogia breviceps)*	4 (13)
Dwarf Sperm Whale *(Kogia simus)*	2.7 (9)
Beaked whales (Ziphiidae)	
Cuvier's Beaked Whale *(Ziphius cavirostris)*	7 (23)
Blainville's Beaked Whale *(Mesoplodon densirostris)*	4.6 (15)
Dolphins and allies (Delphinidae)	
Killer Whale *(Orcinus orca)*	8.6 (28)
*Short-finned Pilot Whale *(Globicephala macrorhynchus)*	7 (23)
False Killer Whale *(Pseudorca crassidens)*	5.5 (18)
Risso's Dolphin *(Grampus griseus)*	4 (13)
*Bottlenose Dolphin *(Tursiops truncatus)*	3 (10)
*Broad-beaked Dolphin *(Peponocephala electra)*	2.4 (8)
Pygmy Killer Whale *(Feresa attenuata)*	2.4 (8)
Rough-toothed Dolphin *(Steno bredanensis)*	2.4 (8)
Striped Dolphin *(Stenella coeruleoalba)*	2.4 (8)
*Spotted Dolphin *(Stenella attenuata)*	2 (7)
*Spinner Dolphin *(Stenella longirostris)*	2 (7)
?White-sided Dolphin *(Lagenorhynchus obliquidens)*	2 (7)
?Common Dolphin *(Delphinus delphis)*	2 (7)

There is some question as to the traditional Hawaiian name for the Sperm Whale. A thick necklace of human hair with a suspended tongue-shaped ornament of ivory (mammalian dentine; in prehistoric Hawai'i that of the Sperm Whale, but historically also that of the walrus or possibly even of the elephant), worn only by some members of the chiefly class, was called *"lei niho palaoa"* (or simply *"lei palaoa"*). *Lei,* of course, is "wreath" or "necklace," and *niho* means "tooth." The final word of this term, however, is sometimes translated as "Sperm Whale," but it may equally well be glossed only as "ivory." In the latter case, *"palaoa"* would not be indicated as the traditional Hawaiian name of the Sperm Whale, as such, and the species would probably have been included with the Humpback Whale in *"koholā."*

In regard to names of smaller odontocetes, it might be noted that the term "porpoise" is frequently used in the place of "dolphin" for some species and also that "Dolphin" is an alternative name for a fish: the *mahimahi (Coryphaena hippurus).* It appears that the collective Hawaiian terms *nu'ao* or, occasionally, *nai'a* are the only two recorded as referring to odontocetes smaller than the Sperm Whale. This particular lack of differentiation in recorded Hawaiian terminology seems unusual because at least a few dolphin species are of common occurrence along Hawaiian coasts and are generally separable by color pattern and, in a few cases, behavior. It appears almost certain that ancient Hawaiians would have known the differences among at least these more obvious Island species, but, if so, the traditional specific names have unfortunately been lost.

SUGGESTED REFERENCES

Balazs 1976, 1980; Balcomb 1987; Banks et al. (eds.) 1987; Beletsky 2000; Ching 1994; Hirth 1997; Hunsaker and Breese 1967; Kramer 1971; Kraus et al. 1999; McKeown 1996; Oliver and Shaw 1953; Tomich 1986; Twiss and Reeves (eds.) 1999; U.S. Department of Commerce 1986, 1997; van Riper and van Riper 1982.

AUDIOVISUAL AIDS

Hawaii: Strangers in paradise.

20

Birds

Like mammals, birds can control their body temperature and thus function satisfactorily in all of the world's climatic regimes. Characters retained from ancestral reptiles that minimize water loss include scaled skin on otherwise bare lower hind limbs, a greatly concentrated form of urinary waste (uric acid crystals), and a shelled egg. These water-conserving adaptations have allowed many birds to occupy diurnal feeding and other activity niches in sun-scorched deserts that companion mammals exploit largely only at night. Evolution of flight by means of the unique feathers and skeletal modifications has also permitted much more efficient exploitation of the aerial environment than has been possible for bats, the only completely volant mammal. Even marine feeding niches not occupied by pelagic mammals are filled by many types of oceanic birds, some on the surface but others well down in the water as in the case of diving ducks and the secondarily flightless penguins (the latter of which, however, still "fly" in underwater activity).

BIOTIC COMPOSITION AND DISHARMONY

Modern representatives of the class Aves are taxonomically divided into twenty-eight orders. Most large continents contain members of perhaps twenty of these orders, but the disharmonic (see chapter 10) native Hawaiian avifauna possesses species from only half this number. The noticeable prehistoric absence in Hawai'i of such orders as those of pigeons and doves, parrots, and kingfishers is surprising because each of these types has colonized many isolated Southwest Pacific island groups. Also, among the ten Hawaiian orders, the endemic and indigenous species belong to only 23 families, even though these same orders contain approximately 120 families worldwide. Such a great taxonomic variety of alien birds has been introduced to the Hawaiian Islands in historic times, however, that this avian disharmony is now seldom appreciated.

The thirty-seven families of oceanic, freshwater, and land birds currently or formerly breeding on a *sustained* basis in the Hawaiian Archipelago are listed in Table 20.1, along with the numbers of species or subspecies of the various native and alien taxa. (The species figures in the tables of this and other chapters may vary somewhat from those of other references because of differing taxonomic decisions of various authorities being followed.)

GEOGRAPHIC SOURCE

Endemic Species

The source areas of founders yielding endemic Hawaiian birds that can be determined with some degree of certainty are listed in Table 20.2. The designation "American" includes both North and South America; "Asian" comprises mainland Asia, Australasia, and all Southwest Pacific islands. The American region seems to have supplied nine founders, and the Asian region six. The remaining twelve founders, however, are of undetermined geographic origin, with two reasons for this uncertainty. A putative founding species may occur on both sides of the Pacific,

Table 20.1. Families of extant and extinct Hawaiian birds. Note that only species and subspecies with current or former *sustained* breeding colonies are included. A dagger (†) indicates taxa prehistorically extinct in the Islands, and an octothorp (#) historically extirpated ones. (Data from various sources.)

Family	Endemic Species or Subspecies	Indigenous Species	Alien Species
Albatrosses (Diomedeidae)		2	
Petrels, etc. (Procellariidae)	†1 + 2	†1 + 4	
Storm-Petrels (Hydrobatidae)		2	
Tropicbirds (Phaethontidae)		2	
Boobies (Sulidae)		3	
Frigatebirds (Fregatidae)		1	
Herons and egrets (Ardeidae)	†1?	1	1
Ibises (Threskiornithidae)	†4		
Ducks and geese (Anatidae)	†8 + 3	†1	1
Hawks and eagles (Accipitridae)	†1 + 1	†1	
Chickens, etc. (Phasianidae)			12
Rails, etc. (Rallidae)	†10 + #2 + 2		
Stilts (Recurvirostridae)	1		
Terns (Laridae)	1	5	
Sandgrouse (Pteroclididae)			1
Doves and pigeons (Columbidae)			4
Parrots (Psittacidae)			1
Barn owls (Tytonidae)			1
Typical owls (Strigidae)	†4 + 1		
Swifts (Apodidae)			1
Honeyeaters (Meliphagidae)	†1 + #5		
Crows (Corvidae)	†2 + 1		
Monarchs (Monarchidae)	1		
Larks (Alaudidae)			1
Bulbuls (Pycnonotidae)			2
Old World warblers (Sylviidae)	1		1
Thrushes (Turdidae)	#2 + 2		1
Babblers (Timaliidae)			4
White-eyes (Zosteropidae)			1
Mockingbirds (Mimidae)			1
Mynas (Sturnidae)			1
New World sparrows, etc. (Emberizidae)			4
True cardinals (Cardinalidae)			1
Meadowlarks, etc. (Icteridae)			1
Finches, etc. (Fringillidae)			
Cardueline finches (Carduelinae)			3
Hawaiian honeycreepers (Drepanidinae)	†14 + #10 + 23		
Old World sparrows (Passeridae)			1
Waxbills, etc. (Estrildidae)			10
Total 37 families	104	23	54
	(†1 + #1 + 35)	(†46 + #19 + 39)	(†3 + 20)

as do, for example, the Common Moorhen and Short-eared Owl (see discussion of their families later in this chapter). Or, in other instances, the Hawaiian derivatives may have evolutionarily differentiated so greatly that the founding species—or even its genus—cannot now be ascertained surely, as, for example, in the case of Stilt-owls of the endemic genus †*Grallistrix*. (In the discussions of Hawaiian birds the dagger [†] preceding a generic or specific name means that the entire taxon is prehistorically extinct in the Islands; the octothorp [#] means that the last Hawaiian species of the taxon became extinct during historic time.)

Indigenous and Other Species

The primary source area among the thirteen Hawaiian land and freshwater birds classified as breeding visitant and indigenous resident, as well as common nonbreeding migrant in Table 20.3 seems to have been the New World (primarily the northern half of it), because six are American and only one is Asian. This cannot be considered entirely definitive, though, because the remaining six cases of unknown source involve species essentially cosmopolitan in temperate and subtropical latitudes. Also, in some cases, conspecific individuals from *both* continents may well have reached the Hawaiian Islands.

The frequent tropical storms moving west from the coast of North and Central America (see chapter 7) might appear to have been most influential in aiding flights of the American birds to the Hawaiian Islands. Most such storms, however, involve quite violent air movements that birds might well not survive, especially since an individual would have to exist in such an environment for the several days it took a storm to reach the Hawaiian Islands. Also, because these meteorological disturbances are almost always limited to a latitudinal band near the equator, they would have had only a small chance of involving most of the American founders, which live primarily well north of this tropical band. It is more likely that the trade winds, relatively consistently blowing from just southwest of North America (Figure 7.1), were the primary factor helping wayward founders from this area reach the Islands. The fact that disoriented migrating North American birds would have a greater chance of reaching Hawai'i than would ones from Asia has already been noted in chapter 13.

ATTENUATION

Within the avian families represented naturally in the archipelago, the drastic attenuation (see chapter 11) in species apparently emigrating from Southwest Pacific areas through island "stepping-stones" to Hawai'i is especially noticeable in the large and varied order **Passeriformes** (perching or songbirds; entries "Honeyeaters" through "Waxbills, etc." of Table 20.1). For instance, although the New Guinea region possesses at least fifty species of the Old World monarch family Monarchidae, the Fiji Islands have only nine, the number drops to three in the Samoan Islands, and only one managed to colonize Hawai'i. Similarly, from North America, the dozen or so typical thrushes (Turdidae) there contributed just a single colonizing species to the native Hawaiian avifauna.

ENDEMISM

The prehistorically extinct and historically recorded endemic forms are here considered a single fauna because most if not all apparently coexisted until late pre-Contact times. On this basis, 104 or 82 percent of the approximately 127 native species and subspecies of sustained-breeding

Table 20.2. Endemic species and subspecies of Hawaiian birds. Numbers of founders and their general geographical sources in terms of sides of the Pacific are also listed. A dagger (†) indicates prehistorically extinct taxa, and an octothorp (#) historically extirpated ones. (Data from various sources.)

Family Species/Subspecies	Founder Number and Source
Shearwaters and petrels (Procellariidae)	
Gracile Petrel (*†Pterodroma jugabilis*)	1 Unknown
Hawaiian Petrel or *'ua'u* (*Pterodroma phaeopygia sandwichensis*)	1 Unknown
Newell Shearwater or *'a'o* (*Puffinus newelli*)	1 Unknown
Herons and egrets (Ardeidae)	
O'ahu heron (*Ardea?* [†sp.])	1 American?
Ibises (Threskiornithidae)	
Maui Nui ibises (*†Apteribis* [4 spp.])	1 American
Ducks and geese (Anatidae)	
Laysan Duck (*Anas laysanensis*)	1 Asian?
Hawaiian Duck or *koloa maoli* (*Anas wyvilliana*)	1 American?
Moa nalo (†4 spp. in †3 genera)	1 American?
Hawaiian Goose or *nēnē* (*Branta sandvicensis*)	⎫
Forest *Nēnē* (*†Branta hylobadistes* and close allies)	⎬ 1 American
Giant Hawai'i Goose (*†Branta* sp.)	⎭
O'ahu Flat-billed "Goose" (†undetermined genus and sp.)	1 Unknown
Lesser Hawai'i "Goose" (*†Geochen rhuax*)	1 Unknown
Hawks and eagles (Accipitridae)	
Hawaiian Hawk or *'io* (*Buteo solitarius*)	1 American
Wood Harrier (*†Circus dossenus*)	1 Unknown
Rails, gallinules, and coots (Rallidae)	
Flightless rails (*Porzana* [†10 + #2 spp.])	2 Asian
Hawaiian Gallinule or *'alae 'ula* (*Gallinula chloropus sandvicensis*)	1 Unknown
Hawaiian Coot or *'alae ke'oke'o* (*Fulica alai*)	1 American
Stilts (Recurvirostridae)	
Hawaiian Stilt or *ae'o* (*Himantopus mexicanus knudseni*)	1 American
Terns (Laridae)	
Black Noddy or *noio* (*Anous minutus melanogenys*)	1 Unknown
Typical owls (Strigidae)	
Hawaiian Owl or *pueo* (*Asio flammeus sandvicensis*)	1 Unknown
Stilt-Owls (*†Grallistrix* [4 spp.])	1 Unknown
Honeyeaters (Meliphagidae)	
Hawaiian *'Ō'ō* (#*Moho* [4 spp.])	⎫ 1 Asian
Kioea (*Chaetoptila* [†1 + #1 spp.])	⎭

(Continued on following page)

Table 20.2. *(continued)* Endemic species and subspecies of Hawaiian birds. Numbers of founders and their general geographical sources in terms of sides of the Pacific are also listed. A dagger (†) indicates prehistorically extinct taxa, and an octothorp (#) historically extirpated ones. (Data from various sources.)

Family Species/Subspecies	Founder Number and Source
Crows (Corvidae)	
Hawaiian Crow or *'alalā (Corvus hawaiiensis)*	
Hawaiian crows (*Corvus* [†2 spp.])	} 1 Unknown
Monarchs (Monarchidae)	
'Elepaio (Chasiempis sandwicensis)	1 Asian
Old World warblers (Sylviidae)	
Millerbird *(Acrocephalus familiaris)*	1 Asian
Thrushes (Turdidae)	
Hawaiian thrushes (*Myadestes* [#2 + 2 spp.])	1 American
Finches, etc. (Fringillidae)	
Hawaiian honeycreepers (†14 + #10 + 23 spp. in †4 + #5 + 12 genera)	1 Unknown
Total 104 endemic species/subspecies	27 founders
(†46 + #19 + 39)	(9 American, 6 Asian, 12 unknown)

Hawaiian birds are endemic (Table 20.1). The data in Table 20.2 reveal that most avian founders yielded only one or a very few descendant species, with the notable exception of the smaller rails (Rallidae) and the Hawaiian honeycreepers (finch family Fringillidae). Even the relatively high average of six derivatives per founder listed for these rails is questionable, because there could have been more than two colonizing species.

The reason for the spectacular diversification of the Hawaiian honeycreepers is unknown, although several possibilities could be offered. For example, their ancestor may have been the first passeriform—or among the earliest ones—to colonize the archipelago. Subsequent adaptive radiation (see chapter 10) of its descendant line into a number of the available ecological niches may have prevented filling of these by potentially evolving descendants of later passeriform immigrants. Or if the Hawaiian honeycreepers' cardueline finch ancestor (see chapter 21) was a relatively late arrival, it may have represented an exceptionally adaptive avian line. The high frequency of mutations in the established cardueline population could then have yielded many forms that were able to evolve relatively rapidly into niches either vacant or only partially utilized by any earlier evolving passeriforms. In regard to the established native land and freshwater bird types other than passeriforms (herons, ibises, ducks and geese, hawks and eagles, rails and allies, stilts, and owls), ancestors of a few may have reached the archipelago earlier than the honeycreeper colonizer, but the relatively specialized ecological requirements of these various nonpasseriforms were not conducive to similar spectacular adaptive radiation.

Table 20.3. Some breeding visitant and indigenous resident Hawaiian nonmarine bird species. (See Table 20.2 for the three breeding indigenous nonmarine species with endemic Hawaiian subspecies, and Table 23.3 for the ocean-related species.) The most common nonbreeding migrants are also included, and the general geographic source of each taxon is listed. A dagger (†) indicates a prehistorically extinct Hawaiian population. (Data from various sources.)

Family Species	Status	Geographic Source
Grebes (Podicipedidae)		
Pied-billed Grebe *(Podilymbus podiceps)*	Formerly breeding visitant	America
Herons and egrets (Ardeidae)		
Black-crowned Night-Heron or *'auku'u* *(Nycticorax nycticorax)*	Currently breeding resident	Unknown
Ducks and geese (Anatidae)		
Fulvous Whistling-Duck *(Dendrocygna bicolor)*	Formerly breeding visitant	America
Northern Pintail or *koloa māpu (Anas acuta)*	Nonbreeding migrant	Unknown
Blue-winged Teal *(Anas discors)*	Formerly breeding visitant	America
Northern Shoveler or *koloa mohā (Anas clypeata)*	Nonbreeding migrant	Unknown
Canada Goose (†*Branta canadensis*)	Formerly breeding resident	America
Hawks and eagles (Accipitridae)		
Hawaiian Sea Eagle (†*Haliaeetus albicilla*)	Formerly breeding resident	Asia
Plovers (Charadriidae)		
Pacific Golden-Plover or *kōlea (Pluvialis fulva)*	Nonbreeding migrant	Unknown
Sandpipers, etc. (Scolopacidae)		
Wandering Tattler or *'ūlili (Heteroscelus incanus)*	Nonbreeding migrant	America
Bristle-thighed Curlew or *kioea (Numenius tahitiensis)*	Nonbreeding migrant	America
Ruddy Turnstone or *'akekeke (Arenaria interpres)*	Nonbreeding migrant	Unknown
Sanderling or *hunakai (Calidris alba)*	Nonbreeding migrant	Unknown

OTHER EVOLUTIONARY PHENOMENA

Founder Effect and Genetic Drift

Because most endemic Hawaiian avian species have differentiated so greatly from their colonizing ancestor, it is difficult now to discern any possible founder effects (see chapter 10). Similarly, the instances of genetic drift that undoubtedly occurred soon after initial colonization are no longer evident. Some more recent instances of this phenomenon apparently taking place as species spread to different islands of the archipelago may be noted, however. The *'Elepaio (Chasiempis sandwichensis)* of the family Monarchidae occurs on Kaua'i, O'ahu, and Hawai'i and has been divided into five subspecies, primarily on the basis of color pattern. The separate subspecies on each of the former two islands, as well as one of the three on the latter are shown in Figure 10.1. The ecology of the various subspecies seems essentially the same, and the differences in plumage are not obviously related to habitat differences; thus the *'Elepaio* color variation is assumed to be largely if not wholly due to genetic drift. Also, in the honeyeater family Meliphagidae, this same type of genetic drift appears to be exhibited by '*Ō'ō* species of the endemic genus #*Moho,* as illustrated in Plate 20.1.

An interesting color change that formerly was sometimes attributed to genetic drift has appeared in an alien species of bird, the House Finch or Linnet (*Carpodacus mexicanus* [finch subfamily Carduelinae]) since its introduction to the Hawaiian Islands over 130 years ago. In its native western North America, the males of this generally brown-striped species typically have heads and throats strongly tinged with red, but in many Hawaiian individuals the red is replaced by orange or yellow. Recent work with mainland populations of the species has revealed that this same differential coloration also began appearing there in the latter half of the twentieth century. Further investigation demonstrated, seemingly conclusively, that the cause is not genetic but, rather, is due to one or more types of physiological stress. Such stress yields a weakened bodily condition that does not allow a bird to metabolize dietary components fully enough to provide the usual red coloration to the plumage, resulting in only orange or yellow feathers. Bird pox was found to be a major cause of this physiological weakening, and, because this disease is common in Hawai'i (see chapter 26), infection by it is likely responsible for the color abnormalities in Island House Finches.

Adaptive Shifts

Apart from the Hawaiian honeycreepers (discussed in chapter 21), most types of passeriforms colonizing the Hawaiian Islands maintained essentially the same ecological niche as their immediate ancestor. Among the nonpasseriforms, however, adaptive shifts (see chapter 10) were made by members of a number of nonoceanic families. Undoubtedly, the most profound was transition from a flighted existence to a nonvolant one, which occurred in three different groups: ibises (Threskiornithidae), ducks and geese (Anatidae), and rails. A further examination of this particular phenomenon, however, is reserved for chapter 22. Another almost equally notable adaptive shift was one from an ancestral diet of a variety of vertebrate prey to one of mostly or entirely birds, which resulted in striking morphological changes in the colonizing lines of both a hawk and an owl. This adaptive shift in these two predatory birds is further examined in the following family discussions of endemic Hawaiian birds.

SHEARWATERS AND PETRELS (FAMILY PROCELLARIIDAE)

A prehistorically extinct member of this family, the **Gracile Petrel** (†*Pterodroma jugabilis*) was named in 1991. Remains of the species are known only from O'ahu and Hawai'i, and on at least the latter island some of the bones were found in an archaeological context, so the bird obviously survived into the Polynesian period. This species, like the Hawaiian Petrel or '*ua'u* (*Pterodroma phaeopygia sandwichensis,* an endemic subspecies of the central and eastern Pacific Dark-rumped Petrel) and the endemic Newell Shearwater or '*a'o* (*Puffinus newelli),* may have been restricted to the Hawaiian Islands, because it has not been recorded elsewhere.

HERONS (FAMILY ARDEIDAE)

A large heron lived on Windward O'ahu sometime between about 800,000 and 120,000 or so years ago; it is commonly recorded from the Ulupa'u Head pond deposits (see chapter 22). Osteologically, this ardeid seems similar to the large North American Great Blue Heron *(Ardea herodias),* an occasional historic vagrant to the Islands, and when the Hawaiian bird is scientifically described it will possibly be placed in this same genus. Incidentally, it seems unusual that the ecologically adaptable Southwest Pacific Reef Heron *(Egretta sacra),* which reaches as far east as Samoa and the Tuamotus, never became a successful Hawaiian immigrant.

IBISES (FAMILY THRESKIORNITHIDAE)

Ibises are typically long-legged continental birds notable for their elongated downcurved bill; some are wetland inhabitants, but many species frequent dry, open country. None is known to be endemic to any insular Pacific locality other than the Hawaiian Islands and Rennell Island in the south-central Solomons. In Hawai'i, the endemic flightless genus †*Apteribis* (Table 22.1, Plate 22.1) evolved on the islands of Maui Nui (Figure 3.3). Presumably, a single colonizing event gave rise to this Island line, and comparison of DNA nucleotide-pair sequences indicates that the immigrant ancestral species was the New World White Ibis *(Eudocimus albus).* There were possibly as many as four species of ibises present on the various Maui Nui islands; this surprising amount of speciation probably was the result of alternating separation and coalescence of these landmasses as Pleistocene sea levels rose and fell (see chapter 3).

The failure of any of the **Maui Nui ibises** to populate other main islands is most puzzling. It may be that the younger island of Hawai'i had not yet developed extensive forest habitat suitable for such a bird before the Maui Nui ibises had become flightless and were thus effectively prevented from occupying it. But the older islands of O'ahu and Kaua'i surely offered varied habitat comparable with that of Maui Nui, and still they were not colonized by the early stillflighted birds.

Because of the scarcity of permanent freshwater impoundments (see chapters 8, 14) and open-land habitats (see chapter 25) before human arrival, the Maui Nui ibises had to have occupied primarily forested areas. Their diet undoubtedly consisted of invertebrates living on and below the surface or in lower vegetation, and this food may well have included many endemic land and freshwater snails (see chapter 18), although this latter possibility has yet to be proven. At any rate, their flightless condition and probing bill morphology may have resulted in a way of life somewhat like that of the similarly nonvolant kiwis *(Apteryx* spp. [Apterygidae; whose ancestor, incidentally, was of unknown family]) of New Zealand. Because the ibises did not disperse from Maui Nui, it is unusual that their distinctive ecological niche was apparently never filled by some other evolving line of birds on the remaining main islands. Perhaps this is one of the theorized occasional examples of an unfilled way of life alluded to at the end of chapter 9.

DUCKS AND GEESE (FAMILY ANATIDAE)

Native Ducks

There were at least four different ancient colonizations of the Hawaiian Islands by members of the Anatidae. One was by a yet-undetermined species of duck (subfamily Anatinae) that yielded the **Laysan Duck** *(Anas laysanensis),* which apparently once occupied all of the Hawaiian Islands, including at least Laysan and Lisianski in the Northwestern chain (see chapter 23). The prehistorically extinct main island populations were not restricted to the few bodies of freshwater, but evidently also ranged extensively through both lowland and upland wooded areas. The extant **Hawaiian Duck** or ***koloa maoli*** *(Anas wyvilliana)* of the main islands is similar in coloration to the Laysan Duck, although skeletally somewhat larger. The two species had long been thought to be very closely related, but recent DNA studies indicate that the Hawaiian Duck is very closely related to the modern Mallard *(Anas platyrhynchos)* or its immediate ancestral line, but the Laysan Duck is relatively quite distinct in relationship from both these anatid types.

Moa Nalo

One or, possibly, two of the earliest other duck colonists of the Islands yielded the four named flightless *moa nalo* (a modern term coined in 1991 from the Hawaiian words *"moa"* [fowl] and *"nalo"* [lost or vanished]). These various *moa nalo* are known from all larger main islands except Hawaiʻi and comprise the genera †*Chelychelynechen,* †*Thambetochen,* and †*Ptaiochen* (Table 22.1), all of which were convergent with true geese (discussed later in this section) in many skeletal characteristics. Because of this similarity, these prehistorically extinct *moa nalo* were originally called "flightless geese" (and even the suffix *"-chen"* in the generic names given them is Greek for "goose"). Discoveries in Maui lava tubes in the 1980s, however, revealed that they were evidently derived from ducks rather than from geese. Accompanying the numerous bones of the Maui Nui *Moa nalo* (†*Thambetochen chauliodous*) and Clumsy *Moa nalo* (†*Ptaiochen pau*) were ossified expansions of the lower windpipe known as syringeal bullae. These structures, which develop only in males, are not found in geese but occur in many kinds of ducks. The recovered bullae closely resemble those of two types of ducks: the genus *Anas,* which includes the suite of familiar Mallardlike dabbling species, and the less well known diving shelducks. The latter have never been reported from the Hawaiian Islands, but at least five species of *Anas* are relatively common yearly visitors. Recent comparisons of DNA characters similarly indicate that the *moa nalo* colonizing ancestor was a duck rather than a true goose and also indicate a probable closest relationship to some relatively primitive now-extinct type of dabbling duck. Use of a "molecular clock" based on amount of divergence in DNA nucleotide-pair sequences suggests that evolution of the Island *moa nalo* began about 3.6 million years ago.

The various bulky, stout-legged, terrestrial *moa nalo* probably weighed between 4.0 and 7.6 kg (8.8 and 16.7 pounds) and had a browsing reach as great as 1 m (3.3 feet). They originally filled the niche of a large **herbivorous** or plant-eating vertebrate in Hawaiʻi, much as do giant land tortoises on the Galápagos Islands, and various hoofed and other large herbivorous mammals on continents. In fact, the distinctive high, short bill of †*Chelychelynechen quassus* (Figure 20.1) from Kauaʻi is so reminiscent of that of a herbivorous land turtle that, as a literal translation of its generic scientific epithet, the common name of Tortoise-jawed *Moa nalo* seems most appropriate. The possible evolutionary effect of *moa nalo* predation on certain endemic lobelioids of the bellflower family Campanulaceae was described in chapter 15.

It is uncertain whether the enigmatic prehistorically extinct Oʻahu Flat-billed "Goose," thus far known only by a single upper jaw-tip fragment and another small skull bone from ʻEwa Plain fossil-reef sinkholes (see chapter 22), will eventually prove to be a *moa nalo* or a true goose. The same is true of the equally puzzling Lesser Hawaiʻi "Goose" (†*Geochen rhuax*), named from a few fragmentary bones found under a lava flow on the southern part of Hawaiʻi Island many years ago.

True Geese

A prehistorically extinct population of true goose (subfamily Anserinae) whose members seem osteologically indistinguishable from the extant North American Canada Goose *(Branta canadensis)* once existed on Windward Oʻahu, although there is no evidence that the population persisted there later than 120,000 or so years ago. This goose is represented by a relatively great

Figure 20.1. Artist's conception of the Tortoise-jawed *Moa nalo (†Chelychelynechen quassus)*. Also shown in the center foreground, is a flightless ibis; and the background (flying, left to right), the Hawaiian Sea Eagle, a raven-sized species of the crow family, the Hoary Bat, and a stilt-owl. All four of the avian taxa are prehistorically extinct, and the extant bat is an endangered subspecies. (Painting by Lawrence W. Duke; unnumbered figure on p. 21 of Royte [1995], used with permission of the National Geographic Society.)

number of bones in the previously mentioned Ulupaʻu Head deposits, so it appears that a sustained breeding colony was involved, rather than simply occasional visitant individuals.

The extant endemic **Hawaiian Goose** or ***nēnē*** *(Branta sandvicensis)* apparently occupied most of the main islands in Polynesian times, although it survived only on Hawaiʻi and possibly Maui at Contact. It is not present in the Oʻahu Ulupaʻu Head deposits of more than 120,000 years ago. DNA studies show that the Hawaiian Goose almost surely evolved from the Canada Goose, so its ancestral stock could have been the Oʻahu population of the latter species. If so, the Hawaiian Goose completed this transformation within only a few hundred thousand years.

Two other types of endemic true geese, both prehistorically extinct, were part of this same Hawaiian *Branta* radiation from a Canada Goose ancestor. Each of these two extinct goose types seems to represent an unsuccessful evolutionary "experiment" in flightlessness within the line. One is the **Forest *Nēnē*** (†*Branta hylobadistes*) from late fossil deposits of Maui, with apparently very close, if not conspecific, relatives on Oʻahu and Kauaʻi. Study of the many recovered skeletons of this form shows that individuals ranged from fully flighted to almost completely flightless. The second prehistorically extinct *Branta* type is the Giant Hawaiʻi Goose. Remains of this bird were only recently discovered in lava tubes of western Hawaiʻi Island, so it has yet to be formally named. The numerous skeletons, however, indicate that it was definitely flightless, stood perhaps 1.2 m (4 feet) tall, and averaged about 8.6 kg (19 pounds) in weight (which is over four times as much as the average Hawaiian Goose). Another interesting aspect of this giant nonvolant bird is its convergence with the *moa nalo* discussed above, not only in postcranial proportions by also in the great strengthening of the cranium itself. It may be remembered from the earlier discussion of *moa nalo* that these birds were apparently lacking on Hawaiʻi, so it appears that the Giant Hawaiʻi Goose filled their niche on that island. There are as yet no radiometric dates available for remains of this flightless species, but, like the various *moa nalo,* it had to have evolved within the lifetime of the island it inhabited, which in the case of Hawaiʻi is no more than 600,000 years (Table 3.1).

HAWKS AND EAGLES (FAMILY ACCIPITRIDAE)

Hawks

The **Hawaiian Hawk** or ***ʻio*** *(Buteo solitarius),* is extant on Hawaiʻi and prehistorically extinct (possibly before Polynesians arrived) on Molokaʻi and Kauaʻi. A somewhat similar species—conceivably directly ancestral to the Hawaiian Hawk—occurred on Oʻahu several hundred thousand years ago. The living bird is a rather typical member of its common widespread genus and, judging primarily from morphological similarities, was evidently derived from a colonizing North American *Buteo* species. Most members of the genus are slow-flying soaring birds, subsisting mainly on rodents, snakes, and lizards, with only one continental species adapted for taking small, active arboreal birds. Before humans arrived in Hawaiʻi, however, there were no ground-living small mammals or land reptiles. This colonizing ancestral hawk line must have been able to shift rapidly to a diet of mostly smaller birds, such as Hawaiian honeycreepers and flightless rails, perhaps also adapting to the dietary inclusion of some nestling forest birds and even larger insects.

Adults of smaller bird species on, at least, Molokaʻi and Oʻahu were also taken by a relatively diminutive **Wood Harrier** (†*Circus dossenus* [the specific name is Greek for "clown" and, as the original describers opined, no circus should be without a clown]). All other members of this essentially cosmopolitan genus are large, long-winged forms that search out varied vertebrate prey while leisurely soaring low over fields and marshes. The Hawaiian species, however, evolutionarily shortened the wings and lengthened the legs: specializations for agilely pursuing and grasping small birds among vegetation. The species thus converged remarkably with swift-flying, bird-catching forest hawks of the common continental genus *Accipiter.*

Eagle

A prehistorically extinct **Hawaiian Sea Eagle** is relatively well represented in various fossil deposits of Oʻahu, Molokaʻi, and Maui. DNA studies show that it is essentially identical to the Old World White-tailed Sea Eagle *(Haliaeetus albicilla).* Although tentatively considered only an indigenous species in Tables 20.1 and 20.3, the Hawaiian population could conceivably have become endemic at the subspecies level. There were no large fish such as postspawning salmon that could be scavenged along Hawaiian streams and coasts, and no mammals except small bats on the main islands before Polynesians arrived. Thus, during their apparent extended existence in the archipelago these large birds must have subsisted primarily on flightless ibises, *moa nalo,* and Forest *Nēnē* or other endemic true geese, at least during that part of the year when rookeries of larger seabirds on which they probably also preyed were not active. This eagle is represented only in Hawaiian fossil deposits less than 120,000 years old, with the single radiometric test yet made on its bones yielding an age of approximately 3,500 years. This lack of more ancient Island records, along with the bird's evident lack of substantial osteological change from the putative ancestor, indicates that it may well have been a relatively late prehistoric arrival.

RAILS, GALLINULES, AND COOTS (FAMILY RALLIDAE)

Flightless Rails

Small, flightless rails, all assigned to the near-cosmopolitan genus *Porzana,* have speciated extensively in the Hawaiian Islands. Ten prehistorically extinct species are recorded from the main islands plus one historically extirpated form each from the islands of Hawaiʻi and Laysan (Table 22.1). The main island prehistorically extinct taxa were fairly evenly distributed, with three on Maui (Plate 22.1); apparently two each on Hawaiʻi, Oʻahu, and Kauaʻi; and one on Molokaʻi, although future fossil discoveries may slightly increase the numbers of both species and islands of occurrence. These rails were apparently very abundant on all main islands, with the exception of Kauaʻi, where their fossil remains are inexplicably scarce. They were undoubtedly **omnivorous** (that is, eating fruit, seeds, terrestrial invertebrates, bird eggs, and probably any other type of ingestible plant and animal matter encountered). These small, nonvolant Hawaiian rails, thus, would have filled the same feeding niche as many types of ground-living small rodents and reptiles in most other parts of the world.

The various flightless Hawaiian rails are generally quite similar skeletally, differing primarily only in overall size and relative degree of reduction of the wing skeleton. For convenience in reference, the twelve known species are currently grouped by investigators into "small," "medium," and "large" size categories. Because all of the Hawaiian flightless rails are short-billed, they are thought to be derived from relatively small continental rails with similar bills (the so-called crakes; all also in the genus *Porzana*). Studies of, primarily, DNA nucleotide-pair sequences indicate that the historically known "small" **Laysan Rail** (#*P. palmeri*) is descended from the Australasian Little Crake *(P. pusilla),* and the "medium" **Common Hawaiʻi Rail** or *moho* (#*P. sandwichensis*) from the Sooty Crake *(P. tabuensis)* of the same general region. Whether or not there were one or more additional ancient arrivals yielding the "large" or other Hawaiian rail species has not been determined. At any rate, in at least one case there was definitely a decrease in body size after colonization, because the **Menehune Rail** (†*P. menehune*) of Moloka'i is the world's smallest known rallid, either extant or extinct, being about the size of a day-old Chicken.

Gallinule

The **Hawaiian Gallinule** or *'alae 'ula (Gallinula chloropus sandvicensis)* is an endemic subspecies of the essentially cosmopolitan Common Moorhen. Its ancestral line has been present on O'ahu for at least several thousand years, judging from fossil remains. The Hawaiian Gallinule historically probably inhabited all main islands, but currently occurs only on Kaua'i and O'ahu. The bird seems especially drawn to agricultural pondfields on these islands, where it eats both invertebrates and wild plants.

Coot

The **Hawaiian Coot** or *'alae ke'oke'o (Fulica alai)* is currently considered endemic at the species level. The remains of a somewhat similar-sized rallid probably referable to the same species date back over 120,000 years on at least O'ahu. Historically, the Hawaiian Coot is found in areas of standing water on most main islands and occasionally visits the hypersaline pond on Laysan Island in the Northwestern chain. It subsists almost entirely on aquatic vegetation. The American Coot *(Fulica americana)* is a regular historic visitant to the main islands and is very likely the ancestor of the slightly differentiated Hawaiian species.

STILTS (FAMILY RECURVIROSTRIDAE)

The **Hawaiian Stilt** or *ae'o (Himantopus mexicanus knudseni)* is an endemic subspecies of the New World Black-necked Stilt. It seems unrepresented in the Island fossil record, but currently is regularly found in wet or muddy habitats of all main islands, where it feeds on small invertebrates.

TERNS (FAMILY LARIDAE)

Recent still-unpublished work on the tropical-ocean Black Noddy *(Anous minutus)* indicates that the individuals on at least the main islands represent an endemic taxon, at either the species or subspecies level. On this basis, the population is here tentatively subspecifically listed as the endemic Hawaiian Noddy or *noio (Anous minutus melanogenys)*.

TYPICAL OWLS (FAMILY STRIGIDAE)

Hawaiian Owl

The only native owls of the archipelago are members of the Strigidae. The **Hawaiian Owl** or *pueo (Asio flammeus sandwichensis)* is regarded as an endemic subspecies of the widespread Northern Hemisphere Short-eared Owl, although morphologically scarcely separable from it. This owl is lacking in Island fossil deposits and, as discussed in chapter 25, like the indigenous

Black-crowned Night-Heron or *'auku'u (Nycticorax nycticorax),* apparently was able to establish in the Islands only after Polynesian-induced ecological change. The owl inhabits grassland areas of all main islands, subsisting primarily on larger flying insects and rodents caught both diurnally and nocturnally.

Stilt-Owls

An undetermined strigid (although possibly of the widespread continental genus *Strix*) gave rise to the endemic genus of **stilt-owls** (†*Grallistrix* [Figure 20.1]), of which a different species is known from each of the larger main islands except Hawai'i. A remarkable adaptive shift occurred in the Islands: a change from an ancestral diet, consisting mostly of nocturnally taken rodents, shrews, and other small mammals, to one of small diurnal birds, possibly supplemented by larger flying insects.

This dietary shift yielded a noticeably long-legged, short-winged, daytime bird catcher obviously convergent with its Island hawk contemporary, the Wood Harrier. It is somewhat of a mystery as to how two endemic bird-catching avian predators as ecologically similar as stilt-owls and the Wood Harrier apparently were could both have evolved and then coexisted in the relatively limited land area of the main islands (they are known to have been sympatric on at least Moloka'i and O'ahu). It would seem that the later colonizing of the two ancestral species would never have evolved into such a niche in the presence of the earlier adapted form. Or, if the hawk and owl originally colonized and evolved on different islands, when one of the two reached an additional island inhabited by the second, it appears that one should have eventually outcompeted the other and caused its extinction there. In the case of this latter distributional possibility, however, it may have been that the two forms were able to coexist by "dividing" the bird-catching niche on jointly occupied islands, with the smaller hawk taking smaller birds, and the owl larger ones.

HONEYEATERS (FAMILY MELIPHAGIDAE)

This family is quite speciose in the Southwest Pacific region, but apparently only one species from there successfully colonized the Hawaiian Archipelago. DNA studies indicate that this immigrant yielded both endemic Island genera. One genus, that of the various **'Ō'ō** (#*Moho*), developed a single historically known species on ancient Maui Nui, as well as one on each of three other larger main islands. All four taxa of this genus were morphologically and apparently ecologically close, with moderately elongated and slightly downcurved bills, as well as rather similar black plumage with minor white markings and a limited amount of yellow feathering (Plate 20.1). The **Kioea** (#*Chaetoptila angustipluma*) represents the family's other endemic genus (note that the Bristle-thighed Curlew listed in Table 20.3 bears this same Hawaiian name). This was a relatively large meliphagid with a fairly elongated bill and streaked brown-and-white coloration. In prehistoric times, it and/or an osteologically very similar relative also occupied Maui as well as O'ahu in fairly large numbers, judging from the relatively great number of fossil remains recovered on at least the latter island. The meliphagids, as their common name implies, are primarily nectar feeding or **nectarivorous** and were quite possibly prevented from any significant adaptive radiation on each main island by competition from the (presumably) earlier radiated Hawaiian honeycreepers.

CROWS (FAMILY CORVIDAE)

The extant **Hawaiian Crow** or *'alalā (Corvus hawaiiensis)* is now known only from the island of Hawai'i, although very fragmentary fossil material from Maui could possibly represent the same species. A slightly larger prehistorically extinct species, the Slender-billed Crow (†*Corvus viriosus*), occurred in the lowlands of Moloka'i and, sparingly, O'ahu. The latter island also once possessed another large corvid, the Deep-billed Crow (†*Corvus impluviatus*), which was apparently quite abundant. Neither of the extinct forms seems clearly ancestral to the living *'alalā*, and it is considered possible that all three taxa evolved from a single colonizing species, which DNA studies suggest may have been the Common Raven *(Corvus corax)* of the Northern Hemisphere.

MONARCHS (FAMILY MONARCHIDAE)

The Old World monarchs are represented in Hawai'i by a single endemic genus and species, the *'Elepaio (Chasiempis sandwichensis* [Figure 10.1]). This bird's ancestral stock was undoubtedly derived from the Southwest Pacific area, where species of this general "fantailed" type are fairly common. Historically, the **insectivorous** (taking a variety of arthropods including insects) *'Elepaio* is recorded only from Hawai'i, O'ahu, and Kaua'i, with identical fossil occurrences. Its apparent absence from all the islands of Maui Nui is puzzling, although it may be that the enigmatic Hawaiian honeycreeper genus of Maui shovelbills (†*Vangulifer* [Figure 21.2]) had preempted the same general "flycatcher" niche there before arrival of the *'Elepaio* or its colonizing ancestor.

OLD WORLD WARBLERS (FAMILY SYLVIIDAE)

The Old World warblers are similarly represented in the Hawaiian Archipelago by only one species, the endemic **Millerbird** *(Acrocephalus familiaris* [the common name originated from the bird's frequent capture of moths often known as "millers"]). Species of the genus are quite common birds in Japan, eastern Asia, and the Southwest Pacific, and it was probably primarily from the last-named region that colonists spread east to many smaller islands of Micronesia and Polynesia. The only Hawaiian Islands ever known to have been occupied by the Millerbird, however, seem to be the two Northwestern ones of Laysan (where it was historically extirpated) and Nihoa.

THRUSHES (FAMILY TURDIDAE)

The **Hawaiian thrushes** *(Myadestes* spp.) underwent a relatively limited amount of speciation into four endemic forms, although the populations of some islands are now extinct. Kaua'i possessed two of the species (one historically extinct), a similarly extirpated taxon occurred on O'ahu and the islands of Maui Nui, and the fourth still inhabits Hawai'i. The single founder was a member of the same turdid genus, a New World group usually known as solitaires. All *Myadestes* are primarily **frugivorous** (fruit eating) and secondarily insectivorous, but may also eat some land snails. In the Hawaiian Islands these thrushes feed primarily in the forest understory, but also occasionally on the ground, including somewhat bare lava flows.

ALIEN BIRDS

Among the great number of avian species introduced to the Hawaiian Islands by humans, the family and numbers of the relatively few successfully established species are listed in Table 20.1. The Red Junglefowl or *moa* (*Gallus gallus* [Phasianidae]), of which the Chicken is a domesticated variety, was the only bird carried in by ancient Hawaiians. After Contact, in addition to a few domesticated forms such as Turkey, Peafowl, Common Pigeon, and so on, numerous wild bird species were imported for three primary purposes: sport hunting, biological control, and aesthetics.

Game birds comprised largely species of Phasianidae and included such forms as wild Turkey varieties, pheasants, Chukar, francolins, and various quail. Larger dove species (Columbidae) and the Sandgrouse (Pteroclididae) were also introduced for hunting. The **Common Myna** (*Acridotheres tristis* [Sturnidae]) was imported in 1865 to prey on armyworms (caterpillars of the lepidopteran family Noctuidae) that were seriously damaging pasturelands. The Common Barn Owl (*Tyto alba* [Tytonidae]) was released in 1958 in the vain hope that it would control various rat species infesting Sugarcane fields. Finally, the Cattle Egret (*Bubulcus ibis* [Ardeidae]) was imported in 1959 to eat insects detrimental to dairy and beef cattle.

The loss of essentially all native land birds in the lowlands of the Hawaiian Islands in the late Polynesian and early historic periods (see chapters 25, 26) prompted a long-continued governmentally sanctioned program of importing for release scores of different songbirds, along with a few other types, intended to provide pleasurable viewing and listening. Even after this type of alien bird introduction became almost entirely prohibited in the latter half of the 1900s, occasional illegal importations added a few more species to the Hawaiian avifauna. For example, both the **Red-vented and Red-whiskered Bubuls** (*Pycnonotus cafer* and *P. jocosus,* respectively [Pycnonotidae]) first appeared in the wild in Hawai'i about 1965, and the former species especially has since been rapidly spreading through the Islands. The numbers of such established alien taxa continue to be augmented by species legally imported as cage birds, but that subsequently either escape or are deliberately (and unlawfully) released. Most of the ten breeding species of **granivorous** or seed-eating waxbills and similar finchlike types of Estrildidae have become part of the Island avifauna in this manner.

SUGGESTED REFERENCES

American Ornithologists' Union 1998; Beletsky 2000; Berger 1981; Fleischer and McIntosh in press; Freed et al. 1987; Harrison 1990; Hawai'i Audubon Society 1996; James and Burney 1997; James and Olson 1991; Olson and James 1991; Pratt et al. 1987; Pyle 1995, 1997; Royte 1995; Sorenson et al. 1999; Ziegler 1987.

AUDIOVISUAL AIDS

Hawaii: An island community; Ke haku hulu: The featherworker; Mānana, Island of birds; Species and evolution.

21

Hawaiian Honeycreepers

This greatly diversified endemic Hawaiian avian group was originally considered a distinct family, with the term "honeycreepers" being applied because it was believed to be derived from one of several New World tropical birds with that name. It seems now accepted that the similarity in morphology and ecology of certain nectar-feeding Hawaiian forms to the American birds is the result of convergent evolution (see chapter 10). More recent anatomical and genetic studies have revealed that the Hawaiian assemblage is derived from a member of the large and widespread finch family Fringillidae, more specifically a species of the subfamily Carduelinae (goldfinches, canaries, and the like). The carduelines are thought to have developed within the fringillid complex about 15–20 million years ago, so the arrival of the Hawaiian honeycreeper ancestor in the Islands necessarily occurred after that event. Analyses of DNA nucleotide-pair sequences suggest that this Hawaiian colonization occurred relatively recently, possibly only some 3.5 or so million years ago. If this date is at least approximately correct, the Island ages given in Table 3.1 indicate that the establishment was very likely accomplished on one of the islands stretching from (West) O'ahu to Necker (Figure 3.1), the only land-masses then large and ecologically diverse enough to have supported an actively speciating bird lineage.

Instead of being classified as a separate family, the **Hawaiian honeycreepers** are now usually considered to constitute the endemic subfamily **Drepanidinae** within the Fringillidae, and some scientists use the term "Hawaiian finches" for the group. Table 21.1 lists the approximately forty-seven historically known and prehistorically extinct species of drepanidines. (Additional fossil material, although too fragmentary to serve in formally naming the taxa, indicates that there are at least ten more species in the subfamily.)

EVOLUTIONARY PHENOMENA

Ecological and morphological shifts occurring during evolution of many Hawaiian nonpasseriform birds are extremely striking (see chapters 20, 22). The adaptive radiation of the Hawaiian honeycreepers, however, is usually cited as the most remarkable evolutionary event among Island birds, largely because so many of these drepanidines survived to be studied in historic times, whereas most highly modified nonpasseriforms did not. This adaptive radiation—and resultant convergent evolution—among Hawaiian honeycreepers has involved substantial changes in several aspects of morphology, behavior, and undoubtedly physiology, although only a few of the more obvious of these can be covered here.

RADIATION IN BILL TYPE

Background

The Hawaiian honeycreepers presumed to be structurally least modified in bill shape and diet from the ancestral colonizer are among those generally termed "finch-billed," with the genera usually included in this informal category segregated from those termed "slender-billed" in Table 21.1. All extant and extinct Hawaiian finchlike species known thus far, however, appear to have evolved larger bills than that of the presumed ancestor, although this structure of the **Nihoa Finch** (*Telespiza ultima* [Plate 21.1, *N*]) is probably only slightly enlarged over that of the original colonizer. Other finch-billed drepanidines such as the Kona Grosbeak (#*Chloridops kona* [Figure 10.4; Plate 21.1, *M*]), however, show especially enlarged bills, and another species of the same genus, the King Kong Finch (†*C. regiskongi*), is among the largest-billed of all the world's finchlike birds. (The octothorp [#] indicates a historically extirpated taxon, and the dagger [†] a prehistorically extinct one.) Primarily responsible for the extensive radiation in drepanidine bill type are, of course, adaptive shifts (see chapter 10) in diet, as detailed in the next sections.

Table 21.1. Genera of Hawaiian honeycreepers. Numbers of species, as well as genera per island are also listed. A dagger (†) indicates genera all of whose species are prehistorically extinct, and an octothorp (#) those for which the last species was extirpated in the historic period. Ly, Laysan; N, Nihoa; K, Kauaʻi; O, Oʻahu; Mo, Molokaʻi; Ln, Lānaʻi; Ma, Maui; H, Hawaiʻi. "F" indicates a fossil record, and "H" a historic one. (Data primarily from Table 14 of James and Olson [1991].)

Genus	Ly	N	K	O	Mo	Ln	Ma	H
"Finch-billed" honeycreepers								
Telespiza (4 spp.)	H	H	F	F	F		F	
Loxioides (1 sp.)				F				H
#*Chloridops* (3 spp.)			F	F			F	H
#*Rhodacanthis* (2 spp.)				F			F	H
†*Orthiospiza* (1 sp.)							F	
†*Xestospiza* (2 spp.)			F	F	F		F	
Melamprosops (1 sp.)							F,H	
Psittirostra (1 sp.)			F,H	F,H	H	H	H	H
#*Dysmorodrepanis* (1 sp.)						H		
Pseudonestor (1 sp.)				F			F,H	
"Slender-billed" honeycreepers								
Hemignathus (2 spp.)			H	F,H	F		F,H	H
#*Akialoa* (5 spp.)			F,H	F,H	F	H	F	F,H
Oreomystis (1 sp.)			F,H					
Paroreomyza (3 spp.)				F,H	F,H	H	F,H	
†*Vangulifer* (2 spp.)							F	
†*Aidemedia* (3 spp.)				F	F		F	
Loxops (7 spp.)			F,H	F,H	H	H	H	F,H
Vestiaria (1 sp.)			H	F,H	H	H	F,H	F,H
#*Drepanis* (2 spp.)					H		F	H
Himatione (1 sp.)	H		F,H	F,H	F,H	H	F,H	F,H
Palmeria (1 sp.)					H		F,H	
#*Ciridops* (2 spp.)			F	F	F			H
Total 22 genera (47 spp.)	2	1	11	14	14	7	18	11

Granivores

Although the ancestral Hawaiian honeycreeper was primarily or entirely seed eating or granivorous, unique environmental circumstances encountered by birds of the evolving lineage spreading among various additional islands of the chain have given rise to quite unexpected permutations of this basic diet. For example, both the Nihoa Finch and the Laysan Finch *(Telespiza cantans)* of the Northwestern Hawaiian Islands supplement vegetable and arthropod food with eggs of the multitude of seabirds nesting there (see chapter 23); they have learned to use their stout bills to crack the shells of such atypical finch fare. The so-called conebills (†*Xestospiza* spp.) had a bill generally reminiscent of that of a finch, but somewhat elongated and with a dorsal profile relatively straight rather than arched. The American cowbirds (*Molothrus* spp. [family Icteridae]) possess a bill much like this and include a substantial proportion of insects in their primarily granivorous diet. Whether this morphological closeness indicates a similarity in food choice between these two avian genera, however, is unknown.

Insectivores-Frugivores

Further radiation in bill shape and use is seen in the Maui Parrotbill (*Pseudonestor xanthophrys* [Plate 21.1, *K*]), which feeds on insect larvae exposed by tearing open live and dead wood with the strong bill. This action, as well as the habit of sometimes hanging upside down while feeding are convergent with those of certain types of parrots (Psittacidae [Figure 10.4]) from other areas of the world. The bill of the *'Ō'ū* (*Psittirostra psittacea* [Plate 21.1, *L*]) is also somewhat lengthened and hooked, as adaptively modified for the arthropod and fruit or insectivorous-frugivorous diet of the species. Quite enigmatic, however, is the Lāna'i Hookbill (#*Dysmorodrepanis munroi* [Figure 21.1]), probably most closely related to the *'Ō'ū* although known from only a single specimen taken in 1913. There are no natural history notes regarding this species, but it may possibly have used its uniquely shaped bill to pluck berries; however, it could conceivably have employed the stout pincerlike structure instead to crush land-snail shells before extracting the gastropods' body. The *Po'ouli* (*Melamprosops phaeosoma* [Plate 21.1, *O*]), although grouped with the finch-billed types, differs from most in having a smaller, somewhat flattened bill, with which it takes land snails, wood-boring beetle larvae, and other forest invertebrates. Incidentally, this endemic Maui species (now near extinction) is the most recently discovered living drepanidine; it was discovered most unexpectedly in 1973 inhabiting dense rain forests high on Maui's Haleakalā.

Nectarivores-Insectivores

Essentially all of the slender-billed Hawaiian honeycreepers feed on nectar and/or arthropods, but there is great variability in the location and manner of obtaining this food. The tongue in nectarivorous birds is often tubular and the tip almost invariably brushlike, both adaptations to aid in extracting this liquid. In these morphological and dietary specializations for nectarivory, the pertinent drepanidines converge wholly or in part with a number of other avian groups, for example the primarily Southwest Pacific honeyeaters (Meliphagidae) and Southeast Asian white-eyes (Zosteropidae). The relatively shorter-billed Hawai'i *'Amakihi* (*Loxops virens virens* [Plate 21.1, *I*]) and *'Apapane* (*Himatione sanguinea* [Plate 21.1, *E*]) probe flowers with short corollas for nectar (or occasionally pierce the base of longer ones to obtain this food) and glean smaller insects and other arthropods from these and other plant parts. Some slender-billed drepanidines with considerably longer and downcurved bills, such as the **Hawai'i *Mamo*** (#*Dre-*

panis pacifica [Plate 21.1, *A*]), are specialized for extracting nectar from flowers with very long, curved corollas, especially those of endemic species in the subfamily Lobelioideae of the bellflower family Campanulaceae (see discussion of coevolution later in this chapter). The similar bill of others, notably the Kaua'i *'Akialoa* (#*Akialoa stejnegeri* [Plate 21.1, *G*]), is typically used for probing deep into moss clumps or similar vegetal substrate to obtain arthropods inaccessible to shorter-billed Hawaiian honeycreepers. Certain Southeast Asian birds such as the long-billed species of spider-hunters (*Arachnothera* spp. [Nectariniidae] [Figure 10.4]) are scarcely distinguishable from the Kaua'i *'Akialoa* in regard to their independently evolved bill morphology and diet.

Gapers

All three **Hawaiian gapers** of the prehistorically extinct genus *Aidemedia* had noticeably elongated retroarticular processes, which are posteriorly directed bony extensions at the proximal end of each lower mandible half. Such processes provide attachment for cranial muscles allowing powerful "gaping," permitting the closed bill to be inserted in various arthropod-containing substrates and forcibly opened to expose this prey. The species †*A. xanclops* had a downcurved

Figure 21.1. The sole known specimen of the Lāna'i Hookbill (*# Dysmorodrepanis munroi*). The photographic inset is an enlarged view of the unique forcepslike bill. (Painting by Nancy Payzant; adapted from unnumbered plate following p. 160 of James et al. [1989], with bill photograph from Fig. 2 of the same reference, both used with permission of Helen F. James and the Wilson Ornithological Society.)

bill at least as long as that of the Hawai'i *Mamo* and Kaua'i *'Akialoa,* but with even more extended retroarticular processes. It quite possibly fed arboreally like one or both of the latter species. The other members of the genus, †*A. chascax* and †*A. lutetiae* (Figure 10.4), had a somewhat shorter bill that was rather straight instead of sickle-shaped, but still possessed substantial retroarticular processes. The Greater *'Amakihi* (#*Loxops sagittirostris*), with a similar bill, was noted by early ornithologists as using it in a gaping action to extract arthropods from at least the confined leaf axils of the climbing Screw Pine relative *'Ie'ie (Freycinetia arborea).* Some like-billed continental gapers such as the meadowlarks (*Sturnella* spp. [Icteridae]) and European Starling (*Sturnus vulgaris* [Sturnidae]), however, feed on the ground, so it is possible that one or both of the straighter-billed *Aidemedia* filled an equivalent ground-foraging ecological niche (see chapter 9).

Other Bill Specializations

Some slender-billed drepanidines have radiated in still other morphological and behavioral ways. The *'Ākepa* (*Loxops coccineus* [Plate 21.1, *H*]) is primarily insectivorous, but is able to

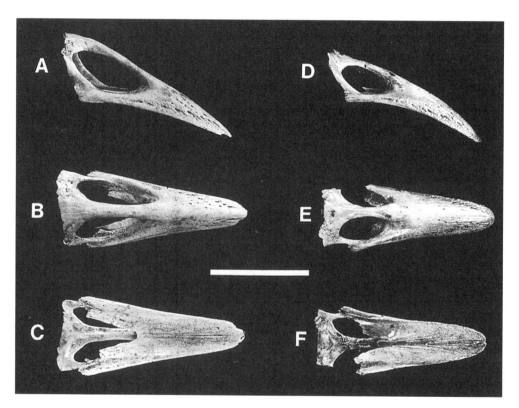

Figure 21.2. Upper bills in the prehistorically extinct Hawaiian shovelbill genus *Vangulifer. A–C,*†*V. neophasis; D–F,*†*V. mirandus.* This odd blunt and shovel-shaped structure may have been somewhat adapted to catching flying insects. (White scale bar is 1.0 cm or 0.4 inches long.) (Photograph by Victor E. Krantz; Fig. 26 of James and Olson 1991, used with permission of American Ornithologists' Union.)

lessen food competition with sympatric (living in the same area) species of similar diet by having tips of the short upper and lower mandibles cross slightly as the mouth is closed. In this manner, leaf buds not easily pierced by other birds may be efficiently twisted open to reveal moth larvae within. Thus, the *'Ākepa* is convergent with continental fringillid crossbills (*Loxia* spp.) that employ a similar "cross-tipped" bill mechanism to extract seeds from between the appressed scales of conifer cones. The so-called creepers of the drepanidine genus *Oreomystis* (Plate 21.1, *J*) do not feed at flowers or foliage, but creep over tree trunks and larger branches using a short, pointed bill to glean insects from crevices and under bark. This foraging behavior is quite similar to that of various nuthatches (Sittidae and Neosittidae, among other families [Figure 10.4]) elsewhere in the world; the shortened tail of many of these continental birds is also characteristic of the Hawaiian species.

Even a reasonable facsimile of a woodpecker (Picidae) is present in the Islands: the **'Akiapōlā'au** (*Hemignathus wilsoni* [Figure 10.4; Plate 21.1, *F*]). This bird uses its stout, straight lower mandible to chisel a cavity in soft or rotten wood while keeping the long, curved upper mandible raised high, then extracts exposed arthropod prey with either the upper or both bill members, although this prey seizing is performed by a long, barbed tongue in the picids.

Somewhat uncertain were the feeding habits of the two drepanidine **shovelbills** (†*Vangulifer* spp.), whose rather broadened, only moderately elongated bills possessed rounded rather than pointed tips (Figure 21.2): a combination not especially closely replicated in any other type of small bird worldwide. It is possible that the bill was used to take smaller flying insects during aerial sallies from forest perches, as is done with wider and more pointed bills by many New World and Old World flycatchers (Tyrannidae and Muscicapidae, respectively), although the structure in the Hawaiian birds seems a little more heavily built than would be necessary solely for catching such insects. The two species of shovelbills are known only from Maui, and it may be recalled from the preceding chapter that the Island monarchid *'Elepaio,* an otherwise widespread endemic insectivore, is unaccountably missing from the Maui Nui islands. It is thus not inconceivable that on Maui Nui one or both of the prehistorically extinct shovelbills could have filled the *'Elepaio* niche.

COLORATION

Selective Advantage

Variation in plumage coloration and pattern among historically known Hawaiian honeycreepers is probably greater than that found among any other passeriform subfamily worldwide. The numerous species of Galápagos finches (Figure 10.2), for example, are all colored shades of black, brown, and buff; the Hawaiian honeycreepers combine greens, yellows, and reds with black, gray, and white (Plate 21.1). Unlike bill morphology, however, plumage coloration is almost never *directly* influenced by food type, although there has unquestionably always been a close causal relationship in many drepanidines between evolution of coloration and place at which food is taken. This food-related selection for particular plumage colors and patterns was probably due mostly if not entirely to the survival advantage of concealing coloration in prehistoric times when these smaller birds were preyed upon by the bird-catching Wood Harrier (†*Circus dossenus*) and stilt-owls (†*Grallistrix* spp.), as well as possibly the Hawaiian Hawk or *'io (Buteo solitarius)* (see chapter 20).

Protective Coloration

Among the two informal honeycreeper groups of Table 21.1, the colors of red and black are restricted almost entirely to certain nectarivorous and insectivorous slender-billed drepanidines. The essentially all red and black **'I'iwi** (*Vestiaria coccinea* [Plate 21.1, *B*]) and *'Apapane* both feed extensively on red flowers in the canopies of *'Ōhi'a lehua (Metrosideros polymorpha),* where they are effectively concealed by their coloration. Even the largely black and gray Crested Honeycreeper or *'ākohekohe (Palmeria dolei* [Plate 21.1, *C*]), which often feeds in the same locations, shows a nape patch of red, but this is perhaps an instance of disruptive rather than concealing coloration.

The *'Ula'aihāwane* (#*Ciridops anna*), extinct for over a century, presents a quite puzzling case in regard to both coloration and feeding habits. The posterior half of the body and shoulder of adults is bright red, with the rest of the plumage showing a bold pattern of gray, black, and white. The considerable amount of red at first suggests that the species may have been another species frequently feeding among *'Ōhi'a lehua* blossoms. The Hawaiian name of this bird, however, seems best translated as "the red [bird] that eats the nuts [*hāwane*] of the native Hawaiian palm [*Pritchardia* spp.]," and a report by an early ornithologist stated that it did frequent such palms. The preserved stomach contents of one of the five known nonfossil specimens were recently examined and were found to be made up of the same general types of insects eaten by flower- and foliage-gleaning drepanidines. Osteological studies of the subfamily have revealed that the exceptional sturdiness of the two more proximal leg bones and associated pelvic region of the *'Ula'aihāwane* (and prehistorically extinct congeners) is unique in the group. Birds elsewhere in the world showing a similar skeletal modification use the feet to remove accumulated dead vegetation from large leaf axils and similar crevices in trees to obtain hidden arthropods. Conceivably, the *'Ula'aihāwane* fed in the same manner and primarily in the axils of Hawaiian palm fronds. If so, its red color may simply have been a selectively neutral character retained from some undetermined Island ancestor.

Slender-billed drepanidine species feeding primarily at arboreal sites other than the exposed red flowers of the *'Ōhi'a lehua* are mostly either green and yellow (for instance, the *'Akiapōlā'au* and species of the now-extirpated genus *Akialoa*) or largely black (the Hawai'i *Mamo* and Black *Mamo* or *hoa* [#*Drepanis funerea*], both color combinations being among those that would seem to provide good concealment for feeding or other activities in the shaded subcanopy.

The predominance of green and yellow in the plumage of generally seed- or fruit-eating finch-billed drepanidines probably represents the selectively most advantageous coloration for foraging activities either in subcanopy situations or at the terminal portion of branches of trees bearing yellow flowers. For example, the **Palila** (*Loxioides bailleui*), with yellow head and greenish upper body coloration (Plate 27.1), feeds largely on the pod-contained green seeds of the *Māmane (Sophora chrysophylla)*. When this tree is in flower a bird perched in its terminal branches is practically indistinguishable among the profuse bright yellow flowers and grayish green pods and leaves.

Sexual Coloration

This generally close correlation between drepanidine coloration and feeding site, however, has several notable exceptions because, some—but by no means all—drepanidines show obvious intraspecific **sexual dimorphism** in color. In all Hawaiian examples of this, the male is more brightly colored than the female, a common although not invariable characteristic among birds worldwide. Presumably, this contrasting sexual coloration is directly related to different aspects of reproduction and must be of greater selective advantage to males of the species involved than is concealing coloration.

Sexual dimorphism in color serves two functions. First, the female, which is most often the member of the pair that incubates the eggs, is less noticeable to predators while on the nest than the male would be. This is well illustrated by the green-bodied 'Ō'ū, in which the head of the male is yellow (Plate 21.1, *L*) and that of the female is green. The second function seems related to female choice of males in mating, because the brighter male coloration usually differs in relatively closely related sympatric species. This difference undoubtedly serves as a deterrent to "gamete wastage" (see chapter 15) in the form of selectively disadvantageous interspecific matings; that is, the female of one species can be induced to copulate only by a male showing the "proper" color pattern of her own species. This may well be the explanation of the noticeable color differences between males of the once sympatric Greater *Koa* Finch or *hōpue* and Lesser *Koa* Finch (#*Rhodacanthis palmeri* and #*R. flaviceps,* respectively), of leeward Hawai'i Island. The females of the two species were almost identical except for the slightly larger size of the former, but the male Greater *Koa* Finch had a deep golden orange head and that of the Lesser *Koa* Finch was yellow.

Presumably, this latter type of color differentiation in males of closely related species develops evolutionarily only when there is a "problem" with interbreeding. If effective sexually isolating characteristics such as major differences in courtship behavior or time of breeding between sympatric species have previously evolved, or if the two potentially interbreeding forms are allopatric (living in different areas), marked variations between male coloration would not be expected.

Occasionally, in a drepanidine species showing sexual color dimorphism and occurring on more than one island, the male coloration differs between or among the islands. This is the case with the 'Ākepa, historically extirpated on O'ahu but extant on Maui and Hawai'i. The O'ahu male was dull dark red, that of Maui is golden yellow to yellowish orange, and that of Hawai'i bright reddish orange (Plate 21.1, *H*). These male color differences may represent solely the independent selective evolution of three separate sexual isolating phenomena, but the fact that all the three islands' males have not evolved exactly the same coloration suggests that genetic drift (see chapter 10) may have been initially involved in the color change after each population reached its respective island.

Another case of sexual color dimorphism may possibly provide information on preferred habitat of species prehistorically extinct on the main islands. The extant finch-billed honeycreepers *Telespiza cantans* and *T. ultima,* historically known only from Laysan and Nihoa Islands, respectively, necessarily live in areas of largely grassy or low brushy vegetation. The females alone have a darker scaled and streaked pattern overlying the basic grayish green-and-yellow coloration (Plate 21.1, *N*). Such patterning is typical of birds (of both sexes) utilizing similar open-land habitats throughout the world (for example, pipits of the family Motacillidae and skylarks of the Alaudidae) and undoubtedly represents concealing coloration. There presumably have never been any avian predators resident on these Northwestern islands since they diminished to their current small size many millions of years ago (see chapter 3). Thus, the color pattern of female *Telespiza* there may well have originally evolved on the predator-inhabited main islands, where both species (along with two extinct congeners) occurred prehistorically on at least Kauaʻi, Oʻahu, and/or Molokaʻi, after which the two extant taxa presumably spread to their current localities. It seems to follow that the original main island habitat of at least these two species was relatively open lowland areas rather than upland forests.

COEVOLUTION OF DREPANIDINE BILLS AND FLOWERS

Background

The term **"coevolution"** signifies mutually advantageous "lockstep" selective changes in characteristics of two interacting organisms, often an animal and a plant. In Hawaiʻi, the phenomenon is presumably illustrated by certain honeycreepers (for example, the historically extinct Hawaiʻi and Black *Mamo*), in which there is a striking similarity in bill length and curvature to the long, tubelike corollas of a number of endemic flowers (primarily Lobelioideae) from which these birds probably obtained nectar. Most of the endemic Hawaiian bird species involved in this alleged coevolution became extinct in either Polynesian or early historic times, so it is not possible to verify that they did feed upon and successfully pollinate long-flowered lobelioids. This question, however, may be approached indirectly. The nectar of most lobelioids is quite rich in 6-carbon or hexose sugars (glucose and fructose) as opposed to sucrose, a 12-carbon sugar characteristic of the nectars of many other plants. Flowers with such hexose-rich nectar are highly favored by (and typically pollinated by) nectarivorous passeriform birds elsewhere in the world. It is true that such flowers are similarly fed upon and pollinated by short-tongued bees of several families as well as by small blossom-visiting bats, but neither of these latter animal types was present in Hawaiʻi before human arrival. Thus, it seems quite likely that the original Island exploiters and pollinators of these flowers with hexose-rich nectar must, indeed, have been primarily long-billed Hawaiian honeycreepers.

Although the scientific literature is replete with descriptions of the *results* of putative coevolution, essentially none of the reports provides a specific explanation of exactly *how* such a process might have occurred. For example, consider that a short-billed Hawaiian honeycreeper originally fed on nectar from a short-tubed flower, fertilizing other flowers of the species during continued feeding by carrying pollen on its bill or head feathers and thus ensuring perpetuation of the plant population. What would be the evolutionary "incentive" for either bill or flower to change in length? It is true that longer flowers typically hold more nectar than shorter ones. Thus, it might be postulated that as variant longer flowers appeared, selection would favor variant longer bills that could successfully exploit (and pollinate) such flowers, leading to continually increasing length of both structures by coevolution. This, however, fails to explain why the bills of *all* nectarivorous species have not lengthened but, in fact, continue to maintain the length appropriate to corolla lengths of the plant species utilized by each.

Hummingbird Example

Relatively recently, scientists in western North America investigating the apparent similar coevolution of the long bills of most hummingbirds (Trochilidae) and the long corollas of the various flowers from which they obtain nectar have advanced a hypothesis as to how such a process may have proceeded. The general findings and conclusions of their study are quite likely applicable to the parallel situation in Hawaiʻi, as is hypothetically detailed in the next section.

Bird Competition

The driving force in coevolution of bill and corolla lengths is apparently provided by competition among *both* the various birds and the various plants involved; that is, without such competition the process would not occur. It may be imagined that on a particular Hawaiian island of long ago the diets of two honeycreepers comprised nectar from flowers of a variety of plant species along with insects from various sources, and that both of these birds possessed bills of no more than moderate length. Presumably, there was persistent competition between these birds for both types of food. One of the bird species happened to be slightly more variable in bill length than the other (or a longer-billed form could have recently immigrated from a neighboring island). The few individuals of the more variable or longer-billed species with bill lengths at the upper extreme of the normal range of variation could successfully obtain nectar from the particular flowers of a variant plant individual similarly situated at the greatest extreme of corolla-length variation.

The other, shorter-billed, bird species would be largely unsuccessful in obtaining nectar from such relatively longer flowers and, through time, there would be natural selection for individual birds within both species that could visually discriminate between flowers with long corollas and those with short ones. The shorter-billed species would find it metabolically advantageous to decrease (through natural selection of "correct" behavioral mutants) its attempts to obtain nectar from the elongated corollas of the particular longer-flowered plant species and progressively utilize more and more the shorter flowers of other plant taxa. Perhaps there would also be selection for individuals of this avian species that included in their diet a greater proportion of arthropods, for whose capture a lengthened bill was not advantageous. Thus, the bill of this latter bird would tend to retain its original moderate length.

The longer-billed species, on the other hand, would similarly be selectively favored if it progressively lessened interspecific competition for nectar through more frequently visiting the elongated flowers that were less often used by the shorter-billed species. And this selective advantage would be further enhanced if, at the same time, the species lessened competition for arthropod food by including in its diet ever-decreasing numbers of such animals, most of which were not efficiently taken by an elongated bill. Continuation of this process would eventually yield a noticeably long-billed bird specifically adapted to feeding almost exclusively on nectar from one (or a very limited number of) plant species with appropriately lengthened flowers.

Plant Competition

Just as both the honeycreeper species were originally always in competition for food, all of the plants fed upon by the two would similarly have been in competition for the most efficient pollinator. From the standpoint of each plant species, the ideal ecological situation would be to have at least one avian feeder/pollinator species that would never fail to visit its flowers, thus assuring the plant species a continued existence. This plant requirement would be satisfied at the time the bills of the two birds had attained (or retained) their most advantageous lengths, and continued selective pressure for "proper" flower length within each plant species would maintain the respective optimal blossom sizes. Mutant flowers of various lengths would, of course, occasionally appear in each plant species, so that, for example, the long-billed birds could feed upon variant short ones of the typically long-flowered species. Mechanically, however, simultaneous pollination in such cases would be unlikely, thus putting individual plants with such atypical flowers at a distinct reproductive disadvantage, consistently eliminating them from the population.

Further, as the corolla lengths in the two plant species were evolving, flowers of variant color might also occasionally appear in one or both species. Any new color that allowed both the long- and short-billed bird species to more easily visually identify a flower as either a relatively suitable or unsuitable food source would be selectively advantageous. Such a color would then be expected to become dominant in the particular plant species involved. Also, other botanical attributes such as position of flowers on the plant, preferred microhabitat of the species, time of flowering, and so on, might then also change evolutionarily for the same reason.

Evolutionary Equilibrium

Presumably, when the evolutionary "need" for changes in pertinent structures of both birds and plants had been satisfied, further morphological modifications would cease or at least remain in equilibrium. As a matter of fact, in the case of at least one of the coevolving pairs, lengthening of both bill and flower necessarily would have to end at some point solely because of physical and mechanical limitations on the gross size of such biological structures.

Overspecialization

Incidentally, if the basic arguments in the foregoing explanation are accepted, it should not be difficult to understand the demise of a coevolved animal or plant species if its mutually reliant partner becomes extinct. This obligate biological interdependence imposed by extreme cases of coevolution is the primary disadvantage of such **evolutionary overspecialization.** In Hawai'i, the extirpation of one member of a number of pertinent pairs has undoubtedly resulted in the loss of its partner, even though the latter was not otherwise threatened.

SUGGESTED REFERENCES

Beletsky 2000; Berger 1981; Fleischer and McIntosh in press; Freed et al. 1987; Grant and Grant 1968; Hawai'i Audubon Society 1996; James and Olson 1991; James et al. 1989; Lammers and Freeman 1986; Pratt et al. 1987; Pyle 1997; Tarr and Fleischer 1995.

AUDIOVISUAL AIDS

Genetics and populations; Hawaii: Strangers in paradise; In the middle of the sea; Ke haku hulu: The featherworker; Species and evolution.

22

Flightless Birds and Fossil Sites

The most radical single adaptive shift that took place among evolving Hawaiian birds was undoubtedly that from a flighted existence to a nonvolant one. In Hawaiʻi the loss of flight has occurred in ibises (family Threskiornithidae), ducks and geese (Anatidae), and rails (Rallidae) (Table 22.1). It was brought about by the reduction of the entire pectoral flight apparatus, which included primarily a marked diminution in size of the wing bones (Figure 22.1) as well as loss of the bony midline keel of the breastbone or sternum. The loss of flight is not, in itself, especially unusual; it has occurred in several well-known types of continental birds, such as the Ostrich of drier regions of the Old World and the rheas of nonforested South America. But a rather special variety of biological evolution appears to be involved in the process on islands, and this is discussed here in some detail.

Darwinian Premises

The original theory of Darwinian evolution is based on three generally accepted premises (see chapter 10). Each of these is reiterated below and illustrated by a hypothetical example.

First, many more young of almost every wild animal or plant species are produced than survive to reproduce. Suppose both sexes of a certain Hawaiian reef fish typically live five years, during which time the female lays half a million eggs. On average, only the individuals from two of these eggs have to survive five years hence to replace their parents; thus, 99.9996 percent of the young fail to reach breeding age. (Further elementary mathematics show that if four instead of two young survived, the oceans would be packed solid with these fish in about four centuries.)

Second, although most offspring resemble their parents very closely, in every generation there are always a certain number exhibiting essentially random variation in morphology, physiology, and even psychology, due to natural genetic mutations (see chapter 10). A few of the fish individuals will be either slightly darker or lighter than the color best concealing the species from its primary predator.

Third, biotic and abiotic selective forces are always present that bring about the near-total elimination of each generation of young. Assume that predation is the primary selective factor in this particular fish species, and that color provides the individuals essential concealing coloration. As long as the predator remains the same, those many individuals most closely resembling their parents in coloration will have the greatest chance of surviving each year, and those few least resembling them the smallest chance.

If, however, because of some changing ecological circumstances this particular predator is gradually being replaced by a new one that uses a different capture technique, the situation changes. Now, one of the formerly detrimental mutant color variations will progressively provide slightly better protection, so that the pertinent mutants have an ever-greater probability of escaping predation each year. At the same time, the probability of a normally colored fish surviving is constantly decreasing. Eventually, these persistently appearing mutants will become relatively so numerous in the population that a few survive to breed, and after many thousands

Table 22.1. Flightless Hawaiian birds. Islands of occurrence are also noted. A dagger (†) indicates pre-historically extinct taxa, and an octothorp (#) historically extirpated ones. Certain birds listed are still awaiting scientific description and naming. Island abbreviations: Ly, Laysan; K, Kaua'i; O, O'ahu; Mo, Moloka'i; Ln, Lāna'i; Ma, Maui; H, Hawai'i. (Data from Olson and James [1991], and Storrs L. Olson, personal communication, September 1999.)

Family Species	Ly	K	O	Mo	Ln	Ma	H
Ibises (Threskiornithidae)							
Moloka'i Ibis (†*Apteribis glenos*)				X			
Lāna'i Ibis (†*Apteribis* [unnamed sp.])					X		
Upland Maui Ibis (†*Apteribis brevis*)						X	
Lowland Maui Ibis (†*Apteribis* [unnamed sp.])						X	
Ducks and geese (Anatidae)							
Moa nalo							
Tortoise-jawed *Moa Nalo* (†*Chelychelynechen quassus*)		X					
Common O'ahu *Moa Nalo* (†*Thambetochen xanion*)			X				
Maui Nui *Moa Nalo* (†*Thambetochen chauliodous*)				X		X	
Clumsy *Moa Nalo* (†*Ptaiochen pau*)						X	
True geese							
Forest *Nēnē* (†*Branta hylobadistes* or close ally)		X	X				
Giant Hawai'i Goose (†*Branta* [unnamed sp.])							X
Anatids of uncertain affinity							
O'ahu Flat-billed "Goose" († [undetermined genus and sp.])			X				
Lesser Hawai'i "Goose" (†*Geochen rhuax*)							X
Rails (Rallidae)							
Small species							
Laysan Rail (#*Porzana palmeri*)	X						
Lesser O'ahu Rail (†*Porzana ziegleri*)			X				
Menehune Rail (†*Porzana menehune*)				X			
Small Maui Rail (†*Porzana keplerorum*)						X	
Small Hawai'i Rail (†*Porzana* [unnamed sp.])							X
Medium species							
Medium Kaua'i Rail (†*Porzana* [unnamed sp.])		X					
Medium Maui Rail (†*Porzana* [unnamed sp.])						X	
Common Hawai'i Rail or *moho* (#*Porzana sandwichensis*)							X
Large species							
Large Kaua'i Rail (†*Porzana* [unamed sp.])		X					
Large O'ahu Rail (†*Porzana ralphorum*)			X				
Large Maui Rail (†*Porzana severnsi*)						X	
Large Hawai'i Rail (†*Porzana* [unnamed sp.])							X
Total 24 species (#2, †22)	1	4	5	3	1	7	5

more generations the variant color will become typical of the entire population. That is, the species will have *evolved* in respect to this character. (It will be recognized, of course, that this is essentially the same process undergone by the English Peppered Moth described in chapter 10.)

Extinction

It may sometimes be that the particular mutant color that would have allowed a sufficient number of fish individuals to survive the newly developing type of predation pressure is not present in the species. Or that the mutation appears with such a low frequency that not enough individuals possessing it ever attain breeding age to allow it to become dominant. In either case, the species will ultimately undergo extinction without leaving a descendant line; this, in fact, has been the fate of a majority of species that have existed on earth.

Horse Evolution Analogy

The evolution of flightlessness in Island birds has involved these same three Darwinian premises, but with a significant deviation from most previously studied cases of biological evolution: the amount of geological time involved. This difference may be illustrated by comparing the diminution of the entire muscle and bone flight apparatus in a flightless insular bird with, for example, the loss of side toes in evolution of the modern single-toed horse.

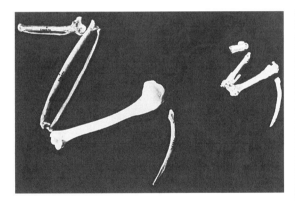
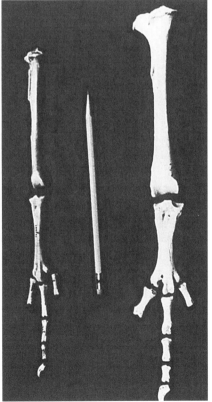

Figure 22.1. Major limb bones of flighted and flightless Hawaiian Anatidae. *Left photograph,* wing skeletons; *right,* leg skeletons. In each photograph, bones of the extant Hawaiian Goose or *nēnē (Branta sandvicensis)* are on the left, and those of the nonvolant prehistorically extinct Maui Nui *Moa nalo* (†*Thambetochen chauliodous*) on the right. All *Moa nalo* bones are isolated elements and represent a number of individuals. (Wing skeletons approximately 75 percent natural size, leg skeletons approximately 30 percent; carpometacarpus of the *Moa nalo* wing modified.) (Photographs by Art Otremba, used with permission of the *Honolulu Advertiser.*)

The ancestral line of the Domestic Horse underwent much of its later development in North America, before it died out there 10,000 or so years ago. About 20 million years previously, ancestral three-toed horses inhabited the area that was to become the Great Plains. The relatively moist conditions of the time selectively favored a three-toed foot that allowed optimal locomotion on the somewhat soft ground while browsing on leafy forest vegetation. The climate of the area, however, was gradually becoming drier, the substrate consequently firmer, and the forests beginning to be replaced by grassland. The three-toed condition, thus, became progressively less advantageous, and a foot with a single more substantial and lengthened middle toe gradually more advantageous because of the greater speed it allowed in running on harder open ground (it must be realized that these animals' predators were similarly undergoing natural selection for more rapid locomotion).

A relatively complete series of fossil horse skeletons spanning this period of evolutionary change shows that the transition to a single toe involved a number of mutations that appeared in either the same individual or, more likely, consecutively in a descendant line. Not only was a mutation leading to production of a longer and thicker middle digit required, but one or two other independent mutations causing progressive reduction and eventual loss of the side toes ultimately had to accompany it. In addition, there had to be companion sequential mutations that modified bones and muscles of the more proximal parts of the foot as well as the leg itself to properly utilize the changing toe structure. (Omitted from this discussion is the important fact that accompanying mutations were also required to change the former low-crowned teeth adapted to leafy food into quite different high-crowned long-wearing structures for adequate mastication of the new more abrasive grass diet.) The one or more descendant lines that chanced to undergo this entire suite of mutations tended to be favored by natural selection, and the surviving population progressively evolved into the modern horse. Paleontologists consider that this phase of horse evolution occurred relatively rapidly in terms of geologic time; but it still took about 10 million years.

Comparative Flightless Bird Evolution

Flightless birds of a particular Hawaiian island must have evolved this condition entirely within the lifetime of that island. With the exception of the occasionally coalesced land units of ancient Maui Nui (see chapter 3), once flightless, birds of an island would be restricted there because they almost surely could not have swum to another. Table 3.1 shows, however, that no main island is old enough to have allowed a land bird on it to undergo reduction of the entire flight apparatus by exactly the same evolutionary process that yielded loss of horse side toes. So, just how Hawaiian birds did attain nonvolancy was long an unanswered question.

The Critical Clue

Storrs L. Olson, while a graduate student at Johns Hopkins University, was confronted with this problem in studying an extinct flightless rail of a geologically young Atlantic island. Upon assembling the bird's skeleton, he noticed that the large obtuse angle formed by two articulating bones (coracoid and scapula) at the shoulder skeleton of the adult flightless island bird was quite different from the acute angle in the adult of a flighted continental species presumed to be its immediate ancestor. Examination of the same bones in a chick of the continental species, whose pectoral apparatus had not yet matured into the adult flighted condition, unexpectedly revealed that the articulating angle was obtuse like that of the flightless island adult rather than acute like that of the flighted continental adult. In other words, as the young continental bird matured and acquired the power of flight, among other related developments, the shoulder-bone angle changed from obtuse to acute. In a flash of insight, Olson realized that the adult island bird was flightless simply because its pectoral region had remained in the juvenile condition.

Neoteny

This general phenomenon of retention of juvenile characteristics in an adult is, in reality, a long-recognized biological fact. For example, in the case of amphibians, the Tiger Salamander *(Ambystoma tigrinum)* of North America usually spends its larval existence in streams and ponds but, as it matures, loses its external gills, develops legs, and leaves the water to spend its adult life on land. Larvae of certain Mexican populations of the species, however, become sexually mature and reproduce while permanently retaining both the juvenile body form and aquatic habitat. The technical name for this maintenance of juvenile features in adulthood is neoteny (Greek *"neos"* [young] and *"tein"* [to extend]), introduced in chapter 15 on flowering plants. It is quite likely the method by which flightlessness was attained by most or all non-volant bird species on various geologically young oceanic islands.

Insular Neotenic Evolution

To apply the theory of neoteny to the development of flightlessness among Hawaiian birds, the following probable scenario is presented. In the distant past a breeding pair of, say, a small continental rail species established a population on a Hawaiian island. Initially, mortality was very low because of abundant food, sufficient activity space, and other favorable conditions, combined with the absence of ecological competitors and predators specifically adapted to taking this new type of Island bird. As the population rapidly expanded, occasional individuals flew to adjacent islands of the chain, and eventually the entire archipelago was colonized. When the carrying capacity for the species was reached and began to be exceeded on each island, however, mortality before reproductive age increased to its typical high percentage. Among the number of random mutations appearing in each generation the ones that happened to be most advantageous in the new insular setting then became strongly favored.

A mutation resulting in the failure of the entire pectoral region to mature properly appeared in a young rail—or perhaps was inherited by an entire brood through mutated ovarian cells of the female parent. In adulthood, all the body systems of these variant rails were normal except for this neotenic flight apparatus. The large breast muscles that power the wing did not grow, the sternum failed to develop the high bony keel providing flight-muscle origin, and the numerous bones of the wing and shoulder retained their juvenile shape and angular relationship.

Perhaps the mutation responsible for this neotenic state caused an insufficient amount of pertinent growth hormone to be produced at the end of adolescence when the pectoral region would normally mature. Or it may have been that one caused the few early embryonic cells destined to yield this entire body region to lack the proper membrane protein-receptor sites that would enable them to take in the growth hormone. Whatever the exact mutational details, the critical fact is that the effective evolutionary reduction of the entire ancestral flight apparatus to a mere vestige involved only a *single* mutation, not the complex suite of individual mutations necessary to produce a single-toed horse. And, equally important, the complete change could occur in *one* generation, rather than requiring hundreds of thousands.

Advantages of Flightlessness

Probably, the general type of neotenic mutation postulated to have appeared in this rail population occurs once in every few million individuals or broods of all bird species around the world. It perhaps sometimes involves the pelvic rather than the pectoral region or affects other parts of the body such as the reproductive or digestive system. Under normal environmental conditions such a mutation would almost invariably be detrimental. If a continental bird remained flightless upon maturing, it would soon fall prey to ground predators such as foxes, cats, and the like. And, when winter arrived, it could not migrate to areas with proper food or survivable climate. But in Hawai‘i before human arrival there were no such predators—at least on the ground—and the climate was equable enough to permit year-round survival without migration.

The flightless rails could not only survive in the Islands, but they were also at a selective advantage over flighted members of their species. The large breast and other pectoral musculature of a flighted bird, along with the associated skeletal elements, average about 15–20 percent of the total body weight. If a bird does not have to support this amount of tissue metabolically, it can survive on notably less food and water than a conspecific flighted individual. Also, it is undoubtedly metabolically more expensive to fly than to walk. Thus, during times when food and/or water became limited in Hawai‘i—especially if the conditions were very severe and persisted for several years—an extremely large percentage of the flighted rails on an island would be eliminated, but a relatively great proportion of the flightless individuals would survive to breed. If such episodes of extended unfavorable environmental conditions occurred several times a century, the population of the original flighted rail species on an island could be transformed from a volant to a nonvolant one in only a few hundred years. Even if this evolutionary process took several thousand years, this is a mere instant in geologic time and, of course, is well within the life span of even the youngest Hawaiian Island.

Pelvic Girdle Enlargement

It is true that the leg skeleton of flightless birds is significantly larger (Figure 22.1) and supports a much larger large muscle mass than in closely related flighted species. Thus, it might seem that the metabolic expense of growing and maintaining this enlarged hind limb (and associated strengthened pelvic girdle) in a flightless bird would have nullified the savings in energy allowed by the reduced pectoral region, and so the individual would not be at any selective advantage in this regard. This would undoubtedly be true if the enlarged leg had developed at the same time as the reduced wing, but it is presumed that in the first brood of young showing the mutant pectoral assembly the pelvic region was of proportions normal for the species. It was only after development of flightlessness, when strong selective pressures had developed among the nonvolant individuals themselves, that there was selection for enlarged hindquarters. It is unknown just what selective advantage the enlarged hind limb region confers on flightless birds. Nonvolant forms throughout the world possess this same characteristic, though, so it may well be related to proper balancing of the body in terrestrial activities not typically engaged in by flighted forms.

Potential Proof

Neotenic flightless individuals in present-day populations of normally flighted bird species have apparently never been reported. This, however, is perhaps due purely to chance, because of the probable relatively low frequency of such a mutation and the undoubted greatly shortened life span of such birds in almost all parts of the modern world. The proffered explanation of the evolution of flightlessness through neoteny, however, does not seem at all unreasonable, and there is a method by which it may someday be verified.

If a complete temporal sequence of fossil remains of one of the flightless Hawaiian species, from original colonization to extinction, could be found in superimposed soil layers (as in the case of the horse), an abrupt morphological change from a fully flighted form in one stratigraphic level to a completely flightless one in the overlying one would strongly support the neotenic hypothesis. If, on the other hand, the bony flight apparatus were seen to diminish only gradually through successively younger layers, the more common evolutionary process like that undergone by the horse would be indicated. Unfortunately, no such suitable stratigraphic deposits bearing bird fossils have yet been located in the Hawaiian Islands, although this obviously remains a most desirable objective of investigators.

Serendipitous Preadaptation

Worldwide, the principal families having numerous and/or notable nonvolant insular members are the ducks and geese (for example, various endemic Hawaiian species); megapodes (Megapodiidae; certain flightless species of the Southwest Pacific); rails (one or more species on each of numerous oceanic islands); and derivatives of doves and pigeons (Columbidae; in the form of the Indian Ocean Mascarene Islands' Dodo, #*Raphus cucullatus,* and Rodriguez Solitaire, #*Pezophaps solitarius,* usually segregated as the extinct family Raphidae). Many flighted species of these families carry out most of their activities on the ground, such as feeding, mating, nesting, and so on. Thus, if such a bird type became flightless on an isolated island without humans, the change from volancy to nonvolancy would entail little if any change from most aspects of the form's previous ecology. In contrast to this effective preadaptation, imagine the hopeless situation of an arboreal nectar feeder such as a Hawaiian honeycreeper if it could not fly upon maturing.

FOSSIL REMAINS

Background

Two-thirds of the original endemic Hawaiian avifauna (Tables 20.1, 20.2) became extinct before written records were kept, but it is surprising that not a single such species can be recognized by any reference in Hawaiian oral tradition. These vanished birds came to be known only through discovery of their remains preserved throughout the archipelago in various types of fossil sites, which are described in the next section.

First, though, it should be noted that the frequently used term "fossil" is actually a rather imprecise one. A few centuries ago it designated any unusual geologic object or ancient biological remnant that was "dug up" (Latin *"fossilis"*), but today is applied only to animal and plant remains of significant age. Many of these have become petrified (Greek *"petra"* [rock]) or **permineralized,** through replacement of the original organic material with harder minerals. Skeletal material buried only a hundred years or so may undergo permineralization if in a periodically or perpetually water-saturated substrate, but bones in a constantly dry matrix will never permineralize. In this discussion, biological remains, whether permineralized or not, are referred to as fossil if they were apparently deposited in the Islands before the time of European Contact (A.D. 1778) *and* are not definitely components of prehistoric archaeological midden (human food refuse and other cultural debris).

FOSSIL SITES

Sand Dunes

In coastal areas, particles of broken coral-algal reef and fragments of marine invertebrate calcareous exoskeletons are often blown inland of the beach high-tide mark (see chapter 5) and cover remains of any dead organisms there. Later, winds may periodically remove portions of this loose sand from "blowouts," revealing previously buried material. Occasionally, some of the containing sand may be lithified or cemented into a type of rock (eolianite) by the joint dissolving and cementing action of rainwater transformed into weak carbonic acid through absorption of carbon dioxide. Blocks of eolianite containing fossils must be removed using rock saws and the remains laboriously dissected out in the laboratory with small electric drills or the matrix surrounding them dissolved away with acetic acid. Although the material from such cemented-sand situations may be partially permineralized, many of the other sand-buried remains are largely unaltered from their original chemical state.

Sandy fossiliferous sites with the remains of birds and other animals have been discovered at **Moʻomomi Beach** of northwestern Molokaʻi, as well as in the more limited **Makawehi Dunes** near Poʻipū on the south shore of Kauaʻi. The first fossil bird remains found at the Molokaʻi locality represented an entire skeleton of the Maui Nui *Moa nalo* (†*Thambetochen chauliodous* [Figure 22.1] [see chapter 20]), exposed by storm waves in uncemented sand beneath an ancient lithified dune. Snail shells accompanying the skeleton radiocarbon-dated at least 25,000 years old, and presumably the bird's remains are approximately the same age. All subsequent bird material thus far recovered at Moʻomomi Beach, however, comes from loose surface sand and dates only from about 5,000 to 7,000 or so years ago. The Kauaʻi locality yielded dates, primarily from land-snail shells and crab claws, approximately the same as those from the surface-sand material of Molokaʻi, certainly no more than 10,000 years. Coastal sites are essentially the only fossiliferous ones thus far discovered on Molokaʻi and Kauaʻi, so the prehistorically extinct bird species that inhabited only their upland areas remain unknown.

Sinkholes

The formation of Hawaiian sinkholes was described in chapter 8. Thus far, significant exposures of emergent ancient reef with such structures have been found primarily on Oʻahu, mostly in the ʻEwa Plain area of its southwestern corner. Wind- and water-transported soil from the uplands gradually accumulated in the developing sinkholes, covering the bones of animals trapped by falling into the deep, flask-shaped cavities. Use of some sinkholes for roosting and nesting by predatory and scavenging birds also contributed partial skeletons of avian prey to the great variety of other biological material present. The buried bones from most sinkholes are chemically unaltered, but in certain levels of a few the sporadic or localized occurrence of ancient water lenses has resulted in permineralization.

There are reefs of two different high-sea stands exposed in the ʻEwa Plain area: the younger Waimānalo and the older Waiʻalae. The surface of the former, with a maximum age of approximately 120,000 years, extends up to about 7.6 m (25 feet) above current sea level. This partially overlies the seaward portion of the latter, formed perhaps 300,000 years ago, whose greatest elevation is about 13 m (43 feet). The stratified soil in the sinkholes of these reefs contains not only the remains of Island vertebrates, invertebrates, and plants before human arrival, but also those of subsequently deposited Polynesian-introduced animals such as lizards, Polynesian Rats (*Rattus exulans* [see chapter 19]), and snails (especially *Allopeas gracile,* formerly known as *Lamellaxis gracilis* [family Subulinidae] [see chapter 18]). This stratification allows at least a relative dating of accompanying fossil bird remains, but specific ages for the bones of most of the various avian species are still much needed. Charcoal from one excavated hearth in an extraordinarily large sinkhole of the Wai'alae Sea Stand reef (Figure 22.2), however, has been radiocarbon-dated as approximately 800 (770 ± 70) years old. This hearth contained a burned bone from each of two prehistorically extinct avian species of the family Anatidae, along with a Polynesian Rat bone, thus showing apparent contemporaneity of at least some of the extirpated avifauna with pre-Contact Hawaiians. Although the sinkholes contain extremely important fossils, these represent only the lowland prehistoric avifauna, so just as in the case of Moloka'i and Kaua'i the ancient bird species of higher O'ahu elevations have yet to be determined.

Lava Tubes

Fossil bird deposits have been found in these structures primarily only on the islands of Hawai'i and Maui Nui, largely because almost all lava tubes on the older islands of O'ahu and Kaua'i

Figure 22.2. An exceptionally large sinkhole on O'ahu's 'Ewa Plain. (State Archaeological Site 50–80–12–9545.) A prehistoric Hawaiian coral-algal rubble wall appears beneath the overhang at the top of the photograph, and a rubble cairn or *ahu* that aided in entrance and exit is visible to the far left center. Dated hearth charcoal and burned bones from the small square test pit to the far right center revealed that humans and at least two prehistorically extinct bird species of the family Anatidae coexisted in this area a little less than 800 years ago. (Photograph by C. John Ralph, used with permission.)

have been obliterated through collapse (see chapter 5). Most lava-tube fossils of flightless birds (Figure 22.3, Plate 22.1) accumulated when the hapless animals fell through collapsed areas of the tube ceiling known as skylights (Plate 5.1). Also present, however, are remains of smaller flighted birds as well as larger predatory and scavenging avian species that probably had fed on them. A few lava tubes without skylights also captured a surprising number of all types of prehistoric birds, along with the two Island bat species (see chapter 19), apparently when these animals proceeded far into the passage and, for some obscure reason, never found their way out. Most bones are found lying exposed on the lava-tube floor and are usually not permineralized, and they are sometimes in a poorly preserved and fragile condition because of the typically damp tube atmosphere.

The lava-tube fossil sites thus far investigated on Maui are all located on the slopes of Haleakalā. They range in elevation from 305 to 1,860 m (1,000 to 6,100 feet), with the exception of a single one near sea level that yielded very few bird remains. Thus, essentially only the upland prehistoric avifauna of this island has been sampled. Many culturally unutilized lava tubes examined on Hawai'i have been disappointingly unproductive, but an exceptional few repre-

Figure 22.3. Skeleton of a *Moa nalo* at its lava-tube death site. The tube is on Kalaupapa Peninsula of northern Moloka'i. The specimen was not collected, so the genus and species of this prehistorically extinct, flightless Hawaiian anatid is uncertain. A leather glove partially visible at the top of the photograph provides scale. (Photograph by Earl "Buddy" Neller, used with permission.)

senting the same general altitudinal range as the upland Maui ones have yielded some spectacular new prehistorically extinct bird species, only one of which is the still-undescribed Giant
Hawai'i Goose discussed in chapter 20. The discovery of many more unknown species may be
expected if more similarly productive lava-tube sites can be found on Hawai'i.

In regard to dating lava-tube bones, the age of the tube-containing lava flow provides at
least a maximum date for their deposition. In most cases, the lack of a soil deposit prevents even
relative age determination for bones of various species based on stratigraphic differences.
Recently, however, newer methods of radiocarbon dating have made possible age determination
of relatively very small quantities of bone, so that a large amount of irreplaceable fossil material no longer has to be destroyed in the process. Some individual bones of extinct birds from
Maui lava tubes so dated have yielded ages ranging between about 8,000 years ago and approximately modern time.

Pond Deposits

Quiet bodies of freshwater usually provide ideal conditions for accumulation and preservation
of fragile material such as bird bones, not only because many nonoceanic species are attracted
to drink and feed, but also because the remains of individuals expiring there often sink undam-
aged to the bottom. Although permanent freshwater impoundments were rare in the Hawaiian
Islands before human arrival (see chapters 8, 14), the craters of many Rejuvenation-Stage volcanic tuff cones (see chapters 3, 5) probably held temporary ponds during each period of unusually heavy rainfall. The fine volcanic ash simultaneously eroded off the encircling crater walls
served to cover and protect any sunken bones while continually building up the pond deposit.

To retrieve fossil material from such an intact site would require deep excavations over an
extensive area, something that is not now possible in many human-utilized tuff cones such as
O'ahu's Diamond Head and Punchbowl. On Kāne'ohe's Mōkapu Peninsula, however, the entire
northeast side of the **Ulupa'u Head** tuff cone has been eroded away by trade wind–driven rain
and waves, so that the profile of a long expanse of crater-pond deposit up to 15 m (50 feet) or
so thick has been laid bare. At the current time of relatively lowered sea level, the deposit is
separated from the ocean by a narrow beach. Bird bones continually weather out of the entire
eroded soil wall and may be collected when noted partially exposed in it or after falling to the
debris slope at its base.

The age of the Ulupa'u Head cone itself is still undetermined but is very likely somewhere
between about 300,000 and 800,000 years. The pond deposits now being sampled must date
between this time and 120,000 years, because their uppermost layers are overlain in places by
the ancient reef of the Waimānalo Sea Stand (see discussion earlier in this chapter). At least the
earlier Ulupa'u deposits, thus, may well constitute the oldest fossil bird locality so far discovered in the Islands, being Late Pleistocene in age rather than considerably younger as in the case
of other known Hawaiian sites.

Other Fossil Sites

Remains of prehistorically extinct Island birds have been found in two additional depositional
situations. On southern Hawai'i, a few fragments of the skeleton of a gooselike bird were fortuitously discovered in 1926 when a water tunnel was being dug under a lava flow 25 m (83
feet) thick at about 275 m (900 feet) elevation, above the town of Pāhala. Apparently, the entire
dead bird or its skeleton had been lying on an ash substrate when it was covered by the lava

flow approximately 10,000 years ago, but, fortunately, not all of the bones were completely destroyed. This specimen, incidentally, represents the first prehistorically extinct bird discovered in the Hawaiian Islands, and it was named in 1943 as a new anatid genus and species of unknown subfamily affinities and ecology: † *Geochen rhuax,* the **Lesser Hawai'i "Goose"** previously mentioned in chapter 20. It is strange that no additional material of this good-sized endemic species has yet come to light in lava tubes or elsewhere on the island.

Finally, along the Leeward O'ahu shore near Mākaha is an undated bank of soil composed largely of material long ago washed down from higher elevations, now being eroded away by rain and storm waves. In these sediments have been found two partial associated skeletons and an occasional isolated bone of the flightless Common O'ahu *Moa nalo* (†*Thambetochen xanion*), along with scant remains of several other prehistorically extinct bird species. Exoskeleton remains of an (apparently historically?) extirpated land crab are also present. The occurrence of, especially, the avian remains in a water-transported accumulation emphasizes that this previously uninvestigated type of deposit on all main islands constitutes a potentially very important source of fossil material.

SUGGESTED REFERENCES

Fleischer and McIntosh in press; Freed et al. 1987; James and Olson 1983; Olson and James 1982, 1991; Sorenson et al. 1999; Ziegler 1987.

The Northwestern Hawaiian Islands

The islands and atolls of this Northwestern chain (sometimes known as the Leeward Islands) stretch almost 2,000 km (1,200 miles) from the main Hawaiian Islands (Figure 23.1) although, for administrative purposes, all except Midway are part of the City and County of Honolulu. Their development is described in chapter 3, and the ages of several are given in Table 3.1. In this chapter the environmental conditions and biological resources of these small land-masses are described, and the human use of them is briefly recounted.

GENERAL DESCRIPTION

Only small basaltic Nihoa and Necker Islands can still be called "high islands" (see chapter 3), with La Pérouse Rock at French Frigate Shoals and Gardner Pinnacles constituting even smaller remnants of former large Hawaiian Islands. The others of the Northwestern chain are "low islands," being rather typical atoll *motu* formed of calcareous sand on coral-algal reef sur-mounting now-submerged ancient Island volcanoes (see chapter 3). The extensive shallow lagoon in and around which the *motu* of each atoll are located usually has many barely sub-merged portions, and these shoals were the site of many shipwrecks in the nineteenth and early twentieth centuries when the Northwestern chain was still incompletely charted.

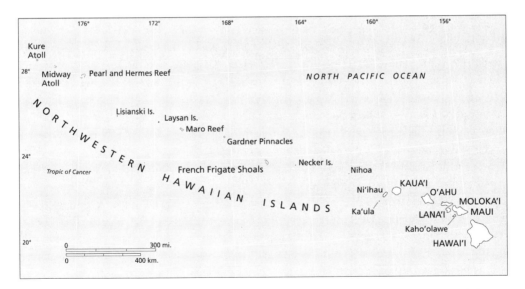

Figure 23.1. Map of the Northwestern Hawaiian Islands. Only Nihoa, Necker, La Pérouse Rock in French Frigate Shoals, and Gardner Pinnacles consist of basalt; the other islands are composed of coral-algal reef sand. Various shallow banks such as Maro Reef and a few similar ones not shown are only occasionally exposed by low tides. (Unnumbered figure on p. 1 of Rauzon [2001].)

Climatology

Rainfall on such low-lying islands is little greater than that of the open ocean or of most rain-shadow leeward areas of the main islands (see chapter 7) and averages between 62.5 and 75 cm (25 and 30 inches) annually. Much of the rain falling on Northwestern chain islands is either trapped by layers of basalt on the high islands or collects as a basal lens underlying the *motu* (see chapter 8). Although sometimes rather heavily tainted with bird excrement, this ground-water has supported humans on certain islands and *motu* in prehistoric and early historic times. On Nihoa, three small seeps collectively produce an average of 38 to 46 liters (10 to 12 gallons) daily, and two on Necker yield only a little less. On most of the low islands, this slightly brackish groundwater can usually be obtained by digging 1 or 2 m (3.3 or 6.6 feet) into the sand at the lowest interior part. Freshwater, however, is not needed by oceanic birds and other vertebrates there, and even the few native land birds seem to survive without constant access to it.

With no forest or other shelter present on most of the Northwestern Islands, the trades and considerably stronger storm winds sweep unimpeded across them, and the latter are responsible for most natural damage. Also, high waves produced by hurricanes are recorded as occasionally killing or injuring biota on the low islands. It would seem that the larger and more powerful tsunamis (see chapter 6) would periodically scour all plant and animal life off these same *motu*, but, evidently, such inundations do not usually occur. The reason for this is obscure, although it is thought that the very shallow lagoon basins and low *motu* shores may offer so little resistance to the tsunami swells that they often fail to crest upon reaching the atolls and continue past in their usual smooth wave form.

Hawaiian Usage

Only Nihoa and Necker are known to have been inhabited by pre-Contact Hawaiians (see discussions of individual islands later in this chapter). Although the name "Nihoa" is used in connection with an undetermined island of the archipelago's western region in at least one ancient Hawaiian chant, as well as in an old proverb, the exact location of that island had been forgotten by the time of European Contact in 1778. In 1822, however, the regent Kaʻahumanu (see chapter 26), knowing of these traditional oral references, requested the sailing-ship captain William Sumner to take her to the north of Kauaʻi in search of Nihoa, which was duly found and annexed to the Kingdom of Hawaiʻi. After this time, there seems to have been little if any sustained human use of Nihoa, although, according to a member of a multigenerational Kauaʻi family, Native Hawaiians from Niʻihau regularly traveled to the island until the early twentieth century. The purpose of such reputed trips was not stated.

Whether the islands to the northwest of Nihoa and Necker were known to ancient Hawaiians is problematical. No prehistoric cultural deposits have been found on any of the *motu*, but there is at least one Hawaiian reference to a small island that could conceivably have been one of this chain. In a traditional chant relating to the northward travels of the volcano goddess Pele (see chapter 5) from distant "Kahiki" to Hawaiʻi, the first island sighted was called "Mokupā-papa" ("flat island"), after which Pele traveled on to "Nihoa." Obviously, in as ancient a context as this legend, the particular "Mokupāpapa" referred to would not necessarily have to have been a Northwestern (or other) Hawaiian Island, but could have been one somewhere between the Society or Marquesas Islands and Hawaiʻi—perhaps one of the Line Islands or even Johnston Atoll (Figure 11.2). And the event of its discovery by ancestral Hawaiians in their travels to and from more southern island groups could, with time, have easily become incorporated into the Pele account. Occasional other vague traditional and early historic Hawaiian literature references to a "Mokupāpapa" indicate that it was sandy and abounded in turtles, which were sometimes hunted there. The two *motu* of Kure Atoll, with occasional turtles on their sandy beaches, were sometimes collectively recorded as "Moku Pāpapa" by early historical informants, but it seems most unlikely that pre-Contact and early post-Contact Hawaiians would have traveled over 1,930 km (1,200 miles) from the main islands to that specific atoll to take turtles.

The occurrence of the Polynesian Rat or *'iole (Rattus exulans)* at Kure could potentially be definitive in ascertaining early Hawaiian presence on the atoll, but here also the evidence is equivocal. This rodent was widely spread throughout the western and central Pacific by ancestral and later Polynesians (see chapter 25). The species is relatively common in certain habitats of the main Hawaiian Islands, but in the Northwestern chain is recorded only from Kure. The time and circumstances of its arrival there, however, are unknown. The atoll's distance from the main islands seems a little too great for colonization by natural "rafting" of the animal, especially because its transport to the latter group only took place during the last 1,500 or so years. Even if such drifting events did happen, it is difficult to understand why only distant Kure Atoll was reached and no closer ones in the Northwestern chain. The improbability of Hawaiians reaching Kure before the era of modern ships was suggested above, but, if they had succeeded, it seems that they would also have reached other Northwestern atolls. And if the Polynesian Rat happened to be on the canoes used, why did it not occupy any of these other places? In fact, the rodent does not even occur on Nihoa and Necker, two Northwestern Hawaiian Islands known to have been inhabited by early Hawaiians. Thus, on balance, it appears most reasonable to assume that the Polynesian Rat was carried to Kure on a post-Contact ship (although the species is not known as a historic "ship rat"). The rodent was present in great numbers on Kure when the USS *Saginaw* went aground there in 1870. It could well have attained the atoll upon the wreck of the British ship *Gledstanes* in 1837 or the 1843 wreck of the American whaler *Parker* (if not some earlier unrecorded grounding of a historic vessel). Unfortunately, however, no accounts of the two earlier shipwrecks that contain information regarding contemporary presence or absence of the Polynesian Rat on Kure have been located.

FLORA

With the exception of an island-endemic Hawaiian palm species of Nihoa and another of possibly the same status from Laysan, as well as an endemic sandalwood reaching small-tree size on the latter, the native terrestrial vegetation of the Northwestern Hawaiian Islands is essentially an indigenous one. It is generally low-growing and quite typical of the Strand and Coastal Zones of the main islands (see chapter 14). Approximately 310 species of ferns and seed-producing plants are recorded as established in this part of the archipelago, and about 256 of these were deliberately or unintentionally introduced by humans. The remaining fifty-five or so species are native to the Northwestern chain, with eight of these endemic to it (although three of these occur on more than one island or *motu* there). The more abundant and obvious of the native seed-producing plant species throughout the Northwestern Hawaiian Islands are among those listed in Table 23.1. Laysan supports the greatest number of native taxa, possessing thirty-two such species. Alien plants are most frequently encountered at Midway Atoll, which is included in the island range of 237 of the 256 introduced species.

Only about half the macroscopic marine algae species (see chapter 11) of the main islands

Table 23.1. More abundant flowering plant species of the Northwestern Hawaiian Islands. All of these apparently occur on at least four of the islands, and a majority are indigenous to the Hawaiian Archipelago as a whole. An asterisk (*) indicates alien species. (Data from Herbst and Wagner [1992] and Wagner et al. [1999].)

Family   Species
Sedge family (Cyperaceae)
Button Sedge or *mau'u 'aki'aki (Fimbristylis cymosa)*
Grass family (Poaceae)
*Common Sandbur or *'ume'alu (Cenchrus echinatus)*
*Bermuda Grass or *mānienie (Cynodon dactylon)*
Lovegrass *(Eragrostis paupera)*
Hawaiian Lovegrass or *kāwelu (Eragrostis variabilis)*
Grass *(Lepturus repens)*
*Bristly Foxtail or *mau'u pilipili (Setaria verticillata)*
*Dropseed *(Sporobolus pyramidatus)*
Fig-marigold family (Aizoaceae)
Sea Purslane or *'ākulikuli (Sesuvium portulacastrum)*
Amaranth family (Amaranthaceae)
Atoll Achyranthes (*Achyranthes atollensis* [now extinct?])
Sunflower family (Asteraceae)
*Hairy Horseweed or *ilioha (Conyza bonariensis)*
Nehe *(Lipochaeta integrifolia)*
Borage family (Boraginaceae)
*Tree Heliotrope *(Tournefortia argentea)*
Mustard family (Brassicaceae)
*Swine Cress *(Coronopus didymus)*
Pepperwort or *'ānaunau (Lepidium bidentatum)*
Casuarina family (Casuarinaceae)
*Common Ironwood or *paina (Casuarina equisetifolia)*
Goosefoot family (Chenopodiaceae)
Goosefoot or *'āheahea (Chenopodium oahuense)*
Morning glory family (Convolvulaceae)
Morning Glory or *koali 'awa (Ipomoea indica)*
Beach Morning Glory or *pōhuehue (Ipomoea pes-caprae)*
Gourd family (Cucurbitaceae)
Puaokama (*Sicyos maximowiczii* [and other species?])
Goodenia family (Goodeniaceae)
Beach *Naupaka* or *naupaka kahakai (Scaevola taccada)*

(Continued on following page)

Table 23.1. *(continued)* More abundant flowering plant species of the Northwestern Hawaiian Islands. All of these apparently occur on at least four of the islands, and a majority are indigenous to the Hawaiian Archipelago as a whole. An asterisk (*) indicates alien species. (Data from Herbst and Wagner [1992] and Wagner et al. [1999].)

Family   Species
Four-o'clock family (Nyctaginaceae)   *Alena (Boerhavia repens)*

Purslane family (Portulacaceae)
    Purslane or *'ihi* (*Portulaca lutea* [and *P. villosa?*])
    *Pigweed or *'ākulikuli kula* (*Portulaca oleracea*)

Nightshade family (Solanaceae)
    Glossy Nightshade or *pōpolo* (*Solanum americanum*)
    Nightshade or *pōpolo* (*Solanum nelsoni*)

Creosote bush family (Zygophyllaceae)   Caltrop or *nohu* (*Tribulus cistoides*)

are also found in the Northwestern chain. At the few high islands this relative impoverishment is undoubtedly because the lava substrate enters the ocean at a steep angle, providing only a small and relatively unvaried amount of shallow-water attachment area for the algae. And, around the *motu,* much of the sandy area apparently does not offer sufficiently firm attachment for most inshore species. Also, the variety of habitats represented on the lagoon reefs themselves tends to be more limited than that of the diverse reef areas around most of the main islands.

MARINE FAUNA

Invertebrates

Although a number of the same shore gastropods commonly found on the main islands may be found on the basalt shores of the high Northwestern Hawaiian Islands (for example, *'opihi* and *pipipi* of the families Patellidae and Neritidae, respectively [see chapter 11]), these are largely missing from the *motu.* This absence is probably due to lack of suitable attachment areas, although it is not clear why areas of "beach rock" (apparently lithified sand [see chapters 5, 22) along the shore of several of these low islands are unoccupied. Perhaps the limited amount of such firm inshore substrate at each *motu* is just too small to support the number of individuals necessary to perpetuate a species' population.

Certain gastropods of sandy bottoms, however, may be relatively common in the Northwestern Islands, as in the case of the Hawaiian Turban or *'alīlea (Turbo sandwicensis).* Bivalves are generally better adapted to life in this sand and reef environment, and such forms as ark shells or *'ōlepe pāpaua* (*Arca* spp.) and rock oysters or *pāpaua momi* (*Chama* spp.) appear abundant around most *motu.* The shallow lagoon of Pearl and Hermes Reef originally supported a very large natural population of the indigenous **Common Pearl Oyster** or *pipi* (*Pinctada margaritifera),* but, for unknown reasons, this species does not seem to have similarly colonized at least other Northwestern chain atolls. In generally deeper water offshore, spiny lobsters or *ula* of the genus *Panulirus* abound, and octopus or *he'e* (*Octopus* spp.) are apparently also common.

Vertebrates

The commonly encountered larger sharks (see chapter 12) around the Northwestern Hawaiian Islands are undoubtedly attracted to, and largely sustained by, the just-fledging young of larger oceanic birds that frequently enter the water, as well as by immature and occasional adult Green Turtles and pups of the Hawaiian Monk Seal. The relative scarcity of seaweeds may limit the types and numbers of herbivorous bony fishes, but members of various primarily carnivorous families tend to be abundant around all of the Islands. Benthic-frequenting "bottom fishes" of the snapper family Lutjanidae, as well as jacks of the family Carangidae feeding higher in the water column, are especially typical of the ocean surrounding the *motu*. Apparently, however, many of these larger "top carnivores"—particularly some carangid species—build up high concentrations of ciguatera toxin (see chapter 12), so human consumption of most good-sized fish-eating species from this area is avoided.

Although the Hawksbill Turtle or *'ea* (*Eretmochelys imbricata*) seems to nest (sparingly) only in the main islands (see chapter 19), the Green Turtle or *honu* (*Chelonia mydas*) lays eggs primarily on Northwestern chain *motu* shores. It is interesting that marine turtles around the world almost never crawl ashore except for female egg laying, but both sexes of the Hawaiian Green Turtle population habitually lie basking for hours during the day on *motu* beaches (Plate 23.1). Ocean waters in the latitudinal band of the Northwestern Hawaiian Islands are relatively cold for the generally tropical ectothermic marine turtles. This sunning behavior thus possibly evolved in the Hawaiian Archipelago because the higher body temperature it produces is adaptively beneficial in accelerating digestion and other critical metabolic processes. The fact that similar "basking" sometimes occurs at night suggests that an additional reason for this behavior may be to decrease the amount of exposure to shark attack.

The final marine vertebrate characteristic of these islands is the endemic Hawaiian Monk Seal or *'īlio holoikauaua* (*Monachus schauinslandi* [see chapter 19]), which, like the Green Turtle, utilizes almost exclusively beaches of the Northwestern Islands for reproductive activities. Nursing females and sleeping individuals of both sexes are common along the sandy beaches of most islands (Plate 23.1), and apparently competing seal males of breeding age often battle in the shallows just offshore. The species seems to feed primarily on smaller inshore reef fish, including eels of several families, along with lobster and octopus, rather than on the abundant snappers and jacks living in deeper water. The seal pups, and occasional older individuals, are preyed upon by sharks, and it is suspected that ciguatera poisoning—perhaps caused by feeding on larger eels—may also play an important part in population mortality. As of 1999, total Hawaiian Monk Seal numbers were estimated at between about 1,300 and 1,400.

TERRESTRIAL FAUNA

Invertebrates

Although a number of mite species have been reported on the Northwestern Hawaiian Islands, these tiny arachnids are seldom apparent to the visitor. The more frequently observed terrestrial arthropods are the insects and, to a lesser degree, a few spiders, centipedes, and millipedes, as well as amphipods and isopods (see chapter 16). At least 163 native species of these various larger arthropod types are known from the Northwestern chain, with over a third being endemic to this part of the Hawaiian Archipelago. Just as in the case of plants, Laysan holds the greatest number of these; fifty-nine are known there. A total of almost 300 alien forms has been introduced throughout the Northwestern Hawaiian Islands, with Midway showing the greatest number, being included in the range of 157 of these.

The only other terrestrial invertebrates likely to be noticed are a relatively few land snails, and it would take close inspection to see these, because all may be characterized as minute. There are probably between one and two dozen native species belonging to seven different genera found throughout the Northwestern chain. No island has more than seven of these species, but sometimes a majority of these is endemic to that particular island. On Nihoa are found two species of the snail family Endodontidae, a group once very common on the main islands, but historically largely extirpated there (see chapters 18, 26). Most of the native snails of the Northwestern chain are apparently ecologically tied to the large clumps of the endemic Hawaiian Lovegrass. About a half dozen tiny species of alien snails of five genera have been introduced among these small islands, mostly to Midway.

Investigations of larger animals such as the turtles, seals, and seabirds tend to dominate animal studies in the Northwestern Hawaiian Islands, but a few interesting observations on the terrestrial arthropods have also been made. A hawk moth, the White-lined Sphinx *(Hyles lineata),* adapted by virtue of its long proboscis to usually feeding on the nectar of flowers with long corollas, was able to establish on florally impoverished Grass Island of Pearl and Hermes Reef by utilizing the short, small flowers of *Alena.* This adaptive shift was probably successful only because the *motu* lacked insects specifically adapted to feeding on this particular type of blossom, which undoubtedly would have prevented the establishment of the hawk moth by outcompeting it in feeding. On Nihoa occur two of the largest Hawaiian insects: the endemic **Nihoa Cone-headed Katydid,** *Banza nihoa,* and the **Giant Nihoa Cricket,** *Thaumatogryllus conanti,* both about 3.5 to 4.5 cm (1.4 to 1.8 inches) long. Possible reasons for insects being able to attain such a relatively large size were discussed in chapter 16.

Vertebrates

At least three species of the presumably alien geckos (see chapter 19) of the main islands are collectively found on most of the Northwestern Hawaiian Islands, very likely carried there primarily in the course of historic human traffic. Alien rodents have undoubtedly traveled in the same manner. The House Mouse or *'iole li'ili'i (Mus musculus)* is historically extirpated on Lisianski and Midway, the only two islands inhabited by this post-Contact species. The historic Roof Rat or *'iole nui (Rattus rattus)* was known only on Midway, before being eradicated in the late 1990s. The earlier-discussed Polynesian Rat was similarly exterminated on Kure during the same period. Domesticated European Rabbits or *lāpaki (Oryctolagus cuniculus)* were introduced to Laysan and Lisianski Islands, as well as Southeast Island of Pearl and Hermes Reef, during the first decade of the twentieth century. All individuals of the species on Laysan and Pearl and Hermes, however, were intentionally extirpated by the end of 1923 and 1928, respectively. And the animals on Lisianski were found to have disappeared by 1923 without human involvement. The Guinea Pig *(Cavia porcellus),* aptly termed "pig rat" or *'iole pua'a* in Hawaiian, was apparently brought to Laysan at about the same time as rabbits, but it is not known whether it similarly established a wild breeding population; at any rate the species does not seem to have still occupied the *motu* when a scientific expedition visited there in 1923.

A few nonmarine birds occur naturally in the Northwestern Hawaiian Islands and are listed in Table 23.2. The five common shorebirds listed as migrants in the table are the same as those most frequently visiting the main islands in the nonbreeding season. All of these may be seen in the Northwestern chain for short periods twice a year as they pause while traveling between their Arctic Region nesting grounds and the main Hawaiian Islands. Some individuals of most or all of these migrants—but primarily the Bristle-thighed Curlew—may occasionally remain on Northwestern Islands for the entire boreal winter.

The dominant birds of the Northwestern Hawaiian Islands are the nesting species of wide-ranging oceanic types as well as several kinds of terns, all of which are listed in Table 23.3. With hundreds of thousands of breeding birds on each island, nesting space is obviously at a premium

Table 23.2. Land and freshwater birds of the Northwestern Hawaiian Islands. An asterisk (*) indicates that the species was historically introduced to an island, and an octothorp (#) indicates either that such an introduced species failed to establish or that a native taxon was historically extirpated there. The myna and canary are alien to the Hawaiian Archipelago. (Data from various sources.)

Family Species	Island(s) of Occurrence
Ducks and geese (Anatidae)	
Laysan Duck *(Anas laysanensis)*	Laysan; Lisianski (#); Pearl and Hermes Reef (* #)
Rails, coots, etc. (Rallidae)	
Laysan Rail *(Porzana palmeri)*	Laysan (#); Lisianski (* #); Pearl and Hermes Reef (* #); Midway (* #)
Plovers (Charadriidae)	
Pacific Golden-Plover or kōlea *(Pluvialis fulva)*	All? (as regular nonbreeding migrant)
Sandpipers, etc. (Scolopacidae)	
Wandering Tattler or 'ūlili *(Heteroscelus incanus)*	All? (as regular nonbreeding migrant)
Bristle-thighed Curlew or kioea *(Numenius tahitiensis)*	All? (as regular nonbreeding migrant)
Ruddy Turnstone or 'akekeke *(Arenaria interpres)*	All? (as regular nonbreeding migrant)
Sanderling or hunakai *(Calidris alba)*	All? (as regular nonbreeding migrant)
Old World warblers (Sylviidae)	
Laysan Millerbird *(Acrocephalus familiaris familiaris)*	Laysan (#)
Nihoa Millerbird *(Acrocephalus familiaris kingi)*	Nihoa
Mynas (Sturnidae)	
Common Myna *(Acridotheres tristis)*	Midway (*)
Finches (Fringillidae)	
Common Canary *(Serinus canaria)*	Midway (*); Kure (* #)
Nihoa Finch *(Telespiza ultima)*	Nihoa; French Frigate Shoals (* #)
Laysan Finch *(Telespiza cantans)*	Laysan; Pearl and Hermes Reef (*); Midway (* #)
Laysan Honeycreeper *(Himatione sanguinea)*	Laysan (#)

(Fig. 23.2), but competition is lessened by partitioning of this critical resource. The ground surface is utilized by nesting albatrosses; the Christmas Shearwater; Red-tailed Tropicbird; Masked and Brown Boobies; as well as Gray-backed, Sooty, and Brown Noddy Terns. Above the ground, shrubs and small trees are used by the Red-footed Booby, Great Frigatebird, as well as Black Noddy and White Terns. Beneath the surface, nesting burrows are excavated by the Bonin Petrel, Wedge-tailed Shearwater, and some Tristram Storm-Petrels. Still other birds such as the Blue-gray Noddy Tern, as well as the majority of Bulwer Petrels and Tristram Storm-Petrels nest mostly or entirely on the high islands, usually choosing rocky crevices available only there. Bulwer Petrels, however, are also found on Laysan, where most nest in burrows dug out by other

Table 23.3. Ocean-related birds breeding in the Northwestern Hawaiian Islands. Estimated numbers of nesting pairs are also listed. (Data from Harrison [1990], with numbers rounded to nearest thousand or lesser multiple of ten.)

Family Species	Number of Nesting Pairs
Albatrosses (Diomedeidae)	
Black-footed Albatross *(Diomedea nigripes)*	36,000–49,000
Laysan Albatross or *mōlī (Diomedea immutabilis)*	291,000–380,000
Petrels and shearwaters (Procellariidae)	
Bonin Petrel *(Pterodroma hypoleuca)*	203,000–331,000
Bulwer Petrel or *'ou (Bulweria bulwerii)*	77,000–103,000
Wedge-tailed Shearwater or *'ua'u kani (Puffinus pacificus)*	174,000–261,000
Christmas Shearwater *(Puffinus nativitatis)*	2,000–3,000
Storm-Petrels (Hydrobatidae)	
Tristram Storm-Petrel *(Oceanodroma tristrami)*	4,000–8,000
Tropicbirds (Phaethontidae)	
White-tailed Tropicbird or *koa'e kea (Phaethon lepturus)*	Occasional pair
Red-tailed Tropicbird or *koa'e 'ula (Phaethon rubricauda)*	8,000–11,000
Boobies (Sulidae)	
Masked Booby or *'ā (Sula dactylatra)*	2,000–2,500
Brown Booby or *'ā (Sula leucogaster)*	350–400
Red-footed Booby or *'ā (Sula sula)*	4,000–5,000
Frigatebirds (Fregatidae)	
Great Frigatebird or *'iwa (Fregata minor)*	8,000–10,000
Terns (Laridae)	
Gray-backed Tern or *pākalakala (Sterna lunata)*	36,000–51,000
Sooty Tern or *'ewa'ewa (Sterna fuscata)*	931,000–1,331,000
Blue-gray Noddy *(Procelsterna cerulea)*	3,000–4,000
Brown Noddy or *noio kōhā (Anous stolidus)*	61,000–93,000
Black Noddy or *noio (Anous minutus)*	6,000–16,000
White Tern or *manu-o-Kū (Gygis alba)*	7,000–15,000

seabirds. Nest-site competition is further lessened by the tendency of a few ground-nesting species (Black-footed Albatross, Christmas Shearwater, and Masked Booby) to utilize primarily the peripheral beach areas, while most other taxa prefer the interior. Also, about one-fourth of all the species nest largely in the boreal winter and spring months, with the remaining three-fourths laying eggs during the summer and fall.

Guano Diggers and Plumage Hunters

The excrement of these millions of birds slowly mixes and possibly chemically reacts with calcareous sand on the *motu*, forming a rather hard, brownish substance known as **guano.** This is an excellent natural fertilizer of high phosphorus content, and around the beginning of the twentieth century, before the development of cheaper chemical substitutes, guano mining on at least Laysan was a thriving—and ecologically injurious—industry. Also during about the same period, fashion styles around the world dictated that women's hats should be adorned with feathers, wings, and even entire stuffed birds. Thus, essentially all of the Northwestern chain *motu* were periodically and illegally occupied by Japanese **plumage hunters,** who killed hundreds of thousands of the nesting birds (especially the extremely abundant Sooty Terns) to supply the French millinery trade. This practice was so abhorrent to many people in the United States that in 1909 President Theodore Roosevelt was led to end the slaughter by designating essentially all of the Northwestern chain as the Hawaiian Islands Bird Reservation. (Incidentally, the plum-

Figure 23.2. Typical nesting colony of the Sooty Tern or *'ewa'ewa (Sterna fuscata).* This is the most abundant breeding bird in the Northwestern Hawaiian Islands, with the birds on Laysan (shown here) alone numbering about a half million pairs. (Photograph by Mark J. Rauzon, used with permission.)

age collection would have ceased soon even without this new protective action, because by that time the vogue in hat ornamentation had shifted from birds to artificial flowers and foliage.) The entire chain is now administered by the U.S. Fish and Wildlife Service as a portion of the Hawaiian/Pacific Islands National Wildlife Refuge Complex.

Albatross Feeding

The various marine-related birds of the Northwestern Hawaiian Islands also avoid competition by utilizing slightly different components of the ocean fauna for food, but a discussion of this subject is beyond the scope of this volume. There is, however, one interesting observation in regard to the feeding of the two albatross species. Adults largely seek pelagic squid or *mūhe'e* (probably primarily *Sepioteuthis lessoniana* and other ecologically similar cephalopods [see chapter 11]) far at sea and return to their single chick every several days or so to feed it this material by regurgitation. The young digests the softer parts of the prey, then in turn casts up the indigestible portions such as horny squid beaks at the nest. In gathering this food, however, the adults have scooped from the ocean surface other floating but often indigestible material, evidently mistaking it for some sort of animal prey. In prehistory this harvested flotsam probably consisted primarily of larger seeds from almost anywhere around the Pacific, along with occa-

Figure 23.3. Indigestible material regurgitated by an albatross chick. This material is from the 1990 nest area of a Laysan Albatross or *mōlī (Diomedea immutabilis)* on Lisianski Island. All of the items were picked up on the ocean surface by foraging adults and fed to the young bird. In addition to beaks of the usual squid prey, dark-colored items include a Candlenut or *kukui (Aleurites moluccana)* and a fragment of pumice. The small lighter-colored pieces are various types of plastic. (Photograph by Alan C. Ziegler.)

sional pieces of volcanic pumice (see chapter 4). In historic time, however, relatively great numbers of smaller buoyant glass and plastic items have supplemented the catch to be fed to the chick.

Thus, such familiar items as small plastic toys, spent ballpoint pens, disposable cigarette lighters, and burned-out miniature lightbulbs may now be incongruously found far inland from the beach of uninhabited *motu* where they have been regurgitated by albatross chicks (Figure 23.3). Subsequent burial of some of this material by the burrowing activities of shearwaters and petrels further compounds the problems of stratigraphic interpretation by archaeologists and paleontologists investigating such *motu.*

THE ISLANDS AND *MOTU*

Nihoa

The first Northwestern chain landmass encountered northwest of the main island of Kaua'i is **Nihoa** (Figure 23.1), a high island 278 m (910 feet) in maximum elevation and 397 by 1,403 m (1,300 by 4,600 feet) in areal extent. The basalt is covered by a thin volcanic soil layer suitable for cultivation of dry-land plants such as Sweet Potato or *'uala (Ipomoea batatas),* and from possibly about A.D. 1000 to 1700 the island supported a prehistoric Hawaiian population of perhaps a hundred or so individuals. The primary impetus for prehistoric family groups to inhabit such an isolated island is conjectural. Perhaps it was for exploitation of the abundant seabirds nesting there, or it could have been for the convenience provided in taking certain of the various kinds of pelagic and larger bottom-dwelling fishes common in Northwestern chain waters. Archaeological evidence in this regard, such as masses of bird and fish bones in middens as well as shell and bone artifacts, is practically nonexistent, according to recent investigators. The volcanic soil's normal high acidity, perhaps enhanced by admixed seabird droppings, has long since completely dissolved most or all deposited bone and shell material, leaving primarily only a few basaltic artifacts in the matrix.

An island-endemic species of Hawaiian palm or *loulu (Pritchardia remota)* is present along with nineteen other smaller native plant taxa, including two more found only on Nihoa. Six alien plant species are recorded as established, but half of these have not been observed there since 1985. There are sixty-one native arthropods (thirty-five of them endemic to the Northwestern chain) other than mites, and fifty-nine alien ones. All of the seven land snail species are native, and represent five genera. The only two land bird taxa, the Nihoa Millerbird and Nihoa Finch, are island endemics.

Necker

This essentially soil-less volcanic remnant is only 153 m (500 feet) wide and 1,220 m (4,000 feet) long, rising to 85 m (277 feet). Ancient Hawaiian use of **Necker** seems to have been largely restricted to temporary visits. These were possibly for religious purposes, because shrines of an apparently early type are extremely common, totaling thirty-three apparently built over a number of years. Also, about a dozen enigmatic male figurines of basalt (Fig. 23.4) were found there and are of a style unknown elsewhere in the entire Hawaiian Archipelago. Possibly, the use of the island involved rituals of worship related to some sort of bird cult, but this is largely conjectural. The island was used during at least the 1500s, judging from two radiocarbon dates, but more such age determinations are needed to aid in deciphering the total time span of human visitation. The island was named after a French minister of finance by Captain Jean-François G. de La Pérouse (see chapter 28), a famous navigator who provided the first historical record of Necker when he sighted it in September 1786.

Necker supports only five indigenous and one alien plant species. Among the arthropods other than mites, fifteen are endemic to the Northwestern chain, twelve are indigenous, and thirty-seven are alien. There is only one land snail, and it is native. No land birds occur on the island (it is probably too small to support the minimum number of pairs necessary to sustain a population), but most of the marine-related bird species of the Northwestern chain nest there.

French Frigate Shoals

This is the first atoll encountered as the chain is traced to the northwest. (The presence of La Pérouse Rock, the last vestige of a volcanic high island [discussed later in this section], means that, technically, French Frigate Shoals is not yet a true atoll, even though it is so termed here.) Its *motu* comprise between five and thirteen named sandy landmasses, of which only Tern Island is not periodically reshaped or erased and redeveloped by wave action because its periphery has been stabilized by bulwarks to protect a small airstrip. This runway was built and used by the U.S. Navy during World War II and occupies most of the island. Tern is approximately 107 m (350 feet) wide and 946 m (3,100 feet) long and rises about 3.7 m (12 feet) above sea level; all of the associated *motu* are smaller. A U.S. Coast Guard Long-range Navigation (LORAN) radio station was built on East Island in 1943, but this facility was moved to Tern in 1952. The military eventually abandoned the entire atoll, and by the 1990s essentially the only human use was that of Tern Island as a base for personnel of the U.S. Fish and Wildlife Service, who mon-

Figure 23.4. Four basalt figurines from a Necker Island shrine. About a dozen such images were found at the numerous religious structures there, but this type is unknown elsewhere in the Hawaiian Archipelago. The tallest figurine shown is just a little over 40 cm (16 inches) in height. (Negative no. CA 787 of Bishop Museum Archives, retouched and used with permission.)

itor the entire Northwestern Hawaiian Islands National Wildlife Refuge. **French Frigate Shoals** received their name from the previously mentioned Captain La Pérouse, who historically discovered the landmasses when the two vessels under his command narrowly escaped running aground there in November 1786.

Twelve species of native plants, and some forty-nine alien ones, grow there. Thirteen native nonmite arthropods occur (three of them endemic to the Northwestern chain), along with thirty-nine alien ones, but land snails seem to be absent. No land birds appear to have inhabited the atoll since it attained its essentially low-island status, and a group of forty-two Nihoa Finches introduced to two of the *motu* in 1967 or 1969 had disappeared by 1980. Most of the marine-related birds of the Northwestern chain may be found nesting at the shoals, and the *motu* collectively support the largest population of Hawaiian Monk Seals in the entire archipelago, as well as the majority of nesting Green Turtles.

The tiny twinned basaltic peak of **La Pérouse Rock** (Plate 23.1) lies about 8 km (5 miles) south of Tern Island and is of geologic interest because it represents the last remnant of the large volcanic island on which the atoll of French Frigate Shoals has developed. The larger portion of the rock is only 24 by 153 m (80 by 500 feet) in extent and 41 m (135 feet) high, and the smaller is 12 by 31 m (40 by 100 feet) and 3 m (9.8 feet) high.

Gardner Pinnacles

Two small and closely approximated volcanic peaks, with the larger 76 by 198 m (250 by 650 feet) in extent and 55 m (180 feet) high, make up this landmass and represent the oldest basalt still exposed in the entire Hawaiian Archipelago. The historic discoverer of **Gardner Pinnacles** was Captain Joseph Allen aboard the New England whaler *Maro,* who came upon them in June 1820. He evidently named them after Edmund Gardner, captain of one of the first two American whaling ships that had reached Hawai'i only the year before. The indigenous Purslane or *'ihi (Portulaca lutea)* is the only plant established on the essentially soil-less substrate, and its population consists of fewer than two dozen individuals. Nine types of terrestrial arthropods have been found, but a species list has not been published. No land snails are known, but a few thousand seabirds of about a dozen species nest on the pinnacles.

Laysan Island

This is the next to largest of the Northwestern Hawaiian Islands and measures about 1,708 m (5,600 feet) in greatest width and 2,867 m (9,400 feet) in length, with the maximum elevation 12 m (40 feet). Geologically, the island is unusual because it supports a pond in its depressed interior, although the continued evaporation of seawater seeping into this has yielded a hyper-saline condition, several times saltier than the ocean. (Note that although this enclosed body of water is often called a "lagoon," it is not the same type of structure as the central shallow reef area of a typical atoll [see chapter 3].) **Laysan** was sighted in March 1828 by a Russian Captain Stanikowitch, who designated it Moller Island after his ship, but the *motu* had apparently already been seen earlier by American whalers, who had bestowed its currently used name, although the meaning of the appellation and other details of this original historic discovery are now unknown. Extensive guano mining and plumage hunting, as well as mass collection of albatross eggs to be exported for human consumption and photographic film-emulsion manufacture were carried out there for a decade or so around the turn of the twentieth century, but since that time the island has had only temporary human visitors.

Apparently, some original plant species (including the endemic Hawaiian Coastal Sandal-wood or *'iliahialo'e* [*Santalum ellipticum*] and a possibly island-endemic Hawaiian palm of the genus *Pritchardia*) were lost from Laysan in the first quarter of the 1900s. This extirpation resulted from the virtual complete devegetation of the island, primarily by rabbits and human activities. Laysan still, however, possesses some thirty-one species of native plants, of which five are endemic to the Northwestern chain. There are also about fourteen alien plant species, including a few Coconuts or *niu (Cocos nucifera)*. Among arthropods other than mites, the seventy-six native species include seventeen endemic to the Northwestern Hawaiian Islands, and ninety-six alien taxa exist along with these. Four native species of land snails of three genera as well as one alien species have been recorded. As noted earlier, European Rabbits and Guinea Pigs apparently brought to the island early in the 1900s were gone by the end of 1923. The surprising total of five endemic land and freshwater bird taxa (three of them historically extirpated, as indicated here by the octothorp #) naturally colonized the island: the Laysan Duck, flightless #Laysan Rail, #Laysan Millerbird, Laysan Finch, and #Laysan Honeycreeper (a race of the common extant main island *'Apapane* [see chapter 21]).

Lisianski

This *motu* is approximately 1,006 by 1,830 m (3,300 by 6,000 feet) in extent, with a highest point of about 12 m (40 feet). The center of **Lisianski** is depressed to near sea level and may possibly once have contained an ocean embayment, but apparently never a hypersaline pond like that of Laysan. An exploring Russian, Captain Urey Lisiansky, historically discovered the island when his ship *Neva* went aground on a nearby lagoon shoal area in October 1805. His crew gave their captain's name to the island (although the alternative spelling used here is almost universally applied), and Lisiansky himself called the dangerous surrounding shoal Neva after his vessel, which survived the grounding to eventually return safely to Russia. Japanese plumage hunters were active on Lisianski during at least 1904 and 1909, but guano never seems to have been mined there.

Fifteen native plant species as well as five alien ones grow on Lisianski. There are eleven native nonmite arthropods, of which four are found only within the Northwestern chain, along with twenty-four alien taxa. Also, four native land snail species of three genera occur, as well as an alien species of an additional genus. The House Mouse was inadvertently introduced to the island upon the 1844 shipwreck of the American whaler *Holder Borden,* and European Rabbits were deliberately released there sometime between about 1900 and 1910. Both mammals apparently became extinct on the *motu* after the rabbits consumed almost all of the vegetation during their brief existence there, because neither species was found on Lisianski by scientists in 1923.

A 2-month archaeological and paleontological investigation of Lisianski in 1990 revealed no certain evidence of prehistoric Hawaiian occupation, but did show that devegetation by rabbits had resulted in the transfer from higher ground of up to 0.5 m (1.6 feet) of windblown sand that now covers the prehistoric ground surface of lower portions of the interior. This work also yielded bones of a formerly breeding native duck taxon that seems indistinguishable from the Laysan one mentioned earlier. The Lisianski population was apparently extirpated for food by shipwrecked whalers in 1844. No remains were found indicating that any other land or freshwater bird species had ever naturally inhabited the island in its atoll state, and a group of forty-five Laysan Rails imported in 1913 apparently survived less than a half dozen years. The usual complement of oceanic birds and terns nests on the island.

Pearl and Hermes Reef

Nine emergent landmasses, arranged in a rough semicircle along the southeastern border of an extensive lagoon, are usually present at this atoll, with only four of these permanent enough to support vegetation. The largest of these *motu* is Southeast Island, approximately 229 by 549 m (750 by 1,800 feet) and standing perhaps 3.7 m (12 feet) high. **Pearl and Hermes Reef** bears the names of two English whaling ships that wrecked on reefs of the previously unrecorded atoll on the same night in April 1822.

The atoll's lagoon supported a thriving colony of the previously mentioned indigenous Common Pearl Oyster, which was heavily exploited in the first third of the twentieth century as raw material for the American pearl button industry. Although a few oysters still exist there, the population has never regained its former density. Native plant species on the vegetated *motu* number sixteen, with one of these endemic to the Northwestern Hawaiian Islands, and there are twelve alien taxa. Forty-four taxa of insects and other land arthropods other than mites occur, including four forms restricted to the Northwestern chain, and there are an additional thirty-four alien species. Three native land snails in two genera, as well as one species of an alien genus, are present. European Rabbits were historically introduced to Southeast Island, possibly from Laysan or Lisianski, about 1908 by Japanese plumage hunters; after a long, concerted effort the last of the animals was finally shot by American military and scientific personnel by mid-1928.

Pearl and Hermes abounds in nesting marine-related birds, but its low-island state supported no land birds until seven pairs of Laysan Rails were released on one of the *motu* in 1929. These failed to survive, possibly because they could not fly above high waves that occasionally sweep the *motu* during storms. An importation of fourteen Laysan Ducks to Southeast Island in 1967 also was unsuccessful, because none was still present a year later. A similar 1967 introduction of 110 Laysan Finches to Southeast and North Islands proved productive, however, resulting in populations that were still flourishing in the mid-1990s.

Midway Atoll

This is the best-known atoll in the Northwestern Hawaiian Islands, and its two *motu* together constitute the largest landmass of the chain. In contrast to most Hawaiian atolls, a considerable portion of the reef rimming the central lagoon at **Midway** extends above the ocean surface, reaching 1.5 m (5 feet) or so. Sand Island is the larger *motu,* being 1,617 m (5,300 feet) wide and 2,440 m (8,000 feet) long, with its highest point 13 m (43 feet); Eastern Island is only a little smaller than Sand. The *motu* were historically discovered in July 1859 by Captain N. C. Brooks, who bestowed the original name of Middlebrooks Island. There were a fair number of early historic shipwrecks there subsequently, and Japanese plumage hunters worked on the atoll during at least 1904.

Intermittent American and European use of the atoll began within a few years after the atoll's discovery because of its strategic location halfway between North America and eastern Asia, and the name was ultimately changed to the more apt Midway. Major events in Midway's busy cultural history during the later nineteenth and early twentieth centuries included utilization as a coaling station for steamships bound to and from the Orient, establishment of a relay station for a transpacific submarine telegraph cable, construction of an airport to serve the "China Clipper" flying-boat service, important service as an American military land and air base during World War II, and subsequent use as a North Pacific station of the American Distant Early Warning (DEW) radar system. By the latter half of the twentieth century, Midway was being used primarily only as a U.S. Naval Air Facility, with up to five hundred personnel and a multitude of related military, residential, and recreational developments. Administration by the U.S. Department of the Navy had begun in 1903 and, officially, the atoll has never belonged to the State of Hawai'i.

In 1996, however, the Navy closed its air facility and vacated Midway in 1997; the atoll was then transferred to the U.S. Fish and Wildlife Service as Midway Atoll National Wildlife Refuge. The Service subsequently entered into a long-term cooperative agreement with a private company, Midway Phoenix Corporation, whereby the latter manages a modest ecotourism enterprise at the atoll in conjunction with the usual refuge operations. In this unique mutually beneficial arrangement, the corporation utilizes the natural- and cultural-history expertise of refuge personnel in part of its tourism operations, and the Service receives a considerable amount of logistic support from the corporation (for example, regular air transportation services).

Both Green Turtles and Hawaiian Monk Seals are currently rare at Midway Atoll, possibly as a result of the relatively great past amount of human activity. About thirty native land plant species, three of them endemic to the Northwestern chain, are present, along with the startlingly high number of 237 alien taxa, the latter's abundance reflecting the long-continued introduction of ornamental and landscaping plants for use in residential and recreational areas. Among this introduced flora, the avenues of towering Common Ironwood are especially noticeable, as are the lawns of Bermuda Grass (Table 23.1). There are forty-four native nonmite arthropods, including eight Northwestern Hawaiian Island endemics, and 157 recorded alien forms. In spite of its relatively great land area, Midway seems to have only a single kind of native land snail, but 111 alien species from each of five genera have been introduced. The importation through past years of over 8,100 metric tons (9,000 short tons) of topsoil from Honolulu and Guam for growing ornamental plants and vegetables undoubtedly provided transportation for a majority of these various alien invertebrates.

Among land vertebrates, the historically introduced House Mouse and Roof Rat had long been common, but these seem to have been successfully eradicated in the later 1990s. The alien Common Myna and Common Canary are both well established (Table 23.2). No native land birds are known to have colonized the two *motu*, but Laysan Finches were introduced to the atoll in 1891 and 1905, establishing a population that survived until the Roof Rats first appeared ashore in 1943, apparently from Navy ships. A thriving colony of Laysan Rails, originating from individuals transported to both *motu* of Midway on several occasions between about 1891 and 1913, was also lost to these same invading rodents. All except four species of the typical breeding oceanic birds and terns of the Northwestern chain nest at Midway.

Kure Atoll

This atoll is essentially a smaller replica of Midway, with two *motu* named Sand and Green Islands encircled by a reef often reaching sea level. The latter *motu* is about twice the size of the former, being 808 m (2,650 feet) in width and 1,617 m (5,300 feet) in length, with the highest point some 6 m (20 feet). The atoll was named for a Russian Captain Kure, who is said to have been the first historic viewer of the atoll, although details of this event seem to have been lost. (It might be noted that the atoll is also referred to as Ocean Island in some early historic accounts, although there is another island bearing this same name in the Gilbert group of Micronesia; the occasional former use of the term Moku Pāpapa for Kure was mentioned earlier in this chapter.) During historic times, there were several major shipwrecks on the reef, the first recorded one in 1837, as also previously discussed. Otherwise, **Kure** was uninhabited until establishment of a U.S. Coast Guard LORAN station with about two dozen personnel on Green Island in 1960, which was abandoned in 1994 (Plate 3.1).

Green Turtles and Hawaiian Monk Seals are much more frequently seen at Kure than at Midway. Nineteen native plant species are found, including three endemic to the Northwestern Hawaiian Islands, and there are also fifty-six alien species. Native arthropods other than mites number twenty-four, of which five are Northwestern chain endemics, and the rather high total of eighty-one alien forms has established. The land snails comprise four native species of three genera. The enigmatic Kure population of Polynesian Rat, mentioned early in this chapter, was eradicated in the later 1990s to protect the atoll's natural environment. No land birds are known to have inhabited the two *motu* since atoll development. Essentially all of the species of marine-related birds nesting on other fair-sized Northwestern chain *motu* also utilize Kure, but for unknown reasons (although conceivably due to depredations of the Polynesian Rats) the numbers of each species have long seemed substantially lower there than at similar Northwestern atolls.

SUGGESTED REFERENCES

Abbott 1989; Apple 1973; *Atoll Research Bulletin* 1971–1977, 1996; Balazs 1976; Beletsky 2000; E. H. Bryan Jr. 1978; Ching 1994; Cleghorn 1988; Conant et al. 1984; Harrison 1990; Herbst and Wagner 1992; Olson and Ziegler 1995; Rauzon 2001; Twiss and Reeves (eds.) 1999.

AUDIOVISUAL AIDS

Beyond Honolulu; Hawaii: Islands of the Fire Goddess; Hawaii's low islands; Hawaii: Strangers in paradise; The Northwestern Hawaiian Islands.

24

Polynesian Origin and Migration

Oceania is the name usually applied to that portion of the insular Pacific comprising the three geographically (but not entirely culturally) delimited areas of **Micronesia** (Greek *"mikros"* [small] and *"nesos"* [island]), **Melanesia** (Greek *"melanos"* [black], in allusion to the relatively dark complexion of the inhabitants), and **Polynesia** (Greek *"polys"* [many]). Most of the almost 290 far-flung islands constituting Polynesia may be enclosed in a map triangle with the Hawaiian Islands, New Zealand, and Easter Island at its corners (Figure 24.1). In addition, there are eighteen so-called Polynesian Outliers outside this triangle, as shown on the map and discussed later in this chapter. This triangle is enormous; its area is twice that of the continental United States. Both the material culture and language differed surprisingly little throughout prehistoric Polynesia, much to the wonderment of the first European visitors who found that Hawaiians could understand much of the Society Island language, even through the latter island group was 4,265 km (2,650 miles) to the south.

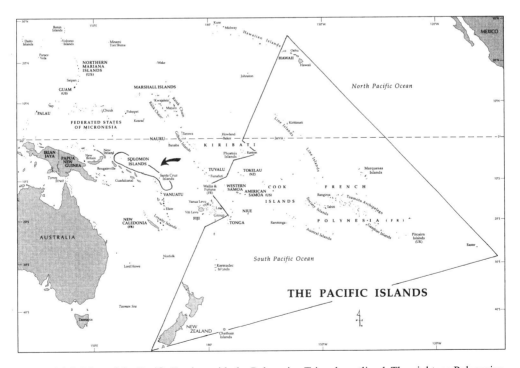

Figure 24.1. Map of the Pacific Region with the Polynesian Triangle outlined. The eighteen Polynesian Outliers (see text) lie in the oval indicated by the arrow. (Base map by Manoa Mapworks from University of Hawai'i Center for Pacific Island Studies, used with permission.)

LAPITA CULTURE

Source

Ancestors of the Polynesians were a group of the **Lapita Culture** (named for a classic archaeological site of these people in New Caledonia of Melanesia). The immediate ancestors of this culture's members, in turn, seem to have occupied the Southeast Asian insular region between Taiwan and Halmahera (off the northwestern end of New Guinea). From here, this cultural stock ultimately expanded east, apparently rapidly skirting most or all of the northern coast of New Guinea proper, but reaching and establishing settlements in the Bismarck Archipelago off the larger island's northeastern end by about 1500 B.C. On the basis of current archaeological knowledge, it appears that the distinctive Lapita Culture first developed in the Bismarcks. Thus, at this geographic and temporal point the members of this culture may now reasonably be called the Lapita People.

Their early and subsequent settlements can be identified by the presence of a particular style of pottery known as **Lapita Ware,** presumably developed—or at least perfected—in the Bismarck Archipelago. This is reddish in color, and throughout all but its latest history certain types of vessels were decorated with distinctive stamped as well as incised designs (Figure 24.2).

Colonization of Melanesia

For the time, the Lapita People were not only relatively skilled seafarers and successful exploiters of at least inshore marine resources, but evidently also accomplished horticulturists and domestic animal husbanders. They carried with them an extensive suite of cultivated plants as

Figure 24.2. A Lapita Ware bowl of probably about 1000 B.C. This was excavated at an eastern Melanesia site. The vessel has been largely reconstructed, but the darker original fragments show the characteristic Lapitan stamped design. (Photograph by Hamish Macdonald in Photo Archive, Department of Anthropology, University of Auckland, used with permission of the photographer and Roger C. Green.)

well as the Pig, dog, and Chicken, all derived from Southeast Asia. The Lapita People continued an extremely rapid eastward dispersal from the Bismarcks through the Solomons and into Melanesia, reaching the eastern end of the latter region by about 1250 B.C. In most or all cases they apparently established settlements on shallow reef flats, small offshore islets, or along the shore of larger already inhabited islands, without encroaching any significant distance inland on lands utilized by the indigenous occupants. In at least the Bismarcks and the Solomons stilt houses were built in the reef areas.

As the Lapita People moved east, they evidently consistently left minor permanent colonies on numerous Solomon and Melanesian islands. In the already occupied Bismarck and Solomon groups the new immigrants were evidently allowed to peaceably remain by the island owners, generally upland-adapted people of Australian–New Guinea origin who had occupied the islands for many thousands of years. The Lapita success in establishing colonies on such inhabited islands was quite possibly because they maintained a trade network among various similar but relatively distant settlements. The Lapita People thus proved extremely useful because, with quite reliable watercraft and considerable skill in their use, the newcomers could consistently provide the original islanders with valuable imported raw materials or finished products not locally available, such as various rare or possibly new types of stone for making cutting tools, as well as the apparently novel item of pottery.

Incidentally, although unrelated to the later colonization of western Polynesia, archaeological evidence indicates that at least one group of Lapita People from Melanesia had colonized the uninhabited islands of central and eastern Micronesia by about 300 or 200 B.C., where their culture evolved into the native one existing in this Micronesian area at the time of historic Contact. One or more other complements of individuals within the Lapita Culture apparently similarly detached themselves to colonize various islands throughout Melanesia. (This dissemination of Lapita Culture to well-separated insular Pacific areas by different member groups has recently led to their being collectively termed the "Lapita Peoples.")

Colonization of Western Polynesia

The Lapita Peoples did not cease their expansion at the eastern end of Melanesia, but quickly continued on to discover and colonize the various uninhabited Fiji Islands bordering western Polynesia around 1100–1000 B.C., before soon moving slightly farther east to Tonga and Samoa. By this time the distances back to earlier colonies had become so great that the traditional extended trade network was abandoned, although local exchanges of various goods continued within this and other Lapita groups. Progressive changes in pottery and other artifacts continued to occur through time and distance, allowing archaeologists to trace and date subsequent human movements, especially those farther east into Polynesia. For example, in this easternmost region of Lapita influence the surface decoration long characteristic of certain Lapita Ware was apparently rather rapidly discontinued, yielding what is known as Polynesian Plain Ware. Also, the former relatively complex variety of vessel shapes became reduced to a few simple styles, before manufacture of pottery itself inexplicably ceased—at least in Tonga and Samoa—between about A.D. 200 and 500.

The design of some stone implements, especially adzes, also changed after Fiji and, especially, the islands of Tonga and Samoa were reached. Such lithic innovation was apparently brought about by different physical properties (for example, flaking characteristics) of the raw material then available. At least the Samoan Islands, for instance, lie outside the Andesite Line or seaward limit of continental-type rocks (Figure 4.1), so the only lithic material locally available in quantity in this group and farther east was basalt (see chapter 4), which is relatively difficult to fashion satisfactorily into implements.

Lapita Culture Transition
Essentially all of the Lapita colonies extending from the Bismarcks through Melanesia gradually lost their original unique status through intermarriage and other cultural amalgamation with any older stock on various islands. Even on previously unoccupied islands, the early culture ultimately underwent at least a few changes, including the loss of manufacture of pottery. Thus, these islands (excluding the Polynesian Outliers) are now ethnographically considered Melanesian. Even Fiji is included in this latter category rather than being classified as Polynesian, although these two major portions of Oceania share a common Lapita ancestry.

POLYNESIAN CULTURE

Beginnings
Once Fiji was reached, it took Lapita People perhaps only another century to discover and colonize the westernmost major Polynesian island groups of Tonga and Samoa (Figure 24.1), completing this possibly by 900 B.C. or so. The interconnected culture of these three island groups then gradually evolved into one that can be recognized as Ancestral Polynesian.

Polynesian Canoes
Some of the Solomon and other Melanesian islands colonized by the Lapita Peoples were within sight of each other, and most of the rest were separated by less than 500 km (310 miles): a maximum of only three or four days' sail in favorable winds. Presumably the watercraft employed for these intra-Melanesian voyages was the **outrigger canoe,** consisting of a single hull with a smaller solid-wood outrigger lashed to two arms extending from one side for stability. This low-set craft could be paddled easily, but was usually equipped with a small sail for longer trips. The discovery of Fiji, however, required a journey of 800 km (500 miles), and it may well be that to accomplish this feat the Lapita Culture had developed at least a primitive form of the **double-hulled canoe.** After the colonization of Fiji and during the discovery and occupation of Tonga and Samoa continued experimentation and progressive improvements to this early version of the twin-bodied craft led to substantially larger and extremely seaworthy vessels that would eventually carry early Polynesians on truly epic ventures farther east into the Pacific (Plate 24.1).

In many parts of Polynesia, hulls of larger canoes were fashioned from planks laced to a keel and to each other. Lashing was done with extremely serviceable braided or twisted sennit cordage of Coconut or *niu (Cocos nucifera)* husk fiber. The cracks between planks were caulked with congealed sap of Breadfruit or *'ulu (Artocarpus altilis).* In the Hawaiian Islands, however, the great number of giant endemic *Koa (Acacia koa)* trees originally available allowed a hull to be formed from a single hollowed-out trunk, some up to 20 m (66 feet) long. To prevent waves from washing into the hull, its gunwales or upper edges were heightened by lashing planks along their length, and wooden endpieces were similarly fastened over bow and stern. For voyaging canoes, two hulls were connected by several lashed-on straight arms (in later versions often upcurved in the middle) bearing a passenger platform, a design perpetuated in modern catamarans.

Such canoes could carry great stores of provisions within the hulls themselves, as well as several families along with their household goods, domestic animals, and plant propagules on the platform between the hulls. However, these voyaging craft had to rely almost entirely on propulsion by wind, because they were too heavy and their gunwales situated too far above the water to be paddled effectively. The one or two large so-called "crab-claw" sails, made of plaited Screw Pine or *hala (Pandanus tectorius)* leaves, were triangular, and repairable at sea in emergency. These sails were spread with the apex downward between a stationary mast and a mobile boom projecting upright from the mast base. Ropework of the rigging consisted of the same Coconut sennit as the lashing. In Hawaiʻi this cordage sometimes had fibers of the endemic nettle *Olonā (Touchardia latifolia* [see chapter 25]) interwoven for increased strength and elasticity. Steering was accomplished with a stern-mounted sweep oar or a pair of them.

Colonization of Eastern Polynesia

From the Tonga-Samoa **Polynesian Homeland** the eastward human movement seems to have paused for somewhere between 500 and 1,000 years. The reason for this interlude is unknown, but may well have been related to the time needed for further experimentation with, and perfection of, an extremely reliable double-hulled voyaging canoe. Learning to use the various sailing winds more skillfully and efficiently undoubtedly also required an extended period of time. At any rate, development of the distinctive Polynesian Culture evidently advanced considerably during this Homeland stay. The initial colonization of East Polynesia was then accomplished, perhaps shortly before the beginning of the Christian Era. The first landing was likely in either the Cook or Society Archipelagos, between 1,800 and 2,400 km (1,100 and 1,500 miles) east of the Homeland islands (Figure 24.1).

This general initial landing area is suggested by a variety of evidence, including very recent studies of mitochondrial DNA nucleotide-pair sequences of numerous insular populations of the accompanying Polynesian Rat (*Rattus exulans* [see chapters 19, 25]), which seems incapable of independently reaching isolated islands by "rafting." The primary archaeological evidence involves the presence of a few Polynesian Plain Ware pottery fragments or shards in habitation deposits of the Cook Islands. Petrographic analysis revealed that the material incorporated in at least a few of these Cook Islands ceramic remains was from Tonga, indicating prehistoric interchange between the two island groups sometime very early in the Christian Era. Pottery shards were also archaeologically retrieved in the Marquesas Islands and were found to include material from Fiji. Recent radiometric dating, however, has shown these to be historic in age, so they were likely from relatively modern Fijian pottery brought to the Marquesas on early Western sailing ships. The very small amount of other ceramic material recovered in the Marquesas proved to be of local manufacture. Extensive archaeological investigations elsewhere in East Polynesia have thus far yielded no ancient pottery.

Other types of artifactual evidence suggest that once a Cook or Society island was discovered and settled, extensive canoe travel soon occurred both within its own archipelago, as well as to and among other centrally located East Polynesian island groups. In addition, longer voyages of discovery were obviously made in all directions out of this nuclear dispersal area. As a result, all of the remaining *inhabitable* Polynesian islands had been colonized within about a millennium, probably before A.D. 1000 or, at the very latest, by 1200 (Figure 24.3).

POLYNESIAN NAVIGATION

The question of what drove the early Polynesians to make these long ocean voyages can never be answered with certainty. It is, however, most interesting to speculate on the matter.

Intentional Voyages

Some workers have postulated that the discovery of new Polynesian islands resulted from either unintentional drift voyages of storm-blown coastal sailors or relatively precipitous departures of ostracized individuals such as those defeated in battle or guilty of breaking taboos. It seems highly improbable, with the prevalence of the easterly trade winds (see chapter 7), that any significant number of drift voyages—at least from west to east—could have occurred. And hasty embarkations would hardly have allowed the extensive provisioning of canoes required to successfully carry out most long journeys.

The time between colonization of a particular large island group (for example, the Marquesas) and emigration of some of the colonists' descendants to initially populate another group (for example, the Hawaiian Archipelago) was often no greater than a very few hundred years. All desirable land of the first island group could not possibly have been occupied in that short

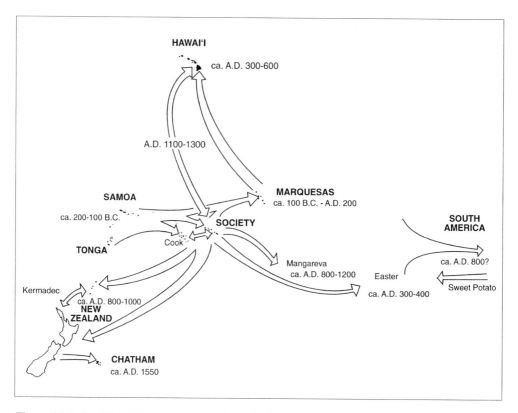

Figure 24.3. Possible settlement pattern of the major Polynesian island groups. A presumed voyage that reached South America and ultimately returned to Polynesia carrying the Sweet Potato is also indicated. (Figure by Keith Krueger.)

period, suggesting that few if any voyages of discovery originating in central East Polynesia were necessitated by such factors as overcrowding, resource shortage, or civil war. Thus, it may well have been simply either a spirit of adventure, the desire for recognition of the ability to discover new lands, or the fact that only the eldest son inherited his father's estate and status that motivated certain islanders or later-born sons to so rapidly and thoroughly explore and colonize all of Polynesia.

It is very likely that not only were most voyages resulting in discovery of new islands carefully planned and executed, but also that the Polynesians were quite willing and even eager to engage in this activity. More than two hundred generations removed from any cultural knowledge of continents, Polynesians undoubtedly envisioned the world as an ocean stretching endlessly to the east in which were imbedded scattered island groups forever available for discovery and settlement. Thus, there was no question in their minds that a multitude of uninhabited islands existed and were just waiting to be found.

To judge from ethnographic accounts of native Hawaiian Culture, undertaking or completion of any major event required performance of specific and frequently complex religious rituals. For example, after the construction of a *luakini heiau* or war temple of the god Kū, a specific requirement had to be met before the *heiau* could be used and the participating chief, priests, and workers released from an onerous *kapu* or restriction that kept them separated from their wives. A mass of floating *limu* or seaweed had to be found and retrieved from far out at sea. Obviously, such a discovery would be extremely fortuitous, so the *kapu* often lasted for many months or even years (reputedly 10 in one instance) before the requisite algal item was located, but this discovery obviously signified that Kū's blessing had finally been received. Similarly, if prospective colonists relied on the occurrence of an equivalent fortuitous event before initiating a discovery voyage, once the event had come about they undoubtedly had no question that their venture would be successful.

Zenith Stars

Still another aspect of ancient Polynesian Culture quite possibly added to the early aspiring colonists' faith that they would surely find new land: the concept of **zenith stars.** There are so many hundreds of relatively bright stars that it is inevitable that at least one of them in its nightly east-to-west passage across the sky will pass essentially directly over each of the numerous Polynesian islands. The one coursing above the island of Hawai'i a thousand or so years ago, for example, was Hōkūle'a ("Clear Star" or "Happy Star"; called Arcturus or the Bear Star by modern astronomers), and the equivalent zenith star of Tahiti was Hōkūho'okelewa'a ("Canoe-guiding Star"; currently called Sirius or the Dog Star). Because the ancient Polynesians had observed a zenith star over every previously discovered island, they would quite reasonably believe that there was a similar bright one passing directly over every other oceanic landmass, each having been divinely placed on such a course to mark the location of that island.

It is not difficult to imagine an ancient Polynesian master navigator pointing out to an apprentice the specific zenith stars that marked known islands or island groups, as well as noting other particularly bright stars under whose overhead trajectories lay islands that had yet to be reached. To arrive at one of these islands, it would only be necessary to sail north or south until its zenith star was passing directly overhead; then, if the island was not sighted at that exact spot, to travel either east or west under the star's course until land was reached. (Successful navigation back to the home island could, of course, easily be accomplished by using this same technique in regard to that island's familiar zenith star.) This means that ancient Polynesians were not just randomly sailing out into the ocean hoping they might be lucky enough to find a new island; they departed not only certain that more uninhabited islands existed and that they had divine blessing to reach one, but also that their particular destination was there just under its zenith star's course. All the voyagers had to do was sail to that new land.

Thus, a journey that would seem prohibitively hazardous to modern humans—and, in reality, was probably indeed that dangerous—was begun by ancient Polynesians with little or no hesitation and trepidation. (It is pertinent to note that even as late as the early 1800s there are at least two reports of the voluntary departure of canoeloads of several hundred potential colonists from the Marquesas in search of new islands; the outcome of these ventures is apparently not known.)

Obviously, most bright stars in the heavens are *not* zenith stars and, during the many centuries of Polynesian settlement, following them without eventually finding land resulted in numerous voyages ending in disaster, with the deaths of probably thousands of hapless travelers through thirst, starvation, and storms. The fact that a journey had ended disastrously, however, would usually never have been known to the communities from which the voyage originated. If the aspiring colonists had not returned in a year or two to report success it was likely assumed they had not yet had enough time in their new home to, perhaps, replace a badly damaged canoe or amass sufficient provisions for a return trip. And, through the next few generations, the unheard-from colonists would gradually fade from memory. Or it may be that many of the voyagers who went in search of new islands were not even expected to return to their original departure point, at least not until their population had increased to such a level that members could be spared for such a return journey.

Use of the Winds

The fact that in both Northern and Southern Hemispheres the persistent trade winds blow from a generally easterly direction means that original colonization of East Polynesia from the West Polynesian homeland region involved sailing into the wind for a major portion of each voyage. In terms of at least the survival prospects of such voyagers, however, sailing into the prevailing easterly wind was distinctly advantageous, as explained here.

The trades typically die down a number of times a year and westerly winds take over, often for only a few days but sometimes for a week or more—or even months during major El Niño episodes (see chapter 7)—thus periodically providing favorable winds for the initiation of a long-distance sailing journey to the east. (Just such winds were utilized by the modern voyaging canoe *Hōkūle'a* during parts of its epic Voyage of Rediscovery, as well as for its rapid transit from central East Polynesia to Easter Island, discussed later in this chapter.) Presumably, a departing canoe would sail east before the westerly wind as long as it lasted, then when the trades returned either tack into them or head north or south, sailing as close as possible to the easterly wind for an additional period of time. By dead reckoning (that is, mentally tracing the previous progress of the canoe as apparently affected by wind and currents) a competent navigator would always know roughly the direction and distance traveled from the point of departure, as well as the approximate number of days it would take to return there. When the canoe's provisions had been depleted to the minimum level necessary for this return time, the colonization venture would be abandoned and the canoe sailed downwind back to the island of origin. On the other hand, if the departure direction had been downwind on the trades (that is, to the west), *timely* return to the east against this usual wind upon finding no land would have been impossible most of the time.

Polynesian Outliers

In regard to possible downwind voyages, however, there are eighteen **Polynesian Outliers** scattered west of the Polynesian Triangle, all in Melanesia except for two in Micronesia (Figure 24.1). Although dual colonizations of most of these islands is obvious from the various degrees of Melanesian or Micronesian traits present, their culture is predominately Polynesian. Variation in, at least, the style of Polynesian-type artifacts excavated on Outliers strongly suggests that many of the individual islands were reached at different periods (and in some cases possibly more than once) during the evolution of Polynesian Culture. Because the Outliers are situated downwind of essentially all Polynesian Triangle islands, it is quite likely that a Polynesian group colonizing any one of them was derived from either an uncontrolled drift voyage or a returning voyage of unsuccessful seekers of new lands missing their home islands.

New Zealand

The arrival time and identity of the first people to reach New Zealand is still unclear. DNA evidence from the islands' Polynesian Rats seems to indicate two or more human contacts, one possibly as early as the time Ancestral Polynesian Culture was developing in the Fiji-Tonga-Samoa area. Whatever the number and date of any such early New Zealand contacts—and the fate of the potential colonists—various lines of cultural evidence indicate that there was almost certainly successful New Zealand colonization from somewhere within central East Polynesia near or shortly after A.D. 1000. Just as in the case of the Polynesian Outliers, this settlement of New Zealand from the east obviously entailed a predominately downwind journey, and the voyage was possibly similarly unintended. There is, however, one New Zealand land bird, the Long-tailed Cuckoo *(Eudynamis taitensis),* that migrates to at least the Cook and Society Islands. People of either group could conceivably have launched a successful New Zealand discovery voyage in the direction of this bird's annual return flight.

DISCOVERY AND COLONIZATION OF HAWAI'I

Source of Colonists

Current evidence based on similarities in the earliest types of Hawaiian artifacts such as fishhooks and adzes, in language characteristics, and in Polynesian Rat DNA attributes indicates that the Hawaiian Archipelago was quite possibly first populated by emigrants from the Marquesas 3,400 km (2,100 miles) to the south-southeast. If this evidence is accepted, the settlement occurred about A.D. 400, if not a century or two earlier (Figure 24.3). This putative Marquesan contact with Hawai'i could have involved only a single nonreturn voyage or, at most, a few round-trip ones. After that, for some reason, Marquesas Islanders do not seem to have engaged in any notable amount of long-distance voyaging, and the archipelago apparently remained a more or less isolated East Polynesian area.

The same general types of evidence that indicated an initial Marquesas-Hawaiian contact suggest that a second important cultural interaction with the Hawaiian Islands began around 1100. This involved people from the more centrally located East Polynesian area to the southwest of the Marquesas, and the Society Islands seem the most likely source on the basis of current knowledge. This alleged Hawai'i-Society contact, however, led to a number of round-trip journeys between the regions (which could eventually have included participation of other island groups near the Societies, such as the southern Cooks). This episode of voyaging evidently lasted until at least 1300, at which time it ceased for unknown reasons. The fact that the channel leading from Maui southward between Lāna'i and Kaho'olawe, which points toward the Society Islands, bears the name KealaiKahiki or "The path to Tahiti or a foreign land" may possibly further attest to the reciprocal nature and relative frequency of such voyages.

This extended period of cultural interaction with islanders of the general Society region is relatively certainly documented in Hawaiian oral tradition, as well as by archaeological evidence. It apparently did not involve any mass immigration of southern people or importations of radically new aspects of material culture. The early arrivals from the south seemingly comprised primarily religious leaders, including the fabled navigator-priest Pā'ao, and individuals from chiefly families, but these relative few leaders significantly changed major features of prehistoric Hawaiian society. By means not clear, this high-status component was gradually able to replace most former Hawaiian religious beliefs and rituals with its own (which apparently included human sacrifice). Also, most of the ruling dynasties encountered by the first European arrivals in the Hawaiian Islands represented these south-central lines, rather than those of the presumed original Marquesan discoverers.

Menehune

As an intriguing aside, the advent of these Society Islanders may possibly provide a basis for the apparently later-developed legend of the **Menehune.** These were the mythical diminutive Hawaiian folk, bands of whom performed often prodigious feats of manual labor overnight (especially on the relatively isolated island of Kaua'i), for which each worker reputedly received only a morsel of food such as a small shrimp. In the Society Islands and neighboring parts of central East Polynesia, the older term *manahune* was applied to people of relatively lower social status. The south-central Polynesians of chiefly rank, in exerting control over parts of the Hawaiian chain, may well have subjugated certain groups of less-privileged residents—or at least regarded them as socially or culturally inferior. These groups could have been forced into essentially slave labor on various public works projects, and the new rulers might reasonably have referred to these unpaid workers by the still-familiar homeland name *manahune.* Any such extreme labor practices were probably eventually largely abandoned in pre-Contact Hawai'i and, as reference to them slowly became legend, the concept of lower social status of the ancient workers gradually changed to one of smaller physical size, with the original appellation becoming the now-familiar Hawaiian cognate *Menehune.*

Hōkūle'a *Success*

For many years anthropologists had questioned whether it was possible for ancient Polynesians to have regularly made intentional voyages between populated island groups such as, for example, Hawai'i and those to the far south. The primary problem envisioned was that to gain enough "easting" to reach the desired islands, the voyaging canoe would have to sail at an angle of less than 90 degrees to the trade winds of either or both Northern and Southern Hemispheres, and this was not thought possible for Polynesian craft. Also, it was debated whether or not ancient navigators without the aid of modern instruments would have been able to consistently find their way between such widely separated island groups.

Both questions were first convincingly answered in the affirmative in 1976. The ***Hōkūle‘a***
(named for the zenith star of ancient Hawai‘i), a newly constructed double-hulled voyaging
canoe of traditional Late Polynesian design, was successfully navigated without modern
instruments from the Hawaiian to the Society Islands. Development of this craft as well as the
undertaking of such a voyage was largely a result of the inspiration and dedicated work of
anthropologist **Ben R. Finney.** Just as postulated by Finney, it was found that *Hōkūle‘a* could
satisfactorily sail as close as 75 degrees to the wind. Because no Polynesian islander was familiar with traditional navigation at that time, *Hōkūle‘a* was guided by **Mau Piailug**, a veteran
Micronesian navigator using the ancient methods of his homeland, with the remaining crew
being primarily Native Hawaiians. The canoe was then safely sailed back to Hawai‘i, although
this time using modern instruments because Piailug was not available for the return. *Hōkūle‘a*
averaged about 185 km (115 miles) daily; the voyages thus each took between 3 and 4 weeks
(Figure 24.4).

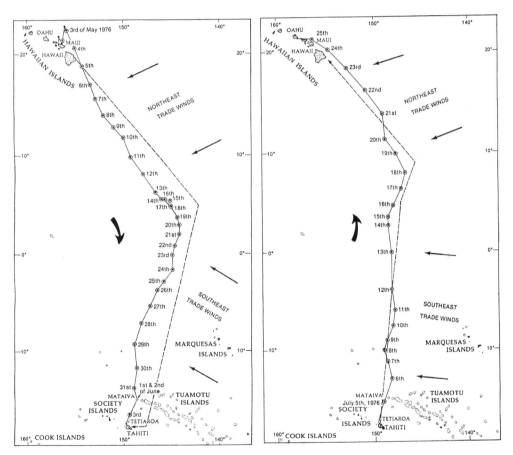

Figure 24.4. First long-distance voyages of the Hawaiian canoe *Hōkūle‘a* in 1976. Projected courses
(at 75 degrees to the prevailing winds) are shown by dashed lines, and the actual courses sailed and
daily noon positions by solid lines and circles. The different trade wind directions north and south of
the equator necessitated the change in course for each area. (Adapted from Figs. 14.4 and 14.6 of
Finney [1979]; copyright 1977, American Association for the Advancement of Science, used with
permission.)

Traditional Navigation

Another round-trip *Hōkūle'a* voyage between the Hawaiian and Society Islands was accomplished in 1980, but this time with noninstrument navigation used on both legs of the journey. The navigator was **Nainoa Thompson,** a young Native Hawaiian who, although he had not been able to sail on the southward leg of the 1976 voyage navigated by Piailug, did crew on the return journey. Thompson was fascinated with traditional navigation, so during the years following the first trip began studying the subject, both at the Bernice P. Bishop Museum Planetarium in Honolulu and with the periodic help of Piailug. He learned that accurate open-ocean navigation was possible by combined observation of such natural phenomena as the position of specific stars as they rose or set, the angle above the horizon of Polaris or the North Star (known historically in Hawaiian as Hōkūpa'a or "Immovable Star," but in ancient Polynesian time describing a small circle in the northern sky), as well as the direction of prevailing winds, currents, and ocean swells. In addition, as undoubtedly known to ancient Pacific navigators, he learned that proximity and direction of islands could often be detected by various means. These included subtle disruptions of a normal swell pattern by a nearby interposed landmass and flights of feeding seabirds and migrating shorebirds. Also, some islands could be located great distances away by lighting of the night horizon during occasional eruptions of large volcanoes or by reflection of the bluish green water of atoll lagoons on the underside of clouds during the day.

Voyage of Rediscovery

The successes of the *Hōkūle'a* and Thompson's navigational efforts eventually led to a plan to sail the canoe traditionally among various major Polynesian island groups: in effect, to recreate many of the same journeys that must have been taken by the ancient discoverers and colonizers of these archipelagos. Thus, between 1985 and 1987 the *Hōkūle'a,* navigated by Thompson using traditional methods a majority of the time, sailed a distance equivalent to halfway around the world in visiting seven major Polynesian groups stretching from Hawai'i to New Zealand before finally returning to Hawai'i on this aptly named **Voyage of Rediscovery.** The great feat led not only to an awakening in Native Hawaiians of justifiable pride in their culture's contemporary and ancestral voyaging accomplishments, but also to a modern revival in many other Polynesian areas of traditional canoe building and sailing by ancient techniques. In late 1999 of this modern era, the final corner of the Polynesian Triangle was reached traditionally when Nainoa Thompson successfully navigated the *Hōkūle'a* on a rapid 17-day voyage from Mangareva in south-central East Polynesia to Easter Island (Rapa Nui).

THE SOUTH AMERICAN CONNECTION

The Sweet Potato

At this point in the discussion of Polynesian migration, it is quite reasonable to ask: if these people had been steadily sailing to the east in progressively discovering new islands, why did they not eventually reach South America? No one knows for certain whether or not an ancient Polynesian ever set foot on the west coast of South America; all that can be said is that *somewhere* there was at least one instance of direct contact between prehistoric people of the two areas. Evidence for this comes from a seemingly improbable source: the geographic distribution and native names of the common **Sweet Potato** or *'uala (Ipomoea batatas).*

The Sweet Potato is the only pre-Contact Polynesian plant (or animal) that originated other than in Southeast Asia or the Southwest Pacific; it is indisputably South American in origin. This species evidently reached most of the East Polynesian islands only after their initial human colonization, but before about A.D. 800. In Hawai'i, at least, association of this cultigen with the putatively late-arriving deity Lono (see chapter 25) tends to strengthen the theory of a relatively delayed prehistoric introduction. Dispersal of the Sweet Potato west through most of the rest of the Pacific was apparently rapid, because it had reached as far west as Samoa, Tonga, eastern Melanesia, and New Zealand by the time of European Contact in the mid-seventeenth and early eighteenth centuries.

This domesticated species does not usually set seed, and vegetative parts other than the tuber are apparently killed by seawater, so it almost surely was not distributed throughout the Pacific by wind, birds, or ocean currents. All of its names in the various Polynesian groups ('*uala, 'umara, ku'ara, kumara,* and the like) are mutual cognates, and there seems no question that their prehistoric origin was in one of the west-coast South American dialectic names *kuala, umala, kumar, kumara,* and so on. This linguistic fact is critically important because it shows that the Sweet Potato did not arrive in Polynesia simply by drifting from the New World in a provisioned but unmanned raft or other vessel, but that *face-to-face* contact between a Polynesian and a South American had to have occurred at some point during introduction of the species to the insular Pacific.

Absence of South American Influence

The trade winds in the Southern Hemisphere would easily allow even a primitive craft to sail west from the South American coast to an island in the southeastern portion of the Polynesian Triangle. This was demonstrated by the Norwegian ethnologist **Thor Heyerdahl** in 1947 through just such a voyage from Peru to the Tuamotu Archipelago in an attempt to support his theory that Polynesia had originally been colonized in this way. (Incidentally, the reason that ancient nonseafaring South Americans might attempt to sail intentionally far out into the Pacific in search of unknown lands is completely obscure.) It seems odd, though, that if colonization of East Polynesia by South American people had been the manner in which the Sweet Potato was first transported from South America, why did the alleged settlers not bring other common New World cultigens (for example, corn, beans, and squash) or any of their domesticated animals (Turkey, Guinea Pig, and so on)? Perhaps, however, such organisms were introduced but all except the Sweet Potato failed to survive on an oceanic island.

Of course, this absence of transported cultigens and animals could have been because the possible South American colonization of East Polynesia was the result of an unintentional drift voyage, on which no great variety of food stores would be expected. But, in the case of either a planned or an unplanned journey, an explanation is lacking as to why no New World artifact styles, weaving or other cultural traditions, and linguistic traits appear in the prehistory of any part of Polynesia. Nor do the skeletal and other biological characteristics of any pre-Contact East Polynesians indicate a mixture of people from the two areas. Although a colonizing group from South American undoubtedly would have been small in numbers, the members surely would have had some degree of observable effect on the cultural and physical characteristics of the rather limited number of Polynesians already on a relatively small island (or who would arrive there later if the New World group had preceded them).

It seems much more reasonable that the contact between the two cultures was made by Polynesians, who while continuing their traditional eastward voyages of discovery through the

Pacific reached the west coast of South America. The various impacts of their small numbers on the substantially larger native population there would have been easily dissipated and quickly lost without significant trace, even if it extended to intermarriage. And any Polynesian plants and animals the newcomers brought may have been of too little local use to have been preserved among the relative abundance of native South American resources. On the other hand, the arriving Polynesians would have been quick to recognize the value of a productive cultigen like the Sweet Potato that could be grown in a variety of soil types and rainfall conditions such as those found among the Pacific island groups. Subsequently, some or all of these Islanders could have left South America on an easily accomplished downwind return voyage to their original area of departure carrying an abundant supply of Sweet Potato tubers—along with the original native name—both of which would eventually become widely distributed in Polynesia.

SUGGESTED REFERENCES

Bellwood 1979; Cachola-Abad 1993; Crawford 1993; Finney 1977, 1979, 1994; Haddon and Hornell 1936–1938; Holmes 1981; Jennings (ed.) 1979; Kirch 1985, 1997, 2000; Kirch and Hunt (eds.) 1988; Matisoo-Smith et al. 1998; Rolett 1993; Sinton and Sinoto 1997; Yen 1974.

AUDIOVISUAL AIDS

4-Butte-1: A lesson in archaeology; Gatecliff: American Indian rock-shelter; Hawaiian fish-hooks; History of Hawaii: Polynesian migration.

25

Polynesian Ecology

Few if any of the small uninhabited islands encountered by the migrating Lapita Peoples (see chapter 24) had possessed native plants capable of supporting substantial numbers of people. They, thus, undoubtedly learned that it was imperative to carry along a particular suite of primarily Southeast Asian food and utilitarian plants. Fishes and other marine resources would certainly be available on new islands reached, possibly along with nesting seabirds at certain times of the year, but as assured supplements to these, three domesticated animals were also conveyed. These familiar plant and animal domesticates allowed them, as well as the descendant Polynesians, to be largely self-sufficient in any new area, to the extent this proved necessary.

POLYNESIAN CULTIGENS

Food Plants

The plants of dietary importance prehistorically carried into the western and central Pacific by the Lapita stock included no grains, but were primarily those that provided sustenance in the form of corms and tubers. All of these plants contain large quantities of starch, and this carbohydrate would eventually form the mainstay of the Polynesian diet. Early in the Lapita migrations many tree species with edible fruits or nuts were also included among the transported plants, but their number decreased markedly as the Lapita migration moved farther and farther east. The major species among the food plants imported by early Polynesians colonizing Hawai'i are listed in Table 25.1. In this particular island group, **Taro** or *kalo (Colocasia esculenta)* was the preferred starchy food, with Greater Yam or *uhi (Dioscorea alata)* and, possibly rather late in the Polynesian period (see chapter 24), Sweet Potato or *'uala (Ipomoea batatas)* as significant secondary sources. Two other yams of the genus *Dioscorea*, Breadfruit or *'ulu (Artocarpus altilis)*, Elephant's-Ear or *'ape (Alocasia macrorrhiza)*, Polynesian Arrowroot or *pia (Tacca leontopetaloides)*, banana or *mai'a (Musa* spp.), and the few remaining food cultigens appear to have been of much less importance.

Some banana varieties could be eaten raw, but other varieties as well as all of the vegetable corms and tubers had to be cooked, in the case of Taro and Elephant's-Ear to break down the microscopic needlelike calcium oxalate crystals that are extremely irritating to the oral membrane. The usual manner of preparing most such plant parts after baking on heated vesicular basalt cobbles in underground ovens or *imu* was to peel and mash them into a thick paste or *poi.* **Kava** or *'awa (Piper methysticum),* although not strictly a food species, was carried throughout, primarily, Polynesia, where it was important as both a mild narcotic relaxant and a ritual beverage.

Utilitarian Plants

A number of nonfood plant species were technologically so valuable to Polynesians that they were unfailingly carried along with the edible ones. The more important of these species prehistorically introduced to the Hawaiian Islands are listed in Table 25.2, along with their primary uses. Certain of those listed were also of secondary importance as food, particularly in times of famine (for example, Coconut or *niu* [*Cocos nucifera*], Ti or *kī* [*Cordyline fruticosa*], and Indian Mulberry or *noni* [*Morinda citrifolia*]). Paper Mulberry or *wauke (Broussonetia papyrifera),* especially, was a most valuable utilitarian species, because its inner bark was used to make tapa cloth or **kapa** for apparel and bedding.

The reasons are problematical for apparently introducing some other species such as the lowland Alexandrian Laurel or *kamani (Calophyllum inophyllum)* and showy-flowered *Milo (Thespesia populnea* [possibly indigenous, instead]), although, because these were commonly found in villages, they may have been favored as shade trees. Or, perhaps, the ancient migrants through Melanesia and then Polynesia consistently carried and planted seeds of one or both of these species to ensure a familiar element in new surroundings, much as is still done today throughout the world in the case of some common ornamental plants.

Table 25.1. Major imported early Hawaiian food plants. Kava provided only a root-infusion beverage. A few of the utilitarian species listed in Table 25.2, such as Coconut, were also of secondary dietary importance. (Data from various sources.)

Family Species	English Name	Hawaiian Name
Aroid (Araceae)		
Alocasia macrorrhiza	Elephant's-ear	ʻApe
Colocasia esculenta	Taro	Kalo
Morning glory (Convolvulaceae)		
Ipomoea batatas	Sweet Potato	ʻUala
Yam (Dioscoreaceae)		
Dioscorea alata	Greater Yam	Uhi
Dioscorea bulbifera	Bitter Yam	Hoi
Dioscorea pentaphyllum	Edible Yam	Pʻia
Mulberry (Moraceae)		
Artocarpus altilis	Breadfruit	ʻUlu
Myrtle (Myrtaceae)		
Syzygium malaccense	Mountain Apple	ʻŌhiʻa ʻai
Banana (Musaceae)		
Musa spp.	Banana	Maiʻa
Pepper (Piperaceae)		
Piper methysticum	Kava	ʻAwa
Grass (Poaceae)		
Saccharum officinarum	Sugarcane	Kō
Tacca (Taccaceae)		
Tacca leontopetaloides	Polynesian Arrowroot	Pia

Prehistoric Weeds

It was not realized until recently that ancient Hawaiians also introduced plant species other than those of specific food or technological use. Examination in the mid-1900s of European herbarium specimens collected by Captain James Cook's botanist David Nelson (see chapter 28) revealed that several "weeds" generally regarded as historically introduced were already present at Contact. Among these are the Primrose Willow or *kāmole (Ludwigia octovalvis),* Yellow Wood Sorrel or *'ihi 'ai (Oxalis corniculata),* and Itchy Crabgrass or *kūkaepua'a (Digitaria setigera).* Throughout Oceania, most of these plants are found in close association with various typical prehistorically cultivated crops, and their spores or seeds were undoubtedly carried along inadvertently with propagules of the ancient cultigens.

Arrival Times

It is unlikely that all of the many different Polynesian cultigens and domestic animals arrived in Hawai'i on the first colonizing canoe. The various species that completed the final inventory

Table 25.2. Major imported early Hawaiian utilitarian plants. *Kou* and/or *pili* could possibly be indigenous instead of alien. A few of the food species listed in Table 25.1 were also of minor utilitarian use. (Data from various sources.)

Family Species	English Name	Hawaiian Name	Primary Use
Agave (Agavaceae)			
Cordyline fruticosa	Ti	Kī	Packaging; baked root sometimes eaten
Palm (Arecaceae)			
Cocos nucifera	Coconut	Niu	Numerous uses; nut eaten
Borage (Boraginaceae)			
Cordia subcordata	Kou	Kou	Ornamental?; wood for artifacts
Gourd (Cucurbitaceae)			
Lagenaria siceraria	Bottle Gourd	Ipu	Containers; percussion instruments
Spurge (Euphorbiaceae)			
Aleurites moluccana	Candlenut	Kukui	Nut kernels for torches, also eaten sparingly
Mallow (Malvaceae)			
Thespesia populnea	Milo	Milo	Ornamental?; wood for artifacts
Mulberry (Moraceae)			
Broussonetia papyrifera	Paper Mulberry	Wauke	Tapa or kapa (bark cloth)
Grass (Poaceae)			
Heteropogon contortus	Twisted Beardgrass	Pili	House thatching
Schizostachyum glaucifolium	Bamboo	'Ohe	Construction; implements
Coffee (Rubiaceae)			
Morinda citrifolia	Indian Mulberry	Noni	Medicinal; tapa dye; fruit for famine food

must have been added as subsequent colonizing events took place. It is interesting that one investigative team has suggested that the relative order in which particular Polynesian plant (and one animal) species arrived can possibly be ascertained from their legendary association with Hawaiʻi gods.

The primary of four major gods of pre-Contact Hawaiʻi is usually considered to have been **Kāne,** with **Kanaloa** and **Kū** often held to be slightly subordinate. The fourth, **Lono,** seems usually to have been regarded as a still-lesser deity, with his priests considered of lower standing than those of at least Kū. Also, in various myths Lono is often portrayed as a human being, and is said to have prayed to Kāne as well as to have been his messenger. He was further alleged to have been the older brother of Pāʻao, a twelfth-century navigator-priest who reputedly led Society Island expeditions to Hawaiʻi (see chapter 24).

Taro, Sugarcane or *kō (Saccharum officinarum),* and one species of bamboo or *ʻohe (Schizostachyum glaucifolium)* are intertwined with the mythology of Kāne. The banana is most often related to Kanaloa, and Coconut and Breadfruit frequently appear in the lore of Kū. Finally, the Sweet Potato and Bottle Gourd or *ipu (Lagenaria siceraria),* as well as the Pig, are closely tied to Lono in much oral tradition (although the Sweet Potato may sometimes be associated with Kū, instead).

It may be argued that the first human arrivals in Hawaiʻi were worshippers of the ancestral Polynesian god Taane (Kāne is the Hawaiian derivative), and the foods brought by this initial group of colonists remaining associated with this all-powerful being. (In support of this alleged primal association of at least Taro, a Hawaiian myth relates that the legendary Hawaiian parents, Papa and Wākea, initially produced Hāloa or the Taro plant and then the first human.) Adherents of the ancestral Polynesian gods Tangaroa (Kanaloa in Hawaiian) and Tuu (Kū in Hawaiian) could have been the next two groups of colonists, and their newly introduced foods respectively entered the lore of each deity. Finally, worshippers of Longo (Lono in Hawaiian) arrived, but so late that their primary deity did not have time before Contact to acquire the fully deified status of the three more venerated beings. Thus, the Lono-related Sweet Potato, Bottle Gourd, and Pig were quite possibly among the last important species to be imported to pre-Contact Hawaiʻi. Other suggestions that the Sweet Potato might have arrived rather late in the colonization of Polynesia were included in chapter 24.

POLYNESIAN ANIMALS

The three domesticated animal species carried by Polynesians and their ancestors were the **Pig** or *puaʻa (Sus scrofa),* **Domestic Dog** or *ʻīlio (Canis familiaris),* and **Chicken** (a domesticate of the Southeast Asian Red Junglefowl) or *moa (Gallus gallus).* All of these species were allowed to roam freely around settlements, although some of the dogs and Pigs were occasionally maintained in pens to fatten them before consumption or, less often, kept as personal pets.

Pig

Polynesian swine were quite small compared with modern breeds, usually weighing only between about 27 and 45 kg (60 and 100 pounds) when mature, but relatively enormous numbers apparently existed throughout the main islands. It was historically related that, not long before Contact, well over a thousand animals would be cooked and eaten at the consecration of an important temple or *heiau.* And, during 4 months in Hawaiʻi in 1778 and 1779, ships of

Cook's expedition were furnished with about six hundred Pigs, and the supply reportedly showed no sign of diminishing.

The multitudinous free-ranging Pigs were often a problem to early Hawaiians because they readily entered agricultural plots and ate substantial amounts of the crop, but they were usually excluded from such cultivated areas by branch or stone fences. The impact on the native ecosystem of any swine that foraged away from settlements was undoubtedly significant, however. They were especially destructive to the endemic Hawaiian tree ferns, *hāpu‘u* (*Cibotium* spp.) and *‘ama‘u* (*Sadleria* spp.), toppling the plants and tearing into the trunk to eat the starchy heart. In addition, any native plants with edible roots (for example, *Alena* [*Boerhavia* spp.]), were rooted out and consumed. The Pig is also a noted predator on smaller vertebrates, and native populations of many of the flightless birds (see chapter 22) as well as ground-nesting flighted species were undoubtedly significantly impacted. The Pig's well-developed sense of smell could also have allowed beach-ranging animals to locate and dig out sea turtle egg clutches.

Domestic Dog

The pre-Contact Hawaiian breed was about the size of a modern fox terrier, and the short-haired animal had rather a long body, short but somewhat slim outbowed limbs, erect pointed ears, and an upwardly curled tail. Dogs were kept primarily for consumption rather than for companionship or any other purpose and were usually allowed to become essentially or fully adult before being killed. They reportedly were fed primarily if not entirely on vegetable food scraps (this supposedly being the reason the term "poi dog" is commonly applied today to any Hawaiian canine of indeterminate breed). It seems reasonable to assume, however, that these basically carnivorous animals would also have been quick to devour any Polynesian Rat (see following discussion) they encountered. Like Pigs, dogs that wandered away from villages undoubtedly also made serious inroads on the populations of flightless and ground-nesting native birds.

Chicken

This adaptable species consistently served as food in pre-Contact times, but apparently only the adults were eaten, with all eggs being allowed to hatch. The enigmatic prehistoric practice of occasionally placing an entire young Chicken in the grave of an adult human female has been noted during archaeological investigations on at least three of the main Hawaiian Islands, although there is no ethnological information regarding this mortuary ritual. Environmentally, Chickens presumably had little effect on native plant and animal species, unless this alien species carried diseases or parasites that were spread to native birds.

Polynesian Rat

A few nondomesticated animals evidently accompanied Polynesian immigrants to the Hawaiian Islands. The **Polynesian Rat** or *‘iole (Rattus exulans)* is often considered to have been simply a stowaway on voyaging canoes, but it seems more likely that the animal was deliberately included with the other alien vertebrates. First, many primitive peoples do not seem to possess the generally widespread modern aversion to having rodents in the vicinity of their habitations; in fact, just as was suggested earlier for importation of nonutilitarian trees, this familiar Polynesian animal may have been taken along as a reminder of a former abode. Second, there was reportedly a sport enjoyed by Hawaiian chiefs in which these rodents were targeted using a miniature bow and arrow, so they may even have been included in the cargo at chiefly insistence. Also, the rats would serve as a "free" protein source for Hawaiian dogs, even harvestable by the animals themselves. Polynesian Rats have been historically recorded as feeding on and killing nesting seabirds in the archipelago, so the rodents undoubtedly contributed to the prehistoric extermination of some native birds on various islands.

Lizards and Snails

Various species of skinks and geckos (Table 19.2) undoubtedly also arrived in Hawai'i on ancient voyaging canoes. At least a few species of lowland endemic insects or other arthropods, having evolved in the absence of such predators, may have been lost to these ubiquitous lizards. A number of land and freshwater snails also habitually accompanied Polynesian voyagers (Tables 18.2, 18.3). Almost all of these are relatively small forms, and the eggs, young, or even adults could easily have been carried unnoticed in bundles of imported plant propagules. None of these alien snails is carnivorous, and so their impact on the native Hawaiian ecosystem was probably minimal. The archipelago already had a diverse complement of selectively adapted herbivorous terrestrial gastropods, and the native plants presumably had long since evolved suitable defenses against overbrowsing and other potential damage by such invertebrates.

NATIVE HAWAIIAN PLANTS

Food Plants

Whatever traditional cultigens the first Hawaiians carried, it would obviously be a number of years before these staples could be produced in large enough quantities to supply all of the human dietary needs. In the meanwhile, a substantial source of vegetable carbohydrate to which Polynesians were accustomed must have been sorely missed. It seems the starch-containing pithy trunk heart of the two genera of native tree ferns may have been the only major source of such a carbohydrate immediately available in the Islands.

Utilitarian Plants

Hau (Hibiscus tiliaceus) was quite important to pre-Contact Hawaiians, for a variety of reasons. The tree grew rapidly and profusely and yielded a lightweight wood useful for canoe outriggers, fishnet floats, and the softwood base of a fire-by-friction kit, as well as inner bark suitable for making rough cordage. It obviously provided firewood, and the smaller limbs and foliage served as mulch for crop production in pits on lava fields essentially lacking soil. The early Hawaiians also discovered that the inner bark of endemic *Māmaki (Pipturus albidus)* could be used to make tapa. But, because this particular type of bark cloth was coarser and less durable when wet than that made from their transported Paper Mulberry, use of the common native species undoubtedly lessened once the cultigen was growing in sufficient quantity. Another endemic Hawaiian plant, however, proved to be of great technological value, because its product had not previously been available. This is *Olonā (Touchardia latifolia),* a shrub from whose bark were extracted long, thin, soft fibers that made excellent cordage for use in fine netting, fishline, and even larger cordage. Even in late historic time, until the appearance of nylon and other synthetic materials in the 1930s, *Olonā* fibers were imported by the Swiss for making rope for mountain climbing.

Constantly increasing exploitation of at least one large native forest-tree species was apparently significant. Ancient Hawaiians preferentially utilized trunks of the endemic *Koa (Acacia*

koa) for making both the smaller single-hulled outrigger canoes *(kaukahi)* and the larger double-hulled ones *(kaulua),* and a relatively enormous number of trees must have been felled for
this purpose. When Cook's ships entered Kealakekua Bay in 1779 his officers are supposed to
have counted between 2,500 and 3,000 various such craft. This heavy usage eventually led to an
interesting anthropogenous change in the morphology of the species. Most *Koa* seen today are
multi- rather than single-boled, and these several trunks are usually relatively so thin or crooked
that they could hardly have served to form the old medium or large Hawaiian canoes. Roughly
1,500 years of selection of only single-trunked straight individuals has resulted in essential loss
of this morphological variant, and the species has evolved into the present multiple-trunked and
somewhat spindly tree. It has even been suggested that the cessation about A.D. 1300 of the
apparent extensive two-way journeying between the Hawaiian and Society Islands (see chapter 24) could have been due to exhaustion of *Koa* massive enough to furnish the large hulls
needed for voyaging canoes.

NATIVE HAWAIIAN ANIMALS

Marine Fauna

In contrast to limited native plant food, abundant sources of marine animal protein in the form
of a variety of invertebrates, fishes, and sea turtles were immediately available to the first Hawaiians. Among the invertebrates, shells of certain mollusks also provided important raw material
for various artifacts. Probably none of these ocean animals was extirpated by prehistoric Hawaiians, primarily because—unlike the terrestrial environment—the marine one was generally
more difficult to overexploit by prehistoric technology. Also, it is extensive enough to hold
repopulating animal stock in cases where certain local populations may have been temporarily
eliminated. In fact, a few marine vertebrate resources seem to have been utilized less by prehistoric Hawaiians than by other peoples of Oceania. To judge from remains recovered during
archaeological investigations, the relatively common species of porpoises (*nuʻao* or *naiʻa* [see
chapter 19]) seem to have been hunted very infrequently in Hawaiian waters. A few of these
small cetaceans must have been taken occasionally, however, because their numerous small,
conical teeth appear in certain traditional artifacts, such as their use in the extensive dentition
of feathered image heads.

Larger cetaceans such as the Humpback or *koholā (Megaptera novaeangliae)* and Sperm
Whale or *palaoa* (and/or *koholā?* [see chapter 19]) *(Physeter macrocephalus)* were apparently
too large to be hunted and killed by any pre-Contact Pacific Islanders. It is curious that in
Hawaiʻi there seems to be no mention of whales in chants and legends, although if the Humpback occurred around the main islands in prehistoric times as it does today it could not have
gone unnoticed by the inhabitants. Nevertheless, ancient Hawaiians were acquainted with at
least the Sperm Whale, as apparent from use of its large, conical lower-jaw teeth for carving the
tongue-shaped pendant of royalty's *lei niho palaoa.* Hawaiian tradition refers to at least two
localities where dead Sperm Whales had reputedly drifted ashore at some time in the past: Point
Palaoa on the southwestern coast of Lānaʻi and Kualoa on Windward Oʻahu. Remains of Hawaiian Monk Seal or *ʻīlio holoikauaua (Monachus schauinslandi)* are not reported from fossil or
cultural sites of at least the main islands. This pinniped is generally restricted to the Northwestern Hawaiian Islands (see chapters 19, 23), although occasional individuals are seen on main
island beaches today and probably also visited them sometimes in the past. Thus, it is extremely
puzzling why none appears to have been taken by ancient Hawaiians.

Terrestrial Fauna

On land, there were initially innumerable nesting seabirds of several types, as well as a great many terrestrial avian species, to provide animal protein. But, at least 46 out of an original avifauna before human arrival of more than 100 native species of land and freshwater birds were lost before Contact (Table 20.1). The easily captured larger flightless forms such as *moa nalo* and Maui Nui ibises (see chapters 21, 22) would have been extensively exploited, and this undoubtedly contributed substantially to their prehistoric extinction. Even if early Hawaiians had placed some sort of *kapu* or prohibition on the taking of such birds whenever their population numbers appeared low, they could still have ultimately been extirpated through the uncontrollable predation by Pigs, dogs, and rats. Nevertheless, because of the long-established Polynesian tradition of Chicken husbandry, it is surprising that at least the gooselike *moa nalo* were not similarly domesticated. Perhaps the particular dietary plant requirements of these large birds made food gathering for them too onerous to merit their husbandry.

In regard to smaller endemic bird species, apparently few if any would have been significantly endangered by direct predation, considering the primitive pre-Contact capture methods. It was undoubtedly the loss of native vegetation (see discussion later in this chapter), on which the coevolved birds (see chapter 21) were entirely dependent for food and shelter, that was primarily responsible for their extirpation. The endemic Hawaiian forest bird taxa that did manage to survive until at least the early historic period were probably either those that lived only in relatively undisturbed upland areas or those with substantial population numbers spread through both lowland and upland regions. With the loss of these smaller species, their highly specialized predators such as the Wood Harrier (†*Circus dossenus*) and stilt-owls (†*Grallistrix* spp. [see chapter 20]) would necessarily also have become extinct.

Featherwork

A widespread Polynesian cultural tradition was the use of feathers in various artifacts used by the chiefly class or *ali'i,* including short capes and longer **feather cloaks** *('ahu 'ula),* headbands or necklaces *(lei),* and royal standards *(kāhili).* The original Polynesian meaning of the derivative Hawaiian term *'ahu 'ula* is "red cloak," and, because birds with red feathers were the scarcer species in island groups through which Hawaiian ancestors migrated, only feather cloaks of this color were formerly considered suitable for royalty. In Hawai'i, however, two of the most abundant forest birds were red (the Hawaiian honeycreepers *'Apapane* or *Himatione sanguinea* and *'I'iwi* or *Vestiaria coccinea* [see chapter 21]). Yellow feathers, however, were much more difficult to obtain, because they occurred (as far as now known) on only two less-common Hawaiian birds (the honeycreeper Hawai'i *Mamo* or #*Drepanis pacifica,* and the honeyeater *'Ō'ō* of the genus #*Moho* [Plate 20.1]), and even on these mostly black species there were only a few yellow feathers per individual. Thus, the traditional Polynesian "red cloak" in Hawai'i was preferably primarily yellow in the case of paramount royalty, although that of individuals of lower chiefly status might often still be largely red—or even black or green.

The birds for featherwork were mostly taken by specialized bird catchers or *kia manu.* The primary capture method involved use of birdlime made from sap of either *Pāpala kēpau* (*Pisonia* spp.), Breadfruit, or a few other plants, and smeared on branches to entrap landing birds. Historic informants said that the bird catchers removed the desired feathers and then released the captured bird, although this is difficult to believe. The removal of any substantial amount of feathers from a bird, especially in the rather cold and wet upland rain forests, would undoubtedly soon cause it to die from body-heat loss, a fact that would not have gone unnoticed by the experienced bird catchers. Also, the usual ancient Hawaiian proletariat diet was undoubtedly too protein-deficient for an isolated bird catcher to resist the temptation to eat a captured small bird. Even though cloaks preserved in museums reveal that many thousands of particular species of small forest birds were taken for each, there is little chance that any of their total populations would have been significantly endangered by this. Each of the types of birds so utilized was widespread on its one or more islands of occurrence, and each bred yearly. Thus, the annual taking of a few thousand individuals probably constituted little threat to the entire species, considering the extremely high mortality rate that occurs naturally in wild organisms (see chapters 10, 22).

HAWAIIAN DEMOGRAPHY

The first few hundred years after colonization of the Hawaiian Islands would have seen relatively low numbers of humans, probably concentrated in a relatively few prime resource localities throughout the archipelago, so they would have caused relatively little overall environmental impact. The small population increased geometrically, however, so that by at least A.D. 1600 or so it had reached a number usually estimated as about 300,000 (although one researcher has suggested that it may have been up to three times that figure). Even at the lower estimate, however, except for Oʻahu and Maui, more people lived on each of the main islands then than are present on them today.

The course of Hawaiian demographic numbers after 1600 is still unclear. Figure 25.1 shows the apparent population changes on Leeward Hawaiʻi and Kahoʻolawe as inferred from temporal variation in numbers of dated habitation sites. There seems little dispute that the Leeward Hawaiʻi and Kahoʻolawe populations' increase up to about 1600 generally held true for all other main islands. The population decrease between that time and Contact in 1778 shown in the fig-

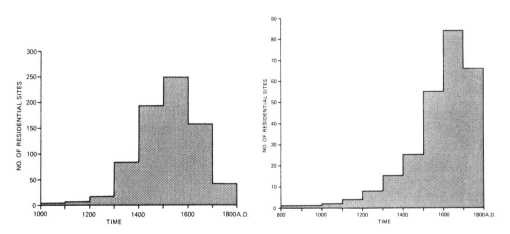

Figure 25.1. Apparent prehistoric Hawaiian population trends. *Left,* histogram of radiocarbon-dated habitation sites of Leeward Hawaiʻi; *right,* the same for Kahoʻolawe. The demographic increase up to approximately A.D. 1600 is quite likely real, but the apparent subsequent drop is now somewhat in question (see text). (Adapted from Figs. 235 and 236 of Kirch [1985], used with permission of Patrick V. Kirch.)

ure, however, is questioned. Certain heavily populated areas of other main islands had more land capable of extensive pondfield Taro production (see discussion in next section) than had been fully put to this use by 1800 (for example, Anahulu Valley on northwestern Oʻahu). Possibly, the post-1600 decrease shown for Leeward Hawaiʻi and Kahoʻolawe is real and could well have been because these two very dry parts of the main islands had reached the maximum number of people that could be supported by dryland agriculture. But, for prime lowland Taro-production areas elsewhere on Hawaiʻi as well as on other main islands, future determinations of their population sizes may show that Hawaiian numbers were still increasing up until the very early 1800s, when introduced diseases began to decimate the native population.

HAWAIIAN CULTIVATION

Methods

Taro, by far the favored Hawaiian starch staple, was the only cultigen for which specialized growth plots were typically prepared: *loʻi* or terraced pondfields, often extensive and continually irrigated with flowing stream water. Numerous varieties of the species were cultivated, almost all of which could also be grown in upland gardens without surrounding water. Any dryland planted areas usually also contained Sweet Potatoes, other tuberous food plants such as various yams, and Kava. Their cultivation consisted of the traditional Southwest Pacific practice of "slash-and-burn" or **swidden agriculture.** A relatively small area of native vegetation would be cleared by cutting and the felled plants burned in place; shading trees too large to conveniently be cut down were killed by girdling their trunks. Mixed plantings were made soon after burning, usually being watered only by rainfall, and crops would be grown until soil fertility had diminished considerably. The area was then abandoned and allowed to revert to native vegetation for a number of years, and the swidden process was repeated at a new or previously used area nearby.

Larger food plants such as Breadfruit, banana, and Sugarcane were most frequently planted along the borders of the pondfields and dryland gardens, as well as around dwellings, often serving a secondary function as windbreaks. Among the nonfood utilitarian plants, Paper Mulberry was usually closely planted in groups for ease in harvesting the large amounts of bark needed for making tapa, and Coconut was sometimes planted in large groves near the shore.

Candlenut

Candlenut trees or *kukui (Aleurites moluccana),* on which pre-Contact Hawaiians were heavily and constantly dependent for nut kernels to burn as torches, grow best in well-watered areas, but these same wet areas were at a premium for lowland Taro cultivation. To help solve this problem, especially as the human population increased, it seems the Hawaiians devised a plan by which this utilitarian species could be grown on inaccessible and otherwise unusable land high on the cliff faces of various islands. The distinctive gray-green Candlenut foliage may still be seen high up in the small hanging valleys of some such basalt ramparts, as on the steep Windward Pali of Oʻahu's Koʻolau Range (Figure 5.3). There appears to be no way that the trees could have reached such places unless the nuts had been "sown" there by Hawaiians walking along the summit ridge and throwing them down the precipitous slopes. Presumably, those nuts that successfully lodged and sprouted along the courses of cliffside streams generated by every rainfall yielded trees, most of whose fallen ripe fruit would be washed down to the escarpment base for periodic gathering.

Pili

Twisted Beardgrass or *pili* (*Heteropogon contortus;* quite tentatively considered prehistorically introduced rather than indigenous) was used extensively for thatching the walls and roofs of Hawaiian houses. This grass was grown in large areas initially cleared of native vegetation by burning and removing shading trees. After the mature crop was gathered each year, the fields were again burned just before the winter rainy season so that stubble was removed and the regenerating grass would grow at a uniform rate. This could then be mass-harvested with a minimum of difficulty when the new stalks simultaneously reached maximum size.

LANDSCAPE ALTERATION

Throughout human existence, people have changed every native environment they have encountered to some degree. A realization of this fact some years ago led to the concept of **transported landscapes:** humans occupying a new area do not change their way of life to fit the landscape; insofar as they are technologically able they change the landscape to fit their way of life. The Polynesians settling Hawai'i were no exception; through necessity they cleared, planted, and otherwise transformed the original Hawaiian countryside into a land approximating as closely as possible that which had allowed survival of their cultural line for several thousand years. Thus, by the later pre-Contact period in Hawai'i the appearance of the occupied landscape was essentially identical to that found on any other long-inhabited Polynesian island.

Expansion of Cultivation

As the prehistoric Hawaiian population grew, the original cultivation methods had to constantly be intensified and modified to support the additional individuals. *Lo'i* in a great many lowland areas were gradually expanded until they filled all suitable space, as has been disclosed by archaeological investigations of the floors of certain amphitheater-headed valleys (see chapter 8) such as Mākaha on Leeward O'ahu and Hālawa on Windward Moloka'i, and as may still be seen in such areas as **Hanalei Valley** of northern Kaua'i (Plate 25.1). Even this great increase in wetland Taro production capability eventually proved insufficient on some islands, though, and earlier small, scattered upland swidden agricultural plots gave way to extensive permanent dryfield systems. Also, the drier leeward parts of the islands began to be populated by the expanding population, and the dryland field systems became especially large and complex there, as at Lapakahi on the west side of Hawai'i (Figure 25.2). One of Captain Cook's officers recorded in 1779 that he walked inland from Kealakekua Bay on Leeward Hawai'i through some 9.6 or 11.3 km (6 or 7 miles) of cultivated fields and that planted bananas extended even farther beyond that point.

Grassland Development

The periodic burning of Twisted Beardgrass described earlier also prevented regeneration of the original forest and other native vegetation. That such anthropogenous grasslands were truly large may be appreciated from several reports of early European visitors, one of whom wrote that on O'ahu his party passed through pure stands of this grass for most of a journey from the general southwestern 'Ewa area east to the vicinity of Waikīkī.

Firewood

One seldom-appreciated major and continuous need of pre-Contact Hawaiians was that for firewood. Most vegetable food, and at least land animals, were cooked over fires in small, stone-lined hearths or *kapuahi* or on heated stones in *imu*. Through centuries of occupation of a particular lowland locality, all native plants constituting potential firewood in the immediate vicinity would be removed, so more and more of the neighboring upland area not already converted to dryfield systems or *pili* grassland would then be similarly denuded. Captain Cook specifically noted in 1778 that on Kaua'i no wood could be found at any distance inland from which it was convenient to bring it to the shore.

Erosion Phenomena

This deforestation for firewood and other purposes led to often severe erosion and land slippage, sometimes with dire consequences for the areas downslope. In Leeward O'ahu's Mākaha Valley, for example, archaeological investigation of ancient Taro pondfields has shown that an enormous landslide from the slopes above buried a portion of the *lo'i* complex under thousands of

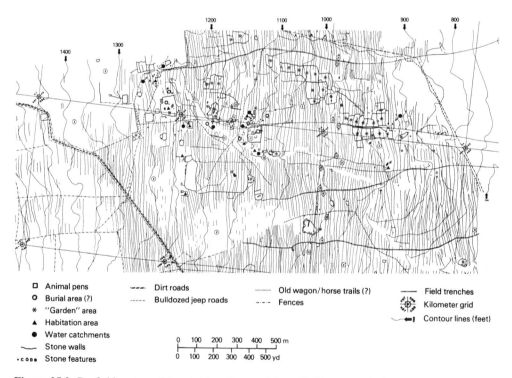

□ Animal pens	--- Dirt roads	.... Old wagon/horse trails (?)	········ Field trenches
○ Burial area (?)	----- Bulldozed jeep roads	--- Fences	Kilometer grid
* "Garden" area			Contour lines (feet)
▲ Habitation area			
● Water catchments	0 100 200 300 400 500 m		
⌒ Stone walls			
·c o ▪ Stone features	0 100 200 300 400 500 yd		

Figure 25.2. Dryfield system of Lapakahi on Leeward Hawai'i. The terraced plots were used for growing primarily Sweet Potato and dryland Taro. In this area, each plot was bordered by a low fence of basalt cobbles or soil generally paralleling the topographic contours to minimize erosion. The land slopes down to the right. (Original map by T. Stell Newman; modified as Fig. 200 of Kirch [1985], used with permission of Patrick V. Kirch.)

cubic meters of earth, after which the inhabitants laboriously dug out the obviously essential agricultural system and returned it to production. Although the Hawaiian forests originally extended down essentially to sea level (see chapter 14), it has been estimated that by A.D. 1600 or 1700 probably 80 percent of all soil-bearing land up to at least 458 m (1,500 feet) on every main island had been cleared of native vegetation.

Habitat Creation

Under certain circumstances, however, erosion might have been advantageous to, and possibly even encouraged by, ancient Hawaiians, as when it formed a more extensive floodplain on which to grow wetland Taro. Scientific studies have revealed that the original shore at the mouth of Kahana Valley on Windward Oʻahu had been extended seaward almost a kilometer (0.6 miles) by soil washed from the heavily cultivated areas higher up the valley, and that as this new land was created it was promptly put to traditional agricultural use. On the other hand, in particular inland areas where it was obviously disadvantageous for land to be lost to erosion, prehistoric Hawaiians apparently went to some lengths to minimize this process, as in the extensive terracing and contoured walling of upland dryfield systems (Figure 25.2). Whatever the methods used, in a few cases they may have been somewhat successful, because recent stratigraphic soil studies at selected areas of Oʻahu that were evidently used for prehistoric agriculture seem to show that erosion was less *after* the initiation of human activities there than it had been when the land was in its original state.

It is interesting that certain environmental changes of pre-Contact Hawaiians seem to have benefited two native birds. The essentially cosmopolitan Short-eared Owl or *pueo (Asio flammeus)* first appears in Hawaiian fossil deposits less than about a thousand years ago. On continents this relatively common owl forages and nests in open country and includes a substantial number of small rodents in its diet. It probably reached the Islands a number of times in the millions of years before Polynesians arrived, but was never able to establish because of the lack of both open fields and rodent prey. The creation and maintenance of extensive *pili* grasslands by ancient Hawaiians, as well as their introduction of the Polynesian Rat, finally happened to produce a favorable environment for the owl, and the bird subsequently became a well-established Island taxon.

Similarly, although the Black-crowned Night-Heron or *ʻaukuʻu (Nycticorax nycticorax)* is a common wetland bird in many parts of the world and is found in some numbers in Hawaiʻi today, it is not represented in the older fossil sites. Presumably, the individuals undoubtedly occasionally arriving in the archipelago before humans could not establish populations because of the shortage and relatively impermanent nature of wetlands (see chapters 8, 14) to provide its diet of aquatic animals. Upon the prehistoric development of the great Taro *loʻi* systems and construction of numerous fishponds (see discussion later in this chapter), ideal foraging habitat was created, and this bird also became a prominent native species.

RESOURCE MANAGEMENT

Although the ancient Hawaiians had to place survival needs above preservation of seemingly nonessential native ecosystem components, certain of their land-management and mitigation measures serendipitously also provided protection for many unutilized endemic species of Island plants and animals.

Ahupua'a

At some unknown but apparently rather late time in prehistoric Hawai'i, the resource-use concept of the ***ahupua'a*** as a basic land unit was developed, quite possibly in response to inland expansion of a growing Hawaiian population. Ideally—although not invariably in practice—each *ahupua'a* consisted of a relatively narrow triangular area of land with its apex at the highest point of an island or proximate mountain ridge (*"mauka"* [toward the uplands]), extending downslope to its base along the coast (*"makai"* [toward the ocean]). Each usually represented a discrete watershed, and its *mauka-makai* range helped to ensure the inclusion of natural resources characteristic of all elevations and even of the marine environment because resident exploitation rights also extended far offshore. (Although the term *"ahupua'a"* as well as certain aspects of its ownership and taxation are uniquely Hawaiian, the same basic concept of dividing an island into wedge-shaped *mauka-makai* land divisions to assure inhabitants of each maximum access to resources is found elsewhere in Polynesia.)

Units of contiguous *ahupua'a* on an island were eventually politically grouped to form a district or *moku* (for example, O'ahu had six districts [with an additional one formed between 1913 and 1932 from parts of traditional *moku*], and the number of *ahupua'a* constituting each ranged from two to eighteen with an average of fourteen). Typically, each main island was ruled by a paramount chief or **ali'i,** and each district by a subordinate *ali'i.* Each *ahupua'a* was managed by an overseer or **konohiki,** usually a trusted relative of the subordinate chief.

The commoners of an *ahupua'a* comprised the **maka'āinana** (people who attend the land), a large percentage of whom might be related. They could usually grow crops, gather various natural materials, hunt, and fish only within the limits of their own *ahupua'a,* thus providing a substantial incentive to properly manage and conserve all introduced as well as native resources of the unit. The *konohiki* also monitored resource status and declared a *kapu* on taking any plants or animals—especially fishes—when the prohibition appeared necessary to prevent overutilization. Surplus food and other materials could be traded with or given to other *ahupua'a,* thus helping ensure maximum usage of the totality of resources within a district or entire island and minimizing the impact of periodic shortages of essential commodities in particular areas.

Fishponds

The several types of constructed **fishponds,** collectively known as *loko i'a,* seem to have been a Hawaiian invention and, like the development of *ahupua'a,* possibly a rather late one in the Polynesian period. Fishes of certain species were raised in the brackish water of naturally impounded ponds just inland from the shore, as well as along with Taro in the flooded freshwater *lo'i.* The most impressive and productive fishponds, however, were the *loko kuapā* ("walled fishpond"), formed by separating an indented portion of protected coast from the ocean with a long wall of basalt boulders and cobbles or coral-algal reef blocks (Figure 25.3). The ocean water of such a large pond was tidally changed through one or more wooden grates set in wall openings *(mākāhā),* but was usually diluted by freshwater flowing from the land so that it often remained brackish. The grates also allowed passage in and out of the pond of small and medium but not large fishes. The fishes most successfully stocked and raised in the various types of ponds were those tolerant of a fairly wide range of salinity, with Striped Mullet or *'ama'ama (Mugil cephalus),* Milkfish or *awa (Chanos chanos),* and Hawaiian Flagtail or *āholehole (Kuhlia sandvicensis)* being the principal species in the walled coastal structures.

It has been estimated that all of the main island fishponds at the time of Contact could have provided each Hawaiian only about 3.6 kg (8 pounds) of fish annually, so the structures were obviously not one of the primary sources of food for the ordinary villager. In fact, it seems the ponds—especially the large, walled ones—were for the exclusive use of the various chiefs, who could demand fishes from them at any time regardless of any seasonal restrictions on fishing that might then be in force on their subjects. Still, this autocratic system was undoubtedly beneficial to the citizenry at large because it relieved commoners of the burden of constantly providing the fruits of their own fishing labors to the *ali'i*. Free-living fish populations probably benefited as well, because the protection of breeding stock as well as the usual supplemental feeding of fishes in the ponds undoubtedly resulted in greater numbers of young of these same species that would leave the ponds and eventually become available for capture by anyone in waters outside the ponds.

Land and Sea Zones
To designate a geographical location relatively precisely, the name of a particular *ahupua'a* within a certain district would be given to indicate the appropriate radial section around the island circumference, and then an altitudinal band (usually indicated by vegetation type) within the *ahupua'a* would be cited. The numerous altitudinal bands so used are listed in Table 25.3, and they are also compared with those of the modern scientific classification of Hawaiian vegetation zones.

Figure 25.3. A large, walled fishpond or *loko kuapā*. This particular structure is located on the south-central coast of Moloka'i. The plants along parts of the pond border are probably historically introduced mangrove *(Rhizophora mangle* or *Bruguiera sexangula);* in ancient times at least the interior of the pond would have been kept cleared of any such vegetation. (Photograph by Marshall I. Weisler; negative no. MO(a)87-18 of Bishop Museum Department of Anthropology, used with permission.)

Table 25.3. Traditional Hawaiian vegetation-zone classification. The apparent approximate and sometimes overlapping elevational relationship of these zones to those of the modern classification presented in chapter 14 on the terrestrial environment is also shown. (Traditional classification follows primarily Malo [1951].)

Traditional Hawaiian Terms		Historic Terms
"kahakai" (mark of the ocean)		Strand
"kula" (plain)	*"kula kai"* (. . . of the ocean) *"kula waena"* (. . . of the middle region) *"kula uka"* (. . . of the uplands)	Coastal
"pahe'e" (slippery [because of mud or grass] zone) *"'ilima"* ([the plant] *Sida fallax* zone) *"'āpa'a"* (arid or dry zone)		Dry Forest
"wao" (wilderness or uninhabited region)	*"wao kanaka"* (. . . of humans) *"wao akua"* (. . . of spirits or gods)	Mesic Forest
	"wao ma'u kele" (. . . of the rain belt) *"wao nahele"* (. . . of the forest)	Rain Forest
	"kuahea" (. . . of stunted trees)	Cool Dry Forest
"kua" (back [= upper portion] of a mountain)	*"kuamauna"* (. . . of higher mountainsides)	Alpine Scrub
	"kualono" (. . . of summit ridges and peaks)	Alpine Stone Desert

An even more extensive system was used to designate ocean regions around the Islands. To give just a few examples of these terms, which are much more numerous than the modern ones used (Figures 11.3, 11.4), the inshore ocean-flat area was *"kai kohola"* (sea of the reef) or, when shallow enough to wade as when spearing fish and gathering marine invertebrates, *"kai hele kū"* (sea of walking upright) or *"kai koʻele"* (sea of thumping [of a grounded canoe hull]). The water just outside the barrier reef where large waves broke and surfing was done was *"kai heʻe nalu"* (sea of wave-sliding), and farther out at greater depths where the water color darkened was *"kai uli"* (sea of deep blue). Various subdivisions of the *kai uli* were *"kai lū heʻe"* (sea of lure-catching octopus), *"kai ʻōpelu"* (sea of *ʻōpelu* [Mackerel Scad]), and *"kai mālolo"* (sea of *mālolo* [flyingfishes]); still farther out was *"kai hī aku"* (sea of trolling for *aku* [Skipjack Tuna]).

MAKAHIKI, LONO, AND CAPTAIN COOK

Makahiki

Theoretically, the *ahupuaʻa* concept should have provided the *makaʻāinana* with a satisfactory though hard-earned existence, but their *aliʻi* were usually notoriously conspicuous consumers and also had to support a large retinue of idle relatives, priests, advisors, and other courtiers. The chiefly demands on their subjects for Taro and other vegetables, fishes, and Pigs, as well as other labor-intensive products such as feather cloaks and tapa, often exhausted the commoners and occasionally brought them to the brink of starvation. A large portion of these levies was collected during the **Makahiki,** a winter festival of the agricultural god Lono. During this time one or more chiefs or their representatives traveled by coastal trail or canoe around an island in a clockwise direction, carrying a stylized symbol of the god and stopping at the border of each *ahupuaʻa* to collect the tribute assembled there. The literal translation of *ahupuaʻa* is "Pig altar," probably because the platform of stones *(ahu)* at each land unit bore either the image of a Pig *(puaʻa)* or the swine and other *Makahiki* tax items for collection.

Lono and Cook

The direction of the annual royal journey around an island was mentioned only because of its relevance to the manner in which Captain Cook evidently came to be regarded as the god Lono. Cook had arrived at the island of Hawaiʻi in 1779 during the *Makahiki* and had sailed *clockwise* around much of the island in full view of the inhabitants before entering the bay at Kealakekua (pathway of the god[!]) on the Leeward coast, where there also happened to be a large temple or *heiau* dedicated to Lono. Further, the symbol of Lono, who legend said would someday return to the Islands, was an upright staff bearing a lashed-on crossarm, from which was hung a sheet or two of white tapa: an artifact to which the masts and sail-bearing yardarms of Cook's ships bore an uncanny though gigantic resemblance. The fact that Cook, like the legendary Lono, had also brought seeds of new food plants and a new animal (Domestic Goat, *Capra hircus;* also deposited the previous year on Niʻihau, which Cook similarly chanced to have visited at the time of the *Makahiki*) seemed the final proof that the obviously powerful stranger was indeed the returned Hawaiian deity.

The captain's perceived identity with Lono, however, soon came into question, and he was ultimately killed during an altercation with angered Hawaiians on the shore of Kealakekua Bay. During his month's stay there, Cook may have prevailed a little too heavily on the hospitality of the local chiefs, but undoubtedly the factors contributing more significantly to his fall from grace were the observed vulnerability of one of his ships to a particularly damaging episode of foul weather just after initiating departure, coupled with his unknowing—but, to the Hawaiians, inexcusable—religious affront in then returning during the period over which the more-powerful god Kū had just become ascendant.

SUGGESTED REFERENCES

Abbott 1992; Abbott and Williamson 1974; Athens et al. 1992; Buck 1957; Crawford 1993; Cuddihy and Stone 1990; Culliney 1988; Handy and Handy 1972; I'i 1959; Kamakau 1964, 1976, 1991; Kepelino 1932; Kikuchi 1976; Kirch 1982, 1984, 1985, 2000; Kirch and Hunt (eds.) 1997; Kirch and Sahlins 1992; Krauss 1993; Malo 1951; Mitchell 1982; Olson and James 1984; Titcomb 1969, 1972, 1978.

AUDIOVISUAL AIDS

4-Butte-1: A lesson in archaeology; Gatecliff: American Indian rock-shelter; Hawaiian fish-hooks; Hawaiian seafood: Limu; Hawaii: Strangers in paradise; Ke haku hulu: The featherworker.

26

Historic Ecology

The English explorer Captain James Cook and members of his 1778–1779 voyages to the Hawaiian Islands were the first non-Polynesians known to have reached the archipelago. In the remainder of the 1700s and the very early 1800s, several other European expeditions also visited the Islands briefly (see chapter 28). Beginning about 1810, however, additional foreigners arrived to spend significantly more time in the archipelago. The series of activities instigated or carried out by them would drastically change the Islands' native social structure and then just as pervasively further modify the natural environment already so substantially changed by the Polynesian discoverers (see chapter 25).

SANDALWOOD TRADE

Captain Cook had found that a most lucrative trade was possible by transporting pelts of North American furbearers, especially those of the Pacific Coast Sea Otter *(Enhydra lutris),* to China, and American ships began this commerce soon thereafter. About 1810, the foreigners' discovery in the Hawaiian Islands of endemic species of the aromatic **sandalwood** or *'iliahi (Santalum* spp.), so desired for Asian furniture and incense manufacture, added another extremely valuable commodity to the China Trade. The Hawaiian chiefs, because they could personally gain vast stores of foreign goods by providing sandalwood for this enterprise, relentlessly forced their subjects to collect vast amounts of this material.

That the more accessible populations of sandalwood on several main islands were almost annihilated by this exploitation between about 1812 and 1830 is of less importance than the fact that this episode was a major early factor in the breakup of the traditional Hawaiian way of life. Commoners compelled to travel far into the uplands to cut seemingly endless amounts of sandalwood had to largely neglect their usual agricultural and other subsistence activities. The old social system based on the *ahupua'a* (see chapter 25) thus began to disintegrate, starvation became commonplace, and eventually the faith of the formerly loyal subjects in their rulers was all but lost. By 1830 sandalwood convenient for harvesting had become so scarce that the chiefs tried substituting the indigenous Bastard Sandalwood or *naio (Myoporum sandwicense),* a relatively common and widespread species whose wood has a scent somewhat like true sandalwood. This substitute did not gain acceptance with the Chinese, however, so populations of this tree were spared overexploitation.

WHALING

Upon the dearth of sandalwood, the former harvesters were able to begin a return to their neglected agricultural plots. But earlier, in 1819, the **whalers** of America and then, within only a year or two, of other nations had discovered the rich Pacific stock of, primarily, Sperm Whales or *koholā* (and/or *palaoa?*) (*Physeter macrocephalus* [see chapter 19]). An ever-increasing number of these vessels began reprovisioning in the Islands each year. Only a few of the traditional Hawaiian utilitarian and food plants were of use to the whalers, but there was a ready market for sennit, the excellent rope made from husk fiber of Coconut or *niu (Cocos nucifera),* as well as sometimes for that made of the fine-fibered *Olonā (Touchardia latifolia* [see chapter 25]). There was also demand for tapa cloth, apparently to be used as ship-hull caulking. Less-perishable primary Hawaiian cultigens such as the Greater Yam or *uhi (Dioscorea alata),* Sweet Potato or *'uala (Ipomoea batatas),* and to a lesser extent Taro or *kalo (Colocasia esculenta)* were also in great demand as ship's food stores.

Thus, in return for factory cloth, nails, and other new foreign products, Hawaiians slighted their traditional *ahupua'a* duties and began concentrating on production of these particular cordages and crops. Pork to be salted for consumption at sea was also greatly desired by the whaling ships, so large numbers of Pigs were taken for trade rather than being available for local consumption and *Makahiki* taxes (see chapter 25). Further, many Hawaiian men left their families and traditional homes on the *ahupua'a* and gravitated to the vicinity of larger developing coastal towns, especially Lahaina on Maui and Honolulu on O'ahu, looking for work there and often shipping out for long voyages on whaling vessels. This urban migration also involved many Hawaiian women, who similarly left their children and country homes, most of them to engage in the lucrative prostitution trade in the bustling seaports. These greatly disruptive influences of whaling on the Islands continued largely unabated until the industry experienced a substantial decline in the 1860s.

PASSING OF TRADITIONAL SOCIETY

In addition to the perturbations to traditional Hawaiian life brought about by the sandalwood and whaling trades (not to mention devastating epidemics of continental diseases to which native Islanders had no immunity), other changes contributed to the irreversible transformation of the centuries-old social system, and these ultimately resulted in domination of Island life by foreigners.

A New Religion

The death in mid-1819 of Kamehameha I, a traditional and respected king who had united all of the Islands under a single ruler, initiated destabilization of the Hawaiian political system. Only months after his death, the new rulers, King Kamehameha II (Liholiho) and the regent Ka'ahumanu, lifted the ancient prohibition on men and women eating together. This signaled abandonment within a very few years of the entire *kapu* system that had ordered the everyday life of Hawaiians for centuries. Then the first **American missionaries** arriving the following year contributed substantially to this upheaval by their attempts—with various degrees of success—to instill in Hawaiians Christian values and strict mores often at odds with traditional ones. Only a relatively short time after arrival the missionaries were successful in converting to Christianity at least the Hawaiian rulers, who decreed that their subjects should also accept this faith's tenets. But the new religion merely substituted a new and puzzling set of taboos for the familiar traditional ones, leaving many Hawaiians unsure of both their present and their future and unable to cope effectively with the changes rapidly occurring on every hand.

Loss of the Land

It would seem that the abandonment after about 1810 of much land formerly devoted to traditional plant production should have proved quite beneficial to the native environment. This would have been so, except for the introduction of new foreign crops and large-scale commercial agricultural methods, as well as the initiation of husbandry of alien hoofed mammals. Both of these activities (discussed further later in this chapter) would do far more environmental damage than traditional Polynesian agriculture and semidomesticated Pigs ever had. Essentially all of the new agricultural and ranching ventures were developed by the **haole** (foreigner), mostly American and British, but for this they needed control of large amounts of land. To their good fortune—and the Hawaiians' great misfortune—the *haole* were able to reach this goal within a few dozen years with only a minimum of effort. A number of foreign immigrants, more secularly oriented than the missionaries, gained positions of increasing influence with the various Hawaiian monarchs, so that by about the mid-1800s government of the Islands was effectively under *haole* control.

Great **Mahele**

In 1848, King Kamehameha III (Kauikeaouli) was persuaded by the resident foreigners to proclaim a highly significant redistribution of all land in the kingdom: the **Great *Mahele*** (Division). A little over one-third was set aside for use and financing of the government. About the same amount was given to the subordinate chiefs or made available for granting to commoners or *maka'āinana* who could satisfactorily demonstrate that they had habitually occupied and worked particular small plots *(kuleana)*. The rest was personally retained by the ruling Kamehameha dynasty as "Crown Lands." (This last-named portion constitutes what are currently known as "Ceded Lands" because, after the 1893 abolition of the monarchy and establishment of the republic, they were turned over to the federal government upon annexation of Hawai'i to the United States as a territory in 1898. Title to most of the Ceded Lands was returned to the Hawaiian government upon statehood in 1959, with 20 percent of the income generated from their use owed to Native Hawaiians. As of 1999, negotiations were still ongoing to settle this debt and, eventually, transfer complete control of such lands to people of Hawaiian ancestry.)

One of several important aspects of this 1848 land reform was that commoners who had managed to gain title to *kuleana* were now free to sell them. Most of these were sold to *haole,* as might be expected, and often only because the Hawaiian owners could not pay the newly imposed real-property taxes. Also, the subordinate chiefs could likewise now either sell or give extensive parcels of their own large holdings to foreigners, which many of them subsequently did. Even members of the royal family sold some of the Crown Lands to *haole* before this particular practice was outlawed by the kingdom's legislature in 1865. Thus, not only domination of the government, but also the equally important control of a substantial portion of the more desirable land in Hawai'i found its way into foreign hands. For example, of the third of all Hawaiian land allocated to commoners and subordinate chiefs at midcentury by the *Mahele, haole* apparently owned about 80 percent by 1900.

Thus, the Polynesian "transported landscape" of the ancient Hawaiians (see chapter 25) was soon largely—and more efficiently—transformed by foreigners (and their introduced plants and animals) into one more typical of a continental area. The remainder of this chapter details some of the primary historic degradations of Hawaiian ecosystems. The following chapter on natural resource protection, however, presents many of the actions that are now being undertaken to repair and, where possible, reverse this damage.

HISTORIC COMMERCIAL CROPS

Sugarcane

Apart from the eventual spread of populous urban areas, a most obvious component of the post-Contact Hawaiian landscape became the vastly increased amount of cultivated lands. The principal historically introduced agricultural plants grown on these lands are listed in Table 26.1. Imported foreign varieties and subsequently developed hybrids of **Sugarcane** (*Saccharum* spp.) had successfully been grown commercially in Hawai'i since about 1835, and 40 years later enough of the economic and horticultural problems of mass cultivation and sugar-mill operation had been overcome to make this plant a major crop over vast areas of most of the main islands. Irrigation and mechanical cultivation methods not possible for pre-Contact Hawaiians resulted in extension of cultivated fields into previously undisturbed areas of both lowlands and uplands (Figure 26.1), with resultant loss of enormous areas of native vegetation and associated animal life. For example, the exposed coral-algal reef making up the extensive 'Ewa Plain on southwestern O'ahu, which originally bore a very thin soil layer and parkland-type vegetation, had been too dry for Hawaiian agriculture. In the late 1800s, however, mechanical drilling techniques produced artesian wells in the area (see chapter 8), so that Sugarcane could then be grown over much of this area, although almost countless wagonloads of topsoil had to be transported from the uplands and laid down first.

The irrigation of higher-elevation fields necessitated drawing water from upper reaches of streams and transporting it long distances through tunnels and ditches to the fields. This de-watering of natural watercourses often caused their lower portions to dry up periodically, resulting in loss of essentially all former native stream biota. Erosion from such fields in certain areas such as northeastern Lāna'i moved the shoreline, already extended by washed-down upland soil during pre-Contact times (see chapter 25), even farther seaward over the coastal reef. This pollution as well as that of trash from cane washing and the bagasse or milling waste of crushed stalks severely damaged nearshore marine resources. The cultivation of Sugarcane continued to dominate Hawaiian agriculture and many other aspects of Island life for another century, although by the 1980s lower labor and other production costs in other world areas such as the Philippines had resulted in a continuing diminution in Hawaiian production. Plantations now remain (with reduced acreage) only on Maui and Kaua'i, and even these operations may well be largely discontinued very early in the twenty-first century.

Pineapple

Early in the 1800s, it was found that historically introduced **Pineapple** or *hala kahiki (Ananas comosus)* could also be grown quite successfully in the Hawaiian Islands, and by 1900 much of the crop was being exported commercially. The plant requires less water than Sugarcane, so by the second half of the 1900s substantial additional, previously untilled, acreage of native vegetation unsuitable for "cane" had been brought into large-scale production of "pine." In fact, in the early 1920s essentially all land on Lāna'i had been purchased from the Hawaiian government and private owners by *haole* commercial interests, and most relatively level upland land there was planted to this crop. At one point during the next 50 years the Hawaiian Islands were providing 75 percent of the world's supply of canned Pineapple. Like Sugarcane, however, Pineapple can now be grown cheaper in less-developed countries, so Hawaiian production appears to be in the process of being gradually phased out.

Additional Crops

Rice or *laiki* (*Oryza sativa;* the Hawaiian name, like that of many historically introduced organisms, is a transliteration of the English one) was first cultivated on the main islands in 1856, in many instances using abandoned Taro pondfields or *lo'i,* so little additional damage was done

Table 26.1. Principal current agricultural crops in Hawai'i. These are listed in order of amount of land devoted to their cultivation in 1997. All of these crops except most Taro plantings represent historically introduced varieties or species. (Data primarily from State of Hawai'i, Department of Agriculture [1999].)

Family Species	English Name	Hawaiian Name	Hectares (Acres)
Grass (Poaceae) *Saccharum* spp. hybrids	Sugarcane	*Kō*	27,480 (68,700)
Protea (Proteaceae) *Macadamia integrifolia*	Macadamia nut	(None)	8,080 (20,200)
Bromeliad (Bromeliaceae) *Ananas comosus*	Pineapple	*Hala kahiki*	7,960 (19,900)
Coffee (Rubiaceae) *Coffea arabica* *Coffea liberica*	Coffee	*Kope*	2,800 (7,000)
Papaya (Caricaceae) *Carica papaya*	Papaya	*Mīkana*	1,620 (4,050)
(Various: corn, sunflowers, etc.) Seed crops	(Various)	(Various)	920 (2,300)
(Various) Miscellaneous flowers and other nursery plants	(Various)	(Various)	865 (2,160)
Banana (Musaceae) *Musa* spp.	Banana	*Mai'a*	640 (1,600)
Myrtle (Myrtaceae) *Psidium guajava*	Common Guava	*Kuawa*	350 (880)
Gourd (Cucurbitaceae) *Citrullus lanatus*	Watermelon	*Ipu haole*, etc.	340 (840)
(Various) Tropical specialty fruit	(Various)	(Various)	260 (650)
Mustard (Brassicaceae) *Brassica oleracea*	Head Cabbage	*Kāpiki*	260 (650)
Aroid (Araceae) *Colocasia esculenta*	Taro	*Kalo*	180 (450)

to the native environment. Production of this grain should have proved a very profitable venture, considering the relatively enormous quantities that are still imported from Japan and California, but by the early 1900s essentially all planting of it had been discontinued. The lack of profitability seems due in significant measure to the large percentage of the crop eaten by immense flocks of such alien granivorous birds as the Nutmeg Mannikin or Ricebird *(Lonchura punctulata)* and other members of the family Estrildidae (see chapter 20).

Coffee or *kope (Coffea arabica* and *C. liberica)* was first introduced for cultivation in 1813 and was being exported in large quantities by 1850. It was eventually found that this crop grew especially well on the leeward slopes of Hawai'i Island with their particular afternoon periods of cloudiness and rain (see chapter 7), and this "Kona Coffee" remains a profitable crop today. Although new areas of upland native forest had to be cleared for cultivation of this crop, the acreage required was relatively insignificant compared with that lost to Sugarcane and Pine-

Figure 26.1. Upland plantations of historic crops on Leeward West Maui. *Foreground,* Pineapple *(Ananas comosus); center and background,* Sugarcane *(Saccharum* spp. hybrids). Modern technology now allows irrigation of such elevated areas, which were too dry for ancient Hawaiian cultivation. (Photograph by David Cornwell, used with permission.)

apple. Macadamia nuts *(Macadamia integrifolia* and *M. tetraphylla)* had been introduced from Australia and grown in relatively limited quantities since the 1890s, but in the last third of the twentieth century much larger orchards of these profitable edible-nut trees (primarily *M. integrifolia*) have been established, and the acreage is liable to continue to increase. Before the 1970s, extensive native forest areas on Hawai'i were bulldozed so that these plantings could be made, but more recently mostly land withdrawn from Sugarcane production has been so utilized.

OTHER HISTORIC PLANTS

Alien Trees

By about 1900, it was decided by the territorial government that steeper upland areas not suitable for agriculture and largely denuded by historically introduced hoofed animals should be reforested to protect them as watersheds. This, of course, was an excellent decision, except that none of the primary trees chosen for the purpose was native. All manner of alien trees, including Australian **eucalyptus** *('eukalikia* or *palepiwa),* Southern Hemisphere *Araucaria* "pines" and Silk Oak or *'oka kilika (Grevillea robusta),* North American true pines and related conifers, as well as various other species such as False *Koa* or *koa haole (Leucaena leucocephala)* and Black Wattle *(Acacia mearnsii),* have been planted.

These tree species were originally intended only as watershed protectors, rather than as commercial timber sources. In recent years, however, there has been a movement on the part of government agencies and private interests to use many of these plantations as well as additional prospective plantings as the basis of an Island timber industry. Even though the endemic *Koa (Acacia koa)* is one of the world's premium hardwoods, and a few of the other native trees are probably almost equally valuable, even areas of native forest containing these have recently been bulldozed to plant potential alien timber trees. It happens that these introduced species grow rapidly under the favorable Hawaiian climatic conditions, but this prevents their wood from developing the hardness and other characteristics required for quality cabinetwork lumber. Thus, apparently no important amount has ever been harvested locally for this potentially very profitable purpose. Now, however, much eucalyptus is being used in the production of wood chips, exported for making paper and certain composite building materials.

Alien Ornamentals and Weeds

In the two centuries since Captain Cook's arrival, between eight thousand and ten thousand taxa of plants have been introduced to the Hawaiian Islands. A great many of these—especially the thousands of orchid species—were imported for commercial ornamental purposes, but a number of others arrived inadvertently with other historic materials. Less than 10 percent of this total alien complement, however, seems to have established self-sustaining wild populations, but about ninety of these species currently pose a danger to the native biota. Table 26.2 lists representative examples of alien species currently regarded as being extremely harmful because they have entered relatively pristine upland forests or are especially injurious to native biotic communities in other ways.

A great many of the historically introduced plants grow only in lowland areas long ago cleared of native vegetation. But these are still detrimental to the native environment because they are preventing reestablishment of still-surviving endemic plant and associated animal species that might otherwise be able to reoccupy their original habitat. It has also been found that certain historic alien plants can change the chemical composition of their substrate relatively rapidly (for instance, by greatly increasing the ground nitrogen content, as in the case of Firetree or *Myrica faya*) so that through time the surrounding soil becomes more favorable for growth of further alien species and less so for that of native ones. As further examples of harm caused to the native biota, the actions of three among the most undesirable alien plant types are discussed here.

Grasses

Broomsedge (*Andropogon virginicus* [Figure 26.2]; a close relative of *pili* discussed in chapter 25), as well as Fountain Grass *(Pennisetum setaceum)* and a few similar historically introduced species have invaded vast areas of open dry woodland both below and above the Rain Forest Zone. These relatively tall upright grasses burn readily, but regrow quickly from the root

Table 26.2. Examples of especially harmful alien plants in Hawai'i. The purpose of introduction is also noted. These species have damaged not only Hawaiian native ecosystems but also agricultural and other commercial interests. (Data from various sources.)

Family Species	English Name	Purpose of Introduction
Mango (Anacardiaceae)		
Schinus terebinthifolius	Christmas Berry	Ornamental
Cactus (Cactaceae)		
Opuntia ficus-indica	Prickly Pear Cactus	Cattle forage
Melastoma (Melastomataceae)		
Clidemia hirta	Koster's Curse	Ornamental; erosion control (?)
Melastoma candidum	Malabar Melastome	Ornamental
Miconia calvescens	Miconia	Ornamental (?)
Bayberry (Myricaceae)		
Myrica faya	Firetree	Reforestation; ornamental (?)
Myrtle (Myrtaceae)		
Psidium cattleianum	Strawberry Guava	Fruit production; ornamental (?)
Passionflower (Passifloraceae)		
Passiflora mollissima	Banana Poka	Ornamental; fruit production (?)
Grass (Poaceae)		
Andropogon virginicus	Broomsedge	Inadvertent (mixed in cattle forage?)
Melinis minutiflora	Molasses Grass	Cattle forage
Pennisetum clandestinum	Kikuyu Grass	Cattle forage
Pennisetum setaceum	Fountain Grass	Ornamental
Rose (Rosaceae)		
Rubus argutus	Prickly Florida Blackberry	Fruit production
Rubus ellipticus	Yellow Himalayan Raspberry	Fruit production; ornamental (?)
Verbena (Verbenaceae)		
Lantana camara	Common Lantana	Ornamental

mass after a fire, unlike the less flammable and slower recovering native understory vegetation. Thus, by fostering relatively frequent burnings these alien species come to dominate an area and eventually lead to a loss of the original tree and ground-cover species of the invaded areas.

Banana Poka

This alien, *Passiflora mollissima,* is an attractive-flowered vining member of the passionflower family introduced as a garden ornamental (reputedly originally to hide a privy) and possibly also for fruit production. It soon escaped cultivation, however, and ultimately spread to the upland forests of Kaua'i, Maui, and Hawai'i. **Banana Poka** is able to climb and essentially cover the tallest trees, after which the dense vegetation shades out the host tree's foliage and causes its death. The vine's elongated fruit drops to the ground and is eaten by, especially, wild Pigs, which then further spread the plant as the seeds pass unharmed through their digestive tract.

Guava

On primarily the windward side of the main islands, **Strawberry Guava** or *waiawī 'ula'ula (Psidium cattleianum)* and **Common Guava** or *kuawa (P. guajava)* have covered extensive areas of upland areas previously cleared by either early Hawaiians or historic hoofed mammals. Strawberry Guava, especially, often forms **monocultures** or single-species stands, preventing

Figure 26.2. Historically introduced Broomsedge *(Andropogon virginicus)*. This photograph shows invasion of an open parkland of endemic *'Ōhi'a lehua (Metrosideros polymorpha)* in Hawai'i Volcanoes National Park on Hawai'i. The flammable nature and dense growth of this grass leads to intense fires that kill or suppress reproduction of native vegetation, thus allowing such a fire-tolerant alien species to eventually dominate the area. (Photograph courtesy of U.S. Fish and Wildlife Service.)

the regrowth of native understory herbs and shrubs as well as shading out seedlings of endemic canopy trees. The numerous seeds in the edible fruits are spread so rapidly and efficiently by alien birds and Pigs that both guavas are practically impossible to eradicate. It is interesting that in the latter half of the 1800s and first half of the 1900s, guava was kept under a semblance of control in some areas by use of great quantities of the favored wood in the Island manufacture of charcoal for cooking purposes. Numbers of now-abandoned charcoal kilns of cemented basalt cobbles and boulders may still be chanced upon in long-overgrown areas, such as along the base of the Windward Oʻahu Pali.

HISTORIC MAMMALS

The preceding chapter included discussions of Polynesian-introduced animals and their early effects on the Hawaiian environment. Also, the principal animals historically introduced to the Hawaiian Islands were listed in earlier chapters devoted to various types of invertebrates and vertebrates. The remainder of this chapter covers the impact of this historic alien fauna on native ecosystems.

Ungulates

Of all the types of terrestrial vertebrates introduced to the Hawaiian Islands following Contact, the herbivorous hoofed mammals or **ungulates** (Latin *"ungula"* [hoof]) have undoubtedly been ecologically most detrimental. The endemic Hawaiian trees and lesser vegetation evolved in the absence of mammalian plant eaters, and in this process most lost any ancestral defenses against fatal herbivore overpredation, such as thorny or poisonous foliage, bitter bark, and resistance of roots to trampling (see chapter 15). Their special palatability to continental herbivores is well recognized by game managers in Hawaiʻi, who term such native forage taxa "ice cream" plants. Game managers usually operate on the principle of "carrying capacity" (that is, there is a certain number of mammals that can be maintained on a given amount of land without overexploiting the vegetation). Although perfectly valid for continental areas with native ungulates, the concept is essentially inapplicable to a place like Hawaiʻi where none of the endemic plants is evolutionarily adapted to coexistence with herbivorous mammals. Thus, the current official state policy of maintaining alien game mammals on a **sustained-yield basis** (regulation of hunting to maintain a constant animal population size) continues to further endanger rarer native plants, prevents regeneration of the others, and assures retention and spread of alien continental flora.

It should be realized that such alien herbivores do not have to destroy an entire native forest to cause the extinction of an endemic bird population. To take a hypothetical but not at all unreasonable case, all that may be required is the mammals' extirpation of a particular small endemic herb that harbors the caterpillar of a similarly endemic moth species. This caterpillar may be utilized by the native bird population as food for newly hatched young during only 2 or 3 weeks each spring. With the plant population gone, the birds, instinctively conditioned to harvest only this particular caterpillar, are incapable of substituting other invertebrate food (even if such were available in the area) and the entire year's crop of nestlings is lost. The life span of the adult birds may possibly extend to a second year of breeding, but the entire reproductive effort of that season will similarly be lost. Thus, the native bird population in this area has become extinct in only 2 years although no individual bird has ever been *directly* harmed by the alien mammals, and the overall appearance of the forest as a whole seems unchanged to every-one except a perceptive terrestrial biologist.

It could be that the unexplained historical disappearance of three finch-billed Hawaiian honeycreepers from their shared and *seemingly* unaltered forested habitat on the Leeward coast of Hawai'i Island represents a case of this type. The Kona Grosbeak (#*Chloridops kona*) as well as the Greater *Koa* Finch or *hōpue* and Lesser *Koa* Finch (#*Rhodacanthis palmeri* and #*R. flaviceps,* respectively [see chapter 21]) were known historically for only 9 years. All three species were discovered by ornithologists between 1887 and 1892, but there is no record of any being seen after 1896. It is unknown when historic ungulates reached the areas inhabited by these three species, but because this habitat is above the range of disease-carrying alien mos-quitoes (see discussion later in this chapter), native plant extirpation by such historically intro-duced mammals must be considered a possible cause of the birds' loss. Contributory factors might conceivably include spread to the area of other harmful historic aliens, for example the Roof Rat (*Rattus rattus* [see chapter 19 and discussion later in this chapter]).

Domestic Cattle or *pipi (Bos taurus),* Domestic Goat or *kao (Capra hircus),* and Domes-tic Sheep or *hipa (Ovis aries)* had all been introduced to the Hawaiian Archipelago by visiting British ships before 1794 (Table 19.3). A royal *kapu* on the imported cattle resulted in enormous numbers of them throughout the Islands by 1823, and a great beef industry was founded, first dependent on free-ranging animals and later on fenced herds. This provided large amounts of salted beef, tallow, and hides to the world market for the next 50 years or so. To handle the ranch animals, experienced cowhands were imported from southwestern North America, pri-marily Mexican nationals of Spanish–Native American descent. Their reply of *"Español"* when questioned as to identity apparently gave rise to the transliterated Hawaiian word for cowboy: *paniolo.*

The effects of, primarily, these three particular ungulate species may currently be seen throughout the main islands in the form of enormous grazed areas in which essentially all native vegetation has been destroyed, with the replacement alien plants including a number of noxious continental species that will not be eaten by these herbivores. Most cattle of **feral** type (Latin *"ferus"* [wild]; free-living individuals of domesticated species) have been removed from pro-tected Hawaiian areas such as Forest Reserves and watershed land. Feral goat populations, how-ever, still infest most of these, being maintained there by the state on a sustained-yield basis at the insistence of the very small proportion (less than 1 percent) of the Islands' population that hunts them. Flocks of ranched sheep, along with goats, were responsible for reducing the island of Kaho'olawe to its current deforested and severely eroded condition. On Hawai'i Island's Mauna Kea, a 150-year-old herd of feral sheep, augmented by numbers of the closely related Mouflon (*Ovis musimon* [state-introduced in 1954 to provide additional hunting]), lowered the original treeline of the Forest Reserve there from about 3,350 m (11,000 feet) to as low as 2,750 m (9,000 feet) in some places (Plate 26.1) before a 1979 federal court order mandated initiation of their removal by the state (see chapter 27 and Plate 27.1).

The feral Pig or *pua'a (Sus scrofa)* is evidently now more numerous in remote areas of the main islands than it was in pre-Contact times, when Hawaiians seem to have fed or otherwise encouraged swine to remain in the vicinity of settlements for ease in harvesting. Even in the early historic period, botanists did not note the presence of the animals, or evidence of their damage to the native ecosystem, in upland forests. Today, however, Pigs are common in many such places, probably retreating there because of persistent hunting in lowland or otherwise more-accessible areas. Also, the average size of wild Pigs has increased markedly over that of the Polynesian animals as larger historic varieties have interbred with the prehistoric stock, thus now making the Pigs' continuing impact on native ecosystems even greater (see chapter 25). Currently, this species probably causes its most significant environmental harm through rooting in native vegetation in search of (historically introduced) earthworms, leaving the thoroughly tilled area susceptible to invasion by alien continental plants evolutionarily specialized for rapid establishment after just such substrate disturbance.

Rabbit

The introduced European Rabbit or *lāpaki (Oryctolagus cuniculus)* is occasionally found feral in lowlands of the main islands, but it seems to do little damage there because its populations are usually never able to build to substantial size in the presence of such carnivores as dogs. Without such predators, however, this species can multiply explosively, as made evident in 1989–1990 on Maui's Haleakalā. Six rabbits released by a pet owner increased to a population of over ninety individuals distributed through an elevational range of 2,100 to 2,500 m (6,930 to 8,250 feet) in only 12 months. Fortunately, upon discovery of the colony, all individuals were able to be located and eliminated with only 9 month's work. Where this species becomes concentrated in a smaller area free of predators, such as Mānana or Rabbit Island off southeastern Oʻahu, as well as Laysan and Lisianski of the Northwestern Hawaiian Islands (see chapter 23), it has the potential of completely eliminating the native and even most of the alien vegetation. Such loss of plants on the two Northwestern *motu* directly contributed to the extinction of three of the five endemic land and freshwater bird species on Laysan, as well as undoubtedly a number of endemic invertebrates. It also allowed the sand exposed on higher ground to be blown into sheltered depressed areas, substantially changing the original topography and limited lower-elevation native vegetation of both *motu*.

Rats

In addition to the prehistorically introduced Polynesian Rat or *ʻiole (Rattus exulans),* two larger species or *ʻiole nui* arrived historically: the Norway Rat and Roof Rat (*Rattus norvegicus* and *R. rattus,* respectively). The Norway Rat tends to remain close to urban structures, but the Roof Rat may be common in both towns and uninhabited areas far from them. It had long been assumed that both of these continental species gained access to the different Hawaiian Islands from some of the earliest European ships visiting the archipelago (that is, during the late 1700s). One investigator has recently proposed, however, that one or both species may not actually have reached land until docking facilities had been constructed on the various main islands. Previous to this time ships had anchored offshore and transferred goods by rowboat, so there was little or no chance of ship rats getting ashore. The first wharfs were constructed at, for example, Honolulu in 1825, and although enough Norway Rats may have come ashore on the island by 1835 to establish populations (their remains appear frequently in certain Oʻahu archaeological excavations of the early historic period), it appears that the Roof Rat possibly may not have done so until the period 1870–1880.

The fact that the dates of extinction of certain small endemic forest birds on a particular Hawaiian island correspond fairly well with the times that shoreside docking facilities became available there has led to the theory that at least the proficiently climbing Roof Rat played a major role in the loss of these birds. Roof Rats have also been implicated in the extinction of some endemic land snail species (see chapter 18), as these are known to be a food of this rodent, and numbers of rat-gnawed shells can be found underneath some arboreal snail colonies.

Carnivores

All three species of *Rattus* cause sometimes severe damage to standing Sugarcane. The Small Indian Mongoose or *manakuke (Herpestes auropunctatus)* had been introduced from India to Jamaica in the Caribbean, where it was reputed to be extremely effective in controlling cane-field rats, so individuals of the species were transported from Jamaica and released on the four largest main islands other than Kaua'i. Mongooses did prove to eat some rodents (even though the former are largely diurnal and the latter nocturnal), but rat populations merely soon reached equilibrium with those of the predator, and both still remain widely distributed on the islands involved. Mongooses, however, also feed on a variety of birds, especially flightless and other ground-nesting native birds, as well as ground-feeding alien game species (see chapters 20, 22). It may not be only coincidence that the formerly abundant endemic flightless Common Hawai'i Rail or *moho (Porzana sandwichensis)* apparently became extinct at about the same time this carnivore—as well as the Roof Rat—were introduced to Hawai'i Island.

The historic varieties of Domestic Dog or *'īlio (Canis familiaris* [which have now obliterated the original Polynesian population of the animal through interbreeding]), as well as feral individuals of the historically introduced House Cat or *pōpoki (Felis catus),* prey on wild birds. In lowlands of the main islands, dogs are particularly harmful to larger avian species that attempt to nest on the ground, such as the Laysan Albatross or *mōlī (Diomedea immutabilis)* and various shearwaters and petrels (all of the family Procellariidae [see chapter 20]). Cats take smaller birds, in the lowlands mostly alien species of doves and other game birds as well as introduced songbirds, but in remote upland areas also a substantial number of endemic forest birds. On upland Maui and Hawai'i these felids also prey upon nesting Hawaiian Petrels or *'ua'u (Pterodroma phaeopygia sandwichensis).*

HISTORIC BIRDS

Historically introduced birds can negatively impact endemic birds and the Hawaiian environment in at least four ways: (1) direct competition, primarily for food; (2) predation; (3) spread of alien plants into native ecosystems; and (4) introduction of exotic pathogens and parasites.

Avian Competition

Fortunately, only a few alien birds seem to have feeding habits similar enough to those of endemic forms to constitute serious ecological competitors. A notable one of these competitors, however, is the **Japanese White-eye** or ***mejiro*** (Japanese *"me"* [eye] and *"shiro"* [white]; *Zosterops japonicus*), currently perhaps the most numerous among alien avian taxa in the Islands (Table 20.1). This small species feeds on fruit, nectar, and small arthropods, and in upland forests where Hawaiian honeycreepers (see chapter 21) and several other smaller endemic birds still occur may compete with them for at least the last two dietary components. The alien Red-billed Leiothrix *(Leiothrix lutea)* is common on some islands in the upland habitat of these same native birds and includes in its diet many small insects that might otherwise sustain certain endemic birds.

Avian Predation

Endemic Hawaiian birds evolved along with at least four native avian predators, all apparently diurnal: a small and a medium-sized hawk as well as a larger eagle and a long-legged owl (see chapter 20). The prey, therefore, presumably evolved adequate behavioral methods of defense against such day-hunting enemies. Three of these original predators became extinct, along with many of their presumed prey species, before the end of the Polynesian period. For various reasons, the still-extant slow-flying Hawaiian Hawk or 'io (Buteo solitarius) of Hawai'i Island does not seem to constitute a major threat to most of the surviving native avifauna. Recently, however, it has been found responsible for the death of captive-reared and released individuals of the Hawaiian Crow or 'alalā (Corvus hawaiiensis). Similarly, the relatively late-arriving diurnal Hawaiian Owl or pueo (Asio flammeus sandwichensis [see chapters 20, 25]) is not usually a significant bird predator. The **Common Barn Owl** (Tyto alba), however, was introduced to various archipelago islands between 1958 and 1963 to reduce rat numbers in Sugarcane plantations. This night-hunting species quickly established and multiplied greatly on all main islands. Because its range includes upland native forests and its diet many roosting small birds (as revealed by contents of its regurgitated pellets), the bird may well now represent a serious threat to remaining endemic bird populations.

Alien Seed Dispersal

Although only a very few of the *surviving* native bird taxa are fruit eaters, a relatively large percentage of the historically introduced bird species are such feeders. The seeds of environmentally harmful alien plants such as Christmas Berry, Koster's Curse, Strawberry Guava, Banana Poka, Prickly Florida Blackberry, and a number of others (see Table 26.2 for scientific names and families) are very easily spread into and throughout native forests by these frugivorous birds. Alien species responsible include primarily the Japanese White-eye, as well as the Red-vented and Red-whiskered Bulbuls (*Pycnonotus cafer* and *P. jocosus,* respectively).

Bird Pox and Avian Malaria

As might be expected, essentially all endemic Hawaiian bird taxa lost their ancestral immunity to continental bird diseases during their long isolation and evolution in the archipelago. A common avian disease worldwide is **bird pox** or "bumble foot," a viral infection indicated by swellings and lesions of unfeathered areas of the body (Figure 26.3). This disease may result in loss of toes, while generally weakening the afflicted individual and leaving it susceptible to other potentially fatal stresses. **Avian malaria,** caused by a blood parasite, may yield only slight illness in continental "carrier" birds, but it usually kills outright species without natural resistance. A reservoir of the agents causing bird pox as well as avian malaria has undoubtedly been at least intermittently present in the Hawaiian Islands for millions of years, maintained in the blood of migratory shorebirds or vagrant continental land and freshwater birds.

The Vector

A terrestrial arthropod species capable of transferring these disease agents, however, did not originally occur in the Hawaiian Archipelago; thus, visiting infected birds once posed no threat to the native avifauna. In 1827, however, Hawaiians living near Lahaina on Maui reported to the area's doctor a strange new itch caused by the bite of a small, flying insect they characterized as "singing in the ear." This proved to be a type of night-feeding mosquito, and it had apparently been introduced the previous year when the whaler *Wellington* drained the dregs of its water casks into a nearby stream before refilling them. The ship had last filled these casks at San Blas on the west coast of Mexico, and the aquatic mosquito larvae and pupae or wigglers inadvertently included there were of a tropical subspecies of the Southern House Mosquito, *Culex quinquefasciatus.* This race, which carries agents of both bird pox and avian malaria, easily survived and reproduced in the similar warm climate of the archipelago and is now found most commonly between sea level and about 915 m (3,000 feet) on all main islands.

Many continental forest birds that live in the range of such mosquito vectors minimize infection with bird pox and avian malaria by behaviorly protecting naked areas from bites of the insects. The birds habitually sleep crouched down on a perch so that feathers cover the bare skin of the legs and feet and also often place the beak and anterior part of the head bearing unfeathered skin under the back plumage. Hawaiian honeycreepers, and presumably most other endemic Island birds, have evolutionarily lost this protective behavior and are thus highly susceptible to bites from mosquitoes carrying disease-causing organisms. Whether one or both of these diseases was the primary cause of the historic extinctions of a number of endemic lowland Hawaiian bird taxa will never be known for certain. It can be said, however, that at least avian malaria is definitely known to be a factor currently preventing most native forest birds from occupying (or reoccupying) mosquito-infested main island areas below about 915 m (3,000 feet) elevation.

Experiments showed that a Hawaiian honeycreeper, the Laysan Finch *(Telespiza cantans),* brought from mosquito-free Laysan Island in the Northwestern chain to lowland Kaua'i, succumbed rapidly to avian malaria there. Half of a group of thirty-six birds were held in mosquito-proof cages, and the other eighteen were placed in cages with mesh large enough to admit the insects. Within 16 days all of the latter group were dead from massive malarial infection, but all birds of the protected group remained healthy. Essentially this same test was repeated by moving individuals of three honeycreeper species native to Kaua'i from the upland forest at about 1,250 m (4,100 feet), which is above the typical range of the mosquito, down to near sea level. A number of alien Japanese White-eyes were also similarly transferred. Again, all of the honey-

Figure 26.3. Bird-pox infection of a Hawaiian honeycreeper. Shown is the 'Amakihi *(Loxops virens),* with a swollen lesion at the base of its upper mandible symptomatic of the mosquito-spread viral disease. (Photograph by Sheila Conant, used with permission.)

creepers exposed to mosquitoes quickly fell seriously ill with malaria, but only one Japanese White-eye was infected, and it developed only a very light case of the disease. In this test, the swellings indicative of bird pox also appeared on the lower limbs of the exposed honeycreepers.

Unfortunately, the fact that the tropical subspecies of the *Culex* mosquito introduced usually lives only below about 915 m (3,000 feet) does not necessarily mean that all endemic Hawaiian bird populations typically living above that elevation are safe from the diseases carried by this vector. At least some upland bird species are known or suspected to migrate temporarily to lower elevations during periods of either severe weather or heavy blooming of lowland 'Ōhi'a lehua *(Metrosideros polymorpha)*. Undoubtedly, some native birds among these are then bitten and fatally infected by mosquitoes. Equally or more troublesome is a 1993 report that numbers of this same mosquito, some carrying the malaria parasite, were found at 1,160 m (3,800 feet) on Maui. It will be fortunate if this particular occurrence of *Culex quinquefasciatus* eventually proves to represent simply an atypical and temporary population movement, rather than a new high-elevation colony of the insect that has recently adaptively evolved to life at that altitude.

Immunity

Given many thousands of years, mutant individual Hawaiian honeycreepers resistant to both avian malaria and bird pox would probably appear on the mosquito-infested Islands, and this could lead to the development of immune native bird populations. The question is whether all of the Hawaiian bird species would be extirpated by one or both of the diseases (or some other relatively new detrimental factor) before this evolution had time to occur. It is interesting that at least some types of endemic birds other than honeycreepers range down to near sea level: for example, the 'Elepaio *(Chasiempis sandwichensis* [family Monarchidae]) and one or more of the four (two unfortunately apparently recently extirpated [see chapter 20]) Hawaiian thrushes *(Myadestes* spp. [family Turdidae]). Such a distribution obviously means that the populations involved must be immune to the two avian diseases. This is very likely not an immunity developed only since historic introduction of the *Culex* mosquito. It quite possibly indicates only that the ancestors of these two bird types arrived in the archipelago more recently than did that of the Hawaiian honeycreepers, and that each of these later-establishing lines still retain the pertinent immunities of their colonizing immigrant stock.

OTHER HISTORIC ANIMALS

Amphibians and Reptiles

Essentially all of the frogs and toads imported during the historic period were intended primarily as either food or biocontrol agents (Table 19.1). Almost all of these inhabit only lowland areas, which have lost most endemic invertebrate and smaller vertebrate species, so possibly only the large Bullfrog *(Rana catesbiana)* is of significant environmental harm, because it may take young of certain native waterbirds. In the 1990s, however, unintentional introduction of at least two small forest-frog species of the genus *Eleutherodactylus* resulted in their establishment in populated portions of three main islands (see chapter 19). If any frog of this genus spreads to areas of largely native vegetation it may cause substantial environmental harm by feeding on native invertebrates.

Most of the established historic reptiles (Table 19.2) represent illegal importations and/or illegal releases. The feeding habits of smaller species such as the anoles (*Anolis* spp.) and historically introduced geckos probably do not significantly increase the environmental impact on native invertebrates already occasioned by Polynesian-introduced geckos and skinks. The effects of larger historic forms, however, especially arboreal types such as the large **Green Iguana** *(Iguana iguana)* and Jackson's Chameleon *(Chamaeleo jacksonii),* can definitely harm tree-nesting endemic bird species. For example, the young of most continental birds crouch down and remain in the nest when the limb on which it is located is disturbed; very likely this is protective behavior evolved in areas where native arboreal vertebrates often cause such disturbances. Hawaiian honeycreepers, however, which evolved in the absence of any nonavian arboreal vertebrates, have young that promptly leap out of the nest upon disturbance, thus falling to the ground where alien ground predators now present may devour any that survive the fall.

Carnivorous Snails

Among the alien nonmarine gastropod fauna, the species that has probably been most destructive to the native Hawaiian snail fauna is the historically imported **Rosy Cannibal Snail** (*Euglandina rosea* [see chapter 18]). This relatively large species was intended to control populations of the vegetation-damaging alien Giant African Snail *(Achatina fulica).* Undoubtedly, the Rosy Cannibal Snail eats some numbers of this lowland herbivorous alien, but it has also spread into the upland native forest zones. There, substantial predation on rare endemic Hawaiian snails of several families has resulted, with the extinction of at least one already reduced population of a species of the family Achatinellidae. This voracious carnivorous mollusk, which was formerly presumed to be completely land-living, has now been found to enter freshwater in Hawai'i to eat endemic aquatic snails of the family Lymnaeidae.

Arthropods

The species numbers and limited other aspects of alien terrestrial arthropods in Hawai'i were presented earlier at the end of chapter 16. Of the 2,550 or so alien insect species, a little over one-fourth were intentionally imported for biological control or pollination of commercial crops. Although such importations were made with all good intentions, quite a number of these invertebrate biological-control agents—much like the Small Indian Mongoose, Common Barn Owl, and Rosy Cannibal Snail already mentioned—have detrimentally impacted either native animal or plant species along with the ones they were intended to control.

In regard to inadvertent invertebrate introduction, during the latter half of the 1900s detailed records began to be kept on the numbers of alien species—mostly insects—found to be newly established. The annual average has been near twenty such taxa. Much of this unintentional importation has resulted since about 1960, concurrent with the great increase in worldwide air passenger and freight traffic, with many of the new invertebrates arriving associated with smuggled illegal fruit, plants, or other untreated vegetable material. Some of the most noxious arthropods, however, arrived much earlier in historic time. Solely in terms of economic losses and nuisances to humans, termites, cockroaches, mosquitoes, and certain true flies, as well as ants are among the most notable of these early inadvertent importations. The original Hawaiian biota contained no such pests as these insects or the sometimes troublesome stinging scorpions and large, biting centipedes.

Some or even many of these types of arthropod pests that merely plague humans may well have proven to be agents of death for certain endemic Hawaiian terrestrial invertebrates and vertebrates, just as the mosquito *Culex quinquefasciatus* discussed earlier. As another example, one or more of the thirty-five to forty species of alien ants are suspected of playing a significant role in extinction of small endemic land snail species of the family Endodontidae by eating the eggs and young individuals.

MARINE RESOURCES

Although historic environmental effects in the terrestrial environment have been more widespread and dramatic than in the marine one, at least some attention should be directed to impacts on the native Hawaiian nearshore environment.

Reef Pollution

Soil eroding from the previously discussed historically cultivated land, as well as various waste material from sugar-mill operations expelled into the ocean, killed coral reefs by partially covering them and increasing water turbidity so greatly that the contained symbiotic algae could no longer photosynthesize efficiently in support of the coral animals (see chapter 11). In addition, fertilizer washing from the fields along with increasing sewage from urban areas spurred the growth of free-living macroscopic marine algae in relatively enclosed areas such as Oʻahu's Kāneʻohe Bay to such an extent that these algae similarly prevented sufficient sunlight from reaching the coral, with devastating cumulative effect on the reef. Pesticides and waste petroleum products entering the nearshore waters also detrimentally affected the entire reef biota.

Commercial Overexploitation

In pre-Contact times, the ability of the *aliʻi* or their *konohiki* to temporarily prohibit taking of marine resources threatened by overexploitation (see chapter 25) provided a great deal of protection to the inshore environment. After loss of this traditional social-system element early in the nineteenth century, however, Hawaiian marine resources generally began to be exploited as heavily as possible, until efforts reached the point of diminishing returns. Each coastal resource was then left to recover on its own, if indeed that was then possible.

Pearl oysters or *pipi* (*Pinctada* spp.) were once common in Oʻahu's Pearl Harbor and at Pearl and Hermes Reef in the Northwestern Hawaiian Islands. These populations were greatly depleted by massive, unregulated harvesting for food, button material, and the occasional contained pearl early in the twentieth century. Neither species shows any signs of recovery after a century of total protection. Also, the amount of *ʻopihi* (*Cellana* spp. [see chapter 11]) limpets gathered for sale in 1900 totaled about 67,500 kg (150,000 pounds), but such continued extensive commercial exploitation reduced the quantity reaching the food market in 1985 to only 8,100 kg (18,000 pounds).

In the Northwestern Hawaiian Islands, sailors of 1891 reported hundreds of marine turtles (presumably mostly or all the Green Turtle or *honu*, *Chelonia mydas* [see chapter 19]) on the beaches of French Frigate Shoals—of which they took large numbers—and thousands more in the surrounding waters. These animals continued to be heavily utilized for food through much of the twentieth century until, by 1975, no more than thirty-five Green Turtles could be found on the shore of any one of the several *motu* of the Northwestern chain. Because turtles hatching on a particular beach usually return only to that beach to lay eggs when adult, on the main islands the early historic overharvesting of eggs and adults is apparently responsible for the current essential lack of nesting in this part of the archipelago.

Alien Marine Fishes

Historic introduction of alien fishes, both intentionally and unintentionally, has also detrimentally affected the native Hawaiian marine biota, as illustrated by two selected examples. Between 1955 and 1959 governmental importations of the **Marquesan Sardine** *(Sardinella marquesensis)* were carried out in an attempt to provide a better source of bait fish for the Hawaiian tuna industry (see chapter 12). This alien species established in the Islands, but its population never attained a great enough size to satisfy that objective, and the small fish may well now be in ecological competition with two similar-sized chumming native bait-fish species: the Hawaiian Anchovy or *nehu (Encrasicholina purpurea)* and Hawaiian Silversides or *'iao (Atherinomorus insularum)*. Further, accompanying the arriving Marquesan Sardines were a few inadvertently included individuals of the so-called "Trash Mullet" or *kanda (Vala-mugil engeli),* an alien that established and very likely now competes for food and other essentials with at least the native Striped Mullet or *'ama'ama (Mugil cephalus)*. It might also be noted—although this is more of an economic problem than an environmental one—that the "Trash Mullet" does not grow large enough to be of commercial value, but the Striped Mullet is an economically important Island species.

SUGGESTED REFERENCES

Atkinson 1977; Beletsky 2000; Cuddihy and Stone 1990; Culliney 1988; Daws 1968; Gagné 1975; Hadfield 1986; Hart 1978; Howarth 1990; Kirch and Hunt (eds.) 1997; Mitchell 1982; Royte 1995; C. W. Smith 1985; Solem 1990; Staples and Cowie (eds.) 2001; State of Hawai'i, Department of Agriculture 1999; Stone and Stone (eds.) 1989; Stone et al. (eds.) 1992; Tummons (ed.) 1990–present.

AUDIOVISUAL AIDS

Cloud over the coral reef; Hawaiian waters: Mauka/makai lifeline; Kalo pa'a o Waiāhole [The hard taro of Waiāhole].

27

Natural Resource Protection

The era of concerted environmental protection in the United States, if not the world, began in the late 1960s. Before this, individuals and organizations striving to protect the natural environment had to work mostly without the support of various laws. Federally, the most important and far-reaching legislation of this period was undoubtedly the 1969 **National Environmental Policy Act,** which was soon followed by similar laws in most states, including Hawai'i. The provision of greatest importance in this act mandated preparation of a formal **Environmental Impact Statement** for any major federal action determined, often upon completion of a preliminary **Environmental Assessment,** to have a significant effect on the social, biological, or physical environment. An Environmental Impact Statement cannot, in itself, stop any contemplated project, but its preparation requirements force the proposer to make the intended action public and to allow for governmental and public input both before Statement initiation as well as at intermediate stages of preparation. Also, all potential environmental effects of the project have to be disclosed, and alternative and mitigating actions must be considered.

Within the subsequent decade a number of other federal (and state) laws were enacted dealing more specifically with particular aspects of the natural environment (for example, those informally known as the Clean Air Act, Clean Water Act, Coastal Zone Management Act, and Superfund [for cleanup of major hazardous-waste sites]). Although all of these pieces of legislation provide some degree of protection to plants and animals, two additional ones are more specifically designed to preserve and restore components of the native biota heavily impacted by human activities. These are the **Federal Endangered Species Act** and, for a far more limited number of species, the **Marine Mammal Protection Act.** On the international level, the United States is also a signatory to the Convention on International Trade in Endangered Species of Wild Fauna and Flora, as well as several other treaties designed to protect biotic resources worldwide.

ENDANGERED AND THREATENED SPECIES

A number of major ways in which the Hawaiian environment has been detrimentally affected by human activities both before and after the arrival of Captain Cook have been outlined in the two immediately preceding chapters on human ecology. Many remedial actions are, fortunately, now being carried out in the archipelago, utilizing the just-mentioned environmental laws as well as various additional ones at both the federal and state level. All of these actions can hardly begin to be detailed in this chapter, so only some of those relating primarily to endangered species protection in Hawai'i are described. This manner of coverage will also serve to elucidate certain measures aiding in rehabilitation of other injured components of the Hawaiian natural environment.

The Federal Endangered Species Act in force today was originally passed in 1973, based on similar legislation of 1966 and 1969. Numerous important amendments to the 1973 Act, as well as many implementing regulations, have since been provided. The Act directs the Secretary of the Interior, through the U.S. Fish and Wildlife Service, to develop a worldwide list containing each plant and animal species that is either **endangered** ("in danger of extinction throughout all or a significant portion of its range") or **threatened** ("likely to become an endangered species within the foreseeable future"). There are presently 379 endangered and threatened Hawaiian taxa, and this is approximately 30 percent of all such plants and animals listed for the entire United States. (These and all other data in this chapter were current as of 1999, but the Fish and Wildlife Service Pacific Islands Ecoregion web site [http://www.r1.fws.gov/pacific/] can be consulted for periodic updates.)

If it is prudent and determinable, the so-called **critical habitat** of each such species is also to be designated at the time of listing, delimiting the area considered essential for continued existence and population recovery of the species. This habitat determination is to be based on the best scientific data available and is also to take into consideration economic and other relevant impacts of such designation. The Service, however, has been notably slow in fulfilling this critical habitat requirement, because such areas have been delimited for only two animals and three plants out of the 379 endangered and threatened Hawaiian taxa.

The Act also provides for advisory **recovery teams** to aid the Service in formulating **recovery plans** for restoring endangered or threatened species to nonimperiled population numbers and status. The teams' members comprise governmental as well as nongovernmental experts and are chosen and reimbursed for necessary expenses by the Service, which is also frequently the lead agency in implementing recovery plans. Thirty-nine such plans covering 333 Hawaiian taxa have been completed and approved by the U.S. Fish and Wildlife Service, and several additional plans are in various stages of development. Essentially all Hawaiian endangered birds, the genus of so-called Oʻahu tree snails *(pūpū kani oe* or *pūpū hinuhinu [Achatinella]),* and over 250 plants are included in the finalized ones. Similarly, the recovery plan for the Hawaiian Monk Seal or *ʻīlio holoikauaua (Monachus schauinslandi)* has been approved by the National Marine Fisheries Service.

The Act further mandates that, with the possibility of a few limited exceptions, no federal or federally funded action may be carried out that would negatively impact an endangered or threatened animal species, and no person (meaning either individual or organization) subject to federal jurisdiction may knowingly cause the death of such a species or carry out any action that further imperils its existence. A most important aspect of the last-named prohibition is that it is not limited to the direct killing of a listed animal, but also prohibits both disturbing an individual to such an extent that it cannot carry on usual behavior and significantly harming its critical habitat. (Plants, unfortunately, receive much more limited protection than do animals under the Endangered Species legislation.) This law contains an important citizen's "right to sue" provision.

Vertebrates

The fifty or more bird species that became extinct on the main Hawaiian Islands during pre-Contact times have been noted in chapters 20, 21, and 22. An additional nineteen endemic bird species, plus seven subspecies of still-extant species, have been lost in the post-Contact period. The enormity of this loss can be appreciated if it is realized that, although the Hawaiian Islands make up less than 0.2 percent of the land area of the United States, fifteen times as many Hawaiian bird taxa have been lost since Polynesians first discovered the Islands as during human colonization of the rest of the nation. Among the surviving fifty or so native Hawaiian land and freshwater avian taxa, the thirty-one species designated as endangered or threatened are listed in Table 27.1. (Note that an occasional subspecies is considered a "species" for purposes of the Endangered Species Act, as in the case of the Hawaiian Gallinule or *'alae 'ula* [*Gallinula chloropus sandvicensis*], a subspecies of the widespread Common Moorhen.) In addition, a seabird that very occasionally visits the Hawaiian chain, the Short-tailed Albatross *(Diomedea albatrus)*, may soon be added to the list of endangered United States species, as will probably also the Oʻahu subspecies of *'Elepaio (Chasiempis sandwichensis gayi)*, a small forest bird of the monarch family Monarchidae. A prehistorically extirpated, undescribed Hawaiian bat was noted in chapter 19, and the extant Hawaiian Hoary Bat or *ʻōpeʻapeʻa (Lasiurus cinereus semotus)* is endangered. The Hawaiian Archipelago is also within the range of fourteen endangered and threatened species of marine vertebrates.

Time is obviously critical for protection of many of the endangered Hawaiian land vertebrates, because a half dozen or more of the small forest birds have probably become extinct since their original listing (for example, the Large Kauaʻi and Molokaʻi Thrushes, *Myadestes myadestinus* and *M. lanaiensis rutha*, respectively, as well as the Kauaʻi *ʻŌʻō, Moho braccatus*, among others).

Invertebrates

Although probably about three-fourths of the 770 or more native Hawaiian species of nonmarine snails (see chapter 18) have been extirpated since humans arrived, the only taxon of this group (or of any other native invertebrate one) listed as endangered is the tree snail genus *Achatinella* mentioned earlier. Perhaps only half of the forty-one officially listed species of this genus still survive. One additional nonmarine gastropod, Newcomb's Snail *(Erinna newcombi)* of Kauaʻi, has been proposed—but not yet listed—as a threatened species, and two Lānaʻi snails are being considered for proposal. Three arthropods have also been proposed as endangered species: the Kauaʻi Cave Wolf Spider *(Adelocosa anops* [see chapter 16]); the Kauaʻi Cave Amphipod *(Spalaeorchestia koloana);* and Blackburn's Sphinx Moth *(Manduca blackburni)*, once ubiquitous among the main islands but now apparently extinct on all except Hawaiʻi, Maui, and Kahoʻolawe. The U.S. Fish and Wildlife Service is currently considering an additional twenty-four Hawaiian arthropod taxa for proposal as endangered or threatened species.

Plants

The historically introduced hoofed mammals discussed in chapter 26 have undoubtedly been the primary reason that approximately one hundred of the nine hundred or so historically known endemic Hawaiian plant taxa have become extinct during the past two centuries. This number of extirpations is startlingly high when it is considered that only about this same number of plants are recorded as having been lost in *all* of the nation's other forty-nine states. Among the remaining endemic Hawaiian plants, 292 are already listed as endangered or threatened, and over 40 are under consideration for proposed listing. Among those already listed, more than eighty are now extremely rare (if not very recently extinct), being known from either fewer than ten individuals or a single surviving population. The family totals of these 292 endangered and threatened Hawaiian plants appear in Table 27.2. Just as in the case of botanical extinctions, this is a relatively enormous number of imperiled Hawaiian plants, as may be realized from the fact that it represents 38 percent of the entire endangered and threatened flora of the United States.

Table 27.1. Endangered and threatened Hawaiian animals. These eighty-seven federally listed taxa include a few central Pacific whales and marine turtles that are seen only very infrequently in archipelago waters. The letter E indicates an endangered taxon, and T a threatened one. (Data from various sources.)

Status	English Name	Hawaiian Name	Scientific Name
	Mammals (10 taxa)		
E	Hawaiian Hoary Bat	ʻŌpeʻapeʻa	*Lasiurus cinereus semotus*
E	Humpback Whale (and 6 other species of baleen whales not usually visiting Hawaiʻi)	Koholā	*Megaptera novaeangliae*
E	Sperm Whale	Koholā (or *palaoa?*)	*Physeter macrocephalus*
E	Hawaiian Monk Seal	ʻĪlio holoikauaua	*Monachus schauinslandi*
	Birds (31 taxa)		
T	Newell Shearwater	ʻAʻo	*Puffinus newelli*
E	Hawaiian Petrel	ʻUaʻu	*Pterodroma phaeopygia sandwichensis*
E	Hawaiian Goose	Nēnē	*Branta sandvicensis*
E	Laysan Duck	(None?)	*Anas laysanensis*
E	Hawaiian Duck	Koloa maoli	*Anas wyvilliana*
E	Hawaiian Hawk	ʻIo	*Buteo solitarius*
E	Hawaiian Gallinule	ʻAlae ʻula	*Gallinula chloropus sandvicensis*
E	Hawaiian Coot	ʻAlae keʻokeʻo	*Fulica alai*
E	Hawaiian Stilt	Aeʻo	*Himantopus mexicanus knudseni*
E	Hawaiian Crow	ʻAlalā	*Corvus hawaiiensis*
E	Nihoa Millerbird	(Unrecorded)	*Acrocephalus familiaris kingi*
E	Large Kauaʻi Thrush	Kāmaʻo	*Myadestes myadestinus*
E	Small Kauaʻi Thrush	Puaiohi	*Myadestes palmeri*
E	Molokaʻi Thrush	Olomaʻo	*Myadestes lanaiensis rutha*
E	Kauaʻi ʻŌʻō	ʻŌʻō ʻāʻā	*Moho braccatus*
E	Hawaiian honeycreepers (6 species in 5 genera)	(Various)	"Finch-billed" Drepanidinae
E	Hawaiian honeycreepers (10 species in 5 genera)	(Various)	"Slender-billed" Drepanidinae
	Reptiles (5 taxa)		
T	Green Turtle	Honu	*Chelonia mydas*
E	Hawksbill Turtle	ʻEa	*Eretmochelys imbricata*
T	Leatherback Turtle (and 2 other threatened species of marine turtles not usually visiting Hawaiʻi)	(Unrecorded)	*Dermochelys coriacea*
	Land Snails (41 taxa)		
E	Oʻahu tree snails (41 species in 1 genus)	Pūpū kani oe	*Achatinella* spp.

California has the next highest number of endangered and threatened plants, but with 164 it hardly begins to approach Hawai'i in this regard.

Many actions in addition to those listed here are obviously desirable to further protect and restore populations of endangered and threatened Hawaiian species to safe levels. A number of governmental and private nonprofit organizations are now cooperating in this endeavor, and the pertinent work of those with offices in Hawai'i is described in the next sections.

FEDERAL AGENCIES

U.S. Fish and Wildlife Service

In the early years of implementing provisions of the Endangered Species Act, recovery teams and plans usually each dealt with a single endangered or threatened species. It soon became evident, however, that not only would handling species in this fashion require an extremely lengthy period of time but also—and much more important—it was realized that it was habitat degradation, rather than direct harm to individuals of a species, that had usually brought about the organism's imperiled status.

Thus, the concept of protecting whole ecosystems, each often containing numerous endangered and threatened taxa, was developed. Many recovery teams formed thereafter were thus charged with considering entire ecologically related groups of organisms (for example, Hawaiian forest birds, Hawaiian waterbirds, and so on). This new view of the problem of conserving endangered biota highlighted the necessity of acquiring suitably extensive areas of native habitat in Hawai'i. With this goal in mind, during the past several years the Pacific Islands Ecoregion Office of the U.S. Fish and Wildlife Service in Honolulu has established a number of additional National Wildlife Refuges. Such Hawaiian areas, managed by the Service, are listed in Table 27.3. That office of the Service also continues its important work of administering and protecting the terrestrial and coral-reef ecosystems of the earlier established [Northwestern] Hawaiian Islands National Wildlife Refuge (see chapter 23) and the recently established Midway Atoll Refuge.

In addition, during the 1990s the U.S. Fish and Wildlife Service has provided well over $14.5 million for conservation projects throughout the Pacific, primarily on state and private lands. For example, the Service provides most of the operating funds for the Keauhou Bird Conservation Center, established in the late 1980s near Volcano on Hawai'i Island property provided by the Kamehameha Schools/Bishop Estate. This facility is now staffed by the Peregrine Fund, a nongovernmental organization. Since 1993 the Fund has been engaged in a quite successful propagation program aimed at captive-rearing and releasing, not only the Hawaiian Goose or *nēnē (Branta sandvicensis)* and Hawaiian Crow or *'alalā (Corvus hawaiiensis),* but also species of smaller endangered native forest birds.

National Park Service

There are five national parks in Hawai'i (Table 27.3), all managed by this Service of the U.S. Department of the Interior. Hawai'i Volcanoes on Hawai'i and Haleakalā on Maui were acquired early in the twentieth century, with the two units being administratively separated in 1961 and subsequently slightly enlarged. The smaller Kalaupapa (Moloka'i), Kaloko-Honokōhau (Hawai'i), and Pu'uhonua o Hōnaunau (Hawai'i) National Historical Parks were more recently obtained. The passage of the Endangered Species Act and similar federal legislation added

Table 27.2. Families and taxa numbers of endangered and threatened Hawaiian plants. These 292 federally listed taxa include ferns and fern allies along with the flowering plants. The letter E indicates an endangered taxon, and T a threatened one. (Data from various sources.)

Family Common Name	Family Scientific Name	Taxa Number
Maidenhair fern	Adiantaceae	1 E
Agave	Agavaceae	1 E
Amaranth	Amaranthaceae	4 E
Parsley	Apiaceae	3 E, 1 T
Dogbane	Apocynaceae	2 E
Ginseng	Araliaceae	2 E
Palm	Arecaceae	8 E
Spleenwort fern	Aspleniaceae	3 E
Sunflower	Asteraceae	30 E, 3 T
Mustard	Brassicaceae	1 E
Bellflower	Campanulaceae	50 E, 1 T
Pink	Caryophyllaceae	22 E, 2 T
Morning glory	Convolvulaceae	1 E
Gourd	Cucurbitaceae	1 E
Sedge	Cyperaceae	5 E
Spurge	Euphorbiaceae	9 E
Pea	Fabaceae	6 E
Flacourtia	Flacourtiaceae	1 E
Gentian	Gentianaceae	1 E
Geranium	Geraniaceae	2 E
African violet	Gesneriaceae	9 E, 1 T
Goodenia	Goodeniaceae	1 E
Finger fern	Grammitaceae	1 E
Mint	Lamiaceae	19 E
Logania	Loganiaceae	5 E
Club moss	Lycopodiaceae	2 E
Mallow	Malvaceae	15 E
Water-Clover fern	Marsileaceae	1 E
Myrsine	Myrsinaceae	1 E, 1 T
Myrtle	Myrtaceae	1 E
Orchid	Orchidaceae	1 E
Plantain	Plantaginaceae	5 E
Grass	Poaceae	9 E
Polypody fern	Polypodiaceae	4 E
Purslane	Portulacaceae	1 E
Primrose	Primulaceae	3 E
Buckthorn	Rhamnaceae	4 E
Rose	Rosaceae	1 E
Coffee	Rubiaceae	10 E
Rue	Rutaceae	15 E
Sandalwood	Santalaceae	2 E
Soapberry	Sapindaceae	2 E
Nightshade	Solanaceae	4 E
Nettle	Urticaceae	5 E
Violet	Violaceae	8 E, 1 T

Table 27.3. Federal and private biotic-protection areas in Hawai'i. The size of each is indicated in hectares (ha) and acres (a). Also given is the approximate number of entire examples of the 150 or so Hawaiian terrestrial natural communities (see the section in text on The Nature Conservancy of Hawai'i) included in each subcategory. The former *Kīpahulu Preserve has been transferred to the National Park Service. (Data from various sources.)

Type	Name	Size ha (a)	Number of Communities
Federal			
	National Wildlife Refuges	**237,252 (593,130)**	**21**
	Hakalau Forest (Hawai'i)	15,212 (38,030)	
	Hanalei (Kaua'i)	367 (917)	
	(Northwestern) Hawaiian Islands	101,767 (254,418)	
	Hulē'ia (Kaua'i)	96 (241)	
	James Campbell (O'ahu)	66 (164)	
	Kakahai'a (Moloka'i)	18 (45)	
	Keālia Pond (Maui)	277 (692)	
	Kīlauea Point (Kaua'i)	80 (200)	
	Midway	119,345 (298,362)	
	Pearl Harbor (O'ahu)	24 (61)	
	National Parks	**102,423 (256,056)**	**61**
	Haleakalā (Maui)	10,940 (27,350)	
	Hawai'i Volcanoes (Hawai'i)	86,919 (217,297)	
	Kalaupapa (Moloka'i)	4,361 (10,902)	
	Kaloko-Honokōhau (Hawai'i)	129 (322)	
	Pu'uhonua o Hōnaunau (Hawai'i)	74 (185)	
	Military Preserves	**240 (601)**	**4**
	Niuli'i Ponds (O'ahu)	35 (88)	
	Nu'upia Ponds (O'ahu)	193 (482)	
	Ulupa'u Crater Booby Colony (O'ahu)	12 (31)	
	National Marine Sanctuary	**358,400 (896,000)**	**—**
	Hawaiian Islands Humpback Whale	358,400 (896,000)	
Private			
	Preserves (via Nature Conservancy)	**10,187 (25,468)**	**48**
	East Maui Lava Tubes (Maui)	30 (75)	
	Honomalino (Hawai'i)	1,608 (4,021)	
	Honouliuli (O'ahu)	1,477 (3,692)	
	'Ihi'ihilauākea (O'ahu)	12 (30)	
	Kaluahonu (Kaua'i)	85 (213)	
	Kamakou (Moloka'i)	1,110 (2,774)	
	Kānepu'u (Lāna'i)	236 (590)	
	Kapunakea (Maui)	506 (1,264)	
	*Kīpahulu (Maui)	359 (898)	
	Mo'omomi (Moloka'i)	368 (921)	
	Pelekunu (Moloka'i)	2,304 (5,759)	
	Waikamoi (Maui)	2,092 (5,231)	

impetus to efforts of Parks' personnel to enhance protection of contained resources in all five, but especially the larger two. This is being done primarily through reintroduction and rehabilitation of Hawaiian biota, as well as through the elimination or control of alien plants and animals. Much of the basic and applied research necessary for this task is carried out by the Cooperative National Parks Resources Studies Unit, headquartered in the Department of Botany of the primary cooperating institution, the University of Hawai'i at Mānoa on O'ahu.

U.S. Military

It is also most encouraging, and extremely beneficial to the native Hawaiian environment, that the various branches of the armed forces have added environmental protection specialists to their personnel since passage of the National Environmental Policy Act and related laws. Table 27.3 lists the three native waterbird preserves set aside on military bases and managed for protection and enhancement of these avian populations, the first by the Navy and the other two by the Marine Corps. The U.S. Army is also carrying out significant and commendable protective ecosystem management in its Island training areas, especially on O'ahu, Maui, and Hawai'i.

National Marine Fisheries Service

This agency of the U.S. Department of Commerce is concerned primarily with maintenance and utilization of oceanic animal resources. The Hawai'i Office of this Service enforces provisions of the Marine Mammal Protection Act and Endangered Species Act in regard to all Island cetaceans, the Hawaiian Monk Seal, and all central Pacific marine turtles. (This Service has jurisdiction over these turtles while at sea, and the U.S. Fish and Wildlife Service is responsible for them on shore.) Most of the resources of the Hawai'i Office are devoted to protection of the breeding population of the migratory Humpback Whale or koholā (Megaptera novaeangliae) while in island waters, as well as to a concerted study of the Hawaiian Monk Seal in the various Northwestern Hawaiian Islands (see chapters 19, 23), including rescue and rehabilitation of orphaned, ill, and injured individuals. Although it is a part of the U.S. Fish and Wildlife Service, the Hawai'i Cooperative Fishery Unit, based at the Department of Zoology of the University of Hawai'i at Mānoa, works closely with the National Marine Fisheries Service and similarly oriented state agencies in study, preservation, and protection of Hawaiian native marine and freshwater aquatic resources.

National Oceanic and Atmospheric Administration

A recent augmentation of Island wildlife protection is the Hawaiian Islands Humpback Whale National Marine Sanctuary, established in general principle by Congress in 1992 and regulated by this Administration. As finally approved by the governor of Hawai'i, the sanctuary encompasses approximately 3,640 km2 (1,400 square miles) and is designed to protect the wintering individuals (including cow-calf pairs) of this cetacean within, primarily, the 100-fathom (183-m or 600-foot) submarine contour around substantial portions of the six largest main islands.

In addition to federal agencies, several state and private organizations now have as their primary objectives either the acquisition and administration of areas containing native Hawaiian ecosystems or the study and management of native Hawaiian biota. As a result of the efforts of these and the previously cited federal groups, approximately 15 percent of the land within the state has now been set aside for protection of native ecosystems.

STATE AGENCIES

Natural Area Reserves System Commission

This official body was established in 1970 to identify and recommend to the governor for designation as natural area reserves state-owned land units throughout the Islands typifying the many kinds of native Hawaiian ecosystems (Figure 27.1). The Commission also sets management policy, which may vary greatly among the different reserves but is designed to allow as many human activities as possible consistent with preservation of the area. For example, hunting of alien game birds and mammals may be allowed in some, but only camping, nonconsumptive actions, and research in others. Nineteen reserves have been officially designated (Table 27.4), and several more are under consideration.

Also, since the early 1990s, the State of Hawai'i—sometimes with federal aid—has initiated three types of management programs aimed at permanently protecting relatively undisturbed native areas on private lands. For example, State Natural Area Partnership agreements provide landowners two-thirds of the funds needed to enhance and maintain suitable lands for the benefit of native Hawaiian biota.

State Division of Forestry and Wildlife

This unit within the Hawai'i Department of Land and Natural Resources primarily manages plantations of alien timber as well as hunting areas containing substantial numbers of introduced game birds and mammals. Funds for the latter task are received largely from the Pittman-Robertson Federal Aid in Wildlife Restoration program, which is administered by the U.S. Fish

Figure 27.1. 'Āhihi-Kīna'u Natural Area Reserve on Maui. This was established as the first such reserve in 1973 and includes portions of a 200-year-old lava flow, anchialine ponds (center of photograph), and the adjoining marine reef area. (Photograph courtesy of U.S. Fish and Wildlife Service.)

Table 27.4. State government biotic-protection areas in Hawai'i. The size of each is indicated in hectares (ha) and acres (a). Also given is the approximate number of entire examples of the 150 or so Hawaiian terrestrial natural communities (see the section in text on The Nature Conservancy of Hawai'i) included in each subcategory. Privately owned areas managed by the state are indicated with an asterisk (*). (Data from various sources.)

Type Name	Size ha (a)	Number of Communities
Natural Area Reserves	43,674 (109,186)	68
'Āhihi-Kīna'u (Maui)	818 (2,045)	
Hanawī (Maui)	3,000 (7,500)	
Honoonāpali (Kaua'i)	1,260 (3,150)	
Ka'ena Point (O'ahu)	14 (34)	
KahauaLe'a (Hawai'i)	6,690 (16,726)	
Kanaio (Maui)	350 (876)	
Kīpāhoehoe (Hawai'i)	2,233 (5,583)	
Ku'ia (Kaua'i)	654 (1,636)	
Laupāhoehoe (Hawai'i)	3,158 (7,894)	
Manukā (Hawai'i)	10,220 (25,550)	
Mauna Kea Ice Age (Hawai'i)	1,558 (3,894)	
Mount Ka'ala (O'ahu)	440 (1,100)	
Oloku'i (Moloka'i)	648 (1,620)	
Pahole (O'ahu)	263 (658)	
Pu'u Ali'i (Moloka'i)	532 (1,330)	
Pu'u Maka'ala (Hawai'i)	4,842 (12,106)	
Pu'u o 'Umi (Hawai'i)	4,057 (10,142)	
Waiākea 1942 Lava Flow (Hawai'i)	256 (640)	
West Maui (Maui)	2,681 (6,702)	
Wilderness Preserve	3,760 (9,400)	8
Alaka'i (Kaua'i)	3,760 (9,400)	
Plant or Animal Sanctuaries	33,572 (83,929)	12
*Kahuku *Nēnē* (Hawai'i)	8,000 (20,000)	
Kamiloloa *Sesbania* (Moloka'i)	4 (10)	
Kanahā Pond (Maui)	58 (145)	
*Keauhou 1 *Nēnē* (Hawai'i)	3,360 (8,400)	
*Keauhou 2 *Nēnē* (Hawai'i)	5,071 (12,678)	
Kīpuka 'Āinahou *Nēnē* (Hawai'i)	15,360 (38,400)	
Koai'a (Hawai'i)	5 (13)	
Manawainui Gulch (Maui)	23 (56)	
Mauna Kea Silversword (Hawai'i)	20 (50)	
Paikō Lagoon (O'ahu)	13 (33)	
Pa'upa'u (Maui)	14 (34)	
Polipoli *Geranium* (Maui)	0.6 (1.5)	

(Continued on following page)

Table 27.4. *(continued)* State government biotic-protection areas in Hawai'i. The size of each is indicated in hectares (ha) and acres (a). Also given is the approximate number of entire examples of the 150 or so Hawaiian terrestrial natural communities (see the section in text on The Nature Conservancy of Hawai'i) included in each subcategory. Privately owned areas managed by the state are indicated with an asterisk (*). (Data from various sources.)

Type	Name	Size ha (a)	Number of Communities
	Pu'uwa'awa'a *'Alalā* (Hawai'i)	1,523 (3,807)	
	Pu'uwa'awa'a *Hibiscadelphis* (Hawai'i)	<0.08 (<0.2)	
	Upper Waiākea Bog Silversword (Hawai'i)	0.3 (0.8)	
	(35 offshore seabird islets)	120 (300)	
Marine Life Conservation Districts		**587 (1,469)**	—
	Hanauma Bay (O'ahu)	40 (101)	
	Honolua-Makuleia (Maui)	18 (45)	
	Kealakekua Bay (Hawai'i)	126 (315)	
	Lapakahi (Hawai'i)	58 (146)	
	Mānele-Hulopo'e (Lāna'i)	124 (309)	
	Molokini Shoal (off Maui)	80 (200)	
	Old Kona Airport (Hawai'i)	87 (217)	
	Pūpūkea (O'ahu)	10 (25)	
	Waialea (Hawai'i)	14 (35)	
	Waikīkī (O'ahu)	30 (76)	

and Wildlife Service. This program was established by Congress many years ago to help mainland states restore depleted stocks of, primarily, *native* game birds and mammals and is financed by a tax on arms, ammunition, and archery supplies. Although the endemic Hawaiian Goose, as well as various endemic waterbirds and indigenous migratory shorebirds were hunted up to the beginning of World War II (the goose almost to extinction), since that time the only birds that may be shot in Hawai'i are introduced game species. Because there are no native mammals to be hunted in Hawai'i, the Pittman-Robertson funds allotted to mammals in the state were originally spent solely to manage and protect alien hoofed game species. By the mid-1970s, however, a changing philosophy on the part of both the state and the U.S. Fish and Wildlife Service enabled part of this money to be spent on research and rehabilitation of endangered and threatened native nongame species, primarily birds. Since that time, the state Division's Wildlife Branch has devoted at least some of its efforts to preserving and restoring the Islands' original biotic resources, often under the pressure of competing demands from variously oriented citizen factions.

The Division is also responsible for a number of state forest reserves (which are managed primarily for hunting and alleged timber production rather than for specific protection of native biota) and the Alaka'i Wilderness Preserve on Kaua'i, as well as for a number of native plant and animal sanctuaries throughout the state (Table 27.4).

An Endangered Species Propagation Facility, similar to the previously mentioned Keauhou Bird Conservation Center near Volcano, was originally located at Pōhakuloa on Hawai'i, but is now located at Olinda on Maui. It was established to carry out captive breeding and release into the wild of the Hawaiian Goose and Hawaiian Crow (Figure 27.2) and was initially a State Division of Forestry and Wildlife facility, maintained with financial and other assistance from the federal government. In 1996, however, its operation was contracted to the private Peregrine Fund, which has now included propagation of small endangered and other native forest birds in the facility's activities.

State Division of Aquatic Resources

This division of the Department of Land and Natural Resources includes among its activities management of alien and native fishes in nearshore waters and freshwater bodies. In a manner analogous to that of the Division of Forestry and Wildlife, substantial funds are received under the Dingell-Johnson Federal Aid in Fish Restoration program for management of sportfishing, including that of introduced freshwater species. Part of this federal money, however, is now being used for basic research and protection of imperiled native freshwater fishes and their associated invertebrate stream fauna. The Marine Life Conservation Districts listed in Table 27.4 also receive significant protection and management attention from the Division, and these sanctuaries are an important component in preservation of native aquatic resources. Also within the Department of Land and Natural Resources is a Commission on Water Resource Management, which is charged with the protection and management of freshwater resources in the state. Working with the Division of Aquatic Resources and other state as well as county agencies, the Commission determines, among other aims, which bodies of freshwater should be protected to adequately conserve native biota.

Figure 27.2. Hawaiian Crow chick hatched at the Keauhou Bird Conservation Center on Hawai'i. The puppeted hand feeding the young bird simulates a parent bird so that the chick will not imprint on humans. This Center and a similar one at Olinda, Maui, produce a variety of Hawaiian forest birds as well as the Hawaiian Goose or *Nēnē,* and offspring are periodically released to supplement wild populations. (Photograph courtesy of U.S. Fish and Wildlife Service.)

State Department of Agriculture

As discussed in the preceding two chapters, one of the greatest threats to the surviving native Hawaiian biota is the presence of alien species of animals and plants. In the past two decades or so, recognition of this fact has resulted in much more rigorous efforts on the part of most governmental agencies to prevent the introduction of additional alien taxa, as well as to eliminate or mitigate the effects of those already present. The Hawai'i Department of Agriculture works with its federal counterpart to prevent the intentional or accidental importation (and exportation) of alien plants and animals detrimental to health, commerce, and native biota. Activities in this regard include inspection of biological material arriving and leaving by sea and air, as well as education of visitors concerning prohibited organisms. In the 1990s, detection and elimination of any arriving individuals of the Brown Tree Snake *(Boiga irregularis)* became of extremely high priority to both the state and federal agencies. Several of these snakes have already been found in Hawai'i, all on O'ahu. Most or all of these apparently entered in aircraft or their cargo from Guam in the Mariana Islands, where extremely dense populations of this alien reptile (evidently inadvertently introduced there about 1950) have extirpated several endemic bird species, in addition to causing serious problems for the human inhabitants.

Application must also be made to the Department by other state agencies and private interests for the intentional importation of most plants and animals (for example, new agricultural crops, pets other than cats and dogs, zoo animals, research biota, and the like). Its Plant Quarantine Branch then seeks advice regarding the advisability of the proposed importation from uncompensated advisory groups comprising state administrators, commercial interests, and nongovernmental scientists. The initial level of advice is provided by one of several specialized Advisory Subcommittees, with the information passed on to an Advisory Committee on Plants and Animals, similarly composed of additional knowledgeable individuals. The Committee's advice as to whether or not the proposed importation should be allowed, and under what conditions, is then submitted to the Board of Agriculture for final action. There is also a similar State Animal Species Advisory Commission that the Division of Forestry and Wildlife may call upon for advice on game birds and mammals whose importation is contemplated by the Division.

The State Department of Agriculture also carries out a program of **biological control** (also discussed in chapters 16 and 26), in which invertebrate predators or microorganisms especially harmful to introduced alien plant and animal pest species are sought in the foreign homeland of the organism and brought to Hawai'i for appropriate testing and potential release. In general, this biocontrol of most pest animals has been much less successful than similar efforts directed at unwanted plants.

PRIVATE ORGANIZATIONS

The Nature Conservancy of Hawai'i

This Island affiliate of the national nonprofit Nature Conservancy is the nongovernmental organization in Hawai'i that has been almost solely responsible for preserving substantial amounts of private land containing native Hawaiian ecosystems, managing eleven preserves on six main islands (Table 27.3, Figure 27.3). The Hawai'i office typically procures protection of such prime areas by either outright purchase, or negotiation of perpetual or long-term conservation easements and management agreements. It may then install its own preserve management staff or arrange a transfer agreement with a federal, state, or private entity. In the case of, for instance, Kīpahulu Preserve acquired on southeastern Maui, essentially all of the area, which is contiguous with Haleakalā National Park, was transferred to the National Park Service, because it seemed logically best managed by Park personnel. Another extremely valuable contribution of the Hawai'i affiliate has been its compilation of a state-wide computerized database (The Hawai'i Natural Heritage Program, at web site http://www.tnc.org) containing the habitat locations of endangered, threatened, and rare Hawaiian plants and animals. From this massive compilation of over ten thousand records, it has been determined that about 150 natural groupings of native terrestrial plants and animals are consistently found together in various parts of the state. These biotic ecosystems are termed "natural communities" and have been geographically delimited by the organization, with the rarest included in the Heritage Program database. Further, by rating such factors as the degree of endangerment or rarity of species and communities, it has been possible to prioritize the communities in regard to necessity of preservation.

Other Private Organizations

Several Island organizations with memberships especially interested in one or more aspects of the native Hawaiian biota should be specifically mentioned for their long-continued stout advocacy of environmental protection. Among their major activities are frequent field trips and pub-

Figure 27.3. Pig-proof fencing at The Nature Conservancy of Hawai'i Kamakou Preserve on Moloka'i. This barrier now limits movement of the damaging alien mammals into a native forest area previously heavily impacted by them. Island hunters have been most helpful in lending their aid to reduce Pig numbers in the Preserve. (Photograph by The Nature Conservancy of Hawai'i, used with permission.)

lic dissemination of Hawaiian natural history information. Also, especially in the case of the first two groups named here, important functions are legislative lobbying, presentation of testimony at public hearings, and comment on environmental documents such as Environmental Impact Statements, not to mention entrance as plaintiffs in lawsuits necessary to enforce environmental protection laws.

The Hawai'i Chapter of the national Sierra Club maintains membership groups on each of the larger main islands. Clearing of alien vegetation from trails, nature preserves, and sanctuaries throughout the state is only one of its several more obvious field conservation activities. The Hawai'i Audubon Society is similarly a local affiliate of a national organization, and its periodic censuses of the numbers and location of native and alien avifauna provide valuable continually updated information to resource managers in the state. The National Tropical Botanical Garden on Kaua'i (formerly the Pacific Tropical Botanical Garden) is perhaps the foremost among several Island botanical organizations preserving and propagating rare native Hawaiian plants, and distributing them for wild planting to augment natural populations. Other important botanical groups involved in propagation and research work are the Harold L. Lyon Arboretum of the University of Hawai'i at Mānoa, Waimea Arboretum and Botanic Garden, and Honolulu Botanical Gardens (including Foster Botanical Garden), all on O'ahu.

Among their other activities, most of the preceding private organizations include various formal or informal educational programs important in increasing awareness and protection of native Hawaiian ecosystems. Additional groups are oriented almost entirely toward such environmental education, especially of secondary schoolchildren and teachers. Foremost among these are Moanalua Gardens Foundation on O'ahu, whose work includes production of instructional guides to major unique natural features on various islands. The Foundation now maintains the privately funded 'Ōhi'a Project, which has produced a series of printed and visual environmental-education units designed for kindergarten through eighth-grade classes. The Hawai'i Nature Center has field instructional centers for school students on both O'ahu and Maui. The Conservation Council for Hawai'i, a local affiliate of the National Wildlife Federation, distributes to Island schools natural history material provided yearly by the Federation, usually adding its own information sheets tailored to Hawaiian biology.

In the category of what might best be considered adult environmental education, the monthly periodical ***Environment Hawai'i,*** established in 1990 and edited by Patricia Tummons, has persistently and meticulously researched and publicized numerous governmental and private actions that currently have—or, if carried out, would have had—significant detrimental effects on the Hawaiian natural environment.

The Bernice Pauahi Bishop Museum in Honolulu is the official State Museum of Natural and Cultural History, but is currently forced by shortage of funds to curtail many of its former activities in public education and scientific research. It was the initial host institution of the just-mentioned 'Ōhi'a Project. In still managing to provide minimal curatorial care for its irreplaceable research and display collections, the Museum provides an indispensable service to protection of the Hawaiian natural environment through the **Hawaii Biological Survey.** This survey, established by the state legislature in 1992 as a program of the Museum, now provides essential basic taxonomic, distributional, and other related information on many groups of Island terrestrial and marine organisms in the form of a comprehensive computerized biological database (available at web site http://www.bishop.hawaii.org/bishop/HBS/hbs1.html). These data are periodically updated, with the research results leading to revisions published annually as Records of the Hawaii Biological Survey in the *Bishop Museum Occasional Papers,* in the form of either original articles or citations to papers published elsewhere.

Earthjustice (formerly Sierra Club Legal Defense Fund), currently with a total of forty attorneys in nine offices nationwide, opened a Mid-Pacific Office in Honolulu during 1988. This organization, administratively separate from the Sierra Club, does not bring suit on its own, but acts as attorney for requesting environmentally aggrieved parties. Without mandatory charge to these plaintiffs, the Hawai'i office has carried out a substantial number of environmental-protection lawsuits involving matters in Hawai'i as well as other parts of the insular Pacific administered by the United States. Among the better known of such legal actions is one of 1978 that the following year forced the Hawai'i Board of Land and Natural Resources to begin removing alien game mammals from Mauna Kea on Hawai'i. These hoofed animals were being maintained there by the state solely for hunting and were steadily destroying not only their own food supply, but also the critical habitat of the *Palila (Loxioides bailleui),* an endangered Hawaiian honeycreeper (which was named as the lead plaintiff in the case [Plate 27.1]). Also, under threat of legal action by the Fund early in the 1990s, the National Marine Fisheries Service agreed to accept its own recovery team's recommended critical habitat for the Hawaiian Monk Seal, rather than a substantially more limited area that high-level Service administrators attempted to designate. More recently, in another out-of-court settlement, the U.S. Fish and Wildlife Service agreed to various actions expediting a more timely listing of most endangered Hawaiian plants and to reconsider nondesignation of critical habitat for dozens of listed Hawaiian plants.

SUGGESTED REFERENCES

Beletsky 2000; Costin and Groves (eds.) 1973; Loope and Juvik 1998; Pratt and Gon 1998; Royte 1995; Staples and Cowie (eds.) 2001; Stone and Stone (eds.) 1989; Stone et al. (eds.) 1992; Tummons (ed.) 1990–present; Turner 1990.

AUDIOVISUAL AIDS

Guided by the Nene; Wilderness.

28

Historic Hawaiian Naturalists

Undoubtedly, a few individuals of each pre-Contact Hawaiian generation were much more conversant than others in natural history matters and probably routinely passed on their accumulated knowledge to particularly interested younger persons. But, unfortunately, these accomplished **prehistoric naturalists** cannot be recognized and accorded the honor they deserve because of the lack of any written record of their observations. Even chants and recited legends have not preserved any significant amount of detailed noncultural natural history information. For example, although occasional names of wild birds and other native animals appear in this traditional literature, there is no reference that can be applied for certain to any of the various prehistorically extinct types of large flightless birds that must have been so common in early Polynesian times (see chapters 20, 22). Similarly, from a botanical standpoint, there is no description of the appearance or composition of the extensive lowland forests that occurred throughout the Islands before their clearing by prehistoric Hawaiians (see chapter 25).

NATIVE HAWAIIAN NATURALISTS

We are, however, fortunate in having at least a partial record of late pre-Contact Hawaiian natural (and cultural) history preserved in the writings of a few native Hawaiians: **David Malo** (born 1795, died 1853 [Figure 28.1]), who wrote between 1831 and 1839; **John Papa Iʻi** (1800–1870), writing between 1866 and 1870; **Samuel Manaiakalani Kamakau** (1815–1876), writing between 1865 and 1871; and **Kepelino** or, as called by the French priests, "Zepherino" (= Kahoalii Keauokalani; ca. 1830–1878), writing between 1853 and about 1869.

Most of these authors produced their works at the urging of resident non-Hawaiians who realized the necessity of recording for posterity as much as possible of pre-Contact Hawaiian history. These Native Hawaiian observations are extremely important, but they represent at best very incomplete accounts of the full range of the prehistoric knowledge of natural history. All four of these observers were born after the arrival of non-Polynesians, so their statements regarding natural history as well as other pre-Contact phenomena were necessarily based solely on second-hand information supplied by their elders. And they were recording this information more than a half century after Contact, after being influenced to various degrees by missionaries and other foreigners. Also, with the apparently relatively limited amount of travel by most commoners among the Islands in the Polynesian and early historic periods, each native historian was primarily conversant with the biota and cultural activities of only parts of one or two main islands.

Thus, most of pre-Contact Hawaiian natural history—and even much of the cultural history—must now be inferred from paleontological and archaeological investigations. In regard to post-Contact natural history, however, more direct information is available, and the major participants who collected the pertinent data are discussed in the remainder of this chapter.

Preface by the Author

I do not suppose the following history to be free from mistakes, in that the material for it has come from oral traditions; consequently it is marred by errors of human judgment and does not approach the accuracy of the word of God.

Figure 28.1. David Malo (1795–1853), astute Native Hawaiian natural historian. His interpretations of pre-Contact and subsequent social and biological conditions are contained in several manuscripts written between 1831 and 1839. (Frontispiece of Malo [1951]; engraving apparently from an original by Alfred T. Agate, first published as Plate III in Vol. 9 of Wilkes [1844–1874].)

HISTORIC FOREIGN NATURALISTS

A great deal of the information on the pioneer naturalists presented here is drawn from a more detailed account by E. Alison Kay (see Kay [1972] entry in References Cited section) and is similarly divided, with slight modification, into three partially overlapping phases. These are (1) the **Explorer-Naturalist Period,** extending from Contact in 1778 to about 1850; (2) the **Resident Amateur Naturalist Period,** from arrival of the first Christian missionaries in 1820 to approximately 1890; and (3) the **Professional Naturalist Period,** beginning about 1870. This last period is still ongoing, of course, but because of spatial limitations, the discussion here is limited to work done up to 1900.

THE EXPLORER-NATURALIST PERIOD: 1778–1850

The Expeditions

All of the great European exploring voyagers of the eighteenth and early nineteenth centuries were instructed by their sponsors to observe and record natural history information relating to any new lands they found. This charge was made primarily with a view toward potential economic gain, but in many cases there was also the secondary scientific goal of learning about natural attributes of previously unknown areas. It was the usual practice on expeditions up to the late eighteenth century to have the college-educated surgeon also serve as naturalist. By about the beginning of the 1800s, however, it was becoming common to include individuals especially versed in biology and geology, whose sole duty was to record natural history observations and collect specimens. In a number of cases, the captain and officers of the expedition ships also proved to be most ardent observers and recorders of biological and cultural information. Quite likely this activity provided them a welcome relief from the boredom that developed on voyages usually lasting between 3 and 6 or more years.

Among the number of exploring expeditions visiting the Hawaiian Islands before 1850, those contributing significantly to the knowledge of the archipelago's natural history are listed in Table 28.1, the English being the leaders in this activity. **James Cook,** on his expedition's third voyage to the Pacific of 1776–1780, captained the first group of non-Polynesians known to have reached the Hawaiian Islands. (The initial historic name of **"Sandwich Islands"** given the archipelago by Cook was to honor the fourth earl of Sandwich, then First Lord of the British Admiralty.)

Although Cook was killed at Kealakekua Bay on Hawai'i early in 1779, upon the expedition's return to England the following year word of this previously unrecorded archipelago quickly reached many other parts of the world. As a result, not only did a number of additional English expeditions to the Hawaiian Islands seek out and record considerably more biological information, but there was at least one visiting expedition each from France, Prussia ("Germany"), and Russia. The Explorer-Naturalist phase was in its last decade before the first non-European exploring voyage reached the Islands. This was the 6-month 1840–1841 scientific visit of the impressive United States Exploring Expedition, comprising six ships under the command of U.S. Navy Lieutenant **Charles Wilkes** and carrying a number of natural history specialists. Also noted in Table 28.1 are the occasional adventurous trained naturalists who worked in the Islands during this early period, often for many months at a time, bearing their own living expenses as well as costs of transportation on whaling and merchant ships.

Expedition Naturalists

The chief observers of Hawaiian natural history sailing on all of these major voyages of exploration and discovery are listed in Table 28.2, along with their primary scientific field. The independent naturalists are also included under their fields. The written records of these early naturalists may not appear to have made a significant contribution to understanding the ecology and, especially, evolution of the Hawaiian biota. It should be realized, however, that their work was carried out before the appearance of Darwin's evolutionary theory of 1859 (see chapter 10). Simple basic recording of the biota found in various parts of the world and brief preliminary descriptions of the multitudinous new species encountered were the necessities of the day. Critical synthesis as well as ecological and evolutionary interpretation of the findings did not come until much later. The plant and animal specimens collected by most of the naturalists of this

Table 28.1. Exploring expeditions and independent travelers to Hawai'i (1778–1850) by nationality. Only those recording significant Hawaiian natural history information are listed. Years of visiting the Islands are also noted. (Data from various sources.)

Nationality Leader	Years in Hawai'i
English	
James Cook	1778–1779
George Dixon and Nathaniel Portlock	1785–1788
George Vancouver	1792–1794
George Anson, Lord Byron	1825
Frederick W. Beechey	1826–1827
David Douglas (independent)	1832–1834
Meredith Gairdner (independent)	1833, 1836–1837
Sir Edward Belcher	1837, 1839
Henry Kellett	1850
French	
Louis C. D. de Freycinet	1819
Auguste-Nicolas Vaillant	1836–1837
P. Adolphe Lesson (independent)	<1842?
Prussian	
W. Wendt	1831
Ferdinand Deppe (independent)	1836
Richard Philippi (independent)	<1842?
Russian	
Otto E. von Kotzebue	1816–1817, 1824–1825
American	
Thomas Nuttall (independent)	1835
John K. Townsend (independent)	1835, 1836
Charles Wilkes	1840–1841

period were not formally described by them, but rather by staff members of various European and American museums, zoological parks, and botanical gardens.

To point out at random the work of just a few of the early expedition naturalists, it might be noted that **Charles Clerke,** although he had to assume command of Cook's third expedition after the latter's death, still found time to record a wealth of information on natural history subjects, especially Hawaiian plants and birds. The biological observations of **William Anderson,** surgeon, provided much of the information used in the official record of the third expedition. Other members of this voyage also made significant biological contributions: the illustrations of assistant surgeon **William Ellis** (not the later missionary of the same name [see discussion later in this chapter]) and artist **John Webber** first portrayed the unique Hawaiian avifauna for the world (Figure 28.2). Their shipmate **John Ledyard,** while unsuccessfully attempting the first foreign ascent of Hawai'i Island's Mauna Loa, set down a good record of the effectively pre-Contact vegetation on the volcano's lower slopes. Some of the plants collected by the expedition's **David Nelson** were reexamined in European collections by the venerable Hawai'i botanist Harold St. John in the mid-1900s. This study showed that several weed species now well known in the Islands had been introduced by ancient Polynesians (see chapter 25) rather than, as had previously been assumed, by early historic immigrants. Although not strictly a natural history endeavor, various Hawaiian coastlines were surveyed by the expedition member **William Bligh,** who years later would become better known as the tyrannical captain of the ill-fated HMS *Bounty* and its mutinous crew.

Botanist **James McRae** (frequently misspelled "Macrae") sailed on the 1825 HMS *Blonde* voyage of **George Anson, Lord Byron** (first cousin and title successor of the famous poet), which had the solemn duty of returning the bodies of King Kamehameha II (Liholiho) and Queen Kamāmalu to Hawai'i after their unfortunate deaths from measles in England. McRae was the first to record a journal characterization of the striking endemic Silversword or *'āhina-hina (Argyroxiphium sandwicense)* for the outside world, although he did not prepare the formal scientific description. The Byron Expedition also collected five species of the terrestrial O'ahu little agate shells or *pūpū hinuhinu,* which subsequently provided the scientific basis of the endemic Hawaiian genus *Achatinella* (see chapter 18). The first sizable numbers of Hawaiian fishes to be received by European scientific institutions were collected by **Jean R. C. Quoy** and **Joseph P. Gaimard** on the 1819 **Louis C. D. de Freycinet** French expedition.

Geologist **James D. Dana,** already partially chronicled in chapter 5, was mineralogist with the Wilkes Expedition. He produced by far the most definitive descriptive work on Hawaiian volcanoes and related geological features of any nonresident natural historian in the Islands. Dana was also one of the few scientists of the Explorer-Naturalist phase to extensively synthesize his observations and present this work in published form.

Early Independent Travelers

Among the early scientific observers not attached to expeditions, the English botanist **David Douglas** is especially illustrious. He had already made important contributions to botanical knowledge of the American Pacific Northwest, and in Hawai'i he carried out similarly valuable studies in botany. In addition to sending many Island plant specimens to England, Douglas provided the first breeding pair of Hawaiian Geese or *Nēnē (Branta sandvicensis)* to reach England alive. In the field of geology, he carried out scientific ascents of Hawai'i Island's Mauna Loa and Mauna Kea. Douglas died under mysterious circumstances in a cattle-trap pit on the slopes of

Table 28.2. Expedition naturalists and independent travelers in Hawai'i (1778–1850) by scientific field. Only those collecting significant amounts of Hawaiian biological material are listed. Any association with the expeditions listed in Table 28.1 is also indicated. (Data from various sources.)

Scientific Field Name	Association
General natural history	
William Anderson	Cook Expedition
Charles Clerke	Cook Expedition
John Ledyard	Cook Expedition
Johann F. Eschscholtz	von Kotzebue Expedition
Ferdinand Deppe	(independent Prussian)
Meredith Gairdner	(independent English)
Richard B. Hinds	Belcher Expedition
Joseph Drayton	Wilkes Expedition
William Rich	Wilkes Expedition
Geology	
James D. Dana	Wilkes Expedition
Botany	
David Nelson	Cook Expedition
Archibald Menzies	Vancouver Expedition
Louis C. A. von Chamisso	von Kotzebue Expedition
Charles Gaudichaud-Beaupré	Freycinet and Vaillant Expeditions
James McRae	Byron Expedition
George T. Lay	Beechey Expedition
Alexander Collie	Beechey Expedition
David Douglas	(independent English)
Thomas Nuttall	(independent American)
William E. Brackenridge	Wilkes Expedition
Charles Pickering	Wilkes Expedition
Berthold C. Seemann	Kellett Expedition
Malacology (and other invertebrate studies)	
George Dixon	Dixon and Portlock Expedition
Franz J. F. Meyen	Wendt Expedition
J. Fortune T. Eydoux	Vaillant Expedition
Louis F. A. Souleyet	Vaillant Expedition
P. Adolphe Lesson	(independent French)
Richard Philippi	(independent Prussian)
Joseph P. Couthouy	Wilkes Expedition
Ichthyology	
Jean R. C. Quoy	Freycinet Expedition
Joseph P. Gaimard	Freycinet Expedition
Ornithology	
William Ellis	Cook Expedition
John Webber	Cook Expedition
Andrew Bloxam	Byron Expedition
John K. Townsend	(independent American)
Titian R. Peale	Wilkes Expedition

Mauna Kea in 1834. His untimely death at 36 possibly deprived the world of an early comprehensive Hawaiian botanical manual, and such a work would not appear for another half century. Douglas is honored by the common name of the native Western American Douglas Fir, *Pseudotsuga menziesii,* the specific name of which similarly commemorates the botanical work of **Archibald Menzies,** who had preceded Douglas to Hawai'i as surgeon on the Vancouver Expedition.

As a result of the work of Douglas, Menzies, and other botanizing naturalists, the world's scientists recognized that a thorough descriptive and interpretive study of the endemic plants of such an isolated island group would be of immense value. In fact, in 1850 Charles Darwin, who was never able to visit the archipelago, offered the then-substantial sum of £50 toward expenses of a botanist to carry out extended plant studies in the Hawaiian Islands. He had no takers at the time, but it happens that amateur naturalists living in the Islands were already engaged in such endeavors (see the next section on Resident Amateur Naturalists).

Among other independent scientists traveling to the Islands during this period were **Thomas Nuttall** and **John K. Townsend,** well-known American botanist and ornithologist, respectively, who together investigated various parts of Kaua'i and O'ahu in 1835. These accomplished observers and collectors provided larger scientific institutions in the United States with most of the first Hawaiian natural history specimens to reach that country, including crus-

Figure 28.2. A typical bird illustration of the Explorer-Naturalist Period. Painting of Thin-billed Prion (*Pachyptila belcheri* [Shearwater family Procellariidae]) of the far Southwest Pacific by William Ellis, assistant surgeon on James Cook's third voyage, 1776–1780. (Plate 37b of Lysaght [1959]; copyright 1959, Trustees of the British Museum, used with permission.)

taceans and mollusks along with plants and fishes. Part of Nuttall's large personal collection of Hawaiian mollusks was also eventually deposited in the British Museum of Natural History (now called the Natural History Museum).

THE RESIDENT AMATEUR NATURALIST PERIOD: 1820–1890

Missionaries

This phase may be regarded as beginning with the arrival in 1820 of seven married couples from New England, who formed the first Christian missionary "Company" to the Hawaiian Islands. By 1844, over seventy more families in eleven additional companies would emigrate to a new life in the Islands. Although the missionaries' primary task was, of course, proselytizing among Native Hawaiians, many had included various natural science classes in their primarily classic education at prominent New England colleges. Although not highly trained in specific scientific fields, once in Hawai'i many took the opportunity not only to accurately record natural history observations but also to collect geological and biological specimens for better-known eastern American college professors and other scientists. Another critical, although indirect, natural history contribution of these early missionaries was their schooling of Native Hawaiians. Their encouragement of the more interested of these (for example, David Malo) to write down or dictate their knowledge of Island culture and natural history resulted in preservation of much pertinent information that would otherwise have been lost.

The missionaries who were especially eminent in describing various aspects of Hawaiian natural science are listed in Table 28.3. Fortunately, many of these missionary observations became widely available to the rest of the world in printed form rather than remaining essentially hidden in handwritten journals as in the past. Among those most eclectic in such observations was **William Ellis** (actually only a visiting member of an English missionary society; not related to the surgeon of Cook's third voyage), who in the company of three resident missionaries spent the summer of 1823 walking around the island of Hawai'i scouting for possible future mission sites. Ellis recorded a relatively enormous amount of information regarding early post-Contact Hawaiian natural history as well as ethnology during this journey. Recognizing the scientific importance of such a record, **Benjamin Silliman,** Yale professor and editor of the respected and widely read *American Journal of Science,* facilitated publication in it of an excerpt of Ellis' Hawaiian observations. For decades to come, this journal remained one of the primary publication outlets for scientific contributions from the Islands.

Among the missionaries who tended to specialize in geological observations, Reverend **Titus Coan** described various aspects of the volcanoes Kīlauea and Mauna Loa in a long series of papers published between 1850 and 1882. His continued attention to the former volcano even gained him the local appellation "Bishop of Kīlauea." An even more interesting recorder of geological events was **Sarah Joiner Lyman** (Figure 28.3), who from 1833 faithfully maintained a record of all earthquakes felt at her Hawai'i Island missionary station in Hilo for over 50 years, often quantifying an earthquake's severity by the number of chinaware pieces shaken off her household shelves. Most of the remaining missionaries did not keep such detailed natural history records, but some still ultimately contributed greatly to advancement of Hawaiian scientific knowledge through their assiduous collection of biological specimens, especially plants and mollusks. These assemblages formed the basis of extensive scientific works by biological specialists in eastern American colleges and museums.

Missionary Sons

If the original missionary men and women in Hawai'i, being engaged primarily in religious work, could not devote a great amount of their time to secular matters, the same did not hold true for their progeny. In very few instances did the latter follow their parents' calling, but, rather, eventually entered and prospered in a variety of other occupations in the Islands. (In fact, a number of the missionary family names mentioned here are still quite familiar ones among the business and professional community of the state.) The missionary children were educated

Table 28.3. Resident amateur naturalists in Hawai'i (1820–1890) by scientific field. Only those contributing significantly to Hawaiian scientific knowledge are listed. The primary vocation or relationship of each is also indicated. (Data from various sources.)

Scientific Field Name	Occupation/Relationship
General natural history	
William Ellis	Missionary
William D. Alexander	Missionary son
Albert B. Lyons	Missionary son
David D. Baldwin	Missionary son
P. E. Th(é)ôdore Ballieu	French consul
Valdemar Knudsen	Rancher
Geology	
Titus Coan	Missionary
Sarah Joiner Lyman	Missionary
Titus M. Coan	Missionary son
Sereno E. Bishop	Missionary son
William L. Green	Businessman
Botany	
Edward Bailey	Missionary
William (originally Wilhelm) Hillebrand	Physician
Isabella McHutcheson Sinclair	Homemaker
E. Jules Rémy	Ethnologist
John M. Lydgate	Minister
Malacology	
John T. Gulick	Missionary son
Wesley Newcomb	Physician
William H. Pease	Surveyor
Ditlev D. Thaanum	Printer
Entomology	
Thomas Blackburn	Chaplain
Ichthyology	
Charles H. Wetmore	Missionary
Andrew J. Garrett	Biological collector
Ornithology	
Sanford B. Dole	Missionary son
James D. Mills	Businessman

at Honolulu's **Punahou School,** an institution established in 1841 expressly for this purpose. At Punahou, while becoming well schooled in the classics, the missionary offspring also took a strong interest in collection and study of Hawaiian natural history specimens. This interest is probably not surprising, considering that there tended to be rather few other recreational outlets among the still-limited foreign community in the Islands (and undoubtedly also because there was a strong parentally instilled work ethic). As an interesting aside, certain of these "Punahou boys" became quite familiar with the volcanic slopes overlooking the Mānoa Valley campus through their spare-time biological excursions in search of land snails and other interesting biota. They are responsible for the historical names of four of the cinder cones or peaks in the area: Round Top (originally Puʻu ʻUalakaʻa), Sugarloaf (Puʻu Kākea), Mount Tantalus (Puʻu ʻŌhiʻa), and Mount Olympus (Awaawaloa).

The children were encouraged by their parents in these natural history studies, and a few were even providing valuable scientific specimens to specialists in the eastern United States before their midteens. The earlier part of the Resident Amateur Naturalist Period overlapped the later of the Explorer-Naturalist one, and it is not surprising that the scientifically inclined among the missionaries welcomed any opportunity to meet these early visiting naturalists. The members of most official expeditions tended to be ashore in the Islands for only limited periods of

Figure 28.3. Sarah Joiner Lyman, a natural historian of the Resident Amateur Naturalist Period. This missionary recorded details of earthquakes affecting Hilo, Hawaiʻi, from 1833 to 1885. She is shown here about 1853 with her husband and four children. (Daguerreotype in possession of Lyman House Memorial Museum, Hilo, Hawaiʻi; used with permission.)

time, but the contemporary independent travelers usually had more opportunity, as welcome houseguests, to discuss natural history matters of mutual interest with missionary families. For example, the Goodrich home in Hilo hosted the botanist David Douglas, and the Gulicks put up Thomas Nuttall and John K. Townsend during their sojourn on Kaua'i. On O'ahu the Baldwin family often engaged in mutually beneficial biological discussions with lodging scientific members of the 1840–1841 Wilkes Expedition. The association with such dedicated naturalists unquestionably did much to fire the enthusiasm and augment the developing biological knowledge of some of the missionary sons.

After finishing Punahou, many of the missionary children (primarily the sons and only a few daughters at this mid-1800s time) traveled to the mainland to attend the same set of New England colleges as had their fathers, two or three taking along their collections of various natural history specimens. There, a number of the missionary sons excelled in the physical and biological sciences, winning awards and joining the various scientific organizations of the large eastern seaboard cities, where they met many of the more eminent American researchers of the day. The graduates returned to the Islands to follow diverse careers, but many retained an interest in natural history, as evidenced by their participation in, or support of, several Hawaiian scientific societies founded during the second half of the nineteenth century (see discussion later in this chapter).

A few of these missionary scions (listed in Table 28.3) devoted a considerable amount of their leisure time to scientific pursuits, publishing their findings in a number of Island and mainland periodicals. Among these resident amateur naturalists might be especially noted **Sanford B. Dole** (a distinguished judge, later president of the Republic of Hawai'i, and eventually first governor of the territory [Figure 28.4]) for his work with birds, and **David D. Baldwin** (a notable Island educator) for his publications on both plants and land snails. **John T. Gulick,** although he spent most of his later life in the Orient carrying on his family's missionary tradi-

Figure 28.4. Sanford B. Dole (1844–1926), a missionary son and resident amateur Hawaiian ornithologist. A jurist by profession, he served as president of the Republic of Hawai'i and first governor of the territory. The basis of the alternative Hawaiian name *'umi'umi o Dole* ("Dole's whiskers") for the historically introduced Spanish Moss *(Tillandsia usneoides)* is perhaps evident. (Photograph by James J. Williams, ca. 1890; unnumbered figure on p. 32 of Rose [1980], used with permission of Bishop Museum Press.)

tion, is the best known of early students of Hawaiian land snails. Some of his publications on these animals contained evolutionary postulates that foreshadowed the later classic theory of Charles Darwin. After the latter's theory appeared, Gulick's land-snail studies and papers were strongly influenced by it. In some instances they supported and even complemented Darwin's ideas, but in others they offered alternative explanations that eventually proved correct and were incorporated into Neo-Darwinism (see chapter 10). In the field of geology, **Titus M. Coan** emulated his father of the same first name in closely observing and publishing papers on Hawaiian volcanism. **Sereno E. Bishop** not only prepared articles on climatology and oceanography, but was also an international award-winning authority on atmospheric effects of volcanic eruptions.

Other Resident Amateur Naturalists

Between about 1850 and 1890, in addition to those investigators in the missionary line, there were a number of other avocational natural scientists who resided in the Islands for various lengths of time.

The active Hawaiian volcanoes understandably still continued to fascinate many such observers and, among these, Island businessman **William L. Green** wrote at least two influential books on the subject. In botany, the first book with color illustrations of Hawaiian flowers was published by the artistically gifted **Isabella McHutcheson Sinclair** of Kaua'i, who carefully obtained or verified the identifications of her specimens by submitting them along with collection notes to Kew Gardens in England. The first real dean of Hawaiian botany, however, was the German immigrant physician and government servant **William (originally Wilhelm) Hillebrand,** who in his spare time between 1851 and 1871 carried out an amazing amount of botanical exploration and collection on all main islands before finally returning to Germany. His 1888 volume on the flora of the Hawaiian Islands is still a classic work on the subject, and the landscaped grounds of his Honolulu residence are now **Foster Botanical Garden.** An Island schoolboy, **John M. Lydgate,** who accompanied Dr. Hillebrand on many of his collecting trips, later entered the ministry but maintained his interest in botany. In addition to publishing in this field, Lydgate eventually deposited his significant Kaua'i plant collection in Honolulu's Bernice P. Bishop Museum.

Wesley Newcomb and **William H. Pease,** physician and surveyor, respectively, were especially interested in collecting and describing endemic Hawaiian mollusks, between them formally describing over 350 new species. Newcomb concentrated on land snails, and Pease on marine forms. A little later than most of the other amateur naturalists, the Danish emigrant and printer **Ditlev D. Thaanum** amassed a great collection of Hawaiian terrestrial and marine mollusks during his 1894–1963 residence. These shells were eventually divided among at least a half dozen major American museums. The native Hawaiian insects were still scarcely known to the scientific world until 1877, when the Episcopal chaplain **Thomas Blackburn** (the "Father of Hawaiian Entomology") began their collection and description in earnest. Most of the immense number of specimens he collected during the next 6 years were sent to the British Museum, where they still form an important source of Hawaiian entomological data. The Kaua'i rancher **Valdemar Knudsen** diligently observed plants and vertebrates of the land and coastal waters of the island over a 40-year period and provided many Hawaiian specimens of these groups to, primarily, the Smithsonian Institution in Washington, D.C.

One amateur ornithologist of this period, **James D. Mills,** has received little attention, primarily because he published no scientific papers and any natural history notes he may have taken appear to be lost. Mills arrived in Hawai'i from England in 1851 and soon went into business in Hilo, also serving in government posts there. He pursued his hobby of taxidermy until at least 1860 and, possibly, sporadically thereafter until his death in 1887. His well-prepared mounted bird specimens include some of the very few preserved examples of now-extinct Hawai'i Island species, and these were most profitably utilized by Sanford B. Dole and later professional ornithologists in their studies. Mills' birds, now mostly in the Bishop Museum, were even loaned to form part of the Hawaiian exhibit in the 1876 Philadelphia Centennial Exhibition. Finally, a rather unexpected source of Hawaiian natural history material for the Paris Museum was the Honorable **P. E. Th(é)ôdore Ballieu** (sometimes misspelled "Bailleu"), French consul in the Kingdom of Hawai'i from 1869 to 1878. This diplomat somehow managed to find opportunities while serving in the Islands to collect and prepare specimens of plants, invertebrates, fishes, and even birds for dispatch to scientific institutions of his homeland.

Expeditions

There were still occasional exploring expeditions that visited the Hawaiian Archipelago in the half century after 1850, but space allows mention of only one. The British *Challenger* **Expedition,** which visited the Hawaiian Islands in 1876, can be considered the first modern oceanographic expedition. This carried a large and varied group of scientists who studied the Hawaiian marine biota extensively. The impressive total of fifty scientific "*Challenger* Report" volumes based on the expedition's collections has appeared thus far, and additional specimens are still warehoused awaiting study.

Early Scientific Organizations and Publications

In the middle and late nineteenth century, the scientifically minded missionary sons, along with other similarly interested Island residents, formed at least three scientific organizations, two of which sponsored the publication of journals. The first group to appear was the **Sandwich Islands Institute** in 1837, which issued varied scientific papers in its *Hawaiian Spectator.* The **Royal Hawaiian Agricultural Society,** with its *Transactions,* appeared later, and this organization eventually became the modern **Hawaiian Sugar Planters' Association.** There was also a less successful, short-lived **Natural History and Microscopical Society,** founded in 1876 at the request of the Hawaiian monarch David Kalākaua.

For the past century, popular periodicals have not been the vehicle for publication of scholarly scientific papers, but those of the latter part of the 1800s commonly served this purpose. Among the various widely read Island publications of this latter sort, the yearly edition of ***The Hawaiian Almanac and Annual*** was especially noteworthy. This was founded in 1875 by **Thomas G. Thrum,** who continuing publishing it until a little after 1900. Even today, scientists sometimes have occasion to consult century-old issues of the publication.

THE PROFESSIONAL NATURALIST PERIOD: 1870–1900

This phase is more or less arbitrarily designated as spanning the period 1870 to 1900, and its primary investigators are listed in Table 28.4. Whatever knowledge of the Hawaiian biota that the first professionals carried with them to the Islands had, of course, all been obtained from publications resulting from the dedicated work of the various types of preceding naturalists. These more recent observers, however, were able to make contributions of much greater scientific importance, not only because they usually had more time to carry out their Hawaiian studies, but also because each had been thoroughly trained in a specific field.

Although the year 1870 is noted as the beginning of this period, a few professional naturalists listed in the table had actually worked in Hawai'i slightly earlier. In 1864–1865, **Horace Mann Jr.,** son of the renowned American educator, and **William T. Brigham** (later to return to Hawai'i to become first director of the Bishop Museum) had been sent to study botany in the Hawaiian Islands by Yale College. Later, several of the other professional naturalists included some of the time's leading scientists (for example, Yale's James D. Dana, who had originally visited the archipelago on the 1840–1841 Wilkes Expedition, and Harvard's **Alexander E. R. Agassiz**). Although such authorities may have worked no more than a year in the Islands, they were still able to make substantial contributions to the knowledge of Hawaiian natural history.

Table 28.4. Professional naturalists visiting or living in Hawai'i (1870–1900) by scientific field. Years in Hawai'i are also indicated. Among the entomologists, Perkins was also quite active in ornithology between 1892 and 1902. (Data from various sources.)

Scientific Field Name	Years in Hawai'i
Geology	
Clarence E. Dutton	1882
James D. Dana	1840–1841, 1887
Botany	
William T. Brigham	1864–1865, 1880, 1888–1926
Horace Mann Jr.	1864–1865
Marine biology	
Alexander E. R. Agassiz	1885
G. D. Sollas	1890s
Malacology	
Charles M. Cooke Jr.	1874–1948
William H. Dall	1899
Entomology	
Theodore D. A. Cockerell	1890s
Henry B. Guppy	1890s
Robert C. L. Perkins	1892–1909, 1912
Albert Koebele	1893–1905
Ichthyology	
Oliver P. Jenkins	1889
Ornithology	
F. H. Otto Finsch	1879
Scott B. Wilson	1887–1888
Henry C. Palmer	1890–1893
George C. Munro	1890–1956

Two of the professionals beginning a long resident career in Hawai'i during this period were **Charles M. Cooke Jr.,** a missionary grandson who had just graduated in zoology from Yale, and **Albert Koebele,** a well-known California professor of zoology specializing in insects. Cooke became the Islands' first resident professional malacologist and would eventually serve for 46 years as curator of pulmonate mollusks at the Bishop Museum. Koebele, as a government entomologist, was best known as an early investigator in biological control, collecting various invertebrates in different parts of the world to introduce to Hawai'i in an attempt to control agricultural insect and other arthropod pests.

The field of Hawaiian ornithology received its first important impetus from work of the young Englishman **Scott B. Wilson** in 1887 and 1888. Upon return to England, his specimens and published studies so enthused the British financier and amateur ornithologist **Lionel Walter, Lord Rothschild** that in 1890 Rothschild engaged another Englishman, **Henry C. Palmer,** to spend almost the next 3 years observing and collecting birds in various parts of the archipelago. Rothschild ultimately also published and illustrated the results of his collector's work in an extensive monograph (Plate 28.1). The background foliage in several of the monograph's color plates was copied by the bird artist from the earlier-mentioned flower book of resident amateur naturalist Isabella McH. Sinclair. A young, trained New Zealand naturalist, **George C. Munro,** assisted Palmer before initiating a long residency in the Islands as a plantation manager and avocational natural historian. Finally, a third Englishman, **Robert C.L. Perkins,** was sent to Hawai'i by the British Royal Society and the British Association for the Advancement of Science to study not only birds, but the entire land fauna. This endeavor, with additional sponsorship of the Bishop Museum, was brilliantly carried out between 1892 and 1902. Perkins ultimately published his results on, primarily, birds and insects, as parts of a still-consulted three-volume scientific classic on the Islands' land fauna edited by David Sharp. After this, Perkins worked in Hawai'i as an economic entomologist and freely shared his almost legendary knowledge of the Hawaiian biota until 1909, when he relocated permanently to England.

Expeditions

Much as the *Challenger* Expedition had done 15 years earlier, the modern American scientific *Albatross* **Expedition** studied Hawaiian waters and their biota on a number of occasions between 1891 and 1902, and a series of monographs was published as a result of those surveys.

The Bernice Pauahi Bishop Museum

Since early in the Resident Amateur Naturalist Period there had been attempts to establish in Hawai'i a museum for properly preserving and displaying examples of the Islands' natural and cultural history. In 1833 a small library and even smaller "cabinet of natural history" had been installed in the Honolulu Seamen's Bethel, at which were later held meetings of the Sandwich Islands Institute scientific society. Apparently, though, within a dozen or so years this collection, which then included "a large black bear" and "poor [David] Douglas' snow shoes," was disbanded with no record of its contents' fate. About 10 years after the 1841 founding of Punahou School, a fair-sized collection of natural biological and ethnological "curiosities" used primarily in teaching had accumulated at the institution. Without professional curatorial care, however, this collection progressively deteriorated and had apparently been completely dismantled and dispersed to unknown locations by the end of the 1890s.

The Hawaiian government had also become concerned about preserving cultural and nat-

Figure 28.5. Princess Bernice Pauahi Bishop (1831–1884) and her husband Charles Reed Bishop (1822–1915). In 1889, Mr. Bishop founded the Honolulu museum bearing his wife's name as a memorial and to house her extensive legacy of Hawaiian cultural and natural history items. (Photograph of Princess Bernice by Menzies Dickson, Honolulu, Hawai'i, ca. 1875, and of Mr. Bishop by B. F. Howland and Co., San Francisco, California, 1866; unnumbered figures on pp. 8 and 11 of Rose [1980], used with permission of Bishop Museum Press.)

ural items unique to the Islands, as it became increasingly obvious that so many of these things were being irretrievably lost. As a result, in 1872 a **Hawaiian National Museum** was authorized by the kingdom's legislature and the current monarch Kamehameha V (Lot). This museum finally opened 3 years later in part of what is now known as the Judiciary Building, directly across King Street from 'Iolani Palace in Honolulu. Its collection contained many priceless ethnological specimens, some deposited by members of the Hawaiian royal family, as well as natural history specimens. A complex series of problems, involving primarily financial support and curatorial responsibility, made worse by continuing instability in government, finally caused the collection to be closed to the public in 1887.

Fortunately, the holdings of this "Government Collection," as it came to be known, were not to be lost like all similar previous assemblages, because construction of the first building of what would become the Hawaiian Islands' premier museum was almost ready to begin. The banker and government official **Charles R. Bishop** (no relation to the missionary family) wished to establish a museum in honor of his late wife **Princess Bernice Pauahi** (Figure 28.5), who had died in 1884. She was the sole heir to the Kamehameha family monetary fortune, heirloom collection, and lands (constituting approximately one-ninth of the area of the main islands, the income from which supports The Kamehameha Schools). The planning for this **Bernice Pauahi Bishop Museum** took 2 or 3 years, and the site finally chosen was on the (then) grounds of The Kamehameha School for Boys in the Kalihi area some distance west of downtown Honolulu. The museum was officially founded in December 1889, with the initial contents comprising not only the sizeable collection of the Kamehamehas inherited by Princess Bernice, but also the entire Government Collection, along with the valuable natural history and cultural item assemblages of a number of Island residents that had recently been purchased by Mr. Bishop.

To ensure the preservation, study, and growth of this new museum's holdings, William T. Brigham was hired as full-time curator and in 1898 was promoted to first director with new curators under him. Brigham had first visited the Hawaiian Islands on a botanical collecting trip in 1864–1865 and, although he was originally trained as a geologist, by the time he assumed his Bishop Museum duties he had become acutely aware of the need to also record and save as much as possible of the endangered Hawaiian natural and cultural heritage. He, thus, was an excellent choice to initiate and guide the course of the young institution, which subsequently engaged in a wide range of research activities in both Hawai'i and other Pacific areas. More recently, the institution was officially designated as the State Museum of Natural and Cultural History (see chapter 27).

SUGGESTED REFERENCES

Buck 1953; Carson 1987b; Dunmore 1991; I'i 1959; Kamakau 1964, 1976, 1991; Kay 1972, 1997; Kepelino 1932; Malo 1951; Olson and James 1994; Rose 1980; Sharp (ed.) 1899–1913.

Glossary of Hawaiian Place Names

The names of most of the main Hawaiian Islands and certain other major topographic features are so ancient that the original meanings have long since been lost. For a number of other places, the interpretive association of the prehistoric name with the locality is no longer known. In some cases, places with identical names occur on two or more Hawaiian islands, but only that island of the locality specifically referred to in the text is listed here. Some information on derivation of selected Hawaiian place names on various main islands is presented in the series of six *Nā ki'i hana no'eau Hawai'i* videos listed in the **Audiovisual Aids** section.

'Āhihi (Bay; Maui). "Entwined."

'Āina Haina (Locality; O'ahu). "Hind's land" (historically named for Robert Hind, who once had a dairy in this area).

'Āinahou (Locality; Hawai'i). "New land."

'Alae (Volcanic crater; Hawai'i). "Mudhen [Hawaiian Gallinule or Coot]."

Alaka'i (Swamp; Kaua'i). "To lead."

'Alalākeiki (Channel; between Maui and Kaho'olawe). "Child's wail" (possibly in reference to frequent roughness of the water here).

'Alenuihāhā (Channel; between Hawai'i and Maui). "Great billows smashing" (this channel is often quite rough).

Āliapa'akai (Lake; O'ahu). "Salt pond" (historically, Salt Lake).

Anahulu (Valley; O'ahu). "Ten days."

Awaawaloa (Peak; O'ahu). As spelled, "Long valley" (historically apparently Mount Olympus).

'Ehukai (Beach; O'ahu). "Sea spray."

'Eke (Bog; Maui). (Meaning unknown.)

'Ewa (Plain, District, and Community ['Ewa Beach]; O'ahu; also used as a directional term on the island). "Crooked" (the stone said to have been thrown here by the two gods Kāne and Kanaloa to determine original district boundaries was misdirected and lost, but later recovered elsewhere).

Hakalau (Locality; Hawai'i). "Many perches."

Halapē (Campground; Hawai'i). "[Possibly] crushed missing" (gourds once growing here are said to have sometimes been lost under windblown sand).

Hālawa (Valley; Moloka'i). "Curve."

Haleakalā (Volcano; Maui). "House used by the sun" (the demigod Māui is said to have once noosed the sun from this mountain).

Halema'uma'u (Volcanic crater; Hawai'i). "Fern house" (*'ama'u* [red tree ferns] grow in the immediate vicinity).

Halepōhaku (Locality; Hawai'i). "Stone house" (historically named for two stone lodges built here in the late 1930s).

Hālona (Blowhole; O'ahu). "Peering place."

Hāna (Community; Maui). (Meaning unknown.)

Hanalei (Valley and River; Kaua'i). "Crescent bay."

Hanauma (Bay; O'ahu). "Curved [*or* Hand-wrestling] bay."

Hanawī (Stream; Maui). (Meaning unknown.)

Hauola (Gulch; Lāna'i). "Dew of life" (dew is said to have been collected here as drinking water).

Hawai'i (State and Island). (Meaning unknown, although in some other parts of Polynesia "Hawaiki" was used as the name of the forgotten homeland of the distant past; in Samoa the cognate "Savai'i" refers to the largest island of that group. In very recent historic time, Hawai'i Island has come to be known as the "Big Island" or "Orchid Isle.")

Hilina (Escarpment; Hawai'i). "Struck [by wind]."

Hilo (Community; Hawai'i). (Perhaps named for either the first night of the new moon or an early Polynesian navigator.)

Honokāne (Bay and twin Valleys; Hawai'i). "Kāne's bay."

Honokōhau (Bay; Hawai'i). "Dew-tossing [or Dew-drawing] bay."

Honolua (Locality and Bay; Maui). "Two harbors."

Honolulu (Community; O'ahu). "Protected bay" (probably in reference to the secure Honolulu Harbor).

Honomalino (Locality; Hawai'i). "Calm bay."

Honoonāpali (Locality; Kaua'i). "Brow of the cliffs."

Honopū (Valley; Kaua'i). "Conch bay."

Honouliuli (Community; O'ahu). "Dark bay."

Hualālai (Volcano; Hawai'i). (Meaning unknown.)

Hulē'ia (Stream; Kaua'i). Originally "Hulā'ia," meaning "Pushed through" (the Pig-demigod Kamapua'a is said to have raped the volcano goddess Pele here).

Hulopo'e (Bay; Lāna'i). (Named for an undetermined man.)

Humu'ula (Saddle; Hawai'i). "Red jasper stone [used for adzes]" (commonly known as the "Saddle Area").

'Īao (Peak and Valley; Maui). "Cloud supreme" (quite possibly in reference to the clouds that usually cover the spirelike summit of the volcanic caldera-fill remnant).

'Ihi'ihilauākea (Volcanic crater; O'ahu). "Wide-leafed *'ihi'ihi* [Water-Clover fern?]."

'Iolani (Palace; O'ahu). "Royal *'io* [Hawaiian Hawk]" (historically named; the high flight of this hawk was considered to typify royalty).

Ka'ala (Peak; O'ahu). (Meaning unknown.)

Kā'anapali (Community; Maui). "Kā'ana cliff."

Ka'elepulu (Stream; O'ahu). "The moist blackness."

Ka'ena (Point; O'ahu). Literally, "The heat," but said to have been named for a brother or cousin of the volcano goddess Pele.

Kahana (Valley; O'ahu). "A cutting."

KahauaLe'a (Locality; Hawai'i). "The *Hau* tree of [*or* The dew of] Le'a" (Le'a was the goddess of canoe makers).

Kahiki (Locality). Literally "Tahiti," but also used to designate a distant mythical land, analogous to Shangri-La of English literature.

Kaho'olawe (Island). "The carrying away [by currents]" (in very recent historic time, occasionally termed the "Forbidden Isle," although this appellation is usually given to Ni'ihau).

Kahuku (Locality; Hawai'i and O'ahu). "The projection."

Kailua (Community, Beach, and Bay; O'ahu). "Two seas [*or* currents]."

Kaimukī (Locality; O'ahu). "The ti oven" (*Menehune* baked roots of this plant here).

Kakahai'a (Fishpond; Moloka'i). "Fish slicing."

Ka Lae (Point; Hawai'i). "The point" (the southernmost part of both the island and state of Hawai'i, as well as, in fact, of all the United States; historically "South Point").

Kalaupapa (Peninsula; Moloka'i). "The flat plain."

Kalihi (Valley; O'ahu). "[Possibly] the edge."

Kaloko (Locality and Fishpond; Hawai'i). "The pond."

Kaluahonu (Locality; Kaua'i). "[Probably] the *honu* [Green Turtle] pit or cavern."

Kaluako'i (A locality term commonly used on most or all main islands). "The adze pit" (fine-grained basalt suitable for this type of implement was usually quarried at places so named).

Kamakou (Volcanic cone; Moloka'i). "The *makou* [undetermined species of either the buttercup or parsley family] plant."

Kamiloloa (Locality; Moloka'i). "The tall *Milo* tree."

Kanahā (Pond; Maui). "The shattered [thing]."

Kanaio (Locality; Maui). "The *naio* [Bastard Sandalwood] tree."

Kāne'ohe (Community; O'ahu). "Bamboo husband" (a wife here is said to have likened her husband's cruelty to the sharp blade of a traditional knife made of bamboo).

Kānepu'u (Ridge; Lāna'i). "Kāne's Hill."

Kapunakea (Locality; Maui). "The clear spring" *or* "The white coral."

Kaua'i (Island). (Meaning unknown; in very recent historic time, termed the "Garden Isle.")

Kauhakō (Volcanic crater; Moloka'i). "[Possibly] dragged large intestines" (sometimes called Lua o Pele).

Kaukonahua (Stream; O'ahu). Probably originally "Kaukōnāhua," meaning "Place fatness."

Ka'ula (Islet; Ni'ihau). "[Probably] the red [one]" (the island is said to have been named for an unspecified seabird, possibly the *koa'e 'ula* [Red-tailed Tropicbird], which along with various other seabirds has a substantial nesting colony here).

Kaupō (Valley; Maui). "Night canoe landing."

Kawaikini (Peak; Kaua'i). "The multitudinous water[s?]" (this general summit area of Mount Wai'ale'ale receives a near world-record high amount of rainfall).

Kawainui (Marsh; O'ahu). "The big water" (this current marshy area was an open ocean embayment perhaps a thousand or so years ago).

KealaiKahiki (Channel between Lāna'i and Kaho'olawe). "The path to Tahiti [*or* a foreign land]."

Kealakekua (Bay; Hawai'i). "Pathway of the god" (gods are said to have slid down a cliff here to cross the bay quickly).

Keālia (Pond; Maui). "The salt encrustation."

Ke'anae (Valley; Maui). "The *'anae* [fully grown Striped Mullet] fish."

Keanakāko'i (Locality; Hawai'i. Also a locality term commonly used on most or all main islands). "The cave of the adze maker[s]" (fine-grained basalt suitable for this type of implement was usually quarried or flaked at places so named).

Keauhou (Locality; Hawai'i). "The new era [*or* current]."

Keonelele (Locality; Moloka'i). "The flying sand" (sand is often blown about this desertlike windward area).

Kīhei (Community; Maui). "Cloak *or* Cape."

Kīlauea (Volcano; Hawai'i. Volcanic cone and Point; Kaua'i). "Spewing" *or* "Much spreading" (presumably, in reference to volcanic activity, at least in the case of the Hawai'i Island volcano).

Kīna'u (Cape; Maui). "Flaw."

Kīpāhoehoe (Locality; Hawai'i). "Much *pāhoehoe* [smooth lava]."

Kīpahulu (Locality; Maui). "Fetch [from] exhausted gardens."

Kīpuka (used in compound locality names). An isolated area of vegetated land left uncovered in the expanse of a lava flow.

Kīpuka 'Āinahou. *See* 'Āinahou.

Koai'a (Plant sanctuary; Hawai'i). "*Koa* [of a particular variety] tree."

Kohala (Volcano; Hawai'i). (Meaning unknown.)

Kohelepelepe (Volcanic crater; O'ahu). "Labia minora" (an imprint is said to have been left here by the flying vulva and vagina of Kapo, a sister of the volcano goddess Pele; this name was historically changed—perhaps during missionary days—to the current name Koko (Crater).

Koko (Head and Crater [two separate volcanic cones]; O'ahu). "Blood" (probably in reference to either the red soil in the area *or* the blood of a shark-attack victim in the ocean nearby); the original name of Koko Crater was Kohelepelepe.

Kōloa (Beach; Hawai'i. Community; Kaua'i). (Meaning unknown.)

Kona (Coastal area; Hawai'i). "Leeward [in regard to the trade winds]."

Kōnāhuanui (Peak; O'ahu). "Large fat kidneys [*or* other internal organs]" (possibly in reference to a legendary giant said to have thrown his testicles at a fleeing woman near here; sometimes now spelled without one or both macrons).

Ko'olau (Volcano and Range [Pali]; O'ahu). "Windward [in regard to the trade winds]" (the features are located on the windward side of the island).

Kualoa (Locality; O'ahu). "Long back [of body or object]."

Kūhiwa (Gulch; Maui). "[Any special chief's] *kapu* [taboo]."

Ku'ia (Valley; Kaua'i). "Obstructed."

Kūkaniloko (Locality; O'ahu). (Possibly named for an ancient chief.)

Kula (District; Maui). "[Topographic] plain."

Lahaina (Community; Maui). "Cruel sun" (said to be in reference to droughts here); the original, correct, spelling for this meaning was "Lāhainā."

Lā'ie (Community; O'ahu). A contraction of the original term "Lau'ie'ie," meaning "Leaf of the '*Ie'ie* [climbing species of the screw pine family] plant."

Lāna'i (Island). "[Possibly] day of conquest" (in very recent historic time, termed the "Pineapple Isle" or, sometimes, the "Private Isle").

Lāna'ihale (Peak; Lāna'i). "Lāna'i house."

Lapakahi (Locality; Hawai'i). "Single ridge."

Laupāhoehoe (Locality; Hawai'i). "*Pāhoehoe* [smooth lava] flat."

Lē'ahi (Volcanic cone; O'ahu). A contraction of the original term "Lae'ahi," meaning "Forehead of the '*ahi* [Yellowfin Tuna]" (said to have been so named when Hi'iaka, a younger sister of the volcano goddess Pele, remarked on the similarity between the cone's profile and the anterior shape of the fish; historically, Diamond Head).

Lehua (Islet; Ni'ihau). "Blossom of the [red-flowered variety of] '*Ōhi'a lehua* tree" (the volcano goddess Pele's younger sister Hi'iaka is said to have once left a *lei* of these flowers on the island).

Lō'ihi (Volcano; off Hawai'i). "Length" *or* "Height" (a historic name, possibly referring to the elevated seamount this active submarine volcano was initially thought to represent).

Lua o Pele (Volcanic crater; Moloka'i). "[The volcano goddess] Pele's Pit" (usually known as Kauhakō Crater).

Mākaha (Valley; O'ahu). "Fierce" *or* "To plunder" (possibly the latter meaning, because the area is said to have been anciently notorious for robberies).

Makapu'u (Point and Beach; O'ahu). "Hill beginning" *or* "Bulging eye" (possibly the latter meaning, because an idol with this name was reputedly kept in a sea-facing cave here).

Makawehi (Dunes; Kaua'i). (Meaning unknown.)

Makuleia (Bay; Maui). (Meaning unknown.)

Mānana (Islet; O'ahu). (Meaning unknown; historically, Rabbit Island.)

Manawainui (Gulch; Maui). "Large water branch."

Mānele (Bay; Lāna'i). "Sedan chair."

Mānoa (Valley; Oʻahu). "Vast" (interpretive association unknown, although this amphitheater-headed valley is quite a large one).

Manukā (Locality; Hawaiʻi). Literally, "Blundering," but said to have been named for a legendary robber.

Maui (Island). Apparently named for the demigod and trickster Māui; in very recent historic time, termed the "Valley Isle" in reference to the large ʻĪao and other valleys of West Maui.

Maui Nui (Island). "Big Maui" (rather recently coined historic name for an ancient large island formed of the current Maui, Molokaʻi, Lānaʻi, and Kahoʻolawe whenever sea level fell at least 140 m or 460 feet below its current stand).

Mauna Kea (Volcano; Hawaiʻi). "White mountain" (a blanket of snow covers the summit in most winters).

Mauna Lei (Community and Gulch; Lānaʻi). "*Lei* mountain" (a cloud ring often surrounds the island's summit area, where these places are situated).

Mauna Loa (Volcanoes; Hawaiʻi, Molokaʻi). "Long mountain" (the summit and gentle-sloped subaerial rift zones of the volcano on Hawaiʻi extend for more than 113 km or 70 miles).

Maunaloa (Community; Molokaʻi). (This is the currently accepted spelling; see Mauna Loa for meaning; a broad, low mountain named Mauna Loa is situated near this town.)

Mauna Ulu (Volcanic cone; Hawaiʻi). "Growing mountain" (first formed in the 1960s on the east rift zone of Kīlauea Volcano and still increasing in size in early 2001).

Moanalua (Locality; Oʻahu). "Two encampments" (reputedly named for two spots here where travelers between ʻEwa and Honolulu are said to have rested).

Moaʻulanui (Peak; Kahoʻolawe). (Original pronunciation and meaning uncertain, but conceivably "Big red Chicken.")

Mōʻiliʻili (Locality; Oʻahu). A contraction of the original term "Moʻoʻiliʻili," meaning "Pebble lizard" (the volcano goddess Pele's younger sister Hiʻiaka is said to have cut up a water dragon here, and the numerous pieces of its body formed a hill).

Mōkapu (Peninsula; Oʻahu). A contraction of the original term "Mokukapu," meaning "Sacred district [*or* island]" (Kamehameha the Great is said to have met with his chiefs here; the area was probably an island up to a few hundred years ago, when sand filled in the shallows between it and the Oʻahu mainland).

Mōkōlea (Islet; Oʻahu). A contraction of the original term "Mokukōlea," meaning "*kōlea* [Pacific Golden-Plover] island" or the enigmatic "*Kōlea* cut."

Mokoliʻi (Islet; Oʻahu). "Little lizard" (the volcano goddess Pele's younger sister Hiʻiaka is said to have killed a water dragon [*"moʻo,"* with *"moko"* being the rarely used complete form of the ancestral word] near here, and its tail became the island; historically, Chinaman's Hat).

Mokuʻāweoweo (Volcanic caldera; Hawaiʻi). "*ʻĀweoweo* [Bigeye] fish section" (in reference to similarity in color between these red fish and molten lava).

Mokulua (Islets; Oʻahu). "Two [*or* Twin] islands" (the closely situated islands are very similar in appearance).

Mokumanu (Islet; Oʻahu). "Bird island" (numerous seabirds roost and nest here).

Mokupapapa or Moku Papapa (Island). "Flat island" (an undetermined—and perhaps only mythical—island, although there is a small islet of this same name off eastern Molokaʻi, and Kure in the Northwestern Hawaiian Islands was formerly sometimes referred to by this term).

Molokaʻi (Island). (Meaning unknown; in very recent historic time, termed the "Friendly Isle.")

Molokini (Islet; between East Maui and Kahoʻolawe). "Many ties."

Mo'omomi (Beach; Moloka'i). (Meaning unknown.)

Mount Ka'ala. *See* Ka'ala.

Mount Wai'ale'ale. *See* Wai'ale'ale.

Nāpali (Coastal area; Kaua'i). "The cliffs" (high sea cliffs and steep valley walls characterize much of this northwestern coast).

Nāwiliwili (Community; Kaua'i). "The *wiliwili* [Hawaiian Coral] trees."

Nihoa (Island). "Firmly set."

Ni'ihau (Island). (Meaning unknown; in very recent historic time, frequently termed the "Forbidden Isle.")

Niuli'i (Reservoir; O'ahu). "Small coconut."

Nu'uanu (Valley; O'ahu). "Cool height" (in at least the early historic period Hawaiian royalty and affluent foreigners often retreated to residences in this valley to escape the summer heat of Honolulu).

Nu'upia (Fishpond complex; O'ahu). "*Pia* [Polynesian Arrowroot] heap."

O'ahu (Island). (Meaning unknown; most Hawaiian-language scholars consider that the often-cited "Gathering place" is not correct.)

'Ōla'a (Locality; Hawai'i). Apparently originally "La'a," probably meaning "Sacred" *or* "Dedicated."

Olinda (Community; Maui). Evidently not a Hawaiian name; quite possibly historically coined from the Spanish *"¡O linda vista!"* (What a beautiful view!).

Olokele (Canyon; Kaua'i). This island's name for the *'I'iwi* [a red Hawaiian honeycreeper].

Oloku'i (Peak; Moloka'i). "Tall hill."

Olomana (Peak; O'ahu). "Forked hill" (probably in reference to the close juxtaposition of this and two lesser peaks, although a giant with this name is said to have leaped from Kaua'i to this place).

'Opihikao (Community; Hawai'i). Probably originally "'Opihikāō," meaning "Crowd [collecting] *'opihi* [marine Limpets]" (it is said that people were once afraid to gather the mollusks alone here because of robbers).

Pāhala (Community; Hawai'i). "[A method of] fertilizing mulch soil by burning *hala* [Screw Pine] vegetation on it."

Pāhoa (Community; Hawai'i). Literally "Short dagger," but in legend this was also the name of a water dragon killed by Hi'iaka, a younger sister of the volcano goddess Pele.

Pahole (Locality; O'ahu). Possibly originally "Pohole," meaning "Bruised" *or* "Scraped."

Paikō (Lagoon; O'ahu). (Not an original Hawaiian name; historically transliterated from "Pico," the surname of a part-Portuguese person who lived nearby.)

Palaoa (Point; Lāna'i). "[Whale] ivory" *and/or* "Sperm Whale[?]" (dead whales are said to have sometimes washed ashore here).

Pali (Escarpment; O'ahu; also used in compound locality names). "Cliff."

Pānī'au (Peak; Ni'ihau). "To touch the midrib [of a Coconut frond]."

Papakōlea (Beach; Hawai'i). "*Kōlea* [Pacific Golden-Plover] flats."

Pauahi (Locality; Hawai'i). "Destroyed [by] fire."

Pauoa (Flats; O'ahu). (Meaning unknown.)

Pa'upa'u (Volcanic cone; Maui). "Drudgery" (servants are said to have been fatigued from carrying bath water here for a chief's child).

Pelekunu (Valley; Moloka'i). "Smelly [for lack of sunshine]" (parts of this damp valley are perpetually shaded by its high walls).

Pi'ihonua (Locality; Hawai'i). "Land incline" (perhaps in reference to its location on the windward slopes of Mauna Kea).

Pōhakuloa (Gulch; Hawai'i). "Long stone."

Point Palaoa. *See* Palaoa.

Po'ipū (Community; Kaua'i). "Completely overcast" *or* "Crashing [as waves]."

Polipoli (Peak; Maui). (Meaning unknown.)

Pololū (Valley; Hawai'i). "Long spear."

Punahou (School and Locality; O'ahu). Originally "Kapunahou," meaning "The new spring" (one pertinent legend relates that the god Kāne thrust his staff into the ground here to create a spring).

Punalu'u (Bay and Community; Hawai'i. Stream and Community; O'ahu). On Hawai'i: "Dived-for spring" (freshwater springs issue from the lower beach and bay floor here); on O'ahu: "Dived-for coral."

Pūowaina (Volcanic cone; O'ahu). A contraction of the original term "Pu'uowaina," meaning "Hill of placing [human sacrifices]" (this ritual is said to have once been commonly practiced here; historically, Punchbowl).

Pūpūkea (Locality; O'ahu). "White shell."

Pu'u Ali'i (Peak; Moloka'i). "Royal hill."

Pu'uhonua o Hōnaunau (National Historical Park; Hawai'i). "Hōnaunau city of refuge."

Pu'u Hou (Volcanic cone; Hawai'i). "New hill" (historically named following formation during an 1868 lava flow of Mauna Loa).

Pu'u Kākea (Volcanic cone; O'ahu). "Kākea [a storm wind] hill" (this particular named wind is said to have been specifically associated with Mānoa Valley; historically, Sugarloaf).

Pu'u Kukui (Peak and Bog; Maui). "*Kukui* [Candlenut] hill."

Pu'u Loa or Pu'uloa (Locality; Hawai'i). "Long hill."

Pu'u Mahana (Volcanic cone; Hawai'i). (Meaning unknown.)

Pu'u Maka'ala (Volcanic cone; Hawai'i). "Vigilant hill."

Pu'u Nānā (Volcanic cone; Moloka'i). "Observation hill" (on clear days it is possible to see great distances from this West Moloka'i elevation).

Pu'u 'Ōhi'a (Volcanic cone; O'ahu). " *'Ōhi'a lehua* tree hill" (historically, Mount Tantalus).

Pu'u o 'Umi (Volcanic cone; Hawai'i). "'Umi's hill" ('Umi was a sixteenth-century chief of this island).

Pu'u 'Ualaka'a (Volcanic cone; O'ahu). "Rolling *'uala* [Sweet Potato] hill" (a rat is said to have bitten a sweet potato here, causing it to roll downhill and sprout; also Kamehameha the Great reputedly raised many of these same vegetables here, and these rolled downhill upon being dug; historically, Round Top).

Pu'u Wa'awa'a (Volcanic cone; Hawai'i). "Furrowed hill" (in reference to the grooved appearance of the slopes).

Pu'u Wēkiu (Volcanic cone; Hawai'i). "Summit hill" (this cone is on the crown of Mauna Kea).

Ulupa'u (Volcanic cone; O'ahu). "Increasing soot" (historically, Ulupa'u Head).

Wahiawā (Community; O'ahu). "Place of noise" (it is said that rough surf could be heard at this far-inland locality).

Waiāhole (Valley; O'ahu). "*Āhole* [Hawaiian Flagtail] fish water."

Waiākea (Locality; Hawai'i). "Broad water(s)."

Wai'alae (Community; O'ahu). "Mudhen [Hawaiian Gallinule or Coot] water."

Waialea (Bay; Hawai'i). (Meaning unknown.)

Wai'ale'ale (Volcano; Kaua'i). "Rippling [*or* Overflowing] water" (a near world-record high amount of rainfall occurs at the summit of this mountain).

Wai'anae (Volcano and Range; O'ahu). " *'Anae* [fully grown Striped Mullet] fish water."

Waiau (Lake; Hawai'i). "Swirling water."

Waikamoi (Locality; Maui). "*Moi* [variety of Taro] water."

Waikīkī (Community; O'ahu). "Spouting water" (probably in reference to the pre-Contact swampy nature of this area).

Wailuku (River; Hawai'i). "Destruction water" (people may possibly have fought over water here.)

Waimānalo (Community; O'ahu). "Potable water."

Waimanu (Valley; Hawai'i). "Bird water."

Waimea (Bay; O'ahu). "Reddish water" (as caused by rust-colored soil suspended in it).

Waipi'o (Valley; Hawai'i). "Curved water" (probably in reference to the meandering course of Waipi'o Stream along the valley floor).

References Cited
(With annotations)

Abbott, I. A.

1989   Marine algae of the Northwest Hawaiian Islands. *Pacific Science* 43:223–233. A recording of 204 green, brown, and red algae species from this area and a brief comparison of this marine flora with the comparable 222 species of Eniwetak Atoll in the Marshall Islands.

1992   *Lāʻau Hawaiʻi: Traditional Hawaiian uses of plants.* Honolulu: Bishop Museum Press. 163 pp. An interesting and well-illustrated account of prehistorically used native and alien plants, both food and utilitarian. Tables giving the Hawaiian and scientific names of all the plants are included.

1999   *Marine red algae of the Hawaiian Islands.* Honolulu: Bishop Museum Press. 477 pp. Descriptions of all of the noncrustose Rhodophyta of the archipelago, with keys to at least the common genera and species. Included are black-and-white photographs of many species, shown primarily in microscopic view.

Abbott, I. A., and E. H. Williamson

1974   *Limu: An ethnobotanical study of some edible Hawaiian seaweeds.* 2d ed. Lāwaʻi, Hawaiʻi: Pacific Tropical Botanical Garden. 21 pp. Primarily a description of Hawaiian names and uses for twelve commonly utilized seaweeds, based on information obtained during interviews with older Native Hawaiians.

Akashi, Y., and D. Mueller-Dombois

1995   A landscape perspective of the Hawaiian rainforest dieback. *Journal of Vegetation Science* 6:449–464. A description of *ʻŌhiʻa lehua* dieback on Hawaiʻi Island's Mauna Loa and Mauna Kea in the 1960s and 1970s, with conclusions about apparent primary and accessory causes.

American Ornithologists' Union

1998   *Check-list of North American birds.* 7th ed. Washington, D.C.: American Ornithologists' Union. 829 pp. A listing of all native and alien birds found from the Arctic through Panama, including the West Indies and Hawaiian Islands. Common and scientific names of all species are given, along with habitat and distribution.

Apple, R. A.

1973   *Prehistoric and historic sites and structures in the Hawaiian Islands National Wildlife Refuge (the Northwestern Hawaiian Islands): A survey.* Honolulu: U.S. Bureau of Sport Fisheries and Wildlife. 111 pp. A relatively exhaustive account of, primarily, the historical utilization of the Northwestern Hawaiian Islands, with many interesting archival photographs. The account of the long-continued human activities on Midway Atoll is especially detailed.

Armstrong, R. W. (ed.)

1983   *Atlas of Hawaii.* 2d ed. Honolulu: University of Hawaiʻi Press. 238 pp. More like an encyclopedia than simply an atlas, and an extremely informative work overall. Most of the chapter subjects of this book are among those treated on pp. 33–92 of the *Atlas* although the depth of coverage among the various topics in the *Atlas* tends to be somewhat uneven. There is a gazetteer, but no subject index.

Athens, J. S., J. V. Ward, and S. Wickler

1992 Late Holocene lowland vegetation, O'ahu, Hawai'i. *New Zealand Journal of Archaeology* 14:9–34. A study of Hawaiian vegetation both before and after Polynesian settlement, based primarily on pollen-core analyses. Important observations are presented on the question of use of fire in Island agricultural activities, as well as the relative rates of natural and anthropogenous erosion.

Atkinson, I. A. E.

1977 A reassessment of factors, particularly *Rattus rattus* L., that influenced the decline of endemic forest birds in the Hawaiian Islands. *Pacific Science* 31:109–133. A review of possible major causes of historic extinctions of Hawaiian endemic birds, with special attention to dates and locations of first appearances of continental rodent species on the various Hawaiian Islands.

Atoll Research Bulletin

1971–1977, 1996 Washington, D.C.: Smithsonian Institution. Individual issues by various authors during the particular years indicated primarily present monographic treatments of all the Northwestern Hawaiian Islands except Midway. The works usually concentrate more on historical and biological matters than on geological ones.

Balazs, G. H.

1976 *Hawaii's seabirds, turtles, and seals.* Honolulu, Hawai'i: World Wide Distributors. 32 (unnumbered) pp. Short descriptions of these vertebrates in the Northwestern Hawaiian Islands, with sixty-nine excellent color photographs by the author.

1980 *Synopsis of biological data on the Green Turtle in the Hawaiian Islands.* Honolulu: National Oceanic and Atmospheric Administration Technical Memorandum, National Marine Fisheries Service. 114 pp. A detailed report on this marine reptile in Hawaiian waters, with an extremely useful, comprehensive bibliography. The author is a long-time scientific investigator of the species and heads the Marine Turtle Research Program of the National Marine Fisheries Service Honolulu Laboratory.

Balcomb, K. C., III

1987 *The whales of Hawaii.* San Francisco: Marine Mammal Fund. 99 pp. A small book, but one filled with descriptive and natural history information on all cetaceans reported from Hawaiian waters. Each species is illustrated by an accurate black-and-white drawing, as well as, usually, at least one color photograph.

Baldwin, B. G., and R. H. Robichaux

1995 Historical biogeography and ecology of the Hawaiian Silversword Alliance (Asteraceae): New molecular phylogenetic perspectives. Pages 259–287 *in* W. L. Wagner and V. A. Funk (eds.), *Hawaiian biogeography: Evolution on a hot spot archipelago.* Washington, D.C.: Smithsonian Institution Press. A cladistic study of this monophyletic group of three endemic genera, based on DNA nucleotide sequences.

Banks, R. C., R. W. McDiarmid, and A. L. Gardner (eds.)

1987 *Checklist of the vertebrates of the United States, the U.S. Territories, and Canada.* Washington, D.C.: Fish and Wildlife Service Resource Publication 166. 79 pp. A compilation of scientific and common names of the covered fauna. Also listed are extinct, endangered, or threatened status; and whether or not human introduced, but no locality data.

Bascom, W.

1960 Beaches. *Scientific American* 203 (8): 80–94. An interesting and informative nontechnical account of many aspects of the dynamics of sand beaches.

Bathen, K. H.
1978   *Circulation atlas for Oahu, Hawaii.* University of Hawai'i Sea Grant Miscellaneous
        Report 78-05. 94 pp. Maps and diagrams, divided into coastal sections, present the
        seasonal directions of wind and various currents around the island, as well as daily
        ebb and flow tidal data.

Becket, J., and J. Singer (eds. and comps.) (with contributions by K. Cachola-Abad,
J. M. Ho, and K. Makanani)
1999   *Pana O'ahu: Sacred stones, sacred land.* Honolulu: University of Hawai'i Press. 186
        pp. An illustrated history of a great number of ancient boulders and stone construc-
        tions on O'ahu.

Beletsky, L.
2000   *Hawaii: The ecotravellers' wildlife guide.* San Diego, California: Academic Press.
        416 pp. A tremendously useful work for environmentally concerned Hawai'i visitors
        and residents. Among the vast amount of information provided are natural history dis-
        cussions of the various main islands and guides to their more significant natural areas.
        The numerous paintings of birds, mammals, reptiles, and amphibians are by H. Dou-
        glas Pratt and those of fishes and marine invertebrates by Colin Newman. Color pho-
        tos include many native and alien plants, as well as selected endemic land arthropods.

Bellwood, P. S.
1979   *Man's conquest of the Pacific: The prehistory of Southeast Asia and Oceania.* New
        York: Oxford University Press. 462 pp. A truly encyclopedic and scholarly work. For
        each general region of continental Southeast Asia and the insular Pacific, the history
        of human culture is covered from earliest times through the latest prehistoric period.

Berger, A. J.
1981   *Hawaiian birdlife.* Rev. ed. Honolulu: University of Hawai'i Press. 270 pp. The stan-
        dard reference source on the subject, but not intended as a field guide or laboratory
        source of detailed morphological data.

Boden, J. F., and E. Emshoff (eds.)
1987   *Hawaii aloha.* Pearl City, Hawai'i: Press Pacifica. 159 pp. A semipopular "coffee
        table" book about cultural and natural history in the Hawaiian Islands. The many
        excellent color photographs illustrate a great many facets of Island life, biota, and
        geology.

Bryan, E. H., Jr.
1954   *The Hawaiian chain.* Honolulu: Bishop Museum Press. 71 pp. A general and quite
        abbreviated overview of Hawaiian natural history, featuring an entertaining and infor-
        mative narrative, with many air photographs of Hawaiian islands.

1978   *The Northwestern Hawaiian Islands: An annotated bibliography.* Honolulu: U.S. Fish
        and Wildlife Service. 190 pp. in four sections. In addition to the exceptionally com-
        plete bibliography, a short (1–4 pages) description and history of each island is given,
        along with tables listing the islands of occurrence of plants and vertebrates.

Bryan, W. A.
1915   *Natural history of Hawaii, being an account of the Hawaiian people, the geology and*
        geography of the islands and the native and introduced plants and animals of the
        group. Honolulu: Hawaiian Gazette Company. 596 pp. The title says it all. A truly
        remarkable compendium based on natural history knowledge available in the early
        part of the twentieth century. The cultural aspects of contemporary Native Hawaiians
        are well covered, and the book contains a myriad of black-and-white photos.

Buck, Sir Peter H.

1953   *Explorers of the Pacific: European and American discoveries in Polynesia.* Bernice P. Bishop Museum Special Publication 43. 125 pp. The scope of the major portion of this interesting and useful work is apparent from its subtitle. The period covered extends back to the first historic voyages anywhere in the Pacific Ocean at the beginning of the sixteenth century and ends with 1850.

1957   *Arts and crafts of Hawaii.* Bernice P. Bishop Museum Special Publication 45. 606 pp. A detailed description of material-cultural items relating to all phases of pre-Contact Hawaiian life, based primarily on the ethological collections of the Bernice P. Bishop Museum. (Reprinted in 1964 by the Museum as fourteen separate sections.)

Burke, K. C., and J. T. Wilson

1976   Hot spots on the earth's surface. *Scientific American* 235 (2): 46–57. Excellent discussions and illustrations of hot-spot phenomena as well as of other plate-tectonic phenomena such as plate formation and volcanic buildup at subduction zones.

Cachola-Abad, C. K.

1993   Evaluating the orthodox dual settlement model for the Hawaiian Islands: An analysis of artefact distribution and Hawaiian oral traditions. Pages 13–32 *in* M. W. Graves and R. C. Green (eds.), *Evolution and organisation of prehistoric society in Polynesia.* New Zealand Archaeological Association Monograph No. 19. 125 pp. A study questioning the long-held theory that Hawai'i received prehistoric immigrants from only the Marquesas and Society Islands and suggesting that there may well have been early contacts involving a number of East Polynesian island groups.

Carleton, J. T.

1987   Patterns of transoceanic marine biological invasions in the Pacific Ocean. *Bulletin of Marine Science* 41:452–465. An initial attempt to determine the means and routes by which historically introduced organisms were—and still are—being spread among islands and continents. (Reprinted as pp. 504–517 *in* Kay [ed.] [1994].)

Carlquist, S. (J.)

1965   *Island life.* Garden City, New York: Natural History Press. 451 pp. Although by now a rather old reference, still one of the few overall discussions of evolution and related terrestrial biotic matters in regard to oceanic islands.

1974   *Island biology.* New York: Columbia University Press. 660 pp. A masterful treatise on methods of biotic dispersal to oceanic islands, as well as ecological, morphological, and behavioral adaptations of terrestrial organisms after colonization. Plants receive by far the most attention, but animals are also fairly well covered.

1980   *Hawaii: A natural history.* 2d ed. Lāwa'i, Hawai'i: Pacific Tropical Botanical Garden. 468 pp. An excellent, profusely illustrated work, although a major portion concentrates on botanical subjects. Included are important discussions of selected ecological and evolutionary phenomena using Hawaiian plant and animal examples, topics usually not found in similar references. The marine environment, and Polynesian culture, are not covered, and the information on geology as well as certain other subjects is unavoidably out of date.

1982   The first arrivals. *Natural History* 91 (12): 20–30. A fact-filled account of how various terrestrial plants and animals may have originally reached the Hawaiian Islands.

Carr, G. D.

1985   Monograph of the Hawaiian Madiinae (Asteraceae): *Argyroxiphium, Dubautia,* and *Wilkesia. Allertonia* 4:1–123. A thorough analysis of numerous aspects of the Silversword Alliance, including foliage and flower morphology, distribution, ecology, chromosome numbers, and hybridization, as well as a taxonomic treatment of the twenty-eight species recognized at the time.

1987 Beggar's ticks and tarweeds: Masters of adaptive radiation. *Trends in Ecology and Evolution* 2:192–195. A greatly condensed overview of certain evolutionary processes yielding the many varied Hawaiian species of two types of plants of the sunflower family Asteraceae. (Reprinted as pp. 292–299 *in* Kay [ed.] [1994].)

Carson, H. L.

1983 Genetical processes of evolution on high oceanic islands. *GeoJournal* 7 (6): 543–547. A very concise review of chromosomal and behavioral evolution in the endemic picture-winged species of the Hawaiian dipteran genus *Drosophila.* (Reprinted as pp. 259–263 *in* Kay [ed.] [1994].)

1987a Tracing ancestry with chromosomal sequences. *Trends in Ecology and Evolution* 2:203–207. A succinct but quite understandable overview of the theory and practical use of chromosome banding in, primarily, the endemic Hawaiian picture-winged flies of the genus *Drosophila.*

1987b The process by which species originate. *BioScience* 37:715–720. An analysis of the writings of John T. Gulick, Hawaiian missionary son and amateur malacologist. It is pointed out that, in terms of twentieth-century Neo-Darwinism, his mid-1800s recognition of the important role of spatial isolation in speciation events complemented Charles Darwin's primary emphasis on natural selection of individuals.

1989 Genetic imbalance, realigned selection, and the origin of species. Pages 345–362 *in* L. V. Giddings, K. Y. Kaneshiro, and W. W. Anderson (eds.), *Genetics, speciation and the founder principle.* New York: Oxford University Press. 373 pp. A perceptive and illuminating discussion of the species concept itself, along with that of speciation methods, including punctuated equilibrium. Special attention is given to the role of behavioral selection in complex mating rituals of such animals as Hawaiian picture-winged flies of the genus *Drosophila.*

1997 Sexual selection: A driver of genetic change in Hawaiian *Drosophila. Journal of Heredity* 88:343–352. A summation of critical portions of this authority's 35-year study of the picture-winged flies, including the role of Island volcanism in speciation within the group. Recent work on the dynamics of genetic change in dispersed populations of *Drosophila silvestris* on Hawai'i is detailed.

Carson, H. L., and D. A. Clague

1995 Geology and biogeography of the Hawaiian Islands. Pages 14–29 *in* W. L. Wagner and V. A. Funk (eds.), *Hawaiian biogeography: Evolution on a hot spot archipelago.* Washington, D.C.: Smithsonian Institution Press. An excellent explanation of the successive formation of the numerous Hawaiian Islands and the interisland dispersal and subsequent evolution of organisms throughout this period.

Ching, P.

1994 *The Hawaiian monk seal.* Honolulu: University of Hawai'i Press. 40 pp. A nontechnical work covering essentially all ecological aspects of this endemic Hawaiian mammal, including paintings by the author as well as a number of photographs.

Clague, D. A.

1998 Geology. Pages 37–46 *in* S. P. Juvik and J. O. Juvik (eds.), *Atlas of Hawai'i.* 3d ed. Honolulu: University of Hawai'i Press. An overview of major geological aspects of the Hawaiian Chain, including formation stages of a volcanic hot-spot island and the phenomenon of submarine landslides. Geology of the individual main islands is also covered, with emphasis on Hawai'i, in both text and geologic maps.

Clague, D. A., and G. B. Dalrymple
1987 The Hawaiian-Emperor volcanic chain. Part I: Geologic evolution. Pages 5–54 *in* R. W. Decker, T. L. Wright, and P. H. Stauffer (eds.), *Volcanism in Hawaii.* Washington, D.C.: Government Printing Office. A complete up-to-date technical report on ages, formation, and basalt characteristics of current and former islands of this entire chain. There is an extensive discussion of such related matters as hot-spot action, ocean-floor spreading, and tectonic-plate fracturing.

1989 Tectonics, geochronology, and origin of the Hawaiian-Emperor volcanic chain. Pages 188–217 *in* E. L. Winterer, D. M. Hussong, and R. W. Decker (eds.), *The Eastern Pacific Ocean and Hawaii.* The Geology of North America. Vol. N. Boulder, Colorado: Geological Society of America. 563 pp. A somewhat abridged, but still quite technical, version of Clague and Dalrymple (1987). (Reprinted as pp. 5–40 *in* Kay [ed.] [1994].)

Clark, J. R. K.
1980 *The beaches of Maui County.* Honolulu: University of Hawai'i Press. 161 pp. A most informative and interesting account of many coastal features around the entire islands of Maui, Moloka'i, Lāna'i, and Kaho'olawe, including references to a number of pertinent Hawaiian legends and historic anecdotes. The author has published similar books (see following) for the three other major counties of the state.

1985a *The beaches of O'ahu.* Honolulu: University of Hawai'i Press. 193 pp.

1985b *Beaches of the Big Island.* Honolulu: University of Hawai'i Press. 171 pp. Covers the coastal features of Hawai'i Island.

1990 *Beaches of Kaua'i and Ni'ihau.* Honolulu: University of Hawai'i Press. 114 pp.

Cleghorn, P. L.
1988 The settlement and abandonment of two Hawaiian outposts: Nihoa and Necker islands. *Bishop Museum Occasional Papers* 28:35–49. A reevaluation of prehistoric human use of these Northwestern Hawaiian Islands, based on a 1984 archaeological reconnaissance by the author, as well as on earlier archaeological findings by others.

Conant, S., C. C. Christensen, P. Conant, W. C. Gagné, and M. L. Goff
1984 The unique terrestrial biota of the Northwestern Hawaiian Islands. *Proceedings, Second Symposium on Resource Investigations in the Northwestern Hawaiian Islands* 1:77–94. (University of Hawai'i Sea Grant Publication UNIHI-SEAGRANT-MR-84-01.) A listing (rather generalized in the case of a few groups of organisms) and discussion of plants, terrestrial arthropods, land snails, and nonoceanic birds of the Northwestern chain, with recommendations for management and protection of this biota. (Reprinted as pp. 378–390 *in* Kay [ed.] [1994].)

Costin, A. B., and R. H. Groves (eds.)
1973 *Nature conservation in the Pacific.* Canberra, Australia: National University Press. 337 pp. Papers from the symposium of this name held at the Twelfth Pacific Science Congress. Most articles deal with western Pacific countries, with less than a half dozen including significant coverage of Hawai'i and other central Pacific islands.

Cowie, R. H.
1995 The land snails of Hawaii: Species richness, species-area relationships, shell shape and vacant niches. *Evolution* 49:1191–1202. A most informative and relatively extensive,

statistically based review of the subjects noted in the title. (This is Hawaii Biological Survey Contribution 1994-012.)

1997   Catalog and bibliography of the nonindigenous nonmarine snails and slugs of the Hawaiian Islands. *Bishop Museum Occasional Papers* 50:1–66. A listing of all alien land and freshwater species recorded from the Hawaiian Islands, whether established or not, including synonyms and islands of occurrence. (This is Hawaii Biological Survey Contribution 1997–001.)

1998   Patterns of introduction of nonindigenous nonmarine snails and slugs of the Hawaiian Islands. *Biodiversity and Conservation* 7:349–368. An examination of the taxa included in Cowie (1997), with special regard to their region of origin, manner of arrival, and reason for deliberate importations. Subsequent effects on native biota are also covered. (This is Hawaii Biological Survey Contribution 1997-012.)

Cowie, R. H., N. L. Evenhuis, and C. C. Christensen

1995   *Catalog of the native land and freshwater molluscs of the Hawaiian Islands.* Leiden, The Netherlands: Backhuys. 248 pp. A listing of all named native and possibly native Hawaiian species (as well as a few selected alien ones), including synonyms and islands of occurrence. (This is Hawaii Biological Survey Contribution 1994-005 [incorrectly stated in the publication as 1994-012].)

Cox, J. H., and E. Stasack

1970   *Hawaiian petroglyphs.* Honolulu: Bishop Museum Press. 100 pp. A relatively extensive information source on petroglyphs statewide, with numerous figures and photographs as well as location maps of all sites discussed.

Crawford, P.

1993   *Nomads of the wind: A natural history of Polynesia.* London: BBC Books. 272 pp. Coverage of primarily the major island groups, but also of a few isolated islands such as Henderson, Pitcairn, and Easter. Probably most useful as an information source in comparing pre- and post-Contact human society among the various Polynesian cultures. This well-illustrated volume accompanied a BBC television series of the same title.

Cuddihy, L. W., and C. P. Stone

1990   *Alteration of native Hawaiian vegetation: Effects of humans, their activities and introductions.* Honolulu: University of Hawai'i Press for Cooperative National Parks Resources Studies Unit, Department of Botany, University of Hawai'i at Mānoa. 138 pp. Probably the best review of the subject, with much detailed historical background information on the effects of both pre- and post-Contact human populations in the main Hawaiian Islands. (Summary on pp. 103–107 reprinted along with pertinent cited references as pp. 467–472 *in* Kay [ed.] [1994].)

Culliney, J. L.

1988   *Islands in a far sea: Nature and man in Hawaii.* San Francisco: Sierra Club Books. 410 pp. A well-written, extensively researched documentary account emphasizing the multitudinous detrimental effects of pre- and post-Contact humans on Hawaiian natural resources. The discussions are generally arranged by major ecological regions, and that on the sea is especially informative. As the author noted, not intended as a college text.

Dalrymple, G. B., E. A. Silver, and E. D. Jackson

1973   Origin of the Hawaiian Islands. *American Scientist* 61:294–308. Application of the plate tectonics and hot spot theory to formation of the Hawaiian Islands and the Emperor Seamount chain.

Darwin, C. R.

1859 *On the origin of species by means of natural selection, or the preservation of favoured races in the struggle for life.* London: John Murray. 502 pp. The initial presentation of the Darwinian explanation of biological evolution.

Daws, G. (A.)

1968 *Shoal of time: A history of the Hawaiian Islands.* Honolulu: University of Hawai'i Press. 494 pp. An extremely readable account of the interactions of Native Hawaiians and foreigners from Captain Cook's arrival in 1778 to statehood in 1959.

Decker, R. (W.), and B. Decker

1997 *Volcano watching.* Rev. and updated ed. Hawai'i Volcanoes National Park: Hawai'i Natural History Association. 84 pp. An inexpensive and entertaining nontechnical account of Hawaiian volcanism and volcanologists' study methods. Examples are also drawn from elsewhere on earth and even from a neighboring planet or two.

Decker, R. W., T. L. Wright, and P. H. Stauffer (eds.)

1987 *Volcanism in Hawaii.* Washington, D.C.: Government Printing Office. 1,667 pp. in 2 vols. An exhaustive report on all aspects of geologic history and recent volcanic activity of the Hawaiian Islands, with contributions of numerous authorities.

DeSalle, R.

1995 Molecular approaches to biogeographic analysis of Hawaiian Drosophilidae. Pages 72–89 *in* W. L. Wagner and V. A. Funk (eds.), *Hawaiian biogeography: Evolution on a hot spot archipelago.* Washington, D.C.: Smithsonian Institution Press. A cladistic study of selected species of various native drosophilid genera, based largely on DNA nucleotide sequences.

Desmond, A., and J. Moore

1991 *Darwin.* New York: Warner Books. 808 pp. An exceptionally complete, well-illustrated biography, covering primarily Darwin's life and scientific work after his return from the *Beagle* voyage.

Devick, W. S.

1991 Patterns of introductions of aquatic organisms to Hawaiian freshwater habitats. Pages 189–213 *in* W. S. Devick (ed.), *New directions in research, management and conservation of Hawaiian freshwater stream ecosystems. Proceedings of the 1990 symposium on Freshwater Stream Biology and Fisheries Management.* Honolulu: State of Hawai'i Department of Land and Natural Resources, Division of Aquatic Resources. A history and tabulation of deliberately and inadvertently introduced freshwater vertebrates and invertebrates other than insects.

Devick, W. S. (ed.)

1991 *New directions in research, management and conservation of Hawaiian freshwater stream ecosystems. Proceedings of the 1990 Symposium on Freshwater Stream Biology and Fisheries Management.* Honolulu: State of Hawai'i Department of Land and Natural Resources, Division of Aquatic Resources. 318 pp. Numerous articles presenting, primarily, current knowledge of vertebrate and invertebrate faunal attributes, as well as certain abiotic factors, of Hawaiian streams and ponds.

1993 *Assessments of the impact of Hurricane Iniki on stream biota and ecosystems on Kaua'i.* Honolulu: State of Hawai'i Department of Land and Natural Resources, Division of Aquatic Resources. 88 pp. Two rather extensive articles describing the physical and biological effects of this devastating 1992 storm on Kaua'i streams.

Doty, M. S.

1967   Contrast between the pioneer populating process on land and shore. *Bulletin Southern California Academy of Sciences* 66 (3): 175–194. Results of a 10-year investigation of plant succession on a new lava flow on the island of Hawai'i. The land portion of the flow receives the most attention in this article, and the relationship of rain to the cooling lava is also considered. (Reprinted as pp. 253–272 *in* Kay [ed.] [1972].)

1973a   Marine organisms—Tropical algal ecology and conservation. Pages 83–196 *in* A. B. Costin and R. H. Groves (eds.), *Nature conservation in the Pacific*. Canberra, Australia: National University Press. A discussion of various ecological and biogeographical aspects of more common seaweeds, primarily in the Hawaiian Islands, but also including comparisons with marine algal floras elsewhere in the insular tropical Pacific.

1973b   Inter-relationships between marine and terrestrial ecosystems in Polynesia. Pages 241–252 *in* A. B. Costin and R. H. Groves (eds.), *Nature conservation in the Pacific*. Canberra, Australia: National University Press. Coverage of somewhat the same subjects as Doty (1967), but with more emphasis on ecology of the marine ecosystem and including both calcareous and noncalcareous Hawaiian algae.

Dunmore, J.

1991   *Who's who in Pacific navigation*. Honolulu: University of Hawai'i Press. 312 pp. Biographic entries of the captains in charge of exploring voyages to the Pacific from the sixteenth to the early twentieth centuries, with brief descriptions of these expeditions. The index allows identification of most naturalists and other scientifically related personnel on these voyages.

Eiseley, L. C.

1956   Charles Darwin. *Scientific American* 194 (2): 62–72. Although there are numerous publications on Darwin, this particular relatively short article rather adequately—and most interestingly—covers the setting and work involved in formulation of the theory of evolution.

Elbert, S. H., and M. K. Pukui

1979   *Hawaiian grammar*. Honolulu: University of Hawai'i Press. 193 pp. A volume for those particularly interested in the language. Notes on the general subject were formerly included as a separate section in each of the three earlier (1957–1965) editions of a Hawaiian-English dictionary by Pukui and Elbert, but now the section has been omitted from the dictionary (Pukui and Elbert 1986) and published as this greatly expanded separate work. (See also Pukui et al. [1975].)

Eldredge, L. G., and S. E. Miller

1995   How many species are there in Hawaii? *Bishop Museum Occasional Papers* 41:3–18. An annotated listing of currently known species numbers of Hawaiian native and alien plants and animals.

Erickson, J.

1992   *Plate tectonics: Unravelling the mysteries of the earth*. New York: Facts On File. 197 pp. A good overall discussion of plate movements and attendant volcanic phenomena, continent formation, and related subjects. A chapter on apparent plate tectonics of other planets is included.

Fielding, A., and E. Robinson

1987   *An underwater guide to Hawai'i.* Honolulu: University of Hawai'i Press. 156 pp. A concise coverage of many types of Hawaiian marine invertebrate and vertebrate animals. The underwater photographs are especially good.

Finney, B. R.

1977   Voyaging canoes and the settlement of Polynesia. *Science* 196:1277–1285. A somewhat shorter, but perhaps more easily accessible version of the following Finney (1979) work. The author originally conceived the idea of construction and sailing of the modern double-hulled Hawaiian canoe *Hōkūle'a* and was a primary participant in every phase of the project.

1979   Voyaging. Pages 323–351, *in* J. D. Jennings (ed.), *Prehistory of Polynesia.* Cambridge, Massachusetts: Harvard University Press. An extensive and highly informative treatment of Polynesian sailing canoes and navigation, concentrating on the recent development of the modern double-hulled Hawaiian canoe *Hōkūle'a* and its subsequent epic voyages between Hawai'i and Tahiti in 1976.

Finney, B. R. (with M. Among, C. Baybayan, T. Crouch, P. Frost, B. Kilonsky, R. Rhodes, T. Schroeder, D. Stroup, N. Thompson, R. Worthington, and E. Yadao)

1994   *Voyage of rediscovery: A cultural odyssey through Polynesia.* Berkeley: University of California Press. 401 pp. A brief review of the recent development and history of two-way experimental voyaging between Hawai'i and Tahiti, followed by a much longer account of the culturally significant 1985–1987 journey of the double-hulled voyaging canoe *Hōkūle'a* from and back to Hawai'i through most of the major Polynesian archipelagos. Methods of traditional noninstrument navigation are also explained in some detail.

FitzPatrick, E. A.

1980   *Soils: Their formation, classification and distribution.* New York: Longman. 353 pp. Only one of a number of good and extensive textbooks on this subject.

Flament, P., S. Kennan, R. Lumpkin, M. Sawyer, and E. Stroup

1998   The ocean. Pages 82–86 *in* S. P. Juvik and J. O. Juvik (eds.), *Atlas of Hawai'i.* 3d ed. Honolulu: University of Hawai'i Press. An extensively illustrated description of certain physical and chemical properties of the central Pacific Ocean around the Hawaiian chain. Characteristics of currents, tides, and waves are also covered.

Fleischer, R. C., and C. E. McIntosh

in press Molecular systematics and biogeography of the Hawaiian avifauna. *Studies in Avian Biology.* A presentation of data based on differences in DNA nucleotide sequences showing the ancestral relationships of many extinct and extant Hawaiian birds. General dates of apparent speciation of a number of endemic species are also provided.

Ford, J. I., and R. A. Kinzie III

1982   Life crawls upstream. *Natural History* 91 (12): 60–67. An illustrated semipopular account of native Hawaiian freshwater fishes and stream invertebrates. (Reprinted, without figures, as pp. 391–395 *in* Kay [ed.] [1994].)

Fortner, H. J.

1978   *The limu eater: A cookbook of Hawaiian seaweed.* University of Hawai'i Sea Grant Miscellaneous Report 79-01. 107 pp. Despite the subtitle, this is much more than just a list of recipes. Natural history data, identification notes, collecting instructions, and seaweed anecdotes appear, in addition to preparation, storage, and cooking suggestions.

Freed, L. A., S. Conant, and R. C. Fleischer
1987   Evolutionary ecology and radiation of Hawaiian passerine birds. *Trends in Ecology and Evolution* 2:196–199, 202–203. A generalized but very informative and useful treatment of the subject, concentrating on the historically known Hawaiian honey-creepers, although some information on extinct species of both passeriform ("perching or songbirds") and nonpasseriform groups is also included. (Reprinted as pp. 335–345 *in* Kay [ed.] [1994].)

Gagné, W. C.
1975   Hawaii's tragic dismemberment. *Defenders* 50:461–469. A semipopular well-illustrated overview of the evolution and current problems of the archipelago's native biota.

Gavenda, R., C. Smith, and N. Vollrath
1998   Soils. Pages 92–96 *in* S. P. Juvik and J. O. Juvik (eds.), *Atlas of Hawai'i.* 3d ed. Honolulu: University of Hawai'i Press. A relatively brief discussion of Hawaiian soil formation, composition, and weathering, accompanied by maps of main island soil types, as well as a chart showing erosion rates of Island lands under different uses.

Giambelluca, T. W., and T. A. Schroeder
1998   Climate. Pages 49–59 *in* S. P. Juvik and J. O. Juvik (eds.), *Atlas of Hawai'i.* 3d ed. Honolulu: University of Hawai'i Press. An excellent comprehensive discussion of Hawaiian climatology, copiously illustrated with explanatory maps, diagrams, and graphs.

Giddings, L. V., and A. R. Templeton
1983   Behavioral phylogenies and the direction of evolution. *Science* 220:372–378. A good review of the mechanics and significance of, especially, the "Kaneshiro model" of sexual behavior and related phenomena in regard to phylogeny and incipient speciation of evolving animal lineages.

Givnish, T. J., K. J. Sytsma, J. F. Smith, and W. J. Hahn
1994   Thorn-like prickles and heterophylly in *Cyanea:* Adaptations to extinct avian browsers on Hawaii? *Proceedings of the National Academy of Sciences of the United States of America* 91:2810–2814. An investigation of the possible relationship of probably neotenic morphological characteristics of a number of species of this endemic genus, and the former presence of large herbivorous flightless birds in the Hawaiian Islands. (This work in part attempts to explain the findings of Lammers [1990].)

1995   Molecular evolution, adaptive radiation, and geographic speciation in *Cyanea* (Campanulaceae, Lobelioideae). Pages 288–337 *in* W. L. Wagner and V. A. Funk (eds.), *Hawaiian biogeography: Evolution on a hot spot archipelago.* Washington, D.C.: Smithsonian Institution Press. A cladistic study of this speciose endemic group, based on DNA nucleotide sequences. The work includes additional information on the prickly foliaged species examined in Givnish et al. (1994).

Gosline, W. A.
1955   The inshore fish fauna of Johnston Island, a central Pacific atoll. *Pacific Science* 9:442–480. A coverage of this animal group, with a zoogeographic discussion that is especially pertinent to origin of Hawaiian fishes.

1965   Vertical zonation of inshore fishes in the upper water layers of the Hawaiian Islands. *Ecology* 46:823–831. A study based on numerous species from forty-eight Island bottom-dwelling fish families, including their occurrence in five different habitats. (Reprinted as pp. 305–313 *in* Kay [ed.] [1972].)

Gosline, W. A., and V. E. Brock

1960   *Handbook of Hawaiian fishes.* Honolulu: University of Hawai'i Press. 372 pp. The most recent comprehensive scientific work on this group. There are keys to families and species, with line drawings, but no color illustrations.

Grant, K. A., and V. Grant

1968   *Hummingbirds and their flowers.* New York: Columbia University Press. 115 pp. Chapter 11 presents a perceptive and persuasive hypothesis of how the coevolution of long hummingbird bills and long tubular flowers of their primary nectar-bearing food plants could have occurred.

Grigg, R. W.

1983   Community structure, succession and development of coral reefs in Hawaii. *Marine Ecology Progress Series* 11:1–14. A detailed study documenting occurrence and density of reef-coral species throughout the archipelago. Reasons for differences in taxonomic representation within communities, as well as varying times necessary for ecological succession are also covered. (Reprinted as pp. 196–209 *in* Kay [ed.] [1994].)

1988   Paleoceanography of coral reefs in the Hawaiian-Emperor chain. *Science* 240:1737–1743. An examination of changes through geologic time in the reef-building coral fauna of the chain, including factors regulating colonization and extinction. (Reprinted as pp. 164–170 *in* Kay [ed.] [1994].)

Gulko, D.

1999   *Hawaiian coral reef ecology.* Honolulu: Mutual. 256 pp. A well-illustrated volume, with good nontechnical discussions of stony corals and the numerous invertebrates inhabiting the coral reefs of the state.

Haddon, A. C., and J. Hornell

1936–1938 *Canoes of Oceania.* Bernice P. Bishop Museum Special Publications 27, 28, and 29. 454, 342, and 88 pp., respectively. An exhaustive, well-illustrated treatment of traditional watercraft throughout the various regions of Oceania. This is the most comprehensive work of its kind, although the conclusions in regard to migrations of Polynesians have been shown to be incorrect by more recent investigations. (Reprinted in 1975 by the Museum as a single volume.)

Hadfield, M. G.

1986   Extinction in Hawaiian achatinelline snails. *Malacologia* 27:67–81. An extensive analysis of numerous life history aspects of, especially, one species each of the achatinellid genera *Achatinella* and *Partulina* by an expert in the field. Early and current historic population numbers for members of the endemic Hawaiian subfamily are also critically evaluated, and reasons given for their current endangerment. (Reprinted as pp. 320–334 *in* Kay [ed.] [1994].)

Hadfield, M. G., S. E. Miller, and A. H. Carwile

1993   The decimation of endemic Hawai'ian [*sic*] tree snails by alien predators. *American Zoologist* 33:610–622. Essentially an amplification of data presented in Hadfield (1986), utilizing field studies of predation on one *Achatinella* species by an alien snail *(Euglandina rosea)* and a rodent *(Rattus rattus).*

Handy, E. S. C., and E. G. Handy (with the collaboration of M. K. Pukui)

1972   *Native planters in old Hawaii: Their life, lore, and environment.* Bernice P. Bishop Museum Bulletin 233. 641 pp. An invaluable encyclopedic treatment of horticulture, animal husbandry, and many other aspects of the commoners' existence in pre-

Contact Hawai'i. (Reprinted in 1991 by the Museum as a 676-page volume, with newly compiled indexes to subjects and chants.)

Harrison, C. S.

1990   *Seabirds of Hawaii: Natural history and conservation.* Ithaca, New York: Cornell University Press. 249 pp. Unquestionably the best single work on the marine-related birds of the Hawaiian Islands, although not intended primarily for species identification. The great amount of natural history data for all species, including the terns, is exceptionally thorough and informative.

Hart, A. D.

1978   The onslaught against Hawaii's tree snails. *Natural History* 87 (10): 46–57. A semi-popular but most informative account of the general ecology, distribution, and threats to snails of the endemic O'ahu genus *Achatinella.*

Hawai'i Audubon Society

1996   *Hawai'i's Birds.* 4th ed., 2d rev. Honolulu: Hawai'i Audubon Society. 112 pp. A relatively brief but extremely useful comprehensive guide to the extant Island native and alien birds, with color illustrations of all species. This guide appears in a revised edition every few years to reflect new information.

Hazlett, R. W., and D. W. Hyndman

1996   *Roadside geology of Hawai'i.* Missoula, Montana: Mountain Press. 307 pp. A useful nontechnical work presenting a brief physical description of each of six main islands, with a profusely illustrated road itinerary pointing out and explaining interesting geological features of each. The introductory chapter consists of a moderately extensive discussion of the formation and geology of the entire Hawaiian chain.

Hedberg, O.

1964   Features of Afroalpine plant ecology. *Acta Phytogeographica Suecica* 49:1–144. A scholarly study of many high-elevation African plants and their adaptations to various montane environments.

Herbst, D. R., and W. L. Wagner

1992   Alien plants on the Northwestern Hawaiian Islands. Pages 189–224 *in* C. P. Stone, C. W. Smith, and J. T. Tunison (eds.), *Alien plant invasions in native ecosystems of Hawai'i: Management and research.* Honolulu: University of Hawai'i Press for Cooperative National Parks Resources Studies Unit, Department of Botany, University of Hawai'i at Mānoa. An account of the nonnative terrestrial plants in this part of the Hawaiian chain, with historical notes on some species, and an island-occurrence checklist of all.

Hirth, H. F.

1997   *Synopsis of the biological data on the Green Turtle* Chelonia mydas *(Linnaeus 1758).* Washington, D.C.: U.S. Fish and Wildlife Service Biological Report 97(1). 120 pp. An exhaustive report on the worldwide natural history of this marine reptile.

Holmes, T.

1981   *The Hawaiian canoe.* Hanalei, Hawai'i: Editions Limited. 191 pp. An extensive, well-illustrated account of all aspects of various types of wooden canoes used in the Islands from ancient through modern times.

Hoover, J. P.

1993   *Hawaii's fishes: A guide for snorkelers, divers, and aquarists.* Honolulu: Mutual. 178

pp. An ecological discussion, along with excellent underwater photographs of a great number of Hawaiian reef fishes. Advice on collecting and maintaining saltwater aquarium fishes of many of the families covered is also included.

Hourigan, T. F., and E. S. Reese

1987   Mid-ocean isolation and the evolution of Hawaiian reef fishes. *Trends in Ecology and Evolution* 2:187–191. A good review of many aspects of inshore fish colonization and evolution in the Hawaiian Islands.

Howarth, F. G.

1987   Evolutionary ecology of aeolian and subterranean habitats in Hawaii. *Trends in Ecology and Evolution* 2:220–223. Hawaiian alpine stone desert and lava tube habitats are notable among those discussed. The author is the leading authority on the Hawaiian fauna of these ecosystems.

1990   Hawaiian terrestrial arthropods. *Bishop Museum Occasional Papers* 30:4–26. An overview of numerous aspects of this fauna, containing helpful tables giving numbers of species in various groups, with counts of the native and alien forms.

Howarth, F. G., and W. P. Mull

1992   *Hawaiian insects and their kin.* Honolulu: University of Hawai'i Press. 160 pp. An examination of the origin, evolution, conservation, and a number of other aspects of Island terrestrial invertebrates, along with a brief history of entomology in the Islands. Half of the book is devoted to outstanding close-up photographs of Hawaiian arthropods by the second author, with capsular accounts of the subjects. (Pages 17–29 of the introductory section reprinted as pp. 370–377 *in* Kay [ed.] [1994].)

Hunsaker, D., II, and P. Breese

1967   Herpetofauna of the Hawaiian Islands. *Pacific Science* 21:423–428. Primarily an updating of Oliver and Shaw (1953).

Hunt, C. D., Jr.

1996   *Geohydrology of the island of Oahu, Hawaii.* U.S. Geological Survey Professional Paper 1412-B. 54 pp. A detailed account of freshwater dynamics on the island, covering many of the same topics as Nichols et al. (1996) and providing many of the specific data for that publication.

I'i, J. P.

1959   *Fragments of Hawaiian history.* Bernice P. Bishop Museum Special Publication 70. 202 pp. Remembrances of Hawaiian cultural and natural history, as recorded by a Native Hawaiian between 1866 and 1870. Translated from Hawaiian by Mary K. Pukui and edited by Dorothy B. Barrère.

James, H. F., and D. A. Burney

1997   The diet and ecology of Hawaii's extinct flightless waterfowl: Evidence from coprolites. *Biological Journal of the Linnean Society* 62:279–297. An examination of preserved excrement of the Maui Nui *Moa Nalo* revealed that at least this species was apparently primarily a plant eater, with ferns being an important dietary component.

James, H. F., and S. L. Olson

1983   Flightless birds. *Natural History* 92 (9): 30–40. A relatively brief but interesting and informative explanation of evolution of flightlessness in Hawaiian birds, especially the large gooselike forms, of which skeletons of flighted and flightless individuals are sketched.

1991   Descriptions of thirty-two new species of birds from the Hawaiian Islands: Part II.
        Passeriformes. *Ornithological Monographs* No. 46:1–88. Formal scientific descrip-
        tions and informative related discussions of sixteen species of prehistorically extinct
        endemic passeriform ("perching or songbirds") whose remains have been discovered
        in the main islands since 1972. Photographs of much of the bill material, as well as
        of a limited number of postcranial elements, are included. (General discussions of pp.
        7–8 and 78–88 reprinted as pp. 456–466 *in* Kay [ed.] [1994].)

James, H. F., R. L. Zusi, and S. L. Olson
1989   *Dysmorodrepanis munroi* (Fringillidae: Drepanidini), a valid genus and species of
        Hawaiian finch. *Wilson Bulletin* 101:159–179. A reexamination of the only known
        specimen of this Hawaiian bird showing that it undoubtedly represents a legitimate
        but historically extirpated species, probably most closely related to the *'Ō'ū (Psit-
        tirostra psittacea)*.

Jennings, J. D. (ed.)
1979   *Prehistory of Polynesia.* Cambridge, Massachusetts: Harvard University Press. 399 pp.
        A classic and extensive compilation of various papers on the subject; the fourteen
        authors of the individual chapters are all recognized authorities on their subjects. Some
        of the data are now outdated by newer discoveries, but the work still contains an enor-
        mous amount of essential information.

Johnson, L. G.
1983   *Biology.* Dubuque, Iowa: W. C. Brown. 1,105 pp. Only one of a number of good and
        extensive college-level texts on this subject.

Johnson, W. H., L. E. Delanney, E. C. Williams, and T. A. Cole
1977   *Principles of zoology.* 2d ed. New York: Holt, Rinehart and Winston. 747 pp. Only one
        of a number of good and extensive textbooks on this subject.

Jokiel, P. L.
1987   Ecology, biogeography and evolution of corals in Hawaii. *Trends in Ecology and Evo-
        lution* 2:179–182. An informative generalized overview of the subjects, limited to
        reef-building species.

Juvik, S. P., and J. O. Juvik (eds.)
1998   *Atlas of Hawai'i.* 3d ed. Honolulu: University of Hawai'i Press. 352 pp. More like an
        encyclopedia than simply an atlas and an extremely informative work overall, with
        the text much revised from the second edition of Armstrong (ed.) (1983). Most of the
        chapter subjects of this volume are among those treated on pp. 34–158 of the *Atlas.*
        There is a gazetteer, but no subject index.

Kamakau, S. M.
1964   *Ka po'e kahiko (The people of old).* Bernice P. Bishop Museum Special Publication
        51. 165 pp. Observations on ancient Hawaiian culture, originally appearing as articles
        in various Hawaiian-language newspapers in the latter third of the nineteenth century.
        Translated by Mary K. Pukui and edited by Dorothy B. Barrère, as were also the two
        following Kamakau references based on the same general type of sources.

1976   *The works of the people of old (Na hana a ka po'e kahiko).* Bernice P. Bishop Museum
        Special Publication 61. 170 pp. (See note under Kamakau [1964].)

1991   *Tales and traditions of the people of old (Nā mo'olelo a ka po'e kahiko).* Honolulu:
        Bishop Museum Press. 184 pp. (See note under Kamakau [1964].)

Kaneshiro, K. Y.

1976   Ethological isolation and phylogeny in the *Planitibia* subgroup of Hawaiian *Drosophila.* Evolution 30:740–745. The original presentation of the "Kaneshiro Hypothesis" relating to disclosure of evolutionary relationships as revealed by differential mating behavior.

1988   Speciation in the Hawaiian *Drosophila. BioScience* 38:258–263. An informative review article on chromosomal and mating-behavior evolution in, primarily, the picture-winged flies of this genus, based on the work of the author and colleagues. (Reprinted as pp. 311–319 *in* Kay [ed.] [1994].)

Kaneshiro, K. Y., and J. S. Kurihara

1981   Sequential differentiation of sexual behavior in populations of *Drosophila silvestris. Pacific Science* 35:177–183. A relatively concise report of use of the "Kaneshiro Hypothesis" in elucidating sequential evolution within populations of this Hawaiian taxon.

Kaneshiro, K. Y., R. G. Gillespie, and H. L. Carson

1995   Chromosomes and male genitalia of Hawaiian *Drosophila:* Tools for interpreting phylogeny and geography. Pages 57–71 *in* W. L. Wagner and V. A. Funk (eds.), *Hawaiian biogeography: Evolution on a hot spot archipelago.* Washington, D.C.: Smithsonian Institution Press. A cladistic study of almost all of the one hundred or more species of picture-winged Hawaiian *Drosophila;* the chromosomal cladograms are based on banding-inversion sequences.

Kay, E. A.

1972   Hawaiian natural history: 1778–1900. Pages 604–653 *in* E. A. Kay [ed.], 1972, *A natural history of the Hawaiian Islands: Selected readings.* Honolulu: University of Hawai'i Press. Descriptions of the major foreign recorders of Hawaiian natural history and their work during the first century and a quarter after the arrival of Captain Cook. (Reprinted as pp. 400–424 *in* Kay [ed.] [1994].)

1979   *Hawaiian marine shells.* Bernice P. Bishop Museum Special Publication 64(4). 653 pp. The current standard reference for the subject.

1987   Marine ecosystems in the Hawaiian Islands. Pages 1–9 (Introduction) *in* D. M. Devaney and L. G. Eldredge (eds.), *Reef and shore fauna of Hawaii, Section 2: Platyhelminthes through Phoronida and Section 3: Sipuncula through Annelida.* Bernice P. Bishop Museum Special Publication 64(2 and 3). 461 pp. A condensed discussion of endemism and biogeography in the Hawaiian marine invertebrate fauna, as well as a more extended one on, primarily, the various Island shoreline ecosystems. (Reprinted as pp. 187–195 *in* Kay [ed.] [1994].)

1997   Missionary contributions to Hawaiian natural history: What Darwin didn't know. *Hawaiian Journal of History* 31:27–51. A detailed account of the Island geological, biological, and related activities and publications of the nineteenth-century Christian missionaries and their children.

Kay, E. A. (ed.)

1972   *A natural history of the Hawaiian Islands: Selected readings.* Honolulu: University of Hawai'i Press. 653 pp. A selection of, mostly, previously published articles by a variety of authors, intended for upper-division university courses in Hawaiian natural history.

1994   *A natural history of the Hawaiian Islands: Selected readings II.* Honolulu: University of Hawai'i Press. 520 pp. A revised version of Kay (ed.) (1972) and intended for the same purpose. Many important more recently published articles have been included, some of which appropriately replace related ones of the 1972 volume.

Kay, E. A., and S. R. Palumbi
1987   Endemism and evolution in Hawaiian marine invertebrates. *Trends in Ecology and Evolution* 2:183–186. An excellent, relatively condensed overview of this biota, with current numerical data regarding faunal composition, endemism, and similar subjects. Distributional aspects of this fauna are also covered. (Reprinted as pp. 346–353 *in* Kay [ed.] [1994].)

Kent, H. W.
1986   *Treasury of Hawaiian words in one hundred and one categories.* Honolulu: University of Hawai'i Press. 475 pp. An extensive compilation of Hawaiian terms, including names for members of various groups of plants and animals, arranged by categories.

Kepelino (= Kahoalii Keauokalani)
1932   *Traditions of Hawaii.* Bernice P. Bishop Museum Bulletin 95. 206 pp. Remembrances of Hawaiian cultural and natural history, as recorded by a Native Hawaiian between about 1853 and 1869. Translated from Hawaiian and annotated by Martha W. Beckwith.

Kettlewell, H. B. D.
1959   Darwin's missing evidence. *Scientific American* 200 (3): 48–53. A good popular account of the author's investigation and explanation of the evolutionary color change of the Peppered Moth population that occurred in England during the Industrial Revolution.

Kikuchi, W. K.
1976   Prehistoric Hawaiian fishponds. *Science* 193:295–299. A concise review of this apparently unique Hawaiian invention.

Kinzie, R. A., III
1991   Hawaiian freshwater ichthyofauna. Pages 18–39 *in* W. S. Devick (ed.), *New directions in research, management and conservation of Hawaiian freshwater stream ecosystems. Proceedings of the 1990 Symposium on Freshwater Stream Biology and Fisheries Management.* Honolulu: State of Hawai'i Department of Land and Natural Resources, Division of Aquatic Resources. A rather extensive review of current knowledge regarding several ecological and taxonomic aspects of the five native Hawaiian anadromous gobies, along with biogeographic information on similar Pacific gobies in general.

Kirch, P. V.
1982   Impact of the prehistoric Polynesians on the Hawaiian ecosystem. *Pacific Science* 36:1–14. An excellent review of the subject, drawing on information from varied botanical, zoological, and cultural sources. (Reprinted as pp. 425–438 *in* Kay [ed.] [1994].)

1984   *The evolution of the Polynesian chiefdoms.* Cambridge, England: Cambridge University Press. 314 pp. An extensive study of Pacific-wide prehistoric Polynesian resource use and its interrelationship with political organization. Tonga, Hawai'i, and Easter Island receive special attention.

1985 *Feathered gods and fishhooks: An introduction to Hawaiian archaeology and prehistory.* Honolulu: University of Hawai'i Press. 349 pp. The standard—and excellent—work on cultural history of ancient Hawai'i, as interpreted from prehistoric evidence.

1997 *The Lapita Peoples: Ancestors of the Oceanic world.* Cambridge, Massachusetts: Blackwell. 353 pp. An excellent and quite detailed study of the Lapita Culture, from its beginnings, through migrations, to final transformation into various Melanesian and Micronesian societies, as well as the entire Polynesian one. The factual information, as well as many intriguing speculations presented, is based on evidence from a great variety of sources: archaeology, linguistics, ethnography, physical anthropology, and ethnobiology.

2000 *The road of the winds.* Berkeley: University of California Press. 446 pp. A scholarly up-to-date chronicle of prehistoric insular Pacific settlement, encompassing Melanesia, Micronesia, and Polynesia. The apparent course of cultural development in these various areas is traced, and the similarities, differences, and environmental effects of the resultant cultures described.

Kirch, P. V., and T. L. Hunt (eds.)

1988 *Archaeology of the Lapita cultural complex: A critical review.* Thomas Burke Memorial Washington State Museum Research Report 5. 181 pp. Papers by several authors giving an overview of current knowledge of this early Southwest Pacific culture, pointing out deficiencies in past archaeological studies and offering suggestions for improving future ones.

1997 *Historical ecology in the Pacific islands: Prehistoric environmental and landscape change.* New Haven, Connecticut: Yale University Press. 331 pp. Thirteen papers on anthropogenous alterations of Pacific island ecosystems, primarily those of Polynesia. Pre- rather than post-Contact phenomena receive most attention.

Kirch, P. V., and M. Sahlins

1992 *Anahulu: The anthropology of history in the Kingdom of Hawaii.* Chicago: University of Chicago Press. 243 and 201 pp., respectively, in two vols. Vol. 1 covers primarily the historical ethnography, and Vol. 2 primarily the pre- and post-Contact archaeology, of this valley on the northwestern O'ahu coast.

Kitayama, K., D. Mueller-Dombois, and P. M. Vitousek

1995 Primary succession of Hawaiian montane rain forest on a chronosequence of eight lava flows. *Journal of Vegetation Science* 6:211–222. A description of vegetational differences on 'a'ā lava substrates ranging from 8 to about 9,000 years old, all located on the northeastern slope of Hawai'i Island's Mauna Loa.

Kobayashi, S. R., and M. G. Hadfield

1996 An experimental study of growth and reproduction in the Hawaiian tree snails *Achatinella mustelina* and *Partulina redfieldii* (Achatinellinae). *Pacific Science* 50:339–354. A comparative examination of the two stated natural history aspects of these species of this endemic subfamily of Achatinellidae. Much of the information may well be at least generally applicable to many other subfamily members.

Kosaki, R. K., R. L. Pyle, J. E. Randall, and D. K. Irons

1991 New records of fishes from Johnston Atoll, with notes on biogeography. *Pacific Science* 45:186–203. Records of additional species from the area, accompanied by informative discussions on various related subjects, including evolutionary phenomena among the atoll's fishes and a comparison of this fauna with that of the Hawaiian Islands.

Kramer, R. J.

1971   *Hawaiian land mammals.* Rutland, Vermont: Charles E. Tuttle. 347 pp. A series of extensive species accounts of all the mammals found wild in the state, exclusive of the cetaceans. A useful complement to Tomich (1986) because so much more life-history information is included.

Kraus, F., E. W. Campbell, A. Allison, and T. Pratt

1999   *Eleutherodactylus* frog introductions to Hawaii. *Herpetological Review* 30:21–25. A presentation of information on the current distribution of three alien species of this genus, their probable method of introduction, ecology and potential environmental effects, and means of possible control.

Krauss, B. H.

1993   *Plants in Hawaiian culture.* Honolulu: University of Hawai'i Press. 345 pp. An exceptionally thorough examination of the food and utilitarian plants used by pre-Contact Hawaiians in essentially all of their activities, including methods of cultivation and preparation of various species. About two-thirds of this volume by a highly knowledgeable and respected ethnobotanical expert is devoted to descriptions of the individual plant taxa, each accompanied by a full-page black-and-white photograph.

Lammers, T. G.

1990   Sequential paedomorphosis among the endemic Hawaiian Lobelioideae (Campanulaceae). *Taxon* 39:206–211. A study indicating that successively younger forms in this subfamily probably evolved increasingly dissected leaves and prickly armament through retention of these characteristics of immediately ancestral juveniles. (The possible selective advantage of this process is examined in Givnish et al. [1994].)

Lammers, T. G., and C. E. Freeman

1986   Ornithophily among the Hawaiian Lobelioideae (Campanulaceae): Evidence from floral nectar sugar compositions. *American Journal of Botany* 73:1613–1619. An investigation revealing that the nectar of many endemic Hawaiian lobelioids of the family Campanulaceae is rich in hexose sugars, rather than sucrose. This supports the hypothesis that these plants were quite likely originally pollinated by endemic birds of the fringilid subfamily Drepanidinae and the family Meliphagidae.

Loope, L. L., and S. P. Juvik

1998   Protected areas. Pages 154–157 *in* S. P. Juvik and J. O. Juvik (eds.), *Atlas of Hawai'i.* 3d ed. Honolulu: University of Hawai'i Press. A brief overview of governmental and private biotic-protection areas in Hawai'i, including a useful map showing the location of most, both on and around the main islands.

Lysaght, A.

1959   Some eighteenth century bird paintings in the library of Sir Joseph Banks (1743–1820). *Bulletin of the British Museum (Natural History) Historical Series* 1:253–371. This article includes the only two bird paintings prepared on Captain Cook's third voyage apparently ever to be published.

Macdonald, G. A.

1972   *Volcanoes.* Englewood Cliffs, New Jersey: Prentice-Hall. 510 pp. An excellent detailed explanation, profusely illustrated, of all volcanic phenomena around the world. A most useful companion volume to Macdonald et al. (1983).

Macdonald, G. A., A. T. Abbott, and F. L. Peterson

1983   *Volcanoes in the sea: The geology of Hawaii.* 2d ed. Honolulu: University of Hawai'i Press. 517 pp. The current definitive work on this Hawaiian subject. Chapter 18 contains an excellent, easily understood, and helpfully illustrated discussion of most aspects of plate tectonics, using examples from Hawai'i and the Pacific whenever possible.

Magruder, W. H., and J. W. Hunt
1979   *Seaweeds of Hawaii: A photographic identification guide.* Honolulu: Oriental. 116 pp. Excellent photographs and short descriptive text, along with ecological data, for 118 of the most noticeable Hawaiian seaweeds. This is by far the best reference currently available for the interested nonspecialist.

Malo, D.
1951   *Hawaiian antiquities (Moolelo Hawaii).* 2d ed. Bernice P. Bishop Museum Special Publication 2. 278 pp. A compendium of Hawaiian social and biological lore recorded by a Native Hawaiian in the 1830s. Originally translated from Hawaiian and annotated by Nathaniel B. Emerson in 1898.

Maragos, J. E.
1977   Order Scleractinia: Stony corals. Pages 158–241 *in* D. M. Devaney and L. G. Eldredge (eds.), *Reef and shore fauna of Hawaii, Section 1: Protozoa through Ctenophora.* Bernice P. Bishop Museum Special Publication 64(1). 278 pp. A presentation of the general biology of reef-building corals, along with identification keys and species accounts for all Hawaiian taxa.

1995   Revised checklist of extant shallow-water stony coral species from Hawaii (Cnidaria: Anthozoa: Scleractinia). *Bishop Museum Occasional Papers* 42:54–55. An update of Maragos (1977).

1998   Marine ecosystems. Pages 111–120 *in* S. P. Juvik and J. O. Juvik (eds.), *Atlas of Hawai'i.* 3d ed. Honolulu: University of Hawai'i Press. An extensive classification of these systems around the Hawaiian Islands. Distribution, environmental conditions, biotic resources, cultural significance, and current threats to each ecosystem are described.

Maragos, J. E., and P. L. Jokiel
1986   Reef corals of Johnston Atoll: One of the world's most isolated reefs. *Coral Reefs* 4:141–150. A study of reef-building corals of this atoll, discussing species composition and habitats, as well as colonization, dispersal, and paleogeography.

Matisoo-Smith, E., R. M. Roberts, G. J. Irwin, J. S. Allen, D. Penny, and D. M. Lambert
1998   Patterns of prehistoric human mobility in Polynesia indicated by mtdna from the Pacific rat. *Proceedings of the National Academy of Sciences of the United States of America* 95:15145–15150. A reconstruction of Polynesian colonization routes and later voyages, based on comparisons of mitochondrial DNA nucleotide sequences from numerous insular populations of the commensal *Rattus exulans.*

McKeown, S.
1996   *A field guide to reptiles and amphibians in the Hawaiian Islands.* Los Osos, California: Diamond Head. 172 pp. An informative guide to the identification and natural history of all extant species in the archipelago, with maps showing islands of occurrence. The color illustrations of each species are excellent. A chapter on the potential threat to Hawai'i of inadvertent introduction of the Brown Tree Snake is included.

Medveden, Z. A.
1969   *The rise and fall of T. D. Lysenko.* New York: Columbia University Press. 284 pp. An account of, primarily, the sociopolitical interactions of geneticists and agronomists in

the Soviet Union between about 1937 and 1964. A number of the specific—and often absurd—Lamarckian practices forced upon Soviet agriculture during this period by the Soviet Union's anti-Darwinian and anti-Mendelian agronomic dictator Lysenko are also briefly described. Translated from Russian by I. M. Lerner.

Miller, S. E., and L. G. Eldredge

1996   Numbers of Hawaiian species: Supplement 1. *Bishop Museum Occasional Papers* 45: 8–17. An update of Eldredge and Miller (1995) by means of a condensed table giving revised totals for endemic and alien species of the Hawaiian biota, but only by very broad groups (for example, "Mollusks," "Insects," "Other Arthropods"). The bases for the numerical revisions are explained in a series of notations.

Mink, J. (F.), and G. Bauer

1998   Water. Pages 87–91 *in* S. P. Juvik and J. O. Juvik (eds.), *Atlas of Hawai'i.* 3d ed. Honolulu: University of Hawai'i Press. An overview of various aspects of freshwater resources of the main Hawaiian Islands, including their location, size, and utilization.

Mitchell, D. D. K.

1982   *Resource units in Hawaiian culture.* Rev. and expanded ed. Honolulu: Kamehameha Schools Press. 301 pp. An extensive and well-researched account of a multitude of cultural activities carried out by both pre- and post-Contact peoples in Hawai'i. Especially useful to secondary-school and other educators because detailed teacher's guides are included.

Monroe, J. S., and R. Wicander

1992   *Physical geology: Exploring the earth.* St. Paul, Minnesota: West. 639 pp. Only one of a number of good college-level texts on the earth's geology. This book is exceptionally thorough and extremely well illustrated.

Montgomery, S. L.

1975   Comparative breeding site ecology and the adaptive radiation of picture-wing *Drosophila* (Diptera: Drosophilidae). *Proceedings of the Hawaiian Entomological Society* 22:65–103. An extensive study of the various egg-deposition sites of many Hawaiian species of the pomace fly family Drosophilidae and how utilization of the larval food at each general site type is partitioned by the different taxa.

1983   Biogeography of the moth genus *Eupithecia* in Oceania and the evolution of ambush predation in Hawaiian caterpillars. *Entomologia Generalis* 8:27–34. A study of this group, many of whose larvae in Hawai'i have adaptively shifted to a carnivorous diet.

Moore, J. G., D. A. Clague, R. T. Holcomb, P. W. Lipman, W. R. Normark, and M. E. Torresan

1989   Prodigious submarine landslides on the Hawaiian Ridge. *Journal of Geophysical Research* 94:17,465–17,484. An investigation of extremely large ancient earth slippages on the ocean sides of Hawaiian volcanoes, as identified by, primarily, sonar mapping.

Moore, J. G., W. R. Normark, and R. T. Holcomb

1994   Giant Hawaiian undersea landslides. *Science* 264:46–47. A synopsis and further explanation of information in Moore et al. (1989), with a map of the ancient landslides along the Hawaiian chain.

Mueller-Dombois, D.

1975   Some aspects of island ecosystem analysis. Pages 353–366 *in* F. B. Golley and E. Medina (eds.), *Tropical ecological systems: Trends in terrestrial and aquatic research.* Vol. 11 (Ecological Studies Series). New York: Springer-Verlag. 398 pp. A good overview of ecological phenomena in plants on the Hawaiian Islands, including original immigration as well as the effects of alien plants and animals on native vegetation. (Reprinted as pp. 131–144 *in* Kay [ed.] [1994].)

1987 Forest dynamics in Hawaii. *Trends in Ecology and Evolution* 2:216–219. The description of plant succession on a new lava flow is of special interest.

Mueller-Dombois, D., and F. R. Fosberg

1998 *Vegetation of the tropical Pacific islands.* New York: Springer-Verlag. 733 pp. A monumental work covering vegetation zones and their plant species of all island groups and isolated islands of tropical Oceania. Japan, the Philippines, Celebes, New Guinea, and New Zealand are omitted. Pertinent climatological and geological information (including soil types) is also presented, along with over four hundred color photographs, primarily of vegetation zones or their major plant components.

Mull, W. P.

1975 Magnificent minutiae. *Defenders* 50:487–490. A semipopular general account of the ecology and evolution of various groups of Hawaiian insects and spiders, illustrated with some of the author's incomparable close-up color photographs.

Nichols, W. D., P. J. Shade, and C. D. Hunt Jr.

1996 *Summary of the Oahu, Hawaii, Regional Aquifer-System Analysis.* U.S. Geological Survey Professional Paper 1412-A. 61 pp. An extensive account of freshwater dynamics on the island, including how this resource is influenced by regional geology and historic usage. Included is a conceptual computer-generated model of groundwater flow in the important South-central Oʻahu aquifer. (See also Hunt [1996].)

Nishida, G. M. (ed.)

1997 *Hawaiian terrestrial arthropod checklist.* 3d ed. Bishop Museum Technical Report 12. 263 pp. A tabulation and species listing of this fauna drawn from a Bishop Museum Hawaii Biological Survey database. The detailed listing gives scientific name, status (endemic, indigenous, and inadvertently or purposely introduced), and island(s) of occurrence. An electronic version may be obtained at the web site: http://www.bishopmuseum.org/bishop/HBS/arthrosearch.html. (This is Hawaii Biological Survey Contribution 1997-016.)

Oliver, J. A., and C. E. Shaw

1953 The amphibians and reptiles of the Hawaiian Islands. *Zoologica* 38:65–95. A listing and review of all these vertebrates reported from the archipelago, as well as discussions of geographic origin, introduction, and postestablishment history. A useful identification key to all species is also included. (Updated by Hunsaker and Breese [1967].)

Olson, S. L., and H. F. James

1982 Prodromus of the fossil avifauna of the Hawaiian Islands. *Smithsonian Contributions to Zoology* No. 365:1–59. An overview of the Hawaiian ecological setting, fossil sites, and types of prehistorically extinct birds discovered on various main islands during the preceding 10 years; intended primarily as an introduction to Olson and James (1991) and James and Olson (1991).

1984 The role of Polynesians in the extinction of the avifauna of the Hawaiian Islands. Pages 768–780 *in* P. S. Martin and R. G. Klein (eds.), *Quaternary extinctions: A prehistoric revolution.* Tucson: University of Arizona Press. 892 pp. A discussion of the evidence that a greater part of Hawaiian avian extinction took place during the Polynesian period (rather than before or after), mostly as the result of anthropogenous alterations of the original habitat.

1991   Descriptions of thirty-two new species of birds from the Hawaiian Islands: Part I. Non-Passeriformes. *Ornithological Monographs* No. 45:1–88. Formal scientific descriptions and informative related discussions of sixteen prehistorically extinct endemic species—other than passeriforms ("perching or songbirds")—whose remains have been discovered in the main islands since 1972. A number of illustrations of diagnostic skeletal elements are included. (General discussions of pp. 7–17 and 81–88 reprinted as pp. 439–455 *in* Kay [ed.] [1994].)

1994   A chronology of ornithological exploration in the Hawaiian Islands, from Cook to Perkins. *Studies in Avian Biology* 15:91–102. A listing of all significant historic collectors of Hawaiian Archipelago birds, and their islands of activity, between 1778 and about 1900.

Olson, S. L., and A. C. Ziegler
1995   Remains of land birds from Lisianski Island, with observations on the terrestrial avifauna of the Northwestern Hawaiian Islands. *Pacific Science* 49:111–125. A review of extinct and extant land and freshwater birds of the Northwestern chain, with notes on the effects of seabirds and alien mammals on the various islands' ecosystems.

Pratt, H. D., P. L. Bruner, and D. G. Berrett
1987   *A field guide to the birds of Hawaii and the tropical Pacific.* Princeton, New Jersey: Princeton University Press. 409 pp. An indispensable guide to field birding in the insular Pacific, covering all of Polynesia and Micronesia (but not Melanesia), with forty-five color plates of extremely accurate comparative paintings of all species by the primary author. An excellent summary of the ecosystems of Hawai'i and certain other Pacific island groups is included, along with many other data ancillary to identification information.

Pratt, L. W., and S. M. Gon III
1998   Terrestrial ecosystems. Pages 121–129 *in* S. P. Juvik and J. O. Juvik (eds.), *Atlas of Hawai'i.* 3d ed. Honolulu: University of Hawai'i Press. A classification of these several native systems on the main Hawaiian Islands, based primarily on vegetation types. Island maps of their distribution (and of a few marine ones) before the arrival of humans, as well as one representing the present time, are included. Also, environmental conditions, biotic resources, cultural significance, and current threats to each are described.

Price, S.
1972   Climates of the states: Hawaii. Pages 94–114 *in* E. A. Kay (ed.), 1994, *A natural history of the Hawaiian Islands: Selected readings II.* Honolulu: University of Hawai'i Press. A relatively extensive but nontechnical account of all aspects of Hawaiian climatology. (This article, reprinted from pp. 155–204 of Kay [ed.] [1972], was adapted by S. Price from D. Blumenstock and S. Price [1967], Climates of the states: Hawaii, *Climatography of the United States* No. 60-51. Washington, D.C.: U.S. Department of Commerce, Government Printing Office. 27 pp.)

Pukui, M. K., and S. H. Elbert
1971   *Hawaiian dictionary.* Honolulu: University of Hawai'i Press. 402 + 188 pp. This is the standard work for translation of the Hawaiian language and comprises separate Hawaiian-English and English-Hawaiian sections. No grammar section is included, nor are the ancestral derivations of most words given (see following two entries).

1986   *Hawaiian dictionary.* Rev. and enlarged ed. Honolulu: University of Hawai'i Press. 572 pp. A revision of Pukui and Elbert (1971), with an updated third printing in 1991. One of the major 1991 innovations is the elimination of hyphens in many terms and varied separation or nonseparation of word parts. No grammar section is included, but ancestral derivations of a number of words are given.

Pukui, M. K., S. H. Elbert, and E. T. Mookini
1974   *Place names of Hawaii.* Rev. and enlarged ed. Honolulu: University of Hawai'i Press. 289 pp. A valuable and quite interesting listing of Hawaiian and historic locality names, with their derivations. The names of many streets and certain modern structures such as buildings, schools, and the like are also included.

1975   *The pocket Hawaiian dictionary, with a concise Hawaiian grammar.* Honolulu: University of Hawai'i Press. 276 pp. An inexpensive abbreviated version of the Pukui and Elbert (1971) dictionary, but with the ancestral derivation of many more words included. The grammar section is relatively short, but extremely interesting and useful (but see also Elbert and Pukui [1979]).

Pyle, R. L.
1995   Birds of Hawaii. Pages 372–375 *in* E. T. LaRoe, G. S. Faris, C. E. Puckett, P. D. Doran, and M. J. Mac (eds.), *Our living resources: A report to the nation on the distribution, abundance, and health of U.S. plants, animals, and ecosystems.* Washington, D.C.: U.S. Department of the Interior, National Biological Service. 530 pp. A summary of species numbers by four categories: native and alien resident, breeding visitor, and nonbreeding visitor. Numbers of extinctions through time, as well as general geographic sources of alien and visitor species are also presented.

1997   Checklist of the birds of Hawaii–1997. *'Elepaio* 57:129–138. An exceedingly useful updated list of the native and alien bird species breeding in or visiting the Hawaiian Islands, with scientific and Hawaiian names as well as various other information regarding status.

Randall, J. E.
1987   Introductions of marine fishes to the Hawaiian Islands. *Bulletin of Marine Science* 41: 490–502. A record of all deliberate and unintended importations of saltwater species to the Hawaiian Islands, and the results of these introductions.

1996   *Shore fishes of Hawai'i.* Vida, Oregon: Natural World Press. 216 pp. The most recent account of Hawaiian reef fishes, listing 340 species. A brief natural-history summary of each family is presented, and all of the more common species are illustrated by an underwater color photograph with accompanying biological information. (Reprinted in 1998 by University of Hawai'i Press.)

Rauzon, M. J.
2001   *Isles of refuge: Wildlife and history of the Northwestern Hawaiian Islands.* Honolulu: University of Hawai'i Press. 205 pp. The only book devoted entirely to the wildlife and human use of this chain of islands and atolls, interspersed throughout with accounts of the author's visits and scientific work on nine of the ten emergent land units there.

Rolett, B. V.
1993   Marquesan prehistory and the origins of East Polynesian culture. *Journal de la Société des Océanistes* 96:29–47. A review and updated account of evidence relating to the putative first settlement area east of the Polynesian Homeland and an interpretation of the subsequent development of Polynesian culture in the Marquesas.

Rose, R. G.

1980   *A museum to instruct and delight.* Honolulu: Bishop Museum Press. 77 pp. An account of the founding of the Bernice P. Bishop Museum in the late 1800s and the role of William T. Brigham, its first director. Other interesting information regarding the founder Charles R. Bishop, other early Island museums, and contemporary sociopolitical events are included.

Rothschild, L. W., Lord

1893–1900 *The avifauna of Laysan and the neighbouring islands.* London: R. H. Porter. 320 pp. in 3 vols. A compendium of Hawaiian birdlife as it existed in the early 1890s, based largely on the specimens and fieldwork of Henry C. Palmer. Paintings by John G. Keulemans and Frederick W. Frohawk.

Royte, E.

1995   On the brink: Hawai'i's vanishing species. *National Geographic* 188:1–37. An overview of the current status of imperiled Hawaiian biota, the alien organisms causing this endangerment, and the various efforts being made to protect and preserve the native plants and animals.

Sanderson, M. (ed.)

1993   *Prevailing trade winds: Weather and climate in Hawai'i.* Honolulu: University of Hawai'i Press. 126 pp. A relatively comprehensive, but not overly long, discussion of the title subjects, as well as of Hawaiian freshwater dynamics. The seven chapters were written by six different authorities, at a level suitable for beginning college students. The Introduction includes ancient Hawaiian weather-related observations and terms.

Scheltema, R. S.

1986   Long-distance dispersal by planktonic larvae of shoal-water benthic invertebrates among central Pacific islands. *Bulletin of Marine Science* 39:241–256. Results of a large number of plankton hauls in Hawaiian and Southwest Pacific waters, along with much information and discussion on current flows, larval life expectancies, and probabilities of island establishment. (Reprinted as pp. 171–186 *in* Kay [ed.] [1994].)

Schroeder, T. (A.)

1993   Climate controls. Pages 12–36 *in* M. Sanderson (ed.), *Prevailing trade winds: Weather and climate in Hawai'i.* Honolulu: University of Hawai'i Press. A good overview of Hawaiian climatology, with an especially useful presentation of the climate and its causes for each main island.

Sharp, D. (ed.)

1899–1913 *Fauna Hawaiiensis, being the land fauna of the Hawaiian Islands.* Cambridge, England: Cambridge University Press. In 3 vols., with the numerous parts published separately on various dates. The sections on vertebrates and a number of the insect groups were authored by R. C. L. Perkins.

Sinton, J. M., and Y. H. Sinoto

1997   A geochemical database for Polynesian adze studies. Pages 194–204 *in* M. I. Weisler (ed.), *Prehistoric long-distance interaction in Oceania: An interdisciplinary approach.* New Zealand Archaeological Association Monograph No. 21. 237 pp. Chemical descriptions of lithic material from thirty-six Polynesian stone quarries (half of them in Hawai'i). Geochemical matching of artifacts and quarry sites allowed tracing of lithic transport within the Hawaiian Archipelago, as well as among Polynesian island groups. (University of Hawai'i at Mānoa, School of Earth Science and Technology Contribution 4560.)

Smathers, G. A., and D. Mueller-Dombois

1972   Invasion and recovery of vegetation after a volcanic eruption in Hawaii. Department of Botany, University of Hawai'i at Mānoa. *US/IBP Island Ecosystems IBP Technical Report* No. 10. 172 pp. An intensive and carefully documented 9-year study of revegetation on various substrates resulting from a volcanic eruption of Kīlauea Iki on Hawai'i Island.

Smith, C. M.

1992   Diversity in intertidal habitats: An assessment of the marine algae of select high islands in the Hawaiian Archipelago. *Pacific Science* 46:466–479. An investigation of the seaweeds of Hawai'i and O'ahu, documenting that a younger main island with relatively limited nearshore habitats supports fewer species than an older one around which a greater variety of such habitats has developed.

Smith, C. W.

1985   Impact of alien plants on Hawai'i's native biota. Pages 180–250 *in* C. P. Stone and J. M. Scott (eds.), *Hawai'i's terrestrial ecosystems: Preservation and management.* Honolulu: University of Hawai'i Press for Cooperative National Parks Resources Studies Unit, Department of Botany, University of Hawai'i at Mānoa. 584 pp. A good presentation of the stated subject.

Sohmer, S. H., and R. Gustafson

1987   *Plants and flowers of Hawai'i.* Honolulu: University of Hawai'i Press. 159 pp. Primarily a photographic collection of the more impressive-appearing flora of the Islands, with a most informative introductory section covering the history of Hawaiian botany, vegetation zones, and various evolutionary aspects of the native flora. (Section on vegetation zones of pp. 38–57 reprinted, without figures, as pp. 145–154 *in* Kay [ed.] [1994].)

Solem, (G.) A.

1990   How many Hawaiian land snail species are left?—and what we can do for them. *Bishop Museum Occasional Papers* 30:27–40. The contents of this article are indicated by its title. A limited amount of ecological information for a number of families is also provided.

Somit, A., and S. A. Peterson (eds.)

1992   *The dynamics of evolution.* Ithaca, New York: Cornell University Press. 325 pp. A rather extensive examination of the recent—and still controversial—evolutionary concept of punctuated evolution by a number of leading students of the subject, including both natural and social scientists. The proposers of the punctuated equilibrium theory, Stephen J. Gould and Niles Eldredge, are among the contributing authors.

Sorenson, M. D., A. Cooper, E. E. Paxinos, T. W. Quinn, H. F. James, S. L. Olson, and R. C. Fleischer

1999   Relationships of the extinct moa-nalos, flightless Hawaiian waterfowl, based on ancient DNA. *Proceedings of the Royal Society of London, Series B* 266:2187–2193. A determination of the relationships of two of the three genera of these duck-derived birds, both to each other and to various possible ancestral continental species.

Spieth, H. T.

1984   Courtship behaviors of the Hawaiian picture-winged *Drosophila. University of California Publications in Entomology* 103. 92 pp. A detailed description of the specific mating behavior of each of a large number of species in this particular group of the pomace fly family Drosophilidae.

Staples, G. W., and R. H. Cowie (eds.)

2001   *Hawai'i's invasive species.* Honolulu: Mutual and Bishop Mus. Press. 116 pp. An exposé of the rapid spread of aggressive macroscopic alien animals and plants over the state's lands and waters, and the various problems caused by them. Uniformly formatted discussions are presented for almost 70 selected vertebrates and invertebrates, as well as 25 plants, and each is illustrated by at least one color photograph. A list of informational websites is included. (This is Hawaii Biological Survey Contrib. 2001-003.)

State of Hawai'i, Department of Agriculture

1999   *Statistics of Hawaiian agriculture: 1997.* Honolulu: Hawai'i Agriculture Statistics Service. 106 pp. A cooperative venture of the state and federal Departments of Agriculture, annually presenting the latest available compilation of Hawaiian plant and livestock information. Among the contents are acreages per island, yields, prices received, and the like.

State of Hawai'i, Department of Land and Natural Resources

1996   *Will stream restoration benefit freshwater, estuarine, and marine fisheries? Proceedings of the October, 1994 Hawaii Stream Restoration Symposium.* Division of Aquatic Resources Technical Report 96-01. 333 pp. Numerous articles concerning, primarily, native Hawaiian stream fishes and other biota in relation to actual or potential restoration of their habitat.

Stearns, H. T.

1985   *Geology of the state of Hawaii.* 2d ed. Palo Alto, California: Pacific Books. 335 pp. Excellent coverage of Hawaiian geology and groundwater resources by a longtime Island investigator, although the role of plate tectonics in formation of the Hawaiian Archipelago receives essentially no attention.

Stemmermann, L.

1981   *A guide to Pacific wetland plants.* Honolulu: U.S. Army Corps of Engineers. 118 pp. Descriptions and illustrations of the numerous plant species found in various wetland areas of Hawai'i, American Samoa, as well as the Caroline and Mariana Islands.

Stone, C. P., and D. F. Stone (eds.)

1989   *Conservation biology in Hawai'i.* Honolulu: University of Hawai'i Press for Cooperative National Parks Resources Studies Unit, Department of Botany, University of Hawai'i at Mānoa. 252 pp. A collection of thirty-four essays covering a variety of current biological conservation topics by research scientists, game managers, educators, and a media representative. A minority of the articles are background descriptions of the various geological and biological resources of the archipelago.

Stone, C. P., C. W. Smith, and J. T. Tunison (eds.)

1992   *Alien plant invasions in native ecosystems of Hawai'i: Management and research.* Honolulu: University of Hawai'i Press for Cooperative National Parks Resources Studies Unit, Department of Botany, University of Hawai'i at Mānoa. 887 pp. An impressive compendium of relatively detailed scientific research papers dealing with, primarily, various means of controlling historically introduced terrestrial plants in Hawai'i. The introduction, distribution, and current status of these, as well as their interactions with alien animals, receive a lesser amount of attention.

Tarr, C. L., and R. C. Fleischer

1995   Evolutionary relationships of the Hawaiian Honeycreepers (Aves, Drepanidinae). Pages 147–159 *in* W. L. Wagner and V. A. Funk (eds.), *Hawaiian biogeography: Evo-*

lution on a hot spot archipelago. Washington, D.C.: Smithsonian Institution Press. A cladistic study of these endemic Hawaiian birds, based primarily on variation in DNA nucleotide sequences.

Time-Life Books
1982   *Volcano.* Alexandria, Virginia: Time-Life Books. 179 pp. An easily understood, well-illustrated explanation of, primarily, continental volcanoes and related aspects of volcanism.

Titcomb, M. (with the collaboration of M. K. Pukui)
1969   *Dog and man in the ancient Pacific.* Bernice P. Bishop Museum Special Publication 59. 91 pp. A general account, based primarily on literature sources, of the association of these two vertebrates during prehistoric colonization of the insular Pacific.

1972   *Native use of fish in Hawaii.* Honolulu: University of Hawai'i Press. 175 pp. An extensive compilation of records from, primarily, the published and unpublished ethnological literature. Hawaiian names and a wide range of information relating to the resource are included.

Titcomb, M. (with the collaboration of D. B. Fellows, M. K. Pukui, and D. M. Devaney)
1978   Native use of marine invertebrates in old Hawaii. *Pacific Science* 32:325–386. An extensive compilation of records from, primarily, the published and unpublished ethnological literature. Hawaiian names and a wide range of information relating to the resource are included.

Tomich, P. Q.
1986   *Mammals in Hawai'i.* 2d ed. Honolulu: Bishop Museum Press. 375 pp. An up-to-date definitive work on the subject. The annotated bibliography is remarkable, including perhaps every published reference to mammals in the Islands.

Tummons, P. (ed.)
1990–present *Environment Hawai'i.* Hilo, Hawai'i. A monthly publication presenting well-documented detailed and incisive examinations of a variety of environmental protection matters in Hawai'i.

Turner, T.
1990   Saving a honeycreeper. *Defenders* 65:10–15. An account of the Sierra Club [now Earthjustice] Legal Defense Fund lawsuit that forced the State of Hawai'i to end maintenance of alien game mammals in critical habitat of the *Palila (Loxioides bailleui),* an endangered endemic Hawaiian bird.

Twiss, J. R., Jr., and R. R. Reeves (eds.)
1999   *Conservation and management of marine mammals.* Washington, D.C.: Smithsonian Institution Press. 496 pp. The nineteen chapters by various authors cover, primarily, the two actions of the title, with only a moderate amount of natural history presented for most individual species. There is however, one chapter devoted to biology of the Hawaiian Monk Seal, as well as another on its management.

Uehara, G.
1983   Soils. Pages 45–47 *in* R. W. Armstrong (ed.), *Atlas of Hawai'i.* 2d ed. Honolulu: University of Hawai'i Press. A succinct but most informative discussion of various aspects of Hawaiian soils, with maps of the main islands showing distribution of the ten soil Orders. (Reprinted, under the title Soils of Hawaii and without maps, as pp. 115–117 *in* Kay [ed.] [1994].)

U.S. Department of Commerce

1986   *Proposed designation of critical habitat for the Hawaiian monk seal in the Northwestern Hawaiian Islands. Final Environmental Impact Statement.* Washington, D.C.: National Oceanic and Atmospheric Administration, National Marine Fisheries Service. 81 pp. + 2 appendices. Pages 25–42 contain an extensive account of the biology and distribution of this endemic Hawaiian pinniped.

1997   *Hawaiian Islands Humpback Whale National Marine Sanctuary. Final Environmental Impact Statement/Management Plan.* Washington, D.C.: National Oceanic and Atmospheric Administration, National Ocean Service. 464 pp. Pages 34–57 contain an extensive account of numerous life-history aspects of this cetacean in Hawaiian waters as well as elsewhere in the world's oceans.

U.S. Department of the Interior

1990   *Hawaii stream assessment: A preliminary appraisal of Hawaii's stream resources.* Honolulu: National Park Service, Hawaii Cooperative Park Service Unit Report R84. 294 pp. A reference work including an inventory of the state's perennial streams (including rivers), along with their associated resources. The availability of a computerized database and guide is noted.

Valier, K.

1995   *Ferns of Hawai'i.* Honolulu: University of Hawai'i Press. 88 pp. A brief overview of the characteristics of ferns and fern allies in general, with good descriptions of over sixty Hawaiian species in twenty-four families. Black-and-white photographs of each of these species are helpfully included, along with color photographs of a dozen and a half.

Van Riper, S. G., and C. van Riper III

1982   *A field guide to the mammals in Hawaii.* Honolulu: Oriental. 68 pp. A relatively brief but very useful guide to the native and alien mammals of the Islands. Color photographs and island maps showing distribution of each species are included, as well as a synopsis of identification characters of sixteen types of cetaceans reported from the archipelago.

Wagner, W. L., and V. A. Funk (eds.)

1995   *Hawaiian biogeography: Evolution on a hot spot archipelago.* Washington, D.C.: Smithsonian Institution Press. 467 pp. Studies of the evolutionary relationships and Island distributions of selected groups of endemic biota by some two dozen authorities. The biotic groups, usually genera, comprise four of insects, one each of spiders and birds, and about a dozen of plants. Analysis is carried out by means of computer-generated phylogenetic trees (cladograms) based on morphological and molecular characters. Much of the text language is extremely technical, but most of the tentative general conclusions are easily understood by the nonspecialist.

Wagner, W. L., D. R. Herbst, and S. H. Sohmer

1999   *Manual of the flowering plants of Hawai'i.* Rev. ed. Honolulu: University of Hawai'i Press and Bishop Museum Press. 1,919 pp. in 2 vols. The current definitive work on the subject. Also included are discussions of such related subjects as geology, climate, and vegetation zones. An Addendum (pp. 1855–1919) updates the botanical information appearing in the original 1990 edition.

Walker, G. P. L.

1990   Geology and volcanology of the Hawaiian Islands. *Pacific Science* 44:315–347. An extensive but generally not overly technical account of the title's subjects, including some speculative ideas on such matters as orientation of Island volcano rift zones. The article offers an interesting and informative alternative to most other inclusive papers that tend to be quite long and involved. (Reprinted as pp. 53–85 *in* Kay [ed.] [1994].)

Wallace, R. A., J. L. King, and G. P. Sanders

1986   *Biology: The science of life.* 2d ed. Glenview, Illinois: Scott, Foresman and Co. 1,217 pp. Only one of a number of good textbooks on the life of plants and animals; this is an exceptionally detailed work on the extensive subject.

Wilcox, C.

1998   *Sugar water.* Honolulu: University of Hawai'i Press. 191 pp. A detailed account of surface-water development by Hawaiian Sugarcane interests, mostly between 1876 and 1920, with much information on the planners and builders of water-transport systems. The illustrations include many historic photographs.

Wilkes, C.

1844–1874 *United States Exploring Expedition. During the years 1838, 1839, 1840, 1841, 1842. Under the command of Charles Wilkes, U.S.N.* Philadelphia, Pennsylvania: C. Sherman. Twenty-one volumes published. An extensive compendium of results from the first American scientific expedition to include work in the Hawaiian Islands. The volumes are by a variety of authorities on biology, geology, ethnology, and other natural sciences.

Yamamoto, M. N., and A. W. Tagawa

2000   *Hawai'i's native and exotic freshwater animals.* Honolulu: Mutual. 200 pp. A photo-illustrated handbook of the vertebrates and many of the more conspicuous invertebrates living in the state's various bodies of freshwater.

Yen, D. E.

1974   *The Sweet Potato and Oceania.* Honolulu: Bernice P. Bishop Museum Bulletin 236. 389 pp. An extensive treatise on all aspects of this plant in the insular Pacific, by the foremost authority on the subject.

Ziegler, A. C.

1987   Island fauna: Of feathers and wings. Pages 59–65 *in* J. F. Boden and E. Emshoff (eds.), *Hawaii aloha.* Pearl City, Hawai'i: Press Pacifica. A popular account of Hawaiian vertebrates, primarily native and alien birds. Explanations of the evolution of flightlessness and adaptive radiation in the Islands are included.

Zimmerman, E. C.

1948   *Insects of Hawaii.* Vol. 1. *Introduction.* Honolulu: University of Hawai'i Press. 206 pp. This introductory volume covers all terrestrial plant and animal groups of the archipelago and contains myriad details of biotic composition, dispersal, evolution, and related matters. Although some of the information in this and several other subsequent volumes (a total of sixteen published as of 2000) is now inevitably somewhat dated, this remarkable collection still remains the best *single* reference available on Hawaiian insects.

1970   Adaptive radiation in Hawaii with special reference to insects. *Biotropica* 2:32–38. An excellent review of ecological and morphological changes undergone by insects after colonizing the Hawaiian Archipelago. (Reprinted as pp. 528–534 *in* Kay [ed.] [1972].)

Audiovisual Aids
(Arranged alphabetically by title; with annotations)

The adaptive radiation of the silversword alliance. 1982?. London: British Broadcasting Corporation Television Service, in association with the University of Hawai'i at Mānoa. 25 min. A presentation of the evolutionary results in three endemic Hawaiian plant genera derived from a single immigrant tarweed species of the sunflower family Asteraceae.

The beach: A river of sand. 1967?. Chicago: Encyclopaedia Britannica Films, in association with American Geological Institute. 20 min. A description of formation of continental quartz-feldspar beaches and methods of measuring beach-sand movements.

Behavior and ecology of coral reef fishes. 1971. University Park: Pennsylvania State University; released by Science Software Systems. 28 min. A study of the feeding and social behavior of fifteen species of the butterflyfish family Chaetodontidae and their ecological relationship with the coral reef. A printed study guide is included.

Beyond Honolulu. 1976. Honolulu: Hawaii Production Center; written and filmed by Bruce Benson. 24 min. A brief examination of four of the Northwestern Hawaiian Islands, their native wildlife, and the need to preserve this wildlife sanctuary.

A bog community in Hawaii. 1984. Honolulu: State Department of Education AV No. V04694 ("Science in Hawaii," No. 21). 20 min. An examination of the special conditions that create bogs and their effects on plant growth and development. Prepared for an elementary school audience.

Cloud over the coral reef. 1971. Mountain View, California: Moonlight Productions, in association with the University of Hawai'i at Mānoa and Lockheed Palo Alto Research Laboratory. 27 min. An explanation of the geological and ecological role of coral reefs and the problems they face from modern pollution and occasional native predators. A printed instructor's guide is included.

Coral. 1991. Evanston, Illinois: Altschul Group Corporation, Journal Films. (Hawai'i Department of Education AV No. V04582.) 15 min. A presentation of coral-reef biology, with close-up footage of coral polyps and their means of protection and food procurement.

The coral reef community. 1977. Culver City, California: Film Fair Communications. 23 min. A well-filmed depiction of the ecology and general habitats of this particular ecosystem, including plants, invertebrates, and vertebrates, with a rather detailed examination of coral anatomy and physiology.

Darwin. 1970. Toronto: Canadian Broadcasting Corporation; released in the United States by Films Incorporated. 28 min. A professionally well-done production covering Charles Darwin's youth and the HMS *Beagle* voyage (especially the Galápagos Islands portion), as well as Darwin's later varied research and writings.

Darwin and the theory of natural selection. 1967. Chicago: Coronet Instructional Films. 14 min. A short—but one of the best—explanations of how Darwin's observations in the Galápagos and elsewhere eventually led him to propose his theory of biological evolution, and how this work has influenced modern biology. A brief printed instructor's guide is included.

Earthquakes: Predicting the big one! 1994. Morris Plains, New Jersey: Lucerne Media. (Hawai'i Department of Education AV No. V06654.) 20 min. An overview of the destructive forces unleashed by earthquakes, and an examination of the causes of earthquakes.

Earth science: Continental drift—theory of plate tectonics. 1980. Chicago: Britannica Films and Video. 22 min. An explanation of continental drift, hot spots, and origin of the Hawaiian Islands.

Earth science: Water cycle. 2nd ed. 1980. Chicago: Britannica Films and Video. 14 min. An examination of the hydrologic cycle and of water erosion in general.

Ecology. 1989. Honolulu: State Department of Education AV No. V04762 ("It's science . . . isn't it?" No. 17). 20 min. A study of Hawaiian pomace flies is used to explain adaptations and ecology of organisms. Prepared for an elementary school audience.

Energy. 1990. Briarcliff Manor, New York: Benchmark Media. (Hawai'i Department of Education AV No. V06095.) 20 min. An examination of the transfer of energy, primarily from the sun, as a biochemical process that includes plant photosynthesis as well as plant and animal metabolism.

Eruption at the sea. 1988. Volcano, Hawai'i: Ka'io Productions. 30 min. A presentation of the various types of eruptions and lava flows of Kīlauea Volcano on Hawai'i Island, including formation of new land at the ocean shore.

Fire under the sea: The origin of pillow lava. 1974?. Mountain View, California: Moonlight Productions. 20 min. Underwater views of lava flowing into the ocean along the south coast of Hawai'i Island, with the resultant production of pillow lava.

Flowing to the sea. 1992. Honolulu: Moanalua Gardens Foundation. 23 min. A portrayal of stream dynamics and stream life in Hawai'i. Prepared for elementary and secondary school audiences.

The food web and energy transfer. 1992. Briarcliff Manor, New York: Benchmark Media. (Hawai'i Department of Education AV No. V06098.) 22 min. A tracing of energy flow in natural food webs—from the sun, through producers and consumers, to decomposers.

4-Butte-1: A lesson in archaeology. 1968. Berkeley: University of California Extension Media Center. 33 min. The planning and execution of an archaeological excavation project in central California, with a perhaps overly long introductory segment regarding possible interpretive use of prehistoric legends. The illustrations of combining historical data with those from excavation of the site are good.

Gatecliff: American Indian rock-shelter. 1974. Washington, D.C.: National Geographic Society. 24 min. An explanation of archaeological investigation methods and artifact analysis, well illustrated by work at a prehistoric Nevada habitation site. (Probably a better and more concise coverage of the interpretation of prehistory than the ***4-Butte-1*** video listed earlier.)

Genetics and populations. 1989. Honolulu: State Department of Education AV No. V04764 ("It's science . . . isn't it?" No. 19). 20 min. An overview of genetics through animated sequences. Introduced are the concepts of genes, mutation, artificial and natural selection, as well as adaptation and hybridization. Prepared for an elementary school audience.

Geology. 1987. Honolulu: State Department of Education AV No. V04769 ("It's science . . . isn't it?" No. 10). 20 min. An examination of selected volcanic phenomena: Hawai'i Island's active volcanism, source of magma, and causes of earthquakes. Prepared for an elementary school audience.

Geology: Science studies the moving continents. 1988. Boca Raton, Florida: Allegro Film Productions. (Hawai'i Department of Education AV No. V01372.) 26 min. An explanation of the earth's lithospheric plates and how their movement rearranges continents, forms mountain ranges, and produces volcanic and seismic activity.

Guided by the Nene. 1974. Berkeley: University of California Extension Media Center.

27 min. A description of efforts aimed at restoring populations of the native Hawaiian Goose on Maui. Also included is a brief explanation of the species' evolution and ecology, as well as a listing of the factors that have caused its current endangered status.

Hawaii: A chain. 1968. Honolulu: State Department of Education AV No. V00524 ("Science in Hawaii," No. 10). 20 min. Primarily a geography of the Hawaiian Islands, including the Northwestern ones, although the main islands receive the most attention. Prepared for an elementary school audience.

Hawaii: A mountain community. 1984. Honolulu: State Department of Education AV No. V04693 ("Science in Hawaii," No. 20). 20 min. A study of botanical and entomological explorations of three elevational levels on Maui's Haleakalā. Prepared for an elementary school audience.

Hawaiian fishhooks. 197-. Honolulu: Cine Pic Hawaii. 10 min. A brief explanation of the use of archaeologically recovered fishhooks to trace migration routes of ancient Polynesian settlers of the Islands.

Hawaii and planet Earth: The Hawaiian geography. 1984. Honolulu: State Department of Education AV No. V04678 ("Science in Hawaii," No. 5). 20 min. A comparative discussion of physical and political geography of Hawai'i by a scientist and an attorney. Prepared for an elementary school audience.

Hawaii: An island community. 1984. Honolulu: State Department of Education AV No. V04682 ("Science in Hawaii," No. 16). 20 min. An explanation of plant and animal dispersal to the Hawaiian Islands and subsequent bird evolution, combining animation and live action. Prepared for an elementary school audience.

Hawaiian seafood: Limu. 1977. Pearl City, Hawai'i: Leeward Community College. 13 min. A portrayal of traditional Island gathering and preparation of edible seaweeds.

Hawaiian waters: House of the shark. 1992?. Honolulu: State Department of Land and Natural Resources, Division of Aquatic Resources. 22 min. A description of general shark ecology around the Islands, along with an explanation of their economic use. Safety precautions to minimize shark attacks are also presented.

Hawaiian waters: Mauka/makai lifeline. 1992. Honolulu: State Department of Land and Natural Resources, Division of Aquatic Resources. 21 min. A documentation of the current status of Island stream ecosystems, factors causing their endangerment, and some of the animals that inhabit them.

Hawaii: Born of fire. 1995. Boston, Massachusetts: Peace River Films in conjunction with NOVA and WGBH. 58 min. A portrayal of volcanism and native biota in Hawai'i, including biotic succession and the Lava-tube Ecosystem.

Hawaii: Crucible of life. 1983. Paramus, New Jersey: Time-Life Video. 57 min. An examination of unique native, and a few alien, insects and other arthropods in Hawai'i, including species of lava-tube crickets, the Mauna Kea Wēkiu Bug, and a carnivorous caterpillar. Biological plant control using the introduced Cactus Moth is also explained.

Hawaii: Islands of the Fire Goddess. 1988. New York: WNET Television. 60 min. A brief description of formation of the Hawaiian Archipelago, along with a discussion of its isolation and evolution of endemic biota. Anchialine ponds and reef fishes receive considerable attention, as do animals of the Northwestern Hawaiian Islands.

Hawaii: Kona storms. 1968. Honolulu: State Department of Education AV No. V00528 ("Science in Hawaii," No. 16). 20 min. An explanation of the causes of this type of atmospheric disturbance, including characteristics of the trade winds, inversion layer, cloud formation, and related atmospheric phenomena. Prepared for an elementary school audience.

Hawaii: Mauka showers. 1968. Honolulu: State Department of Education AV No. V00530 ("Science in Hawaii," No. 15). 20 min. A climatologist's explanation of cloud formation over the main islands, and how orographic rainfall is produced from the trade winds. Prepared for an elementary school audience.

Hawaii's climate. 1984. Honolulu: State Department of Education AV No. V04684 ("Science in Hawaii," No. 10). 20 min. An explanation of the difference between weather and climate, and presentation of the four factors affecting Island climate. Different climatic zones and dangerous weather conditions are also discussed. Prepared for an elementary school audience.

Hawaii's coral: Dead or alive. 1984. Honolulu: State Department of Education AV No. V04686 ("Science in Hawaii," No. 13). 20 min. A description of living coral polyps and their calcareous skeletons, including examination of the features and structure of several coral species. Prepared for an elementary school audience.

Hawaii's forests. 1984. Honolulu: State Department of Education AV No. V04692 ("Science in Hawaii," No. 19). 20 min. A description of three types of Hawaiian forests. Prepared for an elementary school audience.

Hawaii's low islands. 1984. Honolulu: State Department of Education AV No. V04680 ("Science in Hawaii," No. 7). 15 min. A portrayal of the Northwestern Hawaiian Islands and their inhabitants. Prepared for an elementary school audience.

Hawaii's ocean: The Pacific. 1984. Honolulu: State Department of Education AV No. V04677 ("Science in Hawaii," No. 4). 20 min. An explanation of how a scientific expedition maps the ocean floor. Production of tides and erosion of beaches are also examined. Prepared for an elementary school audience.

Hawaii: Strangers in paradise. 1991. Washington, D.C.: National Geographic Society and Hawaii Public Television. 60 min. A general, and beautifully photographed, natural history overview of the archipelago, including the Northwestern Islands. The detrimental effects of introduced organisms are stressed.

Hawaii's streams. 1984. Honolulu: State Department of Education AV No. V04690 ("Science in Hawaii," No. 17). 20 min. A limnologist's discussion of various Maui streams, their native inhabitants, and how Island stream ecosystems have been affected by humans. Prepared for an elementary school audience.

Hawaii: Surf and sea. 1968. Honolulu: State Department of Education AV No. V00532 ("Science in Hawaii," No. 13). 20 min. An examination of North Pacific ocean currents, as well as of shoreline breaker formation and generation and results of tsunamis. Prepared for an elementary school audience.

Hawaii's water resources. 1984. Honolulu: State Department of Education AV No. V04695 ("Science in Hawaii," No. 22). 20 min. An explanation of the hydrologic cycle, along with a description of Island water resources and their importance to humans. Prepared for an elementary school audience.

Hawaii: Volcanoes. 1968. Honolulu: State Department of Education AV No. V00534 ("Science in Hawaii," No. 9). 20 min. An explanation of the different types of volcanoes, along with their origins, shapes, and activities. Footage of 1959 and 1960 eruptions of Hawai'i Island's Kīlauea is included. Prepared for an elementary school audience.

Heartbeat of a volcano. 1970. Chicago: Encyclopaedia Britannica Educational Corporation. 21 min. Descriptions and excellent photography of the various activity stages of an eruption at Kīlauea Volcano on Hawai'i Island, as well as methods of measuring seismic and other activity relating to such a hot-spot volcano.

Heredity and genetics. 1990. Briarcliff Manor, New York: Benchmark Media. (Hawai'i Department of Education AV No. V06100.) 23 min. An exploration of the basic principles of Mendelian genetics, including an explanation of dominant and recessive traits and their inheritance.

History, layer by layer (earth and ocean). 1957. New York: Columbia University Lamont Geological Observatory, distributed by McGraw-Hill Films. 23 min. A description of scientific methods employed in such geological activities as obtaining and interpreting ocean-floor sediment cores, studying past glaciations, and the like.

History of Hawaii: Polynesian migration. 198-. Andy F. Bushnell. 35 min. An excellent illustrated lecture on ancient voyages of discovery among various Polynesian island groups, including the Hawaiian Islands.

The house of science. 1973. Chicago: Encyclopaedia Britannica Educational Corporation. 15 min. An excellent introductory video to most natural science courses, covering fields of inquiry, scientific methods, and the like.

Inside Hawaiian volcanoes. 1989. Washington, D.C.: Smithsonian Institution. 25 min. An explanation of the general mechanics of Island volcanic eruptions and methods of determining subsurface structure and processes of volcanoes.

In the middle of the sea. 1992. Honolulu: Moanalua Gardens Foundation. 18 min. A description of geographic zonation in the Hawaiian Islands, and an explanation of why there are so many endemic organisms. The Silversword Alliance and Hawaiian honeycreepers are featured. Prepared for elementary and secondary school audiences.

Island of Aldabra. 1968. New York: British Broadcasting Corporation Television Service. 25 min. An examination of this Seychelles Islands atoll northwest of Madagascar, which is analogous to a Hawaiian island because a significant proportion of its distinctive native biota has evolved in comparative isolation. Efforts to protect its environment against unnecessary development are also covered.

Islands within islands within islands. 1991. London: British Broadcasting Corporation Television Service (for the Open University and the University of Hawai‘i at Mānoa); distributed by University Media, Solana Beach, California. 25 min. An explanation of biotic dispersal to the Hawaiian Islands. Also covered are a variety of evolutionary phenomena among Island plants and, especially, invertebrates, including lava-tube species. There is some botanical duplication with the video *Succession on lava* later in this list.

Kalo pa‘a o Waiāhole [*The hard taro of Waiāhole*]. 1995?. Nā‘ālehu, Hawai‘i: Nā Maka O Ka ‘Āina. 59 min. A mid-1990s documentary review of the protesting actions of taro farmers and other users of freshwater on Windward O‘ahu relating to water diversion by the Waiāhole Ditch system. The "hard taro" in the title refers to the attribution of great stubbornness to the ancient Waiāhole Valley people. A minor amount of coverage is devoted to native Hawaiian stream ecosystems.

Ke haku hulu: The featherworker. 1985. Honolulu: State Department of Education AV No. V04664 (*Nā ki‘i hana no‘eau Hawai‘i,* No. 21). 20 min. A portrayal of a forest journey by two Native Hawaiians, who describe native Hawaiian birds whose feathers were once used in the traditional featherwork craft. Prepared for elementary and secondary school audiences.

Life at Salt Point. 1978. Chicago: Coronet Instructional Media. 15 min. A comparison of physical conditions in various California inshore and offshore marine habitats and the ecology of their biota. (On same videocassette as following entry.)

Life in Lost Creek. 1978. Chicago: Coronet Instructional Media. 15 min. A comparison of physical conditions in various continental stream and pond freshwater habitats and the ecology of their biota. (On same videocassette as preceding entry.)

Life on the sandy shore and the rocky shore. 1984. Honolulu: State Department of Education AV No. V04688 ("Science in Hawaii," No. 15). 20 min. A description of the ecosystems of two types of Island shoreline habitat. Prepared for an elementary school audience.

Listen to the forest. 1991. Honolulu: Hawai'i Sons. 55 min. A plea for Island rain forest preservation, with much discussion by Native Hawaiians concerning their current attitudes toward the forest and Polynesian-related plants. Probably best suited to school classes below the college level, although comparable coverage of Hawaiian land snails and the Happyface Spider is found in few other documentaries. A program guide is provided.

The living soil. 1992. Evanston, Illinois: Altschul Group Corporation, Journal Films. (Hawai'i Department of Education AV No. V06202.) 20 min. An explanation of the relationship between living and nonliving soil components and the natural cycles of soil formation. The source of soil nutrients and the causes of soil loss are also discussed.

Mānana, island of birds. 1973. Honolulu: Lenra Associates. 25 min. A study of mating and nesting behavior, as well as of the general ecology, of shearwaters, petrels, and terns of Rabbit Island off O'ahu.

Nā ki'i hana no'eau Hawai'i. No. 1 through 6. 1985. Honolulu: State Department of Education AV No. V04732 through V04737. 20 min. each. A series of presentations of, primarily, pre- and post-Contact cultural history of, respectively, the islands of Kaua'i, O'ahu, Moloka'i, Lāna'i and Kaho'olawe, Maui, and Hawai'i. The history behind the names of a number of places on each is also included. Prepared for elementary and secondary school audiences.

Natural selection. 1963. Chicago: Encyclopaedia Britannica Educational Corporation. 16 min. A listing of environmental factors and selective agents involved in natural selection, with an example of evolution of a mosquito strain through selective development of pesticide resistance.

New species from old. 1970. Toronto: Canadian Broadcasting Corporation; released in the United States by Films Incorporated. 16 min. Primarily a vertebrate natural history of the Galápagos Islands, featuring the evolution of many native finches and other birds, as well as lava lizards appearing on the various islands.

The Northwestern Hawaiian Islands. 1983. Honolulu: State Department of Land and Natural Resources, Division of Aquatic Resources et al. 30± min. A coverage of some scientific research methods used in this chain of small islands, along with history of the biota and a very brief explanation of typical atoll and guyot formation.

Oceanography. 1989. Honolulu: State Department of Education AV No. V04758 ("It's science . . . isn't it? No. 12). 20 min. A portrayal of four aspects of ocean science: geological, physical, biological, and chemical. Prepared for an elementary school audience.

The picture wings of Hawaii. 1981. London: British Broadcasting Corporation Television Service, in association with the University of Hawai'i at Mānoa. 25 min. A study of the processes and results of evolution among the numerous species of this ***Drosophila*** subgroup of the pomace fly family Drosophilidae.

Places in the sea. 1994. Evanston, Illinois: Altschul Group Corporation, Journal Films. (Hawai'i Department of Education AV No. V06155.) 15 min. An examination of the major types of marine mollusks, including gastropods, bivalves, and cephalopods.

Pond communities in Hawaii. 1984. Honolulu: State Department of Education AV No. V04689 ("Science in Hawaii," No. 16). 20 min. An examination of the plants and animals of this type of freshwater ecosystem. Prepared for an elementary school audience.

Radioactive dating. 1981. Northbrook, Illinois: Coronet Films and Video. 13 min. An explanation of chemical isotopes and radioactivity and how radioactive potassium and carbon
are utilized in dating ancient materials. A printed discussion guide is included.

The riddle of heredity. 1970. Paramus, New Jersey: Time-Life Broadcast, Inc., released by
McGraw-Hill Book Company. 30 min. An explanation of the role of DNA molecules
and their genes in the transmission of inherited characteristics. Also covered is the
production of mutations and how these lead to individual and populational traits.

Slide bank of Hawai'i's native biota. 1991. Honolulu: Moanalua Gardens Foundation. A set
of two hundred 35-mm color slides, with illustrated explanatory index. The coverage
consists mostly of native terrestrial organisms, including some of the more unusual
plants and animals of the Islands. (Available for loan from each Hawai'i Department
of Education District Office or by special arrangement from any regional Library in
the state.)

Soil and decomposition. 1986. New York: Phoenix/BFA Films and Video. 15 min. A
description of soil formation and fertility, as well as plant nutrition and decomposition.

Species and evolution. 1981. London, British Broadcasting Corporation Television Service,
in association with the University of Hawai'i at Mānoa; distributed by University
Media, Solana Beach, California. (Hawai'i State Department of Education AV No.
B01637.) 25 min. An explanation of several evolutionary aspects of the Hawaiian
biota, including reproductive isolation and hybridization in *'Ōhi'a lehua*. A lesser
amount of information on Hawaiian honeycreepers and the endemic Stream Limpet
Neritina granulosa is included.

Succession on lava. 1970. Chicago: Encyclopaedia Britannica Educational Corporation.
14 min. A description of formation of various types of lava substrates and eventual
successive habitation of them by differing plant forms. The environmental impact of
larger alien animals such as Pigs and goats on these native ecosystems is also covered.

Volcano. 1953. Los Angeles: University of California at Los Angeles Extension Service.
11 min. A portrayal of various growth stages of the typical "continental-plate" Mexican
volcano Paricutín and the destruction caused by its eruptions.

Volcano Surtsey. 1966. Lynn, Massachusetts: North Shore News Company; distributed by
Geoscience Information Services, Reston, Virginia. 26 min. A description of the
growth of an Icelandic hot-spot volcano, from initial sea-level appearance to formation
of a substantial shield volcano.

Wilderness. 1990. Bloomington, Indiana: Agency for Instructional Technology. 20 min.
A discussion of the political, economic, ecological, and social aspects of preserving
and managing wilderness areas.

Index

Boldface numbers refer to tables and illustrations.

Color plates follow page 126.

\# species historically extirpated

† species prehistorically extinct

About the Author

Alan C. Ziegler has lived in Hawai'i for 35 years, spending the first half of this period as head of the Vertebrate Zoology Division at the Bernice Pauahi Bishop Museum in Honolulu and the second as an independent zoological consultant. His academic work includes teaching in the Anthropology, General Science, and Zoology Departments of the University of Hawai'i at Mānoa as well as at community colleges in the state. Dr. Ziegler is the author or coauthor of about three dozen scientific articles and book chapters dealing with both land vertebrates and zooarchaeology, as well as a frequent lecturer and field-trip leader. He has also long been active in Hawai'i environmental protection matters. Before arriving in Hawai'i, after serving 4 years in the U.S. Air Force during the Korean conflict, Dr. Ziegler attended the University of California at Berkeley, where he was named 1957 Outstanding Undergraduate of the Zoology Department and elected to Phi Beta Kappa before going on to receive his Ph.D. from the same institution.

Production Notes for Ziegler/*Hawaiian Natural History, Ecology, and Evolution*

Cover and interior designed by David Alcorn in Times New Roman.

Composition by Josie Herr Graphics in QuarkXPress.

Printing and binding by The Maple-Vail Book Manufacturing Group.

Printed on 60 lb. Text White Opaque II, 500 ppi.